THE EVANGELIZATION OF SLAVES
AND CATHOLIC ORIGINS
IN EASTERN AFRICA

The American Society of Missiology Series, published in collaboration with Orbis Books, seeks to publish scholarly works of high merit and wide interest on numerous aspects of missiology — the study of Christian mission in its historical, social, and theological dimensions. Able presentations on new and creative approaches to the practice and understanding of mission will receive close attention from the ASM Series Committee.

American Society of Missiology Series, No. 38

THE EVANGELIZATION OF SLAVES AND CATHOLIC ORIGINS IN EASTERN AFRICA

Paul V. Kollman

ORBIS BOOKS

Maryknoll, New York 10545

Founded in 1970, Orbis Books endeavors to publish works that enlighten the mind, nourish the spirit, and challenge the conscience. The publishing arm of the Maryknoll Fathers and Brothers, Orbis seeks to explore the global dimensions of the Christian faith and mission, to invite dialogue with diverse cultures and religious traditions, and to serve the cause of reconciliation and peace. The books published reflect the views of their authors and do not represent the official position of the Maryknoll Society. To learn more about Maryknoll and Orbis Books, please visit our website at www.maryknoll.com.

Copyright © 2005 Paul V. Kollman

Published by Orbis Books, Maryknoll, New York, U.S.A.

Manufactured in the United States of America

Library of Congress Cataloging-in-Publication Data

Kollman, Paul V.
    The evangelization of slaves and Catholic origins in eastern Africa / Paul V. Kollman.
      p. cm. – (American Society of Missiology series)
    Includes bibliographical references and index.
    ISBN-13: 978-1-57075-626-9 (pbk.)
    1. Congregation of the Holy Ghost – Missions – Africa, Eastern – History – 19th century. 2. Slaves – Religious life – Africa, Eastern – History – 19th century. 3. Africa, Eastern – Church history – 19th century. I. Title. II. Series.
BV3530.K595 2005
266′.2676 – dc22
                                   2005013700

The publication of this study was made possible in part by a generous gift of the Congregation of the Holy Spirit, USA East Province

For information about the Spiritans and their mission and ministries, visit their Web site: *www.Spiritans.org*

Contents

Preface to the ASM Series

The purpose of the ASM (American Society of Missiology) Series is to publish — without regard for disciplinary, national, or denominational boundaries — scholarly works of high quality and wide interest on missiological themes from the entire spectrum of scholarly pursuits relevant to Christian mission, which is always the focus of books in the Series.

By *mission* is meant the effort to effect passage over the boundary between faith in Jesus Christ and its absence. In this understanding of mission, the basic functions of Christian proclamation, dialogue, witness, service, worship, liberation, and nurture are of special concern. And in that context questions arise, including, How does the transition from one cultural context to another influence the shape and interaction between these dynamic functions, especially in regard to the cultural and religious plurality that constitute the global context of Christian life and mission?

The promotion of scholarly dialogue among missiologists, and among missiologists and scholars in other fields of inquiry, may involve the publication of views that some missiologists cannot accept, and with which members of the Editorial Committee themselves do not agree. Manuscripts published in the Series, accordingly, reflect the opinions of their authors and are not understood to represent the position of the American Society of Missiology or of the Editorial Committee. Selection is guided by such criteria as intrinsic worth, readability, coherence, and accessibility to a range of interested persons and not merely to experts or specialists.

The ASM Series, in collaboration with Orbis Books, seeks to publish scholarly works of high merit and wide interest on numerous aspects of missiology — the scholarly study of mission. Able presentations on new and creative approaches to the practice and understanding of mission will receive close attention.

The ASM Series Committee
JONATHAN J. BONK
ANGELYN DRIES, O.S.F.
SCOTT W. SUNQUIST

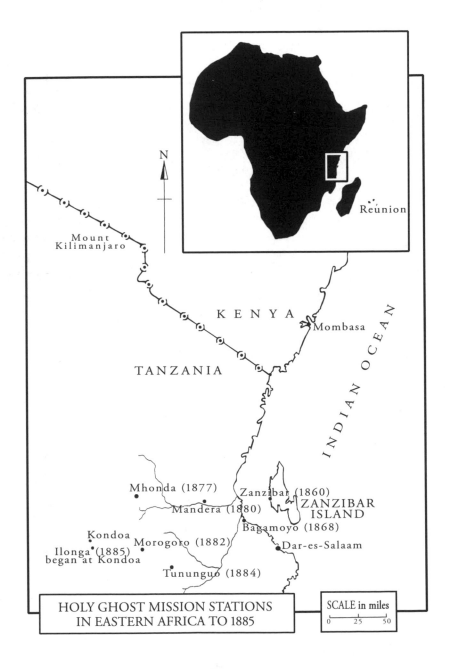

N

Reúnion

Mount
Kilimanjaro

K E N Y A

Mombasa

TANZANIA

I N D I A N   O C E A N

Mhonda (1877)   Zanzibar (1860)

Mandera (1880)   ZANZIBAR
ISLAND

Kondoa   Bagamoyo (1868)

Ilonga (1885)   Morogoro (1882)   Dar-es-Salaam
began at Kondoa

Tununguo (1884)

HOLY GHOST MISSION STATIONS
IN EASTERN AFRICA TO 1885

SCALE in miles

0   25   50

Preface

The twin steeples of St. Joseph Cathedral rise above Zanzibar's Stone Town as one approaches the island port aboard the ferry from Dar es Salaam, Tanzania's largest city. Along with the minarets of prominent mosques, the Anglican church's tower, and blocky administrative buildings abutting the shore, the Catholic cathedral, erected between 1897 and 1900, marks the skyline visible from the Indian Ocean. From within the town, however, the close, narrow lanes and alleys rarely afford any vantage of this place of worship of the first Catholic church in eastern Africa in modern history.[1] The confined thoroughfares of the Stone Town obscure the towers visible from the sea, so that the place eludes the pedestrian on the ground. Though conspicuous, even looming from a distance, the closer one gets physically to the church — locally referred to as *Minara Miwili*, Swahili for "twin towers" — the more it disappears. Photographs of the edifice's facade never quite come out right, for the cramped setting allows no proper view.

The first Catholic mission on the mainland of eastern Africa, Notre Dame de Bagamoyo, presents itself differently to the contemporary observer. The mission property lies a ten-minute walk from the town of Bagamoyo, alone and pristine, surrounded by orchards and fields of crops whose planting consumed the energies of the early missionaries and African Christians. The large buildings of the mission, many of which date from the late nineteenth century, lie at the end of a long, straight, mango tree–lined driveway that runs onto the church property from the road bordering the Indian Ocean. Compared to the Catholic mission at Zanzibar,[2] which sits nearly hidden in an ancient city's maze of streets, the mission at Bagamoyo is approachable and expansive. Open to view well outside of town, the mission inhabits a large compound filled with generously spaced buildings, organized agricultural plots of uniformly spaced coconut trees intercropped with other plants, and open pathways. Bagamoyo's spatial arrangement reflects a comprehensive vision that became the Catholic mission ideal in eastern Africa until well into the twentieth century. That ideal included an ample tract of land; formidable buildings in a clearly defined grid (or at least an open and

---

1. By modern eastern Africa I mean the area covered by the contemporary countries of Tanzania, Kenya, and Uganda since the end of the Portuguese presence in the early eighteenth century.

2. Zanzibar refers to three different overlapping realities, the names of which are often used interchangeably: the set of islands including Pemba and Unguja; the island also know as Unguja; and the largest town on that island.

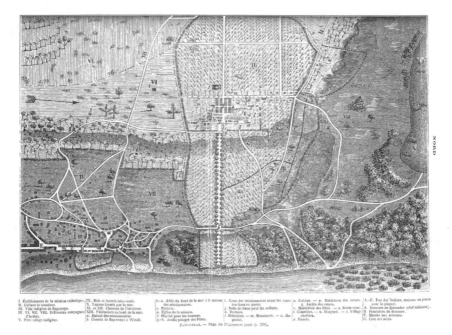

Figure 1. Bagamoyo mission plan from 1880. Originally appearing in *Les Missions Catholiques* 12 (1880): 343. The Indian Ocean shore is at the bottom of the page, and Bagamoyo town lies a ten-minute walk to the left, or south.

bounded area suitable for mapping, as in Figure 1); structured plots for agriculture; industrious Christians tilling the soil, and learning and living their faith in peace and harmony; the entirety overseen by heroic missionaries.

Today the relative quiet of the Catholic parish at Bagamoyo contrasts sharply with the imposing buildings, remnants of missionary ambitions from over a century ago. The large coral-and-stone structures dwarf those who frequent the parish. If Zanzibar's spatial paradox is that of distant prominence coupled with diminishing visibility the closer one gets to the cathedral building itself, Bagamoyo's paradox consists in the contrast between the scope of the architectural remains — reflecting a massive investment of personnel and resources, and once housing a thriving mission community — and the current, comparatively limited state of activity. A museum focusing on the mission's work and Bagamoyo's history attracts a steady stream of visitors,[3] and outlying mission chapels serve

3. The present church at Bagamoyo was built after World War I (Bayo and Nyaki, n.d.). Due to considerable investment, careful historical research, and adroit marketing, mostly by the Spiritans at the mission, over ten thousand people visit the museum each year, which was founded in 1964 but has been expanded considerably over the past four decades (Henschel 2001, 4). A guide to the museum has been published (Nyaki, n.d.), and numerous other pamphlets and periodicals have also appeared in recent years as part of the effort to expand Bagamoyo's profile. These build upon earlier substantial efforts by the museum's founder, Frits Versteijnen, CSSp (1930–92), who served as pastor in Bagamoyo from 1970 until his departure in the early 1990s and whose several publications are

fast-growing Catholic communities composed mainly of recent immigrants to the area. But the structural grandeur of the original mission shelters a comparatively small group of regular worshipers at the main church on the mission compound. Zanzibar, too, has few Catholics compared to the Muslims living nearby, but once in town the large church building recedes from one's vantage. Hence the contrast between previous prominence and the present size of the worshiping community strikes one less sharply than at Bagamoyo.

For the first forty years of their existence these missions stood at the center of the Catholic presence in eastern Africa. Europeans often entered the region via Zanzibar and admired the unselfish dedication of the Catholic missionaries there who ransomed slaves from the slave market (until its closure in 1873) and then sought to make them Catholics. Visitors lavished more fulsome praise still on the heralded Bagamoyo mission, a frequent stop on the trek inland for explorers, traders, military expeditions, and other missionaries. In terms similar to many others, one German admirer wrote in the early 1890s, "It may well be owing to this connection between religious instruction, ordered activity and a civilized life, that the French mission [as the Catholic effort was known, after the nationality of most of the missionaries there] is the only one of all proselytizing institutions here which can look back on real successes."[4] But in the twentieth century, and especially after World War I, the center of Catholic life in eastern Africa shifted away from the coast. Despite their longevity — they are the oldest ongoing Catholic parishes in Tanzania or any of the adjacent countries except Mozambique, with Zanzibar's mission founded in 1860 and Bagamoyo's in 1868 — these Catholic parishes today remain smaller than most others in modern eastern Africa.

The apparent decline in these missions has not gone unnoticed. In 1990, two British reporters preparing a documentary on missionaries for the BBC remarked that Bagamoyo, while evidence of "the grand pretensions and unbounded idealism with which the missionary priests set about their task," was at present "a melancholic place, a sad museum full of the mildewed relics of a more optimistic age . . . [and] a testament both to the romantic illusion and the harsh reality that characterised the missionary occupation of the continent."[5] A far cry, indeed, from the copious praise heaped on the Bagamoyo mission in the nineteenth century.

Most historical accounts of these missions have offered reasons for the small Christian presence in Bagamoyo and Zanzibar. Often invoked to explain the present-day minimal profile of these first places of Catholic evangelization in eastern Africa are the missionaries of the Congregation of the Holy Ghost, or

in the bibliography. Versteijnen's work in collecting and organizing documents and other records has been followed up by Theodore Winkelmolen, CSSp, at Bagamoyo and Morogoro, and later by John Henschel, CSSp, at Bagamoyo (his many works are also in the bibliography). Versteijnen and Winkelmolen appear, along with every other Spiritan who served in eastern Africa up to 1993, in the volume of short biographies by the late Henry Koren (Koren 1994, 437, 555). Henschel arrived later and thus is not included.

4. Cited in Brown 1971a, 209, n. 27. See also Versteijnen 1968a, 26.
5. Pettifer and Bradley 1990, 81–82.

Spiritans, priests and brothers who in 1863 assumed control of the Catholic mission originally founded in Zanzibar in 1860. These missionaries formulated a particular strategy of evangelizing slaves that has been blamed for the supposed lack of vitality of the Catholic Church at Zanzibar and Bagamoyo today. Thus the same British journalists who drew harsh conclusions from what they saw as Bagamoyo's late-twentieth-century seediness wrote:

> ...[F]or the Holy Ghost Fathers their involvement with former slaves dealt a fatal blow to their ambition to spread the faith along the East African coastline. The mission was too closely associated with slavery, and the Muslim population was anxious to distance themselves as far as possible from the slave population. They had no desire to become enmeshed with the new missionary guardians of the ex-captives.[6]

Perhaps the most celebrated recent example of this sort of assessment came from a later Holy Ghost priest who worked in another part of Tanzania a century after the first Spiritans began at Zanzibar. In *Christianity Rediscovered*, an inspiring account of his evangelization of the Maasai, the late Vincent Donovan began his story by criticizing as "sheer folly" the missionary strategy once enacted at Zanzibar and Bagamoyo. Donovan, an American, characterized his earlier confreres as obsessed with the problem of slavery:

> It is easy to understand the feeling of the missionaries who arrived on the scene in the last century, their concern with doing something about the system of slavery which was the cause of all these horrors. They did the only thing they could in the circumstances. They bought the slaves. They bought them left and right, with all the money they could get their hands on. They bought them by the hundreds and the thousands — and they christianized all they bought.

Donovan's verdict was harsh: "They were trying to build the church in the most artificial way imaginable...[and the] apostolate to the slaves had been a miserable failure."[7]

Donovan's assessment replicated the standard view of the Spiritan missionary strategy of evangelizing slaves in eastern Africa, one found already in the early twentieth century. This strategy, such arguments run, had some combination of the following unfortunate effects: it forced Christianity on the unwilling; created a church little prone to attract free peoples who saw Christianity tainted by such slaves; isolated new Christians from surrounding peoples by the creation of separate Christian villages; failed to create an indigenous clergy; or, because of its

---

6. Ibid., 82. Similar sentiments can be found in Sahlberg 1986, 52–53.
7. Donovan 1978, 5, 4. This classic work has gone through many printings and was reissued in 2003 in a 25th anniversary edition by Orbis Books.

paternalism, refused to give sufficient responsibility to the former slaves who became the first indigenous Christians, thus disillusioning them.[8]

This book tells the story of the Holy Ghost evangelization[9] of slaves, a central feature of the missionary strategy at the coast of eastern Africa from 1860 until the late 1880s. As will become clear, I believe that the conventional accounts of this strategy, epitomized by Donovan's views, overlook important parts of the historical record, thus often misrepresenting what the missionaries actually did. Such accounts and the judgments within them also fail to appreciate the situation facing the Spiritans in those years. Donovan's confident claim — "It is easy to understand the feelings of the missionaries who arrived on the scene in the last century" — typifies the common, and dubious, assumption that missionary perspectives are obvious, uncomplicated, and thus transparent to later observers. As a matter of fact, understanding the Spiritan strategy demands specific historical awareness that has eluded previous students of their missionary activity. Like the Africans they evangelized, these Holy Ghost missionaries differed from us — and from other missionaries of the nineteenth century — in important ways.

For one thing, *pace* Donovan, his confreres' earliest missionary efforts did not follow from a desire to "do something" about the horrors of slavery in Zanzibar. They recognized the suffering of those enslaved and sought to ameliorate it, but their purposes and practices with former slaves did not derive from a desire to ransom as many slaves as possible, nor from abolitionist sentiments. The missionaries' strategy derived from other purposes, purposes that are reflected in the spatial arrangements of the two missions at Zanzibar and Bagamoyo whose oddness once caught my eye. The evangelization of slaves was an essential part of the origins of the Catholic Church in eastern Africa, yet like Zanzibar's cathedral it later became hard to see clearly. At the same time, that strategy brought thousands to the Catholic mission at Bagamoyo, all the while with the expectation that the once-teeming mission would gradually become more vacant.

The Spiritan decision to evangelize slaves, and practices they enacted to do so, derived from an easily oversimplified background whose lineaments this book describes. Besides misrepresenting missionary goals, blaming the Spiritans for the small number of Catholics at their coastal missions fails to acknowledge their own quite explicit expectation that these first two missions would never amount

---

8. This strategy has been called *kitumwa* Christianity, from the Swahili word for "slavelike" or "slavish" (slave being *mtumwa*), to distinguish it from later methods (Pels 1999, 66f; Sahlberg 1986, 47f). By the early 1880s, the Spiritans in eastern Africa themselves were slightly apologetic in explaining their focus on slaves, probably frustrated by the fact that the Missionaries of Africa, or White Fathers, had moved with great acclaim to Uganda, leapfrogging the coast (MC 14 [1882], 194–95). Spiritan acknowledgment of the limits of their strategy in eastern Africa was quite overt by the early twentieth century (Walker 1933, 150–51; Ernoult 2000, 141; Sundkler and Steed 2000, 756), though sometimes they blamed colonialism or the damaged characters of the slaves who came to them (Le Roy 1906a, 2, 15ff; Le Roy 1934b, 47). For a later judgment of Spiritan paternalism, see Kieran 1971.

9. This book will use "evangelization" to name the entire process by which missionaries try to make Christians and build the church, aware that other authors prefer distinguishing mission and evangelization. For a discussion, see Bevans and Schroeder 2004, p. 400, n. 8.

to much in terms of numbers of Catholic Christians. They invested in Zanzibar and then Bagamoyo in order to form a restricted number of ex-slaves into Catholics who could colonize the interior, where they saw greater hopes. From the beginning they viewed these coastal missions not as ends in themselves. Rather they envisioned them as preparatory to the more fruitful work of evangelization anticipated inland from the Islamic world of the Swahili coast.

And from today's vantage, one could argue that the Spiritans who enacted this strategy appear more prescient than their critics. The Catholic Church's growth in eastern Africa makes even Donovan's sophisticated and compelling critiques of previous evangelization look outdated.[10] Without defending missionary practices of the past, the Catholics who pray at these places of the Catholic debut in the region worry little about conventional historical judgments. And the Spiritans and others serving the church at Zanzibar and Bagamoyo seem unconsumed by a need to blame their forebears. Tucked away within Zanzibar's maze of streets, and more prominent from afar than from up close, the Catholic mission has had more impact outside Zanzibar than within. Admittedly, Bagamoyo's large buildings dwarf its current parishioners, but the edifices played their foremost role by being grand and imposing a century ago and more. Moreover, new energy arises in both places, as appreciation of the missions' historical importance grows and Tanzania's population migrates.[11] With the Catholic Church burgeoning in eastern Africa today, the comparatively small congregations in these two oldest churches derive their identity from their locations within a still mostly Muslim coast *and* as part of a large and vital ecclesial community at whose origins they played a crucial role. Thus contemporary Catholics at Bagamoyo and Zanzibar feel little inclined to bemoan supposed missionary failures of the past.

If the conventional accounts misconstrue the Spiritan self-understanding of their task, they are crippled by an even more important failure given the subsequent history of Christianity in eastern Africa. Like most studies of missionary work in Africa, previous analyses of Spiritan evangelization have attended hardly at all to the African responses to early missionary strategy. Those responses laid the basis for the Catholic communities at Zanzibar, Bagamoyo, and other places in eastern Africa. Former slaves evangelized by the Spiritans became the first African Catholics since the eighteenth century.

---

10. Barrett et al. 2001; Buhlmann 1979.

11. For discussions of that new vitality, see the following: in *Pentecôte sur le monde* 783 (1999), articles entitled "Un futur de paix" ("A future of peace"), 16–17, which is about Zanzibar and the work of Spiritan bishop Augustine Shao, CSSp, and "Résurrection à Bagamoyo," 18–19; in *Pentecôte sur le monde* 793 (2000), see articles entitled "L'espoir renaît à Bagamoyo" ("Hope reborn at Bagamoyo"), 12–16, by Laurent Grzybowski, and "La liberté pas à pas" ("Freedom step by step"), 17–20, both about Bagamoyo; and *Écho de la Mission*, January–February 2001, articles entitled "Bagamoyo...les premiers 'Villages chrétiens' " ("Bagamoyo: the first Christian villages"), 4–5, and "Se frotter les épaules avec les musulmans: Entretien avec Mgr. Augustin Shao" ("Rubbing shoulders with Muslims: An interview with Bishop Augustin Shao"), 16–17. There have also been videos produced by the mission (Bagamoyo Catholic mission, n.d.; Holy Ghost Fathers, 2000). The establishment of a highly esteemed Catholic boarding secondary school for girls at Bagamoyo has also brought more activity to the mission there in the past few years.

This book describes the origins of the Catholic Church in eastern Africa, and especially the evangelization of slaves that stood at the center of the missionary strategy for the first few decades of the life of that church. It analyzes the interactions between a small group of European missionaries and the Africans they sought to change, portraying the distinctive views of those involved and the particular contexts in which they interacted. The book seeks to understand what the Spiritans did, why they chose to do what they did, how African onetime slaves responded to the Spiritans' missionary practices, and why they reacted in such ways, and considers what the consequences of these interactions were for the shape of the Catholic Church in eastern Africa. The spaces of the church at Zanzibar and Bagamoyo, each unusual in its own way, serve as starting points to pursue answers to these questions about the evangelization of slaves and Catholic origins in eastern Africa.

When I have described my project to others, I have been asked two types of questions. The first type addresses the genre of my effort and its disciplinary orientation; the second queries the subject matter itself. In answering both types of questions, I often find myself contesting the presuppositions behind them. For example, when asked if this study is historical, sociological, anthropological, or theological — or, in a more sophisticated version, when asked if it partakes in the history of religions (the discipline in which I was formed in graduate school), African history, historical anthropology, historical sociology, social history, mission history, or church history — I hesitate to respond. I do not mean to be elusive in refusing to pigeonhole the work; I merely believe that each of these labels has its own perspective, each has its own yield and limitations in appreciating particular aspects of the specific discourses and practices that I want to understand and portray.

A second set of questions concerns the subject matter, and these questions usually betray preconceptions about slavery or the history of the Catholic Church in eastern Africa that this study seeks to undermine, or at least make more complex. Thus I am often asked whether my subject is the Missionaries of Africa, better known as the White Fathers, who became the most famous Catholic missionary society in Africa beginning in the later nineteenth century. As I point out, the Missionaries of Africa, for all their achievements, did not found the church in eastern Africa, nor did they ever constitute a majority of Catholic missionaries working in Africa. Their founder, Cardinal Lavigerie (1825–92), however, masterfully positioned his missionary society into the forefront of international attention through his espousal of abolition and his Vatican machinations, thus increasing its renown.[12] By focusing here on the Spiritans and their earlier missionary efforts, I hope to redress an imbalance in the memories, knowledge, and understanding of many about the history of Christianity in eastern Africa, an

---

12. On Lavigerie, see Renault 1994. His missionary society, officially called the Missionaries of Africa, has long been called the White Fathers because of their habitual attire. There were also White Sisters under Lavigerie's leadership.

imbalance reflected as well in the normative historical works, especially those written in English. Though popular and scholarly perceptions easily recall the impressive work of the White Fathers, the Congregation of the Holy Ghost sent more missionaries to Africa than any other Catholic organization from 1860 to 1960. Moreover, certain places where they established the church (and often continue to serve) have among the strongest Catholic identities on the continent, and produce more vocations to religious life and priesthood than almost anywhere. They deserve better from the dominant historiography of Christianity in Africa.[13]

The questions I have received about slavery are even more common, and concern the status of those whom the Spiritans evangelized between 1863 and the late 1880s. I am often asked, were they free or were they slaves? Did the missionaries liberate them, or keep them as slaves of their own? Again, I usually answer yes, hoping to challenge the assumptions behind such questions. These assumptions are threefold at least: first, that free and slave were clearly understood categories in nineteenth-century eastern Africa and meant what they mean to us; second, that those categories operated as such within the consciousness of the missionaries; and third, that they were held as well by those whom the missionaries targeted for evangelization. As I show, such assumptions overlook the complex circumstances of this evangelization, reading back into the past a clarity that operates only with hindsight.

Though mostly admired in its day, Spiritan slave evangelization is not easy to defend from a contemporary perspective. Taking for granted as we do what philosopher Charles Taylor calls a "modern social imaginary," their strategy appears morally dubious on several counts.[14] First, their choice to evangelize slaves whom they did not unequivocally declare to be free is something that we would reflexively condemn today.[15] Even more troubling were the violent means by which they tried to keep control over those they evangelized, even after some of them sought to free themselves from missionary paternalism once they had grown older. It may be that Spiritan recourse to violence took place because they acted in a world that took for granted racist, ethnocentric, and colonialist prejudices to which they were not immune, prejudices that naturally resulted in actions that in retrospect look indefensible. It may, however, also have arisen

---

13. On the number of missionaries in Africa, see Bevans and Schroeder 2004, 223–24. The late Henry Koren told me this several years earlier. One measure of the historical amnesia about the Spiritan effort in eastern Africa is the absence of the first Spiritan superior at Zanzibar, Antoine Horner, as well as the first Catholic bishop in eastern Africa, Raoul de Courmont, from Gerald Anderson's *Biographical Dictionary of Christian Missions* (1999).

14. By "modern social imaginary," Taylor refers to the presumptions reflexively held by many today about the proper social order. These include the axioms that individuals form society for their own benefit, and that the order formed is meant to secure freedom and thus rejects any fixed social hierarchies. He distinguishes the social imaginary from social theory. The former is not elaborated with analytical language and is the common possession of many instead of the few, so that it is "that common understanding that makes possible common practices and a widely shared sense of [social] legitimacy" (C. Taylor 2004, 19–23).

15. Though, as John Noonan has so poignantly reminded us recently, slavery was practiced for millennia with scarcely any condemnation (2005, 17–123).

from contradictions within their practices themselves, something discussed in the conclusion. Regardless, such means are reprehensible from nearly every angle imaginable, and were condemned by the Spiritans themselves.[16] But the Spiritans were not alone in evangelizing slaves, nor in using coercive and violent means to control them.

Historical awareness of the reasons that they did objectionable things does not excuse the Spiritans, though it may soften the judgments that can come so easily with hindsight. I ask readers to bracket their possible indignation at what the Spiritans did with the recognition that these men operated in a time different from ours, when the actions that arouse our misgivings faced condemnation from very few.

To bracket indignation is not to ignore it, but only to set it aside for the time being. The goal here is not to forego moral evaluation, but to keep it from blinding us to the past. Historical research must be wary of reflexive moral judgments, for they can block the empathy and fellow feeling that can be a hallmark of good historical understanding. Yet the historical research undertaken here, by someone who is also a theologian, does not attempt simply to describe the past without judging it. Along with being historical, this book is self-consciously also missiological inasmuch as it attempts to discern matters of right and wrong from a theological perspective about this piece of the Christian past. Its efforts to do theology with this historical work are mostly bracketed until the conclusion, and throughout I attempt to sharpen the historical edge as a way into the subject, allowing a firmer theological appropriation.[17]

This effort to tell the story of the origins of Catholic Christianity in eastern Africa is not undertaken to defend or indict missionary practices of the past. The hope is to understand the actions here described, both from the perspectives of those involved and in light of their broader significance for Christianity in Africa.

---

16. Their own "second founder," Libermann, condemned violence by missionaries, and later the first bishop of Zanzibar, a Spiritan, forbade the use of violence in the missions (Burke 1998, 50ff; CSSp 195vi: Courmont, circular letter of 1892).

17. I agree with these words of the South African historian and theologian John de Gruchy:

Historians and theologians need each other. Historians seek to establish the way things were and why; theologians are concerned to go beyond the "what" to how things should be. In their different ways both should therefore address the fundamental question, "So what?" If they do not, then the danger of theologians trying to count the number of angels able to dance on a pinhead is likely to be equaled by that of historians trying to recover information about their names.... I am convinced that theologians must endeavor to be good historians in order to do theology. The reverse may often also be true. For those of us with a contemporary concern for the mission of the church, and therefore who regard missiology as a focal point in doing theology, the need for historians and theologians to be engaged in critical dialogue becomes essential. We need to be rooted in the concreteness of history, both past and contemporary, yet exploring the horizons of what should and must yet be (de Gruchy 2003, 225).

Thomas Spear, a historian of Africa, has analogously downplayed the contrasts between theological and secular approaches to the history of Christianity in Africa: "As plain as these differences are [between academic and church history], however, they are ultimately differences of faith and do not intrude on our common concerns for understanding the historical development of Christianity in Africa" (Spear 1999, 20).

The telling is also more concerned with understanding those Catholic origins than with following the normative canons of any single discipline or subdiscipline in the contemporary academic regime. I believe that combined insights from many disciplines can help overcome what E. P. Thompson once called "the enormous condescension of posterity,"[18] something so easy in studies of either missionary activity or slavery. Such condescension is a particular temptation in a study of missionary activity with slaves.

---

18. E. P. Thompson 1968, 13.

Acknowledgments

This book originated as a dissertation in the history of religions at the University of Chicago Divinity School, where I was a student from 1993 to 2001. I owe profound gratitude to the members of my dissertation committee: Frank Reynolds, who served as the chair; Wendy Doniger; John Comaroff; and Martin Riesebrodt. I could not have asked for more supportive and helpful advisors and mentors. Not only are all four superb scholars whose insights improved my scholarship and this text, but they have been generous to me personally as well. Other faculty at the University of Chicago who were of considerable assistance include Ralph Austen, Jean Comaroff, Gary Ebersole, Clark Gilpin, Bruce Lincoln, Stephanie Paulsell, Kathryn Tanner, and David Tracy. I have also benefited from other members of the Divinity School, especially Richard Rosengarten (now dean) and Sandy Norbeck.

In the conceiving and writing of the dissertation and then this book I received financial and academic support from many sources, for each of which I am most grateful. I first learned about the Holy Ghost mission in eastern Africa because of a Foreign Language Area Study fellowship from the U.S. government to study KiSwahili in Zanzibar and Tanzania in the summer of 1995. In support of that language and research trip, I also received assistance from an International House foreign study grant from the University of Chicago. In 1998–99 I was a recipient of a fellowship from what was then the Institute for the Advanced Study of Religion at the University of Chicago Divinity School (now the Martin Marty Center for the Study of Religion). In 1999–2000 I was awarded a fellowship from the Lilly Endowment for Theological and Religious Education at the University of Chicago Divinity School. As part of the Lilly fellowship I taught a course at Catholic Theological Union in Chicago, where I appreciated the still-ongoing mentorship and friendship of Stephan Bevans, SVD. I also received a fellowship from the Erasmus Institute of the University of Notre Dame for 2000–2001, during which I completed my dissertation. I later received financial assistance for research travel from the Institute for Scholarship in the Liberal Arts from the University of Notre Dame. I also thank the College of Arts and Letters at the University of Notre Dame for a leave granted during the academic year 2004–5, during which I completed this manuscript.

I have been fortunate to meet scholars of religion and related topics with whom to discuss my work, and I have presented aspects of my work, much to its betterment, in the following settings: the African Studies Workshop at the University of Chicago; the English Department, the Erasmus Institute, and the Africa Working Group, all of the University of Notre Dame; at the annual meeting of the Midwest Professors of Missiology in Chicago, November 2001; at a conference entitled "Christianity and Indigenous Cultures" at St. Mary's College, Notre Dame, Indiana; at a panel on inculturation at the American Academy of Religion in Toronto; and finally at a conference on the option for the poor at the University of Salzburg. From these various fora, I would particularly like to thank the following: Jon Schofer, Valentina Izmirlieva, Hilda Koster, Hans Kippenberg, Greg Grieve, Hylton White, Mikael Karlstrom, Michael Peletz, Patrick Provost-Smith, Nicholas Creary, Kristin Schwain, Robert Sullivan, Ogbu Kalu, Emily Osborn, Clemens Sedmak, and James Turner.

In writing this book and the dissertation that preceded it, I have relied on the hospitality and assistance of people and institutions in many places, for which I am very grateful. Permission for research and travel in Tanzania was granted by COSTECH, which organizes research in the country. I thank Professor Joseph Safari and Professor Nestor Luanda of the University of Dar es Salaam, the latter of whom served as my official liaison in Tanzania under the auspices of COSTECH. I was also made welcome at the Zanzibar archives. Former vice-chancellor of the University of Dar es Salaam, Professor Daniel Mkude, was also very generous in helping me understand historical issues around Bagamoyo and accompanying me there for a visit.

Most importantly, members of the Congregation of the Holy Ghost on three continents have been most supportive, and this book would not have been possible without their hospitality and cooperation. In Paris, the archives of the Congregation at Chevilly were made available to me by the generous assistance of the late Father Ghislain de Banville, CSSp, in 1996, and the more recent help of his successor, Father Gérard Vieira, CSSp, as well as the director of the Spiritan photograph archives, Geneviève Karg. I also thank the Spiritan community at Chevilly for their welcome to me, despite my halting French.

In Zanzibar and Bagamoyo, I wish to thank the clergy, staff, and people at St. Joseph Cathedral, Zanzibar, and the Catholic mission at Bagamoyo, Our Lady of Bagamoyo. I interviewed some of them, and they were most open and helpful. These included Mzee Barnabas Mkuku of Zanzibar, and from Bagamoyo, the following: Mzee Michael Misheli, Mzee Ferdinand Petro, Mzee Michael Joseph Kabelewa, Mzee Damas Francis, Bibi Leonia Richardi, Bibi Sofia State, Mzee Joseph Ignasio ("Mzee Fisi"), and Bibi Faustina Innocent. Other Spiritans who were supportive in Zanzibar and Bagamoyo included Bishop Augustine Shao, CSSp, and Fathers Valentine Bayo, CSSp, and Jason Ishengoma, CSSp. Of particular help at Bagamoyo were Spiritans priests Daniel Bouju, CSSp, and John Henschel, CSSp. And Father Bouju has been helpful many times since.

Other communities in Tanzania have also given me hospitality and assistance. These include the residence of the Missionaries of Africa in Dar es Salaam, Atiman House, where I was often given a warm welcome. In Morogoro, Tanzania,

Father Theodore Winkelmolen, CSSp, was helpful with food, wit, and wisdom, as well as his house for researching his carefully preserved documents, most of them now at the main congregational archives in Chevilly, Paris. I was also welcomed at the residence of Bishop Telesphor Mkude in Morogoro. Particular help was rendered by the Catholic community at Mhonda in the diocese of Morogoro, especially its then-pastor, the late Father Francis Malati, and his assistant Father James Mpekamoto. I was also able to interview Christians at Mhonda, including Emmanuel Teodori and wife Elizabeth Augusti Nyagwa; Morisi Alberti Msemwa, John Anthony Mzee Kangwati, and the very helpful Ferdinand Nicolas Kabelwa.

Finally, the Holy Ghost archives in Bethel Park, Pennsylvania, have also opened themselves to me, thanks to the kindness of the late Father Henry Koren, CSSp, the able and courteous former director there. I am grateful for him and his confreres for their openhearted hospitality, for the assistance of Virginia Sedor in facilitating my visits, and also to the Spiritan community at Duquesne University, where I stayed when I examined Spiritan materials on microfilm.

I have appreciated the assistance of librarians at the following places: the University of Chicago; the University of Notre Dame (especially Kenneth Kinslow); the University of California, Berkeley; the Graduate Theological Union, Berkeley; and the Billy Graham Center at Wheaton College, Wheaton, Illinois.

Others have read parts of this text and offered helpful comments. These include the following: David Burrell, CSC; Michael Griffin; Joseph Healey, MM; Anita Houck; Carita Kollman; Wilson Miscamble, CSC; Michael Rossmann, Jeff Schneibel, CSC; Pat Gaffney, CSC; and in particular Ken Kollman, Emily Osborn, and Daniel I Issing, CSC.

My friend Jane Pitz shared her artistic ability and technical skill to produce the cover and the map, and to help scan and prepare the photos and drawings. I appreciate her help and her support.

Thanks as well to the communities that have been such warm homes for me since I began my doctoral work at the University of Chicago, where I lived at the house of formation of the Society of the Divine Word in Chicago and then at St. Thomas the Apostle Catholic Church. Later I lived in communities of my own religious order, the Congregation of Holy Cross: André House, in Jinja, Uganda; Moreau Seminary, at the University of Notre Dame; and Holy Cross Center, Berkeley, California. In each place I have been made to feel very welcome.

Finally, I thank most heartily the USA East Province of the Congregation of the Holy Ghost, which generously offered a subvention for the publication of this book. Anthony Gittins, CSSp, was helpful in this endeavor, which was approved by several provincials. I thank, too, my editor, William Burrows, who has been most generous in accepting this book for publication and assisting in the process at every stage.

Abbreviations

See the explanation of how citations of the various archives are used in references at the beginning of the bibliography on p. 293.

AA	*Annales Apostoliques de la Congrégation du Saint-Esprit et du Saint Coeur de Marie*
APF	*Les Annales de l'Association de la Propagation de la Foi*
BG	*Bullétin Général de la Congrégation du Saint-Esprit et du Saint Coeur de Marie*
CSSp	Holy Ghost Archives, Chevilly, Paris
LERE	*Livre des Enfants Rachetés de l'Esclavage.* Bagamoyo mission, 1884–94
MC	*Les Missions Catholiques* (Lyon)
MS	*Mémoire Spiritaine*
ND	*Notes et Documents relatives à la Vie et à l'Oeuvre de Vénérable François-Marie-Paul Libermann, Supérieur Général de la Congrégation du Saint-Esprit et du Saint Coeur de Marie*
TNR	Tanganyika Notes and Records
UMCA	Annual reports of the Universities' Mission to Central Africa, 1860–1900

Figure 2. St. Joseph Cathedral, Zanzibar. Photo by author.

Chapter One

Introduction

Disclosures: An Unnerving Appeal, an Anxious Guideline, a Revealing Memory

In 1883, serious worries consumed a group of missionaries in eastern Africa. They were Spiritans, priests and brothers belonging to the Congregation of the Holy Ghost, the religious order that had spearheaded Catholic evangelization in the region for two decades. Now that effort and their missionary strategy faced unprecedented challenges. They were uneasy.

From the outside, the program of evangelization envisioned since the mission's founding in 1860 seemed to be unfolding as planned. The move from the first mission on the island of Zanzibar to the coastal mainland at Bagamoyo in 1868 and from there to other stations in the interior of present-day Tanzania by 1882 had apparently proceeded smoothly, and Spiritans staffed five missions in eastern Africa. European admirers gushed over the orderliness of these missions, often viewed as islands of civilization and proper religious observance in a sea of savagery and paganism. The foremost Catholic mission periodical of its day, *Les Missions Catholiques*, in its annual overview of Catholic missionary activity at the beginning of 1882 saluted "the model Christendom [or Christianity] of Notre Dame de Bagamoyo, nursery of several Catholic villages." It described the missionary work there and the rest of the ecclesiastical region of *Zanguebar* — as the district was known in the Latinized terms of official Catholic discourse — as honoring the church and France.[1]

Such praise notwithstanding, the priests and brothers on the ground knew something was wrong. The behavior of the Christians of these stations, whose formation had been the mission's preoccupation since its inauguration, worried the missionaries. At Zanzibar, Bagamoyo, and the interior stations these African Catholics, almost all of whom had once been slaves, were failing to live up to Spiritan hopes. They chafed at the restrictions on their behavior and complained that they were not paid for their labor. They often refused to carry out their expected work for the mission. Escapes from the missions, almost unheard of

---

1. MC 14 (1882), 1–4.

before the move from Zanzibar to Bagamoyo in 1868 and rare in the late 1870s, grew rampant.[2]

One of the events most disturbing to the missionaries occurred in early 1883. Two men who resided at the Christian village located at Mhonda, the first Catholic mission established inland from the coast in 1877, had escaped the mission and fled to Zanzibar. There these former slaves, Léon Matelala and an unnamed companion, wrote a letter to the French consul asking for what the missionaries called "liberty."[3] The two villagers, prominent African Catholics of the first generation in eastern Africa, no doubt wanted some enhancement of their situation, and they represented the other villagers as they made their appeal. In doing so, Léon and his companion chose to go over the heads of the social authorities closest to their day-to-day lives, the Spiritan missionaries. Yet unlike most eastern Africans, including protesting slaves, they did not appeal to the sultan of Zanzibar, the obvious political overlord at the coast.[4] They invoked instead the French consul, who had little formal power at the coast. He did share, however, the nationality of most of the missionaries who ran the Catholic community to which they belonged, which apparently in their eyes made him the proper recipient of their complaint. Their appeal to him showed that they thought of themselves as Catholics (and maybe, by implication, French, a language that Léon certainly spoke) and thus worthy of the attention of the French consul. They saw the consul as someone who could potentially override missionary refusal to respond to their demands.

Father Amandus Acker (1848–1923), then local superior at Zanzibar, admitted that the question raised by the appeal was most painful and full of dangers for the future of the mission. This "black spot," as he called it, fortunately occurred while the man who was consul "valued dearly the French influence of our missions in the interior." The consul thus ordered the two escapees returned to Mhonda. This set what Acker described as a very fortunate precedent: "Thanks, therefore, to his decision, the children know that upon arriving at the consulate they will be returned to the mission." Acker recognized the threat the appeal to the consul represented. Under another consul, he felt, these former slaves might have been accorded what he referred to dismissively as "rights," and the missionaries would have faced a general debacle in the mission stations.

Acker's evident relief at the consul's actions disclosed the anxieties felt by the mostly French Spiritans, who viewed the appeal with alarm. This alarm

---

2. As we shall see in chapter 4, there were also a number of escapes in 1873. The later unrest is discussed more fully in chapter 5. For escapes in 1883 see the following: Bagamoyo journal, 12i83, 2ii83, 27vi83, 1vii83, 3vii83, 25vii83, 6viii83, 12ix83, 20x83, 22x83, 23x83, 25x83, 27x83, 28xii83; Mhonda journal, 15xii82, 8iii83.

3. Mhonda journal, 15xii82; CSSp 197ai: Acker to Emonet, 21ii83; ibid., Baur to Emonet, 26iv83; ibid., Machon to Emonet, 13vi83. For a brief discussion, see Kieran 1966, 122. The other Christian might have been Adrian, who fled Mhonda not long after Léon, then returned from Zanzibar in mid-January with a note from the superior, which might well have informed the Mhonda mission of the escapees' actions (Mhonda journal, 22xii82, 16i83).

4. Glassman 1995, 111.

stemmed from two realities. First, their missionary hopes looked increasingly fragile since their new Catholics seemed so fickle. Second, the actions of these Africans threatened to undermine their sometimes tangled relationship with the French diplomatic presence in Zanzibar. The appeal to the consul also, however, indicated something about those who made the appeals. It showed that these two African Catholics had appropriated aspects of the evangelization the missionaries provided even as they refused simply to acquiesce to missionary expectations. After all, they thought of themselves as *able* to appeal to the French consul because of who they were, and also believed they would likely receive a hearing. Besides typifying the unrest at the Christian villages in the 1880s, the appeal thus also points toward the complex identity forged in these African Christians, an identity that eluded the missionaries' self-conscious goals.

The appeal of Léon and his unnamed companion was one of many incidents that disturbed the Spiritans in the 1880s.[5] The missionaries reacted to what was perceived as African obduracy with fear, frustration, racial denigrations, and even violence. Anxiety and anger filled the correspondence and journal entries of 1883 and 1884, as the missionaries pondered a precarious future for their beloved enterprises. In August 1883, after more than twenty escapes already that year from the Bagamoyo mission, one missionary asked, "When will these frequent escapes end?" Several months later the same chronicler remarked that the ongoing mutinies raised fears about the viability of the mission. Another Spiritan said that Mhonda, the mission from where Léon had fled, felt like a prison.[6]

Along with these laments about the mission's state and tenuous future appeared blanket condemnations of the African character, denunciations much more severe than judgments made twenty years before when the Spiritans had first arrived in eastern Africa. The missionaries drew increasingly on racial characterizations to explain the supposed ingratitude of these ex-slaves. They elaborated the deleterious effects of "the curse of Ham" — the supposed consequences of the sin by Noah's son Ham described in the book of Genesis, sometimes ascribed to Africans who were prototypically seen as Ham's descendants[7] — that afflicted the ex-slaves at their missions. They also relied more than before on physical force to keep the Christians in their villages. They built prisons, secured gates, hunted down those who had fled, and flogged repeat offenders.[8]

Yet the missionaries did more than grumble and crack down before the perceived defiance of these African Christians; they also reconsidered their strategy. They were led to this reconsideration by their difficulties, but also by a change in status for their mission. For 1883 was both a year of crisis for the Spiritans and also the year when their mission achieved the status of an apostolic vicariate,

---

5. We discuss Léon again in chapter 5.
6. Bagamoyo journal, 6viii83, 22x83; CSSp 197ai: Machon to Emonet, 13vi83.
7. Genesis 9:20–26. On the origins of this idea, see Goldenberg 2003.
8. These measures are described in chapter 5.

the equivalent of a Catholic diocese in mission territory. In November, Propaganda Fide[9] first named a bishop to the region. The accession to episcopal office of Raoul de Courmont (1841–1925), a Spiritan, led to a number of reports on the state of the mission. In order to understand his new responsibility, Courmont relied especially on the opinions of Alexandre Le Roy (1854–1938), a Spiritan priest who had first arrived in Zanzibar in December 1881. Le Roy was in Paris recovering from an illness before returning to the mission when he met the new soon-to-be-bishop preparing to assume his new assignment.[10] Le Roy, later a prominent intellectual and churchman,[11] prepared several reports during this period.

Struck by the difficulties he and his confreres faced at their missions, Le Roy decided to rethink aspects of the Holy Ghost missionary strategy. One report requested by Bishop Courmont concerned the Christian villages, where Léon and the other village had fled from, and where other serious disruptions had occurred. To remedy the situation, Le Roy suggested revisions in the organization of the villages, emphasizing their necessary evolution toward independence from missionary control and offering strategies to encourage responsibility and self-sufficiency among the Christian households there.[12]

In the midst of introducing his opinions about the proper evolution of such villages, Le Roy makes a revealing point about the journey from Bagamoyo to a new interior site:

> An important remark about what is to be done. From the time that the children [as the former slaves were called: *les enfants*] leave the orphanage [in Bagamoyo] in order to go found a village [in the interior], the missionary who directs them must allow *no lapse* in their habits of regularity and piety: in the caravan, at the station the prayers will be made, the sacraments practiced, etc. [emphasis in the original][13]

In the background of Le Roy's guideline lies the comprehensive missionary strategy of the Spiritans in eastern Africa until the late 1880s. For three decades, the Spiritans sought to form freed slaves at the coast, first at Zanzibar and later at

---

9. Propaganda Fide was the office that organized Catholic missionary activity since 1622, taking responsibility for mission areas not covered by other papal arrangements. Since the fifteenth century, the Spanish and Portuguese monarchies had their own accords with the Vatican, called the *patronato* or *padraodo*, that gave them authority over the church's activity in their territories.

10. Courmont was ordained a bishop in December in Paris and arrived in Zanzibar with Le Roy on March 23, 1884 (Koren 1994, 65; BG 13:260). Le Roy had left Zanzibar after being hospitalized with ophthalmia, an inflammation of the eyes, probably caused by the sun (Zanzibar journal, 12iv83, 6v83).

11. Le Roy was the first chairman of the history of religions at L'Institute Catholique in Paris and spoke on his then forthcoming book, *La Religion des Primitifs* (1909), during a series of lectures there in 1907 (BG 24:412). Further discussion of Le Roy appears in chapters 5 and 6.

12. CSSp 391aiii: Le Roy 1883; CSSp 196ax: Le Roy to Propagation of the Faith, 15ix83; CSSp 195v: Le Roy 1884.

13. CSSp 391aiii. Translations from French, German, and Swahili are mine unless otherwise noted.

Bagamoyo, before settling them in the interior at new stations. The missionaries envisioned these ex-slaves as colonizers of the interior, a nucleus of dependable Catholics around whom they would then build up the church by attracting the surrounding people to the prosperity and good order of the mission. Because of their importance, the missionaries set their sights on doing all they could to make these onetime slaves into the best Catholics possible. That process began at the coast, but Le Roy drew attention to the environment during the journey to the interior stations as well.

A central feature of Spiritan strategy is revealed in Le Roy's emphatic caution to "allow no lapse in their habits of regularity and piety." From the beginning, the key to the evangelization of freed slaves was not considered by the Spiritans the message they tendered, a message that could then be refused or accepted. Instead, slave evangelization was a social experience or embracing environment to be imposed or fostered, an environment that required constant maintenance. Le Roy's emphasizing was most telling about the sociological assumptions within Spiritan strategy.

Le Roy's directive also betrayed contradictory assumptions about that strategy. In the first place, Le Roy assumed that a certain change in the Africans had already been effected at Bagamoyo, the station at the coast where the Spiritans moved the bulk of their mission beginning in 1868 and from where the caravans to establish interior missions originated. Léon and many others had helped compose those caravans after years at Bagamoyo, and Le Roy presumed that changes in these early African Catholics had occurred at least partially because of the missionary environment there. Compared to the original mission site on Zanzibar, which lacked land for an agricultural project and where the heavily Islamized milieu supposedly threatened the faith of the new Christians, the Spiritans considered Bagamoyo a better site for the "cultivation of the land, as well as the hearts and minds" of the mission's children.[14] There on the mainland coast the Spiritans developed an agricultural showpiece at their mission with more than one hundred species under cultivation, many of which were then transplanted to other missions.[15] Yet not only plants were transplanted after successfully sprouting; Bagamoyo was called a *jardin d'acclimation* (or horticultural nursery) for people, too. It was also likened to a beehive, from where "swarms" would emerge to colonize the interior of Africa.[16] The guideline to "allow no lapse" in prayerful habits indicated Spiritan confidence that these ex-slaves had already changed under missionary tutelage to become a suitable swarm of bees ready for a new hive or thriving fresh shoots ready for transplanting. Something had happened to make them proper colonists for the Catholic Africa the Spiritans hoped to

---

14. Zanzibar journal, 10xii68.

15. BG 11:717. For a discussion of the crops cultivated at Bagamoyo, see Vogt, n.d. and Kieran 1966, 406–27.

16. CSSp 196axi: Courmont to Propagation of the Faith, 2x84; CSSp 194ai: Marras 31x86: BG 14:643ff; CSSp 196ax: Le Roy to Propagation of the Faith, 15ix83.

construct. This process had taken place in the space and time marked out by the mission at Bagamoyo, and the change was for the better.

Yes, Léon and many others had changed. But besides implying missionary optimism, Le Roy's guideline also betrayed the cautious voice of missionary realism in its wariness about the reality and permanence of the change. Lurking as well was the shadow of missionary failure, embodied in the escape and appeal of Léon and his companion. Le Roy worried that the "cultivation" acquired was fragile, so that the arduous journey from the coast to the interior could potentially undo the process already achieved.

Le Roy's emphasis shouts: "This must not be allowed to happen!"

Instead, the missionaries needed to buttress these still-fragile products of Bagamoyo's carefully shaped space and time with an uninterrupted regularity in life — especially in liturgical practice — during the caravan journey to the new station. The environment that had formed the future Catholic colonizers at Bagamoyo must, he insisted, become portable. It must not unravel. Catholic liturgical and devotional life, he added later in the same report, must continue to attack "the superstitious and materialist spirit of *les noirs* and [keep them directed toward] God and the truth." According to Le Roy, the missionaries should strive to make the Christian life natural and internalized among the Christians, eventually obviating the need for external oversight. But they were not there yet.

This book examines the first decades of Spiritan missionary work in eastern Africa, when they largely evangelized freed slaves. As Le Roy's guideline suggested, missionary processes geared toward formation of freed slaves depended upon control of space and time so that in the arena of evangelization there would be no lapse in the embracing environment of the mission. The Spiritans wanted their mission to be a constant environment impinging upon the Africans they evangelized. The escape and appeal of Léon and his companion, along with the other unrest at the Catholic missions in the 1880s that generated Le Roy's guidelines, indicated that African responses to such formative processes did not always fulfill the missionaries' hopes. And in a conversation over a century later, I learned that aspects of the missionary strategy still lingered in the memories of present-day Catholics in the region.

I was at Bagamoyo speaking with two now-elderly granddaughters of the first generation of African Catholics in eastern Africa, when I heard an echo of the earlier Spiritan strategy. While we shelled beans together, Bibi Leonia Richardi and Bibi Sofia State discussed their parents and grandparents. As they remembered their forebears, among whom most had been slaves, these two women bemoaned the loss of *utawa* at the mission in Bagamoyo. I was puzzled, for I knew that the Swahili word *utawa* referred to the experience of the cloister for those aspiring to be members of Catholic religious communities in modern eastern Africa. But these women had not said they had once wanted to be sisters. It became clear that they used the word to designate not formation to become nuns, but to name their own experiences of boarding school during their childhood at the mission.

Utawa was the local term for the enclosure or cloistering that existed in missionary practices of education in the 1930s for boarders. These women spoke as if it had deep roots in local Catholic experience. Their use of *utawa* was the historical remnant of Le Roy's anxious "allow no lapse" during his suggested reforms from the 1880s. Unlike Léon and his fellow escapee, these latter-day African Catholics embraced this strategy, or at least valued it in hindsight to the extent of lamenting its passing.[17]

Le Roy's guidelines and the appeal to the French consul by the escapees from Mhonda occurred twenty years into the Spiritans' evangelization in eastern Africa. *La Congrégation du Saint-Esprit et du Saint-Coeur de Marie*, the Congregation of the Holy Ghost and the Holy Heart of Mary, like other Christian communities — including Methodists, Quakers, Lutherans, different groups of Anglicans, as well as other Catholics like the Missionaries of Africa — sought to establish Christianity in the region by evangelizing slaves in the later nineteenth and early twentieth centuries.[18] Beginning in 1863, these mainly French missionaries sought to save souls and establish the church in this unevangelized area. To this end they gathered potential church members by ransoming slaves, taking in the abandoned, and receiving once-captive slaves from Europeans who had freed them from slave-ships and slave-caravans. To forestall the anticipated eternal punishment of those they encountered, they tried to baptize and convert the dying as well as those whose death was not imminent. They changed the landscape by building churches; organizing agricultural colonies; running workshops for industrial training; and establishing Christian villages, schools, and hospitals They sought the transformation of African consciousness and habits by planning and carrying out elaborate liturgies and other devotional practices, learning and codifying indigenous languages, confronting African customary practices, educating Africans old and young, mediating local disputes, and training future church leaders. In these efforts the Spiritans faced complicated and changing political and ecclesiastical circumstances that created conflicting demands from a number of different authorities. They suffered financial pressures that forced them repeatedly to raise money at their missions, as well as to advertise their needs and legitimate their activity in order to continue the flow of funds. And they were plagued by frequent ill health and occasional natural disasters. These formidable obstacles did not prevent them from undertaking a variety of works in their efforts to make Catholics out of the Africans they sought to evangelize.

These three anecdotes — Léon's appeal, Le Roy's guidelines, and the lamenting of *utawa*'s end by two contemporary Catholics — are episodes in the

---

17. Interviews with Bibi Leonia Richardi and Bibi Sofia State, Bagamoyo, August 2, 1998. Le Roy wrote some time after 1928 that many of the missions had moved away from the strategy of *utawa* (CSSp 420a: Le Roy, n.d.).

18. No single volume covers the evangelization of slaves in eastern Africa. For summaries see the relevant sections in the following: W. B. Anderson 1977; Oliver 1952; Nwulia 1975; Hastings 1994; J. Baur 1994; Isichei 1995; Sundkler and Steed 2000. On Anglican slave evangelization, see Strayer 1978; Small 1980; Reed 1997. On later Quaker efforts, see Newman 1898.

historical processes that this book describes. Only the first two took place directly within the span to be depicted here, roughly from 1860 to the late 1880s. And both Le Roy's reforms and Léon's appeal occurred in the 1880s, toward the end of the story. By that time the evangelization of slaves was about to leave the center of Spiritan strategy, having run its course. The book seeks to make comprehensible their (and similar) actions by Africans and Europeans in the 1880s by depicting the processes that led up to them, processes in which missionaries and freed slaves were both active participants. Besides looking back from those events of the 1880s to understand the historical forces making them comprehensible, this story also looks *forward* from them to understand their longer-term significance for Christianity in Africa.

In the history of Christianity in Africa, slave evangelization was an important, if rather short-lived missionary strategy. Its importance has not always been recognized, likely due to moral misgivings and because it ended in the colonial period. This has meant overlooking, to a great extent, the beginnings of the church in eastern Africa. Slave evangelization generated African Catholics whose responses to evangelization and whose evolving identities fundamentally determined the unfolding Christian life enacted at the missions and continuing into the present life of the church.

In the midst of portraying the story of the evangelization of slaves and the beginnings of the Catholic Church in eastern Africa, this book makes points about the missionary strategy and the way that strategy was received. First, it shows that the slave evangelization carried out by Holy Ghost missionaries was not an attempt at *conversion* aimed at individuals sharing a particular *culture*. The Spiritans evangelized slaves who shared no common culture, and they sought to form them from childhood, not convert them as adults. From such slaves the Spiritans tried to create new persons and communities through control of the environment and practical activities designed for formation and transformation. Their practices relied upon particular theological and sociological assumptions, and they attached special importance to the organization of space, time, and labor. They sought to reshape individuals, and yet at the same time they also tried to construct the church as fully as possible. Over time, contradictions in their strategy between their theological impulses and the sociological roots of their practices showed themselves, thus revealing a very distinctive, and in practice unwieldy, nineteenth-century Catholic approach to freedom and subjectivity. Those contradictions were only exacerbated by their decision to evangelize slaves in the context of eastern Africa between 1860 and the beginning of colonial overrule.

Second, African responses to that evangelization likewise did not depend on their culture — as that term is normally understood — nor on their acceptance or refusal of conversion. Those evangelized entered the missions as slaves and often as children, and they could not help but be deeply affected by missionary practices directed at them. In fact, the mission helped create an identity in them. Yet missionary attempts to form them did not always have the results the missionaries envisioned, for the Africans at the Spiritan missions appropriated missionary practices on their own terms as they sought to enhance their lives in the broader world of nineteenth-century eastern Africa. African responses to evangelization exposed the contradictions in the Spiritan strategy. In addition, they responded with collective protests in the 1880s that marked an important historical achievement: the emergence of a shared identity as Catholics evangelized by the Spiritans. Though these and other African responses to slave evangelization often frustrated the missionaries, many became Catholics and thus their reactions marked the beginning of the Catholic Church in the region.

Making sense of slave evangelization requires understanding those engaged in it and the circumstances they faced. It demands a respect for the Africans whom eager missionaries tried to change and the Europeans who sought to do the changing, as well as the dynamic conditions under which they met and interacted. This is not the first study of missionary activity in Africa to attempt this kind of understanding, yet certain features of slave evangelization make this a privileged subject for the appreciation of certain normally underappreciated realities.

First, attention to slave evangelization allows unprecedented insights into nineteenth-century French Catholic missionary practices and their roots in European social traditions. The distinctive strategy pursued by the Spiritans derived from precise historical circumstances and reflected a revealing mixture of theological and sociological currents to which they were exposed. In particular, their evangelization drew upon practices and discourses operative in European juvenile reformatories, something not before recognized.

Second, this effort to understand the experiences of evangelized slaves charts a new approach to the relationship between missionary practices and resulting African Christian identities. Léon was neither the first nor last former slave whose way of being a Catholic frustrated the Spiritans. This book seeks to interpret an admittedly spotty and problematic historical record to understand how Africans responded to slave evangelization. Unlike other similar studies, here the concept of culture is not of much use in grasping African responses. The slaves evangelized did not share a culture in the usual sense. Instead, many were socialized at the mission itself, and thus the challenge is to appreciate their identity as it emerged in the wake of evangelization.

Third, this case investigates the relationship between missionary practices and a resulting church. It argues that the Catholic identity that arose among former slaves depended upon missionary practices but cannot be attributed to the work of the missionaries. Though unthinkable without Spiritan actions, the Catholic communities that emerged from slave evangelization represented a collective African achievement that in fact required resistance to missionary preconceptions of what it meant to be Catholic.

Slave Evangelization and African Mission History

The study of Christian missionary activity in Africa has passed through stages of interpretive practice. These stages have mirrored those operative in the field of

African history more generally. The first historical studies of Christian missionaries in Africa appeared in the colonial period, usually with colonialist assumptions. They featured the heroic exploits of self-sacrificing European Christian spiritual warriors fostering social regeneration and personal salvation. Colonial-era mission history thus often resembled missionary hagiography. In reaction, new narrative conventions arose in the period immediately before and after many colonized parts of the world achieved nationhood. In such works, the *telos* of the nation often governed the storytelling. Thus the activity of missionaries was considered from the perspective of their hindering or helping the task of nation building, and the Africans were often depicted with more historical agency than the missionaries. Other recent studies have shown how missionary activity fostered the historical emergence of ethnic identities.[19]

Today the limitations of both of these approaches to the history of missionary activity — the colonialist/heroic and the nationalist/ethnic — are evident. Sophisticated mission history now favors critical analyses that stress the need to render carefully the distinctive perspectives of the agents involved, both those who carried the message and those who received it. Along with close attention to the participants, a growing consensus also emphasizes an understanding of the dynamics at work in the settings where evangelization was pursued.[20]

Better historical practice in analyzing what some call "the missionary encounter" has certainly been welcome. But another shortcoming of the earlier stages of interpretive practice in historical studies of Christian missionary activity has become apparent, especially in light of the growing importance of Christianity in contemporary Africa. Previous historical studies of evangelization in Africa have often failed to address adequately the experience of African Christians *as* Christians.[21] Reflecting on the "rapid and exhilarating" shift from the colonialist to nationalist modes in mission history in Africa, the late Adrian Hastings noted that by focusing on missionaries' roles in abetting or hindering independence, historians have failed to attend to African church history. It was, he continued, "obvious . . . in retrospect that each required the other and that African church history cannot be written without a great deal of careful missionary history . . . " He also observed that the "search for African initiatives" meant that so-called African independent churches received fuller scholarly attention than the churches he calls "historic," that is, those traceable to missionary work and with ongoing international ties. Understandable resistance to previous colonial-era models of mission history has meant that African Christianity,

---

19. For these ideas, see the following: Comaroff and Comaroff 1991, 7ff; Strayer 1976; Strayer 1978, 1–3; Vail 1991; Shenk 1996; Peel 1996: Arnold and Bickers 1996; Pels 1999, 16f; Petersen and Allman 1999.

20. For an important study that adopts a similar strategy to that espoused here, see Pardo 2004.

21. By "experience" I mean to suggest that different participants in social action have different ways of viewing it. Thus, the category usually represents an attempt to appreciate what Africans underwent in slave evangelization. In using the category I do not intend to ground an essential identity (like "the African experience" or "the missionary experience") nor to privilege unobservable intrapsychic activity as especially important to personal identity.

especially that embodied in the churches with self-conscious ties to European missionaries, has been understudied.[22]

Emblematic of this inattention to the African targets of missionary evangelization is "The Holy Ghost Fathers in East Africa, 1863 to 1914," a 1966 dissertation by John A. Kieran written at the University of London. Kieran's dissertation has been the main source for understanding the works of the Congregation of the Holy Ghost in eastern Africa in this period for nearly four decades, and for good reason. His research was prodigious, his analysis clear and usually compelling. Like other students of the Spiritans in eastern Africa, I have drawn upon his work a great deal, not only to guide me through the archives of the past but in the setting of questions for analysis. It is hard to imagine anyone soon matching the breadth of archival research that Kieran achieved.

Even if it represents the best single source on the Spiritans in nineteenth- and early-twentieth-century eastern Africa, Kieran's work nonetheless has its limits. First, it remains a rather traditional documentary history and thus is open to challenges from a more critical perspective. Kieran also focused a great deal on determining the success or failure of the Spiritan efforts by relying on a certain notion of conversion. By conversion he meant the growth of Christian communities and the number of baptisms. One problem with this way of assessing missionary activity is that it makes dubious assumptions about conversion as a self-explanatory analytic category in its own right, something now increasingly difficult to uphold, as we shall see. Second, it takes as a measure of missionary success something whose value the Spiritans themselves disputed. Some expended a great deal of energy in caring for the dying and baptizing them before they expired. Others had misgivings about such emphasis on "saving souls" even if they admired those whose zeal sent them in that direction. Thus, Kieran judges the Spiritans by a standard that neither external observers today nor all the participants themselves would have accepted.

Predictably, dependence on Kieran's sources and research has also led to reliance upon his interpretations of those sources, and some of his interpretations are suspect. Kieran divides Spiritan missionary strategy into two parts, conceived more or less temporally, which he calls the Closed Society and the Open Society. The first, in Kieran's description, involved the ransoming of slave children, the reception of slaves freed by the British and the Germans, and the creation of Christian villages as they married. The Open Society, by contrast, entailed the abandonment of the Christian village scheme in favor of schools as a means of evangelization. Kieran correctly describes a very broad pattern, but he overplays the contrast between these two approaches and ignores the complex forces at work in the production, implementation, and defense of these strategies.

This book shows that the shifting nature of Spiritan slave evangelization cannot be so easily categorized. It depended upon a variety of factors, not least

22. Hastings 2000, 31–33. For similar observations see Willis 1993, 127; Pels 1999, 16; and Spear 1999, 3–4.

of which was the nature of the African responses to that evangelization. And this raises the major problem with Kieran's analysis, and that of previous studies of the Spiritans' work in eastern Africa.[23] They have paid almost no heed to African responses to evangelization. Kieran himself admitted the limits in his sources, lamenting Spiritan inattention to the cultural characteristics of those they evangelized.[24]

But the intervening years have produced other scholarly tools that allow insight into African experiences of evangelization like those considered here. Better historical and anthropological research has shed new light on the pasts of African peoples, showing the complex ways their identities evolved in relation to a variety of historical forces, including colonialism and Christian evangelization. Others have illuminated the historical realities of subject peoples such as those born into slavery in eastern Africa. In addition, scholarship in the past few decades has also cast further light on social processes organized for the disciplining of populations in nineteenth-century Europe, processes that influenced slave evangelization. With the help of such research, I have delved more deeply than Kieran could into the anthropological and cosmological assumptions of both Africans and Europeans in order to describe better the evolving missionizing strategy and its reception over time. Yet I humbly acknowledge my debts to his formidable archival digging and clear exposition.

Like the earliest mission histories of the colonial era, this book emphasizes the missionaries a great deal. The goal is neither to make them heroes nor to vilify them, but to recognize that their practices of evangelization had profound effects on the Africans who came to their missions as well as on the broader history of Christianity in Africa. Like mission history in its African nationalist phase, this book also focuses on the Africans who were evangelized. Here, however, the goal is not so much to understand how evangelization prepared them for independence or helped create their ethnic or national identity. Instead it aims to understand how their identities — as Christians, and as agents and subjects of their own history — evolved under the impact of evangelization and in light of other circumstances that affected them.

This is thus a study of the history of Christianity in Africa, as well as an inquiry that, because of its willingness to ask theological questions, fits within the discipline of African church history. Indeed, it represents an effort to undermine the presumptions often held to obtain between mission history and church history, presumptions that reinforce a center-periphery model of church that is dubious both historically and theologically.[25] At the same time, interpreting missionary

---

23. The same criticism could be made of Bennett 1963a, and could be applied as well to Oliver 1952, which remains the canonical study of missionary work in eastern Africa. For a similar judgment, see Pels 1999, 17.

24. Kieran's claim can be found in his preface (Kieran 1966, ii) and is seconded by others (Bennett 1963a). But several Spiritans proved themselves quite adept ethnographers for their time, as we shall see.

25. Kollman 2004b.

practices of evangelization and their reception in this way also places this study within the disciplinary ambit of the history of religions.[26]

In order to tell the story of Spiritan slave evangelization, this book proceeds as follows. The next chapter describes in some detail the two parties most intimately involved in slave evangelization: the Spiritan missionaries and the slaves whom they targeted for their missionary practices. These descriptions establish a basis upon which to narrate the unfolding of slave evangelization in the three chapters that follow. The missionaries' backgrounds lend themselves to extensive generalization, since their training pursued the formation of uniform dispositions among members of their congregation. Compared to the missionaries, generalizing about these ex-slaves is difficult, because of the paucity of direct, first-person testimony and also because of the varying circumstances that brought them to the coast of eastern Africa. Still certain generalizations can be drawn about this group, out of whom the missionaries sought to make the church.

Building upon the descriptions of the two groups, chapters 3, 4, and 5 describe the Spiritan evangelization of slaves in eastern Africa and the discernible African responses to that evangelization from 1860 to the late 1880s. Each chapter corresponds with an approximately ten-year period during the mission's history. The chapter delineations, however, are more spatial than temporal, charting the movement of slave evangelization from the Indian Ocean island of Zanzibar in chapter 3, to the coastal mainland at Bagamoyo in chapter 4, and to the interior of eastern Africa in chapter 5. The spatial structure is deliberate and reflects a central contention of the book: that both Spiritan strategy and African responses to their strategy depended upon mutual perceptions of the opportunities available in the locales where evangelization was pursued. A time line introduces each chapter and certain events will mark the narrative, but there will be no detailed event-history of the mission's progress. Instead, chapters 3 to 5 trace the evangelization of slaves and its reception as a social process of interaction. These chapters address both structural aspects of that unfolding and the ways particular human decisions determined its shape. In these chapters the anthropological and cosmological predispositions of the missionaries and those they evangelized — the basis for which is laid in chapter 2 — become apparent. In particular, African experiences of evangelization became more evident over time, and emerging African Catholic identity can be better discerned.

Chapter 3 describes the original Catholic mission at Zanzibar from its beginnings in 1860 up until the foundation of the second mission at Bagamoyo in 1868. After depicting the mission's foundation, the chapter offers a detailed analysis of the Spiritans' strategy after they assumed responsibility in 1863. Chapter 4 focuses on the Bagamoyo mission, which after its founding became the center of Catholic missionary effort in the region, a position it held into the twentieth century. Chapter 5 covers the spread of the Catholic missions to other places

---

26. By locating this project within the history of religions I seek to connect it to the discipline in which I was trained, which rarely has analyzed Christian missionary activity.

away from the coast beginning in 1877 until the late 1880s, and especially the growth of collective identity among the Africans at Bagamoyo and the newer interior stations.

In the move from Zanzibar to Bagamoyo and then to missions in the interior, two themes in particular marked the evolution of Spiritan slave evangelization. First, the role of physical labor changed. Labor began as a central part of the effort to *form* small children at Zanzibar, then became a *resource* on which the missionaries depended at Bagamoyo, and finally developed into a *commodity* that earned remuneration for the African Catholics at Christian villages. The second theme that marked evolving Spiritan missionary practices was the missionaries' organization of the space of evangelization. At Zanzibar they enacted a regime based on *enclosure*, while at Bagamoyo their mission featured a more open approach to space appropriate for a mission with large plantations. Finally, at the interior missions the spatial arrangements depended upon the Christian villages where the former slaves settled.

African responses to Spiritan evangelization also changed, often in reaction to missionary attempts to organize labor and space for evangelization. Like the Spiritans, the former slaves had operative convictions about persons, labor, and space that emerged over time. At Zanzibar, the former slaves' reactions to evangelization are difficult to understand since the historical record provides little evidence, but a few telling indications nonetheless appeared. At Bagamoyo and the interior missions greater African agency can be discerned. Certain individuals appeared vividly in the historical record, and a collective African Catholic identity also emerged in the 1880s. This identity drew upon various sources: African backgrounds before coming to the mission, evangelization itself, and the broader environments where evangelization took place. African reactions helped determine the eventual shape of the Spiritan mission that initially targeted them, and also forged the first African Catholics in eastern Africa.

The concluding chapter synthesizes what slave evangelization's history tells us about Spiritan missionary practices, about the African Catholics who emerged from such practices, and about the relationship between the history of missionary evangelization and that of the church. The Africans who came into the church after enslavement, I argue, showed the effects of slave evangelization, but also displayed religious identities that eluded the Spiritans' own desires. They emerged as Catholics, though not in ways that the missionaries could immediately appreciate, even though that identity was unthinkable without the practices the missionaries enacted.

Before entering the more narrative part of the story, however, this chapter concludes by addressing three issues that face historical studies of its sort. First, what is the subject matter here to be considered and how is it related to other similar studies? Second, what is the nature of the sources upon which this study relies and how should they be interrogated? Third, what are the important broader historical forces that must be recognized in order to properly situate the subject to be studied?

**Beyond Culture and Conversion: The Practices and Effects
of Slave Evangelization**

Contemporary studies of missionary activity — whether historical, anthropological, or theological — regularly invoke the terms "culture" and "conversion."
Culture has been the prerogative and specialization of anthropologists, while
conversion is attended to by sociologists and theologians. Sociologists tend to
focus on conversion as a change of religious identity in an external, observable sense, while theologians emphasize such change in an internal, spiritual, or
psychological sense.

In attempts to understand Christian mission, these terms are often put in relation to each other. Generally a given people's culture names what it is that
those who are or were evangelized share or shared, envisioned as an integral and
essential reality held by insiders, thus as something prototypically *local*. Conversion names the process desired or achieved by missionaries in making people
of the given culture into Christians (or some other new identity). The missionaries in turn are usually prototypical outsiders *not* sharing the culture in question.
They come from a distance and bring a religion that is conceived of as *global*.
In the ensuing interaction between the missionaries and those evangelized, the
local people's culture might be the reason for the success, failure, or other more
complex outcome of missionary activity. Or the missionaries' ignorance of or
familiarity with the local culture, as well as the clumsiness or carefulness of their
attempts at spreading their message, becomes a major reason that conversion is
or is not successful.

The subject of this book poses analytical questions surrounding what is referred to by the terms culture and conversion differently than most studies of
missionary activity. The Spiritans did not initially focus their energy on a group
defined by its culture in the normal sense, nor did they seek to convert those
whom they evangelized. Furthermore, the insider/outsider and local/global relationships often at work — between those evangelizing and those evangelized —
also fail to apply. Both the Spiritans and the slaves they evangelized were outsiders at the coast of eastern Africa where slave evangelization took place, the
missionaries by choice, the slaves unwillingly. Neither group was local. Indeed,
before long the Spiritans had often been in the Swahili coastal region years longer
than the Africans they evangelized.

Deliberate choices within the Spiritan strategy led to such circumstances. The
Holy Ghost missionaries in eastern Africa conceived of their strategy as evangelizing Africans of two distinct types, and in successive order. Ultimately, they set
their sights on the more or less settled peoples of the interior who increasingly
drew their attention as the twentieth century neared. The Spiritans worked with
such peoples at their missions near and away from the Swahili coast beginning
in the late 1870s. As discernible ethnicized units, these groups resembled the
more typical subjects of mission history. They differed from one another in the
variety of ways obvious to even the most cursory student of Africa's historical

and anthropological record. This book does not much concern itself with Holy Ghost evangelization of this group of Africans, for its historical compass ends before such evangelization assumed priority in Spiritan activity.

The focus here is on the first group evangelized by the Spiritans, those designated slaves. These Africans, the targets of the earliest concerted Catholic evangelization in eastern Africa, lacked the collective identity deriving from a shared language and social experience that the label "culture" seeks to capture. Instead, for nearly all of them the designation "slave," a political or economic term suggesting someone who exists in a property relation to another and thus whose life and labor belong to another, aptly describes their social situation prior to contact with the Holy Ghost missionaries.[27] In the midst of this shared distinction as slaves they spoke a variety of languages, came from disparate places, suffered differently in relation to slavery and other social unrest, and brought diverse religious beliefs and practices to the experience of evangelization. They may have shared certain attributes, but they did not share a common culture in the usual sense.

This book shows that over time their common experiences of missionary evangelization at the Swahili coast, which built upon varying foundations, generated something like a collective identity among them, emerging in the 1880s especially. Was this a culture? Not in the usual sense. The historian William Sewell distinguishes between culture understood as pluralizable and nonpluralizable. He notes that culture as normally used is pluralizable. It attaches itself to existing groups, often defined by language, and indicates a systematic and coherent bounded whole that a given group shares. But Sewell prefers to view culture in a nonpluralizable way. He accepts that certain understandings generated in practices conduce to create affinities between people, though these might have only what he calls a thin coherence. Borrowing Sewell's distinction, this book tries to understand the "thin coherence" — culture in his second sense — shared by the ex-slaves at the mission, especially in the 1880s. But with other contemporary approaches to the idea of culture, I want to emphasize the contradictory, loosely integrated, contestable, changing, and weakly bounded aspects of any culture, especially one like that appearing due to slave evangelization.[28] Undoubtedly, the Spiritans shared a culture, as the term is normally used, more than those they evangelized.

---

27. The designation "slave" generally suggests someone who is owned by another or exists in a relationship of absolute political dependency on another. Nieboer's classic definition, of which mine is an adaptation, is preferred by Anthony Reid: a slave is one "who is property of another, politically and socially at a lower level than the mass of the people, and performing compulsory labor" (Nieboer 1910, 5; cited in Reid 1983b, 1). Defining the term "slave" generates contentious debate, broadly speaking between those who believe it most helpful to consider slavery as a social or political status and those who prefer to view it as an economic relationship generating a social condition. Claude Meillassoux distinguishes these two in helpful ways (1991, 9ff; see also Glassman 1995, 79ff).

28. Sewell 1999. For a fuller discussion of the limitations of the culture concept, see Kollman 2001, 20–22.

If normal uses of culture do not easily apply in this case, neither do those associated with conversion. The Spiritans did not seek to convert these slaves in the ordinary sense of the term. Conversion, in common language linked with Christianity, derives from the Greek notion of *metanoia*, and its model in the West has been St. Paul's conversion on the road to Damascus recounted in the Acts of the Apostles (9:1–19; 22:6–16; 26:12–18). Filtered through the analyses of William James and A. D. Nock, conversion has been envisioned as individual, sudden, profound, irreversible, and centered in religious beliefs.[29] As Jean and John Comaroff have argued, conversion understood in this fashion has usually joined two other assumptions: teleological beliefs in the inevitable advance of so-called world religions like Islam and Christianity, and intellectualist views on the need for macrocosmic worldviews when previously "microcosmic" peoples get thrust into more "modern" and "historical" situations. Used in this sense, conversion tends to explain what it purports to describe, substituting theological opinion for sociological analysis.[30]

Many scholars who study the spread of Christianity share the Comaroffs' views of the limitations of the concept of conversion in understanding practices of evangelization and their effects. Religious identities can change, but conversion, with its emphasis on interior beliefs, misrepresents what usually happens, which is best understood at the level of practices. A growing consensus also stresses the essentially dialectical nature of the process. Those subjected to evangelization selectively appropriate the missionary message, which is itself always a selective transmission of Christianity. If missionaries initiate the process, they quickly lose control of it. Thus most of the important transformations in those missionized occur beyond the historical record, while the effects of such changes go often unnoticed for decades and rarely fulfill missionary goals in any direct sense. Though missionaries dreamed of both complete once-and-for-all conversions of individuals (a prototypically Protestant hope) and of conversions of large groups led by their ruler (one prototypically Catholic), neither fantasy occurred very often, at least in recent times. Yet people often took on other things that came along with missionization, such as literacy and other trappings of so-called European modernity. The last few decades have seen particular appreciation of the role of translation, an act that shaped local peoples' languages while it also generated new manifestations of Christianity.[31]

Regardless of how one conceives of conversion — and I accept the Comaroffs' objections to the ordinary uses, though I would argue that the term can be used in a more rigorous sense — conversion was not the Spiritans' self-conscious goal

29. James 1902; Nock 1933.

30. The Comaroffs' target is primarily Robin Horton's influential theory of conversion (Horton 1971, 1975). For the Comaroffs' opinions, see the following: Comaroff and Comaroff 1991, 250–51, and 1997, 117–18. For a discussion of the limitations of the notion of conversion as usually conceived, see the conclusion of this book and Kollman 2001, 20–22.

31. For a recent collection of essays discussing conversion, most of which recognize the limitations of the concept, see Mills and Grafton 2003. In addition, see the following: Sanneh 1989; Hefner 1993; Etherington 1996; van der Veer 1996b; Spear 1999.

with freed slaves in eastern Africa. They only rarely used the term themselves.[32] Instead of seeking conversion, they tried to begin the church by *forming* slaves into Christians *from childhood*, believing that this was the best way to establish the church in a Muslim environment. Later, when such people grew older, they continued to trust practices similar to those implied by the idea of formation or, as we shall see, the idea of *reformation*. Later still, they sought something more akin to conversion of interior groups of so-called pagans.[33] In the beginning, however, they tried to *make* or *form* Christians out of former slaves, who had intrinsic value as God's creatures and also instrumental value for the missionary hopes of evangelizing the interior.[34]

The term "formation," even if it captures Spiritan goals better than "conversion," is less able to explain the emerging identity of those subjected to slave evangelization. What actually happened in the minds and hearts of the Africans evangelized by the Spiritans did not cohere with missionary goals. Despite the fact that slaves initially experienced evangelization in ways that we would describe as unfree, the effects of such practices depended on how those former slaves appropriated them as much as on the missionaries' own purposes. Yet if the Africans whom the Spiritans sought to form into Catholics did not automatically adopt the identities the missionaries wanted them to embody, neither did they face the missionary message as a disembodied choice whose advantages and disadvantages they could weigh in some objective fashion. Their experience of evangelization thus featured — to use categories familiar to contemporary social theory — *structures* that the Africans did not choose, but also depended on their own historical *agency*.[35]

There were and are a variety of ways to approach the nature of religious identity emerging from missionary activity. In the sacramental and theological language of official missionary self-understanding, becoming Catholic meant being baptized and not having left the church in a formal act. But even the Spiritans knew that such approaches were profoundly limited, hence their recourse to formation as a missionary strategy. Despite their apparent sociological realism, however, they continued to harbor presumptions that there was one proper

---

32. Interestingly, the French word *conversion* appears on forms that the Spiritans had to fill out annually in their reports to the Propagation of the Faith. There it refers to adults, either "pagans" or "heretics" (Protestants), who became Catholic, the number of which the Spiritans had to give (CSSp 196ax, passim).

33. In those circumstances they asked questions about how to facilitate the process, how to adapt to different peoples, and how to determine sincerity (Kieran 1966, 174ff).

34. The anthropologist Peter Pels prefers the notion of initiation to describe Spiritan missionary goals (Pels 1999).

35. By "agency" this book refers to the ability to act on one's own, which in the light of historical efforts to understand those actions, can as well be understood here as a "generalized ability to represent oneself in meaningful ways" (Comaroff and Comaroff 1997, 48). The Comaroffs distinguish agency from voice, the latter being a subset of agency. For a fuller discussion of structure and agency, see Giddens 1979, as well as important recent works by Margaret Archer (1996, 2000, 2003). Pierre Bourdieu's works have also been very influential (1977, 1990).

way to be Catholic: baptized, pious, hard-working, obedient — as defined by the Spiritans.

This book resists that missionary view on historical as well as theological grounds. Instead, Catholic identity had no univocal meaning equally shared by both the missionaries and African Catholics. Being Catholic was not a fixed essential facet of identity (even if sacramentally effected) but an interactive and historical process marked by social performances, a process shaped both by the missionaries and those they tried to bring into their fold.[36] As a consciousness held by Africans themselves, it was a relationship of belonging, and thus depended on their own self-awareness and attributions by others. It took a variety of forms, and possessed symbolic and material components. Due to the historical circumstances, at the heart of being Catholic for these former slaves was a belonging to the mission defined by a certain relationship to the Spiritans themselves.

Two constructs, put into relation with each other, constitute a loose framework to help make sense of African responses to slave evangelization in this book. They try to capture the dynamic, relational, and negotiated quality of the Catholic identity that constituted one outcome of Spiritan missionization. The first is the late social historian E. P. Thompson's influential notion of the *moral economy*. Thompson used this term to describe the basis for generalized outrage that led to food riots in early modern England. Thompson found that such riots occurred when certain expectations that were supposed to have been guiding the relations between the different classes of society were not met. Such riots were a sign that lower classes felt that obligations assumed to be traditional and customary went unobserved by those accorded social authority and prestige. He labeled those expectations — rarely stipulated but nonetheless embodied in values and approximating a rough consensus — the "moral economy." The nature of that economy was usually best appreciated when it was felt to have been violated, because then the expectations, otherwise implicit, found expression in protest.[37]

The use of "moral economy" here represents an attempt to name one aspect of the many effects of slave evangelization on those evangelized, one part of the perceived reality or thin coherence that evolved in African Catholic consciousness due to material and symbolic changes in the lives of those evangelized. In a way analogous to Thompson's formulation, the moral economy of the mission describes the internalized sense of expectation within Africans at the mission about how the Spiritans and the program itself *should* have treated them. As noted earlier, those evangelized developed a sense of being Catholic that presupposed a profound relationship to the mission and the Spiritans, a relationship that over time generated certain expectations. As with Thompson's food riots, such

36. As the political scientist Anne Norton has it, "Identities are performed," and Catholic identity in eastern Africa emerged from — and evolved in relation to — numerous social performances (Norton 2004, 47–49).

37. Thompson 1971. I am aware of Thompson's own reluctance to use the term outside the context in which he developed it (Randall and Charlesworth 2000, 19, 23).

expectations appeared most vividly in the historical record *when they were felt to have been violated.*

Yet Africans acted as Catholics in other ways as well; even their responses to perceived violations of the mission's moral economy took many forms. To make sense of the ways that the Africans evangelized reacted to the mission's message, and especially to differentiate among their reactions to perceived violations of their evolving moral economy of the mission, this book uses a second theoretical construct: the now-quite-dated threefold typology of *exit, voice,* and *loyalty* developed by political scientist Albert O. Hirschman. Hirschman developed these concepts in order to analyze the interrelationships between preferences individuals take in situations that present them with economic or political choices. His terminology attempts to relate personal choices to perceptions held by those choosing, perceptions about the circumstances in which they make such choices.

By *exit,* Hirschman means decisions by which individuals choose against preferences they had once seen as desirable. They thus leave the political stance or party (or the buying preference) that they once favored.[38] Hirschman uses "voice" to indicate an effort to try and change the context that presents options to a potential customer or political supporter.[39] In order to specify the notion of voice beyond explicitly economic and political contexts, "voice" here follows the formulation of Jean and John Comaroff: "a self-conscious ability to [act as a human agent] through discursive means."[40] "Loyalty," in Hirschman's formulation, is the willingness to stick with a given product or political position over time, and thus not let oneself be easily tempted to exit.[41]

Hirschman's terms acknowledge the ways the world is always experienced as presenting both constraint and opportunity. As possible options facing people, exit, voice, and loyalty relate to one another dialectically. Thus certain types of voice can be among the best evidence of loyalty, for they show that the agent in question desires to improve the product or political position instead of exiting the situation. Indeed, if loyalty is generated, then voice becomes the regular response to situations that present options felt as limiting. Yet if exit is not available, then voice is the only option available to those who make economic and political decisions, so that it is not always simply a sign of loyalty. And if exit is too easy, then voice atrophies.[42] As social theorist Anne Norton writes, "Belonging may be expressed as affirmation or rebellion," and Hirschman's terms invite investigation of the nature of belonging and its expressions.[43]

An evolving consciousness about one's sense of belonging resists easy historical analysis. Attaining identity, personal or collective, is always a relational

38. Hirschman 1970, 21ff.
39. Ibid., 30ff.
40. Comaroff and Comaroff 1997, 48.
41. Ibid., 76ff.
42. Hirschman 1970, 30f, 43.
43. Norton 2004, 61–62.

achievement, taking place with and through others, yet it happens in distinctive and often hidden ways. Aspects of that identity thus often appear most clearly when expectations that were part of it are unfulfilled. And this is where Hirschman's categories come in handy. By linking his terms to the notion of the moral economy, I want to suggest that the kinds of human action that are most revealing of the moral economy — in this case, at least — took forms approximated by exit, voice, and loyalty. The use of Hirschman's terms here thus reflects a desire to do two things at once: acknowledge the agency of these Africans as they appropriated the mission's discourses and practices of evangelization, and also take account of the situated way in which that appropriation took place. African Catholics like Léon and his companion could flee the mission, thus apparently seeking to exit. Yet at the same time they could exercise their voice, as they attempted to do with the French consul. And it is clear, given Léon's long time at the mission and his exercise of voice, that some loyalty had been forged in him. Actions like his exit and his exercise of voice show how he was internalizing something like a moral economy of the mission.

Different challenges face the discernment of Hirschman's options. Loyalty, for example, is not so much an action as a sentiment that ushers forth in action. Thus evidence for it is often due to the absence of exit and the presence of voice. This is admittedly thin evidence, especially in light of the scant historical sources on African experiences of slave evangelization. For that reason, exit and voice — actions inasmuch as these can be discerned — are taken as clues to determine the presence or absence of loyalty, as well as the form of the moral economy that developed within the Africans at the Spiritan missions. But they allow inferences to be drawn, not certainty to be attained.

In particular, as will become clear, the argument is made that voice represents the clearest evidence that a certain moral economy has been achieved, a certain identity internalized, a certain loyalty forged.[44] Though the missionaries disliked exercises of voice, often interpreting them as disloyalty, they appear in retrospect to have been the best evidence of loyalty. Belonging to the mission could entail a variety of behaviors and feelings, beliefs and practices, some of which were observable and most of which could not be observed. Discerning exit, voice, and loyalty allows historical insight into ways in which the moral economy of the Spiritan missions evolved, and thus into the ways that eastern Africans came to be Catholics through slave evangelization.

And collective voice, voice enacted by a group, represented even more. Léon's appeal was a singular act, but it existed as part of a trend. Patterns within collective actions in turn show a collective identity emerging, one that, by analogy, can be considered to reflect a collective moral economy of the mission. These categories thus allow the historical imagination to push beyond the biographical

---

44. The category of voice is used in other contexts to indicate authenticity within human discourse. I am not using voice in this way, and am wary of such notions of the authentic, especially in something as contested as African Christian identity. For a similar perspective to mine, see the essays in Cox and ter Haar 2003.

details of individuals and into the collective experiences of those evangelized by the Spiritans. Discerning collective decisions to exit or to exercise voice allows discernment of a collective loyalty that, I argue, signified the appearance of a church that was achieving independence of missionary approval.

The crudeness of these categories, especially Hirschman's, can be off-putting at first. Exit, after all, can be impulsive or planned, temporary or permanent. Loyalty can be feigned or real, wholehearted or carefully couched. And voice can take many forms and mean many things. I beg the reader's forbearance for the time being. These terms gain more specification over the next chapters, as historical evidence accumulates. The anthropologist Ann Stoler has defined working concepts as those that "promote analytical openings and are subject to change."[45] It is in that spirit that this book offers this conceptual framework of terms that seek to make sense of slave evangelization and responses to it. Over time, both the Spiritans and ex-slaves were forced to structure and restructure their stance in relation to the other, in order to reflect their changing senses of mutuality and belonging. These terms attempt to gain some purchase on those evolving relationships.

•

Can historical research grasp something so elusive, vague, and mutable as an emerging moral economy or the thin coherence that emerged in Africans subjected to slave evangelization? Can a spotty historical record yield insight into practical approaches to personhood, time, and space, epistemological presuppositions held by Europeans and Africans that ordered this attempt at evangelization and responses to it? If so, any such understanding requires critical methodologies that interrogate a variety of historical sources for insight into the past.

Sources for Slave Evangelization and Their Interpretation

To understand slave evangelization, I visited most of the places discussed in this story and tried to interpret those sites and settings where that might be profitable. More importantly, I spoke with the descendants of witnesses of some of these events — both the biological descendants of African witnesses as well as the contemporary Holy Ghost missionaries and other religious leaders who carry on the work begun by the congregation in eastern Africa. On the whole, unfortunately, such conversations were limited in their capacity to cast light on the nineteenth-century events and processes here considered. Several reasons can be adduced for their limited helpfulness. First, the simple passage of time has meant that the original witnesses have all died, as have nearly all of those who knew firsthand those who participated. The last surviving slave evangelized by the Spiritans, Maria Ernestina, who had been enslaved in the Congo in 1890 and entered the mission later that year, died in 1974.[46] Second, the years since

---

45. Stoler 2002, 206.
46. Nyaki, n.d., 19.

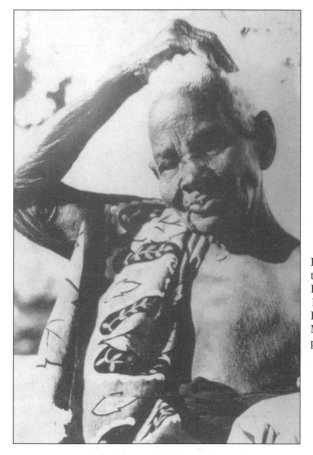

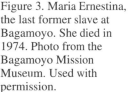

Figure 3. Maria Ernestina, the last former slave at Bagamoyo. She died in 1974. Photo from the Bagamoyo Mission Museum. Used with permission.

these events have witnessed tremendous changes in Zanzibar and what is now Tanzania. As a consequence, the descendants of the former slaves who became the first African Catholics in eastern Africa often now live far from the missions once inhabited by their forebears. Most descendants are very difficult to trace. Third, since slave evangelization more or less ended in the early twentieth century, the members of Catholic communities where it occurred developed new ways to think of themselves that did not dwell in that past. Despite these limitations, certain of those conversations generated real insights into slave evangelization, and I am grateful for the time and efforts at remembering.[47]

Nonetheless, *texts* have been the richest type of source for this study. And most of these written sources, especially those most revealing, were written by the missionaries themselves. Unlike J. D. Y. Peel's stunning recent study of the

---

47. Especially helpful were conversations carried out near the Catholic communities at Zanzibar, Bagamoyo, and Mhonda.

emerging Christian identity of the Yoruba in Nigeria,[48] this book cannot rely on extensive writings by those evangelized, of which there are few. Frustrating, too, is the absence of comparable writings by the Catholic nuns who, from the beginning, cooperated with the Spiritans. When possible, missionary writings were supplemented by other contemporaneous records, but those rarely showed much depth, nor did they usually add significantly to the missionary accounts themselves. The Spiritans themselves wrote the most thorough and extensive sources describing the evangelization of slaves that they undertook.

Types of Spiritan Writings

The Holy Ghost missionaries in eastern Africa described what they were doing for a number of audiences: their friends and families, European mission support agencies, the numerous contributors to such funding sources, their own confreres, their religious superiors, local political leaders, European political leaders, Vatican officials in Rome, private benefactors, and each other. They wrote articles (in different kinds of journals), books, appeals for money, monthly and annual reports, daily entries in mission journals, and private letters. At least one Spiritan even kept private notebooks, *carnets*, that contain materials he later reassembled for publication but also notes not meant for public consumption.[49] They wrote with a myriad of purposes, including to fulfill religious obedience, in an effort to be and remain holy, to legitimate their missionary strategy, to explain difficulties, to complain about their circumstances, to gain subsidies, and to maintain friendships.

Despite this variety of audiences, genres, and purposes, nearly all Spiritan depictions of their missionary work in eastern Africa can be found in one of the four typical forms of writing: comprehensive reports, letters, the mission journals, and sacramental records.[50]

First, their ties to Europe meant that the Spiritans often described their mission's scope and emphasized its needs and promise in formal *comprehensive reports*, the most complete accounts available. The Spiritans prepared annual descriptions of their mission's works (*oeuvres*) for a number of their benefactors, especially the Holy Childhood Society and the Society of the Propagation of the Faith. They produced reports of similar thoroughness for those who had sent them to eastern Africa: Spiritan authorities in Paris and Vatican officials at Propaganda Fide in Rome. They felt particular duty to report often and thoroughly to their Holy Ghost superiors in Paris, to whom they owed religious obedience. Ignatius Schwindenhammer, who served as superior general from 1852 until his death in 1882, made accurate and complete reporting an important religious duty of his

---

48. Peel 2000.

49. These were by Courmont, the first bishop of eastern Africa, who is discussed more fully in chapter 5 (CSSp 198b).

50. For a fuller discussion of Spiritan writing, see Kollman 2001, 37–50.

missionaries, part of his efforts to centralize Spiritan authority in Paris.[51] Less comprehensive reports went to other recipients.

These reports for external authorities or benefactors, often accompanied by lists of expenses and requests for future funding or personnel due to challenges facing the missionaries, reflect the tactical purposes that produced them. These included the need to legitimate the mission in order to procure the funding to maintain or expand it, or to show an obedient spirit. Such reports are far from valueless because of these mitigating circumstances. In fact, the obvious self-interest of such sources can make interpreting them less problematic than sources whose biases might be harder to identify. Still, it is important to recognize that they corresponded to an official style aimed at legitimation and the garnering of support.[52] For example, in the effort to receive an annual subsidy from the French government, irregular Spiritan reports to the Ministry of Foreign Affairs took pains to emphasize that their missionary work extended French influence in the region, raising the esteem of France in the eyes of the sultan, other Arabs, and the indigenous Africans. The first Holy Ghost superior at Zanzibar, Antoine Horner (1827–80), played upon the French-English rivalry in such funding requests, raising the specter of the expanding Anglican (and English) mission in Zanzibar, no doubt in order to loosen French purse strings.[53] Such nationalistic sentiments are less obvious in letters to their religious superiors in Paris, or in descriptions of the missionary effort directed to Propaganda Fide in Rome.

Yet reports directed toward fund-raising agencies in France and elsewhere analogously drew attention to the affinities between the mission's own practices and the particular ideals inspiring the agency in question. Conversely, they avoided descriptions that might undermine the mission's perceived fulfillment of the agency's self-understanding. Annual reports prepared for the Society for the Propagation of the Faith, for instance, stressed the number of souls saved through baptism in line with that group's dedication to *le salut des âmes* (the salvation of souls), and featured accounts of the gathering of the abandoned who received baptism before dying. Likewise, reports prepared for the Holy Childhood Association underscored the congruence between the organization's focus on ransoming and educating slave children and Spiritan efforts.[54]

But comprehensive reports also have their advantages as historical sources. Such reports generated a panoramic perspective on the mission rarely found in other more occasional written records, since the missionaries gave overviews of their activities to encourage ongoing financing and satisfy their superiors. They featured more or less exact counts of the personnel at the mission, the children

---

51. See Kollman 2001, 161–62.

52. Arnold and Bickers 1996, 4.

53. CSSp 194aii: Horner to Ministry of Foreign Affairs, 13iv67; CSSp 196biii: Horner to Ministry of Foreign Affairs, 23ix73; CSSp 195v: Emonet to Ministry of Foreign Affairs, 3xii83.

54. The reports and other correspondence between the Spiritans in eastern Africa and these agencies can be found as follows: reports to the Propagation of the Faith up to 1883 in CSSp 196ax and after 1883 in CSSp 196axi; reports to the Holy Childhood Society up to 1883 in CSSp 196axii and after 1883 in CSSp 196axii.

and families living there, and the sacramental activity in the preceding year, information rarely found elsewhere. These reports need to be balanced by other sources to be sure, yet they display Spiritan commitments to institutions such as hospitals, orphanages, schools, and industrial and agricultural works.

In addition to comprehensive reports, the missionaries produced a second important type of historical source, *letters,* some of which went to those for whom they produced the comprehensive reports. Letters differed from the comprehensive reports in two important respects. First, unlike such reports, they were usually written for personal (or at least limited) consumption, thus lending them a certain frankness. Second, because of their occasional nature, they offered insight into what was preoccupying the writer at the moment he was writing, lending them immediacy. This correspondence can be very revealing in offering a window on a particular circumstance occupying the attention of the writer of the letter — a personal grievance against a peer or superior, a recent tragedy, the need for a certain kind of supply at the mission, advice on a disputed point. In addition, the trajectory of a missionary's writings can show that with some correspondents he was more frank than with others. Such an awareness into his patterns of concealment and revelation lends specificity to his view of things.[55]

In addition to formal reports and correspondence, the missionaries at each station kept a *mission journal,* a third source. The journals were designed to recount day-to-day events at the mission. Though under the vow of religious obedience to maintain them, the Spiritans kept these journals irregularly. Moreover, the task of being chronicler often fell to the most recently arrived missionary, who lacked a perspective in which to place the events described. They can be, therefore, frustratingly incomplete. Crucial journals are missing as well, from the 1870s in particular, and have been gone since early in this century.[56] The journals' value consists in their uncovering the daily activities at the mission. The contents are often mundane, even numbingly repetitive, listing, for example, the liturgical details of mission life and the routines of agricultural labor. Even then, however, they reveal what the missionaries cared about recording. More importantly, African agency appears to a great extent in the mission journals, which often are the only record on escapes from the mission, punishments accorded, and African grievances. For obvious reasons, such difficulties at the mission did not usually feature prominently in reports for funding agencies. Even with their superiors in Paris the missionaries could be less than forthcoming about such things.

Like the mission journals, the *sacramental registries* at each mission station, a fourth source by which the missionaries represented their work, were supposed

---

55. For example, in his initial correspondence upon arriving in Zanzibar, Horner is much more frank with his superior in Réunion than with his superior in Paris, describing his difficulties with the sisters for the former, not the latter. Compare CSSp 196bii: Horner to Duboin, 24–28vi63, with ibid.: Horner to Schwindenhammer, 24–28vi63.

56. They were lost by the early twentieth century (Vogt, n.d., which also appears as CSSp 391a: Vogt, Resume of Bagamoyo mission, 1868–1918). According to personal communication from a Spiritan in Morogoro, Father Theodore Winkelmolen, they might have been taken in order to describe the visits of Livingstone and Stanley to the mission in those days.

to remain at the missions. There are three types of these sacramental books at Catholic parishes: the *Liber Baptizorum* (or *Liber Baptizatorum*), a volume listing baptisms (and other sacraments received afterward, especially confirmation and marriage); the *Liber Defunctorum*, which lists the dead; and *Liber Conjugatorum* (or *Liber Matrimonorium*), the book recording marriages. At the beginning of a mission's existence, all three were often kept in one volume. Over time they became three separate books at most of the mission stations. Each developed within a few decades into a several-volume collection as missions expanded. Though subject to review by visiting bishops and also of course opened when new entries were made, such books were not prepared for public consumption, and their contents were supposed to be more or less secret.

These sacramental registries are limited as historical sources, but can be very revealing. They often supplement other records that described African Catholics. This is because the names of those who receiving sacraments and of those served as sponsors for sacraments — for example, as godparents for baptisms or witnesses for marriages — were recorded. These sponsors could have been invited to do so by those marrying, being baptized, or, as the case may be, presenting their child for baptism. At times the Spiritans themselves chose certain trusted people to take such roles. Regardless, a sponsor's participation meant she or he had the permission of the missionaries to serve in that capacity, an important sign of some confidence. Godparents and marital witnesses, therefore, were active Christians at the time of these sacramental celebrations, at least in the eyes of the Spiritans. They also usually had the esteem of those who requested their participation.

The sacramental registries yield other clues, too, for some of the early Christians could sign their names while others simply marked a cross or had their names written in by the missionaries. In addition, curious missionaries in intervening years have added notes to these sacramental books, following up on some of the African Catholics listed there to fill out their personal histories. Unfortunately, as with the mission journals there are often volumes missing, so that we have Zanzibar's earliest sacramental registry but no records after the late 1860s until several decades later. At Mhonda, records of baptisms and marriages are complete, but the records of deaths before 1910 are missing. Bagamoyo's records are the most complete and, since more former slaves passed through there than anywhere else, the most valuable.

The Spiritans made concerted efforts to describe their work for the interested public. But very little of what appeared in public appeared as the Spiritans produced it. Much of what they wrote underwent deliberate (and sometimes very telling) revisions at the hands of editors in Paris and elsewhere. The traces of these editorial processes can be observed at times, since the originals, marked by editors, still exist. Editors rearranged the order, softened aspects deemed problematic, downplayed or enhanced particular themes, and embellished details or created them ex nihilo. The missionaries' annual reports to funding agencies also underwent recopying and editing at the congregation's Paris headquarters, a process that often altered them considerably.[57] They then were often edited again by those agencies if they appeared in a periodical for the public. Certain of the Spiritans in eastern Africa, especially Horner, Le Roy, and Courmont, became regular contributors to the *Annales* of the Propagation of the Faith and their more popular *Les Missions Catholiques*. Articles appearing there underwent an editorial process at the Spiritan mother house as well as at the journals' offices themselves.

A more comprehensive source on all the Spiritan missions, including the one started at Zanzibar, came from the congregation, and it, too, was the result of editorial processes. In 1857, the Spiritan mother house in Paris began to produce a quarterly bulletin for members worldwide, the *Bullétin Général de la Congrégation du Saint-Esprit et du Saint Coeur de Marie* (BG). Besides being an excellent repository of data on the missions in eastern Africa and elsewhere, BG also revealed what Paris thought was important about events at the missions. From all the reports and letters they received — hundreds of pages monthly — the mother house prepared an extensive publication approximately every three months. Comparisons between the original letters and reports with what eventually appeared suggest that writings from mission fields underwent several stages of editing prior to appearing in BG. The original writings sometimes bear the marks of that process.[58]

Interpreting the Spiritans' Writings

This book attempts to attend as fully as possible to the Spiritans *and* those they evangelized as it makes sense of their interactions over time. Understanding the missionaries and their decisions is complicated enough, for they drew upon no preset plan for their evangelization. Instead they enacted missionary practices that depended upon assumptions of various sorts, many of which they took for granted and thus rarely mentioned. Their practices also evolved over time, in response to changes in the world around them and in relation to their perceptions of the opportunities at hand for forming the kinds of Catholics they wanted.

The near-absence of African writings from this period, however, creates even more formidable limitations to understanding their experiences of slave evangelization. This book nonetheless shows that insights into the specifically African

---

57. Their superiors in Paris also criticized the Spiritans in eastern Africa when their reports were unsatisfactory (CSSp 196bi: Schwindenhammer to Horner, 19i79; ibid., Schwindenhammer to Baur, 14xi81).

58. On BG, see Ernoult 2000, 41–42, and Kieran 1966, 70. Letters from the Spiritan missions addressed to their superior general apparently first went through the hands of someone who highlighted certain portions before handing them on, for some letters have marginalia indicating their content. Other markings show an obvious editorial hand that governs what eventually appears in either BG or other public writings, and Horner knew and trusted the mother house's editing (CSSp 196bii: Horner to Schwindenhammer, 24vi64).

origins of Catholicism in the region are possible despite the overwhelming reliance on missionary writings. These missionary texts allow the discernment of an emerging moral economy of the mission that developed among these former slaves. This book shows that African exercises of voice and exit, African resistance and loyalties, African Catholic historical agency and identity can be discerned within a historical record mainly produced by missionaries.

It should be admitted, however, that the extensive and well-catalogued archives of the Congregation of the Holy Ghost (and those of similar missionary societies) generated little homogeneity in missionary discourse. The diversity of authors, genres, and purposes at work in their writings meant that there was no unanimity among the Spiritans, nor a single missionary perspective.[59] Certainly, the Spiritans rarely described their efforts in order to deceive; there should be no doubt that they usually sought to present the truth as they knew it. But their writings, though an incomparable boon for the researcher, are not objective reservoirs upon which to draw for a picture of the mission's activity.

And this book seeks to know more than merely what happened at the Spiritan missions. It also pursues an appreciation of the worldviews and other assumptions that motivated the missionaries and those they evangelized. Those motivations, the complex anthropological and cosmological assumptions that inspire human practices, would be difficult to grasp even with much more complete and unproblematic sources than those available for this study. Such assumptions often go unsaid, so naturalized are they within human discourse.

Consequently, relying on sources like those available here — especially for such underlying and usually implicit presuppositions — has demanded critical practices, such as close attention to the broader contexts in which these sources were produced. It has also entailed interpretive risks. These included drawing tentative conclusions from maddeningly incomplete evidence and allowing many puzzling aspects to remain puzzling for a long time before they began to become comprehensible.[60] It also required comparisons of sources over stretches of time with no intervening evidence, especially in efforts to follow the lives of the former slaves whom the Spiritans evangelized. Most importantly, it has meant accepting that imaginative inference is a legitimate method of historical inquiry, as long as it is acknowledged.[61] No doubt many of the interpretive decisions made in the effort to make sense of Spiritan slave evangelization escaped my own awareness. Others among those decisions are on display in the chapters ahead, as the historical practices entailed in this book's own production are laid bare. All this is to say that the available sources, mostly found in missionary archives, were *interpreted*, for they are not ready-made windows on the past.

---

59. Arnold and Bickers 1996, 1.

60. I agree thus with Peter Hulme, who argues that discourse must sometimes be read not only for its objective truth value. He admits the need to "... [bracket] particular questions of historical accuracy and reliability in order to see the text whole, to gauge the structures of its narrative, and chart the interplay of its linguistic registers and rhetorical modalities" (cited in Pels 1997, 168).

61. For a good discussion, see Deutsch 2000, 57, which depends on Wright 1993.

There was no other choice. In fact, given the one-sided nature of the sources, an appreciation of African experiences of evangelization and discernment of African agency requires a thorough understanding of how those sources were produced, as well as the practices of missionary evangelization they described.

Such appreciation is not always apparent. Many of those who draw upon missionary records to understand African history pay insufficient attention to the critical demands of reading missionary writings. One rarely reads anything like the humility expressed by a historian of German colonialism in Tanganyika: "Nor did I use missionary records to an especially wide extent. What I saw of them convinced me that I would have needed years more to undertake a proper study."[62] And I would argue that glib assumptions about the perspectives of missionaries and lack of attention to African Christians are related. Previous studies failed to situate the Spiritans within their historical context, a context that included awareness of their practices of self-representation. They have also, partially because of such inattention, underplayed the African side of the origins of Catholic Christianity in eastern Africa.[63] Thus I am convinced that understanding the so-called missionary perspective on evangelization does not mean ignoring the so-called African perspective on the same process, or vice versa. In fact, to appreciate one supports an appreciation of the other.

The point cannot be stressed enough: intimate familiarity with missionary sources in all their historical and representational complexity, far from obscuring the former slaves' experiences, is a necessary, though not sufficient, precondition to grasping them in any depth. It is necessary since missionary sources are the best window on the past, and properly interpreted can be rich indeed. Yet such knowledge is insufficient because no historical source interprets itself. Instead, the available evidence creates a larger pattern in the midst of which — and only in the midst of which — individual parts make sense.

Certainly there are profound limits to a comprehensive appreciation of the African experiences of evangelization in circumstances like those described in this book. African Catholic identities emerging under the impact of evangelization do not rise intact from written records by the missionaries. As historian Steven Feierman says more generally, "The European sources hang like a veil between the historian and African actors. . . . "[64] And in this case the veil can appear particularly opaque, since "slave-ridden Africa" was a ubiquitous European

---

62. Koponen 1994, 679.
63. On the need to construct an archive through self-conscious historical practice, see Comaroff and Comaroff 1992, 34, as well as more recent comments by Gaurav Desai (2000, 4ff). Given the demands of properly interpreting missionary writings, it is surprising to see how blithely and uncritically many historians rely on them. Others find them biased and thus unusable. In a recent study, Kenneth Mills and Anthony Grafton attack such a view. They urge critical attention to missionary sources, the kind of attention that should be accorded any historical source, and attack the indefensible dichotomous historiographical tendency to view missionary records as of less value because they are especially tainted (Mills and Grafton 2003, xiii).
64. Feierman 1999, 186.

representation of the continent and its peoples and thus shaped depictions.[65] Yet veils, even if they shield, also reveal things behind them if one understands the nature of the veiling in question. In this case, that requires familiarity with missionary practices of representation. The goal is not to pretend that one can see behind the veil of such texts, but to interpret them in such a way that the veils are pulled and prodded. This helps uncover the shapes and voices of African agency behind them, allowing a glimpse into the ways Africans internalized missionary practices.[66]

This book thus joins other historical efforts to uncover what has often been overlooked in the past, in Africa and elsewhere. Elizabeth Isichei, a historian of Africa, says that Africa's poor have profound experiences worth recovering. But she admits, "Unconsciously, however, academics — myself among them — have selected their evidence according to preconceived notions of the possible." In a recent work, however, she tries to uncover those "subjugated knowledges" by reading archival materials with an eye to linking oral and other evidence with archival materials themselves.[67] Other historians who study colonialism suggest that those who were colonized always lurk within colonial archives, as subjects who engaged colonizers even when those colonizers did not directly acknowledge their presence in their writings.[68]

At times this book also pursues such covert presences of African Catholics within missionary texts. But Africans do not always hide in Spiritan writings, for the missionaries often directly discussed those whom they evangelized. The Spiritans and the Africans at the mission lived in close proximity with one another and interacted in intimate ways on a regular basis. Since much of the missionaries' sense of themselves was bound up with changing these former slaves in ways deemed productive of the church's future thriving, they described them often. Their writings revealed their impressions of the success and failure of their work, generating appreciation and frustration, and producing different registers of discourse ranging from simple observations to implicit and explicit evaluations.

The Spiritans never acted in a vacuum, but worked very hard to create something akin to what Hirschman calls loyalty in those at the mission, having ambitions of internal transformation as they tried to make them into Catholics. Thus evangelization was always an interactive process. And those evangelized made their own decisions in light of the practices to which they were subjected, so that the Spiritans regularly faced reactions to their activity that puzzled and annoyed them. Of course, the record on African responses is incomplete, and it

---

65. Cooper 2000, 115.

66. At the same time, like many I am wary of a search for "an authentic African voice" undisturbed by foreign influences, some essentialized reality behind the veil Feierman identifies. For pointed rebukes to such attempts to isolate an essential African identity, see Mudimbe 1988 and 1994. See also recent essays in Cox and ter Haar 2003 with regard to African Christianity in particular.

67. Isichei 2002, 1, 9ff, passim.

68. Desai 2000, 4ff; Olsen 2004.

is very difficult to attend to both sides of interactions with such an imbalance of sources. In particular it is difficult to portray a co-present in which each of the characters operated, without favoring the evolution of one at the expense of the other. Predictably, evolutions within Spiritan thought are much easier to chart than comparable developments in those they evangelized.[69] Yet the world inhabited, whether of colonizer and colonized, or evangelizer and evangelized, was one world, with both groups producing and reproducing representations of themselves and the others.

Literary clues can be important for generating the kind of understanding sought here. Unexpressed presuppositions and underlying preoccupations often appear within discourse as assumptions that shaped desires expressed or objectives frustrated. In my reading of these sources, I have sought to pay special attention to the tensions within them, tensions between the official discourse and the private, among individual missionaries, between those in and under authority, between life in this world and the next, between Spiritan assumptions and African reactions.

If there was an official missionary approach among the Spiritans — something that is itself debatable — there were also different operative missionary views of the human person and the world. These emerged in Spiritan writings. The *obvious* aspects of evangelization, on the other hand, lent themselves to a less freighted discursive presentation and suggest aspects of their missionary ideals that the Spiritans and their audiences could more self-consciously acknowledge and endorse. Differentiating one from the other requires understanding the world these missionaries, individually and collectively, came from, as well as the world where they expressed their convictions.

Anxiety in missionary discourse is one clue to this missionary world. It is also a privileged avenue to discern the nature of the veiling in missionary representations. Examples of anxiety as a clue already seen include Le Roy's concern to "allow no lapse" in spiritual practices, a point he emphasizes in his own draft, and Acker's relief at the French consul's eventual rebuff to Léon. Such signs alert the attentive reader to missionary assumptions, as well as to missionary doubts about their efforts. Such anxiety or ambiguity is often a clue to African agency, for one can discern Africans acting in ways that disturbed missionary composure and self-assurance. African voices — to use Hirschman's term — often expressed loyalty, but did so in ways that unsettled missionary expectations and thus appeared in missionary frustration. Spiritan anxieties thus revealed an emerging African Catholic identity, as former slaves developed their own moral economy of the mission.

The Dynamic Setting of Slave Evangelization

The Spiritan evangelization of slaves carried out at Zanzibar, Bagamoyo, and the interior of what became Tanganyika took place in the midst of ongoing

---

69. Pels 1999, 27; Cooper 1994.

transformation in the region.[70] Such transformation was nothing new given the long-standing dynamism characterizing eastern Africa, but the Catholic mission began as the region increasingly attracted the renewed attention of groups from outside Africa, mostly Europeans. These included individual explorers, large-scale geographical organizations, and other scientists; humanitarians bent on the abolition or amelioration of slavery; other missionary societies, Protestant and Catholic; traders eager for slaves, spices, and ivory; and European governments intent on abolition and/or taking territory, whether for economic gain, imperial rivalry, or some combination of the two.

This European incursion dramatically changed the nature of political authority in eastern Africa during the decades of Spiritan slave evangelization. When the Catholic mission began at Zanzibar in 1860, permission for the foundation was granted by the sultan of Zanzibar, who laid claim to the political loyalties of the slaves whom they sought to evangelize, as well as to much of the rest of eastern Africa. Though there remained a sultan officially ruling over Zanzibar until the revolution of 1964, by the early 1890s the political power of this once-formidable ruler had dwindled significantly, replaced for the most part by European control.[71]

The particular nations composing the prominent European presence in the region also changed in this period. During the middle of the century, and thus at the start of the mission, the French and the British jockeyed for power with the sultans of Zanzibar, but in the mid-1880s the Germans entered eastern Africa with a series of dubious treaties that supported claims to territory. The process leading to formal European overrule began with this sudden and unexpected German incursion in 1884 and 1885, which prompted British responses in kind. By this time French colonial ambition had looked elsewhere, so that the so-called scramble for Africa was in this region an Anglo-German affair.[72]

---

70 This historical survey relied on many sources, including: Abungu 1998; Alpers 1975; Atmore 1985; Beidelman 1962; Bennett 1963b, 1964, 1966, 1971, 1973, 1974, 1978, 1986; Bhacker 1991, 1992; Boahen 1985; Burton 1872; Chrétien 2003; Cooper 1977, 1980; Coupland 1938, 1967; Curtin 2000, 112–15; Deutsch 2000, 2003; Flint 1963, 1976; Freeman-Grenville 1988; Gann and Duignan 1969; Gifford and Louis 1967, 1971; Glassman 1995; Gray 1962, 1963; Guillain 1856; Iliffe 1979; Kimambo 1989; Liebowitz 1999; Lonsdale 1985; Meritt 1978; Middleton 1992; Mutoro 1998; Mwanzi 1985; Nicholls 1971; Ofcansky and Yeager 1997; Oliver 1952; 1991; Pearson 2000; Pétré-Grenouilleau 2004a, 2004b; Ranger 1985; Robinson and Gallagher 1961; Sheriff 1987; Sheriff and Ferguson 1991; Sunseri 1993, 1996, 2002; Unomah and Webster 1976; Valey 2004; Wirz and Eckert 2004; Wright 1985. A helpful overview can be found at Kieran 1966, 16–22.

71. On Zanzibar in particular, see Amory 1994; Bennett 1978; Fair 1994, 2001; Gilbert 2004; Hamilton 1957; Hollingsworth 1953; Ingrams 1967; Lodhi 1984; Lyne 1969; Nicolini 2002; Sheriff 1987, 1995; Sheriff and Ferguson 1991. For an overview of Omani history, especially in relation to Zanzibar, see the following: Bennett 1978, 14–123; Bhacker 1991, 1992; Lodhi 1984; Middleton 1992, 35–59; Owtram 2004, 29–50; Pearson 2000; Risso 1986; Sheriff 1987. On the world of the Indian Ocean as it affected eastern Africa, see the following: Clarence-Smith 1989b; Pearson 1998; Risso 1995. For excellent discussions of the Islamic history of the region, see the relevant articles in Levtzion and Pouwels 2000a, especially those by Pouwels, Pearson, Sperling, Alpers, and Chande (2000). Useful surveys of the historical literature on the politics of the period in question can be found in Adas 1993 and Bridges 2000.

72. On the German presence in eastern Africa, see Iliffe 1969; Iliffe 1979, 89ff; Koponen 1994; Wirz and Eckert 2004.

European overrule certainly affected the Holy Ghost mission in eastern Africa, but other political, economic, religious, and even environmental processes distinguishable from the coming of colonialism also shaped in profound ways the Spiritan evangelization of slaves. Most importantly, a number of factors enhanced or restricted the availability of slaves for the purposes of evangelization. Aggressive British attempts to interdict the slave trade prior to colonial overrule brought many potential Christians to the missionaries, for example, as those freed from slave ships found themselves handed over to the missionaries by the British. The closing of the Zanzibar slave market in 1873 at British insistence ended the Spiritan practice of ransoming (or buying[73]) slaves at that venue. Other smaller markets sprang up and those freed at sea continued to arrive, but British decisions later limited the number of those delivered to the missions from maritime seizures of slave ships.

More properly economic changes in eastern Africa also affected slave evangelization. The missionaries watched the prices of slaves fluctuate due to market forces.[74] In addition, higher prices for commodities lowered the number of potential new Catholics-to-be because limited missionary funds could feed and shelter only so many. Finally, famine conditions could lead African families to turn over their vulnerable members to mission care.

Religious changes such as the expanded Christian missionary presence meant that the Spiritans found themselves facing other rivals for the hearts and souls of African peoples. Not only did they feel threatened by Protestants and Muslims, but Vatican decisions restricted the scope of their mission by handing over responsibility for some regions to other Catholic missionary societies. Finally, a series of ecological crises in the 1890s — locust swarms, drought, epidemics that killed cattle and people — forced many local peoples to turn to missionaries for help, again affecting missionary activity.[75]

This is not to say that European colonialism per se had only a slight effect on Spiritan evangelization, but only to place colonialism within a number of factors that shape missionary activity of any sort, not least the origins of the Catholic Church in eastern Africa. Indeed, contrary to much received wisdom, it could

---

73. Most of the time the word used for the purchasing of slaves at the slave market was *rachat* or *racheter* ("ransom," "redemption"; "to repurchase"). From time to time, however, missionaries employ *achat* or *acheter* ("buying"; "to purchase"). I have tried to follow the varying instances in order to discern if there is difference between the use of the terms, but I have found no pattern. They could be used interchangeably, though there is one late instance where the mother house in Paris crossed out the "r" in *rachats* in order that the truth of the matter not be lost (Kieran 1966, 129; CSSp 195vi: Circular letter draft by Courmont, 2i92; revision by mother house, vii–viii93).

74. One difficulty in comparing prices over time is that the currencies in use changed. Henschel estimates that prices for slaves were around fifteen francs in 1863 but climbed to seventy-four francs in 1874. Slaves cost between twenty-seven and fifty rupees in the 1890s (2001, 17).

75. Koponen 1994, 157–66. Iliffe raises the issue of whether the ecological difficulties of the 1890s might be related to the onset of the colonial economy rather than simply environmental factors not subject to human control (1979, 123ff, esp. 163–67). Giblin has raised similar questions (1992, 1996), as have recent essays edited by Beinart and McGregor (2003).

be argued in this case that official colonialism in fact hindered the Catholic mission in a variety of ways, at least initially, by spurring resistance to things seen as European. More to the point of the subject matter here considered, colonialism in its formal manifestation appeared when Spiritan attention to freed slaves was declining. The upshot of all this is simple: official European colonialism, much conventional historiography about the relationship between colonialism and Christian missionary activity notwithstanding, was not the necessary and sufficient soil in which Spiritan evangelization took place, but one prominent aspect of a complex and dynamic setting for that evangelization.

More important for the history of Spiritan slave evangelization than colonialism itself were the variety of forces that affected the number and types of freed slaves who came to the mission, and the manner in which they came. Two forces in particular shaped slavery in eastern Africa during this period: first, the consolidation of Omani power at Zanzibar, beginning in the early nineteenth century; second, the increasing European presence, in which Christian missionaries played a prominent role.

Omani Expansion, Christian Missions, and European Colonialism

The departure of the Portuguese in the late seventeenth century had left eastern Africa mostly outside of European political dynamics and without Christian missionaries until the mid-nineteenth century. By that time, the preeminent political figure at the coast of eastern Africa was the sultan of Zanzibar, scion of the BuSaidi dynasty originally from Oman at the Persian Gulf. The Omanis had long traded in the Indian Ocean and for centuries had been a political force at the coast of eastern Africa. Their powerful ruler Said Said, who ruled from 1804 until his death in 1856, solidified their place by moving the capital of his empire from Muscat to Zanzibar in 1840. His son, Majid, was the sultan who allowed the establishment of the Catholic mission at Zanzibar. Majid had come to the throne after his father's death precipitated a dynastic crisis, the upshot of which was that the sultanate was split in two. One son, Thuwain, remained in power in Oman, while Majid in 1856 assumed control in Zanzibar, where he ruled until his death in 1870.

As part of Omani expansion in eastern Africa and the growing power emanating from Zanzibar, the sultans' reach extended farther inland into eastern Africa, where caravans went for the trade that grew dramatically through the first half of the nineteenth century. Beginning in the early nineteenth century, the increased world demand for African ivory, seen as superior to that from India, had brought Swahili- and Omani-led trading caravans as far as the Great Lakes region after herds of elephants, tying eastern Africa more into the Indian Ocean economy.[76]

---

76. On trade in eastern Africa, see the following: Chrétien 2003, 195ff; de Vienne 1872; Nicholls 1971; Iliffe 1979, 40–52; Kimambo 1989; Glassman 1995, 55–78; Rockel 1995, 2000; Sheriff 1987, 155–200; Pearson 2000; Sperling 2000; Middleton 1992, 15–20.

Both Zanzibar's growing authority and the trade buoying it drew the interior and the coast more tightly together, economically and politically.

Under the sultans' leadership, Zanzibar town became an international city, with consulates of several countries as well as a number of international trading companies' offices within the Stone Town, the part of the city where the Omani presence and culture were most marked.[77] Large quantities of ivory, slaves, and spices were traded there, the last mostly cultivated at the coast, the first two gathered farther inland. Control over much of the trade from the interior allowed Zanzibar in the mid-nineteenth century to eclipse Kilwa as the main entrepôt for Indian Ocean trade at the coast, and the sultans grew rich by controlling trade through Zanzibar and other coastal ports.[78]

While their nations' traders and diplomats came to Zanzibar, the region's growth also led European Christian missionaries to take an increasing interest in eastern Africa in the mid-nineteenth century. Missionary beginnings were inauspicious. In 1844, the Church Missionary Society (CMS) of the Anglican Church had sent the German Johannes Krapf, who was joined in 1846 by his compatriot Johannes Rebmann. The two settled near the coast at Rabai in what is today Kenya, learning languages and customs as well as exploring the coast and interior of eastern Africa. Their attempts to convert local people produced few results.[79]

Catholic attempts at evangelization in the region had been even less noteworthy. In an effort to evangelize in Ethiopia, Propaganda Fide had sought a new way into the area in the middle of the nineteenth century. Two Capuchins who arrived in Zanzibar in 1857 as part of that attempt created a controversy by purchasing and baptizing a young slave girl, who they then tried to remove from Zanzibar via a slave ship. This action led to conflict with Sultan Majid — who feared British reprisals at a possible violation of the treaties suppressing the slave trade that he had signed with them — as well as with the French consul, who was the natural local authority for Catholic missionaries. The consul, however, was also anxious to keep Zanzibar from becoming a port from which laborers would go to the French island of Réunion in contravention of France's own restriction on contract labor agreements.[80] Eventually the missionaries were expelled from Zanzibar, and Majid forbade other missionaries to enter his capital several times later in the 1850s.[81]

This episode showed the importance of the French and British consuls, who represented their countries in the ongoing economic and political competition be-

---

77. Morton 1998; Sheriff 1987, 147f; Sheriff 1995; Fair 1994, 2001.
78. Sheriff 1987, 137–54.
79. Stock 1899, 2:124ff; Bennett 1964; Strayer 1978, 3f; Sahlberg 1986, 23–30.
80. The consul's refusal to allow the movement of workers from eastern Africa stood in contrast to other French interests. Some of his countrymen saw the need for labor at the French colony of Réunion, the place where the Catholic mission assumed by the Spiritans originated. The colonial regime at Réunion helped sponsor the initial foundation, with funding and transportation. See Bennett 1973 and 1974, as well as the recent discussion in Valey 2004.
81. Kieran 1966, 17–20; Bennett 1963a, 54ff; Bennett 1974; Bennett 1986, 21, 41.

tween their governments. Eastern Africa was one of many theaters where the two sought influence, trade, and the countering of the other's ambitions. The French Second Empire's foreign policy — until its end in 1870 — sought to check British advances wherever it could, a tendency begun even under the Guizot regime of the July Monarchy (1840–48). The British, meanwhile, besides pursuing trade, saw Zanzibar as crucial in their efforts to enforce existing treaties to curb the slave trade, as well as to counter perceived French advances.[82] Each wooed the sultan to gain economic and political advantages.

The foundation of the Catholic mission in 1860 was an important episode within the evolving relationships among the British, the French, and Zanzibar. It may also have been the consequence of Majid's strategy in relation to these European powers. Like the French and British, the Catholic Church also pursued its goals in the region, and Majid's refusals to allow missionaries into Zanzibar did not end Catholic attempts to found a mission there. In 1858, Bishop Armand Maupoint of St. Denis in Réunion was named apostolic delegate for the region by the Vatican. His designation bore fruit two years later when his vicar, Father Armand Fava, founded the Catholic mission at Zanzibar in December 1860. In his official accounts, Fava claimed that he overcame the sultan's objections with pledges to help develop the area and refrain from preaching openly.[83]

Others have surmised that Majid also accepted the Catholic (and thus French) mission in an effort to encourage even stronger British support for his regime, playing upon the anxieties within the rivalry. If this was so his ploy worked, for the large building purchased by the French mission alarmed local British officials, who suspected that French troops would eventually be housed there. The Foreign Office received news of the large potential barracks with concern, and British agents protested to the Ministry of Foreign Affairs in Paris. The appearance of the Catholic mission thus led to negotiations culminating in the March 1862 treaty between the French and the British that finally ended the long-simmering, low-level conflict between the two over influence at Zanzibar. According to the treaty, each side committed itself to support the Omani regime and not interfere in the region.[84] It was this mission that the Congregation of the Holy Ghost assumed two and a half years later, in June 1863.[85]

The noninterference treaty did little to stem the growing British influence at Zanzibar, an ascendance that was to have significant consequences for the

---

82. In an 1822 treaty the sultan had accepted British demands that he limit the slave trade, and that treaty was modified and made stricter by revisions in 1839, 1845, and 1850 (Bennett 1986, 21–22). On the British focus on Zanzibar to stop the slave trade, see McCaskie 2004, 175f. For French considerations, see Valey 2004, 200–202.
83. CSSp 196bii: Fava to Schwindenhammer, 18vii60.
84. See Kieran 1966, 27–30; Kieran 1968; Bennett 1974; Coupland 1967, 33–34; Groves 1948, 2:285–87; Nwulia 1975, 270ff. For a description of the house after some modifications by the Spiritans, see CSSp 196axii: Horner to Gaume, 1vii69. For the British correspondence in this period, see the Zanzibar Archives, Foreign Office correspondence, files AA1/5, AA1/6, AA1/7, AA2/3, and AA2/4.
85. Soul 1936; Versteijnen 1968a, 3.

economic and, eventually, the political fortunes of the Zanzibari sultan, as well as for the Spiritan mission. In 1870, Sultan Majid died, and his brother Barghash acceded to the Zanzibari sultanate. Three years later, the abolition-minded British Parliament sponsored the visit to the region of the former governor-general of India, Sir Bartle Frere, commissioning him to investigate the slave trade and enforce existing treaties in order to end it.[86] Frere's tour resulted in the closing of the slave market at Zanzibar in April 1873, an episode that went against French wishes, again demonstrating French weakness and ending any hope that France would play a significant part in the region's future.[87] The end of the open trade in slaves at Zanzibar along with the stricter enforcement of restrictions on slave trading that ensued also had another consequence. These measures eroded the financial backing and political authority of the still-new Sultan Barghash, thus loosening his hold over other Arab and African authorities in the region.[88]

Meanwhile, broader European interest in Africa grew. King Leopold II of Belgium hosted the International Geography Conference in 1876, where the participants laid the ground rules for concerted exploration of the continent and stipulated conditions for so-called legitimate European occupation. In late 1884, claiming rights from that conference, a new European presence entered eastern Africa: the German empire, anxious for overseas possessions equal to its ambitions. Hard-pressed, Sultan Barghash acceded to German and English pressure and withdrew from direct control of most of the mainland.[89]

Beginning in the late 1880s there was a great deal of anticolonial fighting in what would become Tanganyika.[90] German entry into the region aroused the resentment of both Arab and African peoples, who responded with armed resistance, probably without direct support from the sultans. The most notable such action has been called the Bushiri war, after the leader of the heterogeneous group of Africans and Arabs who fought the Germans. The war began in 1888 and lingered even after Bushiri's hanging at German hands in December 1889. It was the first of a number of armed conflicts between the Germans and local peoples beginning in the late 1880s and continuing into the twentieth century. As a result of these conflicts — most of which were more ethnically localized than the Bushiri war — the Germans cemented their grip on the mainland through

---

86. Frere's correspondence relating to his visit to eastern Africa can be found in the Zanzibar Archives, Foreign Office correspondence, file AA1/10.

87. As we shall see in chapter 4, the Spiritan missionary Baur was part of those conversations. He and the French consul vainly sought to forestall Barghash's capitulation before Kirk's threat (BG 9:518; Bennett 1973, 1974).

88. His income diminished and his concessions before British threats made manifest his dependence upon them. In light of the various opponents of his regime in Zanzibar, this situation made him even more dependent on the British, who weakened him financially but supported him politically, preferring the order he maintained to the potential chaos they expected should he be deposed (Sheriff 1987, 201–44).

89. See Meritt 1978 and Wirz and Eckert 2004. The Zanzibar journal (20xii85) speaks of a conference on the sultan's possessions, details about which can be found in Bennett 1986, 133–39.

90. Bennett 1986; Glassman 1995.

military conquests of different peoples and chiefdoms. At the same time, British control over Zanzibar itself also expanded after Barghash's death in 1888. He was followed by a series of short-lived sultans who presided, rather helplessly, over the emasculation of the Omani regime in eastern Africa before European colonial domination. An 1890 treaty between the Germans and British split control in the region between the two, the Germans gaining rights to Tanganyika and the British assuming responsibility for what would become Kenya and Uganda, as well as Zanzibar.[91]

Despite the fact that it eventually retreated before European colonial ambitions, accounts of nineteenth-century eastern Africa have often underestimated the power of the Omani regime. As a recent overview of the historiography of eastern Africa covering the years prior to European colonialism argues, historians have usually written the story of that "prelude" in such a way as to allow the eventual imposition of European control to determine its telling.[92] Such history writing places Africans and other non-Europeans out of the picture. It also often unfairly caricatures the Omani regime centered in Zanzibar as weak when in fact its political reach was extensive.[93]

This tendency to downplay Omani power makes contextualizing Spiritan evangelization in this period difficult, for the Omani presence shaped their strategy. Unlike many historians of eastern Africa affected by what Roy Bridges calls the "mesmeric effect" of eventual colonialism,[94] the Spiritans saw the sultan of Zanzibar as a major figure, and they acted with a deep awareness of his power until the 1890s and even beyond. They mentioned rumors that the sultan would hand over his territories to Europeans, and they could look forward in hope to European control of Zanzibar,[95] but they did not fully anticipate the supplanting of the sultan and the imposition of European colonialism.

Omani rule in Zanzibar and at the coast was thus an ever-present context within which the missionaries evangelized slaves in the period covered in this book. Indeed, the Spiritan near-exclusive focus on slaves as targets of evangelization, at least until the less Islamized areas of the continent were reached, finds its explanation not in missionary precedent but in the Islamic political situation in which they operated. Fava had been allowed to begin the Catholic mission, he thought, because christianizing slaves did not trouble the sultan. Open preaching to Muslims, however, could endanger their permission to carry out missionary activity,

---

91. In 1891, the German government assumed control over the German East Africa Company, which had been founded in 1887. See Kollman 2001, 58–66.

92. Bridges 2000. See also the articles in Pétré-Grenouilleau 2004a, each of which also underscores the haphazard and unpredictable course that eventuated in the so-called scramble for Africa.

93. Bennett 1986, 14f. Bennett also insists that the sultan's power stretched inland more forcefully than is usually acknowledged (ibid., 121–22).

94. Bridges 2000, 105.

95. In April 1865 Horner wrote of rumors that the French were going to take control of the coast and the British the island of Zanzibar (CSSp 196bii: Horner to Schwindenhammer, 16iv65; BG 4:563ff). For his hopes in this regard, see CSSp 196bii: Horner to Schwindenhammer, 7i67.

and the Spiritans avoided it out of fear of arousing their hosts' antagonism. It
later endangered Muslims who converted to Christianity.[96]

The Expansion of Slavery in Nineteenth-Century Eastern Africa

The Omanis and Europeans did not bring history to eastern Africa. Both
the interior and coast of the region had long been subject to large-scale political and social transformations. The coastal region had for centuries belonged
to the mainly non-European commercial system centered around Indian Ocean
trade.[97] The interior was never dormant but had witnessed political consolidation,
technological advances, and religious movements centuries prior to prolonged
interaction with outsiders.[98] Indeed the interior was in the midst of profound
social and political change in the early nineteenth century when the trade from
the Swahili coast first began to increase. Populations in the region were moving in the wake of the Ngoni invasions of southern-eastern Africa, themselves
possibly the result of the *mfecane* in southern Africa. There were also conflicts
among the Maa-speaking peoples of what is today north-central Tanzania and
southern Kenya.

One crucial consequence of the deeper penetration of transregional trade into
eastern Africa in the nineteenth century was a significant expansion of the slave
trade.[99] The taking of slaves in conquest or as pawns due to indebtedness had
long been part of life in the region, and slaves had been exported to Arabia
and Asia in relatively small numbers for centuries by the Persians, Omanis, and
others. Yet new trade triggered and catalyzed religious and political changes that
increased the traffic in human beings. Different access to trade goods, especially
firearms and certain luxury goods that could be traded for firearms, created power
imbalances among local authorities, enabling large-scale political consolidation

---

96. The Zanzibar journal records two situations in which Muslim converts to Christianity were
jailed (9i86, 17iv86). See CSSp 197aii: Acker to Emonet, 18i86.

97. Prestholdt 2004.

98. For a discussion of technological changes and the evolution of political consolidation in
Africa, see Miller 1999a, 13–18.

99. For overviews of slavery in eastern Africa, see the following: Beachey 1976a, 1976b; Cooper
1977, 1–23; Cooper 1980, 19ff; Davidson 1980, 175–202; Delpechin 1991, 21ff; Ewald 1998;
Middleton 1992, 24–25; Morton 1998; Nimtz 1980, 40–43; Sheriff 1985; Sunseri 1993. On the
pre-nineteenth-century slave trade, see Oliver 1991, 142ff; Nwulia 1981; Scarr 1998. On the expansion of the trade in the nineteenth century, see the following: Alpers 1975, 234–38; Glassman 1995;
Sheriff 1987, 33ff; Manning 1990, 52–54, 136–42; Daget 1989; Gordon 1989, 128ff; Renault 1989;
Unomah and Webster 1976, 298ff; Kimambo 1989, 235ff; Morton 1990; Cooper 1977, 1980. Sheriff
(1987, 49ff) sees the shift from export to internal slavery as the key change in Zanzibar's economic
history in the nineteenth century, while Campbell (1989) emphasizes the connection between the
Zanzibar-centered slave trade and that farther south, connecting Kilwa, the interior, and Madagascar.
The most sophisticated and influential recent studies of slavery at the eastern African coast are by
Glassman (1991; 1995, 79–114) and Deutsch (2000, 2003). Important insights also can be found with
regard to Madagascar in Larson 2000. An intriguing study of the role of slavery and emancipation
in the formation of ethnic identity is dealt with in Isaacman and Isaacman 2004. See Kollman 2001,
115ff.

for some and making turmoil for many. Powerful chieftains used the new weapons and military strategies derived from the Ngoni to draw together larger polities, especially in the Great Lakes region. These processes of political consolidation often occasioned violence, as polities became subordinated to one another, thus increasing the taking of captives, a regular feature of political incorporation in the region.[100]

Such captives became slaves for export when demand for their labor increased at the coast. New demand for human cargoes had arisen from Europeans some years before, first in the eighteenth century as the French sought to buy human labor for their sugar-producing islands of the Indian Ocean.[101] Mid-nineteenth-century British abolitionist pressures in western Africa also led the Portuguese and Cubans to seek labor for Brazil and the Caribbean in the eastern part of the continent. The growth of large new markets for slaves at the coast combined with the political changes of the eighteenth and nineteenth centuries to foster slave-raiding in the interior, which grew in frequency and ferocity. As one study of slavery puts it, "The 1860s, 1870s and 1880s were times of incredible danger and insecurity in central Tanganyika, where people could easily fall prey to warlords, kidnappers or slave traders."[102] As slavery increased, Zanzibar became the most important site for slave-trading by the middle of the nineteenth century, as well as a trading center for ivory, spices, and goods from outside such as cotton cloth.[103] Local demand for slaves continued even after the Europeans had renounced slavery and forbade the slave trade.

A variety of interrelated and mutating terms described the increasingly diverse local population of Zanzibar, which jumped from an estimated twelve thousand in town in 1835 to perhaps seventy thousand by the end of the 1860s.[104] At the apex of the social hierarchy since 1830 were the Arabs, who comprised three groups: the Omanis, who were Ibadhi Muslims and in overall control since the 1830s; the Hadrami, who had been at the eastern African coast prior to Omani control and were Sunnis; and a group from the southern Arabian peninsula who arrived every year to trade, staying several months. Parallel to the Arabs in social power but somewhat apart in social interaction were Indians from south Asia, who served as financiers and shopkeepers in the city. These Indians also broke down into

100. Thus George Deutsch points out that Unyamwezi, a region several weeks' journey from Zanzibar, imported more slaves than they exported (Deutsch 2000, 25).
101. Alpers 1967; Stein 1979, 119–26.
102. Deutsch 2000, 272.
103. Erik Gilbert has recently suggested that Zanzibar's growth in the nineteenth century reflected interest from the Atlantic Ocean economy in the goods coming there from the interior, for the island had already long been central to the Indian Ocean economy (2004, 31–34, 58).
104. See Sheriff (1987, 138) for a table of the population of Zanzibar town from 1835 to 1910. For information on the Zanzibari population, see the following: Burton 1872, 1:105ff; Dale 1969; Nimtz 1980, 29ff; Middleton 1992, 10–15; Mazrui and Shariff 1994. The first Holy Ghost superior in Zanzibar, Antoine Horner, also wrote a description of Zanzibar's population and cultures that appears in the Holy Ghost mission's Zanzibar journal after the entry for December 1866. For the most recent analysis of Zanzibar's racial history, linking early categories to postcolonial politics, see Glassman 2004.

several groups: Hindu "Banians," Shi'ite Muslim "Khojas," Ismaili Muslims, and Portuguese citizens from Goa, who were Catholic. After the middle of the century the first three groups of Indians took control of the finances of the region. Many Arabs became indebted to them due to fluctuations in world prices of local commodities caused by abolitionist pressures, changing supply and demand, and natural disasters.[105]

Below the Arabs and Indians in status were the nonslave Africans of Zanzibar, represented by a series of terms that approximated ethnic identities in the precolonial world. At the apex were those designated the Shirazi, an ancient term that had been used at the coast to indicate (probably fictive[106]) Persian ancestry. The Shirazi in traditional lists of Zanzibar's ethnic groups are often glossed as "Afro-Arabs." Recent analyses show the way the term served to distinguish some Africans from other Africans, giving the Shirazi a higher status either through association with the town, the coastal region, Islam, or nonslave origins. The term "Swahili" itself changed in its uses and references through the nineteenth and early twentieth centuries. On the one hand it signified the variegated language of the coast, KiSwahili, a Bantu tongue one-third of whose words are borrowed from Arabic. It also could indicate, however, a certain achieved state of civilization associated with the coast, and could thus elevate one person above another who was seen to be associated with the less civilized interior. There were other Africans whose roots were considered more "local," and who were also not seen as slaves. These included the Wahadimu, Watumbatu, and Wapemba, each of whom spoke a different Swahili dialect and shared particular customs and locales.[107] Recent studies of the historical uses of terms such Shirazi and Swahili (and there were others[108]) — suggests that they should be seen more as status markers than ethnic identities. Africans could aspire to be Swahili, then Shirazi, who themselves could become "Arab." In the midst of this fluidity, the most important political change in the nineteenth century among the influential classes consisted in Omani Arab supersession of the Shirazi as the dominant class along most of the eastern African coast.

The largest change, however, occurred at the bottom of this social world, among those usually designated slaves. By the middle of the nineteenth century these composed two-thirds to three-quarters of the population, or some 40,000 in Zanzibar town, and an even greater number, perhaps 250,000, on the islands

---

105. Sheriff 1987, 105–9.

106. John Middleton discusses the nature of "Shirazi" identity, showing how claims to Persian ancestry reflect attempts at increasing social prestige (1992, 186–87). See also Amory 1994, 103ff, and Glassman 1995, 22–24.

107. For the fullest discussion of these ethnic groups, see Gray 1977.

108. Thus the terms *mwungwana* ("gentleman," with connotations of free and not slave status) and *mmrima* ("townsperson") became labels to distinguish one from someone from the interior. These could even be appropriated by slaves to distinguish them from slaves more recently arrived from the interior, who could be called *mshenzi* ("barbarian") or *mjinga* ("fool"). For fuller discussions of the term "Swahili," see Glassman 1995, 61–64, 81f; Amory 1994, 51ff.

of Pemba and Zanzibar as a whole.[109] They served in a variety of roles but increasingly labored in burgeoning clove plantations.

Claude Meillassoux claims that Africa has had in its history a wider variety of servile relationships than anywhere else,[110] and the nineteenth-century eastern African coast certainly epitomized that variety. People designated as slaves had long carried out diverse tasks in the region: as domestic servants, dockhands, concubines, agricultural workers, and fishermen. Such people, labeled by a variety of terms, were not "free" in the modern Western sense of possessing personal autonomy and the possibility of self-determination, but few were alienable commodities, as were African American slaves in the nineteenth-century American South.[111] They were outsiders within the dominant hegemony by which coastal elites might seek to define themselves — hence their slave status — yet other ties of dependency and reciprocity could exist alongside that status. Such relationships could be conceived in a variety of ways, so that dependency could bind them to their masters (or lords, or owners) by fictive (or extended) kinship,[112] debt obligations, overt clientage, patron-client relations variously conceived, even marriage. Many analyses of slavery distinguish this sort of "open" or "absorptive" system of unfree labor from the "closed" systems typical of extractive plantation slave systems like the American South and the Caribbean.[113]

This "open system" or institutionalized "rights-in-persons"[114] did not cease in the nineteenth century. But it was joined (and sometimes replaced) beginning in the early and mid-nineteenth century by a new kind of less paternalistic, more "closed," more economized personal servitude — sometimes known as "chattel slavery" to distinguish it from other forms of unfree labor. This much more clearly resembled slavery in the sense common to most Western readers. The increased demands from Europeans and others helped stimulate chattel slavery, but changes in the political economy of eastern Africa itself also generated this new form of servitude. With the establishment of the clove plantations at Zanzibar and Pemba beginning around 1830 an increasing number of unfree laborers in eastern Africa had become *internal* plantation slaves. Thus the slaves living in Zanzibar town and its environs increasingly took on the status of commodities,

---

109. Ewald 1998; Morton 1998. Serge Daget (1989) argues that there were 200,000 slaves exported into the Indian Ocean region in the eighteenth century, and from 1860 to 1870, 30–35,000 per year passed through ports controlled by Zanzibar. In 1870, he says, 13,000 were exported to Oman alone. Kimambo (1989) says that in the 1860s, Zanzibar and Pemba absorbed 10,000 slaves per year, and that 70,000 passed per year through the Zanzibar slave market. His figures rely on Alpers 1967.

110. Meillassoux 1991, 7.

111. The distinctiveness of Caribbean and North American slavery has long been recognized in comparison to other forms of social domination or unfree labor. For a thoughtful comparison of the culture of slavery in the United States and Zanzibar, see Cooper 1977, 241, 253–54, as well as his more general thoughts in Cooper 1979.

112. Thus, in the language of the Yao, the word for free is "of the family" (Small 1980, 35).

113. Glassman 1995, 81ff; Cooper 1979; Cooper 1981, 272–78. For a good discussion of the varieties of slave experiences in eastern Africa, especially a helpful distinction between coastal and interior slavery, see Deutsch 2000, 15–92.

114. The term was popularized by Miers and Kopytoff (1977).

liable to be bought and sold in the slave market. Growing trade between coast and interior also led to new demands for porterage, creating new sorts of labor relations, even likely helping to create a new ethnic identity, the Nyamwezi, who were said to be "cheaper than slaves."[115]

Even more insidiously still, beginning in the 1850s plantation agriculture also spread to the coast, for sugar production in the Pangani River valley and to grow grain near Malindi, north of Mombasa. There the vivid horrors of plantation-type slavery developed in eastern Africa. The slave market at Zanzibar reached its height between 1859 and 1872, at which time fifteen to twenty thousand slaves were sold there every year, of whom perhaps one-half left the island for other destinations on the coast of eastern Africa or other places in the Indian Ocean or beyond. Whether or not the economy at the eastern African coast can be judged a "slave mode of production" in the Marxist sense, all witnesses agree that slaves constituted the majority of the population on the islands of Zanzibar and Pemba for most of the nineteenth century. They came from a number of different parts of eastern and central Africa, but by 1860, 13 percent were locally born. Most came from the hinterlands behind Kilwa, thus south of Zanzibar away from the coast. They were roughly balanced between males and females and of a variety of ages, with the males younger than the females.[116]

•

It was in this setting, with its growing slave population and its changing political and economic realities, that the missionaries of the Congregation of the Holy Ghost pursued the evangelization of slaves.

---

115. Sheriff 1985, 1987; Glassman 1995, 60–61, 81–85; Rockel 2000; Deutsch 2000.
116. Sheriff 1989, 140–44.

Chapter Two

The Spiritans and the Africans They Sought to Change

The Spiritans and the slaves they evangelized met in the same place and time, yet they imagined themselves very differently. Like most Christian missionaries, the Spiritans arrived in eastern Africa imbued with zeal for evangelization. They were intent on making Christians from the local inhabitants, who would then form a new ecclesial community to bring Christ to the interior of Africa. The nature of the changes they sought in individual Africans and the type of community they tried to establish derived to a great extent from the world from which these priests and brothers had come and where they had been socialized. After 1863 and before 1890, about eighty-five Spiritan priests and brothers served in eastern Africa.[1]

The targets of their missionary zeal, Africans who found themselves at the Catholic mission through various means, came to Zanzibar in the reverse direction and against their will. They brought to their interactions with the missionaries their own predispositions, forged through diverse experiences prior to and during what was almost invariably at least a short period of enslavement. Most arrived at the mission through one of two means: after ransoming by the Spiritans (from Zanzibar's slave market or less formal situations) or after being freed at sea (usually through British interventions). A small number came to the Spiritans from the streets of Zanzibar or other places where they probably either escaped from, or were abandoned by, their masters.[2] Later the Spiritans received refugees and orphans from war, the children of families suffering famine, and those released by the Germans from slave caravans. Perhaps four thousand such slaves passed into the Spiritans' hands between the early 1860s and the early 1890s, though up to a third might have died soon afterward.[3]

---

1. Koren 1994.

2. Those whom the Spiritans gathered from the streets and brought to their mission would thus have usually spent some time enslaved at the coast, but it is difficult to determine the length of their exposure to coastal slave realities. Such *abandonées* might have been part of the system of unfree labor that existed prior to, and perhaps apart from, chattel slavery or the growth of export slavery, but that is hard to determine.

3. The Spiritans at Bagamoyo began a formal list of those they ransomed or received from slavery only in 1884 (LERE). It is a large booklet, listing the name of the ex-slave, age, place of

45

Generalizations can be made about both the Spiritans and those they evangelized. Both were made up primarily of individuals who had come from rather restricted geographical areas: eastern Africa and France. Both were composed of individuals who had undergone significant shared experiences: formation in their religious congregation and enslavement. But neither group was homogeneous, nor did either group or the individuals composing them act from a fixed set of rules that governed their behavior in any automatic or predetermined way. The lack of culturally or socially prescribed blueprints ordering human action, however, does not entail the absence of generalizable traits structuring such action. This chapter describes the two groups in order to begin to appreciate those habits of mind, heart, and body that organized their sense of themselves, others, and the environment in which they lived. After drawing a portrait of each group, the chapter concludes by discussing their immediate concerns upon arriving at the mission, especially their approach to slavery, the institution that enabled their coming together. Predictably, they approached the reality of slavery quite differently.

The Spiritan Missionaries Who Came to Eastern Africa

The Holy Ghost missionaries who came to eastern Africa emerged from within several encompassing historical trajectories that shaped their approach to evangelization. In the first place, they rode the crest of a nineteenth-century Catholic missionary reawakening. This gave them zeal, connected them with the universal church centered in Rome, and led them into aggressive fund-raising efforts. At the same time, their (mostly) French background caused them to view the political world through the prism of French church-state relations in that period. These national origins generated an ambivalent loyalty toward the French colonial presence in Zanzibar, and affected their relations with the Omani regime as well as other European powers. They also came from a rather narrow geographic and socioeconomic segment of France. The aspects of their background that most shaped the practices enacted in the evangelization of slaves, however, derived from social experiences while they were in formation to become Spiritans. These included their seminary training itself, which alerted them to Catholic missionary practices and also shaped their approach to slavery. Finally, there was a factor not before appreciated: nearly all the Spiritans were exposed to nineteenth-century penal institutions designed for the reform of juveniles.

---

origin, as well as the benefactor who sponsored their purchase or support. A huge number of ethnic groups and designations found their way into the list. Many of those entered were very young. The book was kept until 1894. By then, 1,580 slaves had been ransomed and received.

The total of 4,000 comes from the total in LERE combined with a figure given by Henschel (2000a, 5), who counted those received from 1870 to 1884 and came up with 1,765. In addition, I estimate that between 500 and 1,000 slaves were ransomed at Zanzibar prior to 1870. If anything, the estimate of 4,000 is low, for it does not count those who came to interior missions beginning in 1877.

Nineteenth-Century Missionaries and Africa

Founded in 1703, the Congregation of the Holy Ghost had long served the church in France and in French colonies. Soon after its founding it took responsibility to train colonial clergy for the expansionist prerevolutionary French state. After almost disappearing in the wake of the French Revolution, the Spiritans revived and expanded in the mid-nineteenth century under the leadership and inspiration of François-Marie-Paul Libermann (1802–52).[4] Libermann, an Alsatian-born Jewish convert, had founded another congregation in 1840, the Congregation of the Holy Heart of Mary, the expressed purpose of which was evangelizing *les noirs*. The vitality of this new congregation contrasted with the desultory postrevolutionary state of the Spiritans, so in the 1840s Libermann's group took over missions in French possessions in the Caribbean, the Indian Ocean, and western Africa, with the approval of the French state and the Vatican. In 1848, the burgeoning newer movement joined the struggling older congregation at the suggestion of Catholic authorities in Rome.[5] Libermann dominated the group after the merger, serving as superior general until his death in 1852, by which time the majority of the members owed their allegiance to the congregation to his dynamism.

Libermann's revitalization of the Spiritans took part in a trend with epochal importance for our world today: the remarkable missionary expansion of the Christian churches outside of Europe beginning in the nineteenth century.[6] The Catholic part of that expansion derived predominantly from France, where numerous religious orders were founded, and others, like the Spiritans, were revitalized. These new communities increasingly imbued the church as a whole with a missionary spirit. Catholic zeal, which paralleled at least equally strenuous efforts by Protestant missionary groups initially mostly from Great Britain, drew upon the general renewal of the French church during the Restoration period (1815–30) and afterward.[7]

As part of that missionary growth, in 1822 the Society for the Propagation of the Faith — often confused with the Vatican office Propaganda Fide but actually a separate organization though it was put under the direction of Propaganda Fide after 1922 — was founded in Lyon, to gather and encourage contributions to support Catholic missionaries around the world. Twenty years later the Holy

---

4. For the history of the Spiritans and Libermann's role in their revitalization, see Le Roy 1921, Koren 1958, and Koren 1983. For a more recent account of the Spiritans in France, see Ernoult 2000, which has an excellent summary of the pre-Libermann years on pages 17–24.

On Libermann's thought see the following: Burke 1998; Kelly 1955; Gay 1943; Briault 1946; Goyau 1948, 151f, 177f, 207–20; Van Kaam 1959; Koren 1958, 157–84; Koren 1983, 247–64. For brief summaries see Kieran 1966, 11ff; Sundkler and Steed 2000, 102–3. The most reliable and critically valuable material can be found in the articles contained in Coulon and Brasseur 1988.

5. For a recent discussion of the merger, explaining the history of interpretation of the events, see Legrain 2000. See also Kollman 2002, 84ff.

6. Kieran 1966, 4ff. For recent studies that appreciate the importance of the missionary movement, see Walls 1996, 2002.

7. Baumont 1984, 216f; Prudhomme 1996; Giglioni 2001.

Childhood Society was established to encourage missionary support and enthusiasm among Catholic children. These two organizations established local chapters all over the Catholic world, including in Zanzibar, where the mission had chapters of both before the Spiritans arrived.[8] They also published regular, widely circulated newsletters informing the faithful about the deeds of men and women serving in mission lands. Horner claimed that his missionary vocation came from reading about the exploits of French missionaries in the periodical of the Society of the Propagation of the Faith, *Les Annales de la Association de la Propagation de la Foi* (APF), which began publication in 1826. He later inspired others by his writings in APF as well as in *Les Missions Catholiques* (MC), a journal added in 1868 by the Propagation of the Faith in order to speak to a more popular audience about Catholic missionary activity.[9]

French Catholic missionary zeal drew upon nationalistic pride in earlier missionary activity and helped generate an obsessive urgency to reclaim lost souls.[10] This drive for *le salut des âmes* (the salvation of souls) joined the spiritual virtue of abandonment into the hands of providence as hallmarks of the missionary spirit in Libermann and others who sought to inspire missionaries.

Such zeal would certainly mark the Spiritans in eastern Africa, a zeal at once for souls and for founding the church. A few days after arriving in Zanzibar, Horner wrote the Spiritan superior general on the need to move to the coast, closing with this plea: "Strive, on your part, most reverend father, to obtain resources for us and send us zealous confreres to begin a new mission on that immense mainland coast from where we hear great cries!"[11] Another Spiritan wrote joyfully of the baptisms of the dying he was able to perform at Zanzibar:

> In the midst of all of our trials, the good Lord grants us plenty of consolations, and the sweetest for the heart of a missionary. What makes our joy supreme is to be able to receive and save poor abandoned slave children; and we have this good fortune often, myself in particular, for nearly everyday I have the good luck of making these precious discoveries.[12]

Catholic missionary zeal reached Africa, and eastern Africa in particular, comparatively slowly. Only long-established missions in Asia and America were discussed in the Propagation of the Faith's journal *Annales* until 1839. After that the coverage of African missions grew steadily, reflecting the fact that by the end of the century Africa drew the lion's share of French Catholic missionaries.[13] Yet until the late 1830s, only North Africa merited discussion, and in the

8. Zanzibar journal, 3xii62.
9. CSSp 196bii: Horner to Schwindenhammer, 24–30xiii63; BG 6:443–44. The Holy Childhood Society's journal began in 1849 and was entitled *Annales de l'œuvre de la Sainte-Enfance*.
10. See Kollman 2001, 88–89.
11. CSSp 196bii: Horner to Schwindenhammer, 29vi63.
12. CSSp 196bii: Baur to Schwindenhammer, 3v65; BG 4:635ff.
13. Libermann's congregation joined other mostly French groups like the Oblates of Mary Immaculate (who worked primarily in southern Africa), the Society of African Missions (also known

early 1840s were added Liberia, the Cape of Good Hope, Madagascar, Guinea (the coast of western Africa), and Central Africa. Only in the 1850s were French subscribers able to read about eastern Africa, where the ecclesiastical prefecture Zanguebar appeared in 1860.[14]

Such missionary efforts brought Africa to the attention of Europeans, but they often presented Africa as an object of particular pity. The Spiritans described eastern Africa as the most abandoned place in the world with regard to truth and proper religion. "Where," Horner asked, "is there such an abandonment of souls as here?" The famous French cleric Monsignor Gaume, a friend of the Spiritans, opened an 1872 book on Catholic missionary work in Africa with the assertion that "of the five parts of the world [Europe, Asia, the Americas, Australia, and Africa], Africa is the most unfortunate and abandoned." He then proceeded to describe the deleterious effects of the "curse of Ham": slavery, idolatry, savage customs like infanticide and cannibalism, as well as fierce beasts and an inclement climate.[15]

In going to Africa, Spiritan missionaries self-consciously did so in union with the Catholic Church centered in Rome. Their mission in eastern Africa, like their entire congregation, lay under that central authority, which had sought to organize and direct missions in unevangelized areas through Propaganda Fide since the office's founding in 1622. Though the existence of Propaganda Fide testified to the Catholic Church's desire for direct control over its missions without interference from nation-states — especially the Spanish and Portuguese, who had arrangements with the papacy for religious control over their colonies beginning in the fifteenth century — French appointment of bishops in France and its colonies persisted through the nineteenth century. In addition, only in the twentieth century were some of the stipulations of the Portuguese and Spanish treaties with Rome, called the *patronato* and *padraodo*, undone. Indeed, in eastern Africa the Spiritan mission several times faced challenges from the Portuguese-controlled church in Mozambique, which occasionally claimed authority over the entire region on the basis of a papal bull from 1612.[16]

The decisions of Propaganda Fide affected the Spiritans more directly when these altered the ecclesiastical authority of the mission. This first occurred when

---

as the "Lyon Fathers," who worked in western Africa), and a number of religious orders of women, all of whom sought to spread the gospel in Africa.

From a broader perspective than only missionary activity, Philip Curtin says that European interest in Africa, which had focused on western Africa beginning in the 1780s and southern Africa from the 1820s, shifted toward eastern Africa only in the 1850s (Curtin 1964, v–vi).

14. The best single account of eastern African Christian missionary history remains Oliver 1952, though its limitations are considerable mainly due to the fact that Lutherans and Catholics restricted the sources at Oliver's disposal on their works, as he admits (Oliver 1952, x). A brief summary is given by Kieran (1966, 17ff).

15. Gaume 1872, 1, 2–4. Horner often did the same (CSSp 196ax: Horner to Propagation of the Faith, 31xii66, 29xii67).

16. The 1885 visit of the archbishop of Mozambique, Reed da Silva, laid bare Portuguese ecclesial ambitions, prompting Courmont to press Propaganda Fide for clear boundaries to his apostolic vicariate. See Kieran 1966, 284f, and Kollman 2001, 74f.

the death of the bishop of Réunion in 1871 led Propaganda Fide to place the mission under direct Spiritan control. Then in 1883 Rome agreed to a Spiritan request to advance the Zanguebar mission from an apostolic prefecture to an apostolic vicariate, by which decision Bishop Courmont was appointed to direct the mission. Finally, by Propaganda Fide's decisions, areas originally assumed by the Spiritans as part of their ecclesiastical jurisdiction were assigned to other Catholic religious orders. These decisions caused profound frustration to the Spiritans.[17]

Their missionary vocation not only connected the Spiritans to a global church centered in Rome, it also made incumbent upon them raising money to support their mission. From the beginning of their service in eastern Africa, finances distracted the missionaries and caused them much worry. In order to support their mission with funds from agencies in Europe, the Spiritans had to issue the regular reports noted earlier.[18] They also published accounts of their work, even dramas to be performed in Europe, to raise money.[19] Money was a constant concern of the Spiritans, and raising it and using it responsibly occupied a great deal of their energy. As we shall see, financial pressures determined Spiritan practices in their evangelization of slaves, as the need for the labor of the former slaves grew in Spiritan awareness and shaped missionary strategies.[20]

The Spiritans did not only seek money from overseas. They also tried a number of different revenue-producing activities in eastern Africa, especially the raising of crops and livestock.[21] Courmont in particular made self-support a high priority at the mission stations after his arrival in 1883. During his tenure, the Spiritans expanded the coconut and copra production at Bagamoyo, tried mining and rubber cultivation, and experimented with vanilla, cotton, clove, and coffee. They also sold plants and animals to European zoos and botanical gardens. Courmont urged his confreres not to share new species with strangers; the glory (and the money) should instead flow into the Congregation.[22]

Financial pressures certainly affected practices at the mission. They also shaped how missionaries represented their missionary work. Missionaries have not infrequently overestimated the misery of those they serve in order to raise money, something the Spiritans may well have done.[23] More commonly, anxieties

---

17. Courmont's frustrations and fears of being supplanted by other Catholic missionaries can be found in the 1887 letters found in CSSp 197aii. For the territorial arrangements in the late 1880s, see BG 14:369ff, and a fuller discussion in Kieran 1966, 40f. Henry Koren prepared, but never published, a very helpful comprehensive schematic presentation of the evolving jurisdictions of the church in eastern Africa (Koren 1992).

18. Kieran 1966, 396–98. On Horner's success as a fund-raiser, see BG 10:50, 95, 117.

19. These included Suéma, to be discussed in chapter 3 (Gaume 1870). In addition, in 1886 Le Roy produced a play, *Douze Sous*, to encourage young people to save one *sou* per month for the missions (CSSp 196axiii).

20. For a thorough discussion of this issue, see Kieran 1966, 394–427.

21. Kieran 1966, 400–427.

22. CSSp 196aiv: chapter of 1884; Kieran 1966, 401–2.

23. Kieran 1969, 348–49. As we shall see in chapter 3, however, there were limits to this tendency, because the Spiritans also want to ensure the promise in those they evangelized.

about the fiscal circumstances of the mission constantly intrude upon missionary discourse and manifest themselves in a bewildering variety of legitimations in funding requests and annual reports. The rhetorical strategy of the Spiritans commonly involved punctuating their accounts of their work with a *conditional* tone, emphasizing both threats to their mission and potential opportunities. Both the possible boon and the looming danger varied: they could be external force or opportunity, physical threat or fiscal promise. Ironically, the same external forces, especially Islam and Protestant missionary activity, could appear both as reasons for fear or hope, as carrot or stick. Regardless of the contradictions that appeared over time, the conditional discourse functioned rhetorically to encourage generous donations, underscoring the promised benefits to the mission should funding continue or a requested grant be given, and threats of harm to come should funding be cut or a plea be denied.[24] The political changes in the 1880s eventuating in European overrule, like the presence of Islam and Protestantism, featured in missionary fund-raising requests as reason for both hope and fear, the threat of Protestant powers imposing their will balancing the potential benefits of European control.[25]

It was not only external forces — Muslims, Protestants, or Germans — that legitimated missionary requests for funding because of the conditions they created. The Spiritans paraded their mission's promise in the work of civilizing the wretched or Christianizing the condemned and emphasized the esteem in which the mission was held by others — for instance, the French consul.[26] The missionaries also proclaimed financial incentives for timely giving: a current investment in land at Bagamoyo, for instance, would create revenue long into the future, but land would not be available forever.[27] The same conditional tone was struck, as we shall see, in descriptions of the Africans who came to the missions.

---

24. For Horner's warnings about the consequences of lack of funds, see CSSp 196ax: Horner to Propagation of the Faith, 13xii71; CSSp 196axii: Horner to Laverriere, 7ii78.

Islam both justified slave ransoming, since no conversions of Muslims were possible, and also legitimated new buildings because of its polluting threat to the fragile faith of the new converts. But it also guaranteed that donations would be well used because of its promise of social order and religious toleration, especially when the sultan favored the mission. For examples of this contradictory discourse, see the following: CSSp 196aii: Horner to Notre Dame des Victoires, 24xi64; CSSp 196ax: Horner to Propagation of the Faith, 29xii67; CSSp 196axii: Horner to Gaume, 1vii69; CSSp 196axii: 31xii71, *compte-rendu*; ibid., Baur, *compte-rendu*, 31xii80; CSSp 196ax: Baur to Propagation of the Faith, 6xi82; CSSp 195iii: Duparquet to Schwindenhammer, 9iv72.

The Protestants were even more common in this legitimating discourse. Their Englishness (and later Germanness) was often emphasized, with the possibility implied that what had been achieved might be undone by those deemed heretics (and non-Frenchmen) if the next gift was not granted (CSSp 196aii: Horner to Notre Dame des Victoires, 24ix64; CSSp 196axii: Horner to Holy Childhood, 30xi65, 31xii66).

25. CSSp 196axi: Courmont to Propagation of the Faith, 23xi86, 31xii86, 31xii94, 31xii95, 31xii96; CSSp 196axiii: Courmont to Holy Childhood, 23xi86. CSSp 196axi: Courmont to Propagation of the Faith, 8vi88.

26. CSSp 196ax: Horner to Propagation of the Faith, 31xii66.

27. CSSp 196axii: Horner to Holy Childhood, 30xi65; CSSp 196ax: Horner to Propagation of the Faith, 31xii66, 29xii67.

These contradictory legitimations appeared in reports to their large benefactors such as the Propagation of the Faith and the Holy Childhood Society, from whom they received thousands of francs per year. Yet perhaps the most important aspect of Spiritan fund-raising in the nineteenth century was another feature that at least one observer has called an innovation arising from Horner: namely the use of personal sponsorships whereby individual European benefactors gave money for the ransoming of a slave child, who then would be named according to the donor's wishes.[28] Horner used trips to Europe to drum up such sponsors, and their monies — twenty-five francs per child or so — supplemented the larger benefactions. Lists of the donors appeared in mission periodicals.

Whether or not Horner actually began this practice — continued in our day by many agencies that seek funding for disadvantaged children the world over — his use of it was extensive.[29] In retrospect, one can admire Horner's acumen (especially if he was the pioneer), for African slave children represented an ideal group for such purposes. Their misery was increasingly known in Europe, and they became an easy way for the pious to contribute to the *salut des âmes* that increasingly characterized nineteenth-century French piety. At the same time, such practices also encouraged a global awareness in European Catholics, who thereby connected their own generosity to new believers thousands of miles away. Horner wrote often that the mission's children prayed for their benefactors daily. He urged his benefactors to offer ongoing support for the Catholic boys and girls in eastern Africa, saying that the mission's children were their adopted children, too: "You've already given them liberty of the body and [liberty deriving] from the profession of faith." Now, he wrote, the new adoptive parents must not stop donating to their religious offspring's upkeep.[30]

The "French Mission" and Relations with Omanis and Others in Zanzibar

Along with their participation in the missionary upsurge of nineteenth-century Catholicism, an upsurge in which the French church played the predominant role, the national origins of most of the Spiritans affected their missionary activity with slaves in eastern Africa. The Spiritans had been founded and then renewed by Libermann's vigor in France, maintained their headquarters in Paris, and recruited most of their members from France, including those who came to Zanzibar and its environs. In Zanzibar and Bagamoyo the Spiritan mission came to be known as "the French mission," with French the language spoken by the missionaries among themselves and taught in their schools at least until the early 1880s.

28. CSSp 194bii: Stegmaier, Sr. Ortrud, 1980, *"L'Acheteur Blanc sur le March aux Esclaves"*: *Pour le Centenaire de la Mort du Père Antoine Horner, CSSp.*

29. Numerous letters between Horner and the Holy Childhood Society discuss these practices (CSSp 196axii). Horner also listed the names of sponsors and the names they requested in Zanzibar's sacramental book in 1866, and similar records of sponsorship appeared in the list of slaves ransomed kept from 1884 to 1894 (LERE).

30. APF 44 (1872), 425.

Their French and missionary identity affected the Spiritans' interactions with the Omani regime in Zanzibar, as well as with the European political authorities there. The Catholic mission's relationships with its neighbors naturally varied over time. Relations between the missionaries and Omani authorities tended to be cordial, especially in the first decade of the mission's existence when Majid was sultan. Mutual visits were common, and the missionaries praised the freedom of religion they enjoyed under the sultan's rule. Still, they also felt the tug of their missionary zeal and complained at the limited scope of evangelization. Horner spoke of the circumspection needed in an infidel land.[31] Islamic "moral degradation" also featured prominently in missionary discourse and preoccupied the missionaries who were anxious to preserve the faith of their young Christians from corrupting influences. Their discomfort at evangelizing under a Muslim regime only increased under Majid's brother and successor, Sultan Barghash, who showed less favor than his predecessor toward the Spiritans after his 1870 accession to power following his brother's death. Barghash sought to purchase back their mission properties and blocked Spiritan attempts to buy new land. Later Barghash refused a request for land in Zanzibar town for a church.[32] Barghash's successors, beginning with Khalifa in 1888, had much less ability to act independently in Zanzibar due to encroaching European domination. Partially as a consequence of these later sultans' weaker position, land for the church in the town was granted to the French consul in order to be given to the mission in 1889.[33]

The years just prior to the onset of European colonialism distanced the mission from Sultan Barghash and his successors. Increasing European and missionary vilification of Islam combined with the mission's growing identification with colonial authority to work against the previous détente. Anticolonial wars, especially Bushiri's war of 1888–89, cemented distrust that only grew in the early twentieth century. Arabs welcomed the beginning of World War I, according to the Spiritan journal of the mission at Zanzibar, because it might represent a chance to chase away the Europeans.[34]

From its origins, the Zanzibar mission imagined itself as especially close to France, and in their relations with the French consulate, the Spiritans maintained courtesy, and occasionally friendship.[35] Of course this relationship could not ignore that the nineteenth century was a difficult period for the Catholic Church in

31. APF 36 (1864), 128.

32. Kieran 1966, 260. The missionaries could speak well or ill of Barghash, but generally they were uncomfortable (BG 8:748; CSSp 196biii: Machon to Schwindenhammer, 4vi71; Horner to Schwindenhammer, 8x70, 4ii71, 15ix71, 25ix71; CSSp 197ai: Baur to Schwindenhammer, 14x80 and Acker to vicar general, 23ix81; Bagamoyo journal, 14ii85). He did, however, help defend the mission at Bagamoyo against feared Wazaramo invaders in 1875 and the Mhonda mission against its invaders in 1881 (CSSp 196biv: Baur to Horner, 21ix75; Zanzibar journal, 15iii81). Most importantly, he gave them freedom like his predecessor (BG 13:35).

33. Zanzibar journal, vi89; CSSp 197aii: Courmont to Emonet, 3vi89, 10vii89; Kieran 1966, 260–62.

34. Zanzibar journal, 3viii1914. See also Njoroge 1999, 39.

35. For a summary of Spiritan relations with the French consul in Zanzibar, see Kieran 1966, 262–73, and Kollman 2001, 68ff.

France, which had to negotiate its identity with a series of French governments that succeeded one another after the end of the revolutionary and Napoleonic eras. Fortunately for the missionaries, relationships between the Spiritans and the French state in eastern Africa and other non-European settings were rarely as contentious as the relationships between Catholic institutions and the national government within France itself.[36] The French mission at Zanzibar began during the Second Empire (1851–70), when church-state relations in France enjoyed relative calm. Later, during the rise of French religio-nationalism that followed the catastrophic French defeat in the Franco-Prussian War (1870–71), the founder of the Spiritan mission in eastern Africa, Antoine Horner, spearheaded a drive to have a chapel devoted to the missions placed in the new basilica, Sacré-Coeur in Montmartre, an important symbol of national reconstruction.[37]

During the period of the Third Republic (1870–1914) that succeeded the Franco-Prussian War, the fall of Napoleon III's Second Empire, and the Paris Commune, revolutionary sentiments and anticlericalism periodically made institutional Catholic life in France very difficult. But strident anti-Catholic feelings rarely surfaced with similar energy abroad, where religious groups like the Spiritans served French interests in a variety of ways. Thus the national Republican government and its colonial offices usually saw missionaries abroad as helpful allies in various national efforts: to expand French commercial and political dominion; to counter perceived or real attempts by other European powers, especially Britain, to broaden their role and reach; and, increasingly, to spread the virtues of French culture in a *mission civilisatrice*.[38]

In Zanzibar, conflicts arose occasionally with local French diplomats, but the mission almost always felt the support of the French consul and his office. The missionaries reciprocated, publishing works praising France for its cultural and religious accomplishments.[39] The French colony at Réunion supported the foundation of the mission at Zanzibar materially and financially, likely with the hopes of gaining laborers from the region. Afterward, the Spiritans sought government subsidies for their mission, and received large sums for most of the century. In making such requests they emphasized the mission's spread of the virtues of the French nation.[40] Until the end of the Second Empire in 1870,

---

36. For a fuller discussion, see Kollman 2001, 92–98.

37. BG 10:649, 651, 687; CSSp 196iv: Horner to Schwindenhammer, 13xi75 and 12i76; APF 52 (1880), 387; MC 7 (1875), 552.

38. There were exceptions to the relative absence of anticlerical sentiment abroad. For example, Réunion was a site for antichurch violence, and the Spiritan institution at La Providence was burned by an angry crowd in 1872 (BG 3:329–30, 353f, 383; Koren 1983, 275). "Mission civilisatrice" was a concept that they used, but not with the regularity it would later assume in French colonial thought (Brunschwig 1966). As Kieran suggests (1966, 267–68), it was articulated primarily to curry favor with the French government.

39. Several missionary dramas written in the 1870s include praise of the Catholic Church in France and the virtues of the French people (CSSp 196axiii: Le Roy 1884, 1886).

40. Kieran 1966, 266–68. For the Spiritan requests to the Ministry of Foreign Affairs for money, as well as the grants from the ministry, see CSSp 194aii.

the mission hosted a national celebration for the intentions of the emperor on August 15, often attended by French naval personnel and the other consuls at Zanzibar.[41] The French consul also sought practical help from the missionaries at times.[42] In fact, Spiritan French identity and national loyalties were never really in doubt until the twentieth century. The missionaries mourned as Frenchmen, and even more as (mostly) Alsatians, after the French defeat at the hands of the Prussians in 1870. The French government printed early texts prepared by the mission in KiSwahili and donated books for the seminary.[43] In their relations with the sultan, the Spiritans often allied themselves with the French consuls, most of whom saw the mission's value as a bearer of French presence in the region.

Despite their shared national sentiments, conflicts erupted periodically between the missionaries and French colonial officials in Zanzibar.[44] As the appeal by Léon and his fellow escapee showed, the occasionally uneasy relationship between consulate and mission was not lost on African Catholics, who at least one other time also appealed to the consul against the mission's treatment of them.[45] For their part, the missionaries feared the Third Republic that followed the Second Empire, and watched nervously as anticlerical sentiments waxed and waned in France over the next decades. The Spiritans were almost all Ultramontanists, and their congregation had founded and then staffed the French seminary in Rome beginning in 1853.[46] They took control in Zanzibar when the Gallicanist legacy of the French church was waning, only increasing tensions between church and state, with ramifications overseas at times.[47] The annual celebrations of July 14 (Bastille Day) at the French consulate occasioned soul-searching among the missionaries during the period of the Third Republic as they considered whether or not to attend. The Spiritans also lamented the appearance of the notorious pro-Republican and anticlerical Masons in Zanzibar, many of whom were French. Later the missionaries resisted a consul's demand to sing a song

---

41. They also approached the French consul when they felt the need for physical protection at their missions, requests to which the consuls responded by petitioning the sultan for action (Kieran 1966, 265–66).

42. When rumors spread of the death of French explorers, the French consul asked that one of the Spiritan brothers at Zanzibar go discover the truth, and reimbursed the mission for his trouble (BG 8:746).

43. On the gifts of books from the French government, see CSSp 194aii: Baur to Ministry of Public Instruction, 8ix71, and BG 8:752.

44. Horner wrote that one consul used to read the letters he sent to Paris without permission, so that Horner could only express his pleasure at the fellow's departure once he had left. In addition, the same consul had prodded Horner to petition Rome to name him Duke of Zanzibar (CSSp 196bii: Horner to Schwindenhammer, 22v69). Another consul was described as an embarrassment, a marked regression from his predecessor (CSSp 196biv: Baur to Schwindenhammer, 13xii76; Zanzibar journal, 24ix78).

45. A similar appeal apparently came the next year (Bagamoyo journal, 30vii84).

46. See Koren 1983, 276–77, for the details of the founding of the French national seminary.

47. The Vatican and French Navy clashed in the 1860s over who had authority to appoint clergy in the French colonies, after Rome rejected the government's choice for vicar apostolic of Martinique (BG 5:632f).

with Republican overtones at Mass, eventually relenting after Bishop Courmont's accession in 1884.[48]

The French consulate grew anxious about its relationship with the mission as the German presence increased beginning in the mid-1880s.[49] They feared that the Spiritans might surrender their French identity and their connection to the French consulate in an effort to gain benefits for the mission under the Germans, whose domination of the mainland was becoming obvious.

In fact, the missionaries initially observed German encroachment with trepidation. The Franco-Prussian war of 1870–71 had soured the Alsatian-dominated Spiritans to German nationalism, for many had mourned over the suffering of their home, speaking of the cruel testing of "our Alsace."[50] In the aftermath of the war and German annexation, the Alsatians among them faced the choice of acquiescing to the new political reality or clinging to their French citizenship though their homeland was officially part of the German Empire.[51] During the ensuing Kulturkampf of the 1870s, official German policy sought to marginalize Catholicism in the country and forced the Congregation of the Holy Ghost to leave Germany and suspend their recruitment there.[52] Naturally, the missionaries viewed with foreboding the incursion into eastern Africa of the power that had usurped their homeland.

Despite Spiritan misgivings about the German incursions, the French consuls were right to feel the need to ensure the loyalties of the missionaries. German commercial and then political officials sought assiduously to build a relationship with the Spiritans as they established control over what would become Tanganyika beginning in 1885. The newcomers guaranteed military protection of mission stations and an annual subsidy in exchange for considerations such as the teaching of German in mission schools, the appointment of German-speaking Spiritans to the mission on the mainland, and promises of informal support for the German colonial presence.[53] In response, the French consulate asserted its priorities in relation to the mission, even threatening the Spiritans with retaliation in France should the missionaries in eastern Africa support German rather than French interests.[54] Eventually Courmont rejected French subsidies as well

---

48. The song in question, *Domine salvam fac*, was a traditional hymn sung at Mass for the ruler. In 1870 the archbishop of Paris had ordered it sung for the Republic (Dansette 1961, 1:319; A. Mitchell 1984, 126).

49. Kieran 1966, 269–70; CSSp 194aiv.

50. CSSp 196biiii: Baur to Schwindenhammer, 6x70; ibid.: Horner to Schwindenhammer, 8x70. The entire congregation faced the issue of the French defeat and the loss of Alsace to the Germans.

51. Several were culturally Germans. Baur, for example, was described as a German by Bishop Maupoint in a letter of 1867 to Cardinal Barnabo (CSSp 195bii: Maupoint to Barnabo, 19viii67), and his accent when speaking KiSwahili was criticized by Horner and Sacleux for its Germanic tone (CSSp 196bii: Horner to Schwindenhammer, 18xi64; CSSp 194bii: Dubourget 1941). Felicien, one of the two brothers who arrived in the beginning, was also described as a German (CSSp 196aii: Horner, August 1863).

52. BG 9:560.

53. See Kieran 1966, 287–91 and Kollman 2001, 72–73.

54. CSSp 197aii: Courmont to Emonet, 29ix87; Kieran 1966, 270, 289–90.

as German support in order to maintain the mission's neutrality, claiming that they were Catholic missionaries doing apostolic work, and nothing more. "Our only flag must be that of Jesus Christ," he wrote.[55]

The increased German presence beginning in 1884–85 culminated in warfare with Arabs and local peoples in the late 1880s, creating dangers for several Spiritan missions. Such unrest led to the temporary evacuation of some missions, and generated orphans and displaced persons whom the Spiritans sheltered and received at other missions. In addition, slave caravans moving through German-claimed territory were stopped, with those freed given to the mission. The German military and economic presence also probably stimulated an upsurge in Islamic activism beginning in the late 1880s, and anticolonial Islamic activism hampered Catholic evangelization. Frustrations with the new resurgence led the missionaries to welcome the colonial presence despite their initial contention that the Islamic surge itself was the result of European, and especially German, incursions. As Juhani Koponen says, the missionaries became "colonial allies in spite of themselves"; that is, despite initial suspicion they eventually embraced European overrule.[56]

Throughout this period, the British were the most powerful Europeans at Zanzibar, and until the German incursions they also had the most influence on the mainland. Spiritan relations with the British consulate tended to be respectful and courteous, though Horner from the beginning recognized the need to be prudent with the British consul.[57] The British consuls helped protect the mission's right to exercise its ministry, and in turn the mission appreciated the order that British naval strength provided. Their service to each other was also more direct. From the beginning the mission's hospital cared for British sailors, and at times the British consulate provided direct assistance to the Catholic mission. They supplied huts for the Catholic couples who moved from Zanzibar to Bagamoyo in 1871, for example, and Horner reported that one consul, John Kirk, had offered him land and freed slaves to start a new mission in 1872, a move supported by the head of the Anglican mission. Later the Spiritans felt that the British authorities in Kenya also welcomed them warmly, when they sought to establish a mission in Mombasa in 1888.[58]

---

55. Zanzibar journal, 17xii87; cited in Kieran 1966, 271. For more details on the relations between the mission and the French and German authorities in the late 1880s, see Kieran 1966, 270–73, 287–91. After suspending the Spiritans in Germany during the Kulturkampf, the German government allowed them to return to active ministry and recruitment in 1895, and the activities of Spiritan missionaries from eastern Africa in support of German colonial ambitions were instrumental in effecting the permission to reenter (BG 17:412–14; Koren 1983, 315–19). On German relations with the mission in the decades following the establishment of German East Africa — a period that saw war with local inhabitants, the disruption of many of the interior missions, and conflicts over the place of education and labor migration in the new colony — see Kieran 1966, 287–337.
56. Koponen 1994, 157ff.
57. CSSp 196bii: Horner to Schwindenhammer, 28vi63. For a summary of Holy Ghost relations with the British, see Kieran 1966, 273–84, and Kollman 2001, 67.
58. Bagamoyo journal, 19i71; CSSp 196biii: Horner to Schwindenhammer, 15iv72; Zanzibar journal, 22xi88. The Anglican UMCA mission of High Churchmen naturally forged even closer ties with the British consulate, yet, in the beginning at least, the Spiritans felt that their mission had

Though political considerations deriving from the Spiritans' mostly French identity occasionally affected their missionary activity, more important in shaping their practices of evangelization were three other features characteristic of the missionaries. First, their geographic origins and social-class status within France led them to emphasize the formative capacities of agricultural labor in evangelization. Second, their religious and clerical formation into the Congregation formed them in certain social practices and made them familiar with models of missionary activity. Third, their participation in French juvenile reform institutions exposed them to other practices that shaped their approach to forming Catholics from former slaves.

Spiritan Social Origins

These missionaries came from a rather narrow slice of nineteenth-century Europe.[59] They often shared geographical and ethnic origins, so that the first superior, Antoine Horner, his assistant and successor Etienne Baur, and about one-half of the Spiritans who served in eastern Africa during the nineteenth century were, like Libermann himself, from Alsace.[60] Alsace was one of the regions of France that had remained predominantly religious during and after the French Revolution, and it came in the nineteenth century to be acknowledged as "the homeland of missionaries" within the French and even European Catholic church.[61] The nineteenth century also saw Alsace industrialize, mostly under Protestant leadership, which left the mostly rural Catholics suspicious of the effects of industrialism.

In addition to their Alsatian origins, the Spiritans tended to be of a similar socioeconomic background. Like most members of other religious orders in Europe in the later nineteenth century, they came mainly from rural areas and from the peasantry or lower middle class.[62] Catholics in Alsace were predominantly rural anyway, and the Spiritans rarely hailed from the landed gentry. Those from other parts of Europe also shared a similar background. About half were brothers, about half priests, though the percentage of brothers fell off as the nineteenth century progressed.[63] The less educated brothers, who tended to do either skilled

---

the greater respect of most visitors, the British included. This judgment was confirmed by Frere's glowing report on the Spiritan work at Bagamoyo, a stark contrast to his criticisms of Methodist and Anglican initiatives, to be discussed in chapter 4. See Kollman 2001, 210–14.

59. For a description of the geographic distribution of religious practice and piety in nineteenth-century France, see the following: Dansette 1961, 1:112f, 2:11f; Jedin 1981, 8:98f; Cholvy and Hilaire 1985, 1:259–312; R. Gibson 1989, 111f, 158–80. See also Kieran 1966, 81–82.

60. According to Henry Koren's *Spiritan East African Memorial* (1994), 70 of 144 of the Spiritans who served in the region in the nineteenth century were Alsatians.

61. On religious practice in Alsace, see Dansette 1961, 2:60, and Cholvy and Hilaire 1985, 1:269–73. The Spiritans recognized Alsace as a fertile site for vocations, especially for work with *les noirs* (BG 3:429–30).

62. R. Gibson 1989, 68f, 112f; Kieran 1966, 81f; Perrot 1990, 506.

63. Again following Koren 1994, brothers made up 67 of the 144 who served in the twentieth century, not counting the 5 Africans, yet 30 of the first 50 to come were brothers.

labor or elementary school teaching whether serving in Europe, Africa, or else-where, could almost certainly be counted on to have origins in the peasantry or the lower or lower-middle classes of European society, regardless of their country of origin. Most of the priests came from similar social classes and backgrounds, and few had any advanced education before entering the seminary.[64] There were exceptions, among them some of the more notable Spiritans who served in east-ern Africa.[65] Most of the Spiritans who came to the region, however, came from modest, pious rural backgrounds. Given the many who came from Alsace, not a few had a marked suspicion of the effects of industrialism on faith, a suspicion that, as we shall see, shaped their evangelization of former slaves.[66]

Formation in the Congregation of the Holy Ghost

If the Spiritans in eastern Africa shared a number of common traits before coming to the congregation, the deepest bond uniting them became their shared participation in the process to become members: years of study, spiritual training, physical work, and supervised discernment in a series of structured stages within institutional settings, mostly in France.[67] These missionaries experienced what was supposed to have been a uniform program of formation into the life of their religious order.

Seminary education loomed as an important part of the self-understood mis-sion of the Congregation of the Holy Ghost both before and after Libermann's group joined.[68] The original congregation had been founded to prepare clergy for the foreign missions, and the founder, Father Claude Francis Poullart des Places, had established a seminary for that purpose in Paris in the early eighteenth cen-tury, the Seminary of the Holy Spirit. Libermann, too, showed concern about the formation and training of clergy, and he assumed charge of the seminary at the time of the merger in 1848. Libermann's successor as superior general, Ignatius Schwindenhammer, also founded a number of seminaries, both for the Spiritans themselves as well as to train diocesan clergy.[69]

---

64. Gibson 1989, 80ff; Dansette 1961, 2:6f.

65. Fr. Etienne Baur, for example, who arrived with Horner in 1863, was the son of a colonel in the Imperial Army of Napoleon, though his education was undistinguished and the economic background of his childhood unclear. He lived and served in eastern Africa until 1913 and through that lengthy tenure may have shaped the Spiritan missionary presence more than any other single individual (CSSp 194bii: Noel 1983 and Dubourget 1941). Father Charles Duparquet, who served at Bagamoyo and Zanzibar from 1869 until his departure in 1872, was the son of a wealthy widow in Normandy and studied classics and philosophy before entering the seminary. Though he served only a few years in eastern Africa before achieving renown as a missionary in central Africa, his strong personality shaped the indigenous seminary founded at Bagamoyo (G. Anderson 1999, 189; Koren 1994, 31–33). And the first bishop of Zanzibar, Raoul de Courmont, came from French nobility and was educated at a college in the Pyrenees (Koren 1994, 65).

66. Kieran 1966, 82–83.

67. Ernoult 1992. Documents from those early years can be found in CSSp 105bi.

68. Koren 1990, 111–49, 186–91.

69. Koren 1958, 9–25, 111–26.

The process of formation was relatively standardized through the nineteenth century and took place at a number of different institutions in France.[70] In its guiding philosophy, Spiritan formation during the nineteenth century followed the Sulpician model that dominated French seminary education at the time. This model built upon the reforms of the Council of Trent and prevailed in Catholic seminary formation into the twentieth century. Studies, according to this model, were deemed important but less essential than proper spiritual formation, which depended on developing self-control, personal asceticism, a spirit of obedience to one's superiors, and habits of prayer. To effect such personal reformation, the Spiritans fashioned their houses of formation like other seminaries of the day, as tightly structured communities cut off from the external world and regulated by a schedule of prayer, work, and study. The seminary program emphasized withdrawal from one's previous life and complete entry into the regimented life of the religious order, understood as a new family. Holy Ghost seminarians were closely observed by religious superiors, who wrote quarterly evaluations assessing their demeanor, personal habits, and performance in ritual behaviors. Perceived irregularities or lack of proper decorum were recorded. Maintaining one's vocation demanded continued vigilance and ongoing enclosure, careful restriction of movement, and care in relating to one's family and women. One was to be in the world as a servant, but apart from it at the same time.

Besides such spiritual expectations, the program of formation at seminaries also valued in a particular way agricultural labor in the gardens around the seminary.[71] Physical work was believed to inculcate the proper spirit of humility and industriousness, especially for those preparing to be brothers. Such predilections in favor of agricultural labor overlapped as well with values emerging from the Catholic culture of Alsace, where industrialism was linked with Protestantism and anticlericalism.

The academic seminary curriculum followed that established by the Council of Trent, a mix of dogmatic theology, moral theology heavily influenced by the demands of the sacrament of confession, Bible, church history, and the practical skills priests needed for presiding at sacramental and liturgical occasions. Missiology, the academic discipline within theology that, among other tasks, prepares missionaries for their work, did not appear on the seminary curriculum, developing only gradually in the later nineteenth and twentieth centuries.[72] As a consequence, within the academic training the Spiritans received, there was nothing that focused on specific preparation for missionary work overseas, except for spiritual exhortation toward self-abnegation and discipline.

---

70. Kieran 1966, 83–85; Ernoult 1992, 2000; Kollman 2001, 98–102.

71. For evidence of this emphasis, see CSSp 106aiv.

72. On the seminary training for missionaries, see the following: Koren 1990; Spindler and Gadille 1992; de Montclos 1984, 323; Comby 1992; Lange 1992; Zorn 1992; Prudhomme 1996. As the founder of Catholic missiology, Joseph Schmidlin, wrote in the early twentieth century, "Only during the most recent times has the custom of training the future missionaries in special mission colleges become universal" (1931, 201–12).

The absence of specific missionary training, however, did not mean that the Spiritans lacked shared convictions about the goals for that work. All sought the salvation of souls and the establishment of the church, the long-standing goals of missionary work.[73] It did mean, however, that the means to those goals were neither systematically elaborated nor widely shared through a common discursive tradition. Despite this absence, however, the missionaries did not create their missionary strategy ex nihilo, but drew quite consciously upon a missionary tradition. Making up this archive of potential missionary models and policies were heroic narratives culled from past missionary activity, contemporary missionary projects in which Spiritans worked among African peoples, certain Vatican guidelines, and the missionary theories of Libermann, their "second founder."

In their seminary education and Catholic upbringing more generally, Spiritans had encountered stories of great missionaries and missionary movements of previous centuries in the church's history. Among those that appear in Spiritan discourse in relation to missionary strategy were the Jesuit *reductiones* in South America and the monasteries of medieval Europe, both of which were seen to have civilized and Christianized. More proximately, Holy Ghost missionaries had been in present-day Gabon and Senegal since the 1840s, and Aloyse Kobès, bishop of the vicariate in what was to become Gabon, oversaw a famous mission there when the Spiritans arrived in eastern Africa. The *Bullétin Général* of the society kept Spiritans everywhere aware of the achievements in other places, and accounts of the strategy of Kobès appeared in the bulletin in the years before the Spiritan undertaking at Zanzibar.[74] The missionaries in eastern Africa knew of their confrere's attempts to create a *civilisation chrétienne* through settlement of nomadic peoples and agricultural endeavors instilling a spirit of work.

Besides the past and present examples they emulated as models, these early Spiritans also had specific ideas and instructions from ecclesiastical authorities. Over the previous centuries Rome had issued a body of well-known practical missionary guidelines. Though some of these, such as calls to adapt the Christian message to local circumstances and the admonition to cooperate with local authorities, had been contested in practice, most, like orders to learn local languages, appeared prominently in Spiritan discourse.[75] In addition Catholic missionary activity had received new impetus by the accession to the papacy of Gregory XVI (Bartolomeo Cappellare), who had been prefect of Propaganda Fide. In an 1839 apostolic letter, *In Supremo Apostolatus*, he condemned the slave trade and reiterated a long-standing official teaching that Africans were not inferior to other peoples. The 1845 papal instruction *Neminem Profecto* acted on a complaint that native clergy were not being created quickly enough in the new Catholic churches

---

73. Their goals prototypically embodied what Bevans and Schroeder identify as the missiology emerging from Type A theology (Bevans and Schroeder 2004, 38–49).

74. On Kobès and his work, see summaries in Koren 1997 and Noël 1988, as well as relevant sections from Koren 1983. For specifics see BG 2:485ff; BG3:89ff, 381; BG 4:615ff; APF 26 (1854): 438f; APF 36 (1864): 105ff; APF 38 (1866): 32–43.

75. CSSp 196bi: Schwindenhammer to Horner, 18i72; BG 2:591; BG 6:85f.

and called for intensified efforts to create indigenous leadership. Promising young men were to be taken and formed in seminaries set up for this purpose.

These Vatican directives against slavery and in favor of indigenous clergy filtered to the Spiritans primarily through similar and even more emphatic injunctions in the thoughts of Libermann, whose personal witness and leadership had attracted Horner and many of the others in eastern Africa to the Spiritans. The Holy Ghost missionaries revered Libermann's voluminous writings, especially his 1846 Memorandum to the Prefect of Propaganda Fide, as guidelines for missionary action. More of a plea than a set of practical suggestions, Libermann's memo urged the church to serve Africa's peoples, on the continent and elsewhere. He criticized suggestions that Africans were inferior by nature to other peoples, believing instead that any perceived immorality or disorder derived from slavery and other degradation in which they had been raised. African intellectual and moral potential were undeveloped because of stagnating circumstances.[76] He wrote:

> When we look at the condition of black people anywhere in the world today, we may be tempted to think that they are cursed by God from the outset and oppressed beneath a burden of ignorance and suffering. Everywhere, they are in [a] truly miserable condition of ignorance and superstition. Nobody stretches out a hand to free them from the infernal power that holds them in bondage.... And yet, they are made in the image of God like all other people, and they are ready to welcome the gift of Faith that they have never known.[77]

Libermann was a committed abolitionist, and he called for the church to raise up African leaders as clergy, members of religious orders, teachers, and catechists. He also decried European domination of Africans, recognizing that his own missionaries could be tempted to such a stance. In a famous statement he outlined his missionary strategy in light of his confidence in the potential of Africans:

> Do not act according to what you have seen in Europe nor according to European customs. Get rid of Europe, its customs and its spirit. Become black [*nègre*] with the blacks [*les nègres*], and then you will know them as they should be known and not the way they are known by Europeans. Let them be themselves. Become their servants. As servants, adapt to their customs and their way of life. Do all this with the aim of improving them, sanctifying them, ennobling them, and gradually forming them into God's people.[78]

---

76. Koren 1958, 162–77; Koren 1983, 251–64; Burke 1998, 50f.
77. ND VIII, 233. Cited in Burke 1998, 50.
78. ND IX, 330, trans. Burke 1998, 80.

Libermann's missionary teachings covered a number of issues in missionary practice: the need for collaborators from the local people, the importance of language ability, the need to cooperate with local authorities. Yet they did not constitute a coherent set of systematic guidelines. They were ad hoc principles in response to particular situations, which Libermann himself insisted required careful application to specific circumstances.[79]

These various sources, therefore, formed no coherent missionary strategy, but constituted part of a long-standing diversity in Catholic missionary theory and practice. Such sources represented a virtual repository, or a "trade store," as a student of missionary activity in Mexico has put it, one which the Spiritans knew implicitly and then deployed selectively depending on the circumstances.[80]

The Spiritan Approach to Slavery

Due to their backgrounds, the Spiritans came to Zanzibar predisposed to view slavery in certain ways. Their opinions derived first of all from those of the broader Catholic Church, which were in flux in the nineteenth century but slow to embrace abolition.[81] Such views drew upon broader anthropological assumptions that were steeped in official theological pronouncements undergirded by a Christianized moral order. The Spiritan approach to the institution also reflected French Catholic experiences with abolition.

In the first place, as its official representatives, the Holy Ghost missionaries shared the beliefs of the Catholic Church about the human person. This official anthropology had two ideals about personhood: first, an ecclesiological notion of the ideal person as one within the visible church; and second, a conviction about the ultimate value of the soul. These two ideals generated their twofold missionary strategy, at once to save souls and establish the church.

Today the theological limitations of the implicit anthropology and ecclesiology operative in the nineteenth-century version of this approach are widely recognized. Such a view had a dualistic view of the human person, so that the body's value derives from its role as a vehicle for the soul. This anthropology had ecclesiological consequences too, according to which the church was the only institutional milieu in which proper personhood could be formed and then lived; outside that environment was the almost-certain danger of losing the promise of eternal life. Within the church, on the contrary, one knew one's place within a hierarchical order and worked out a personal salvation through the moral life appropriate to an individual vocation, strengthened by sacramental participation.

---

79. Burke 1998, 35–48.

80. On the diversity in Catholic missiology, see the recent study by Bevans and Schroeder (2004), as well as older studies by Schmidlin (1931) and Daniel (1975). For the notion of missionary ideas as a "trade store" see Pardo 2004, 4–5.

81. In an unsatisfactory literature on Catholic approaches to slavery, perhaps the least biased study in English of the history of Catholic opinions of slavery remains Maxwell 1975. See also a judicious, recent discussion by John Noonan (2005, 112ff), and further information in Kollman 2001 (168ff).

The church in this vision was almost absent from theological reflection, because its supposed perfection shaped the evaluation of everything else, on earth and in the heavens.[82]

One consequence of this ecclesiology was a strict interpretation of *extra eccle-siam, nulla salus*, or "outside the church no salvation." Proper human personhood and the means for eternal life were thus in the church, and nowhere else. A re-lated complaint from contemporary missiologists about previous approaches to missionary activity links such ecclesiocentrism to a lack of appreciation for Jesus' attempt to proclaim the reign of God rather than to establish the church.[83] This approach to ecclesiology and its related theological anthropology helps explain the Spiritan reluctance to condemn slavery, which they saw as acceptable in light of natural law and which disallowed neither church membership nor eternal life. Indeed, as we shall see, the Spiritans in eastern Africa saw slavery as provi-dential, at least for the time being, since it brought Africans into the church's embrace.

In addition to their ecclesial goals, there were also historical reasons for the Spiritan missionaries to look askance at strident calls for abolition. Catholic am-bivalence about — and often resistance to — abolition in France was, in part, the aftermath of the Revolution.[84] Slavery had been declared illegal in 1792 during the revolution, championed by the bête noire of Catholics, the revolutionary priest l'Abbé Grégoire (1750–1831), only to be reimposed under Napoleon in 1802.[85] After Napoleon's downfall the abolitionist movement reconstituted itself, with Grégoire remaining a prominent figure until his death. The slave trade was de-clared illegal in 1818, and abolition proclaimed in 1848.[86] Though the Catholic Church declared the slave trade contrary to church teaching in an unequivocal manner in 1839, the abolitionists in France tended to be strongly anticlerical in their outlook. As a consequence there was little incentive, sociologically speak-ing, for Catholics to sympathize with the movement. Thus the Spiritans joined many Catholics in considering slavery unfortunate and its violence and cruelties unconscionable, but they were not abolitionists.

There were thus understandable reasons that, unlike other missionary groups in Africa at the time, the Spiritans did not establish their mission proclaiming a desire to end slavery.[87] Yet their reluctance to embrace abolition meant that

---

82. de Lubac 1967; McCool 1977; Himes 1997; O'Meara 1997. Yves Congar says that the Catho-lic Church in the nineteenth century was conceived as follows: "not as the Body of Christ animated by the Spirit but 'as a society or an organization where Christ intervenes at its origins as the founder and where the Holy Spirit guarantees authority. Since they [Christ and the Spirit] had given once and for all a superterrestrial quality to the institutions, more interventions were not needed' " (cited in O'Meara 1997, 179).

83. Bevans and Schroeder 2004.

84. Drescher 1980; Cohen 1980, 181ff.

85. Drescher 1980, 49; Klein 1998, 19f.

86. Federini 1998; Motylewski 1998: Dorigny 1999.

87. Nwulia 1975. In his effort to highlight the complex motivations of escaped slaves, Glassman disputes common missionary claims that such slaves were choosing "individual liberty over personal dependence." I agree with his skepticism. But he mistakenly lumps all missionaries together when he

the missionaries parted company with important elements in their own Congregation's background. As noted earlier, Libermann had been convinced by the pope's condemnation of slavery in 1839 and became a committed abolitionist, one of the few French Catholic churchmen to call for an end to slavery.[88] Some of Libermann's early associates had worked hard on the behalf of slaves in Réunion and elsewhere at the time of abolition in French colonies after 1848. In contrast, the Spiritans in eastern Africa, though purportedly the "sons of Libermann," did not call for abolition. They objected to the cruelty of slavery, and especially of the slave trade, but feared the social upheaval abolition could cause. They also tended to see "Islamic" slavery as rather mild compared to slavery in the Americas, with brutality the exception rather than the rule.[89]

When British pressure culminated in the closing of the slave market at Zanzibar in 1873, the local Holy Ghost superior Horner rejoiced to see what he called "his hopes fulfilled," but he had not pushed for abolition, only widely proclaimed the cruelties of enslavement and the horrors of the market.[90] Later the Spiritan constitutions embraced abolition much more fully, stating that their missions sought to ransom as many as possible,[91] but nonetheless Cardinal Lavigerie's campaign to abolish slavery in Africa of the late 1880s was felt by at least one Spiritan to be too aggressive, and none expressed marked abolitionist sentiments.[92] Lacking evidence to the contrary, one could guess that they would have defended their refusal to call for abolition on the grounds that slavery was defensible according to natural law. Catholic theology had done so for centuries.

Spiritan Exposure to Social Reform

Nearly all the Spiritans in eastern Africa also shared a final characteristic that affected their evangelizing practices with slaves: exposure to, and often service in, very distinctive nineteenth-century juvenile penitentiaries and detention centers in France or Réunion prior to coming to Zanzibar.

---

continues as follows, explaining the missionary mistake as their willing blindness encouraged by their own goals: "The missionaries were fighters on the front lines of abolitionism, zealous propagandists of the liberal ideologies of triumphant capitalism in which the free individual was placed at the center of the 'natural' social order" (Glassman 1995, 107). Like so many, he homogenizes the missionaries and distorts the historical record.

88. On Libermann's connection to abolitionism in France, see Brasseur 1988 and Burke 1998. Prudhomme shows that in the period before he took over the Spiritans, Libermann's missionaries in Bourbon pushed abolition in ways that were unprecedented in French Catholic practice. The theological consequences of this change were profound, for the missionaries directly linked worldly freedom and the possibility of eternal life, something not often done up to then (Prudhomme 1999b, 16–17). On abolitionism in France during the eighteenth and nineteenth centuries, see the articles by Drescher and Daget in Bolt and Drescher 1980. For a fuller discussion of Catholic responses to slavery in the French colonies during the July Monarchy, see Delisle 1995.

89. Though asserted by many historians past and present, the supposed "gentleness" of Arab slavery has been contested (Morton 1990; Azumah 2001).

90. Kieran 1966, 115–17; CSSp 195iv: Horner to Geography Society of Paris, 28iv73; MC 5 (1873), 343.

91. Cited in Henschel 2000a, 8.

92. CSSp 197aii: Acker to Emonet, 1xii89.

Spiritans coming to eastern Africa would have been exposed to such facilities because the Spiritans made a practice of establishing orphanages and similar social works near their houses of formation, especially when Schwindenhammer was superior general between 1851 and 1881.[93] In addition, Spiritan assumption of control over many such facilities in France and elsewhere also led many members to serve directly in them. The superior general and his associates saw in such works not only ways to serve the church but also sources of potential vocations for the congregation, and the government during the Second Empire (1852–70) was happy to turn over such institutions to their care.[94] A number of the Spiritans who came to Zanzibar and Bagamoyo had served at either one or the other of the two most prominent of the institutions assumed in France, the agricultural and industrial colonies for juveniles at Saint-Ilan and Saint-Michel.[95] Such exposure profoundly shaped Spiritan slave evangelization in eastern Africa.

A similar foundation for troubled youth existed at La Providence in Réunion, which gave its name to the early mission at Zanzibar. La Providence had been turned over to the congregation in 1858, and almost half of the priests and brothers who arrived in eastern Africa before 1873 worked there before crossing over to Africa.[96] Judging from its predictability, it appears there was an unarticulated but regular pattern by which Spiritan missionaries from Europe, especially brothers, became acclimatized to the tropics and to working with people of African descent at La Providence in Réunion before coming to Zanzibar and Bagamoyo. Even after the closure of La Providence, however, many Spiritans continued to come to eastern Africa from having worked at similar institutions in France or elsewhere. Several of the brothers served both at reformatory institutions in France and at La Providence. One was Brother Polycarp, who afterward served in the mission workshops of eastern Africa from 1870 until his death in 1894.[97]

This widespread exposure to orphanages and juvenile detention facilities places the Spiritans within a historical trend: the dramatic increase in state-sponsored institutions designed to intervene in order to promote the welfare of families and individuals in France and elsewhere. This trend occasioned the emergence of differing forms of social disciplining that are increasingly appreciated for their significance in epitomizing and helping to forge the so-called modernity supposedly distinctive to Europe.[98]

---

93. Koren 1958, 305. Cellule, where most of the brothers spent time in formation, housed an orphanage after 1856, as did the mother house and home of the Seminary of the Holy Spirit at Rue Lhomond, beginning in 1860. In the early 1870s the large property at Chevilly, first the novitiate and later the site of the senior seminary for the Spiritans, had an orphanage (Ernoult 1992, 25, 27f).

94. The congregation assumed control over more than forty such institutions in the second half of the nineteenth century, many of them only for a short while (Ernoult 1992, 4).

95. For story of Levavasseur's founding work at Saint-Ilan, see Koren 1958, 146f, and Koren 1983, 274ff. On the history of this institution, see Ernoult 1992, 23f.

96. According to Koren (1994), nine of the first nineteen Spiritans in eastern Africa worked at La Providence.

97. Koren 1994, 34.

98. Sudhir Hazareesingh argues that a "profound social and economic revolution was set in motion sometime between 1850 and 1875, fundamentally and irreversibly altering individual and

Important aspects associated with this sort of modernity were also resisted officially by the Catholic Church. Thus the Spiritan notion of ideal personhood, with
its characteristics of membership in a hierarchical spiritual community and virtues
of obedience, faith, and institutional loyalty, on the surface contrasts sharply with
the notion of selfhood driving nineteenth-century secular reforms, a notion that
many have often identified as "modern" — the self-regulating, self-reflective,
autonomous individual, whose commitments derive from voluntary choices.[99]
By contrast, theological assumptions rooted in a vision of proper human life as
obedient church membership motivated the Spiritans and constituted the official
explanation of their missionary work. In their ecclesiological anthropology the
virtues of obedience and acceptance of one's proper role in the essentially hierarchical nature of the church, far from standing in opposition to freedom and
human flourishing, helped constitute it.

Yet practices from these overtly modern institutions no doubt affected Spiritan
missionary activity, as we shall see. Insights into European social history from
studies of colonialism in Africa and elsewhere have related these European social transformations to European colonial policy.[100] So, too, Spiritan practices in
evangelizing slaves only make sense if the connection between the missionaries'
exposure to such social interventionism — exposure from their own formation but
also in many cases by their own work — and their later efforts to make Catholics
out of ex-slaves is recognized.

The Africans Evangelized by the Spiritans

Compared to the Spiritans, who had undergone similar comprehensive processes of formation before coming to eastern Africa, it is difficult to make
extensive generalizations about those they evangelized. The firmest generalization is that, until the late 1880s, the Africans at the Spiritan missions in Zanzibar
and Bagamoyo were almost invariably slaves before their arrival at the mission. Their enslavement usually derived from the nineteenth-century processes
described in the previous chapter that had created turmoil in some parts of eastern Africa, concentrated political and economic power at Zanzibar, and expanded
slavery in the region. Those coming to the mission usually thus passed through
alienation and violence in an era when plantation slavery and the commoditized
markets for slaves expanded. The standard narrative of the few first-person accounts from those evangelized depicted a settled life in their homes of their birth

---

collective mentalities in France," with the 1860s as the turning point (1998, 21). The rise in social
discipline was part of this transformation.

99. Certain Protestant missionaries quite deliberately have sought to convert Africans into Christians much more akin to this prototypical modern individual and to inculcate freedom on this model.
These included the Non-Conformist Protestants missionizing among the Tswana of southern Africa,
whom John and Jean Comaroff have described as "the most ambitious ideological and cultural agents
of empire" (Comaroff and Comaroff 1992, 236).

100. T. Mitchell 1988; Rabinow 1989; Comaroff and Comaroff 1991, 1997.

unsettled by the event (or series of events) that culminated in their arrival at the mission.

Those coming to the Spiritan missions had usually been subject to socialization processes to some extent before their enslavement (or, if born slaves, before they arrived at the mission). For many that process had been comparatively brief, since the missionaries sought children when they could, their preferred age being four or five years.[101] Others came to the Spiritans more fully socialized, as adolescents or adults. Drawn from an extensive geographic area and a variety of locales in eastern and central Africa, they were exposed from birth to diverse cultural and social realities distinctive to their homes. Reflecting that diversity and its local determinations, the Spiritans called them by many ethnic labels, so that by the mid-1880s the missionaries had described those at their missions using hundreds of terms, many of them precursors for colonial-era tribal designations.[102]

Yet if those who came to the mission often were first socialized in settings where the comparative lack of differentiation created largely shared social experiences, and where identity came from local relations based on kinship and lineage systems, they left those places when enslaved and entered another milieu. And enslavement at the coast, even if brief, constituted the most significant shared experience prior to their arrival at the Spiritan missions.

Undergoing and Representing Slavery in Eastern Africa

Understanding slavery in nineteenth-century eastern Africa faces difficulties, namely the few first-person accounts and the problematic nature of most descriptions. Numerous European witnesses described the horrors of slave raiding, slave caravans, the slave market at Zanzibar, and the slave ships that took away these unfortunates. But there are reasons to suspect such accounts. One can see in retrospect that they were put to political uses by Europeans. Even if they were produced in good faith, they are inextricable from what seems the inexorable attempt by the West to draw Africa into a moral context where the case for systematic intervention — religious and political — could be made, an intervention that culminated in colonial overrule. A crucial part of that process was presenting Africa as a "slave-ridden continent" deeply in need of care from the outside, an image that was "a major component of the knowledge of Africa available to the reading publics of Europe."[103]

Missionary accounts such as those of the Holy Ghost missionaries partook in this process, and at times epitomized it. Their descriptions of their missionary work commonly featured the misery at the customs house of Zanzibar or the slave market, both contrasted with the bustling harmony of the mission's schools,

---

101. CSSp 195aii: Horner to Barnabo, 25i68. Children were often enslaved.
102. See, for example, the numerous such designations of former slaves in LERE.
103. Cooper, Holt, and Scott 2000, 27f; Cooper 2000, 115.

workshops, and plantations.[104] Thus Antoine Horner, first Spiritan superior at Zanzibar, wrote that his descriptions of the Zanzibar slave market brought tears everywhere to his hearers in Europe during his tour in 1867, and his accounts are self-consciously calculated to move emotions.[105]

Yet one need not choose between attending to slave realities and attending only to the politics of slave representation. In fact, attention to the problems inherent in representations of slavery helps one to understand just what slaves suffered, materially and otherwise. And despite the biases deriving from the political uses of representations of African slavery, it seems undeniable that enslaved people suffered terribly. Certainly people could become slaves through a variety of means, their circumstances once enslaved varied considerably, and descriptions of those circumstances were never without rhetorical purposes. Yet all descriptions of the slave market at Zanzibar are ghastly. In addition, freed slaves' accounts of their seizure and liberation show a striking degree of correspondence. The content of such descriptions cannot merely be laid at the feet of compelling narrative convention or legitimation for future political or religious domination. Yes, those stories were constructed. And many, whether by Europeans or Africans who became Christian, often took a narrative form that emphasized the liberation that came with contact with missionaries.[106] Such construction does not mean, however, that the products so distorted the facts as to render them unbelievable. It does mean that such accounts require critical interpretation.

Such accounts certainly disturb, whether they be of seizures of Africans from their natal homes, of the press-marching to the coast, of the slave market, or of the slave ships. The Spiritans themselves published several such accounts, as did other witnesses in this period.[107] Freed-slave narratives took regular forms, though with many permutations. They tended to stress the harmony before the narrator (or protagonist, in a non-first-person account) was uprooted, a harmony disturbed by raiders, indebtedness caused by some tragedy like the death of a parent, or, less commonly, a more amicable transaction that led to a departure to the coast in payment of a debt. In the raid many were killed, often members of the narrator's family, and the narrator then describes the harrowing journey to

104. See, for example, the following summaries found in the *Bullétin Général:* BG 3:461f; BG 4:119–20, 346, 563f, 635–39; BG 5:149f, 498. Other sources for descriptions include: CSSp 196aii: Horner to Notre Dame des Victoires, 24ix64; CSSp 196ax: Horner to Propagation of the Faith, 12ii65; CSSp 196axii: Horner to Holy Childhood, 15i69; Spiritan correspondence speaks of the crowds for sale at the slave market those years. See for example, CSSp 196iii; Baur to Sundhouse, 22xii66, and Baur to Horner, 14v67. Gaume 1872, 256f.

105. CSSp 196bii: Horner to Schwindenhammer, 14viii67; CSSp 196ax: Horner to Gaume, 1vii69.

106. Wright 1993, 1–2; UMCA 1861, 28.

107. For descriptions of the slave market, see the following: Burton 1858, 200–206; BG 8:756–58; CSSp 196ax: Horner to Propagation of the Faith, 12ii65, 29xii67; ibid.: Horner to Gaume, 1vii69; CSSp 196axii: Andalouma, 1883; APF 42 (1870): 48–55; Beachey 1976a, 8ff; Beachey 1976b, 37–66; Cave 1909; Lyne 1969, 83–89; Segal 2001, 145–49. For narratives by freed slaves, see CSSp 196aiv: Isa, 1876; Madan 1886; AA 1887: 71–76; Alpers 1983; Le Roy 1888; Bagamoyo Catholic mission, n.d. For descriptions of slave seizures, see UMCA 1861, 18; CSSp 196axiii: Courmont to Holy Childhood, 5x84; CSSp 196axi: Courmont to Propagation of the Faith, 8vi88. For caravan horrors, see Elton 1874 and Charmetant 1882, 141ff.

Figure 4: A slave caravan depicted. From *Les Missions Catholiques* 14 (1882): 457.

the coast, during which more were killed or abandoned to die. Adults on such marches had their necks placed in forked branches or were chained together. Once at the coast those surviving found themselves forced to the market at Zanzibar, where liberation was (eventually) found at the hands of benevolent missionaries or other kindly souls. Or perhaps they entered a slave ship that was attacked by the British and its human cargo freed.

European accounts of the slave market at Zanzibar emphasized the unhurried pace of the sales, the intimate inspections of bodies (the salaciousness of Arab traders and buyers features prominently in descriptions of inspections of the women), the rough manner of sellers and purchasers, and the empty eyes and skeletal bodies of many of those sold. Horner, for example, described the gruesome arrival at Zanzibar of slaves brought via ship from Kilwa: the stench, blood, and other bodily fluids; the dead among the living; others driven mad by the conditions. Perhaps most vivid were the vicious conditions on sea voyages, reminiscent of Atlantic slavery from western Africa, with the dead and dying tossed overboard or lingering, shrieking, and moaning, while chained with the living, and slaves drowned when slave traders sensed that British naval forces were near.

In general, accounts that derived from the period after colonial overrule, as well as accounts produced by those, like the Spiritans, who did not push for abolition, also stressed the relative mildness of internal slavery at the coast itself.[108]

108. Beech 1916; Cave 1909.

Earlier accounts, especially those composed by abolitionists, emphasized more the violence of seizures, marches, and markets. Both contained an element of truth, and both packaged that truth for certain reasons. Slavery in eastern Africa arose in the context of preexisting relations of patronage, unlike the enslavement of Africans in the Americas. It thus contained within it vestiges of that earlier paternalism, sometimes Islamic, that justified domination and subordination but usually without the profound dehumanization of slavery in Jamaica or South Carolina, at least before the rise of the plantation system. The growth of the plantation system and extractive slave exports, however, created a market at the coast that, coupled with political upheavals, led to huge profits in the trade of human beings, and corresponding strenuous efforts to capture and transport people from the interior. Thus there is no contradiction between the violence of slave raids, slave marches to the coast, and the dehumanization evident at the Zanzibar slave market, on the one hand, and, on the other hand, the mildness of much of the slave experience in eastern Africa compared to what happened in the African diaspora to the New World. In fact, the variety of terms used to describe those who were enslaved to some degree or another, and the fluidity of such terms, highlights the varied experience of slavery in the region.

Naming Slavery in Eastern Africa

In the KiSwahili language of the nineteenth century, a variety of terms described the different types of people who fit under the large rubric of slave status at the coast. These terms classified slaves based on their perceived relation to their master, occupation, religious participation, place of birth, whether or not they had arrived recently to the coast, and their degree of assimilation into Islam and hegemonic coastal society. Placement within this complex and shifting hierarchy could also be indicated by other markers of status such as dress.[109] These terms (and other identifying practices) generated a fluid continuum of statuses, what George Deutsch calls "subtle gradations of unfreedom," which were grounded in everyday practices, especially in places of residence and work. Labels indicated degrees of personal autonomy, but also particular places within the social world.

The generic word in KiSwahili for a slave was and is *mtumwa* (pl., *watumwa*), which means "one who is sent" (from the verb *ku-tuma*, to send). In certain contexts, however, the term could also mark outsider status in relation to some designated ethnic group.[110] Slaves who had just arrived from the interior of Africa

---

109. For the various terms used to describe types of servility in eastern Africa I have relied on the following: Akinola 1972, 216ff; Lodhi 1973, 4–7; Cooper 1977, 34–37, 183, 199f, 219; Deutsch 2000, 57ff; Morton 1990, 2–11; Glassman 1991, 288ff; Glassman 1995, 85f; Middleton 1992, 23ff, 116ff; Horton and Middleton 2000, 134f. Not all these witnesses agree, suggesting that significant local variations existed and continue to persist in terms for these sorts of ascribed status.

110. Kopytoff and Miers 1977, 17–18. See also Kollman 2001, 126–29.

to the coast were called *watumwa wajinga* (fools), *washenzi* (savages[111]), *waja* (from the verb *ku-ja*, "to come," so "those who have recently come") or, especially if they were in the process of being sold or transported, *mateka* (booty). Europeans often referred to such new arrivals as "raw" or "deracinated" slaves, to indicate that they were uprooted from their place of origins and had not been assimilated into Swahili society. Those who were not newcomers but assimilated to some degree had several designations. If born into slavery they were called *wazalia*, while those raised in slavery after being brought to the coast as children were *wakulia*. These two terms took their meaning from the verbs "to give birth" (*ku-zaa*) and "to grow up in/at" (*ku-kulia*). The label *mswahili* could have similar connotations, at least into the twentieth century, indicating one who was assimilated but not free, at least as the Arabs were free.[112]

There were two rather rough but serviceable distinctions at work in the language of slavery that became important for the story to be recounted in this book. The first distinction was between the two primary ways that enslavement was talked about. As Deutsch notes, slavery was described with kinship terms for the most part away from the coast in the interior of Africa. This language reflected the paternalistic understanding in which unfree relations were legitimated and, occasionally, euphemized throughout Africa. At the coast, however, kinship terms, while not unknown, increasingly gave way to patron-client types of language as the nineteenth century proceeded and slavery grew more harsh.[113]

The second distinction was not unrelated to the first. It was between field slaves who worked on plantations (*watwana* or *washamba*) and other sorts of unfree labor. Field slaves were usually "raw" *wajinga* or *mateka*, whose integration in Swahili culture was marginal. This was especially true of those who served in the brutal plantations appearing after the middle of the century. Field slaves also received plots of land for their own use called *makonde* (singular, *konde*) and enjoyed two (or more) days per week when they did not have to work on their owner's land. The yield on the slaves' *makonde* was their own. While the relationships between owners and both types of slaves could be defined using either kinship or patron-client language, field slaves rarely were designated with kinship language.

Other sorts of slaves, sometimes referred to simply as *watumwa* without another adjoining term, by implication had some sort of personal relationship — often defined through kinship terms — with their owner, unlike the field slaves. *Watumwa* often were paid, and from what they earned paid *ijara*, a rent or subsidy. They thus had a certain degree of personal autonomy, but they did not have

---

111. One indication of the difficulty with such terms can be seen in the fact that the first UMCA bishop, Tozer, treated the Washenzi ("savages") as a tribe (UMCA 1868).

112. Beech 1916, 146, n.2. Others claim that to be Swahili meant one was "free," in terms of no longer having the burden of true outsider status, though not free in the Western sense of possessing individual autonomy. Like the term *mwungwana* ("civilized"), *mswahili* thus marked a new higher status (Glassman 1991, 296–97).

113. Deutsch 2000, 15ff.

a regularized "free time" as did the field slaves. Nor did they generally possess the plots of land for their own use called *makonde*. They were, however, more integrated into Swahili society and could more easily aspire to higher status, even to the purchasing of their freedom. They tended to be *wakulia* or *wazalia*— born or raised at the coast—and worked in town or in the household.

Both of these distinctions became important as slave evangelization proceeded. In the first place, the Spiritans defended their relationship to their African converts using paternalistic language from the beginning. They were fathers to their children, while the sisters were mothers. Over time, however, aspects of the more typical coastal language of patronage and clientage also appeared. Second, many of those whom the Spiritans evangelized received plots of land that resembled *makonde*, and the possession of land created affinities between them and slaves at the coast. As we shall see, African Catholics recognized the ways that missionary language changed over time, and they also acted in light of their self-identity as landowners.

A large slave population often overlooked in the past were the *watoro*, or escaped slaves, who of course overlapped with these other categories. A number of colonies of such slaves existed at the eastern African coast beginning in the early nineteenth century, testifying to the frequency with which those enslaved fled their bondage.[114] The rise of the plantation system in the middle of the century led to more brutal forms of enslavement and flight grew even more common, as did slave revolts. Large-scale revolts occurred in 1840 and 1872–73.

The Complexity of Slave Experiences in Eastern Africa

In the past several decades, historians have sought to understand the consciousness and experiences of slaves in nineteenth-century eastern Africa, part of a larger movement in African historical studies to accord greater attention to African experiences and agency. Such work has generated appreciation for the variety of experiences associated with the different categories of enslavement, as well as the ways slaves adapted to political and economic changes in the region. Special attention has been accorded slaves' responses to plantation slavery and the promise of abolition, slave resistance as shown through flight and other forms of resistance, and the strategies of women under slave conditions.[115]

Such studies have emphasized the pragmatic nature of the strategic choices made by those enslaved in coastal eastern Africa. Despite their unfree status, slaves in eastern Africa did not entirely lose their ability to shape their lives. In fact, the variety of roles and terms used within the coastal slave system suggest that the line between slave and free was not clear and obvious to all, and such fluidity was typical in African slavery.[116] This uncertainty generated possibilities for

114. Recent studies of slave flight in eastern Africa include the following: Morton 1990; Cooper 1977; Cassinelli 1987. See also Glassman 1995.
115. Cooper 1977, 1980; Morton 1990; Wright 1993; Deutsch 2000, 2003.
116. Iliffe 2005, 120.

social mobility and status adjustments within the slaves' strange and potentially dangerous environment. In the face of these conditions, slaves were inclined to take steps in pursuit of their interests, in order to mitigate the effects of their forced marginalization.[117] One way to reduce one's marginal status included attempting to attach oneself to a patron who would be less brutal rather than more. Other efforts directed the creation of social ties among those held in unfreedom like themselves.[118]

Joseph Miller's appreciation of what he calls "the necessarily spontaneous, opportunistic, *bricoleur*-like, integrative quality of constructing new identities under the constraints of slavery" in Brazil is echoed in the most influential work on slave consciousness in eastern Africa, that of Jonathon Glassman. Glassman has analyzed the Swahili crowd that resisted and periodically rebelled against the powerful, beginning with the Arabs and most dramatically against the Germans in the late 1880s. Building upon previous studies of slavery at the coast of eastern Africa like those of Frederick Cooper, Glassman attributes to the Swahili crowd what he calls a "contradictory consciousness." By this he means that slaves could simultaneously resist their own experiences of enslavement without rejecting the hegemonic worldview that created enslavement in the first place. Such worldviews could be contested, wholesale or in part, and were not simply internalized by all who partook in them. Yet most resistance did not attack the system. Instead, Glassman underscores the strategic ways those designated *watumwa* or slaves used patron-client ideology — or other ideologies by which slavery was justified, such as paternalistic idioms — to subvert, or at least ameliorate, the worst consequences of their outsider status without contesting that ideology directly.[119] Thus slaves at the Swahili coast, even in their most rebellious state, did not strive after something like Western freedom. As Glassman (1995, 94; 1991, 281ff) puts it, "... in societies such as those of preconquest East Africa, where most people relied on ties of personal dependency to provide social security and social identity, it would be difficult to find an equivalent of the modern western concept of 'freedom.' "

Glassman's descriptions of the Swahili crowd and its "contradictory consciousness" ring true in connection to much anthropological literature on African peoples. But by interpreting slave escapes not as a way out of coastal society, Glassman contests interpretations by many other previous African historians, as well as the contentions of many of the early missionaries and colonizers. These emphasized the loss of freedom and dignity suffered by the enslaved. Such views, though understandable given their humanitarian motives, often robbed Africans

---

117. See Deutsch 2000, 58ff, as well as Glassman 1995. For more general discussions of the possibilities within the slave state, see the following: Kopytoff and Miers 1977; Wright 1993, 1–22, 43.

118. J. Miller 2003, 83, 108–9.

119. Glassman 1991, 1995. Similar arguments have been made more recently with regard to slavery before and then under German colonialism by Jan-Georg Deutsch (2000, 2003), and with regard to slave strategies after abolition at Zanzibar by Laura Fair (1994, 2001). See Kollman 2001, 126–29.

of their capacity to determine their own situations, and thus overlooked the ways Africans acted as agents of their own history, even in conditions like slavery. Glassman's contrary position appreciates African agency but situates it. By arguing that slaves rarely sought to escape "the system," but worked for a better life within it, he admits that they were often firmly socialized into the Swahili world as slaves. The ideal self in the slave imaginary, then, was not the free autonomous individual, but rather one with a considerate patron who abided by the coastal codes of proper behavior in relations with his clients.

Despite his insights, Glassman's Swahili crowd fails to serve as a direct template for those at the Catholic missions, whose experience only approximated that of those he analyzes most closely. The *mateka* (booty) slaves ransomed or received by the Spiritans — those recently enslaved — would not have possessed such a contradictory consciousness upon their arrival at the mission, as he himself recognizes.[120]

Nonetheless, Glassman's careful work lays a basis for understanding a group like the slaves who came to the Holy Ghost missions at Zanzibar and Bagamoyo in the nineteenth century. Previous historians, as well as the missionaries, often imagined that such a "deracinated" group — to rely on problematic colonialist terminology that assumed an essentialized tribal identity whose loss supposedly spelled social anomie and created nightmares for colonial administrators — had nothing in common. They thus experienced evangelization in a way only analyzable on an individual basis. They were so uniquely constituted by their experiences prior to evangelization, such an argument has often run, that no shared "freed slave experience" can be theorized. This admission of unknowability becomes even more tempting in light of the nature of the sources, which show a very uneven curiosity about the collective experience of the Africans at the mission.

Glassman's analysis gives one resources to fight such skepticism. He shows how living in coastal society could generate in other slaves a desire to participate within that hegemonic society, that is, to improve their lot within it, and not simply to flee it. By analogy, his work encourages attention to the kind of collective identity forged by Africans once at the mission, the kind of belonging that emerged through slave evangelization, one aspect of which was the moral economy of the mission. Adapting Glassman's ideas, one can say that those who participated in the missions' activities developed certain shared sentiments, or a culture understood as a "thin coherence," to use Sewell's term. And Hirschman's options of exit and voice allow us to make sense of the Catholic identity that emerged at Spiritan missions.

---

120. Glassman 1995, 107. At the same time, the other group of slaves whose circumstances have been studied at some length in eastern Africa, the *watoro* who fled slavery, also little approximate those who came to the mission, at least those who spent much time there. Thus Morton's 1990 study is also of limited use as a study of those at the missions.

The Spiritans and Slaves upon Arriving at the Mission

Both the Spiritans and those they evangelized were new to coastal society, outsiders within the dynamic and complex system of patronage and clientage, domination and subordination, operative in the Swahili environment where most Spiritan slave evangelization occurred. Together they adapted to that world, which itself underwent profound economic and political changes in the late nineteenth century. Yet if they occupied the same place and time, the two groups faced very different circumstances within that setting. In particular, the reality of slavery impinged upon them in very different ways.

The missionaries came to the coast of eastern Africa in pursuit of their vocation. They arrived at Zanzibar after taking a long voyage in order to participate in evangelizing a continent. Upon arriving they were eager to fulfill their calling, and they looked for opportunities to do so within their new environment. The missionaries saw eastern Africa as pregnant with opportunities for evangelization, and overdue for the processes they came to enact. Elements of the spirituality that the Spiritans inherited from their second founder Libermann only reinforced their spatial consciousness of being on the edge of a needy continent and the temporal urging to act with dispatch. Libermann wanted the Spiritans anxious to plunge ahead into the unknown on noble and possibly dangerous missions, into places where — as explorer and Spiritan chronicles portrayed — cannibalism, sorcery, and other examples of "pagan savagery" or "Muslim corruption," as well as dangers to health, were rife. Cartography itself partook in their spirituality. The missionaries had maps that presented the coast of eastern Africa as the gateway to the interior — an interior often depicted as dark and in need; they felt themselves poised for the spiritual work of regenerating benighted peoples.[121]

In light of their missionary zeal, slavery was one important feature of the environment in which they were to act. They came with certain feelings about slavery due to their backgrounds prior to arriving in Zanzibar, but they faced the issue primarily in light of their overall missionary goals in eastern Africa. The missionaries thus took a pragmatic approach to slavery. Slavery was a tragedy, they admitted, yet it was also a missionary opportunity. They recognized that slavery prevented a fruitful exterior ministry at the coast but did not dare risk offending the sultan, upon whose permission the Catholic mission depended. When asked, they emphasized the gradual abolition that would come with Christian and European civilization.[122] Eventually they refused to receive escaped slaves as the Anglicans did at Freetown, their establishment for freed slaves established

---

121. The Spiritan mother house in Paris urged the missionaries to draw maps when entering new territories, and maps often appeared in missionary publications, including those the Spiritans produced for themselves (BG 3:136).

122. CSSp 196ax: Horner to Propagation of the Faith, 29xii67; CSSp 195iv: Horner to Geography Society of Paris, 28iv73; CSSp 195iii: Courmont to Simeoni, report on slavery, 1896. By contrast, the Anglican Universities' Mission to Central Africa stated, in its constitution, that among its goals was "the ultimate extinction of the slave trade" (UMCA 1861, B).

near Mombasa in 1875.[123] In fact Horner himself considered employing slaves in 1864 but was afraid of public pressure. The correspondence with his superiors weighing the question shows no sign that moral qualms shaped his decision.[124]

Slavery's place in the missionary program was complex and at times self-contradictory. Most importantly in light of their missionary vocation, slavery in eastern Africa afforded the Spiritans the chance to carry out their missionary goals of saving souls and establishing the church. Slaves were, in their minds, first and foremost potential future Catholics. At the same time, slavery as an issue helped support the mission by generating European funds. As noted earlier, slave children in particular became useful symbolically to connect European Christian benefactors with the missionary project through sponsorship. The Spiritans also used slavery in rhetorical attempts to generate moral indignation and attack Islam, thus reinforcing the alleged superiority of European and Christian values. Finally, the Spiritans honestly felt compassion for those enslaved and were moved by the pathetic scenes they witnessed. Helping slaves fulfilled their desire to alleviate suffering.

The Africans who came to the Spiritan missions, of course, had no luxury to consider slavery from such an external perspective, nor was it one feature among many shaping their lives. Most had been forcibly taken from the interior to the coast, and faced violence and misery in that uprooting and the transport that followed.[125] They had suffered as slaves and knew intimately the violence of the practices of slavery. They had come to the mission in the opposite direction from the missionaries — not from the sea, but toward it, from the interior of eastern Africa to the coast. And they had come not out of zeal, but against their will.

Unlike the Spiritans, the former slaves lacked a shared overarching collective moral framework with which to evaluate the changing economics and legitimating moral reasoning that fostered practices like slavery. They did not share the legacy of Europe's religious and social conflicts, out of which certain notions of freedom had been and were being formed, an evolution that affected even those, like the official Catholic Church, which tried to resist some of its implications that favored liberal versions of freedom. Also unlike the missionaries, they had no shared and coherent theological vision of personhood that presumed to lay claims to an even deeper notion of freedom, a theological notion that did not entail an embrace of abolition.[126] Thus the former slaves' experiences likely did not conduce to

---

123. CSSp 196biii: Scheuermann to Horner, 2vi73; BG 9:525; Bagamoyo journal 2viii86; Mhonda journal 1viii79; Strayer 1978; Morton 1990.

124. CSSp 196bii, Horner to Duboin, 24vi64; CSSp 196aii: Horner to Schwindenhammer, 10x66. As we shall see, Horner may even have had four slaves working on the mission at Zanzibar in 1866, though he could be referring to former slaves not part of the mission community properly speaking.

125. Enslavement could occur through many means, but Deutsch identifies four main avenues leading to enslavement in nineteenth-century eastern Africa: through capture or defeat in war or raiding; through a judicial process by way of punishment; due to impressment due to indebtedness (or voluntary enslavement in times of famine); or because one was born into slavery (2000, 58ff).

126. Thus African Catholics, themselves former slaves, held slaves at the Spiritan missions into the 1890s. This practice is obviously very revealing, and I take it up in chapters 5 and 6. For details, see Kieran 1966, 129; Mandera journal, 4v87; Mhonda journal, 17xi88, 8vii92, 8xii95; Bagamoyo

consideration of the institution of slavery as a whole. Lacking substantive views of freedom in common, the slaves would likely not have been able, early on at least, to articulate something like either the liberal Western notion of freedom or the Christian freedom espoused by the missionaries.

That being said, however, the slaves likely had been socialized in places with a moral order legitimating what the social collective, or some part of it, could demand of any individual. Such communities, mostly decentralized, also no doubt had terms for freedom and its opposite. These were likely embedded in forms of "implied obligation and assumed self-restraint," expectations lodged in political practices that were incumbent upon social authorities like parents, chiefs, and elders, as well as those under them.[127] As Crawford Young writes, "Thus freedom, understood as absence of unaccepted power from above, was the unarticulated norm." Yet he adds that such freedom was not linked with owning property in the Lockean sense, since land was available and harnessing labor and social relationships, rather than territorial control, signified social power.[128] In the kinds of polities from which most of those evangelized by the Spiritans had come, there might well have been circumstances approximating slavery that were so legitimated, something like social pawning or temporary labor expectations connected with indebtedness or marriage. The seizures that had eventuated in their having come to the coast as slaves, however, probably violated the local moral order. They certainly did so if slave raiders had come from outside. At other times, a series of locally legitimated but progressively disempowering interactions had culminated in individuals being drawn into the growing slave trade, one node of which stood at Zanzibar. Slave narratives of those received by the Spiritans depicted just such downward spirals, ending only with ransoming by the missionaries.[129]

Those who came from the slave market had been liable for export or transport to some other unknown destiny after purchase. These were not the locally born *wazalia* or locally raised *wakulia*, who were sometimes simply called *watumwa*. These were newcomers, *mateka* or *watwana*. Similar designations would have fallen upon those rescued at sea by the British, who composed the majority of those who arrived at the missions in the 1870s. Many had endured a march to the coast, and they knew that others like them had died on the way, while some had gone to places unknown, perhaps through sales to slave owners.

Such people, many of them children, found themselves in a place that was new, foreign, and frightening. The harsh new circumstances of enslavement coupled with incomprehensible languages and estrangement from home only increased

---

journal, 27i90. When the missionaries criticized the Christians for the way they treated "their" slaves, and reminded them that they had servants, not slaves, the Christians were displeased (Mhonda journal, 22xii95).

127. R. Taylor 2002, 1, 4; C. Young 2002, 16ff.

128. C. Young 2002, 17–18.

129. For examples see the story of Suéma in chapter 3, as well as the stories collected by A. C. Madan 1886 and Le Roy 1888.

their felt dislocation, fear, and vulnerability. Prior to their enslavement, they might have considered the coast an exotic destination signaling excitement and newness, religious innovation and economic potential. But being taken there against one's will did anything but conduce to that excitement.[130] The missionaries told of slave fears of being sent across the sea, or of being eaten by those to whom they were sold. For most slaves, the coast represented a place of precarious exile.

These circumstances thus did not initially encourage former slaves at the mission to dream ambitiously about a future, any future, much less the Christian one that transfixed the missionaries. They sought instead more immediate and concrete goals, like finding the means of survival, and then forging relationships with mild rather than harsh patrons. Eventually they would seek to enhance their chances for social reproduction, but they had no grandiose visions to do so, at least upon coming to the mission.[131] Instead their circumstances likely induced a fearful longing for security.

Unlike the missionaries, these Africans did not have printed maps with them. Thus their self-location was more *relational* than spatial. Above all they sought settings and relationships that fostered security and, eventually, might offer them a chance to thrive in ways they understood. The various forms of servitude at the coast encouraged the new arrivals to become aware that some situations were better than others for material reasons, some circumstances more conducive to the possibilities of social reproduction and others less, some regimes of labor more onerous than others. That socialization might even have begun before seizure by slave raiders, or on the way to the coast itself. But the process was inchoate and uneven, only to be complicated by the mission's own ambitious agenda.

The slaves' first encounter with the missionaries came through a process of transaction, a process effected by the decisions of the missionaries to purchase them, to receive them (mostly) from the British, or to gather them. Upon arriving at the mission, the slaves procured by the mission were probably prone to obey those deemed above them, especially if they were children. They had usually been socialized to some degree in hierarchical societies where social identity derived from personal dependency. For this reason, one can imagine that they easily assimilated the missionaries to the other social authorities they had known, whether in previous enslavement or in their natal homes.

Due to the way they came to the mission, older slaves likely considered missionary *rachat* (repurchase; ransom) or reception as reenslavement, at least in the beginning. The Spiritans simply resembled new masters upon whom their well-

---

130. The coast did not have dreadful connotations for all eastern Africans in this period. In fact, for a growing number in the nineteenth century, the coast represented opportunities, and porterage on caravans even assumed a role as a rite of passage for young men (Glassman 1995, 55ff; Rockel 1995, 2000).

131. Thus Frederick Cooper says that those who could claim their freedom beginning in 1897 made their decisions on whether to do so not because they preferred one state to another in some abstract sense, but because they assessed the advantages and disadvantages of staying with their master or leaving (Cooper 1980, 72–76).

being to a great extent depended. Perhaps they appeared as some combination of patrons, masters, and enemies, in line with other sorts of authority operative in their African homes and Swahili society.[132] As socialization into the mission and the Swahili coast progressed, the Africans at the mission gradually saw the missionaries in two overlapping ways. First, the Spiritans represented religious authorities in a way more akin to the missionaries' own self-perceptions, especially if the Africans themselves were targeted as potential future elites. Second, the missionaries also appeared in relation to other social authorities at the coast, who included African and Arab landowners as well as formal political figures in the Omani and European elites.

Later, as they grew more accustomed to coastal society, the former slaves understood that their situation differed in important ways from that of those purchased by other landowners at the coast. Still, they likely continued to compare the missionaries to other patrons in a slaveholding society, and their own circumstances to those in unfree situations that approximated their own. Other observers considered the Africans at Spiritan missions in relation to unfree laborers in the region, as we shall see. If Glassman sees enslaved Africans to have been open to selectively embracing the hierarchized world of the coast, where deference and subordination were the norm, freed slaves held at the missions likely strategized in a similar fashion, especially as their socialization progressed, both at the mission and in its broader environs.[133]

Missionary and African Approaches to Labor and Space

Slavery as an institution was predicated on the control of the movement and labor of some people by others. The evangelization of slaves also implicated space and work in important ways. As we shall see, the Spiritans trusted physical labor as an essential part of the formative processes they sought to establish. They also put great emphasis on the proper spatial organization of the mission for evangelization. The Africans, too, approached physical labor and space in ways reflective of their backgrounds.

For the missionaries, labor's role in forming and reforming the Africans at the mission derived from their religious and cultural background. Monks had long argued for the formative value of physical labor in the cultivation of virtue, and Spiritan seminary formation also featured labor in gardens and orchards. Libermann himself had emphasized the importance of work in regenerating those recently freed from slavery.[134] Secular developments in Europe encouraged attention to labor as well, for in the European political economy of the modern period human beings increasingly were conceived as *homo laborans*. In places

---

132. Wright 1993, 1–2.
133. Giblin 1996, 134–36; Sundkler and Steed 2000, 515.
134. Libermann, n.d. 528–29, 569f.

like the juvenile reformatories where the Spiritans served, the programs of reform tried to inculcate proper working habits, linking gainful productivity with self-enhancement.[135]

Valuations of work had particular resonances in nineteenth-century France, where the assessment of industrial work in particular often depended on one's religiously inflected politics.[136] Robert Locke, for example, has shown how the French Legitimists who wanted a return of the monarchy had a "politics of moral order," an approach that not only saw religion as essential in the maintenance of society, but also praised peasants, rural life, and the family. These mostly Catholic conservatives held deep suspicions of urbanism, industrial workers, and artisans, whom they associated with radicals and revolutionaries.[137] Such valorization of labor on the land at the expense of industrial toil, also common to Alsatian Catholics from whom the missionaries were so often drawn, increasingly figured in Spiritan strategies.

Since labor takes its meaning from its place in a larger social system, thus gaining its value in relation to other cultural realities, Africans naturally approached it differently. Prior to colonial contact and extensive commoditization, African approaches to labor tended to derive from a pastoralist-cultivator economy characterized by a familial or kinship-centered mode of local production. Labor was not isolated as a distinctive area of human concern but existed as a social practice that generated subsistence and perhaps a small surplus for the purposes of limited forms of exchange. This does not mean that Africans merely adapted to their environments in some mechanical way, but it does mean that labor was not an abstract category differentiated as particularly productive apart from other processes associated with social reproduction. If there was a "work ethic," it likely did not derive from a religiously inspired obligation or from some external sanction, but from practices of subsistence production and the expectations of locally constituted forms of social reproduction. As the Comaroffs write of the Tswana, "Work . . . was the positive, relational aspect of human social activity; of the making of self and others in the course of everyday life."[138]

Regarding approaches to space, recent studies of landscape suggest that Europeans and Africans, generally speaking, have appropriated space in different ways, thus pointing to further important differences between the missionaries and the targets of their evangelization.[139] Though both Africans and Europeans, like most peoples, have "constructed" landscapes so that neither group has a more objective approach than the other to conceiving of spaces, they do so in distinctive ways.

---

135. Gronemeyer 1992, 58.

136. For insightful studies of work in France in the nineteenth century, see Sewell 1980 and the essays in Kaplan and Koepp 1986.

137. Locke 1974, 140, 170f.

138. Comaroff and Comaroff 2001, 273. For similar ideas, see the following: Sahlins 1968; Bundy 1979; Atkins 1993; Luig and von Oppen 1997, 28–29.

139. Cohen and Odhiambo 1989; Ranger 1999; Luig and von Oppen 1997; Neumann 1998.

For their part the Spiritans placed great store in their ability to shape environments that fostered the reforms they sought. Their attention to the instrumental value of spaces derived from their formation to religious life and other experiences. In contrast, African peoples tended to evaluate land in relation to social practices associated with it rather than to stress its instrumental potential for the shaping of individuals. Recent studies have shown that in creating environments perceived as suitable for habitation, however, Africans developed a variety of practices in connection to settlement, cultivation, worship, and burial.[140] Such research has challenged the colonial commonplace that Africans mismanaged or ignored the land. That claim is now seen as a politically useful contrast justifying colonial rule by establishing an "implicit call for Western-induced 'rationalization' of landscape."[141] Compared to the missionaries, however, most Africans showed less self-consciousness about shaping their environment for the formation of persons.

Part of the European attention to landscapes involved its intense visualization.[142] By contrast, Africans, especially in the precolonial period, tended to situate themselves in certain places through use and practical activity rather than aesthetic considerations. As one recent overview puts it, "In African discourses, spatial terrain is turned into landscape first and foremost by human practice."[143] This does not mean lack of sophistication, for African languages have complex lexicons for land that refer to its usage, distinguishing between various sorts of field, bush, wilderness, or forest. Many African societies differentiate sharply between land for human habitation and nonhabitable sites, which might be viewed as unsuitable for ritual or historical reasons.[144] Nonetheless, intensive visualization of land was not common in a precapitalist economic and social world characterized by a familial mode of production of food, a relatively unelaborated division of labor, limited surplus production, and the importance of kinship ties in self-definition.[145]

•

Both the Spiritans and the Africans they evangelized were people who lived in moving streams. The missionaries came to Zanzibar from a Europe that was itself undergoing transformation, and they discussed their missionary strategy in

---

140. Kopytoff 1987; Maddox, Giblin, and Kimambo 1996; Luig and von Oppen 1997, 7, passim.
141. Luig and von Oppen 1997, 27. At the same time, African approaches to land ownership and use confused Europeans, especially colonizers who sought control of land (Giblin 1996). The Holy Ghost missionaries were no exception. Their attempts to gain access to land to found their mission stations ran into repeated trouble, beginning in the late 1860s at Bagamoyo. There the Spiritans faced challenges to their claims to land from local African authorities who disputed the grants made by the sultan and other Arabs, as we shall see in chapter 4.
142. See Green 1990, who highlights nineteenth-century France as particularly obsessed with the visualization of spaces (2ff). Beinart and McGregor also link European approaches to landscape with a particular way of seeing (2003, 4).
143. Luig and von Oppen 1997, 24, 27.
144. Ibid., 21, 24–26.
145. Bundy 1979, 4–25.

reference to a number of the issues of the day, including theological controversies connected with Catholic identity, educational reforms, and the role of the pope in the church and among other European powers. The Africans who came to their missions also emerged from a world in transition. They stood among those who most suffered because of those transitions, for enslavement had brought them to the coast in the first place.

With different views of the world and of their place in it, the generalizable goals of the two groups who met in evangelization thus differed considerably. The missionaries sought their personal sanctification along with their twofold aims in evangelization: to save souls and build the church. This entailed fervent obedience to ecclesial authorities and zeal for their mission. They strove to construct an environment to pursue these goals.

For their part, the Africans had no clearly defined collective purpose driving their presence at the mission. After all they were there, initially at least, against their will. In view of their limited choices, especially if they were children, they sought to make the best of what were very trying circumstances. This usually meant pursuing the most helpful relationships possible. Given that many had already internalized assumptions of hierarchy and subordination, they had pre-dispositions that, at the outset, fit neatly into missionary assumptions about proper personhood, which were also essentially hierarchical because they were ecclesi-ological. It pleased the missionaries that those arriving at the mission usually did what they were told.

What deeper (and more immanent) notions of human thriving the Africans possessed were probably connected with procuring the means of social reproduc-tion, and such means derived first from their experiences prior to enslavement. Upon arriving in a new place like Zanzibar, their impressions about the possibil-ities within their new surroundings would have developed in relation to that past but also in light of particular social practices carried out in the new environment, at least if their relationships to some identity before arriving continued to have any hold on them.

As we shall see in the chapters ahead, the former slaves at the Spiritan missions reacted to Spiritan evangelization in a variety of ways. In the 1880s, they fled in large numbers and protested the conditions at the missions, leading the mis-sionaries to reconsider their strategy. Even before the Spiritans faced this crisis, however, missionary records show that many of the Africans evangelized under-stood their circumstances and acted self-consciously to improve them, though in less collective ways. The interplay between missionary practices and African ac-tions, to be discussed as the next three chapters trace the evangelization of slaves and responses to it, produced the Catholic Church in eastern Africa.

Chapter Three

Forming the Christian Nucleus at Zanzibar

The Catholic Church Returns to Eastern Africa, 1860–68

Timeline

1858	Father Armand-Joseph Fava, vicar general of Bishop Maupoint of Réunion, visits Zanzibar in June.
1860	Holy See approves apostolic prefecture of *Zanguebar* and entrusts it to Bishop Maupoint.
	December 22: Fava arrives to start the mission, called *La Providence.*
1862	March: French-British treaty to respect the territorial integrity of Zanzibar.
	August: Spiritans accept responsibility for apostolic prefecture of Zanguebar.
1863	June 16: Four Spiritans arrive at Zanzibar along with three sisters.
	August 2: Horner visits Bagamoyo and celebrates Mass at 5:00 a.m. on August 6, 1863.
1864	June 24: Anglican UMCA mission arrives at Zanzibar.
	October 18: Horner visits Réunion for medical leave, returning on July 4, 1865.
1865	February: Baur travels to Bagamoyo with Casimir, one of the older boys at the mission.
1866	January: Death of Sister Marie-Pierre at Zanzibar and a huge funeral.

February: Attempted escape from the mission by Casimir and Josephine.

September/October: Horner visits the mainland, chooses Bagamoyo as site for the mainland mission.

1867   January: Horner's sickness sends him to Europe, where he raises money.

Baur prepares French-KiSwahili catechism.

July 1: Bishop Maupoint visits Zanzibar.

August: Baur leases a local house for African Christian couples; they marry September 2.

December 1: Horner returns with funds sufficient to discharge the mission's debts.

1868   January: Horner and Baur visit Bagamoyo and rent a house.

A New Beginning

In early 1868, Father Antoine Horner, the first Holy Ghost superior in eastern Africa, wrote Cardinal Barnabo, head of Propaganda Fide, the Vatican office organizing missionary activity. He described the strategy of the Spiritan mission, then five years underway at Zanzibar:

> Instead of beginning in the interior [of Africa] with a preaching hampered in a thousand ways and generally unproductive for years, we apply ourselves to implanting there in one fell swoop fully formed Christian communities. . . . Is this not a far more effective Christianizing influence than a word thrown in haste by a passing missionary?[1]

To enact this strategy, which he oversaw from 1863 until his departure from eastern Africa in 1879, Horner and his confreres needed Catholics to implant in the interior of Africa. They chose to evangelize slaves for this purpose. Believing that public proclamation of Christianity threatened to undermine their friendly relations with the sultan of Zanzibar and dubious about conversions among Muslims anyway, they opted for what seemed the only approach to molding Catholics for Christian communities of the interior: obtaining slaves, either through purchase at the slave market of Zanzibar or other means, and forming them into Catholics for the future.

This chapter describes the first eight years of that effort, when the Catholic mission in eastern Africa, begun in 1860 and assumed by the Spiritans in 1863, was restricted to Zanzibar. There the Congregation of the Holy Ghost developed an ambitious missionary strategy that sought to form onetime African slaves into

---

1. CSSp 195aii: Horner to Barnabo, 25i68.

Catholics. From Zanzibar the Spiritans founded a larger mission at Bagamoyo in March 1868.

As Horner's letter suggests, the Spiritans planned eventually to use the ex-slaves raised, educated, and prepared at Zanzibar and Bagamoyo to found missions in the interior. Away from the coast where their formation had begun, such complete Christian communities would, Horner believed, cooperate with the missionaries in the task of evangelization. Horner foresaw some in direct cooperation as priests, brothers, and sisters (and later, as catechists); others would attract surrounding nonslave peoples because of their virtues and prosperity. Reformed individuals would compose a new branch of the universal Catholic Church. What Horner derided as "unproductive" preaching in the interior, "a word thrown in haste by a passing missionary," signifies his typically Catholic perceptions of the Protestant missionary model to be shunned. Horner depicted that model as viewing potential believers as soil awaiting a seed, soil that might or might not be fertile. The Spiritans at Zanzibar and Bagamoyo focused their efforts on the formation of communities of the faithful designed to emigrate inland together as a Christian *noyau* (French for "nucleus" or "kernel") for the new mission stations to which they would be sent. Those African Catholics would be the seed.

Beginning in 1863, the Spiritans established a comprehensive missionary program even though the number of missionaries remained comparatively small — only a handful of priests and brothers along with nuns who collaborated with them under their direction. Circumstances such as the availability of slaves, the young age of most of the Africans who came to the mission, Zanzibar's stability combined with the sultan's beneficence (especially until Majid's death in 1870), missionary doggedness, considerable funds from overseas, and the support of the European community in the town allowed the Spiritans to institute an ordered program approximately in line with their semiarticulated missionary strategy. Later, as we shall see, obstacles arose from within the missionaries themselves, from outside forces, and from the Africans they targeted for evangelization. Consequently, their ability to shape the practices of evangelization on their own terms decreased. But the early years allowed the Spiritans considerable scope for putting their mark on the Zanzibar mission.

Besides establishing certain practices on the ground, Horner and his confreres also wrote voluminously about their mission in those early years. Mindful of the complex nature of the historical records upon which our understanding of slave evangelization relies, this chapter, after a summary of those first years, examines the rhetoric within the missionary writings that represent our best source on those years. Then follows an analysis of the central features of Spiritan evangelization of slaves at Zanzibar. The analysis emphasizes two facets of the Spiritan program: the regime of enclosure aiming at comprehensive formation of Catholics, and the emerging salience of physical work. A look at the limited but revealing discernible African responses to missionary evangelization in this early period concludes the chapter.

The Early Years of the Catholic Mission
at Zanzibar

The Catholic mission in Zanzibar began on December 22, 1860, when Father Armand-Joseph Fava (1826–99) arrived with two other priests, a surgeon from the French Navy, industrial workers for a forge and a carpentry shop, and six sisters of the *Filles de Marie*, or the Daughters of Mary, a religious community founded at the Indian Ocean island of Réunion in 1849.[2] On November 29 the group had embarked from Réunion, where Fava served as vicar general for Bishop Armand Maupoint of the diocese of St. Denis, who had recently been named by the Vatican as apostolic delegate for eastern Africa. Fava brought funds from the governing Council General of Réunion (fifteen thousand francs) and the Propagation of the Faith (twenty thousand francs). He also carried household furnishings, implements for agricultural work, and equipment for the other establishments planned for the mission. These included a large chapel, a hospital/clinic for the poor of Zanzibar, a hospital for European sailors, a bandaging room, a pharmacy, a forge, and a carpentry/joinery shop. Fava had gathered these materials in fulfillment of the promises he had made to Majid, the sultan of Zanzibar, during negotiations to gain permission for the mission before arriving. The sultan's refusals of previous requests to establish Christian missions in the 1850s meant that Fava received permission with clear expectations governing the mission's conduct. Eschewing the goal of converting the local Muslim population, in the short term at least, he accepted the challenge to win the confidence of the people through Christian charity. The Catholic mission came to Zanzibar to help the sick, feed the poor, and instruct and teach the children in trades.[3]

Two days after arriving, Fava visited the sultan and in short order fulfilled his promises. He established the workshops and two hospitals, one for Europeans and the other for Zanzibar's indigenous population. Soon came three schools, one for Zanzibar's Arabs, one for the Indians, and one for the former slave children who soon came to the mission. Historians of the politics of this period highlight the diplomatic dispute between the French and British that the so-called French mission's establishment touched off, the size of the mission's central building and residence igniting British fears that French sailors might bivouac there. This dispute culminated in the noninterference treaty of 1862, which officially governed European interactions with Zanzibar until the mid-1880s. Fava hardly mentioned such concerns, instead depicting in his reports the goodwill won by the mission's small-scale activities.

---

2. The Daughters of Mary had been founded by Libermann's friend and cofounder of the Congregation of the Holy Heart of Mary, Frédéric Levavasseur (1811–82), who later served briefly as superior general of the Congregation of the Holy Ghost before his death (Dussercle 1974; Eve 1999).
3. Zanzibar journal, 22xii60; Kieran 1966, 26ff; Versteijnen 1968b; CSSp 196bii: Fava to Schwindenhammer, 28vii60.

Soon the mission property hummed with activity, hosting daily Masses, caring for the sick, providing esteemed technical repairs, educating children, and imparting vocational training to the former slaves old enough to learn.[4] The workshops earned a reputation for excellent service, with the forge and joinery repairing various official and commercial ships, and ensuring that the sultan's machine for making sugar operated properly. The mission's hospitals and schools also garnered praise. Fava wrote the sisters' superior in Réunion describing the awe he felt before their devotion and hard work, an esteem he claimed was shared by all of Zanzibar.[5] Europeans expressed thanks for the care they received from the sisters in the hospital reserved for them, while the hospital for non-Europeans, meant particularly for those of African descent, was soon the busiest part of the mission, receiving between forty and fifty patients per day.[6] The largest room of the dwelling that alarmed the British housed a chapel for Catholic worship catering to the European Catholics and few Goans of Zanzibar, as well as the mission's African children.

Fava claimed the mission's most important work centered around such children who came to the mission, but he followed no systematic approach to increasing their number. Some arrived after ransoming at the slave market, while others came to the mission through a transaction such as debt payment or were gathered from the streets after having been abandoned. These totaled sixteen in August 1862, among whom four of the boys and four of the girls had been baptized. Local Europeans (especially the mission doctor) and the sisters served as godparents.[7] Fava, pleading prudence, defended the low number baptized, but he praised the group's heart and intelligence. All had been slaves before coming to the mission, and four, he reported, had been stolen from their parents near Lake Nyanza (today Lake Victoria). The boys of teachable age attended an industrial training school located at the workshops to learn a trade, while girls had their own workshop (*ouvroir*) where they were trained as seamstresses under the tutelage of the sisters. Besides this industrial training, the mission also offered more scholastic education in what was called alternately the orphanage or the school. There catechism, reading, writing, and arithmetic were imparted. Fava described the attraction of the mission for those who came to work and learn there:

---

4. For descriptions of the founding of the mission and its early days, see especially Fava's July 1861 letter to Bishop Maupoint (reprinted as Fava 1933) and his July 1862 letter to the Society of the Propagation of the Faith, reprinted in APF 35 (1863), 124–41.

5. Eve 1999, 174–75.

6. In early letters Fava described the crowds waiting at the hospital before 7:30 a.m., when the doors opened and the French naval surgeon began seeing the sick (Fava 1933; APF 35 [1863], 127–29; also CSSp 196bii: Fava to Schwindenhammer, 19vi61). In December 1862, one of the sisters also wrote the mother general in Réunion describing their service in the hospital (Marie du Sacré Coeur to M. M. De la Croix, 3xii62; summarized in CSSp 196aviii: Secretariat of the Mother House of the Daughters of Mary, St. Denis, Réunion, November 1981). She also said they housed seven girls whom they were educating.

7. The mission at Zanzibar baptized twenty-six before the Spiritans assumed control in June 1863. Most of the baptisms were carried out not by Fava, but by the other two priests who came with him, Fathers Jego and Schimpff. Several of those baptized were Europeans, but probably over twenty were Africans. In that same period, there were five burials (Zanzibar sacramental registry).

Figure 5. Sisters with the sick. Photo from the Bagamoyo Mission Museum.
Used with permission.

> Those whom we snatch from slavery have followed us. In vain we have
> told them that they are free and they can leave us; they respond in their
> language: "Here, good eating, we remain here, we are quite content working
> here. You, my father, my mother, my brother, my sister, all."[8]

Fava presented the Catholic mission as a new family for the mission's once-
slave children, who, he reported, readily embraced the mission's care and the
expectation to work.

Fava called the mission *La Providence* after the large and famous social institution that the Spiritans had assumed in 1858 in Réunion, and where the Daughters
of Mary also served.[9] In the types of services offered, the Zanzibar mission resembled not only La Providence at Réunion but also other Christian missions
established earlier in Africa, mostly in the western and southern parts of the
continent. Unlike most such places, the Catholic mission at Zanzibar was not a
"mission village" or "missionary island" in a rural setting. It took a more modest
shape in a large building and walled-in small property within an ancient town.

---

8. Fava 1933, 118. See also: APF 35 (1863), 130; CSSp 196bii: Fava to Maupoint, 12viii62,
and Fava to Schwindenhammer, 6xii62; Zanzibar journal, 19iii62, 21xi62.

9. Eve 1999, 225ff; BG 2:97f, 187ff, 232ff.

Fava's descriptions of the town emphasized its narrow, dirty streets and the agony of those abandoned who found themselves thrown into them, or into other desolate spots like the ocean's shore or the cemetery. He blamed Islam for such indifference to suffering, portraying it as a religion that, despite all its pious practices, failed to generate compassion for those in misery. When they saw the mission's services, offered free of charge because of faith in Christ, Fava wrote that the Arabs and other residents of the town stood in awe of such self-sacrifice and unrewarded service. He epitomized the Catholic impact by describing the sisters' response to those who asked about remuneration for their medical care: "On earth no one pays us."[10]

Fava and Maupoint recognized that their colonial diocese lacked the resources to continue sponsoring the promising mission in Zanzibar, called the apostolic prefecture of *Zanguebar* by Propaganda Fide in Rome. They sought to turn the mission over to the Spiritans, who were well known and active in Réunion. After refusing several times, the congregation finally accepted in August 1862. Under the terms of the agreement between the congregation and diocese, Bishop Maupoint remained the vicar apostolic or episcopal head of the mission until his death, at which time the superior general of the Spiritans would assume the title, with the local superior of the mission named vice-prefect apostolic.[11]

The Spiritans at Zanzibar

The first Spiritans in Zanzibar — the superior Antoine Horner (1827–80), his fellow priest Etienne Baur (1835–1913), and two brothers, Félicien Grüneisen (1838–78) and Célestin Cansot (1840–1922) — arrived in June 1863 and assumed the mission Fava had established two and a half years before.[12] Horner was thirty-five at the time and had spent the previous eight years ministering to the church at Réunion, developing a reputation as a compassionate priest with the lepers he served at their settlement. Baur, twenty-seven and newly ordained, arrived at Zanzibar in his first assignment, as did the twenty-five-year-old Brother Félicien. Brother Célestin was younger still but had already worked at La Providence in Réunion for six months before Zanzibar. The four newcomers moved into the large residence Fava had purchased, near where all the works of the mission were located and where the Zanzibar cathedral residence still remains.

The Spiritans initially maintained what Fava had begun: the workshops, schools, and hospitals. They also ransomed children from the slave market with funds supplied by missionary support agencies in Europe. Regretting that the

---

10. Fava 1933, 115–17.

11. After Maupoint's death in July 1871, Horner took that title, which he held until he left eastern Africa in 1879. The relevant documents pertaining to the agreement between the Spiritans and the bishop are to found in CSSp 195ii and 195iv. While *Zanguebar* became the customary ecclesiastical term for the region, Zanzibar was used for the island and city (MC 21 [1889], 10).

12. Zanzibar journal, 18vi63; Koren 1997, 22; Versteijnen 1968a, 3, and 1968b, 364; H. Gibson 1886, 198; Comerford 1978, 53. Fava had been called back to Réunion in October 1862 to direct the diocese while Bishop Maupoint went to Europe for medical care (Kieran 1966, 31).

market existed at all, Baur nonetheless observed its advantages as "a way to up-root these slaves from hell," implying that without the slave market none would obtain the salvation conferred by baptism.[13] The priests grew the beards Fava insisted were necessary to be received as men (and not women) among the Arabs of Zanzibar. They also took their place among the European contingent of the city, hosting and attending dinners with the European consuls and businessmen, and welcoming French and other naval vessels. Like Fava and his companions, they presided over the Catholic liturgical life and supervised the pastoral care of the few Catholics on the island.[14]

The Spiritans also followed Fava's example by gathering the abandoned, often baptizing them before the death that shortly followed in most cases. Their zeal for souls even led them to employ a man to watch the cemetery for people thrown there still alive whom they could baptize. The Spiritans never doubted that Africans had souls and the capacity to get to heaven, and they sought to ensure their destiny. Baur in particular gathered children from the streets and cemeteries of Zanzibar, and he filled his letters with moving descriptions of their plight. In 1865 he wrote the Spiritan superior general in Paris, telling of his encounters with such children, one of whom looked "half human, half animal," another of whom had been badly burned and abandoned by her master. He described such experiences as welcome consolation for "the heart of a missionary."[15]

Baur narrated another tale of one youth who resisted the missionary's urgings to be baptized. As his death neared, Baur grew more and more insistent, promising heaven if he submitted and threatening hell if he refused. The youth took to belittling such promises, even wondering if the missionary in fact wanted his death. Having asked the sisters to pray for him in the chapel, Baur then took another tack:

> Seeing my gentle arguments useless, I took hold of his throat, squeezing it a little, and said to him: "Listen, you wretch, if I wanted to kill you I would hardly have recourse to baptism. You know how the Arabs do it; I would strangle you like them, I would cut off your head, and for that I have no need of my other remedy [baptism]."

Baur's severity worked, according to his story:

> Suddenly entirely stupefied, he remained tranquil a moment, and then, over-come by grace, finally let escape from his lips these words which I had awaited for so long: "Indeed! It's true! You don't want to kill me! Give me your cure for my soul, so that I can go to the good Lord...."[16]

---

13. CSSp 196bii: Horner to Duboin, 24vi63; ibid., Horner to Schwindenhammer, 24xii63; BG 4:118–25.

14. For summary descriptions of the early Spiritan days in Zanzibar, see APF 36 (1864), 122–29, and BG 3:331–33. Both derive from CSSp 196bii: Horner to Schwindenhammer, 29vi63.

15. For descriptions of Baur's baptisms of the dying, see the following: BG 4:563ff, 635ff; CSSp 196bii: Baur to Schwindenhammer, 3v65; APF 39 (1867), 37f.

16. BG 5:639; see also CSSp 196bii: Horner to Schwindenhammer, 24vi64.

Horner and later Spiritans also extolled missionary efforts to baptize the dying in extremis, which were described in mission journals as well as correspondence and reports.[17]

The Spiritans also assumed the superiorship of the nuns at Zanzibar, the Daughters of Mary. They numbered thirteen sisters, four others having joined the original six who had come with Fava in 1860 and three new sisters accompanying the Spiritans from Réunion. Two of the new arrivals augmented the community already active in the hospitals, as well as in the school/orphanage and workshop for girls. In addition, the mother general had sent her own biological sister and first councillor, Sister Marie Thérèse, as her own representative to assist in dealing with difficulties facing the community. The precise problems remained unspoken, but in early August, two of the group returned to Réunion. Marie Thérèse remained for nine months, embarking for the mother house in March 1864.[18]

Unfortunately, our understanding of the experiences of these women remains limited because of a lack of sources. In official Catholic parlance of the time, the term "missionary" applied only to the men, usually only to the priests, and priests penned all the official reports, as well as the vast majority of the unofficial records. That the nuns' life was difficult is not surprising. Some were of European origin, but most were designated creoles. They likely came from families freed from slavery in 1848, when French colonies like Réunion experienced emancipation. In Réunion, these nuns served in elementary schools and hospitals, as they did in eastern Africa. Their life in the racially charged circumstances of Zanzibar, with the open selling of African slaves featured at the public market, was no doubt quite complicated. A few weeks after arriving, Horner wrote their mother general, extolling the virtues of the sisters and underscoring their importance for the future Catholic communities of eastern Africa. In a more revealing letter to his Spiritan superior at Réunion, however, Horner spoke of difficulties in the sisters' community, indicating the "sobs in the confessional" that he endured as they told of their experiences in the cloister. From their superior general's sister and envoy, the community of nuns in Zanzibar received orders to organize better their communal life, part of which entailed a weekly spiritual talk given by Horner.[19]

---

17. For examples, see Zanzibar journal, 21xii64, 20xi66, 25iii68; CSSp 196bii: Horner to Schwindenhammer, 24vi64, 26vii66; CSSp 196axii: Horner to Holy Childhood, 31xii77; BG 11:706; BG 13:1102.

18. Bengt Sundkler tried to discover details about these nuns in the early 1980s and received some limited information about them. The letter admits, however, that little can be gleaned (CSSp 196aviii: Secretariat of the Mother House of the Daughters of Mary, St. Denis, Réunion, November 1981). That letter was the source for Sundkler's published description of the first six sisters who came with Fava, repeated by Henschel (Sundkler and Steed 2000, 522; Henschel 2000a, 6).

19. CSSp 196bii: Horner to Mère Marie Magdeleine de la Croix, 13vii63; ibid.: Horner to Duboin, 24vi63; Eve 1999, 175. Between 1849 and 1889, 413 women entered this congregation, mostly from Réunion. They welcomed candidates from any racial background and served mostly in Réunion itself (Eve 1999, 113ff). For Spiritan correspondence about the sisters, see CSSp 196aviii. See also Kollman 2001, 229, n. 1.

On their second day in Zanzibar, the Spiritans called on Sultan Majid, who welcomed them warmly and accepted their invitation to visit the mission some days later. Horner portrayed the sultan's court's flowery costumes and its inhabitants' impassive gravitas, as well as the sultan's friendly questioning of the missionaries and esteem for the mission's workshops and chapel decorations. He also described his intense admiration for the noble sultan and his sadness that Majid was not Catholic.[20]

These first letters do more than inform and entertain. Horner's and Baur's earliest reports to their superiors in the Congregation and the mission's benefactors also contained fervent pleas for money. Privately to their superiors they detailed their debts. More public reports luridly portrayed the brutalities of the slave market, "these poor beings looking at us with longing sighs on their lips, and telling us, 'White man, buy me!' [*Blanc, achete moi!*]." The Spiritans described their own profound heartbreak at their inability to ransom more children due to limited funds. They sent Paris photos of the wretched children gathered from the streets or bought from the slave market — they called them "living skeletons" — to arouse pity and loosen European purse strings.[21]

Fiscal concerns filled their reports and also directed Spiritan choices about the mission's institutions. The precarious financial situation in which Fava had left him soon led Horner to close the school for the Indians, which he claimed irrelevant to the mission's goals of saving souls and establishing the church. Horner sought to economize as much as possible. Within weeks of arriving he also experimented with crops on the parcel of land owned by the mission, seeking thereby to save the mission money.[22]

Yet not every activity at the mission suffered cutbacks equally, the reason being that, compared to Fava, the Spiritans declared an even more ambitious and explicit hope in the group called "the children of the mission." Most of these boys and girls at the mission had been ransomed from slavery. Prior to the Spiritans' arrival, the mission's priests had employed a man who alerted them when children suitable for missionary purchase arrived at the slave market.[23] Whether the new missionaries continued this practice of having such a scout on retainer is not clear, but the Spiritans augmented the purchases of boys and girls on sale there. A few other young Africans came to the mission some other way: sent there by Europeans, found in dire straits, or after fleeing their masters.

Horner saw these children as the basis for a bright future for the mission. Six weeks after arriving, he wrote, "The hope of the mission is the children of the schools.... Formed and then gathered in villages of Christians, they will

---

20. On their visits to the sultan, see CSSp 196bii: Horner to Schwindenhammer, 29vi63. This was revised for BG 3:394ff and then again before appearing as APF 36 (1864), 122–29.

21. CSSp 196bii, Horner to Schwindenhammer, 26xii63; APF 39 (1867), 37–39; APF 42 (1870), 48; CSSp 196axii: Horner to Gaume, 1vii69; BG 7:273ff; Versteijnen 1968b, 4.

22. For a fuller discussion of the mission's financial state at the time the Spiritans took over, as well as the reasoning behind the closings of the various facilities and mutual accusations of impropriety between Fava and Horner, see Kollman 2001, 225, especially nn. 15–20.

23. CSSp 196aviii: Marie Thérèse of Jesus to Marie Magdeleine, 18vi63.

Figure 6. Father Antoine Scheuermann, CSSp, with two boys at Zanzibar. Photo from the Spiritan photo archives in Paris. Used with permission.

contribute to the regeneration of Africa."[24] Clearly such unfortunates stood in obvious need, and the missionaries depicted them as eager recipients of the mission's care. In addition, the missionaries felt called toward them by their zeal for souls. But most importantly, the Spiritans saw hope in such children for the church they came to build, a church they imagined taking place most fully in the interior of the continent, away from the Islamic coast. Works bringing prestige to the mission but *not* helping to form such children into Catholics — such as Fava's workshops, the hospital for Europeans, and the school for Indians — the missionaries deemed tangential to that purpose and thus expendable, unworthy of equal consideration in allocating the mission's meager resources.

Decisions to close some of the mission's institutions, though explained by way of financial concerns, thus also supported overall Spiritan strategy. In late 1863, Horner articulated a sentiment that underlay their efforts: "We must before everything work to create an enduring and solid foundation; trying to form children already advanced in age would be like wanting to bend large trees." The missionaries deemed adults already formed as pagans or Muslims no longer fully open to the Gospel. Most of the older children and few adults at the mission in the 1860s arrived before the Spiritans took over, or survived after being gathered

---

24. CSSp 196bii: Horner to Schwindenhammer, 1viii63.

from the streets. Adults at the slave market the Spiritans passed over. Young children held special promise for evangelization and represented the hope for the future.[25]

In the months after their arrival, Horner and Baur both extolled the children of the mission, who were good raw material out of whom they planned to build the church. Their reports for funding agencies gave names and personal details, depicting how their young lives had been interrupted due to seizure by slave traders. They described how they had then been ransomed at the slave market and now displayed joyful openness to their new life at the mission. Sweet and agreeable, simpler, more docile, and harder working than the "descendants of Ham" in Réunion, these youngsters were depicted as showing the effects of grace in their disinterest, devotion, and charity, all reminiscent of the early Christians. They rarely needed to be punished.[26] Horner referred to these young Africans as "Swahilis," Baur as "Kaffirs" (or *caffres*), generic terms that distinguished them from the Arabs and Indians of Zanzibar and also revealed how missionary language could homogenize them. Over time such descriptions ascribed more particular designations that anticipated later ethnic labels.[27] Though missionary paternalism pervades these descriptions, they lack the explicit racial denigrations that would appear in the 1880s amidst missionary frustration and growing European racialist thinking.

By contrast, conversion among the Muslim population of Zanzibar was deemed by Fava and the Spiritans both hopeless and also dangerous for the mission's future. Besides, the missionaries in Zanzibar felt that Islam was waning on its own before Western advances and Christian missionary contact. To proselytize among the Muslims might not only imperil the permission granted them by the sultan but also imprudently awaken "Arab fanaticism," something no Europeans wanted. The evangelization of Zanzibar itself, Horner felt, had to wait until a fuller European presence in the future because of Islam and slavery.[28] The children, either abandoned or ransomed, represented the best hope for establishing the church.

The number of such children grew steadily. Fava had gathered sixteen children by August 1862, and twenty-six children lived at the mission when the Spiritans arrived, fourteen boys and twelve girls. Very quickly that number was augmented through the official action of a European diplomatic representative, the first of many such to come. Two days after their arrival, Henri Jablonski, a French consular official and important early friend of the mission, sent La Providence eight

25. CSSp 196ax: Horner to Holy Childhood Society, 16xi63.

26. Ibid. CSSp 196bii: Horner to Maupoint, 29xi63; ibid.: Baur to Schwindenhammer, 24xii63; BG 4:118f; BG 6:416.

27. CSSp 196bii: Horner to Schwindenhammer, 24–30xii63; CSSp 196ax: Horner to Propagation of the Faith, 4iii69; CSSp 196biii: Duparquet to Barillec, 17vii71; MC 4 (1871), 76–77.

28. CSSp 196bii: Horner to Schwindenhammer, 24vi64; CSSp 195aii: Horner to Barnabo, 25i68. Libermann and the Vatican also urged upon missionaries cooperation with local governments (Burke 1998, 72–73). As late as 1889, the Spiritans claimed that they had no expectation of making Catholics from Muslims and did not aim their efforts at them (Mackay 1889, 23).

young African boys. These were taken from a French ship carrying so-called contracted laborers from eastern Africa to Réunion, a violation of French laws prohibiting such activity as thinly disguised slavery. Horner applauded the fact that Jablonski had sent the mission those who were of a young age, "capable of being formed to the principles of Christianity."[29] Jablonski's handover of those freed at sea initiated a practice whereby the now-Spiritan mission received those emancipated by Europeans. That number expanded dramatically beginning in the late 1860s when British abolitionist zeal led to frequent seizures of slaves at sea.

Before that time such bestowals by Europeans were few. Usually the mission's population grew through ransoming at the slave market. Thus the same nun who wrote of Jablonski's handover herself soon added to the mission's population. A few days later she ransomed four girls with funds brought from a women's group in Réunion for that purpose. She continued what had been Fava's practice, braving the appalling scene at the slave market in order to bring children to the mission. The Spiritans carried on this practice until the market's closing in 1873, after which ransoming continued sporadically in other venues. Letters to Europe and Réunion, whether to superiors, friends, or funding agencies, spoke of the sufferings of those at the slave market or abandoned in the street. An increasing number were purchased after the Spiritans headed off to the market in their black cassocks, purses of money for ransoming in hand. Through ransoming and, to a lesser extent, gathering the abandoned, the number of children at the mission climbed quickly: 52 by late 1864, 60 by early 1865, 128 by the end of 1866, 162 by August 1867.[30]

Spiritan writings in those days also revealed their awareness of larger events around them, many of which they learned about due to their participation in the social life of Zanzibar's small European diplomatic and commercial set. Horner keenly observed the world around him and eventually produced an impressive (and unjustly ignored) description of Zanzibar's diverse peoples and customs.[31] He and his confreres also struggled to learn KiSwahili. Their growing facility eventuated in a change of Baur's local name to *Père* Etienne, since Baur was too close to the KiSwahili vulgarity *ku-baua*, "to piss." Of more practical consequence, one Spiritan, admitting that not all the mission's children spoke the language, prepared a KiSwahili children's catechism in 1865, but his efforts failed to gain the support of the others. Baur, who seems to have been the most assiduous

---

29. The precise number of children in those early days is unclear. Horner wrote that the original number was fourteen, soon becoming twenty-six, but elsewhere Horner, Fava, and a sister give higher numbers (CSSp 195i: Horner to Maupoint, 29xi63; APF 36 [1864], 126; CSSp 196bii: Fava to Maupoint, 12viii62; CSSp 196aviii: Marie Thérèse of Jesus to Marie Magdeleine, 18vi63; Kieran 1966, 109).

30. On the sister's purchase, see CSSp 195i: Horner to Maupoint, 29xi63, and CSSp 196axii: Horner to Holy Childhood, 16xi63. On later numbers of children at the mission, see CSSp 195i: Horner to Maupoint, 12ix64; CSSp 196ax: Horner to Propagation of the Faith, 12ii65, 31xii66, 29viii67; CSSp 196bii: Baur to Schwindenhammer, 30vi65; BG 5:494.

31. The original draft of Horner's essay, over thirty poorly preserved pages, appears in the Zanzibar journal at the end of 1866.

student of the language in those early years, produced a French-KiSwahili catechism in 1866, which was published some years before more celebrated works
in the language by the Anglican mission and others.[32]

Besides organizing and overseeing the works at Zanzibar, the Spiritans also
looked across to the mainland. Their early letters and reports from Zanzibar
revealed that Horner and the other Spiritans self-consciously saw themselves
poised on the precipice of a continent in need. Their eyes went inland as soon as
they arrived, lending their zeal and sense of moral obligation a geographic cast.
This spatial awareness also generated an urgency to move inward that became
a ubiquitous feature of Spiritan discourse for the next several decades. Updates
on progress toward the heart of Africa or obstacles to such progress featured
in nearly every letter back to the mother house in Paris or to mission support
agencies.[33]

This rhetoric of desire and anxiety about the need to pass over to the mainland
manifested itself almost immediately. Less than two weeks after arriving, Horner
begged his Parisian superiors for more money and manpower. He never let up.
His urgency derived from the supposed plaintive cry of the unevangelized, but
the missionaries also saw practical advantages in a move to the mainland. More
land might allow the cultivation of crops to lessen the mission's expenses. More
importantly, the Spiritans heard the footsteps of rivals, and competition lent their
zeal for the interior only deeper urgency. Fava and the Spiritans who replaced
him longed to cross over before their rivals. They feared the advances of the
UMCA missionaries who had arrived in Zanzibar in 1864 and Muslims, who not
only polluted the coast but also moved inland to settle.[34]

Fava's zeal had also been geographic. His perceptions of eastern Africa's
desperate need generated churning emotions during his first Mass at Zanzibar, at
midnight on Christmas Eve, 1860. Fava wrote, "Jesus Christ descended for the

---

32. On the decision for Etienne, see CSSp 196bii: Horner to Schwindenhammer, 16iv64. Baur
was known by that name ever after in eastern Africa. Henry Morton Stanley referred to him as
Père Etienne, and contemporary Zanzibari Catholics remember him by that name (Stanley 1890,
2:457, 459; Barnabas Salvi Mkuku, Zanzibar interview, 3ix1997, 4ix1997, 29vi1998). Father Charles
Steurer, who arrived in Zanzibar in October 1864, tried to prepare the first children's catechism
(CSSp 196bii: Steurer to Levavasseur, 31iii65). Though Horner criticized Baur's German-accented
KiSwahili (CSSp 196bii: Horner to Schwindenhammer, 18xi64), he was slow to master the language.
As late as 1878, Horner gave a talk to the mission's children that, though stirring, could not be
understood because it was in French (Zanzibar journal, 2ii78).

Baur's catechism (Baur 1867), one of the first full-length books ever published in KiSwahili (at
least with the Latin alphabet still in use), deserves more discussion than it has received and that I can
give it here.

33. Among the many Spiritan letters and reports describing their zeal for the interior, see the following: CSSp 196bii: Horner to Schwindenhammer, 28vi63, 3x63, 15xi63, 24xii63, 26xii63, 24vi64,
18xi64, 12ii65, 25vi66, 3xii66, 24ix67; ibid: Horner to Duboin, 1vi64; ibid: Baur to Schwindenhammer, 24xii63, 3v65; ibid: Baur to Horner, 11viii67; ibid: Horner to Collin, 12x68; CSSp 196axi:
Horner to Holy Childhood, 16xi63; CSSp 196axii: Horner to Holy Childhood, 30xi65; CSSp 196ax:
Horner to Propagation of the Faith, 12ii65, 31xii66, 29xii67; CSSp 196aii: Horner to Notre Dame
des Victoires, 24ix64; BG 4:566–67. For further discussion, see Kollman 2001, 136–42.

34. CSSp 196bii: Horner to Schwindenhammer, 29vi63, 3x63; ibid. Baur to Schwindenhammer
24xii63; BG 3:400; APF 42 (1870), 54.

first time in our midst, we who had come from France to this lost island [*l'ilôt perdue*]." Ambitious hopes buoyed him: "The mission is the instrument God will use to place Jesus in a church consecrated to him, at the entrance of these vast regions of Africa still unexplored." The future beckoned with promise of civilization and prosperity, for Christian and European contact would awaken the African coast and the even larger interior from "its lethargic sleep."[35] Horner's thoughts were similar as he celebrated Eucharist for the first time on the mainland, on August 6, 1863, the Feast of the Transfiguration:

> How my heart swelled with emotion as the King of heaven and earth descended into our humble cabin! How earnestly I implored Him to pity these unfortunate people and to apply to them the fruits of the Sacrifice of Calvary! It is impossible to express the feelings of hope and holy joy which I then experienced. A single moment of such happiness suffices to erase the memory of years of tribulation.

Horner saw explorers as models to be followed. He wrote the superior general in 1863, urging "that Christians passionate for God and for the church must feel [called to] emulation of the ardor of explorers who confront the same climate for the love of science."[36]

Zanzibar was well-placed for a mission to eastern Africa, poised at its edge. In the missionary imagination, the 1860s also represented an opportune time for reestablishing the church where it had been absent since the removal of the Portuguese in the early eighteenth century. Besides lacking a Christian presence, their region on the needy continent was also blessed by circumstances no longer existing in Europe. The missionaries knew that such circumstances might be temporary in Africa, only reinforcing the propitiousness of the opportunity and the need to act decisively. Thus they praised the freedom of religion that the sultan of Zanzibar afforded them, a freedom they contrasted with the restrictions on Catholic religious practice in France and, later, Germany. In addition, the tolerance of the brand of Islam practiced in the region allowed evangelization — at least among slaves — while the widespread use of KiSwahili made spreading the faith easier, one language obviating the need for years of learning a variety of tongues.[37]

The presence of slaves also struck the Spiritans as an opportunity afforded them by providence. They recognized the tragedy of the slave trade and often described its horrors. Nonetheless, the availability of the children and the distance between them and their parents — if these still lived — created an openness to evangelization that contrasted with what the missionaries saw as baneful anticlerical social pressure young people often suffered in Europe. The mission could

35. Fava 1933, 112, 120.
36. CSSp 196bii: Horner to Schwindenhammer, 15xi63; H. Gibson 1886, 203; APF 39 (1867), 32.
37. On Zanzibar's advantages for evangelization, see CSSp 196bii: Horner to Schwindenhammer, 24–30xii63; CSSp 196ax: Horner to Propagation of the Faith, 12ii65; CSSp 196aii: Horner to Notre Dame des Victoires, 24ix64; Gaume 1872, 21; MC 9 (1877), 580.

in effect replace the parents of such children, which the Spiritans saw as a special advantage for the seminary they began in the late 1860s. They contrasted the mission's own paternal care with the discouragement to clerical vocations supposedly exerted by European parents eager, the missionaries claimed, to be grandparents.[38]

Imbued by this sense of being on an edge and endowed with an opportunity, the Spiritans visited the mainland soon after their arrival. Fava had explored the area around Bagamoyo in May 1862 and purchased a plot for the planned future mission. Horner inspected that property when he visited in early August 1863, as did Baur when he crossed to Bagamoyo in February 1865. A lengthy visit to the coast in September and October 1866 to review possible new sites settled Horner on Bagamoyo as the place for the next mission. Debts remained an obstacle to any expansion, however, and to raise money the superior toured Europe for most of 1867.[39]

Those early years also saw the appearance of difficulties that would plague the mission for decades. In October 1864, new Holy Ghost missionaries arrived. Interpersonal conflicts, already present in Spiritan correspondence, only grew in intensity. Disagreements over missionary policy catalyzed and magnified mutual personal dislikes, and Spiritans complained about each other's shortcomings. Often overlooked within histories of Christian evangelization, these fractious relationships loomed in Spiritan consciousness. They not only reflected significant and revealing differences of opinion about missionary strategy, as we shall see. They also bespoke apostolic failure since the Spiritans viewed their communal life as part and parcel of their missionary vocation. An unsettled life behind the walls of their community house represented a problem meriting focused attention.[40]

Along with these internal difficulties, the Spiritans faced together challenges to their missionary goals from other directions. After the 1864 arrival of the Universities' Mission to Central Africa (UMCA), rivalry with the Anglicans consumed the Catholic missionaries ever after. Both Baur and Horner soon spoke of rumors of an imminent British takeover of the island. These rumors turned out to be unfounded, at least in the short term, but the Protestant mission preoccupied the Spiritan imagination nonetheless. Protestants represented competition for the esteem of Europeans in Zanzibar and the sultan, besides threatening the Spiritan

---

38. CSSp 196aii: Horner to Notre Dame des Victoires, 24ix64; CSSp 196axii: Horner to Holy Childhood, 3xii66; CSSp 196axiii: Horner to Propagation of the Faith, 28x69.

39. On Fava's 1862 visits to the coast, see CSSp 196bii: Fava to Maupoint, 12viii62; Zanzibar journal, 12v62, 27viii62; APF 35 (1863), 135–41; Brown 1971a, 201. For Horner's visits in August 1863 and 1866, see these accounts: BG 3:463, 5:832ff; Zanzibar journal, viii63; CSSp 196bii: Horner to Schwindenhammer, 24–30xii63; APF 39 (1867), 23–36; Gaume 1872, 112ff. On Baur's 1865 visit, see Zanzibar journal, 23ii65, 27ii65; BG 4:567.

40. Libermann had stressed the importance of communal life for missionaries (Gay 1943, 122; Burke 1998, 26, 71). CSSp 196aii and CSSp 196aiv contain Horner's formal reports on his personnel sent to Paris in the 1860s and 1870s, which detail the shortcomings the superior found in his confreres. For a fuller listing of Horner's complaints, see Kollman 2001, 228–30, which lists, among many similar observations, Horner's scorn for the "sissies" and *"papier-maché* missionaries" he received.

dream of evangelizing the interior.[41] Beginning in 1864, illnesses led to Holy Ghost departures from Zanzibar, either for short breaks or permanently. Malaria was chronic, and later years saw epidemics of cholera and smallpox, both taking the lives of many children of the mission. The first of the mission's personnel to die was in 1866, and a host of Spiritans succumbed starting in the 1870s.[42] Fires and hurricanes later destroyed years of missionary effort. Finally, the changing political circumstances at Zanzibar and the region as a whole in the years to come forced the Spiritans to adapt to new power brokers such as the Germans and the British, all the while pursuing their missionary goals.

Already in the fall of 1864, an ill and exhausted Horner returned for recuperation to Réunion, remaining there nearly nine months. He returned in July 1865, his health and spirits for the time being restored. The first death of one of the sisters at the mission the next January, though sad, nonetheless displayed the mission's sterling reputation, for a huge crowd representing Zanzibar's diverse population came to commemorate the passing of Sister Marie-Pierre of the Filles de Marie.[43] The 1866 trip to the mainland that decided Horner on Bagamoyo, however, exhausted him further. In early 1867 he went to Europe, to recover his strength and also to raise money for the future mission.

In July 1867, while Horner was in Europe fund raising and recuperating, Bishop Maupoint made his only visit to his mission at Zanzibar. Baur readied a warm welcome with banners and a procession, and Maupoint took dinner with the sultan at his palace, an honor, the Spiritans claimed, not accorded a European in six years. Besides celebrating the first confirmations of forty-two of the mission children, the bishop also bestowed a thousand francs for the purchase of twenty boys and twenty girls at the slave market. His report to Propaganda Fide praised what he saw and predicted great success in the future.[44]

Horner returned in December with more than enough money to pay off existing loans. Over the next few months, he and Baur negotiated to secure land at Bagamoyo for the mission, which was founded in March 1868.[45] A few weeks after returning, he wrote his first of many reports to be published in the new weekly journal of Propagation of the Faith, *Les Missions Catholiques.* He described the Zanzibar mission, depicting its personnel and their good efforts, the 150 children mostly purchased at the slave market, the horrors of that market, and the esteem in which the mission was held by all segments of the town and

---

41. For a fuller discussion, see Kollman 2001, 231f. The UMCA strategy, like that of the Spiritans, targeted slave children whom they received from the sultan, from British authorities, and at the slave market. They also saw Zanzibar as a base for missions in the interior, which began in 1868 (Sahlberg 1986, 34ff).

42. See Kieran 1966, 184–85, and Henschel 2000a.

43. Zanzibar journal, 15i66; BG 5:145, 211; APF 39 (1867), 43.

44. Zanzibar journal 1–8vii67; CSSp 196bii: Baur to Schwindenhammer, 5vii67; 11viii67; CSSp 195i: Maupoint to Barnabo, 19viii67; BG 6:291f; Soul 1936, 50–51; MC 1 (1868), 67.

45. Zanzibar journal, 29i67, 1xii67; BG 6:301. Horner apparently returned at the end of 1867 with sixty-eight thousand francs, which enabled him to pay the forty-thousand franc debt on the house.

all visitors. He claimed that Zanzibar differed from other missions where Christianity emerged from the indigenous people. Muslims will resist until later, he wrote, and thus the Spiritan strategy was forced upon them by circumstances: to raise children purchased from the slave market, to initiate them to the habits and works of the civilized life, then to marry them and settle them in Christian villages under missionary supervision. He foresaw Bagamoyo as a place where an agricultural establishment would soon take the mission to its next stage, and asked for support from subscribers for the move to the mainland.[46]

The Rhetoric of Spiritan Slave Evangelization

Horner's extensive report for *Les Missions Catholiques* was one of many written descriptions of the Zanzibar mission. Within a few years the Spiritans, mostly Horner, produced hundreds of pages about their work. The Spiritans also assumed responsibility for maintaining the mission journal at Zanzibar, which may or may not have been kept prior to their arrival. Despite the diverse purposes, authors, audiences, and circumstances of this missionary discourse, the corpus as a whole shows remarkable single-mindedness, even obsessiveness.

Not every topic entered all writings equally, but some themes were ubiquitous. Thus every audience important to the mission's future heard about the financial concerns of the mission, underscoring the debts and needs still unmet. Spiritans also shared freely the flourishing state of the mission's works and the esteem in which the mission was held by Zanzibar's various constituencies, often listed in order of perceived importance: first the sultan and/or the European consuls; then European visitors and other European residents of Zanzibar; next Arabs and other non-African residents of Zanzibar; and finally Africans.[47] Frequent mention was made of the health of the missionaries, often linked to an argument as to the healthy or unhealthy nature of Zanzibar, something that would become a prominent issue as the mission developed. Denigrating Protestant evangelization, especially after the 1864 founding of the UMCA mission at Zanzibar, also became a constant for all audiences. Equally ubiquitous were the zeal for the move to the mainland and the promising nature of the mission's children as Catholics of the future.

The Spiritans reserved other topics for select interlocutors. For example, if Horner wrote everyone about the latest party at the French consul's and the praise the mission received there, or about the virtues of the mission children, only his superiors in Paris read his litany of complaints — and those in the few letters penned by other Spiritans that have come down to us from those early years — addressed to the mother house. Horner highlighted his confreres' shortcomings,

---

46. MC 1 (1868), 65–67.
47. Libermann and Vatican guidelines urged missionaries to cooperate with local authorities (Koren 1983, 262–64; Burke 1998, 83). Thus Horner's regular assurances about good relations with Zanzibar's elites demonstrated the mission's faithfulness to expectations (CSSp 196bi: Schwindenhammer to Horner, 18i72; BG 2:591; BG 6:85f).

Figure 7. Father Antoine Horner,
CSSp. Bagamoyo Mission
Museum. Used with permission.

ranging from laziness to impracticality to habitual drunkenness, and contrasted
the disappointing personnel he received with the sterling characters supposedly
sent to other missions. He groaned about the burdens of superiorship, a role he
claimed ill befit him, and asked repeatedly to be relieved of the responsibilities.
The threefold multiplication of superiors to whom he was at first beholden — the
bishop in Réunion, his Spiritan superiors there, and then also those in Paris —
led to unfortunate confusions and a burdensome amount of writing.

Horner's willingness to grumble coexisted, however, with a fervent desire
to remain united spiritually to his superiors in Paris. Soul searching about his
motivations, frequent requests for what look like very trivial permissions, and
obsequious apologies for taking liberties before permission was granted suggest
his occasionally tortured distress on this score. Despite this self-conscious anxiety
to remain in proper obedience, Horner's rants against his superiors in Paris could
take caustic turns at times, bringing down their wrath.[48]

For nearly two decades Horner's vision guided the Spiritan mission. His role
as superior meant that he penned the vast majority of Spiritan writings in the
1860s and 1870s, so that his rhetorical patterns and modes of representation
also shaped later understandings of the mission's activity. The obsessions of the

48. For details, see Kollman 2001, 162–63 (nn. 17, 18), 165–66 (n. 20), 228–33.

correspondence were often his obsessions. He was a very thorough correspondent, driven by a sense of responsibility for the fiscal and spiritual health of the mission, and for the fulfillment of his vocation. While he lacked the stylish rhetorical polish of later Spiritans like the intellectual Le Roy and Courmont, the first bishop, his vigorous handwriting, assertive demands, blunt criticisms of his superiors, and heartfelt self-doubts portray a strong and volatile personality. Witnesses described him as tall and imposing, but often quiet and frequently compassionate. His words suggest a man alternately pious and resentful, visionary about an anticipated noble future and trapped by present burdens, appreciative of his confreres yet biting about their shortcomings, long-suffering before his fevers and quick-tempered before perceived slights.[49]

The Spiritan Shape of the Zanzibar Mission

Horner's early decision to truncate some of the mission's works and concentrate on the mission's children demonstrated the Spiritan conviction that young former slaves were the hope for the future.

His predecessor Fava had thought differently. He focused on educating children but also valued other activities at the French mission. In his eyes, the workshops in particular brought the mission prestige and provided employment for the workers from Réunion. Fava deemed such workers essential for the new mission, believing that Christians from the Indian Ocean island would serve as an anchoring witness at the beginning of the church in the unevangelized area. He thus sought close ties between Zanzibar's mission and Réunion, so that new Catholics would grow through mimesis of already existing Catholics. Fava dreamed of the day when outsiders, from Réunion or elsewhere, would come as a Christian *noyau* to teach Africans "two things that make the man and the Christian: work and religion."[50]

The Spiritan program shared some of Fava's assumptions. The new missionaries also valued work and believed in mimesis; they, too, used the image of *noyau* to explain their strategy. Yet there were important differences. While Fava hoped for a Christian *noyau* of workers from Réunion whom the mission's children would emulate, Horner counted on missionary evangelization itself to create such a nucleus *from* the children. They would then become a Christian *noyau* and leaven in the interior of eastern Africa. Seeing no immediate need for the example of other Christians, the Spiritans trusted their own paternalistic care to direct the mission's activities to shape the former slaves into the nucleus of the

49. On Horner's personality, see Moulinet 1998, 112; Maupeou 1932; Ricklin 1880; APF 52 (1880), 382–88; Kieran 1966, 58f; BG 11:796–809; CSSp 194bii: Stegmaier, Sr. Ortrud, 1980, *"L'Acheteur Blanc sur le March aux Esclaves": Pour le Centenaire de la Mort du Pere Antoine Horner, CSSp.* Apparently a short biography of Horner exists, written by Joseph Simon (*Pater Anton Horner* [Knechtsteden, 1932]), but I have not located it. Probably it derived from the obituaries in APF 52 and BG 11.

50. CSSp 196bii: Fava to Maupoint, 24x58; ibid., Fava to Schwindenhammer, 19v61, 7xi61; Fava 1933, 119–20.

future church in the interior. Shunning Fava's appeals for workers from outside, Horner quickly sent back to Réunion the workers Fava had brought, and only partly because they were a financial burden on the heavily indebted mission. Mostly he found them unnecessary, even a dangerous example. Horner saw Zanzibar as a corrupting influence on the workers and feared they in turn would corrupt the mission's children.[51] To replace them, Horner implored his superiors in Paris for Spiritan brothers to oversee the workshops and supervise the children. Distrustful of outsiders to provide instructive models for their young charges, the Holy Ghost missionaries set themselves to the task of providing the right kind of environment to form future Catholics.[52]

The Spiritans' rhetoric of urgency and zeal not only looked to the mainland, therefore, but also at those they considered the hope of the mission's future. They took deliberate and practical steps to shape the growing number of children at the mission into the pious and obedient Catholic nuclei for the imagined church. In their imagination, the mission's children resembled the African interior. Poised on the edge of Africa, the Spiritans were called to evangelize the "dark continent." Poised as fathers to these children, they were called to the action of formation to save souls and create Catholic coworkers for that evangelization.

Early descriptions of the mission's children prepared for outsiders reflected a number of purposes, but they invariably struck what was earlier described as a *conditional* tone that often featured in Spiritan writings that legitimated their work. The structure of their discourse was such that the church's future looked bright *if* certain conditions were met. Thus the Spiritans were unstinting in their positive depictions of the promise the mission's children represented, and they also expressed confidence in their own ability to fulfill the promise they detected. Yet their descriptions couched their positive appraisals within invocations of the vulnerability of that promise. This reflected missionary paternalism (and often implicit or explicit racism) while it legitimated support for the mission. Readers of these reports could not miss the implied message: here was an opportunity to build the church, and the Spiritans were capable of succeeding, but missionaries needed their benefactors' support to take advantage.[53]

This conditional tone created contradictions within descriptions of African capabilities. Similar contradictions within portrayals of Africans appear in the writings of their foremost source for missionary strategy, François Libermann, and are common in missionary discourse more generally. Latent in Libermann's missionary principles is the tension between "civilizing" (or "assimilation") and "adaptation" that has long characterized Christian missionary practice and theory.[54]

---

51. The majority of the workers left for Réunion at Horner's orders on June 29, 1863 (Zanzibar journal, 29vi63). See Kollman 2001, 237.

52. BG 4:119–20; CSSp 196bii: Horner to Schwindenhammer, 28vi63, 1viii63.

53. CSSp 196axii: Horner to Holy Childhood, 16xi63.

54. Missionaries stress the newness of Christianity and thus at least implicitly denigrate the past that must be left behind, on the one hand, and, on the other, uncover and build on evidence

In eastern Africa, such contradictions appeared, for example, in Spiritan discussions of African intelligence. Though they praised the children, both Baur and Horner saw their charges as less intelligent than Africans in Réunion. Baur complained about the difficulty of "getting the ABCs into the heads of these Kaffirs," and Horner said that in no way were they as intelligent as whites. This lack, however, far from an obstacle to missionary work, spurred it on. Horner was quick to add that they were certainly intelligent enough to become Christians, and Baur spoke often of his satisfaction of working with them, thus avoiding a conclusion that might question the mission's viability. The descriptions themselves urged upon the readers of Spiritan reports the necessary generosity to fulfill the conditions to develop the inherent promise in such children. The mission children were fit to be the future colonizers of the African church of the interior if they received the proper missionary attention. In a letter that answered questions supposedly posed to him by the Holy Childhood Society, Horner described the intelligence of *les noirs*, which he labeled "imitative" in contrast to the "inventive" intelligence of whites. Again, such perceived deficiencies were presented carefully, so that they did not undermine African potential for Catholic identity. Certain children, especially one called Patrice whom we shall discuss in the next two chapters, showed particular aptitude, thus presenting the likelihood that an indigenous clergy could be formed in the future.[55]

Spiritan confidence that their mission could forge Catholic identity if the proper circumstances were set in place derived from their background. They had been immersed in a number of formative processes themselves and exposed to other social institutions aimed at personal formation and transformation, especially juvenile reformatories. Their participation in such institutions, increasingly part of the taken-for-granted horizon of modern life in France, not only gave them a tacit confidence but also shaped the methods they undertook to change the African ex-slave children at Zanzibar. They rarely discussed this directly, but the missionaries sought for such children a setting where the operative space and time remained separate from the surroundings, in which processes of prayer, education, and training in habits of work could be properly inculcated. Slave evangelization depended first of all, therefore, not on a set of beliefs that prospective Catholics could accept or reject by an act of the will, thus effecting their conversion; it was instead a complete *environment* created for former slaves who found themselves within the mission's care, an enclave or enclosure designed to shape them in ways conducive to hoped-for Catholic identity.

---

of God's goodness already present (Kieran 1969, 342f; Burridge 1991). Similarly, Andrew Walls says all Christian missionary activity presumes both the "indigenizing principle" (Christ is already present) and the "pilgrim principle" (Christ transforms; Walls 1996, 7). Libermann and his followers articulated and practiced both.

55. CSSp 196bii: Baur to Schwindenhammer, 24xii63; CSSp 196aii: Horner to Notre-Dame des Victoires, 24ix64; BG 5:498; CSSp 196axii: Horner to Holy Childhood, x67. Patrice was baptized in 1866 (Zanzibar sacramental registry, 20v66).

Enclosure

As noted in chapter 1, to this day certain older Catholics at the Spiritan mission of Bagamoyo recall with wistful nostalgia the missionary practice of *utawa*, KiSwahili for "staying in the house, seclusion," or "a chaste, religious, pious life and character." They also vividly remember *les dortoirs* (the dormitories), a French word they knew. In dormitories at boarding school many of them had experienced the practices of *utawa* — likely the original translation of the French *clôture*, or enclosure — until the practice had ceased in the 1930s. Women and men now in their seventies and eighties had been boarders in the schools at Bagamoyo until the time for their marriage. For some, *utawa* recalled missionary idealism and zeal, sentiments they now felt were in short supply in the church. It signaled the proper upbringing of young people, a feature of the past life at the mission. Judging from their comments, *utawa* represented an aspect of missionary evangelization that pervaded Spiritan discourse and practice into the twentieth century.[56]

Spiritan writings show that the ideal of *clôture*, later *utawa*, was enacted as soon as they arrived in 1863. It was the precondition for the practical steps the Spiritans undertook to create the "fully formed Christian communities" that Horner desired. At the edge of the continent and in the enclosed spaces of Zanzibar's mission, in its chapel, schoolrooms, and workshops, the children could be formed through spiritual and physical practices under the eyes of watchful missionaries.[57] Spiritan practices sought to make the mission resemble the "total institutions" made famous by Erving Goffman's study of asylums, military training facilities, and religious communities like monasteries. Goffman defined a total institution as "a place of residence and work where a large number of like-situated individuals, cut off from the wider society for an appreciable period of time, together lead an enclosed, formally administered round of life." He described other features of such places:

> First, all aspects of life are conducted in the same place and under the same central authority. Second, each phase of the member's daily activity is carried on in the immediate company of a large batch of others, all of whom are treated alike and required to do the same thing together. Third, all phases of the day's activities are tightly scheduled, with one activity leading

---

56. On *utawa*, see Johnson and Madan 1939, 457. I heard about *utawa* during interviews with Bibi Leonia Richardi and Bibi Sofia State at Bagamoyo, August 2, 1998.

57. Though Spiritan recourse to enclosure derived from the repository of sources from which they drew their missionary strategy as a whole, not all the sources upon which they relied would have supported it. Libermann, for example, was a Jewish convert from Alsace whose experience made him wary of any notion of creating a Christian ghetto in Africa. He expressly resisted the missionary ideal of creating a "small Christian corner," wanting instead the evangelization of entire peoples (Burke 1998, 43). Libermann's missionary principles, however, appeared in response to particular situations and he himself admitted the need to apply them prudently, not follow any blueprint (Gay 1943, 120; Libermann, n.d., 526ff). This allowed recourse to enclosure, especially in an Islamic environment like Zanzibar.

at prearranged time into the next, the whole sequence of activities being imposed from above by a system of explicit formal rulings and a body of officials. Finally, the various enforced activities are brought together into a single rational plan purportedly designed to fulfil the official aims of the institution.[58]

Spiritan experiences in the seminary and at juvenile facilities in France and Réunion reinforced the tendency for enclosed and regulated spaces as described by Goffman. An 1859 newspaper article from Réunion described the guiding philosophy of La Providence, the large social institution in Réunion after which Fava originally named the mission at Zanzibar, where the Spiritans and the Daughters of Mary both served. The guiding philosophy at La Providence, according to the article, was formed from both "charity" *and* attention to "the social question." These two — charity and the social question — were nineteenth-century French euphemisms for Catholic and more secular approaches to social welfare, respectively, reflecting Spiritan reliance on overtly religious and also secular sources in their missionary practices. The newspaper account acknowledged the perceived divisions between the two, while maintaining that they were not irreconcilable, as La Providence showed. According to the article, the policy there was "a proper combination" for the formation of wayward young men. Discipline and surveillance figured strongly both in the schools and the penitentiary. Time and space were controlled by a rigid daily schedule, control of movement, and well-guarded walls and doors.

Both institutions, especially the penitentiary, had a clearly defined interior and exterior. Within the walls the regulations derived from the penal code, which rigidly controlled the inmates' movements. Outside the walls, La Providence had a farm where people worked, learning habits of industry. The one observed shortcoming, the article noted, lay in the short time that juvenile offenders spent in the penitentiary. They contrasted the brief internment with practices at the four reformatories staffed by the Spiritans in France, where stays were longer. At La Providence the boys left too soon, so that reform began but remained incomplete: "Without enclosure (*clôture*), discipline and propriety are nearly impossible."[59]

One of the first tasks undertaken by the Spiritans at Zanzibar was to shape their own common life in line with *clôture*, an expectation incumbent upon them as members of their congregation. Fava, they complained, had run the house like a tavern or casino, with regular soirées. They quickly transformed the internal organization of their residence and its activities to support their missionary religious identity with a structured common life. They set up a daily and weekly timetable to govern their lives together, specifying hours for common and personal prayer, meals, and recreation. Besides shaping the time, they also

---

58. Goffman 1961, xiii, 4ff, 11. Of course the parallel is not exact, for Goffman's keen description depends on such institutions being set within his society, in which case the indignities of such places are felt by those used to their previous life in the so-called modern West.

59. *The Monitor*, Réunion, 29xi59; see BG 2:98ff, 187ff, 232ff.

reorganized the space, separating themselves from the sisters and controlling access to their residence, so that visitors, especially Europeans, did not disturb their cloister.[60]

Examining the mission's state, the Spiritans also grumbled that proper conditions for training the children had not been established by their predecessors. Horner observed that under Fava's administration the children had "done what they wanted." He set about to order in a proper way the formation and supervision by drawing on the practices that had formed him and the other Spiritans. They organized the mission to create the enclosed, regulated environments they knew from the seminaries, schools, and juvenile reformatories where they had served. They were convinced that just such an environment was best for their own religious vocation. It would also allow the supervision to best nurture their future Catholics.[61]

The organization of time was a missionary preoccupation, and this took place within a daily, weekly, and a more encompassing register. Thus the Spiritans sought to have work and rest, prayer and study, sleeping and eating all regulated by the clock each day. In addition, they established the seven-day week in which Sunday represented the day of highest worship, a Christian orientation that clashed with local Muslim custom in Zanzibar. If zeal for the interior meant that the missionaries felt the burden to move quickly and establish new stations, at Zanzibar their practices suggest that they trusted time, patiently and properly used, to form Christians out of the former slaves. Time, they felt, could be "a great teacher,"[62] and their passion for timetables that organized practices at once liturgical, economic, and educational highlighted their conviction that the flow of time within the enclosed space had to be regulated.

In addition, these daily and weekly activities took place in a larger cosmology shaped by the annual Catholic religious calendar with its formal liturgical seasons, special periods dedicated to certain Catholic devotions, and days shaped by the observation of feasts. Journal entries compulsively recorded feasts celebrated and other devotional practices, while letters and reports also recounted special liturgical moments.

Horner and the others showed a great scrupulosity about the liturgical calendar and the practices it enjoined upon them.[63] In addition to the normative liturgical

---

60. Zanzibar journal, 12vii63; CSSp 196aii: Horner to Schwindenhammer, 18ii66; CSSp 196aiii: Bauer, floorplans, June 1864; CSSp 196bi: Horner to Schwindenhammer, 3x63; CSSp 196bii: Baur to Schwindenhammer, 24xii63; ibid.: Horner to Schwindenhammer, 26xii63; BG 4:118–25.

These strictures on contact with outsiders did not mean that the Spiritan missions in Zanzibar and Bagamoyo were completely closed off from their surroundings. Libermann urged his missionaries to forge and maintain cordial relationships with local authorities wherever they served (Koren 1983, 262–64), and the Spiritans in eastern Africa worked hard to follow his advice, beginning at Zanzibar (Zanzibar journal, 18vi63, 29viii63, 15viii64, 16viii64, 16x64, 26xii64, 28xii64).

61. Horner used the word *surveillir* to describe his goals (CSSp 196bii: Horner to Schwindenhammer, 1viii63).

62. CSSp 196biv: Horner to Schwindenhammer, 12vi75.

63. The missionaries often asked advice about the proper observances of feasts, and argued among themselves in order to standardize their observances. See Kollman 2001, 256ff.

calendar, however, the missionaries also observed special months whose character was devotional, deriving from certain feasts proper to the month in question. Thus May was the month of Mary, the mother of Jesus, and observances included special prayers at statues of Mary during Mass and at other hours of prayer. Though May was the month of devotion most regularly observed by the mission, beginning even before the Spiritans took over the mission, the missionaries also occasionally marked other months with special significance, often announced at the month's beginning in the mission journals.

Such feasts and devotional months not only shaped the life of prayer and work within the community, but also served as reference points and legitimation for larger decisions of missionary strategy. Fava earlier had opened the schools at Zanzibar on March 19, 1862, the feast of St. Joseph, seeking the patronage of the Holy Family. Likewise, the move to Bagamoyo and other milestones in the evolution of Catholic evangelization took place on dates determined by the Spiritans to be propitious for symbolic reasons deriving from the liturgical calendar. All this was part of an implicit practice that connected the present Christians in eastern Africa with Christians of the past. These children were to be new saints and new missionaries.[64]

While organizing the mission's time, the Spiritans also pursued the production and maintenance of the space of evangelization. The Spiritans recognized possible sources of pollution that made Zanzibar and later the African mainland dangerous places where the fragile faith of these children could be lost. Chief among these was Islam. The missionaries saw it as heartless and cruel, but also particularly appealing to *les noirs* because it gave religious support for their sensuality. It limited the attraction of Christianity, which the missionaries saw as more demanding. The missionaries also saw threats to their Christians in the urban society of Zanzibar and, later, Bagamoyo, as well as in industrial workers, even when these were in their own workshops.[65] In light of these threats, the Spiritans tried to separate the mission as much as possible from the rest of Zanzibar and its population, in order to create a defined place in which to educate, train, and catechize the future Christians. Such practices established an interior in which formation could occur, and also defined an exterior containing influences that could ruin the evangelization envisioned.

Within the self-enclosed mission, the missionaries also practiced what Michel Foucault calls "partitioning" and the creation of "functional sites." This meant, first, creating distinctions in space and then, second, identifying sublocations

---

64. APF 35 (1863), 130. When one such child died, the missionaries could at times purchase a new child at the market and give them the same saint's name as the deceased (Zanzibar journal, 19vi65).

65. Fava 1933; CSSp 196bii: Horner to Schwindenhammer, 1viii63, 3x63, 7i67; CSSp 196ax: Horner to Propagation of the Faith, 12ii65; CSSp 196biii: Horner to Schwindenhammer, 15vi70, 22ix73; ibid.: Horner to Duparquet, 27iv71; CSSp 196aix: Duparquet to Schwindenhammer, 18i72; CSSp 197ai: Baur to Schwindenhammer, 8ii80; ibid.: Machon to Schwindenhammer, 7iii80; ibid.: Horner to Schwindenhammer, 6iv80. Later, as we shall see in the chapters ahead, the Spiritans saw threats from European explorers and pagan practices.

within the enclosed area for particular practices, activities, or observation. The Swahili home was already a heavily partitioned space, as it was an enclosed one, and the Spiritans reinforced the distinctions architecture had already created between themselves and others, between men and women, boys and girls. Upon arriving they reordered their residence to separate themselves more clearly from the sisters. The missionaries partitioned their children, separating girls and boys, as well as the primary school students from the older children for reasons they called at once hygienic and moral. Those spaces were in turn defined by the activities taking place in them, so that each function had its proper place. The mission's children were to sleep in the dormitory, pray and practice singing in the chapel, take meals in the refectory, work in the workshop or the field, and receive instruction in the classroom.[66] Tellingly, Horner belittled the Anglican mission for their chapel was "a room like any other."[67]

Enclosure was organized so that the former slaves could, as Libermann wrote, "share in the benefits of Christianity and the civilization of the people of Europe."[68] It allowed the proper functioning of three main practices constituting the comprehensive formation for the mission's children: indoctrination into Catholic liturgical life, vocational training, and schooling.

Liturgical Prayer and Sacraments

Upon their arrival at the Zanzibar mission, the children began to participate in the liturgical life of the small chapel there. They visited the chapel several times every day for Mass and a variety of other prayers, along with the Spiritans, the sisters, and other Catholics who chose to join. Since they were beholden to the mission and its routines — routines established and maintained by the missionaries for their own common life of prayer — the children's exposure to Catholic liturgical celebrations was considerably more extensive than ordinary Catholics in Europe at the time. The mission became to a profound extent the world in which they lived, with practices of common worship perhaps the most abiding feature of that world. Such practices oriented them to the Catholic faith by exposing them to the sacramental and devotional life of the church. They also learned bodily disciplines in chapel: sitting quietly, responding to liturgical directions, singing and acting in harmony. The common prayer in which they shared constituted a powerful influence in their experience of the mission.

Given its certain prominence in the missionary program, the missionaries rarely mentioned the formative aspects of this liturgical structure in shaping these

---

66. Foucault 1977, 143–44; 196axii: Horner to Holy Childhood, 30xi65; CSSp 196aiv: chapter of 1870; BG 6:616f. On the architecture of Swahili homes, see Blais 1916, 507; Middleton 1992, 63f; M. Horton and Middleton 2000, 116f. At the time of the first recorded escape, to which we soon turn, Baur expressed concern about the nighttime sorties of boys and girls, and later reported that repairs had been made to allow for better surveillance (CSSp 196bii: Baur to Schwindenhammer, 9ii66).

67. BG 4:349.

68. ND VIII, 318: trans. Burke 1998, 79.

ransomed slave children. They commented on the piety of the children in letters and reports, and the journals in particular recorded liturgical observances and devotional practices, but the Spiritans did not elaborate in theoretical discourse what they were hoping to achieve by such practices. Such absence reflects the taken-for-granted nature of these practices, which implicitly sought to construct a Christian identity in these children by immersing them in the Christian narrative. Though they may not have been able to articulate it, in practice the Spiritans understood what Paul Ricoeur has described as the way human identity emerges as narratives take temporal shape. By creating new identity-producing narratives through the sacralizing of time, they sought the creation of Christians who could embody the church.[69]

Liturgical prayer in the chapel also reinforced the social distinctions that operated in every aspect of the life at the mission. Gender and rank ordered those present. Boys and girls prayed on opposite sides of the chapel, and both the liturgy of the hours and the Mass enacted and thus reinforced missionary authority, situating the priests, brothers, and sisters in hierarchical fashion. Unless none were present, the priests led the common prayer and by ordination stood *in persona Christi* at the Masses celebrated daily, with the brothers nearby and the sisters separated.

Sacramental celebrations also tied individual processes of transformation into the daily communal liturgical practices. At a certain age, usually estimated by the missionaries to be between seven and ten, the mission children were invited to be baptized, in which case they entered a more intense process of preparation with others, culminating in a retreat before the ceremony. After baptism their participation at the liturgies increased. Similar preparation took place before celebrating their first communion, which often followed close upon baptism, after which the boy or girl was fully participating in the Eucharistic celebrations. They also confessed their sins to the priests regularly. By being confirmed, which first happened with Bishop Maupoint's visit in July 1867, they became even more deeply embraced by the church's official processes of incorporation.[70] These events became goals after which the children strove, though again the missionaries felt little need to describe their underlying presuppositions in fostering such piety.

69. Ricoeur 1984, 3. If Ricoeur identifies the role of such narratives — here understood as unfolding within the context of Catholic liturgy — in the formation of new identities, the late anthropologist Roy Rappaport emphasized how such ritual experiences establish the narratives that order that identity (Rappaport 1999, 169, 190). Kieran criticizes the Spiritan approach to liturgy as too intellectual, claiming that they did not appreciate or trust its pedagogical value (1966, 161f). I contend that they did not mention the effects desired from liturgical observances because they took them for granted. Their close attention to common prayer suggests a profound, though implicit, appreciation that such practices taught the faith and forged identity.

70. The absence of some of Zanzibar's sacramental books makes determining certain sacramental numbers, such as marriages, difficult. The journal records the baptisms of around 80 people, 20 or so of them at death, before the end of 1868, while the Zanzibar sacramental registry records over 150 (Zanzibar sacramental registry; CSSp 196bii: Horner to Schwindenhammer, 24vi64; Zanzibar journal, 6i64, 28viii64, 2ii65, 15iv65, 25iii66, 9ix66, 16vi67, 1–7vii67).

In official Catholic self-understanding, baptism formally effected the church membership that liturgical practices symbolized and supported. The Spiritans preferred to celebrate baptisms in groups and on the occasions of feasts such as the Transfiguration (August 6), the Assumption of Mary (August 15), the Immaculate Conception (December 8), Epiphany (January 6), the Presentation of the Lord (February 2), Easter, or Pentecost, as had Fava before them. The numbers baptized at Zanzibar in those years were considerable, the vast majority of whom were African children who came to the mission after being ransomed:

Zanzibar mission sacraments, 1860 to 1868[71]

	Baptisms	Deaths
1860	–	1
1861	4	–
1862	18	3
1863	6	3
1864	29 (12 adults[72])	13
1865	18 (2 adults)	13
1866	32	12
1867	29	6
1868	35	–

The earliest sponsors for baptisms were Europeans in Zanzibar. These included the mission's friend and French consular official Jablonski, as well as the Spiritans or the sisters. Beginning in 1863, some of the Africans already baptized started to serve in that role.

School

Besides liturgical practices in the chapel, the Zanzibar mission in the 1860s also pursued regular scholastic education of a rudimentary sort. To what extent the girls were included in this early education is not clear, but a classroom for the girls was planned in December 1863, and they certainly had catechism before that, for Baur remarks finding them better than the boys. By 1866, Horner spoke of 128 children in the primary school, girls included.[73]

The Spiritans' "second founder," Libermann, had emphasized the importance of education. He had stressed that African potential could only be released by formal classroom work, which would "improve, sanctify, and ennoble" them.

---

71. These figures come from the Zanzibar sacramental registry book, which only records baptisms and deaths from 1860 to 1868.

72. Horner kept a separate list of the adult baptisms and added short descriptions, such as "two lepers" or "young man fallen from tree, the slave of a Zanzibar resident."

73. Zanzibar journal, 15xii63; CSSp 196bii: Baur to Schwindenhammer, 24xi64; CSSp 196ax: Horner to Propagation of the Faith, 31xii66.

Libermann did not specify the details of such "civilizing" education, recommending instead the need to adapt general missionary principles to particular circumstances on the ground. But he was suspicious of any simple catechizing, favoring instead comprehensive education. Any substandard education only reinforced the inferiority that plagued Africans, he thought: "The civilization that consists of a mediocre knowledge of agriculture and trades and small business could not really take root among the people nor be of any great advantage to them."[74]

Most of the Spiritans in eastern Africa had been produced by the church's school system in France, and the Daughters of Mary, several of whom taught in the school, had come from Réunion, a French colony. Thus the mission's educational practices followed those of the French Catholic education of the day, as refined through their experiences of seminary education and formation to religious life. Most such classrooms in France relied on the "simultaneous method" of instruction, a method increasingly preferred by Catholic pedagogues in the nineteenth century. This method, pioneered in missionary settings by the religious community of Libermann's friend Anne-Marie Javouhey (1779–1851), a famous French nun whose sisters served in French colonies, allowed a single teacher to supervise a large number of children by "turning schoolhouses into highly disciplined and hierarchical spaces." As Sarah Curtis suggests, in her study of nineteenth-century French education, this met teachers' "moral need to protect and watch over schoolchildren and simply to cope with more crowded classrooms."[75]

The few descriptions of the Zanzibar mission's schooling and other comments from the missionaries suggest parallels with practices in French education, indicating the mission's indebtedness to French educational models. Catholic educators in France shared Spiritan confidence in their ability to shape the young. Both "viewed the child as a malleable creature" and linked moral and religious education. Curtis has shown, for example, how Catholic educational advocates trusted education to shape individuals not prone to revolutionary violence and immune to the disruptive effects of industrialism.[76] In Zanzibar, the Spiritans also showed great faith in the pacifying and moralizing effects of education, especially in this early period, and displayed suspicion of industrial work, as we shall see.

Nineteenth-century French Catholic schools also featured timetables along with closely supervised and enclosed classrooms, spatial and temporal practices resembling those operative throughout the Spiritan mission at Zanzibar, which Curtis has called "a pedagogy of watchfulness." Curtis also underscores the centrality of the catechism in the Catholic schools. As noted earlier, the Spiritans soon dedicated themselves to preparing a Swahili catechism for the children's

---

74. ND VIII, 248: trans. Burke 1998, 88.
75. Curtis 2000, 83, passim. On Javouhey, see Kollman 2001, 105.
76. Curtis 2000, 83, 88f. See also Feay 2003, 16–17.

Figure 8. A sister teaching at the Spiritan missions. From the Bagamoyo Mission Museum. Used with permission.

religious formation, a process completed in 1866. Missionary accounts also described curricula much in line with the French schools of the day.[77] Finally, both the missionaries and French Catholic teachers used paternal and maternal imagery to describe their work with students.[78]

Learning to Work

Along with learning to pray and rudimentary education, learning to work was prominent in the missionary strategy designed to make Catholics from the former slaves. Before the arrival of the Holy Ghost missionaries, Fava had written that two things made "a man": work and religion. Horner agreed:

> I am convinced that the success of the African missions will depend greatly on the love of and respect for work... joined to elementary instruction and knowledge of Christianity.... Work develops intelligence, fortifies the will, allows the support of one's dreams, makes for appreciation of true happiness, and finally multiplies the sources of material prosperity.

---

77. Curtis describes a curriculum consisting of reading, writing, French, simple mathematics, and religion. Horner mentioned the same subjects as well as KiSwahili, a program seconded at the chapter of 1870, to be described in the next chapter. See the following: Curtis 2000, 95–96; CSSp 195aii: Horner to Barnabo, 25i68; CSSp 196aiv: chapter of 1870.

78. Curtis 2000, 94–95, 100–101. Feay shows that Javouhey's sisters used similar images and practices (2003, 17–18).

He hoped that "native indolence," which he considered "the only obstacle" to African willingness to embrace Christianity, would be overcome by a love of work inspired from childhood. He wrote the bishop of Réunion in 1864: "Moralizing the blacks by work appears to me, bishop, the only hope [*planche de salut*] of this mission."[79]

This occurred most publicly in Zanzibar's workshops. The Spiritans expanded the workshops in the first few years after their arrival, adding lathes, a grain mill, and a creamery to the carpentry and forge that Fava had established.[80] There the Spiritans tried to both encourage industrious habits within the boys and girls. While the boys spent their days in the workshops learning a trade under the supervision of the Spiritan brothers, the girls went to an *ouvroir*, or sewing school, overseen by the sisters. The *ouvroir* served as the primary site for the girls' training, providing them with "motherly skills" such as sewing, washing, and repairing linens.[81]

Work not only forged individual habits. It also distributed the mission's children in line with expectations of the ecclesial polity of the future, reinforcing gendered distinctions in study and prayer. Such distinctions reflected the missionary goal of fostering dispositions for the proper families that would be building blocks for the Christian nuclei by which the continent would be evangelized. In the missionary understanding, women primarily needed training to assume their role as mothers in such households. To the sisters' superior in Réunion, Horner described the sublime vocation of the Daughters of Mary, "destined to become mothers to these girls, to regenerate them . . . and . . . to collaborate in the regeneration of Africa."[82] The girls did not need as much formal education as the boys to fulfill their roles in the ideal Christian communities of the future. The mission's task was to provide them with the tools considered proper for their future circumstances.[83]

The Spiritan program was thus oriented toward individuals, in whom it sought to inculcate certain habits and values associated with proper personhood, and also to the envisioned future church. The missionaries drew considerable inspiration for their practices from the social assumptions of their ecclesiology, so that distinctions proper to the church — men from women, members of religious orders

---

79. Fava 1933, 120; Versteijnen 1968a, 19; CSSp 196aii: Horner to Notre Dame des Victoires, 24ix64; CSSp 195i: Horner to Maupoint, 12ix64.

80. CSSp 196ax: Horner to Propagation of the Faith, 31xii66.

81. On the workshops, see the following: CSSp 196bii: Fava to Schwindenhammer, 6xii62; CSSp 196aii: Horner to Notre Dame des Victoires, 4ix64; CSSp 196ax: Horner to Propagation of the Faith, 31xii66.

82. CSSp 196bii: Horner to Marie Magdeleine, 13vii63; CSSp 194ii: Horner to Propagation of the Faith, 28x69; BG 8:761ff.

83. The Spiritans also claimed to want to conform to Zanzibar's Muslim-inspired expectations about feminine demeanor, which reinforced their own predilections about preferred limits to girls' education. Up to 1867, at least, education of girls remained very rudimentary, ostensibly so as not to offend local sensibilities, and the missionaries defended their decisions to Rome on this basis (CSSp 195ii: Maupoint to Barnabo, 19vii67; ibid.: Horner to Barnabo, 25i68).

Figures 9 and 10. Children in mission workshops. From the Bagamoyo Mission Museum. Used with permission.

from laypeople, clergy from other religious elites — operated in daily life and in other formative experiences of the former slaves. In that ecclesial worldview, differentiation by gender, distinguishing boys and girls, Spiritans and nuns, joined the practiced distinction between laypeople, on the one hand, and priests and religious, on the other. The work of the latter was in turn also defined by their gender and their state as lay or clerical religious. Thus the Spiritan brothers occupied themselves with manual work and the teaching of small children, while the

better-educated priests invariably served as superiors, presiders over the sacraments, preachers, and instructors for the older children. Physical work was not,
officially at least, part of the priests' lives. The sisters, for their part, worked
as nurses in the hospitals and educated the girls, with the religious superiors
and well-educated doing less physical work than the others. In contrast to what
they saw as their own well-ordered mission, the Spiritans disdained the gender
confusion at the UMCA school. There the boys and girls dressed the same, the
Spiritans reported, creating "chaos" that later forced the Anglican missionaries to
send their four oldest girls to the Indian Ocean islands of the Seychelles because
of "pell-mell relations with the boys."[84]

The Salience of Agricultural Labor

But the workshops had their limitations. Already at Zanzibar agricultural work,
in contrast to skilled labor, grew in importance in the missionary program. This
occurred in part because the Spiritans faced two competing and irreconcilable
desires. On the one hand, they wanted to establish the church in as thorough a
manner as possible, which entailed targeting small children who could be raised
within the care of the mission. They liked receiving those young enough to be "capable of being formed to the principles of Christianity," as Horner had remarked
approvingly of the first eight boys sent by Jablonski just after they arrived in
Zanzibar. Five years later, in his letter to Cardinal Barnabo in Rome, Horner
wrote that they sought to receive or ransom children between four and five years
of age. At that age they could be formed fully in order to establish the church of
the future on a firm footing.

At the same time, however, the Spiritans felt the burden of Fava's debts and
tried to support their mission as much as possible with internal resources. This
directed them to use the children's labor when possible to generate income. But
this was impossible with those they thought most promising for the future church.
On the contrary, young children demanded a great deal of care after arriving. In
addition, the missionaries faced the practical problem of simply occupying the
boys and girls unable to attend school or the workshops. Within a month after
arriving, the Spiritans moved the workshops to allow for larger gardens on the
mission's property, not only for crop experimentation but also to provide the
possibility for the easy work and play that might occupy the younger children.[85]
They helped with gardening on that land, but the gardens were still quite small
compared to the growing number of children at the mission. Moreover, once the
land was cleared there was little someone small could do.

The developing awareness of the importance of physical work eventually
called into question the importance of the workshops at Zanzibar. In this early

84. CSSp 196bii: Horner to Duboin, 25vii65; CSSp 196bii: Horner to Schwindenhammer,
22viii66.
85. Zanzibar journal, 12vii63.

period, however, Spiritans maintained and even expanded the workshops Fava had founded. The older children worked at such shops, supervised by the brothers and the sisters.[86] The missionaries recognized the value of the workshops in raising the mission's profile, and in 1865 Horner even contemplated preparing a pamphlet extolling the workshops to assist his fund-raising efforts in Europe.[87] Yet the limitations inherent in such technical training for those whom the Spiritans considered the ideal members of the future church — those whose young age made them open to proper formation — led the Spiritans to long for the large agricultural work projected for Bagamoyo. Meanwhile they sought to develop agricultural work at Zanzibar.

The workshops continued to attract the admiration of many visitors and the sultan of Zanzibar, who sent his own steamship for repairs. But the Spiritans saw their shortcomings. In November 1864, Baur wrote Paris and admitted that the workshops he supervised might not be the best means to form Christians in Zanzibar. The Africans with skills became proud, he wrote, like whites. Meanwhile, at Zanzibar the older children spent many days in 1865 away from town, and hence from their classes, working in the countryside preparing the modest agricultural establishment to employ the younger children.[88]

The trajectory was such that in early 1867 Horner wrote that workshops were only a secondary means of evangelization. Not only were industrial workers poor role models for the mission's children, but he felt the workshops themselves would be eclipsed by competition when Zanzibar had a fuller European presence. He also felt that the workshops disturbed the cloistered life, for the outside business drew the brothers especially into external relations injurious to their vocations. The shift toward agricultural work, which Horner spoke of as his goal from the beginning, inexorably moved ahead. A few days later at a council meeting, the Spiritans in Zanzibar decided to expand the agricultural work with a rabbit warren, which the children spent February constructing. Horner was in France on a fund-raising tour, and Baur wrote him, declaring his conviction that work was more important than study in the formation of the children: " . . . manual work moralizes more than studies."[89] When Bishop Maupoint visited Zanzibar in 1867 he, like other European visitors, was amazed by the workshops. His report to Propaganda Fide, however, emphasized that the agricultural work planned at Bagamoyo was the best hope for the mission's future. The mission there, foreseen

86. CSSp 196bii: Horner to Schwindenhammer, 26ix63, 3x63, 30x63; ibid.: Baur to Schwindenhammer, 24xii63; CSSp 196aii: Horner to Notre Dame des Victoires, 24ix64; CSSp 196ax: Horner to Propagation of the Faith, 31xii66.

87. I have found no evidence that such a pamphlet was ever printed, but his effort did eventuate in a supposed account from one of the mission children, Suéma, to which we soon turn. On Horner's plans for the pamphlet, see the following: CSSp 196aii: Horner to Notre Dame des Victoires, 24ix64; CSSp 196bii: Horner to Schwindenhammer, 12ii65, 12iii65, 15iv65.

88. CSSp 196aii: Horner, 18iii66; Kieran 1966, 402–4; Versteijnen 1968a, 6; BG 4:564; CSSp 196bii: Baur to Schwindenhammer, 2xi64; Zanzibar journal, April, May, June 1865.

89. CSSp 196bii: Horner to Schwindenhammer, 7i67; ibid.: Baur to Horner, 21iii67; Zanzibar journal, 11i67, 28ii67.

by Fava and anticipated by the Spiritans, would, he felt, better train the children and support the mission, mainly because of the extensive plantations planned.[90]

Spiritan awareness of the labor's economic value grew over time. Upon their arrival, it will be recalled that Horner sent Fava's workers from Réunion back home, deeming the latter more burden than benefit for the mission. Spiritan brothers were more reliable and also less expensive. Given the mission's needs for cheap labor, Zanzibar's slaves also represented a possible cost-cutting strategy. Soon after arriving, Horner had observed that abolition of slavery, though he did not push for it, would help the mission.[91] In 1864, however, Horner considered using slaves at the Zanzibar mission to generate income on the agricultural works in place and to clear new ground on those that the Spiritans were planning. In the end, Horner decided not to buy slaves for this purpose, at least initially. The reasons he gave in explaining his decision showed the complicated missionary perspectives on slavery as an institution.

He had been advised not to use slaves, Horner wrote in letters to Paris and Réunion, because they might escape once the mission moved to Bagamoyo. More importantly, he admitted there would be no chance to evangelize them. He continued, "I pass silently over the fracas that would ensue," and then admitted the bad light that slave keeping would cast on the mission in the eyes of the Arabs. Instead he planned to employ Nyamwezi porters, "who worked for almost nothing," and rely for other needs on the mission children.[92]

Horner's awareness of possible escapes once at Bagamoyo and his openness about the expenses entailed suggest that he imagined holding and using slaves as would any other Zanzibari landowner. His awareness of the likely "fracas" occasioned by any slave keeping showed that he attended to the mission's reputation among Arabs and Europeans. His claim that owning slaves would remove the possibility of evangelizing them is puzzling, for it is not clear why owning them would prevent seeking to form them in the faith. In the context of his explanations of why he did not buy slaves, however, his sensitivity to the evangelizing imperative perhaps puts his decision in the best possible light.

Soon, however, the mission apparently did have slaves, with no explanations given for the change. Horner's 1866 annual report to the Spiritan mother house on the mission's activities listed among the mission's employees four slaves — two males and two females. Given that they were listed among the employees, it is not clear what Horner meant by calling them slaves. It may have been his way to say that they, like the mission's children, had once been slaves, but that they were not children of the mission. Instead they simply worked there.[93]

90. Zanzibar journal 1vii67; CSSp 195ii: Maupoint to Barnabo, 19viii67.

91. CSSp 196bii: Horner to Duboin, 24vi63. He later said that abolition would allow for more conversions (CSSp 196axii: Horner to Propagation of the Faith, 12ii65).

92. CSSp 196bii: Horner to Duboin, 1vi64; ibid.: Horner to Schwindenhammer, 24vi64.

93. CSSp 196aii: Horner to Schwindenhammer, 19ix66. The mother house's rewritten version of Horner's report notes four slaves employed at the mission, stipulating that they are two married couples (CSSp 196aii: Barillec, 10x66).

Horner's 1864 flirtation with using slaves and his reasoning for not doing so also showed that he did not think that the mission's children were slaves, for they certainly *were* able to be evangelized. But the Spiritans also never designated the children who came to the mission as "free." Fava's views had been quite different, at least in one of his reports. Recall that he described the attraction of the mission for the children who came to work and learn there, and who protested when reminded of their freedom to leave the mission: "Those whom we snatch from slavery have followed us. In vain we have told them that they are free [*libre*] and they can leave us. . . ."[94] Such sentiment never appeared in Spiritan writings of this period.

Though the idea of the moral economy was not invoked to appreciate in particular the missionaries' own horizon of expectations, the Spiritans also possessed what could be called an operative moral economy. In the missionaries' view, those they designated the "children of the mission" belonged to the mission in some capacity, and thus could be expected to behave in certain ways. One looks in vain for a clear legal articulation of that relationship, which was complicated given the changing political circumstances in eastern Africa, yet certain events revealed how the missionaries thought about it. For instance, as we shall soon see, the Spiritans punished one of the mission children as if he were a French citizen subject to French law, and sent him to Réunion for incarceration. Despite this act, the legal status of those at the mission was never made explicit, and the mission's children represented an anomalous category within the legal circumstances of Zanzibar as well as European laws at the time.

For their part, the Spiritans envisioned the Africans who came to them first and foremost as potential Catholics, and they saw their task as making their mission into an environment that effected that anticipated future role. Those evangelized primarily embodied members of the future hoped-for church, and the missionaries ascribed them no clear status, as free or slave. It seems that the legal basis of the relationship between the missionaries and the former slaves at their missions was not much on the missionaries' minds. The Spiritans praised the children's potential as future Christians, stressing their humility, gentleness, and openness to the Christian message. They saw to it that they prayed regularly, worked, and attended classes. They supervised them and organized their behavior so that they no longer "would do what they wanted." Such descriptions of their work contrasted what they saw as the chaos that preceded their arrival with the order that missionary evangelization established. In their eyes, true freedom for the former slave children meant not moral autonomy apart from mission's authority but incorporation into the life of the mission.

•

The first stage of the Spiritan evangelization of freed slaves witnessed the attempted creation of a sacralized cosmos, an enclosed place differentiated from

94. Fava 1933, 118.

the surrounding space and ordered by a liturgical calendar and various timetables. As such it represented an attempt to create a new Christendom. Yet that cosmos was also a profoundly disciplinary space, shaped by surveillance and other techniques with affinities to secular traditions as much as Catholic ones. The day for the young Christians-to-be was carefully structured with prayer, education, meals, and rest following each other in an orderly procession. The Spiritan program thus featured the compulsive, temporal, and spatial reorientation identified by one anthropologist as typical of modern penitential practices.[95] This combination of ideals at once theological and sociological in the formative practices at the mission shows that such practices derived from ecclesiological hopes in the missionaries as well as the disciplinary practices in their backgrounds in school, seminary, and juvenile reformatories. In the practices and imaginations of the missionaries, the freed slaves were assimilated in two different directions — in their official discourse, as neophytes to Christianity preparing for the sacraments, but in their actual practices also as students and juvenile offenders reformable through a disciplinary regime.

Within the regime of enclosure enacted at the mission, physical labor soon assumed a particular importance, both in Spiritan practices and discourse. Like the regime of enclosure, which could be legitimated in both overt theological and tacit sociological terms, labor's valuations in missionary discourse also showed the presence of a double narrative. Physical work simultaneously had formative and economic benefits. It both forged the proper habits within the mission children and, potentially at least, generated income for the mission. The evolution of labor's role within Spiritan evangelization reflected both missionary predilections and the constraining circumstances facing them in Zanzibar, especially fiscal urgency.

The complications and contradictions of these overlapping narratives of legitimation — at once theological, sociological, and economic — were not lost on all the mission's children, even in this early period.

Africans in the Missionary Archive:
The Insights of Young Workers, Piety, and Escapes

Horner's first formal report to the Holy Childhood Society in November 1863 contained a scene that featured regularly in Spiritan descriptions of the mission children in following years. Horner wrote that the pathetic state of the children coming from the slave market had motivated the boys already at the mission to gather together their own money — coins received from visitors to the mission — for ransoming others. According to Horner, Casimir, one of the boys, said that he and his fellows wanted thereby "... to make them [the boys to be ransomed] as happy as we ourselves, to make them Christians and send them to heaven." The Spiritans saw the value of such scenes. Willingness to sacrifice to ransom

---

95. Rhodes 2001.

other children showed the children's inherent goodness — Horner suggested that most children of that age would instead buy candy — and also their instinctive appreciation for the missionaries' commitment to slave evangelization. Unsurprisingly, the generosity of the children became ubiquitous in descriptions of the mission for outsiders, suggesting its perceived usefulness to the Spiritans as they represented their missionary work.[96]

More striking in this instance than the children's generosity, however, were other details surrounding that generosity. In a mixture of French and KiSwahili, Horner reported that the boys' request had specifically said that the mission not buy any *small* children. Why? Because, Casimir claimed, "These small ones not good [sic], they cannot work." Horner described this request as "some conditions that our benefactors imposed on me." He meant to be ironic, aiming his remarks at his benefactors in the Holy Childhood Society, who certainly imposed conditions on *their* gifts to the mission.[97] He then addressed his readers: "Poor little ones! You see how they understand already that it is not enough to ransom children, for it is still more difficult and expensive to feed and care for them." He said he responded to Casimir and the others: "A big child is not good, because they are already too lively and instead of becoming good themselves will end by spoiling all of you." Then switching to address the readers once more, Horner wrote that Casimir's complaint had a logic to it, for the mission spent years and considerable money nourishing and sheltering young children who produced nothing. Horner, however, saw no alternative, and here proclaimed the sentiment earlier noted: "We must above all aim to make a work solid and durable: trying to form children already advanced in age would be like wanting to bend large trees." Horner continued, adding that another of the larger boys working in the workshops said he wanted his coins used to buy a heavy (or strong) child (*mtoto mafuta*) who could wield a hammer and help him at the forge. Horner urged the young forger to consider that the three slaves to be bought with the children's money would grow into his fellow workers eventually. He reported that when the three arrived after purchase at the slave market, the boys already at the mission rejoiced. They then said they wanted to ransom more boys and promised to work hard to do so.

In the same letter, Horner reported that one of the children had the habit of theft. This mortified the others, who decided to watch him carefully. One day he

---

96. CSSp 196axii: Horner to Holy Childhood Society, 26xi63. For other accounts depicting this behavior, see CSSp 195i: Horner to Maupoint, 29xi63; Zanzibar journal, 18vi65; BG 4:563–64; BG 5:498; BG 7:265. The generosity of those ransomed, in one form or another, also appeared in nearly every annual report to the Propagation of the Faith or the Holy Childhood Society in CSSp 196ax and 196axii. That such descriptions legitimated the mission is not to say that they did not happen, for such behavior was recorded at least once in the Zanzibar mission journal written for missionary eyes only and thus indicating authenticity.

97. Such conditions included that the money be spent only for ransoming, as well as the writing of regular reports, which had to specify the kinds of things the agencies themselves wanted to hear. The agencies complained when the reports did not meet their expectations and at times threatened to withhold contributions (CSSp 196aii: Barillec to Horner, 10x66). For a good example of an agency specifying its demands, see CSSp 196axii: Holy Childhood to Maupoint, 30vi63.

was caught taking a fig and brought to Horner for punishment. Horner punished him, but the habit of theft was "so rooted" that his punishments did not suffice. Thus the superior let the boys themselves carry out the punishment, which was sufficiently harsh to break the habit of stealing. Horner wrote, "Now he is one of our best children."

Horner used this report to make a heartfelt appeal to the Holy Childhood Society to continue and, if possible, increase its annual gift to the mission. In describing the children, he emphasized their promising qualities and wanted to make clear to benefactors the challenges facing the mission. Yet much more interesting than Horner's conscious aims in writing, historically speaking, are the voices of the mission children that can be heard within this missionary text. First of all, the report showed children eager to prove their virtue to the missionaries and also able to act in concert. They corrected each other's shortcomings, and collaborated to pool their money to purchase other children for the mission. Such actions showed that Casimir and the other boys at Zanzibar had achieved two important things: first, the ability to articulate a single voice; and second, the ability to project that voice to those in authority over them.[98]

The most revealing aspect of Horner's account, however, lies in the specification of the kind of child that those already at the mission wanted to purchase. Their request for older and stronger children showed their awareness that their workload increased because of the presence of nonproductive younger peers in their midst. At least some of these children saw themselves as workers for the mission, workers who had interests that were best served by having the missionaries ransom older and stronger children. The requests, by Casimir and the unnamed boy at the forge, to purchase other strong children from the slave market represents the first hint of real African agency among the former slaves in the Holy Ghost missionary archive.

Horner recognized the boys' realism and used it to make his plea to European benefactors: "You see how they understand that it is not enough to ransom children, for it is still more difficult and expensive to feed and care for them." But only slowly did he and his fellow Spiritans themselves face squarely the contradictions arising from their twin goals of supporting the mission through the children's own labor and seeking young children to evangelize. Horner's account shows that the contradictions in the missionary strategy were not lost on the mission children already at Zanzibar. In a remarkable foreshadowing of tensions to be faced in the future, the boys' reaction to the arrival of ransomed children suggests that they saw the Spiritan dilemma because they felt themselves burdened by the need to work on the mission's behalf to support these others.

Even if the piety of the children looks suspiciously like missionary wishful thinking — their desire that other children be ransomed and so made "as happy as we ourselves, to make them Christians and send them to heaven," for example —

---

98. These achievements, labeled by Guillermo O'Donnell "horizontal voice" and "vertical voice," respectively, are discussed more fully in the next chapter (O'Donnell 1986).

their demand for older and stronger children showed prescient insight along with the piety. Their "conditions" — which Horner described ironically — indicated an awareness of tensions within the missionary strategy that even Spiritans could not directly acknowledge very readily.[99] The labor of the former slaves at the mission, which the Spiritans emphasized for its role in forming proper habits, was recognized by those former slaves themselves as a resource. This anticipated Spiritan recognition of labor's resource value, which only appeared in the later 1860s.

This episode, revelatory as it is, underscores the limits to our ability to understand African experiences of evangelization to this point. Most of those at the mission were children whose capacity for self-representation and agency in a form interpretable by historical scholarship was rather undeveloped. In May 1862, the sacramental registry at Zanzibar recorded the baptism of Henri-Joseph Casimir, the boy called Casimir in the above account, and estimated that he was twelve years old. Most of the children were even younger when baptized, and those unbaptized were younger still. As a consequence, nearly everything known about these former slaves in this period comes from records produced by others, usually Europeans and missionaries.

But the door on their experience is not completely closed, as the above example suggests. Missionary writings, though crafted to underscore the conditional promise found in the mission's children and thus establish the viability of the mission for potential benefactors, can nonetheless reveal those same children's experiences of evangelization as well. Such evidence is often oblique, for the missionaries themselves were not always aware of the significance of what they revealed. In addition, the meaning of such accounts sometimes only becomes clear by comparison to later accounts of the same people, which cast light on individuals first introduced years before. But missionary records can disclose African experiences of evangelization when approached with an awareness of both the Spiritan worldview that produced them and an imaginative, informed, and admittedly hypothetical awareness of what the world of the mission's children might have been like.

And there are things we can safely presume about that world. For example, the means by which most of these children came to the Catholic mission at Zanzibar are clear. The majority were purchased at the slave market by the missionaries; a smaller number came to the mission after abandonment by their masters or mistresses; and others, at this point quite a small number, came after being released into the mission's care by European or other authorities who had freed them. Some may have been born into slave status, but most entered it unwillingly in childhood. They arrived at the mission in a variety of states, but often in wretched condition. Witnesses described the children ransomed coming to the

---

99. Only in 1866 did Horner make his first request that funding given by the Propagation of the Faith for ransoming be available for use in the upkeep of those ransomed (CSSp 196bii: Horner to Schwindenhammer, 25vi66).

Zanzibar orphanages completely nude and ravenous. Once at the mission they were in the mission's care, with little opportunity to do other than to follow the mission's routines of education, prayer, and work. Even that was a challenge for many. Horner wrote that some who recently had been on caravans had grown accustomed to eating dirt on those journeys, an occasionally mortal habit a few continued at the mission.[100]

Given their fragile circumstances, the children who came to the mission likely looked to get along as they could in their new setting. Having quite possibly left their own family quite recently, they reached the mission bewildered, with a combination of fear and confusion. They looked for safe and supportive relationships with those who seemed more powerful, and they were quickly defined by relationships with the priests, brothers, and nuns, relationships that were literally and self-consciously constructed as paternalistic and maternalistic rather than merely patronal. In light of the intimate contact with the Spiritans and the sisters, it is not surprising that ritual experiences like those associated with the Catholic liturgy and the sacraments attracted the former slaves at the mission. Thus prayer and sacramental participation probably seemed a natural progression of incorporation into the mission's life, the appropriate filial response to their circumstances.[101]

Missionary reports about the children, though designed to legitimate missionary work, should be interpreted in light of the likely conditions in which such children found themselves. Thus it is not surprising that the missionaries stressed the openness of the new arrivals to the Gospel message, their sweetness and docility, and their piety, especially if they had not been "spoiled" by living among Arabs. The missionaries saw these children as manifesting Christian promise, for example, by the seriousness with which they prepared for the sacraments. Thus Baur wrote Horner, then in France, about the first communion of sixteen of the mission's children in August 1867. He named all those who participated, then described their exemplary behavior on the five-day retreat before the celebration, during which they confessed their sins. He reported that during the Mass, but before the reception of Eucharist, one girl screamed out, "I dare not receive; I've forgotten a sin." Baur repaired to the confessional during the liturgy in response to this pious declaration, which he took as a sign of sincere fervor. Comparing reports for funding agencies with letters to their superiors in Paris — the latter usually not as carefully crafted to reassure benefactors of the fruitfulness of their contributions — suggests that the Spiritans' views were not merely contrived for external consumption. This story, for example, though replicated in more public arenas — suggesting recognition of its rhetorical usefulness as a demonstration

---

100. CSSp 196axii: Horner to Holy Childhood, x67.

101. Of slaves in early modern Brazil, Joseph Miller writes, "The Catholic sacraments restored the hope of personal security, in death as well as in life, that enslavement had cost its victims.... [T]hey would have struck arriving Africans as offering responsible patronage of the sort that enslaved persons might have sought in Africa" (Miller 2003, 97).

of the mission's deserving promise — had its origins within an internal letter, pointing to its authenticity.[102]

A similar judgment of likely accuracy can be made of a common feature in missionary descriptions of the slave market: the plaintive cries the Spiritans claim to have heard as they passed by with their money, *"Blanc, achète moi!"* ("White man, buy me!"). Though their reporting legitimates the good the missionaries did by their ransoming, such cries were also comprehensible self-interested action. A black-clad European with a bag of coins might have struck a contrast with the mostly Arab buyers. Those for sale at the market might well have thought that he, at least, would not take them overseas — likely a strong slave fear. In another similar account, an abandoned child brought to the mission received the visit of his mother, probably still a slave. He responded, according to Horner, "My mother is here." Another child, when told that God was in charge of the mission, responded, "This God must be a good master."[103] These representations legitimated the mission by dramatizing the hunger for the mission's message in such children. They also distinguished the mission's merciful care from Arab callousness and violence. Yet they might well have described events that occurred.

In light of what can be inferred about how the Africans came to the mission at Zanzibar, as well as firmer conclusions about the regime the Spiritans established, one can thus hazard some cautious conclusions about Africans' experiences at the mission. First, the mission's activities kept the children busy. Before too long the shared experiences of evangelization likely forged a common identity among the mission's children as they together underwent schooling, work, and liturgical practices. They were exposed to the rhythms of the mission and a common Christian narrative punctuated with sacramental moments of initiation and celebration. Most of them no doubt developed a sense of belonging to the mission and an identification with its rhythms. In light of the vulnerable helplessness in which they usually arrived, they became beholden to the mission quite quickly. It became the place where they belonged; its routines defined the life they led; and the priests, brothers, and sisters represented the clearest authorities within their lives.

Second, though in intimate contact with the Spiritans and the sisters, the children also lived together in dormitories where they likely created their own operative patterns of interaction — sometimes dubbed subcultures — outside missionary surveillance. No matter how keen, missionary control could not eliminate personalizing strategies like the typical reactions in the much stricter total institutions described by Erving Goffman. Goffman observed in such places how some withdrew, others cooperated and conformed, still others "worked the system" by

---

102. For Baur's story from the first communion Mass, see CSSp 196bii: Baur to Horner, 11viii67; Gaume 1872, 111.

103. APF 42 (1870), 48; CSSp 196axii: Horner to Gaume, 1vii69; BG 7:273ff; CSSp 196aii: Horner to Notre Dame des Victoires, 24ix64.

adopting strategies that allowed them to hide their deeper selves while maintaining a loyal exterior. In fact, Goffman theorized that total institutions, far from merely creating conformism, naturally foster a high level of self-concern in the inmates, who constantly consider how to gain small advantages within the evident constraints.[104] Eager Spiritan attempts to control the children's behavior, beginning at Zanzibar and persisting later at other missions, indicated Spiritan zeal for control in those circumstances. They also suggested that the mission's children learned to manipulate the environments created to secure places from which to achieve some semblance of individual agency. The children also no doubt developed relations with one another that buoyed their sense of themselves.

The broader embracing environment of Zanzibar was also part of the world to which the mission's children adapted. Despite the confining regime, Spiritan efforts to control their boundaries could not keep the outside world at bay, and it was a dynamic world. Europeans, Arabs, and Indians of all sorts interacted with the missionaries, and the mission's children grew aware of such people and the larger environment in which they lived. But the setting gave the mission children few obvious ways to assert themselves, and many were too young to have much capacity for defiance or self-determination anyway. Thus the children probably also soon learned that flight from the mission was risky; Zanzibar's confining streets and the sultan's authority there meant that unattached Africans easily fell under suspicion as *watoro*, escaped slaves, and were subject to seizure.

Adapting to the mission was a complex affair, and historical certainty about it impossible. Over time, the initial bewilderment of those arriving at the mission probably gave way to feelings that oscillated between appreciation of where they were and a longing to be elsewhere. At the same time, both the missionaries and those who came to them developed certain expectations of each other. These mutual expectations constituted part of the evolving moral economy that emerged at the mission. The missionaries had certain preconceptions about those they targeted as Catholics. Meanwhile the African boys and girls developed within themselves a felt sense of what belonging to the mission, and thus becoming and remaining Catholic, entailed. Given the realities of the setting, however, the moral economy that developed in the Africans at the Spiritan missions cannot be reduced simply to what the missionaries wanted to inculcate. It drew upon the former slaves' backgrounds prior to coming to the mission, their experiences after having arrived, and broader circumstances in eastern Africa. This evolving consciousness was part of the historical identity and the historical agency possessed by the Africans at the missions.

Indeed, almost certainly Spiritan strategy itself, even in the seemingly constrictive guises enacted at Zanzibar, still had spaces and opportunities for personal self-assertion and individual action. Goffman claims that total institutions generate self-concern. If he is right, then one natural way to adapt to the mission at Zanzibar was reinforced, for the official ideology of the mission also legitimated

---

104. Goffman 1961, 66f.

self-worth. The Christian narratives in which the mission's children were sub-merged, enacted daily or more often at liturgical prayer, declared the great value the mission placed on the individual soul's relationship to God. Of course, the internalization of this sense of self-regard, whether spiritual or practical or some combination of the two, took place outside historical scrutiny.

Some have drawn attention to the mixed implications of such internalization. As one observer has suggested, one role of Christianity is to instill "personal responsibility of the individual before God," a tendency that, he says, "could not fail to contribute to the collapse of traditional collectivist values and institutions in African societies."[105] Christianity automatically does no such thing, since any new ideology can be put to many different uses. But it seems clear that in the case of slave evangelization, Christian narratives had no preexisting larger collective identity to undo. Instead, such narratives helped create an identity in those at the mission. And there is ample evidence that those evangelized appreciated the liturgical experiences and especially the sacraments that helped forge their sense of themselves.

The direct historical traces of African experiences of slave evangelization are few in this period, but they are not absent. In addition to generalized descrip-tions of Africans at the mission, two characters appeared distinctly as individuals within missionary writings in these early years. They represent in different ways potential responses to the Spiritan message moving beyond the conventional ac-counts that constitute most of our descriptions of the mission children. One is Casimir, already introduced, whose debut in the Spiritan archive demonstrated a prescient awareness of the mission's needs for labor and the complexities of ransoming children too small to work. His later actions, however, occasioned greater Spiritan consternation. The other is a girl later named Madeleine, who, Horner claimed, arrived at the mission as Suéma.

Suéma: Fact and Fiction

Beginning in 1870, European Catholics interested in the Catholic mission in eastern Africa had the chance to read an account purportedly written by Suéma, one of the former slave girls then at the mission.[106] Horner claimed to have tran-scribed her story in the mid-1860s, and in the announcement of the publication added that she still lived at the mission. Publication was sponsored by Monsignor Gaume, a friend of the Spiritans and prominent French cleric, whom Horner had written not long before.[107]

---

105. Koponen 1994, 581–82.

106. Gaume 1870. The name Suéma is almost certainly the French form of Siwema, a KiSwahili/Bantu name meaning "not good" (*si*, a prefix for "no" or "not," *wema*, a form of good or goodness).

107. The original text can be found in CSSp 194v. The notice of release appeared in BG 7:659–60. See also CSSp 196axii: Horner to Gaume, 1vii69; Horner to Duparquet, 16vi70, private communication from Daniel Bouju, CSSp.

Suéma, which Horner had subtitled "The story of a small slave buried alive; or filial love," unfolds as the first-person life history of a young African slave girl who found her way to the Catholic mission at Zanzibar. She belonged to the Yao, whose origins are in contemporary Malawi and southern Tanzania. Suéma begins by describing the tragic circumstances in her home that led to her enslavement. After a serene early childhood, her father's sudden death sank her family into steep debt. Suéma and her mother were then seized in payment of the debt and led on a harrowing trek to the coast. On the way her mother was murdered before her eyes, and her daughter watched helplessly as birds picked at her dead body. Suéma and the others then embarked upon a horrible sea voyage to the island-coastal slave market at Zanzibar.

Upon arrival in Zanzibar, Suéma was thrown into a garbage heap by a slave trader disgusted by her ill health and angry at his lost revenue. There a jackal picked at her weak body until, rescued by a young man from Réunion and conveyed to the Catholic mission, she entered the care of the sisters there and recovered her strength. She entered the life of the mission along with other children. Her baptism, however, was delayed because she could not "forgive those who trespassed against (her)," namely the Arab slave-caravan leader who struck down her mother. One day, as Suéma volunteered in the hospital staffed by the sisters, this leader himself was brought in on a stretcher, mortally wounded by the British who had interdicted the slave boat on which he had been serving. Recognizing her mother's murderer, Suéma resisted treating him, but relented at the mother superior's command. Her heart moved as she cleaned his wounds. Later in prayer she felt herself bathed in life-giving water as she pardoned the now-dead slave trader. Baptized, she took the name Madeleine, and Horner reported that she entered the sisters' congregation as a postulant.

The published account of *Suéma* contained a brief introduction by Horner, where he asserted that this tragic story was true, that he only had translated her KiSwahili telling into French. The girl arrived at the mission in 1860 when she was around nine years old, he wrote, and slowly she told the other children her story, beginning around 1864. Horner claimed that she was very pious and compassionate, refusing to marry several times and showing a mother's tears at the deaths of children during an epidemic, meanwhile caring tirelessly for the sick. He in turn published it so that his European readers would be grateful to God for not undergoing such experiences. No doubt he also saw its potential as what one historian calls "a Christian metaphor," with an innocent person suffering, being buried, rising, and then undergoing conversion. Finally, Horner no doubt appreciated the funds it brought Zanzibar, since already by 1870 *Suéma* was making money for the support of the mission. Three editions were published in French, the last one illustrated, as well as one in English. A play based on the story was prepared by a woman in Grenoble and performed there.[108]

---

108. Moulinet 1998, 116f; BG 8:754–55; BG 13:62; Vogt n.d., 28.

In introducing the story, Horner referred to a certain Madeleine, then at the sisters' community in Réunion, claiming that she was the girl whose story was related. There is no doubt that Madeleine existed. A girl of that name (Marie Madeleine Vallet, the surname probably from a European sponsor) was baptized in October 1862 at Zanzibar and received her first communion in 1867. She also served as a baptismal sponsor for other children baptized at Zanzibar through the decade, indicating that the missionaries trusted her. She continued to do so at Bagamoyo beginning in the early 1870s.[109] Later Horner mentioned her as a witness to a dispute between two Spiritans, and another friend of the mission wrote that she took the name Antoinette in religious life.[110] We return to her in the next chapter, to examine letters she wrote to Monsignor Gaume in Paris that revealed her pious articulations of the mission's ideals.

Gaume accepted Horner's attribution and thus it made its way into print. But that Madeleine was the Suéma who narrated the story published by Gaume and defended by Horner is another matter.

There are several reasons to be suspicious of Horner's claim that he merely transcribed *Suéma*. In the first place, Horner detailed in letters the process of its production, never mentioning that he was telling someone else's story. He first mentioned the writing of such a tale while in Réunion convalescing in 1865. He had, he wrote his superiors in Paris, first imagined preparing something on the children's workshops at Zanzibar, but then instead wrote this short piece, which he planned as the first of a volume of thirty such edifying stories. After sending a draft to Schwindenhammer, he claimed to have finished his account in February 1866 while in Réunion. Apparently the draft, by now called "Madeleine," was returned with suggestions, because he sent what he called a final version several months later. He confidently predicted that it would generate support for the mission in Maurice and Réunion, and described how the French consul praised the accurate portrayal of Zanzibar and eastern Africa. Horner was anxious that the Spiritans in Paris not change any details, except stylistically, in order not to distort his careful work, "for things are different here than in Europe." He trusted that the story would increase the mission's reputation and attract vocations to the congregation.[111] At no point in the earlier correspondence did he assert the story's veracity.

Perhaps most damning to Horner's claims of authenticity are two of his colleagues' words soon after *Suéma* appeared. In 1872, Father Charles Duparquet,

---

109. Zanzibar sacramental registry, 19x62, 28viii64, 6viii65, 31x65, 20v66, 6i67; CSSp 196bii: Baur to Schwindenhammer, 11viii67; Bagamoyo sacramental registry, 1871, passim. In the Bagamoyo record, her name is given as Madeleine Akimboka, which might be the name she had at birth among the Yao.

110. Gaume 1872, 35, 55; Ricklin 1880, 130ff; CSSp 196bii: Baur to Schwindenhammer, 11viii67; CSSp 196biii: Horner to Schwindenhammer, 19xi74.

111. CSSp 196bii: Horner to Schwindenhammer, 12iii65, 15iv65, 12ii66, 26vii66. These letters make peculiar Alpers' claim that in determining the story's veracity he was "[l]acking any evidence other than Swema's story itself" (Alpers 1983, 186).

who served in eastern Africa from 1869 to the early 1870s and who is discussed in the next chapter, attributed what he called *le roman* (the novel) *Suéma* to the mission's friend Jablonski. He spoke of his repugnance at Horner's farce and charlatanism, regarding it as undignified for the head of a mission. Around the same time, Baur, who worked with Horner closely from 1863 to 1878, also found Horner's assertions about the story's veracity ludicrous. He pointed out in a private letter to a Spiritan friend that Madeleine's mother — the mother who, according to the story, had been killed on the way to the coast by the ruthless caravan master whom Suéma eventually forgave, and whose body Suéma saw eaten by crows — lived at the sisters' house at Bagamoyo. "What a sham!" he wrote.[112]

Broader consideration of the rhetorical uses to which Spiritans put their descriptions of the mission children also suggests that *Suéma* was likely the result of Horner's or someone else's creativity. Though numerous scholars have believed otherwise, this text was not an account deriving from the girl herself. Its purpose was originally to promote the mission, though gradually it assumed the status of a historical account.[113] Horner's letters, as well as other claims by his confreres, suggest that Horner began the story of Suéma as a work of fiction for didactic and fund-raising purposes, then affixed a real person to it. Antagonism between Horner and his confreres Baur and Duparquet, which grew over time, likely led the latter two to belittle what they saw as Horner's ruse. Though she was not the source of the story of Suéma but probably merely the surrogate subject of Horner's tale, the novice Madeleine died at Réunion in 1878.[114]

---

112. Recent correspondence with Father Daniel Bouju, a Spiritan working in Tanzania, has uncovered the 1872 letter from Duparquet, whose views were seconded by François-Xavier Vogt, a prominent Spiritan in the early twentieth century and bishop of Bagamoyo (Vogt n.d [also CSSp 391a: Vogt, Summary of the Bagamoyo mission]; Duparquet, 6ix72, from Bouju, private communication). Father Bouju also alerted me to an earlier letter in which Horner gives more details on Madeleine/Suéma in response to questions from Gaume (Horner to Gaume, 15vi70).

Baur's letter is a litany of complaints against Horner (CSSp 196biii: Baur to Collin, 15viii72). Both he and Duparquet had bitter conflicts with Horner over Spiritan strategy, to be discussed in the next chapter. On Horner's conflict with Duparquet, see Coulon 1999.

113. For nineteenth-century sources that treated the story of Suéma as a nonfictional account, see Gaume 1872 and Ricklin 1880, 130ff. More recently, the story has been treated as nonfictional in an article about Gaume, and in a radio broadcast of the story in Tanzania prepared by the Holy Ghost priests at Bagamoyo (Moulinet 1998; personal communication from Joseph Healey, MM, and Daniel Bouju, CSSp). A play entitled *Siwema* was prepared from *Suéma* with the help of Father John Henschel, CSSp, and performed at the *Chuo cha Sanaa* (Art School) at Bagamoyo. A video has also been produced from the stage play (Holy Ghost Fathers 2000). Henschel also prepared a recent book in Swahili and English based on the story (Henschel n.d.D).

Historian Edward Alpers examined the story of Suéma in a collection of studies about women and slavery in Africa (Alpers 1983), and since then many scholars have referred to it as an important slave-produced narrative from the nineteenth century. Alpers defends the historicity of the story — and Horner's accounts of its origins as a transmission and then translation of the girl's own story — from internal evidence as well as convictions about Horner's reliability. Similar assumptions of the story's veracity can be found in Hoppe 1993 and Larson 2000, 19–20, each of whom refers to Alpers. For further details see Kollman 2001, 279f.

114. Gaume 1872, 35; Ricklin 1880, 130f; CSSp 196biii: Horner to Schwindenhammer, 19xi74; ibid., Baur to Collin, 15viii72; CSSp 196biv: Horner to Schwindenhammer, 24viii78.

Suéma was one of several stories the Spiritans produced for popular consumption in the mission journals in France in the nineteenth century. Such stories revealed how the missionaries wanted their ideals to be embodied in the freed slaves they sought to evangelize. Suéma in this story represents the ideal missionary product, the former slave who became a committed Christian, the proper outcome of the missionary evangelization carried out in Zanzibar. Suéma, baptized Madeleine and professed under the name of Antoinette as a sister, showed herself a hard-working and pious girl, desiring to become a nun in order to evangelize her brothers and sisters who remained in darkness. Her gratitude to the mission and her dependence upon it were obvious. She prayed often in the story and forgave the one who had harmed her. These actions proved that she had been effectively evangelized, justifying the missionary enterprise. No wonder Horner was so keen to claim her story as real.

Records of Casimir within the missionary archive are very different than Horner's reports on Suéma. They are both more reliable historically and at least as valuable as a window on African experiences of slave evangelization.

Casimir

A little over a year after his first appearance in the missionary archive in Horner's November 1863 letter, where he voiced the desire that the Spiritans ransom strong boys, Casimir accompanied Baur on an exploratory journey to Bagamoyo made in Horner's absence. Baur likely chose him because he was the boy at the mission seen to be most reliable and helpful for such an important role. This trust is not surprising given the leadership he showed among the boys already in Horner's earlier account, not to mention his self-awareness about the situation in which the mission's children found themselves as laborers. Like Madeleine, he was often a baptismal sponsor for other children in those early years, listed in the sacramental registry as Casimir Sopor. He did not sign his name, evidence that he probably could not write.[115] His exact age is impossible to determine, but if he was around twelve at his baptism in May 1862 — as it says in the sacramental registry — then he was fifteen or so when he was with Baur.[116]

Three years after his first appearance in the historical record and one year after he accompanied Baur to the coast, Casimir appeared again in the Spiritan archive, this time for a very different reason. By 1866 it seems he was no longer in a mood to acquiesce eagerly to the demands of the mission. In February, Casimir, at this point described by Baur as "the first boy received at the mission," escaped from the mission along with Josephine, one of the larger girls in the sisters' care.

---

115. Zanzibar journal, 23ii65, 27ii65; Zanzibar sacramental registry, 22xii63, 2viii64, 28viii64, 1v65, 17ix65.

116. Given that he was older than most of the children, Casimir was probably one of those on Horner's mind when he wrote in 1863 of the need to move to the coast within two years because some of the mission's children would need to marry soon (CSSp 196bii: Horner to Schwindenhammer, 3x63).

Apparently he had escaped before and was also on previous occasions guilty of introducing women into the dormitory. Captured when betrayed by a confidant and found to be hiding at the local launderer, Casimir was confined and then discovered concealing a knife while he was chained up.[117]

This was the first recorded instance of many escapes from Spiritan missions by former slaves in the years ahead. Baur was apparently quite shaken by the turn of events, for Horner accused him of overreacting. Casimir, according to Horner's explanation in the wake of his escape and recapture, was quite practiced at pretense. He had been the slave of an Arab but was given to Fava in payment of a debt. Josephine, who was baptized in December 1861 at what the missionaries estimated was only seven years old, had also served as a sponsor for several baptisms afterward. She had been given to the mission by an Arab woman jealous of the attentions her husband had shown her — altogether horrifying, if she came to the mission at seven years old. Both, Horner emphasized, were already at the mission when the Spiritans had arrived, too old to be formed or reformed, and he asserted that he would not have accepted them had he been in charge at the mission.[118] After their capture, Horner sent Casimir to a penitentiary at Réunion, conceivably to La Providence, the reformatory there, while Josephine remained at the mission, though Horner doubted her sincerity. Despite Horner's misgivings, Josephine served as a baptismal sponsor several more times at Zanzibar and then received her first communion the next year, along with Madeleine and fourteen others.[119]

The legal basis according to which Horner sent Casimir to Réunion and to a penitentiary must have been that Casimir was under French, not Zanzibari, authority as a member of the mission community. According to Zanzibari law, he was no doubt a slave of the mission, but the French state, officially at least, would not have recognized that relationship after 1848. If he was still considered a child, then perhaps that was the basis of Horner's power over him in French law. There is no evidence, however, that the legal status of the act was considered at all, and Horner's action shows he presumed that Casimir remained under his control. No one apparently contested that presumption.

Needless to say, *this* story did not find its way into reports for donor agencies as had Casimir's earlier enthusiasm for the mission's practice of ransoming slave children. It was for the mission journal and superiors in Paris only. Instead of prompting pious support in donors faraway, it was for select consumption. It represented the Spiritans' worst nightmare: the oldest children at the mission, among those longest under missionary tutelage, showing by their behavior that the enclosed and regulated spaces, the rigorous timetables, the careful liturgical

117. CSSp 196bii: Baur to Schwindenhammer, 9ii66; Zanzibar journal, 3–4ii66.
118. CSSp 196bii: Horner to Schwindenhammer, 25vi66. If Josephine was indeed only seven when she came to the mission, then Horner is being disingenuous, probably wanting to blame troubles at the mission on the children whose arrival preceded the Spiritans' own.
119. Zanzibar sacramental registry, 20v66, 7vii67; CSSp 196bii: Baur to Schwindenhammer, 11viii67.

practices, and the education and industrial training had not formed the ideal Christians desired. Fortunately for the missionaries, Casimir and Josephine were the exceptions, at least for a while. But their actions showed that responses to Holy Ghost evangelization could already disappoint and alarm the missionaries, with dramatic change possible in at least one individual over time.

One might imagine that incarceration at Réunion ended Casimir's relationship with the Catholic mission, but such was not the case. When he returned to Zanzibar is not exactly clear, but on an 1870 journey to Ukami, a region inland from Bagamoyo, Casimir again accompanied the Spiritans, as he had when Baur had gone over the coast in 1865. The caravan visited the king who invited them, finding him ill with paralysis. Here Casimir appeared in the record: "The strong hand of Casimir, a robust boy who accompanied us, soon raised the skin of the arms of Kingaru, and the royal nerves were reanimated."[120] Apparently he left the mission soon after, for in 1873 he came to Bagamoyo as a soldier with the expedition of a famous British explorer, Lieutenant V. L. Cameron. While at Bagamoyo, apparently, he assaulted the mission's children for showing him insufficient respect. He then fled Cameron's caravan after being accused of theft. Later in 1882 he turned up at one of the Spiritan missions in the interior as a soldier for the sultan, visiting several times in a way that suggested a cordial relationship. Finally in 1884, the new bishop of Zanguebar, Courmont, arrived to find Casimir, whom Courmont says, "had left the mission four years ago," present among those whom he met at the dock.[121]

Others among the older "mission children" appeared intermittently in the Spiritan writings from Zanzibar in those early years. One of the children who worked at the forge, Alfred, moved back and forth between Zanzibar and Réunion several times. Perhaps he was the other unnamed boy in the earlier report by Horner, in which Casimir appears so prescient. The other boy, Horner wrote, requested the ransoming of a big boy who could help him with the hammer at the forge.[122] Another, Charles Denis, had been part of a voyage of the explorer Baron de Decken, which ended in the German's death in 1862. Like Alfred, he too had come to the mission while it was under Fava's administration.[123] Many other names appeared in the sacramental books as sponsors for baptisms of the other children who came to the mission, names that would continue to feature over the next few decades of Catholic life in eastern Africa.

---

120. MC 5 (1873), 622. Casimir may have returned to Zanzibar in December 1867, for Horner returned from Réunion at that time with two of the mission children who, the journal at Zanzibar reads, "were in Bourbon for various reasons" (Zanzibar journal, 1xii67).

121. CSSp 196biii: Scheuermann to Horner, 8iv73; Mhonda journal, 15iv82, 26vi82, 28vi82, 22viii82, 28x82; CSSp 198b, Courmont, 30iii84.

122. CSSp 196axii: Horner to Holy Childhood, 16xi63.

123. It may well be that these are the same person. Zanzibar's baptismal registry records a Charles Denis baptized around the age of twelve in 1862. He was a frequent sponsor for baptisms at Zanzibar in the 1860s. Later there was a prominent mission resident at Bagamoyo named Charles-Alfred, to be mentioned in the chapters ahead. Many names are used for more than one child, so keeping them straight is often difficult. On Alfred, see the Zanzibar journal, 7x64, 17iii66.

In considering the few glimpses of the Africans at the mission within the historical record to this point, it is worth noticing that many appeared when Horner was away from Zanzibar. Horner's absences meant that Baur communicated with Paris in the expected reports and regular updates, and his writings created new possibilities for historical understanding. He also kept Horner apprised of the mission's state. The younger man's letters contained fewer complaints about personnel and Paris's decisions — he was, after all, not the superior — and much more willingness to betray his own frustration and uncertainty about how to proceed with the mission's children. He recorded, for example, Casimir's escape. Later, writing to Horner in March 1867, Baur mentioned the other mission children's misbehavior when not supervised and noted that the Holy Ghost brothers did not understand the need for surveillance.[124]

A few months later Baur wrote Horner again, telling of pressure he faced from some of the older children who wanted to marry.[125] He acquiesced to their pleading, and the first eastern African Catholic marriages in modern times took place on September 2, 1867. They paired those whom Baur claimed were the four oldest boys in the mission at Zanzibar with the four oldest girls. Most had probably received their first communion only a few weeks earlier. To house them, Baur rented another residence, thus establishing a new Christian community of Africans in Zanzibar apart from the orphanages or dormitories for the other children.[126] These couples continued to work in the workshops of the mission at Zanzibar, and Baur praised their piety and faithfulness.[127] Later some served as first residents of the Christian village at Bagamoyo, while others remained at Zanzibar for years.

One wonders, however, whether the mission's children would have been so bold to push for permission to marry had Horner been present, and whether Horner would have agreed to their request. When Horner wrote that Baur overreacted to Casimir's escape, he underscored his own experiences with Africans, contrasting it with Baur's callowness and sensitivity. The fact that the marriages

---

124. CSSp 196bii: Baur to Horner, 30iii67.

125. CSSp 196bii: Baur to Horner, 14v67.

126. Zanzibar journal, 5viii67, 2ix67; CSSp 196ii: Baur to Schwindenhammer, 11viii67, 13x67; BG 5:826f; BG 6:293f. Unfortunately, the book recording marriages at Zanzibar in this period is lost, and only the names of the boys were listed in the Zanzibar journal: Athanase, Louis, Charles, and Edward (5vii67). Boys with the first two names were baptized in 1862 (Zanzibar sacramental registry: Athanase, 8xii62, age thirteen; Louis, 11v62, age ten). Athanase and Louis also served as sponsors often in the mid-1860s (ibid., 28viii64, 17ix65, 31x65, 20v66). Louis reappears in the next chapter. Due to a later entry in the baptismal record it is clear that the Charles who married was not the Charles (or Charles-Alfred) mentioned earlier, but Charles Malberouzi, baptized at Zanzibar only in 1867 (ibid., 8vi67, age nineteen; Zanzibar journal, 8vi67). He is also the only one whose wife is identified. He and his wife, Henriette, the first African baptized at Zanzibar, soon had a child, Marie-Joseph, who was baptized in May 1868. Edward is harder to identify, since there are several people baptized with that name in the 1860s.

127. CSSp 196bii: Baur to Schwindenhammer, 13x67, 6v68; BG 6:616f. Baur continued to call those who lived at the mission "children" until his death in 1913 (CSSp 194aii: Mauberge 1882). Since it is burdensome to keep placing the term in quotes, I will use "children" to refer to the former slaves who make their home at the mission, whatever their age. When I want to draw attention to their age I will specify them as adults or not.

occurred when Horner was away raises the possibility that Baur was not only more sensitive to African refusal to go along with the missionary program, as in the case of Casimir, but also more open to African requests for greater autonomy than Horner. Evidence that Baur was, in comparison to Horner, less strict might also be found in an 1873 upsurge in African escapes from the mission, to be described in the next chapter. These also occurred when Horner was away and Baur was in charge. Though in the 1880s, as we shall see, Baur showed a great deal of firmness before African demands for reforms, before that he looked more willing to countenance African desires than Horner. Perhaps the escape of Josephine and Casimir — which apparently disturbed him more than Horner — encouraged him to accept the requests to marry of the eight oldest children at the mission. He might well have been anxious to avoid a larger debacle and sought to domesticate, quite literally, the children's desires.

•

All who came to the Catholic mission at Zanzibar adapted in their own way to the circumstances in which they found themselves, and very little about those processes can be recovered with certainty.

Admitting the hidden nature of African adaptations to the mission, the Spiritans nonetheless recorded glimpses of African behavior that approximated what Hirschman called exit, loyalty, and voice. These actions indicated that some sense of a moral economy was developing at the mission. Casimir's case is particularly suggestive in light of these categories, since he seems to have embodied all three of Hirschman's options. He showed what the missionaries felt was loyalty already in late 1863, by his desire to ransom other children. His service as a baptismal sponsor and Baur's inclusion of him on the voyage to the mainland in 1865 confirmed that the Spiritans sensed Casimir's loyalty. His effort to have Horner ransom older children epitomized what Hirschman calls voice, inasmuch as Casimir sought to change the conditions in which he found himself. Finally, he attempted to flee the mission to which he had once shown some commitment, opting for exit, a choice suggesting that he no longer saw efforts at voice to be so promising. Yet his return to the mission after his incarceration suggests some degree of ongoing loyalty. His attachment, even if thin, remained into the 1880s.

Casimir and Josephine had both been enslaved at the coast prior to coming to the mission. Unlike most of those at the mission, they had thus been socialized to some degree into the Swahili world before coming into Spiritan hands. Horner claimed they were "too old to be formed," while Baur said that Casimir was "the first boy who had come to the mission." Josephine apparently had been old enough to attract the sexual attentions of her mistress's husband, or at least to arouse the jealousy of the mistress. Prior to coming to the mission both had lived in something like a patron-client relationship with their master or mistress. Probably the missionaries assumed the place of patrons in their own imagination when they arrived. In this, too, they differed from the other mission children, for whom the paternalistic and maternalistic images that the Spiritans used to define their role might have had more appeal.

Casimir and Josephine initially experienced evangelization at Zanzibar — the practices of work, education, and prayer, enclosure, and timetables — in light of those prior experiences. They pursued their interests and were anxious to get along. If they were like those whom Goffman observed in total institutions, they joined the other children at the mission in adapting to the new environment through adjustments of their behaviors. Judging from Horner's description of Casimir as someone adept at pretense, he likely generated some sort of a double sense of himself, a strategy Goffman found typical in total institutions. He developed both a "public self" that sought to satisfy the missionaries and a coexisting personal sphere outside of the missionaries' purview.[128]

Horner's 1863 report indicated that Casimir reacted to the possibility of new labor as one might expect, given predictable hopes that his own labor might be lessened by newly ransomed children. He was working hard in the workshop where he had been for two years already. He wanted his monies used to ransom someone who could lessen his burden, not a small child who could offer no help. His voice was probably articulated within the context of his own preferences for less demanding work. That voice also had a pious cast in line with missionary hopes, which is how Horner seems to have heard it, but one can also discern very pragmatic interests at work. The Spiritans discerned in Casimir an incipient loyalty, hence Casimir's participation as a baptismal sponsor and later as assistant on Baur's journey to the mainland.

Lacking direct evidence about their state of mind, we cannot know in any definitive way what led Casimir and Josephine to try and escape. Their flight indicated their dissatisfaction with their circumstances at Zanzibar, but it is very difficult to make sense of that dissatisfaction because their sense of themselves cannot be grasped with much confidence. Baur wrote of "the passions under the skin of Cham," and remarked that large *caffres* caused trouble, desiring "to breathe the pestilential air of liberty."[129] The two may have wanted to elope, or felt angry at their treatment, or they saw a chance at a new life. They may simply have sought some privacy to pursue sexual intimacy, even temporarily. Yet something made Casimir go from a willing contributor to ransoming others — even though he wanted them big, so they could help him work! — to a violence-threatening escapee. And Josephine, baptized at Zanzibar five years before and with the sisters most of the days since, also fled.

The sparse evidence cannot answer important questions with any certainty, but it can allow educated inferences. One wonders the extent to which Casimir and Josephine continued to think of themselves as slaves, *watumwa*, in the sense of other slaves at the Swahili coast. How had five years within the liturgical, educational, and labor regime of the mission changed their self-identity? The

---

128. Goffman 1961, 54ff.
129. CSSp 196bii: Baur to Schwindenhammer, 9ii66.

Spiritans who discerned loyalty in these two young people and accorded them responsibility within the life of the mission were not blind or naive. Maybe after five years of more or less enthusiastic participation at the mission, however, Casimir and Josephine concluded that the Spiritan program, with its strict regime of enclosure and its growing emphasis on labor, constricted their future. Recall that Hirschman related his options to one another dialectically, so that voice becomes the regular response of those who develop loyalty, while it can be the only option when exit is not possible. And if exit is too easy, then voice does not develop. Perhaps Casimir and Josephine fled because they concluded that exit was their best recourse. The mission offered no possibility for the exercise of voice to ameliorate their circumstances.

Did their flight indicate a desire to leave the mission forever, or did they simply seek some privacy? As Glassman suggests of fleeing slaves, most did so not to leave forever but to return with concessions made, so that their circumstances within it would be better. The aftermath suggests that some sort of loyalty had been forged in Casimir and Josephine. Their return to the mission and the later confidence shown by their participation — Casimir's later accompaniment of another caravan to the interior and Josephine's role as a sponsor — indicate the mission's abiding effect on them. That Casimir was still present to some degree into the 1880s means that slave evangelization forged some connection in him.

Others among the mission's children were also internalizing their own moral economy of the mission. To this point in the telling of this story, however, most of the children of the mission were, in fact, children. Their capacity for exit or voice, and their ability to articulate their frustration at any unfulfilled expectations of the moral economy of the mission, was small. That would change, as we shall see, for in the years to come, the historical record showed an increasingly wide range of responses to the mission's message. Casimir and Josephine thus anticipated the responses to come. Changing African voices, as they can be discerned in the historical archive, reveal the shape of the developing moral economy of the mission, the set of presumptive opinions and values that the former slaves produced and internalized in the context of missionary evangelization. Thus were Catholics emerging, and thus was the Catholic Church being born in eastern Africa.

Chapter Four

Claiming La Grande Terre *for Christ*
The Move to Bagamoyo, 1868–77

Timeline

1868	March 4: Horner and Machon open the mission at Bagamoyo.
	July 16: Blessing and dedication of the Bagamoyo mission property.
	December 10: Horner brings fifty boys from Zanzibar to Bagamoyo.
1869	Opening of the Suez Canal eases travel from Europe to eastern Africa.
	April–August: Bagamoyo land disputes.
	Before December: Beginning of the minor seminary at Zanzibar.
	November 4: Forty-six girls of the Zanzibar mission transfer to Bagamoyo.
1870	February 17: Twelve *latinistes* move to Bagamoyo with Father Duparquet.
	June 6–20: First chapter of the Spiritans in eastern Africa at Zanzibar.
	August 11–September 22: Visit to Ukami by Horner, Baur, and Duparquet.
	October 7: Death of Sultan Majid, followed by accession of his brother, Barghash.
	November 1: Sisters' novitiate begins with six girls at Bagamoyo.
1870–71	Franco-Prussian War and subsequent Commune in France.
1871	January: Beginning of construction of the Christian village at Bagamoyo.

February 5: Henry Morton Stanley visits Bagamoyo mission for the first time.

March 11: Baur goes to Europe for the first time since 1863, returning January 9, 1872.

July 10: Death of Bishop Maupoint of Réunion.

1872   April 5: Hurricane destroys the Bagamoyo mission.

April 30: Death of Brother Isaac Guillerme, first Spiritan to die in eastern Africa.

May 24: Seminarians return to Zanzibar from Bagamoyo.

September: Horner named apostolic vice-prefect of the Zanguebar mission.

October 25: Sultan Barghash visits Bagamoyo.

1873   February: Horner ill, leaves for Europe, traveling with Ferdinand (later Philippe).

January: Sir Bartle Frere arrives in eastern Africa sponsored by the British Parliament.

March 17: Frere visits the Bagamoyo mission.

June: Slave market in Zanzibar closed.

1874   February 24: Body of famous missionary/explorer David Livingstone arrives at Bagamoyo.

Sisters' novitiate moved from Bagamoyo to Zanzibar.

June: Horner arrives and moves to Zanzibar, while Baur goes to Bagamoyo.

1875   July: Horner to Europe, brings African candidates Benoît and Joseph with him.

December: Three sisters' novices killed in accident at Zanzibar. Horner returns from Europe.

1876   February: Horner dismisses most seminarians at Zanzibar. Julien and Dieudonné (or Isidore) leave for France and the novitiate, arriving March 18.

July or August: Baur visits Freretown, the CMS mission near Mombasa.

Summer: Horner at Réunion.

October/November: Death of Benoît and Joseph (Godfrey and Aureline) in France.

December: Julien and Dieudonné return from France.

1877   Suéma/Madeleine and two other girls go from Zanzibar to the sisters' novitiate at Réunion.

June: Patrice returns from France.

August: Latin discontinued at Zanzibar.

August 1–20: Visit to choose Mhonda by Horner, Baur, and Brother Oscar Schwedding.

Horner returns to enter the new hospital at Zanzibar as its first patient.

October 18: Caravan leaves for Mhonda, mobilized by Protestant plans.

November 5: Arrival at Mhonda.

The Spiritans at Zanzibar and Bagamoyo:
A Reputation for Practical Evangelization

Spiritan efforts at Zanzibar and Bagamoyo to form Catholics from the slaves they took in drew considerable praise from nineteenth-century Western observers. In *How I Found Livingstone*, Henry Morton Stanley lauded the work at the two missions of "the French missionaries":

> The French missionaries [the Spiritans] have proceeded actively to work in a true practical spirit. They not only endeavour to instil into the minds of their numerous converts the principles of religion, but also to educate them in the business of life. They teach their young disciples various useful trades; they produce agriculturalists, carpenters, blacksmiths, boat-builders, and mechanical engineers among them. Their various departments of instruction have able, efficient, and laborious teachers. Their shops at Zanzibar form one of the sights which a stranger would wish to see. At Bagamoyo, on the mainland, their mission station is on an extensive scale. The estate adjoining the mission station, cultivated by their young pupils, is a model of industry; and the products serve to more than support the institution with all the necessaries of life. The converts and pupils they are educating exceed more than two hundred.... There are some ten padres engaged in the establishment, and as many sisters, and all find plenty of occupation in educing from native crania the fire of intelligence. Truth compels me to state that they are very successful, having over two hundred pupils, boys and girls, in the Mission, and, from the oldest to the youngest, they show the impress of the useful education they have received.[1]

---

1. H. M. Stanley 1872, 43–44.

142 Claiming La Grande Terre for Christ

A common feature of such praise was what Stanley called the Spiritans' "practical spirit." This practical approach was contrasted with Protestant missionary activity, characterized as "attempts to make gentlemen" or work for "conversion." In a later work, for example, Stanley belittled Anglican efforts as follows:

> Instead of attempting to develop the qualities of this practical human being, [the missionary] instantly attempts his transformation by expounding to him the dogmas of the Christian Faith, the doctrine of transubstantiation and other difficult subjects, before the barbarian has had time to articulate his necessities and to explain to him that he is a frail creature requiring to be fed with bread, and not with a stone.[2]

Sir Bartle Frere disparaged in similar terms the work of the Anglican Church Mission Society (CMS[3]) in his report to the British Parliament after his 1873 visit to the region to stop the slave trade: "It has been longer at work, with less apparent result, than any mission on the coast."

Of the Anglican UMCA mission at Zanzibar not far from the Spiritans, Frere wrote, "If I might presume to advise the Bishop and the missionaries, I would introduce a far larger industrial element in their schools." A similar judgment fell on the Methodists in Kenya: ". . . [T]he most conspicuous defect seemed to me the want of a larger admixture of the industrial element, of more direct teaching how to live in this world, as well as how to prepare for that which is to come."

In contrast, Frere lauded the Catholic mission at Bagamoyo, suggesting

> . . . no change in the general arrangements of the institution, with any view to increase its efficiency as an industrial and civilizing agency, and in that point of view I would recommend it as a model to be followed in any attempt to civilize or evangelize Africa.[4]

This chapter describes slave evangelization in the years following the move to Bagamoyo in March 1868 until the establishment of the first mission in the interior in late 1877. This nine-year span saw considerable transformation in the Catholic mission in eastern Africa. Bagamoyo quickly eclipsed Zanzibar, becoming a larger center for Catholic evangelization than the original mission. Its renowned practical approach made it a showpiece of the missions in eastern Africa for Catholics as well as other visitors.

The move to the mainland, however, meant more than an expansion in scope. Despite reports from the Spiritans and others that suggested a single model with freed slaves in which evangelizing and civilizing went together, the history of Spiritan slave evangelization and its practical program followed no blueprint.

---

2. Stanley 1878, 80.
3. The UMCA mission at Zanzibar represented so-called high-church or Anglo-Catholic Anglican missionary interests, while the CMS represented evangelical or low-church Anglicans.
4. Frere 1873, 121–23; also cited in Bennett 1964, 161. As late as 1896, observers still complained of the lack of industrial training at UMCA missions (Small 1980, 45). For further examples and contrasting estimates of Catholic and Protestant missions, see Kollman 2001, 212ff.

Instead, the move from Zanzibar to Bagamoyo occasioned different emphases and considerable evolution in Spiritan activities and discourse, even though expressed principles remained constant. New aspects of Spiritan missionary work at Bagamoyo included institutions such as the Christian village and the seminary, both implemented as the Spiritans developed their program on the mainland.

In addition, the Bagamoyo mission featured new approaches to space and labor in evangelization. Zanzibar had already witnessed spatial and laboring practices that simultaneously relied on both theological and sociological assumptions, with missionary goals being both formative and financial. This doubled approach only deepened at Bagamoyo, and also took on new facets that located the Spiritans even more firmly in Europe's evolving practical social theory. The new features manifested in the move from Zanzibar to Bagamoyo drew upon profound theological commitments as well as a single but not undifferentiated tradition of social disciplining in nineteenth-century France, one that in practice was amenable to, but not identical with, theological foundations. Understanding those developments both sharpens our appreciation for the missionaries and allows greater insight into the diverse African appropriations of slave evangelization.

The Missionary Foundation at Bagamoyo

As he looked forward to the move to the mainland in late 1867 and early 1868, Horner's evident pride in the Spiritan mission did not keep him from admitting that Zanzibar failed to provide the circumstances for the ambitious program he foresaw:

> It is not possible for us to keep all our children with us at Zanzibar. The upkeep in the town is too costly and we lack work to occupy all of them. ... And yet to abandon them to themselves in the midst of this Muslim population would be to expose to loss all the fruit of their Christian education. To avoid this great evil, I had the thought of founding at Bagamoyo an agricultural colony [*colonie agricole*].[5]

The town of Bagamoyo, believed by some to mean "to lay down one's heart,"[6] sat across the sea a three hours' trip by dhow — *un boutre* in French, the sailing

---

    5. Versteijnen 1968b, 7. See also CSSp 196ax: Horner to Propagation of the Faith, 29xii67; CSSp 195aii: Horner to Barnabo, 25i68; MC(1), 65–67.

    6. The meaning of Bagamoyo has generated a great deal of discussion. The KiSwahili verb *kubwaga* means "to throw off" and *moyo* means "heart," but the name could indicate, among other hypotheses, the relief felt by caravan personnel upon arriving at the coast, or the lament of slaves upon reaching their destination. The Spiritans also offered different meanings, with Baur and Horner suggesting "into the heart," while Courmont offered "rest your heart" (CSSp 196ax: Horner to Propagation of the Faith, 4iii69; MC 14 [1882], 194–95; MC 17 [1885], 548). See the following for discussion of the meaning of the word: Brown 1971a, 3ff; Donovan 1978, 2f. According to John Henschel, in 1884 Bagamoyo had around five thousand inhabitants, among whom were two thousand local indigenous Africans, one thousand slaves, one thousand Shirazi, five hundred Arabs, and five hundred Indians. He estimates that ten thousand to twenty thousand porters arrived every year (Henschel n.d.A).

vessel so common at the Indian Ocean then and now — from Zanzibar to the coast. It was the closest caravan endpoint to Zanzibar itself and grew in importance with Zanzibar's trade in the nineteenth century. The permanent indigenous population numbered several thousand, but that number multiplied several times when caravans arrived with porters from the interior, bearing mostly ivory and slaves. To the Spiritans, it seemed to lack the large Muslim population of Zanzibar and possessed a less populated hinterland of promising fertility. It therefore offered the conditions for both of Horner's earnest hopes still unrealized at Zanzibar. First, he planned a large *colonie agricole* for the more thorough formation of the mission children as well as the financial health of the mission. Second, he foresaw the mainland mission as the site for a seminary to prepare indigenous clergy.

On March 3, 1868, Horner and Father Pierre Machon (1842–98), who came to Zanzibar in 1866, crossed to Bagamoyo to establish themselves. They settled in a primitive and vacated hut on the property that Fava, the founder of Zanzibar's mission, had earlier purchased.[7] Soon the Spiritans established the two new institutions Horner had envisioned to further their work of forming a *noyau* for the anticipated missions in the interior of eastern Africa.

Bagamoyo's Agricultural Colony

The Spiritans claimed to have chosen March as the month for establishing the mission at Bagamoyo to gain the help of St. Joseph, whose feast fell on March 19. As patron of workers, Joseph was the perfect symbol for the agricultural establishment Horner envisioned. On December 10, 1868, fifty boys from the orphanage at Zanzibar arrived at Bagamoyo, reversing the direction by which most had come from the mainland to the slave market and into missionary hands. This installment of the mission's children at Bagamoyo, like March's initial establishment, continued the pattern of connecting the mission's activities with the sacred calendar. The feast that day, Our Lady of Loretto, commemorated a miraculous medieval event when the house in which Jesus grew up appeared in Italy. This was a telling analogue to the beginning of the move of the center of the Spiritan mission in eastern Africa from Zanzibar to the mainland. Bagamoyo, too, was imagined as a place where holy families — composed of hard-working, now (or soon to be) Christian former slaves — might live, and from where they might go into the interior as Catholic colonizers.[8]

The boys settled into rudimentary dormitory-style living similar to Zanzibar, but on a site the Zanzibar chronicler described as "a better place to cultivate the

---

7. For details on the settling at Bagamoyo and the first months of the mission, see the following: Bagamoyo journal, 4iii68; Zanzibar journal, 4iii68, 8iv68, 10iv68, 16iv68, 19iv68, 27iv68, 7v68, 28v68, 5vi68, 23vii68, 21viii68, 19xi68, 25xi68; BG 6:623ff; APF 42 (1870), 49ff; MC 2 (1869), 3–5; Walker 1933, 148ff.

8. Bagamoyo journal 4iii68, 10xii68; Zanzibar journal, 10xii68.

land, and the hearts and minds of the children."[9] The missionaries established a daily schedule with five hours of work in the fields and about the same period in the classroom, interspersed with regular prayers and devotions. Their reports emphasized the harmony and order of the mission, with the boys happy learning and working in the fields. The timetable — a routine of labor, prayer, and instruction — furthered the clearing of the property of the mission as the agricultural colony took shape. Soon extensive areas were under cultivation.

The boys arose at 5:00 a.m. and went to prayer at 5:30, then to work "singing with great spirit," with a break for food at 9:00 a.m. Work followed until the late morning, unless it was very hot in which case there was schooling and chapel practice. At noon came lunch, followed by catechism and lessons, with work resuming in the afternoon at 3:30 until around 5:00 p.m. (perhaps later, according to some accounts), at which time there was supper, followed by evening prayers and sleep. "Such is the day for our Swahilis," wrote Horner, "shaping habits of regularity and a working life." With confidence, he informed the Propagation of the Faith, "This patriarchal life fits these small blacks perfectly, and carries them naturally to Christian civilization." He reported great progress.[10]

In November 1869, forty-six girls came to Bagamoyo from Zanzibar. The girls also settled into a dormitory and followed a daily schedule with about five hours of catechism or scholastic lessons directed by the sisters and an equal time of work in the fields. Sometime that year the Bagamoyo mission also began a creche to take in infants who were abandoned or whose parents could be convinced to sell them to the mission instead of committing infanticide.[11]

Besides working in the large plantations of the mission, each of the boys who first came to Bagamoyo also received his own garden to manage.[12] Whether the missionaries continued to allot each boy his own plot as the numbers grew in the years to come, and whether the girls who came received such a plot, is unclear. Regardless, agricultural labor constituted a large part of the day for the children at the two orphanages at Bagamoyo.

The Minor Seminary (Le petit séminaire)

Bagamoyo soon also housed Horner's second hope, a scholasticate or minor seminary program. The formation of indigenous clergy stood at the center of the

---

9. Zanzibar journal, 10xii68.

10. CSSp 196ax: Horner to Propagation of the Faith, 4iii69, 29x69. There are many descriptions of the early life at Bagamoyo, for example: CSSp 196bii: Horner to Spasser, 11x68; ibid.: Horner to Schwindenhammer, 29xi68; BG 6:1009ff; CSSp 196axii: Horner to Holy Childhood Society, 15i69; CSSp 196axii: Horner to Gaume, 1vii69; CSSp 196bii: Horner to Collin, 12x68; ibid.: Machon, journal of Bagamoyo, 28vi69; APF 42 (1870), 49; APF 44 (1872), 416–26; MC 4 (1871), 32–33. Other descriptions include Brown 1971a, 213ff; Ricklin 1880, 327–28; Versteijnen 1968b, 17.

11. Bagamoyo journal, 4xi69; Zanzibar journal, 7xi69; BG 7:660f. Horner wrote the Propagation of the Faith that he had heard that the mission would be able to buy hundreds of children per year for the creche (CSSp 196ax: Horner to Propagation of the Faith, 4iii69). The children surviving in the creche then moved into the orphanages.

12. BG 6:1009ff; Zanzibar journal, iii69.

Figure 11. Panorama of the Bagamoyo mission, "the girls' side." From *Les Missions Catholiques* 7 (1875): 401.

missionary strategy of the Vatican and Libermann, and the Holy Ghost missionary in western Africa, Kobés, had made it a priority in his renowned mission.
The Spiritans in eastern Africa endorsed this goal wholeheartedly as part of their
vision of fully formed Christian communities planted in the interior. Already in
1866, Horner had optimistically reported that among the 128 children in primary
school at Zanzibar there were some future clergy, and by late 1867 he anticipated
the teaching of Latin to the brighter boys. Envisioned as an agricultural colony,
Bagamoyo also promised to be, in Horner's words, "a nursery for indigenous
priests." Training indigenous clergy not only fulfilled the expectations in their
official missionary strategy, but reflected Spiritan assumptions about Africa's
climate, which was seen to be dangerous for outsiders. They imagined that indigenous priests would fare much better than European missionaries as "evangelizers
of those suffering in the interior." Horner spoke of the minor seminary as the
chief hope for the mission's future.[13]

Some time in 1868, after the March foundation at Bagamoyo but before the
December move of the agricultural section of the boys to the mainland, the Spiritans at Zanzibar established a special educational program for those young men
whose intellectual gifts indicated that they might have the promise to be future

13. See the following for such references: Kieran 1966, 134; CSSp 196ax: Horner to Propagation
of the Faith, 31xii66, 29xii67, 28x69; CSSp 196axii: Horner to Holy Childhood Society, 15i69,
29xii69; ibid.: Horner to Laverriere, 16vii75; Gaume 1872, 45ff. On Kobés, see APF 26 (1854): 449,
451. On Libermann's calls for rapid creation of an indigenous clergy, see Gay 1943, 132; Burke
1998, 59, 84–85.

Figure 12. Father Scheuermann with a group of mission children receiving their first communion. From the Spiritan photo archives, Paris.

clergy. In December, Father Antoine Scheuermann (1841–83), the first director of the seminary program, had four students in their own classroom with a distinctive curriculum. They had Scheuermann for their teacher and Latin in the curriculum, unlike the others who were instructed in French by less-educated sisters or brothers. The seminarians did physical work outside, a facet of the program reckoned healthful and also part of an explicit concern to keep these young men "simple," that is, unaccustomed to luxuries that would later burden the mission with unneeded expenses. But such work was less than that expected of the other children. Scheuermann soon bragged that their academic abilities equaled those of any similar students in Europe.[14]

Under the leadership of Scheuermann's replacement, Father Charles Duparquet (1830–88), the seminary, then with twelve students, moved to Bagamoyo in February 1870. Duparquet, well-educated, sought to strengthen the academic quality of the educational program at the seminary, asking for books from Paris to that end. He also established a Confraternity of the Holy Spirit for the *latinistes*, as the seminarians were called, as a way to unite them to the Congregation of the Holy Ghost. Such lay confraternities, social organizations designed to enhance the piety of ordinary Catholics, were common in nineteenth-century France, and this one had two goals: the sanctification of its members, in this case the seminarians, and the conversion of "the black race." In his letter enrolling the eight members,

14. MC 3 (1870), 307. See also CSSp 196bii; Horner to Collin, 12x68; BG 6:1015.

Duparquet listed their origins, using terms designating places, peoples, and/or languages mostly away from the coast. The Spiritans eagerly anticipated that the *latinistes* would become priests or brothers and assist them in evangelizing their places of origin.[15]

Duparquet also had a chamber (*chalet*) placed in the midst of the seminarians' sleeping quarters, from where he could observe (*surveillir*) their behavior. The program of enclosure at Zanzibar was thus supplemented by surreptitious direct supervision in the scholasticate.[16] The seminarians were not only separated from the other students, subjected to more demanding studies, and given less physical labor. They also were seen to need special surveillance. Duparquet and others who observed them sought signs of their suitability for their future role: seriousness at their studies, earnestness at prayer, and regularity of personal habits. Time and space were, if anything, more sharply regulated for them. If the program of spiritual formation resembled that in Europe (which is likely, though we lack records to confirm such an assumption), self-examinations of consciousness and regular confession featured prominently.[17]

Liturgy and Boundaries at Bagamoyo

Along with the specialized program for seminarians, the Spiritans continued to offer instruction for the other boys and girls at Bagamoyo as they had at Zanzibar. Catechism and other religious lessons accompanied basic arithmetic, reading, and writing lessons. In addition, the Spiritans organized splendid liturgical celebrations, especially at Christmas, the feast of Corpus Christi, and Holy Week, as well as on the occasions of papal pronouncements such as the appearance of the encyclical declaring papal infallibility, *Pastor Aeternus*, in 1871. The children learned to sing well enough to impress Henry Morton Stanley, who "was astonished to hear the sounds issue forth in such harmony from such woolly-headed youngsters." Liturgical practices, especially dramatic celebrations, reflected the goal of "causing the love and practice of our holy religion to enter strongly into their habits and manners."[18]

A few months after the Spiritan arrival at Bagamoyo, the missionaries carried out the first dedication liturgy of a new mission, a ritual they repeated at

---

15. Versteijnen 1968a, 44. Duparquet was already well known for work in French Guinea (MC 1 [1868], 14ff, 23ff), and he would later achieve renown as a missionary in central Africa (Gittins 1999a). For his reflections on the seminary, see BG 8:758ff; CSSp 196biii: Duparquet to Schwindenhammer, 12vi70; ibid., Duparquet to Peureux, 9viii70; ibid., Duparquet to Schwindenhammer, 9ix71; ibid., Duparquet to Barillec, 17vii71. When their conflict eventuated in Duparquet's departure, Horner accused Duparquet of taking books that belonged to the mission (CSSp 196biii: Horner to Schwindenhammer, 3vii72).

16. CSSp 196biii: Horner to Schwindenhammer, 15vi70; CSSp 196aix: Duparquet to Schwindenhammer, 18i72.

17. CSSp 106A, n.s. 2G11.2.

18. Stanley 1872, 44; MC 4 (1871), 76–77; BG 8:744, 762–63; BG 9:263; BG 10:721f; BG 11:705, 720, 735; BG 15:714, 741. The Bagamoyo journal often recorded intricate details about liturgies (e.g., iii69, 14xi69).

later missions established in the interior. The elaborate ceremony included the singing of the *Veni Creator*, Mass, a procession, blessings of still-rudimentary buildings, the marking of boundaries, and the firing of guns and cannons.[19] This event established a place for the church, marking a stage for the missionary progression from the coast inward and establishing an enclave within a non-Christian population. The choosing and marking off by separating, blessing, and naming enacted the practices of enclosure begun at Zanzibar in the new setting, further dramatizing the transition from the edge whence the Spiritans came into an enclosure they wanted to create. In the missionary imagination, such ceremonies established a bounded location for a future Catholic community composed of people properly formed, obedient, and supervised. They inaugurated a sacralized cosmos where time would be different, where souls and bodies could be contained and saved. The missionaries also established barriers against pollution, monitoring the boundaries between the mission and the outside world around Bagamoyo, as they had in Zanzibar's Stone Town. They tried to keep the children in the orphanages free from contamination so they could be formed into — and maintained as — effective Christian colonists of the interior.

Spiritan efforts at claiming and protecting what they saw as their property at Bagamoyo soon impinged on local understandings of land ownership and use, and conflicts erupted with their neighbors. Looking across from Zanzibar, Horner expressed confidence about the ease of obtaining land on the mainland, claiming that there "one takes land by possession as in the time of our [French] ancestors." Upon arriving in Bagamoyo, however, he found settlers on property supposedly allotted to the mission. In response he carried out what he called a coup, creating a path that forced their withdrawal. In July 1869, however, a crowd of the local people, the Wazaramo, appeared at the mission, threatening to seize land they claimed belonged to them. A fight was narrowly averted, and Sultan Majid, responding to the French consul, intervened on the mission's behalf. Horner recognized that the Wazaramo refused to accept Arab claims to allot land they considered their own. After the sultan paid a sum to calm local complaints, a meal at the mission with Arab and African elites ended the dispute over land for the time being.[20] These incidents revealed ongoing conflicts between local African elites and the Arab power emanating from Zanzibar, whose sway over the region around Bagamoyo required constant negotiation. They also showed

---

19. Bagamoyo journal, 16vii68; Mhonda journal, 5xi77; BG 6:1009f; CSSp 196ax: Le Roy to Propagation of the Faith, 15ix83. The *Veni Creator* was (and is) a Catholic Latin hymn asking for the blessing of the Holy Spirit, usually chosen to inaugurate a new work of some sort.

20. For Horner's confidence regarding land acquisition, see CSSp 196ax: Horner to Propagation of the Faith, 31xii66. On his coup upon arriving, see CSSp 196bii: Horner to Schwindenhammer, 10x68; BG 6:626, 1011; BG 7:270f; MC 2 (1869), 3–5. On the Wazaramo "invasion" and subsequent negotiations, see Bagamoyo journal, 14vii69, 22vii69, 7viii69, 26viii69; Zanzibar journal, 14vii69, 7viii69, 10viii69, 15viii69, 21viii69, 23viii69; CSSp 196bii: Horner to Schwindenhammer, 8x69, 19x69; ibid.: Baur to Schwindenhammer, 26viii69; CSSp 196ax: Horner to Gaume, 4iii69; MC 3 (1870), 299–301. Difficulties over land returned in 1871 and periodically thereafter (Kieran 1966, 228ff).

European misunderstandings of African land practices exemplified by most of the Spiritans.[21]

These difficulties did not diminish the fact that the new institutions at Bagamoyo fulfilled Horner's hopes. A Catholic presence had appeared on the mainland of eastern Africa for the first time in centuries. The move, however, also catalyzed disagreements among the Holy Ghost missionaries in the late 1860s, and Horner arranged a meeting in June 1870 to address the conflicts.

The Chapter of 1870

This meeting, convened at Zanzibar, came to be considered the first chapter of the Spiritan mission in eastern Africa.[22] Four of the five priests then serving in the region met for two weeks, discussing many aspects of their mission's activity. While Scheuermann remained at Bagamoyo, Horner, Baur, Duparquet, and Machon examined the new institutions at Bagamoyo and revisited abiding concerns since the original foundation.[23]

Already Horner had declared the seminary and Bagamoyo's agricultural work the keys for the future of the mission. In the aftermath of the chapter of 1870, those priorities only intensified, to the detriment of the hospitals and the workshops at Zanzibar. The chapter's deliberations described both of these older institutions as too expensive. They were also deemed ancillary to the *salut des âmes* (salvation of souls) for which the mission's benefactors such as the Society for the Propagation of the Faith sent their money. In response, the delegates entertained suppressing both in order to speed ahead the move into the interior.[24]

The discussion of Zanzibar's workshops at the chapter became heated due to personal disagreements between Horner and Baur. By early 1870, the two had quarreled over a number of issues, not least Horner's opinion that Baur's role as superior at Zanzibar led the younger man to infringe on his overall authority. Their interpersonal tension appeared in their correspondence as well as the chapter's proceedings six months later.[25] More substantively, they were in open disagreement about the value of the Bagamoyo mission, which Horner lauded but

---

21. As Walter Brown observes, the Spiritans were often unknowing participants in the longer struggle over land between Zanzibari and local peoples (Brown 1971a, 235ff).

22. Bagamoyo journal, 31v70. The word "chapter" in this context refers to meetings of religious congregations. They can be of many different types, but they usually have some sort of juridical power in the life of the congregation in question. In the Congregation of the Holy Ghost, the constitutions gave rules for such chapters, including the fact that only priests participated as full members and that freedom of speech was allowed (Kieran 1966, 68). The Spiritan priests had already had numerous formal meetings at Zanzibar to discuss their work before this, but usually for only one afternoon or evening. Those proceedings can be found in the Zanzibar journal, after 1866.

23. For details on the chapter's proceedings, see CSSp 196aiv: chapter of 1870 and BG 8:744f, as well as Kollman 2001, 321ff.

24. CSSp 195aii: Horner to Barnabo, 25i68; CSSp 196ax: Horner to Propagation of the Faith, 28x69; BG 8:751.

25. Baur had remained at Zanzibar while Horner directed Bagamoyo, and their conflict stemmed, in part at least, from the fact that all information, money, and supplies came from Zanzibar, subject to Baur's control, while Horner had all the official power. See Kollman 2001, 165, 324–27.

which Baur felt had few advantages over Zanzibar. The chapter had stated clearly that neither coastal site was appropriate for the evangelization of pagans, which all agreed was the fundamental goal of the mission. All present also accepted the impossibility of converting Muslims at the two present stations, declaring both Zanzibar and Bagamoyo preparatory works or staging areas for the more serious evangelization in the interior.

During the chapter Horner wrote the superior general in Paris, saying he had called the meeting in order to counter his confrere's condemnation of Bagamoyo and concomitant championing of the Zanzibar workshops, which made them too prominent in accounts of the mission. Horner admitted, "If I have too much dislike of the workshops, I admit this antipathy: I observe that pure industrial work breaks down the moral sense and leads to a failure of probity." It was, he claimed, "always prudent to keep at arm's length men of machines." His goal was to close the workshops in order to reach the interior more quickly, which was the chapter's ultimate recommendation. He even considered renting the Zanzibar mission house — in effect closing the mission there — in order to speed the move to the interior.[26]

The missionaries at the chapter of 1870 also carried on an extensive discussion of the education offered at the mission. They reaffirmed the need to separate the younger and older children as well as to keep the *latinistes* from the others, continuing the practices of partitioning that accompanied the strategy of enclosure. They insisted that all children must at least receive elementary academic instruction. Their reasoning revealed something of how they conceived of those in whom they vested their hopes: if simply sent to the fields without any instruction, the mission's children would receive treatment accorded slaves, something the missionaries insisted they were not. The priests present also discussed at length the curricula in both the primary school and the indigenous seminary, a discussion that invoked educational disputes very much alive in mid-nineteenth-century French Catholic circles. Finally, the chapter decided that Baur's French-Swahili catechism, published in 1867, was too full of errors to be useful, and they opted to use the French colonial catechism in their religious instruction.[27]

In one final important decision of the chapter of 1870, the Spiritans approved a program to form women religious, which began in November with six girls under the day-to-day direction of the sisters. Horner himself oversaw their formation, giving them a spiritual talk in French every day, something that he felt the sisters could not do.[28]

---

26. CSSp 196biii: Horner to Schwindenhammer, 15vi70, 8viii70, 12ix71.

27. See Kollman 2001, 323–24. The proceedings of the chapter of 1870 do not name the "errors" for which the catechism was rejected, but several features may have led to its rejection. In the first place, there are many grammatical errors, especially in the noun classes that are one of the features of Bantu languages like Swahili. Second, there are word choices that might have been controversial. Horner even spoke of Baur's work as having heresies, though he does not specify them (CSSp 196biii: Horner to Schwindenhammer, 15vi70). This may simply reflect their antagonism.

28. Bagamoyo journal, 1xi70; BG 8:760–61. Apparently there was already such a program at Zanzibar in June 1870, for Horner wrote that Madeleine, the putative narrator of *Suéma*, was at

St. Joseph Village

In addition to the agricultural colony and the programs of specialized formation for young men and women, the missionaries established another new
institution at Bagamoyo after the 1870 chapter. This was the Christian village,
where married Christians settled after completing school and other training at
the mission's orphanages. The weddings of 1867 at Zanzibar had created a small
settlement of married Christians within the town. This was a forerunner of the
larger village of married people on the mainland, which the Spiritans named after
St. Joseph. Established at Bagamoyo with the help of huts supplied by the British
consul, St. Joseph village began with eighteen couples in 1871, reaching forty
families by 1876.

Though it stood apart from the other mission buildings, about three hundred
yards from the Spiritan residence, St. Joseph village remained within the mission
property. It was thus separated from the surrounding pagan and Muslim populations, with movement in and out restricted at night as well as a curfew to keep the
villagers from untoward mingling with their non-Christian neighbors. The village
eventually had four streets, two pairs of parallel lanes crossing each other. At the
center stood a chapel and, later, a residence for the priest. Life in the village was
organized like the Spiritans' own religious community, with a bell marking time
and hours for meals, work, choir practice, free time, and common prayer. For
five days a week the villagers worked for the mission in its fields in exchange
for food and clothing, following a timetable resembling, though less strict than,
that at the orphanage. Each family also received its own land, a plot no doubt
larger than the small one given each of the boys in the orphanage in 1868. The
weekly schedule reserved Thursdays as a day when no work was required for the
mission, and on that day the villagers cultivated their own crops. Idleness with
one's land was not allowed; a plot not cultivated was given to another. A priest
was assigned to pastoral care of the villagers.[29]

In the broader missionary strategy for eastern Africa, Horner foresaw similar
villages at the interior stations, each composed of a *noyau* of former students
from the mission schools at Bagamoyo who would evangelize Africa's non-
Christian population. Such villages fulfilled several practical and strategic goals.
They represented safe places for the Christian couples formed at the orphanage
and the married couples already at Zanzibar, several of whom moved to the new
village. In the villages, such couples could raise their children as Catholics for,
as the Spiritan constitutions insisted, such villages represented the best way to
protect the Christians from surrounding threats to their faith and thus to build

---

"the novitiate" (Horner to Duparquet, 15vi70; Bouju, private communication). See Kollman 2001,
318–29.

29. On the village, see the following: Kieran 1966, 120ff; Kieran 1971, 25f; Versteijnen 1968a,
17–18; Brown 1971a, 217ff; CSSp 196bii: Horner to Spasser, 11x68; ibid.: Horner to Collin, 12x68;
Bagamoyo journal, 17i71, 19i71; CSSp 196biii: Horner to Schwindenhammer, 1vi71; CSSp 196axii:
Horner to Holy Childhood, 31xii77; CSSp 196axi: Baur to Propagation of the Faith, 15xi80; CSSp
194aii: Mauberge, 2ii83. See Kollman 2001, 318ff.

the church. The villages also allowed the Spiritans to promote domesticity on a European model, a particular feature of the formation and education offered to the girls by the sisters. At the same time, the missionaries imagined that the agricultural prosperity and the domestic ideals practiced by the Christian villagers would attract surrounding peoples to the Catholic mission.[30] Finally, the villages also became a place to put the adults received by the mission as well as the children in the orphanages who approached adulthood. The tight regime of work and discipline enacted in these institutions chafed those who were older than the majority of the residents, who were under fifteen years of age.

From Bagamoyo to the Interior

By the end of 1871, therefore, the Spiritans staffed two missions, one in Zanzibar and a newer and more elaborate venture in Bagamoyo. They oversaw two programs training potential leaders for the church of the future, each with a small number of students receiving specialized education for their anticipated responsibilities. Their orphanages housed 172 children in the elementary school and agricultural work section of the Bagamoyo mission, while a Christian village sat adjacent to the other buildings at Bagamoyo. In November 1870, the first coconut palms had been planted at Bagamoyo, and the missionaries dreamed of profits when the trees would begin bearing fruit, ideally eight years later. The British consul was sending the mission large numbers of slaves liberated from slave ships stopped in the Indian Ocean, responding to criticisms that sending them as so-called freed laborers to British possessions outside of Africa only perpetuated the slave trade.[31] The Spiritans tried to shape Catholics for the future colonization of the interior of Africa from these new arrivals, from others ransomed at Zanzibar and elsewhere, and from those already present. They saw their plan fulfilled when two couples went with the Spiritans to found the new mission at Mhonda in 1877.[32]

Given the constant refrains expressing their desire to move into the interior, the Mhonda foundation was a long time coming. Had the Spiritans been told that the new station would only appear in 1877, those at the chapter of 1870 would have been astounded at the delay. Only two months after the chapter ended, several missionaries visited a potential new mission site, prompted by the arrival at Bagamoyo of the sons of a chief in nearby Ukami (or *Oukami*). The sons came in a series of visits over a couple of days, carrying messages from their father inviting the missionaries to their territory. Though the site was finally judged unsatisfactory, nonetheless the visit encouraged Spiritan hopes for a move in the

30. Kieran 1966, 121.
31. BG 8:760–61.
32. BG 9:714ff; BG 11:125f, 730f; Zanzibar journal, 23ix77, 29ix77; Mhonda journal, 5xi77; MC 9 (1876), 604; MC 10 (1877), 189–91.

near future.[33] They could not anticipate, however, the difficulties to be faced in the years following. Though they sought to create an enclosed environment for the formation of the future Catholic colonists of the interior, the Spiritan program was anything but immune from surrounding realities, and the 1870s saw great changes of various sorts that hindered their expansion.

First, in 1870 Sultan Majid died, to be replaced by his brother and one-time rival Barghash, who never embraced the Catholic mission like his brother. Two years later, on April 15, 1872, a hurricane struck the coast, causing slight damage to the mission at Zanzibar but almost destroying the still-emerging Holy Ghost agricultural colony at Bagamoyo and its nearly fifty buildings.[34] The mission was rebuilt, but it took years to restore what was lost. Soon thereafter the first Spiritan brother died, and many fell after him beginning in 1872. Most likely the mortality increased because of Bagamoyo's rudimentary shelter and the demanding program of rebuilding.[35]

The hurricane hurt the economy of the entire region, weakening Barghash's grasp by decreasing trade and lessening his profits from duties levied on goods in and out of Zanzibar. This only made him more vulnerable the next year, when the British Parliament sent the aforementioned Sir Bartle Frere to eastern Africa to suppress the slave trade. His visit eventuated in the closing of the slave market at Zanzibar in 1873, only further weakening the sultan's financial situation. Frere's visit also placed the Holy Ghost missionaries in what Horner called a "delicate" position. Though not supporting slavery in a direct sense, the Spiritans recognized the convenience of the slave market for obtaining, in a Muslim environment, future Christians for the evangelization of the interior.[36] At the same time, however, they anxiously pursued friendly terms with all the principals involved. These included the sultan, who sought to resist British pressure and keep open the slave market, an important source of revenue for him and many other leading citizens of Zanzibar upon whose support he relied; the Englishman Frere and the acting British consul, John Kirk, who were committed to closing the slave market; and the French consul, Charles de Vienne, who, like the Spiritans, found himself in a difficult spot, at once no friend of the slave trade but also worried about undue British influence in the region should the slave market be closed, and thus who sought to support the sultan in the face of British pressure. Horner's absence at the time of Frere's visit meant that responsibility for negotiating these conflicting relationships fell to Baur, who attended meetings where the French consul failed

---

33. Bagamoyo journal, 17vii70, 21vii70, 24vii70, viii70; CSSp 195i: Horner to Maupoint, 8viii70; Horner 1873.

34. On the hurricane, see the following: MC 4 (1871–72), 370; APF 44 (1872), 416–26; BG 8:889; BG 9:271f; CSSp 196biii: Baur to Schwindenhammer, 16iv72; ibid.: Duparquet to Schwindenhammer, 16iv72; ibid.: Horner to Schwindenhammer, 22iv72.

35. BG 9:272; BG 11:695. Seven brothers and five sisters died at Bagamoyo between 1870 and 1877 (Versteijnen 1968a, 15; Henschel 2000a, 10ff). On the rebuilding of Bagamoyo, see the comprehensive discussion of the dates of construction in Vogt, n.d.

36. On Frere's visit to eastern Africa, see Coupland 1938, 184f; Gavin 1962; MC 5 (1873), 61–63; W. B. Anderson 1977, 9ff. For Spiritan reflection, see BG 9:271ff, 515–24.

to buttress Barghash sufficiently. Eventually the hard-pressed sultan capitulated to British demands.[37]

Frere visited the Catholic missions at both Zanzibar and Bagamoyo. Along with his fulsome praise of the Holy Ghost efforts, he gave two hundred pounds in support and promised to seek ongoing financial assistance for the mission from the British government. So impressed was Frere by the mission at Bagamoyo that he encouraged his country's naval officers to continue to turn those liberated over to the Catholic mission as well as to the Anglican (UMCA) mission in Zanzibar. Thus despite Spiritan concerns about losing their steady supply of potential converts from the slave market, Frere's visit in fact initially increased the number of slaves coming to the mission. Horner even found himself temporarily forced to request the British to send no more freed slaves to the Catholic missions due to overcrowding. Once the Anglican Church Missionary Society (CMS) followed Frere's suggestion and in 1874 established Freretown, their own colony for freed slaves near Mombasa, it became the destination for most freed by British interdiction.[38]

Spiritan ties to the church in Europe meant that changes outside the region itself also impinged upon their plans in these years. In particular, the aftermath of the Franco-Prussian war attenuated the financial support upon which the mission relied and heightened Spiritan concern for the mission's fiscal self-sufficiency.[39] The 1876 African conference presided over by Leopold II of Belgium signaled Europe's increasing interest in Africa, and many explorers came to eastern Africa in the 1870s. Changes in church policy also affected the Spiritans, disrupting older routines and forcing adjustments. The death of Bishop Maupoint of Réunion in 1871 meant that the Spiritans took direct control over their mission, and Horner was named vice-prefect apostolic of the apostolic prefecture of Zanguebar.[40]

The delay of the move into the interior did not mean the years before 1877 were idle ones. Despite the hurricane, Bagamoyo's fields took shape and the Spiritans solidified the operative regime at the mission: in the orphanages, the formation programs for future priests and nuns, and in the Christian village. Yet the many Spiritan illnesses and deaths in the years after the hurricane took their toll on Spiritan energies for expansion. Horner's health and congregational responsibilities took him to Europe several times in the 1870s, and his absences made concerted action difficult.[41] Then in 1875 the entire region waited in fear of

37. CSSp 196biii: Baur to Schwindenhammer, 11iv73; ibid., Baur to Horner, 7vi73, 4vii73; Bennett 1966, 1974; BG 9:515; MC 5 (1873), 327. For the Zanzibar Protestant mission's view of these events, see Wilson 1936, 31f.

38. On Frere's visits to the Holy Ghost missions, see Bagamoyo journal, 17iii73; BG 9:515, 809; CSSp 196biii: Scheuermann to Horner, 8iv73; Frere 1873; MC 5 (1873), 61–63, 234, 266f, 295, 327, 416–17, 428.

39. The Holy Ghost missionaries anticipated decreases in their funding after the war: CSSp 196biii: Horner to Schwindenhammer, 8x70, 28xii70.

40. On the death of Maupoint and the passing of authority into Spiritan hands, see MC 4, 1871: 18–19, 659–60; BG 9:118. The official documents can be found in CSSp 195iv.

41. On the outbreaks of disease at Zanzibar and Bagamoyo, see Kieran 1966, 184–85, and Kollman 2001, 232. On Spiritan deaths, see Versteijnen 1968a, 15; Comerford 1978; Henschel 2000a.

an anticipated attack by a nearby band of Wazaramo raiders. The sultan's show of force kept them from attacking Bagamoyo town, but in anticipation the mission armed itself.[42]

Through it all, Bagamoyo steadily regained what had been lost due to the hurricane. There the Spiritans welcomed the corpse of the famous explorer and missionary David Livingstone, carried hundreds of miles from the interior to be sent to Westminster Abbey. They also struggled to master KiSwahili, preparing a limited grammar.[43] In the end, though Horner and the others longed to move to the interior, only the imminent move of Protestants into the area around Mhonda finally mobilized them to effect the new foundation, for Horner spoke of the shame if Protestants had arrived there before Catholics.[44] They were plenty occupied at Zanzibar and especially Bagamoyo, which grew into what a British observer in 1877 called "a flourishing mission" set on a "splendid estate."[45]

The Spiritan Strategy at Bagamoyo

"Notre Dame de Bagamoyo" is situated about a mile and a half north of Bagamoyo. . . . Thrift, order, and that peculiar style of neatness common to the French are its characteristics. The cocoa-nut palm, orange, and mango flourish in this pious settlement, while a variety of garden vegetables and grain are cultivated in the fields; and broad roads, cleanly kept, traverse the estate.   (Henry Morton Stanley 1878, 79)

In July 1871, Horner made a very revealing request from Bagamoyo to the Spiritan mother house in Paris. He asked for clarifications about the Catholic liturgical calendar, a common enough subject for missionaries who valued the ways liturgical prayer forged spiritual connections with the hierarchical church in Rome and their congregation in Paris. The question in this case was unusual, however, for it concerned more than how to remain in proper relation to ecclesiastical authority. Instead, Horner sought permission to take advantage of a discrepancy between liturgical theologians about obligatory feasts. He wanted to follow the opinion that allowed fewer rather than more such observances. Horner wrote of the lengthier list, the one from which he sought dispensation: "Such a multiplication of feasts is a heavy burden to a poor mission like ours, which relies on freed slaves who live by the work of their hands." Horner sought to interpret the church's laws in such a way as to harness the labor of the former slaves at

42. On the near-attack, see BG 10:724; MC 6 (1875), 521; Brown 1971a, 270–71.

43. See Kollman 2001; the grammar is Daull 1879.

44. BG 11:125, 730; Zanzibar journal, 19ix77; CSSp 196biv: Baur to Schwindenhammer, 7ii77 and 7v77; ibid., Horner to Schwindenhammer, 24viii77, 20ix77, 18x77, 13xii77 ("the English were prowling around like lions"); CSSp 196ax: Horner to Propagation of the Faith, 31xii77; MC 9 (1877), 604. In fact, there were already Protestant missions away from the coast, though not in the areas inland from Bagamoyo (UMCA 1876).

45. The observer was Arthur Dodgshun (1847–1879), whose journal has been edited by historian Norman Bennett (Bennett 1969, 22–23, 77).

the mission in good conscience, lessening the time allotted to liturgical prayer and holidays and allowing more hours for Bagamoyo's fields.[46]

A second letter to Paris not long after Horner's request exemplified a second overriding missionary concern of those years: the concern for proper milieus in the formation of the mission's children. In early 1872, Father Charles Duparquet wrote his Paris superiors about the location of the seminary program. Maintaining his suspicion of Bagamoyo voiced at the chapter of 1870, Baur had urged that the *latinistes* should return to Zanzibar while he was in Paris in 1871. In response to the mother house's second-guessing prompted by Baur, Duparquet — who had already endorsed the mainland's healthy climate and was now directing the seminary — wrote to defend the present setting at Bagamoyo.[47]

Duparquet's reasoning betrayed his and his confreres' immersion in nineteenth-century European arguments about the importance of environment in fostering personal reform. Eloquently he argued that Zanzibar's stifling urban setting, with less space, air, and sun than Bagamoyo, represented a poor location for the ambitious task of forming seminarians. Citing a famous 1851 treatise on education by a noted French Catholic educator, Bishop Felix Dupanloup, Duparquet warned that so-called confined children suffer and become sad, melancholy, solitary, and "inclined to impurity."[48] Against what he called this *régime cellulaire*, Dupanloup had praised the effects of exercise and manual work in the open air. He praised the uncluttered atmosphere at the mainland coast for moral and hygienic reasons, extolling the effects of seminary formation in open spaces in France, too, as opposed to the confining regimes at some of the seminaries there.

Duparquet's elaborate arguments and Horner's unusual request highlighted two aspects of the Spiritan strategy enacted at Bagamoyo that distinguished it from the program underway at Zanzibar. First, at Bagamoyo the Spiritans practiced a new approach to space, revealing both a close attention to formative milieus and also their embrace of a different emphasis within the evolution of penitential practices in Europe. Second, at Bagamoyo, the Spiritans showed a heightened awareness of labor's economic value within the missionary strategy.

The New Place of Formation: Climate and Space in Bagamoyo's Milieu

From the beginning, the Spiritans held convictions about the role of surroundings in the proper formation of persons, believing that Africans could be changed through the right practices within the right environment. Two features of such environments drew heightened attention from the Spiritans after the move to

---

46. CSSp 196biii: Horner to Schwindenhammer, 1vii71, 12vii71. Horner noted a disagreement between theologians whom he named as Gury and Ballerini, and he wanted to follow the former. The indult (church permission) was received (BG 9:535).

47. CSSp 196biii: Duparquet to Schwindenhammer, 31i70; CSSp 196aix: Duparquet to Schwindenhammer, 18i72. Scheuermann, too, feared a move of the scholasticate back to Zanzibar, believing that all the seminarians would leave and marry if it occurred (CSSp 196biii: Scheuermann to Schwindenhammer, 26i72). See Kollman 2001, 368ff.

48. On Dupanloup, see McManners 1972, 28ff.

Bagamoyo: the climate and the arrangement of space. Their references to both reflected their nineteenth-century French roots.

Slave evangelization reflected Spiritan exposure to the effects of early environmentalism and developing ecological consciousness in eighteenth- and nineteenth-century Europe, and especially in France. Recent studies of these trends underscore the growing fascination with weather and the ways it shaped species. As part of this trend, the word *milieu* came to denote an environment that was proper for a certain species, as scientists gathering species from around the world developed sophisticated theories of acclimation. Yet biology was not the only realm in which this discourse of acclimation operated, for nineteenth-century French intellectuals linked human and nonhuman species so that ecology and social thought developed alongside each other. Thus the concern to shape the environment through control of landscapes went together with efforts to control society through social interventions.[49] The mid-nineteenth century witnessed a number of such interventions, what Paul Rabinow calls "experiments in social paternalism." Rabinow contends that by the 1860s, when the Spiritans arrived in Zanzibar, "French faith in progress [achievable through such interventions] was at its pinnacle."[50]

Though they would not share that faith in progress to the exclusion of super-human agency, Spiritan rhetoric reflects their immersion within the emerging biologization of practical social theory. Nascent environmentalist discourse in Europe generated two totemic tropes that organized this new perception of nature and society: the garden and the island. Both became prototypical sites for intervention and protection, offering a potential structure for a social and moral world in which interactions between people and nature could be defined and described. The Spiritans invoked both images as they discussed their missionary strategy, indicating confidence in their abilities to shape an environment conducive to personal and social transformation. The missionaries sought to make their mission at Zanzibar an island in an Islamic world through practices of enclosure, and they referred to Bagamoyo as a *jardin d'acclimation*, or horticultural nursery, regularly drawing parallels between the proper cultivation of plants and people. Such metaphors were part of the taken-for-granted world from which the missionaries came.

As time went on, an idiom of what might be called "competitive salubrity" became a regular feature of missionary correspondence, and debates among

---

49. On the development of theories of acclimation, see Osborne 1994. Richard Grove (1995) has linked the rise of environmentalism with the economic theories of the physiocrats and emergent French colonialism. Paul Rabinow, in his study of the development of French perceptions of the social environment from the 1830s into the twentieth century, has offered a genealogical account of the evolution of environmental consciousness and social control as operative in French colonial settings (1989). Borrowing the insights of Georges Canguilhem and Louis Chevalier, he shows that in the eighteenth century the word *milieu* became a biological term under the influence of Lamarck. For Rabinow, the urban planning characteristic of French colonial policy in North Africa and Southeast Asia emerged from a process dating at least back to the Paris cholera epidemic of 1832.

50. Rabinow 1989, 82f, 104. See Kollman 2001, 202ff.

Spiritans over the advisability of different sites often turned on the perceived healthfulness of one place or another. Many features of the missionary strategy depended on interpretations of the weather, as letters to and from Paris indicated. For example, an indigenous clergy was needed because of the ill health of the region for Europeans, with Duparquet arguing, "We can't live there." In explaining the move to Bagamoyo, Horner told the Holy Childhood Society about the epidemics that afflicted Zanzibar due to its climate. Horner defended the purchase of property at Zanzibar by saying it was in the healthiest part of town, and later adduced Mhonda's salubrity as the reason for its choice as the first interior mission. The Spiritan superior general himself weighed in on the advisability of certain proposed sites for new missions, complaining about illnesses and deaths.[51]

Competitive salubrity appeared most starkly in the dispute between Baur and Horner over the comparative merits of Zanzibar and Bagamoyo. Their disagreement persisted because the chapter of 1870 created no lasting consensus. Baur claimed to have no irrational dislike for the mission at Bagamoyo, about which Horner was enthusiastic, but felt it had few advantages over Zanzibar. Unlike Horner, he saw little hope for a solid Catholic future in the former slaves then at the mission and felt the agricultural work at Bagamoyo was doomed because of likely lack of workers. He disputed Horner's confidence that freed slaves would continue to flow to Bagamoyo, doubting the mission would receive even one hundred freed slaves per year from the British, much less the three hundred Horner anticipated. Once slave ransoming was over due to the anticipated closing of the slave market at Zanzibar, Baur believed labor would be hard to come by. He thus questioned the ambitious building projects undertaken after the hurricane of April 1872, overseen by Scheuermann.

Horner's refusal to accept Baur's pessimism about the possibility of Christianizing Africans of "the first generation" after slavery was connected to his hopefulness about Bagamoyo's healthy possibilities for formation. Horner also countered Baur's contention that the closing of the slave market would end the arrival of slaves at the mission, arguing that there would be little change in the mission's activities after the market's end. Baur countered that instead of dependence on an unreliable labor supply from former slaves, it would be better to trust the revenue that could come from Zanzibar's workshops. He complained that he needed to hire temporary workers to keep them going since the mission children were unavailable to him. They were (as he saw it) fruitlessly toiling at Bagamoyo.[52]

51. CSSp 195iii: Duparquet to Schwindenhammer, 9iv72; CSSp 196axii: Horner to Holy Childhood, 15i69; CSSp 196bi: Schwindenhammer to Horner, 3v77; ibid.: Schwindenhammer to Baur, 5iv77. MC 7 (1875), 201; MC 9 (1877), 604.

52. CSSp 196biii: Horner to Schwindenhammer, 17ix71, 22ix71, 28i72, 17v72, 29vii72, 22ix71, 9i73; ibid.: Baur to Schwindenhammer, 18xii72, 26ix73, 15i74, 10iii74; ibid.: Baur to Horner, 7vii73, 14vii73, 30viii73, 26ix73, 24x73, 18xi73. For temporary workers, Baur uses the word *vibarua*, which is still the KiSwahili term (Glassman 1995, 61, 87f).

In 1874, Horner's health required him to switch with Baur and transfer to Zanzibar, while Baur replaced him at Bagamoyo. Each assumed the move would prove the correctness of his own judgment as to the comparative salubrity of the two spots. Horner begrudgingly admitted Bagamoyo's unhealthiness, especially in the face of numerous missionary deaths in the mid-1870s that led Schwindenhammer to protest. Yet his shrillness and acrimony toward Baur only increased and broadened. The many deaths at Bagamoyo, which Baur highlighted as evidence of its insalubrity, were not due only to the climate, Horner claimed, but to unwise decisions (by Baur and others) to drink only water when fevers hit. Even when admitting its insalubrity, he claimed that the places Baur favored were even less healthy.

If their feuds showed an obsessive attention to climates in eastern Africa, Spiritan practices at Bagamoyo displayed even more vividly a new approach to the arrangement of space itself. This was best typified by the striking difference in spatial organization and layout between the new mainland mission and Zanzibar. As Duparquet's letter suggests, the mission in Zanzibar lay within the labyrinth of streets in the Stone Town of that centuries-old city, hemmed in by a mosque, residences, and shops. In contrast, the large tract of land that Fava purchased at Bagamoyo sat outside of a much smaller town on a broad plain near the Indian Ocean.

Bagamoyo's arrangement reflected a deliberate Spiritan strategy. The Spiritans received the mission at Zanzibar already established, with little chance to change the setting they inherited. At Bagamoyo, on the other hand, they had freedom to arrange the layout as they saw fit. And its visibility and openness suggest that the Spiritans organized the Bagamoyo mission to be the antithesis, spatially speaking, of their mission at Zanzibar.

Upon coming to Bagamoyo, there were obvious financial, strategic, and historical reasons that the missionaries organized their new mission as they did. Given the constant financial pressures faced by the mission, they envisioned Bagamoyo as self-supporting. They thus planned large plantations to feed the many children and Christian villagers who would eventually live there. They also trusted physical work in the formation of the Christian nucleus, and the ample room for plantations promised scope for such training. In addition, Bagamoyo's location meant that evangelization took place at a greater distance from the dangers so present at Zanzibar and also to a lesser extent in the town of Bagamoyo. Separation from possible pollution by Muslims further ensured the proper formation of Christians through work, prayer, and education. Historical precedent also supported the creation of a large plantation-style mission set apart from surrounding populations. Their confrere Kobés had established large missions dedicated to agriculture in western Africa, following many other Christian missions in nineteenth-century Africa.[53]

---

53. On Kobés, see APF 36 (1864), 109–10, and APF 38 (1866), 32–43. On similar works by the Sisters of St. Joseph in French Guiana, see Koren 1997, 43f, and Cornuel 1999.

Despite these obvious reasons that the Holy Ghost missionaries might have organized Bagamoyo as they did, it is important to recognize that the missions at Zanzibar and Bagamoyo exemplified two different stages in the evolution of penitential practices in nineteenth-century Europe, especially France. Zanzibar's concern for enclosure reflected attention to carefully circumscribed spaces that predominated in early-nineteenth-century penitential practices. Duparquet, in his letter defending Bagamoyo as the preferred site for the seminary, called this first stage the *régime cellulaire*, following Dupanloup. But a different strategy grew in prominence in French prisons beginning around the middle of the century. In self-conscious contrast to the earlier stage, this later style, found prominently in juvenile correction, downplayed the value of overt physical enclosure in the reform of individual habits. In this second stage, space was bounded but also organized to render people legible or available to surveillance, *without encroaching upon them*. In prison and reformatory regimes this second sort of practice was defended as more effective in fostering the normalization and rehabilitation of those incarcerated, for it fostered the growth of internal resources of self-contol. Experts conversely saw limits to the regenerative capacities possible in regimes of confinement for such internal changes toward a self-policing subject.[54]

Changes in reformatory practices appeared piecemeal and gradually; thus, the Spiritans who came to eastern Africa between 1863 and 1890 may well have been exposed to both models in their formation: the earlier one emphasizing enclosure *and* the later concern for openness and legibility. Bagamoyo's organization, with surveillance maintained yet overt enclosure relaxed, suggests that the Spiritans followed this second notion in constructing their mission. The two types of spatial organization at Zanzibar and Bagamoyo thus corresponded with different stages in the evolution of French penology in the nineteenth century.

Tracing missionary strategies in Africa to evolving penal practices in Europe may appear far-fetched and indefensible. After all, Spiritan descriptions of their work in eastern Africa did not attribute their practices to strategies of juvenile reform in Europe. Contemporary Spiritans, however, do not hide the connections between missionary strategies and practices of juvenile reform, connections that nineteenth-century missionaries never felt the need to mention. As a recent study of Holy Ghost facilities in France states of one of their houses of formation, near which was located a home for abandoned children and where many who came to eastern Africa served, "At Cellule, future missionaries were able to make their apprenticeship working at the education of young *abandonées*."[55] Still, the

---

54. This early stage, which began before the nineteenth century, has been called "the rise of discipline" (Foucault 1977), "cellular" isolation (Petit 1990), and a concern for encapsulation (Rhodes 2001). For a fuller discussion, see Kollman 2001, 348ff. According to Petit, another reason that the second style became prominent was quite similar to one reason the Spiritans opted for its spatial organization at their new mission at Bagamoyo: in order to generate income at such institutions. Petit argues that the later set of practices derived from efforts by prison officials to make their institutions income-producing through productive labor, something a confining regime did not allow (Petit 1990, 315ff).

55. Ernoult 2000, 354–55.

specific ways in which practices first encountered in France became enacted by Spiritans in Zanzibar and Bagamoyo cannot be charted. Such habits of mind and ways of seeing the world were taken for granted, internalized through years of formation in religious houses and work in reformatories that shaped thought and physical predilections. Such social experiences generated implicit expectations that were reinforced through repetitions in observation and practice so that they needed no discursive rearticulation. But there is other evidence that what they saw and practiced in European reformatories, Spiritan missionaries in turn put into practice in Zanzibar and Bagamoyo.

The name given Bagamoyo's mission itself suggests this underlying inspiration. Horner called Bagamoyo a *colonie agricole*, the same label adopted by his confrere Kobés for his largest establishment in western Africa. To twenty-first-century ears, this term sounds innocuous enough, an agricultural colony. Yet *colonie agricole* was not merely a descriptive term in mid-nineteenth-century France, unmoored from other discourses. It referred to Mettray, a famous juvenile facility near Tours with direct connections to the Spiritans. Mettray was famous as an innovative place for encouraging reforms in young people, the foremost example of the second stage of penal reform in the nineteenth century, that which encouraged open, not closed, environments.

Spiritan connections to Mettray may have been many, but they certainly came through St.-Ilan in Brittany, a reformatory the congregation took over in 1855. St.-Ilan had been founded in 1842, and its first residents were twenty boys who had come from Mettray as *colons*, colonizers, for the new establishment.[56] The parallels between the colonizing of St.-Ilan from Mettray and the Spiritan strategy of colonizing the interior of Africa with Christian communities formed at Bagamoyo are already striking. Further insight into Mettray's program — St.-Ilan's has not been studied in such depth, though due to its origins as Mettray's colony one can assume a resemblance — only reinforces the connections.

Mettray was founded in 1839 as a new style of alternative juvenile reformatory, one that kept young offenders apart from adults and trained them through close attention to their habits. It soon became the most famous juvenile reformatory in mid-nineteenth-century Europe. It served as a model for many others, especially in Britain, where praise of Mettray resounded in the middle of the nineteenth century, inspiring other so-called cottage reformatories. Boys and young men came to Mettray to be reformed through a comprehensive and systematic program of supervised physical work, elementary education, extensive religious teaching, and agricultural or industrial training. For Michel Foucault, Mettray represents the prototype of the second strand of disciplinary practices that focused on normalization of behavior and reform through surveillance, and downplayed overt enclosure. Yet what made it distinctive and indicative of an epochal shift in the history of prison reform for Foucault was the fact that not only offenders, but

---

56. The founder of St.-Ilan in 1847 inaugurated a religious order, on whose habit was written *In labore virtus*, Latin for "in work lies virtue" (Ernoult 1992, 23; 2000, 352ff).

also those acquitted (but unable to find another home) and those abandoned went there. Thus nonoffenders underwent the same regime as those convicted of crime as techniques previously reserved for prisoners began to move into regimes for the nonincarcerated.[57]

They also moved into missionary practices in Africa, due to the Spiritans' exposure to Mettray-like regimes at places like St.-Ilan. As at Bagamoyo, a strict timetable governed the days for the *colons* (colonizers) at Mettray, with hours devoted to a series of carefully supervised activities. Three other aspects of the Mettray program became noteworthy, each of which paralleled practices enacted at Bagamoyo. First, the *colons* were organized into thirteen groups of forty or fifty boys, each under the supervision of adults, an attempt to create family-like structures. The ideology of family was also an important part of Spiritan self-understanding. The Holy Ghost priests often cast themselves as fathers of the mission's residents who, regardless of age, were usually called children. References to the future role of the mission children as parents within Christian families also appeared prominently in descriptions of the mission.[58] Second, at Mettray outdoor labor became the preferred way to "inculcat[e] the boys with a sense of moral purpose, thus saving them from the perils of idleness." As we have seen, the mission at Bagamoyo, too, centered itself around agricultural labor.

Perhaps the most striking similarity between Mettray and the mission at Bagamoyo, however, lay in the architecture, especially the physical layout of the two compounds. This points to the third distinctive feature of Mettray: the absence of obvious physical restraints on the boys' movements. No walls kept the residents inside the compound. One description reads,

> The architecture of the buildings and their surroundings dominated the open elevated site that avoided high walls and the usual prison structures, but still made the surveillance and control of inmates an easy matter.... [The founder] had given his architect precise instructions emphasizing the need to avoid structures that enhanced the escape possibilities of inmates while at the same time giving them the feeling they were not within a prison.

In addition, corporal punishments were prohibited. Instead the program pursued the internalization of obedient behavior through meticulous supervision and a strict program of rewards and punishments for following or disobeying detailed codes of conduct: "... [T]he principle is, that no part of the boy's conduct, however inconsiderable, be unnoticed or overlooked." In fact, "The least act of disobedience is punished and the best way of avoiding serious offences is

---

57. For descriptions of Mettray and its influence, see the following: *Quarterly Review* / 1856, 42–47; Carpenter 1969 (1851); Latham 1869; *Penn Monthly* 1881, 478–80; Foucault 1977, 293–97; Ramsland 1989, 1990; Driver 1990. Foucault names Mettray the completion of what he calls the carceral system. He calls it, "the disciplinary form at its most extreme ... [and] the first training college in pure discipline" (1977, 293 and 295).

58. On the ideology of family at Mettray, see Carpenter 1969, 326. For Spiritan claims to the status of fathers to the mission's children, see, among many examples: CSSp 196axii: Horner to Holy Childhood, 3xii66; BG 11:718f.

to punish the most minor offences very severely; at Mettray, a useless word is punishable." According to a report in 1852: "... the entire parapenal institution, which is created in order not to be a prison, culminates in the cell, on the walls of which are written in black letters: 'God sees you.' "[59]

Bagamoyo had no official architect, but its setting and the organization of its buildings point toward the same implicit principle: open spaces to create at once high visibility without encouraging escapes. In such a setting,

> The absence of walls and other visible means of confinement ... became a potent symbol of the methods of the colony, the "prison" without walls. At Mettray, it was claimed, the spaces of liberty and of discipline were no longer distinct; in the words of one of its disciples, "The little colonists are, as it were, imprisoned only by their free will; Mettray has neither armed force, nor iron bars, nor walls, and ... the only key to this colony is the key of the open fields." Discipline was not simply or even primarily a matter of physical confinement; it lay essentially in the moral training of individuals.[60]

At Bagamoyo, too, the spaces of liberty and those of discipline were not distinguished from one another, at least in the beginning. The hope of the Spiritans lay in the cultivation of the habits of these freed slaves by their comprehensive formation. One of the commonly repeated praises of the mission children was that they worked "without supervision."[61] True liberty was to come not through escape from authority but from discipline, created by the proper practices.

The different spatial orientations thus pointed toward subtly different emphases within the strategies of evangelization between the Spiritans' first and second missions. At Zanzibar, the Spiritans relied on practices of enclosure to ensure the properly formative behavior of the mission's children and the supervision of that proper behavior. But Bagamoyo's open architecture derived from European practices designed to effect more vigorous internal changes rather than simply the modification of behavior. Mettray sought the creation of a self-monitoring spirit within its inmates, and Bagamoyo sought the same for its young Catholics. On the mainland, strict enclosure gave way to new spatial practices in which the missionaries maintained their concern for boundaries, but tried to inculcate a spatial experience in the children in which the impositions of such boundaries were not as obvious.

In relying on two different approaches to space, the missionaries drew upon interrelated, even if competing, theories of how best to effect their goals. Both Zanzibar and Bagamoyo sought to habituate the mission's children for their formidable responsibilities as colonizers of the interior. To that end the Spiritans

---

59. Carpenter 1969, 327; Foucault 1977, 294. See also Kollman 2001, 354ff.
60. Ramsland 1990, 31; Driver 1990, 276.
61. See, for example: BG 5:498f, 827; BG 8:759; CSSp 196ax: Horner to Propagation of the Faith, 28xii70.

formed environments designed to forge the virtues of the ideal Catholic Christian: hard-working, obedient, pious.

Yet the missionaries had more at stake in the future clergy. Thus it is not surprising that Duparquet's 1872 letter, with its denigration of the effects of confinement and its espousal of Bagamoyo's "open" environment, addressed the seminary program. Earlier he had built the *chalet* for surveillance within the seminarians' dormitory at Zanzibar. In that setting, missionary interest in the formation of proper and internalized habits among the mission children was most pronounced. Duparquet's explicit environmentalist arguments about the location of the seminary were echoed the next year, when, in response to later difficulties with those seminarians, two other missionaries clashed over the source of the trouble, and each invoked environmental logic in his own defense.

The hurricane of April 1872 destroyed most of the structures at Bagamoyo and led the Spiritans to transfer the seminary to Zanzibar, as Baur had desired. After the May return to Zanzibar a spate of escapes and insubordination followed in early 1873. By then Duparquet was gone, yet his penchant for environmentalist attentiveness persisted. Disappointment with the seminarians, some of whom appeared as ringleaders among those perceived as troublemakers, led to an argument over the causes for the difficulties. Baur traced the problems to the environment at Bagamoyo and all the physical work that the children had done there, characterizing the program before the move back to Zanzibar as a system that neglected proper formation of good habits. Scheuermann, on the other hand, who oversaw the building at Bagamoyo after he relinquished control of the seminary to Duparquet in 1870, isolated Zanzibar's corrupting environment as the culprit. In the wake of Baur's reports and crackdown on his former pupils, Scheuermann despaired of the formation he had supervised when in charge of the seminary, now that some of those boys were in chains. We return to this episode below, as it points to African experiences as well as missionary preoccupations. Here the point to note is that, though each Spiritan in effect blamed the other for the problems, both Scheuermann and Baur presumed that the lack of missionary oversight created an environment conducive to reprehensible behavior.[62] According to both missionaries, African misbehavior derived from European failures to ensure the proper milieu for the supervised formation of Christian habits.

Probably not coincidentally, around the time that the Spiritans in eastern Africa moved the bulk of their mission from Zanzibar to Bagamoyo, the Spiritans in Paris also moved their primary major seminary from the city of Paris to a suburb outside the city, where there were large agricultural plantations, wide rows between crops, and a rural environment far from the city. Tree-lined paths marked out a classical French garden. In moving to Bagamoyo, therefore, the Spiritans not only responded to conditions in eastern Africa, but also acted in accord with spatial preferences operative at the center of their Congregation.[63]

---

62. CSSp 196biii: Scheuermann to Horner, 8iv73; ibid.: Baur to Horner, 11iv73.
63. Ernoult 2000, 32; Kollman 2001, 352.

Along with their close attention to the proper milieu for forming the Catholic *noyau*, Spiritans' words and deeds also indicated new approaches to labor in this period.

Labor after the Move to Bagamoyo

Three developments occurred with regard to labor after 1868, each of which reflected the changing circumstances facing the Spiritan mission.

In the first place, adults came to the mission in larger numbers, so that labor's role in *forming* working habits in the young also gained a reforming function. Beginning in 1869, British officials began to give the Spiritans freed slaves taken from slave ships, among whom were adults who then worked either at Bagamoyo or the workshops in Zanzibar.[64] These slaves liberated at sea became the largest group of new residents at the mission, so that in 1876 Horner wrote that most of the four hundred children at Bagamoyo had come from the British.[65] In addition, the move in March 1868 to the mainland at Bagamoyo placed the mission at the site where many trade caravans to the interior started and stopped. This connected the Spiritans with sick or unemployed porters as well as others who became attached to the mission through a variety of means less possible in the crowded environment of Zanzibar. This was never a large group, for the overwhelming majority at the mission remained former slaves, yet many were adults.

The presence of a larger group of adults to be evangelized and formed into the Christian nucleus affected Spiritan discourses and practices of evangelization. At this time the language of regeneration entered Spiritan descriptions of their evangelization in relation to work. The term had already been used to describe the spiritual effects of the sacrament of baptism, but in this new context regeneration (or reformation) suggested that personal habits, especially habits of work, had been damaged by slavery. Thus in the same way that formation indicated that the missionaries sought to shape Christian habits from the beginning in the mission children, regeneration in relation to work indicated missionary awareness that the mission had to undo harm caused through the slave experience in this new adult population.[66] Besides forming a proper Catholic character, work could also heal or repair damage.

The aftermath of the Franco-Prussian War witnessed a second change in this period, when a new kind of labor relation shaped by remuneration was forged between the ex-slaves and the missionaries. This came about when the missionaries, anticipating a marked decrease in financial support from Europe in the wake

---

64. The missionaries report receiving forty to one hundred at a time, e.g., CSSp 196bii: Baur to Schwindenhammer, 29viii69; CSSp 196biii: Horner to Schwindenhammer, 2vi71, November 1872; ibid.: Baur to Schwindenhammer, 10iv74; Zanzibar journal, 14ii76, 17iii76; Bagamoyo journal, 28xi70, 15i71, 11x72. Adults freed at sea went to the Christian village, children to the orphanages (BG 9:277).

65. Kieran 1966, 106; CSSp 196biv: Bulletin of Zanzibar community, 4iv76.

66. CSSp 196bii: Horner to Schwindenhammer, 24vi64; BG 6:1009f; BG 8:758f; BG 9:522ff.

of the disastrous French defeat, sought to cut their expenses. They thus started to pay the married couples for their work in Zanzibar's workshops, "rather than furnishing all they needed, as before." Spiritan defense of this innovation was revealing:

> This system is preferable. Before, we were never able to satisfy them and they on their part squandered what they were given. Now, besides the savings from this system, it has the advantage of teaching our young men the practical cost of life, something to which their nature scarcely disposes them.[67]

This moment stands alone in the documentary record before the 1880s, a single witness from this period that the Spiritans could see *compensation for work* as educative.[68] Only in the 1880s did the Spiritans accept that ex-slave labor deserved financial remuneration. Pressure to make the Christians' labor a commodity was coming, but the missionaries did not accept such an understanding without the prodding of the African Christians themselves.

The third and most important change in the way labor was approached at Bagamoyo compared to Zanzibar lay in the Spiritans' much keener appreciation of the economic value of work. Horner's request to truncate liturgical observance in order to increase available time at work in the fields was one of many indications that the missionaries saw the value of labor as a resource upon which the mission depended. The previous chapter noted the conditional tone in which the Spiritans described the mission's children, who at once showed vulnerability and potential in Spiritan writing. It also noted that Casimir and the other boys had recognized that their labor was a resource, and that ransoming larger boys would ease their burden. The move to Bagamoyo produced Spiritan descriptions of the mission children that prioritized their instrumental value under the influence of the mission's labor needs. In particular, Spiritan writings show two interrelated innovations in the ways work was understood, changes with long-lasting effects on the mission's history. Both presage a shift in work's role away from the effects it had on the mission's residents toward its importance for the mission as a whole.

First, Spiritan writings indicate that they were actively confining the mission children and preventing their leaving. This suggested a refinement in the missionaries' perception of the legal status of the work the ex-slaves performed and in the status of those who had been ransomed. It was noted earlier that in an 1861 letter, the mission's founder, Fava, wrote that those ransomed had been told they were free to leave, but that they responded that they were happy to remain. Though the Spiritans had not, in the intervening years, designated the children as free — indeed, they bragged about changing the conditions whereby the children,

---

67. BG 8:752.
68. Concern for proper remuneration characterized efforts to reform freed slaves carried out by Quakers in the region some decades later (Newman 1898).

who had been "doing what they want" now came under better supervision — neither had they called them slaves. They still did not call them slaves. Seven years later, however, the Spiritans wrote of the skilled workers at Zanzibar, "They work in our shops *sans pouvoir nous quitter*" ("without being able to leave us"). By 1868, the freedom to leave, freedom that Fava claimed was a consequence of ransoming, was no longer the operative missionary assumption. Indeed, the ransomed slaves were now apparently deemed to remain in a state of (at least) contracted labor to the mission after they had been purchased at the market, and their work was part of the mission's property.[69]

Interpreting just what the 1868 Spiritan phrase meant, however, is not easy. It could simply refer to the fact that on an island with so many African slaves, where labor was in huge demand especially during the harvesting of cloves, leaving was inconceivable; an African who was foreign to the coast and not attached to some patron might face enslavement, even imprisonment. Perhaps, too, Fava's report several years before misrepresented what was actually the case, and the children really never could leave the mission even before the Spiritans arrived. Given the ways that the labor of these ex-slaves was seen later, however, the suspicion that coercive force lay behind the phrase *sans pouvoir nous quitter* seems likely. This interpretation is supported in light of the 1866 episode already discussed in which the escaped Casimir was apprehended and sent to a Réunion penitentiary. Not only were the children not called free; it appears that within the space of a few years the missionaries could and did publicly say — for this appears in the quarterly congregational magazine, not only in a private letter — that those ransomed could not leave their civilizing care, while previously Fava had said they could.

In addition to confining the mission's children, Spiritan writings betray a growing awareness of the labor of the mission's children as something that could run short and thus threaten the mission's future.[70] The strict timetable, with five hours of work outdoors per day, suggested careful deployment of labor at Bagamoyo. The awareness of dependence on ex-slave labor was even more clearly reflected in different descriptions of the reception of slaves at Zanzibar, where the Spiritans received most of those handed over by the British Navy. Before the move to the mainland, those ransomed were never described as a labor pool in Spiritan writings. In 1869, however, a British naval captain's promise of one hundred children from his next capture was greeted with an unprecedented enthusiasm suggesting acknowledged dependence on this projected labor. Higher prices at

---

69. Fava 1933, 118; BG 6:617.

70. The labor force at the new agricultural colony was also initially not only the children of the mission from Zanzibar. Horner had admitted that to develop the agricultural work required, the children of the mission were insufficient and other labor was needed (BG 6:1014f). In the first year, therefore, Horner's reports on the new mission contain apologies for hiring local workers for the task of clearing the land, an expense he considered an unfortunate use of donations to the missions, for such donations should only have been for the salvation of souls. The progress of the agricultural colony, however, required men strong enough to clear the brush on the property, something initially beyond many of the boys from Zanzibar (CSSp 196axii: Horner to Holy Childhood Society, 15i69; CSSp 196ax: Horner to Propagation of the Faith 4iii69; ibid.: Horner to Gaume, 1vii69; CSSp 196bii: Machon, excerpt from Bagamoyo journal, 28vi69; BG 8:761; BG 13:30–31).

the slave market had lowered the number of children the mission had ransomed and the report reads, "[W]e need a large number for the agricultural work" (*il nous en faudrait en grande nombre pour l'œuvre agricole*). The same sentiment found expression a few months later when the British consul gave six slaves to the mission. These were taken from a local Indian who, being a British subject, could not legally keep them. The missionaries wrote to their Paris generalate, "The work of these men will be useful to us" (*Ces hommes nous seront utiles par leur travail*). By the early 1870s, Horner was confident that the mission would receive three hundred slaves per year from the British, and he wanted to plan accordingly.[71]

The new valuation of work as a resource reflected Spiritan perception that their growing mission at Bagamoyo — full of children, many of whom could not support themselves — faced a shortage of money unless they took advantage of the laborers they had. Already before the move to Bagamoyo, Horner recognized that problems arose from conditions placed on donations to the Propagation of the Faith and the Holy Childhood. These conditions stipulated that monies designated as such only be used for ransoming slaves, a harsh restriction for a mission that also had to feed the children it ransomed. In the wake of the Franco-Prussian War, the Spiritans requested permission to use such funds for maintaining those already at the mission. When hypothetically asked how much it cost to support a ransomed slave, Horner wrote the Propagation of the Faith that it was sixty francs per year for an agriculturalist (as those who worked on the plantations were called) and one hundred francs per year for a student, since the latter generated less support for himself through labor. Eventually the destructive hurricane led to permission for the Spiritans to use funds stipulated for ransoming for the upkeep of those at the mission.[72]

As more land was put under cultivation, the growing plantations of Bagamoyo required a larger and more reliable labor reserve. Horner touted the self-sufficiency of the mission, but meanwhile he and his confreres grumbled over the high prices for ransoming, a practice that continued after the slave market at Zanzibar was closed in 1873, though on a smaller scale and in less public ways. They also complained when promised deliveries of slaves liberated from slave ships did not materialize, often because they went to the newly founded Anglican settlement for freed slaves at Freretown near Mombasa.[73] In addition,

---

71. BG 7:268, 658; CSSp 196biii: Horner to Schwindenhammer, 19ix71, 22xi71.

72. For Spiritan worries about the restrictions on funding, see CSSp 196bii: Horner to Schwindenhammer, 25vi66; CSSp 196biii: Horner to Schwindenhammer, 1vii71, 15iv72; CSSp 195iii: Duparquet to Schwindenhammer, 9iv72; BG 8:941; MC 3 (1870), 307; MC 4 (1871–72), 370; MC 5 (1873), 164. The permission from the Propagation of the Faith to switch the use of the funds away from donors' original stipulations for ransoming came after Horner's account of the hurricane's destruction (MC 4 [1871–72], 370). Horner tried to economize in other ways as well, including ending the mission's support of the sisters, whose shortcomings annoyed him (CSSp 196biii: Horner to Schwindenhammer, 12vii71).

73. For missionary grumbling about British failures to deliver on promises of newly freed slaves, a failure blamed on "envious and greedy" Anglican missionaries as much as on British officials, see BG 9:272; CSSp 196biv: Thorax to Horner, 22ix75, 21x75.

as the British navy handed over slaves freed at sea, the missionaries evinced increased concern over the health of those they accepted, a sign that they considered the economic value of the freed slaves before taking them.[74]

The amount of physical work for the majority of the ex-slaves particularly increased after the 1872 hurricane destroyed most of the buildings at Bagamoyo. As a consequence, commitment to Libermann's ideal of education that "civilized," in which physical work was but a part of a more comprehensive formation, lessened. Evidence from the Bagamoyo journal suggests that work frequently replaced school classes, especially during periods of harvest or intense building. The missionaries also canceled planned vacation periods because of urgent needs for workers. Religious holidays, normally days off from work, increasingly went unobserved. In addition, punishments were administered to those who resisted work. In 1873, Baur wrote from Zanzibar to Horner, then in Europe raising funds, and alerted him that Horner's earlier fears that work would eclipse the education at Bagamoyo were well-founded. There were, Baur complained, 140 children carrying stones from the sea every day to construct walls for the new buildings, so that in the year in question there had been only three months during which classes had been held.[75]

The growing awareness of labor's instrumental value as a resource did not entail the disappearance of the formative value of labor from Spiritan considerations of those they received at their mission. They did not merely accept everyone they were offered, but continued to emphasize their desire for younger children whom they could form into Catholics. When they received nine from the British consul from a slave ship, they took only five, those who seemed "amenable to our style of life."[76] Yet even if the Spiritans saw work's value in other ways, a trend toward an instrumental understanding of the labor of the mission's children nonetheless was evident after the move to Bagamoyo.

Did the Spiritans Keep Slaves at Bagamoyo?

These signs of increased awareness of the ex-slaves' labor value again raise the question of whether the missionaries thought of their charges as slaves.[77] Judging from their rhetoric, the Spiritans did not consider any group at the missions of Zanzibar and Bagamoyo as slaves — neither the children in the orphanages, the industrial workers, the villagers, and certainly not the seminarians or African

---

74. After the slave market was closed, Baur asked Horner whether he was still obliged to receive the freed slaves from the English. He was reluctant to continue the practice if the children were not healthy or numbered too many to be supported (CSSp 196biii: Baur to Horner, 7vi73). That his question did not signal reluctance to receive them in all circumstances is shown by his joy when he received the healthiest forty children from the English consul (CSSp 196biii: Baur to Schwindenhammer, 10iv74). See Kollman 2001, 340 n. 58.

75. CSSp 196biii: Baur to Horner, 24x73.The entries in the Bagamoyo journal of 1872–73 show many days marked "carrying stones from the sea."

76. BG 9:522f.

77. Historian Roland Oliver wrote of Bagamoyo and its "inmates" (Oliver 1952, 21f).

girls in formation for the sisterhood. Yet they did confine their movement. In addition, the mission's children now possessed a value quite distinct from their capacity to embody the church of the future. Their capacity to labor ensured the ongoing well-being of that still-infant church. Their work was thus not only part of the formative or regenerating process but also the mission's own right, its just recompense because of the act of ransoming and/or supporting them. Whether or not the missionaries saw the former slaves as *property* — spiritual or legal — is difficult to tell; the nature of the obligation owed by those ransomed, or the missionary view of the tie that kept them bound to the mission, was not explained. Certainly the missionaries did not consider themselves as slaveholders, at least in the ordinary sense. They felt an obligation was owed them, however, so that they had an expectation about those they received.

Evidence that the missionaries did not see the mission children as slaves can be gleaned from their language. For example, Horner wrote of dying Africans who *offered* to become the mission's slaves due to the kindness they had received. He also spoke of the double slavery of the children *before* they were ransomed by the mission. Both examples suggest that he considered the mission children in another category.[78] At the chapter of 1870, the delegates had mandated that all children go to primary school and receive a certain amount of instruction per day, an indication that such training distinguished them from slaves. Also at the chapter, one of Horner's complaints about the workshops was the lack of proper remuneration of the workers, so that the workshops perpetuated slavery.

An even clearer indication of Horner's view of the mission's children came a few months later in a letter Horner wrote to the superior general. Frustrated by a lack of personnel, he complained that he could not form the children at Bagamoyo as they deserved, for they missed classes too often. His conscience stung him, he wrote, and he threatened to take those in the orphanages at Bagamoyo to Bourbon in the Indian Ocean unless Holy Ghost brothers with skills to teach came soon. He could not abide treating the mission's children "like ordinary slaves."[79]

The use of the word "ordinary" in this context suggests the possibility that these children at Bagamoyo were "extraordinary" slaves. It seems that in Horner's eyes they did represent something like a third category. They were not ordinary slaves, but neither were they workers for a wage like those at Zanzibar's workshops. For missionary purposes they were better than either, and Horner certainly had higher hopes for those at Bagamoyo who worked in the fields than the workers at the workshops. He predicated his missionary strategy on the conviction that agricultural workers were more likely to develop the loyalty the missionaries wanted. Their status as nonslaves did not derive, however, from the fact that they were paid for their work. Instead, in the Spiritan imagination because they were the mission's children they were not slaves. To have paid them would admit

---

78. CSSp 196ax: Horner to Propagation of the Faith, 28x69; CSSp 196axii: Horner to Holy Childhood, 31xii75.

79. CSSp 196biii: Horner to Schwindenhammer, 8x70.

that the relationship binding them to the mission was economic, and the Spiritans sought a deeper relationship than one predicated on money. They sought loyal Catholics who placed their work on the mission's behalf within the context of their faith and discipleship.

Spiritan writings after the move to Bagamoyo show the persistence of the double narrative around work that already emerged before the move to the mainland. On the one hand, physical work remained formative, part of the spiritual program by which slaves became Christians in the official ideology of evangelization and moralization of the missionaries. This was the place of work in the majority of mission descriptions of work prepared for outsiders, especially fund-raising agencies. In this narrative, young children represented the preferred objects of missionary attention, and labor was a crucial component of the comprehensive formation sought for them. This approach to work hearkened back to Christian monasticism, in which work and prayer, *ora et labora*, helped compose the proper orientation toward the virtuous life, especially for those who sought a specialized vocation approximating Christian perfection. In support of this understanding, the missionaries attended to the individual characters of the children at the mission, especially those marked for special service like the seminarians. They recognized and identified, for example, their cultural background with ethnic terms still used today.

At the same time, however, there was another narrative that, instead of being spiritual, derived from the pragmatic and material realities facing the mission. This second narrative, likely that of everyday discourse at the mission but also at times found in writing, envisioned the labor of such children not merely as formative but increasingly also as a necessary part of the mission's economic well-being. Indeed, after 1868 these two narratives became even harder to distinguish from one another, for Bagamoyo's economic structure depended on the labor of the children in the orphanage to a much greater extent than the mission at Zanzibar. This second narrative gradually subsumed the first, especially when the seminary closed in the mid-1870s, with a consequent lowering of interest in the ethnographic or cultural particularity of individual former slaves.

While Spiritan approaches to work relied on this double narrative, another double narrative operated in language justifying broader practices of enslavement in eastern Africa. As noted in chapter 1, such practices relied on a variety of metaphors to name the relationship between slaves and those to whom they were bound. Two types were most common: terms associated with kinship, and those reflecting ties between patrons and clients. While patron-client language predominated at the coast, kinship language predominated in the interior of eastern Africa in the nineteenth century.[80] The Spiritans' own language describing their relation to the Africans at the mission never lost its primary location within kinship terms: they were fathers to their children. One assumes that the Daughters of Mary used maternal terms to describe their position in relation to the

80. Deutsch 2000, 15–56.

mission's children, too. Yet the move to Bagamoyo generated expectations about the labor of these children that began also to betray the language more typical of patron-client relations. The implications of this change became clearer in the 1880s, as we shall see.

The 1874 founding of the Anglican CMS colony for freed slaves at Freretown, near Mombasa, created unavoidable comparisons with the Spiritan works further south. In 1876, Baur visited the Protestant mission, which became the destination of most slaves freed by the British Navy. His telling comments indicated how the Spiritans thought of their own work as well as their rivals'. He wrote of Freretown that it was rightly more famous for the resources it consumed than its results, and noted the hatred for the mission in Mombasa itself. The British consul even criticized the CMS mission, according to Baur. One resident supposedly told Baur, "Our masters are Protestant at the mission and Muslim in town." This suggested a harshness that stood far from the paternalistic approach that the Spiritans favored, officially at least, and by which they justified their actions.[81]

Laboring, Learning, and Fleeing:
African Experiences at the Catholic Missions, 1868–77

The move to Bagamoyo that occasioned evolution within Spiritan strategies also fostered a predictable increased diversity within African experiences of slave evangelization. As the former slaves lived their lives in the new *colonie agricole*, their identities — as Africans and as Catholics, as objects of missionary attention and pursuers of their own interests — emerged more sharply over time in the historical record. Greater evidence of all three of Hirschman's categories — exit, voice, and loyalty — can be discerned. Thus the move to Bagamoyo saw an increase in the number of Africans who seemed to opt to flee the mission, while others developed demonstrable loyalty along the lines that the Spiritans wanted. Still others manifested what Hirschman calls voice — the effort to change one's condition — that can be discerned clearly. These reactions suggest the further development of a moral economy associated with the mission within the consciousness of these African Catholics.

But the new evidence also makes clear the limits within Hirschman's concepts in capturing African responses to slave evangelization. In the first place, Hirschman developed his framework particularly for contexts in which participation in an economic or political relationship depended on personal choice, more or less uncoerced. Even if the missionaries did not consider them slaves, the Africans at Bagamoyo and Zanzibar were not free of coercion. In addition,

---

81. Zanzibar journal, 19viii76; BG 11:724–25; CSSp 196biv: Baur to Schwindenhammer, 24viii76. Courmont later wrote admiringly of the Protestant missions at Bonde and the "superb" station at Mombasa, which he visited with the Anglican bishop, indicating perhaps that Spiritan disdain had softened. Perhaps this came about due to their own frustrations with the ex-slave Africans at their missions (CSSp 198b: Courmont, 8x87).

as we shall see, exit, voice, and loyalty took a variety of forms, so that responses to slave evangelization resist simple categorizations into one of the three.

While there are a few letters written by Africans at the missions from this period, the missionaries themselves continued to produce almost all such sources. Moreover, the historical sources closest to the events and thus usually the most revealing about the daily life at the missions — the mission journals — are missing for large periods, from 1874 to 1877 for Bagamoyo and from 1869 to 1875 for Zanzibar.[82] This loss is acute because other Spiritan writings revealed little interest in African perspectives on missionary evangelization. What interest the missionaries showed in African perspectives aimed at measuring the former slaves' demonstrated promise for Christian life, especially the promise of potential future priests and nuns. Yet even that interest usually meant little attentiveness to subjective experiences of evangelization.[83] The missionaries had even less invested in the formation of the mass of the former slaves, those not in specialized education, and attended to their experiences hardly at all.

Recognizing the limitations imposed by the sources, one can surmise that African experiences of evangelization depended on several things new compared to Zanzibar. First, compared to the earlier period, the newly arriving Africans now were older, due to the sizeable handovers from the British. More, therefore, arrived after having been socialized in other environments. Consequently their appropriation of the practices of the mission depended more on prior experiences than those in the 1860s at Zanzibar, who were almost all children. Second, the Africans at the mission, whether new arrivals or having arrived from Zanzibar, found themselves in increasingly differentiated positions within the missionary program. After all, Horner sought to build what he called "fully formed communities" for the interior, and this meant formative experiences specifically designed for different positions within those anticipated communities. At Zanzibar, the boys and girls had stayed in a rather homogeneous program, but at Bagamoyo the orphanages were joined by the village, as well as the specialized formation programs for the boys and girls. These differing positions within the mission meant quite different experiences of evangelization. Third, the mainland at Bagamoyo was less circumscribed and more politically volatile than the island and town of Zanzibar. The Mettray-like spatial organization allowed more openness, while the mission's land troubles indicated uncertain sovereignty in the area. In addition, despite Spiritan attempts to maintain a separate environment, the Africans at the mission could not help but consider their lot in relation to that of their neighbors, especially those also working the

---

82. They were lost in the early twentieth century, and, according to a Spiritan in Morogoro, Father Theodore Winkelmolen, might have been taken in order to describe the visits of Livingstone and Stanley to the mission in those days (Vogt, n.d., also appearing as CSSp 391a; Vogt, Resume of Bagamoyo mission, 1868–1918).

83. Such attention did not feature in seminary reports from Europe either, which also emphasized observable criteria (CSSp 106a).

land in positions of servility, something that Bagamoyo's porousness encouraged more than Zanzibar. Observers also considered the mission's children using local categories.

The mission's Africans fell into three rather coherent groups besides those in the creche. The largest group consisted of those younger persons in the orphanages at Bagamoyo, boys and girls who worked in the fields and followed a rudimentary educational program. Given their numbers, the children in the orphanages took the most energy from the missionaries, but Spiritan depictions of these boys and girls give few details. The married Christians living in the village at Bagamoyo (or the smaller number remaining at Zanzibar, many connected to the workshops there) constituted the second group. The villagers as a group emerged with particular clarity beginning in 1880, as we shall see in the next chapter, but in this period they featured little in Spiritan correspondence and other writings. Comprising some thirty families in 1875 and forty by 1876, they probably numbered somewhere around one hundred people by the latter 1870s.[84] In the near absence of other sources, the sacramental books at the Bagamoyo mission provide a limited glimpse into their participation in the mission. Finally, the smallest group, and the one whose experiences can be most known because the Spiritans reported on their progress and promise, was composed of the young women and men in formation programs for a future as priests, brothers, or sisters. In contrast to the other two groups, those marked off for special formation appeared often in the historical record, offering the most thorough glimpse at how some of the mission's children appropriated Spiritan evangelization in this period.

The Children at the Orphanages and the Christian Villagers

There were 172 children at the mission's orphanages in December 1869, a number that climbed to 322 three years later and remained around that level through most of the 1870s. Shiploads of freed slaves came to the mission courtesy of the British consul, who saw the Catholic mission as a place to put those released by the British Navy, especially before 1874. In addition, Horner continued buying children at the slave market during his trips to Zanzibar, sometimes as many as forty at a time, until the closure of the slave market in 1873.[85] All of those ransomed and many of those received from the British were of the age to end up in the orphanages:[86]

---

84. BG 10:723; BG 11:718.
85. CSSp 196axii: *Compte-rendu* for Holy Childhood Society, 29xii69, xii72; CSSp 196bii: Duparquet to Peureux, 9viii70.
86. The figures in the table come from Henschel 2000b, 5, which borrows from Vogt n.d., as well as other sources. The absence of figures for slaves ransomed after 1873 reflects the closing of Zanzibar's slave market and lack of sources. The drop-off in slaves received from ships after 1873 reflects the founding of Anglican CMS mission at Freretown, where many of those freed from slave ships by the British went, as well as an expansion of the Anglican UMCA mission founded at

Number of slaves ransomed by year		Number of slaves from ships by year	
1870	170	1871	36
1871	200	1872	63
1872	324	1873	185
1873	325	1874	25
1877	220	1875	29

Our insights into these children's experiences come almost exclusively from missionary writings and inferences we can draw from them and other historical understanding of the Swahili coast of the time. Alongside occasional complaints about "African laziness," the Spiritans reported regularly on the good spirit within the "agriculturalists" and praised their progress in scholarship and work habits. Yet other evidence fills in the picture a little, suggesting that the children at the orphanages might have had reasons to complain. In the first place, the number of those ransomed or received in the 1870s far outnumbered those ever at the mission. This suggests that many departed from the mission's oversight quickly. Deaths due to disease were common, but they do not account for most of the shortfall.[87] Shortage of priests and brothers likely contributed to the ease of flight, given the large number of children present at any one time. Horner admitted several times in 1870 that the absence of personnel led him to cancel classes because he did not have time to teach the children. He complained of being consumed by the supervision of agricultural work that should properly have been the responsibility of brothers. As we saw earlier, he even threatened to send the children to Réunion because without instruction they remained in the state of ordinary slaves, something his conscience could not abide. They sometimes went weeks without class, he admitted.[88]

Spiritan writings yield other clues about the life for those in the orphanage, suggesting the difficulties these young people faced. The Spiritans were not always model instructors. Horner complained that one priest lacked the aptitude for forming children and could not be trusted with them. He admitted that another Spiritan, a brother who was often in conflict with his confreres, beat the children and left wounds that "did not heal quickly."[89] The mission's journals and timetables that were so prominent in missionary reports also indicated that

Zanzibar, which had interior missions by this time. The UMCA mission received 453 slaves between Frere's visit in 1873 and 1877 (UMCA 1878, 16).

87. For accounts of the mission's suffering from cholera in 1869 and 1870, which killed a dozen children and a sister, see the entries in the Bagamoyo journal through December 1869 and January 1870, as well as Henschel 2000a, 9. Gangrene killed twenty in the early 1870s, but they were mostly newly received from the British (BG 9:277). Smallpox killed many in the early 1880s (Vogt n.d.; Bagamoyo journal, 30v82). Other children died regularly from unspecified illnesses, probably malaria and dysentery.

88. For Horner's comments on the work regime at Bagamoyo, see CSSp 196bii: Horner to Schwindenhammer, 8x70, 12ii71, 1vi71.

89. CSSp 196biii: Horner to Schwindenhammer, 22v69, 28vi69.

the regimen of work was demanding. This was true from the beginning, so that Horner had to hire outside workers to do the heavy work of clearing the property since it was beyond the capacities of the mission's children fresh from Zanzibar. But work became unrelenting after the 1872 hurricane and the ensuing rebuilding campaign that continued through the mid-1870s. The mission's journal of 1872 and 1873 lists day after day in which the children carried stones from the sea, mostly done by those in the orphanages.[90]

Given these conditions, attempts to flee were understandable. In October 1870, one girl escaped the Bagamoyo mission and was recaptured,[91] a foretaste of a spate of escapes in 1873 and a flood in the early 1880s. The large numbers of children, with sizeable groups added all at once as the British discharged those who came into their possession, no doubt made accounting for all of them difficult.

The experiences of those in the villages also resist easy understanding, since the Spiritans' daily interaction with them was even less marked than with the children in the orphanages. Of the African Catholics at Zanzibar, around eight couples and others, the missionaries made almost no comment except to speak of the numbers at Mass, which usually numbered around twenty Africans, a few Goans (whom the missionaries called "the Portuguese"), and the Europeans, who were few except when a French or British naval vessel came to port.[92] The sacramental books from this period are also missing, though they likely would have recorded little since most of that activity had moved to the new mainland mission.

At Bagamoyo, however, the sacramental records from this period signaled the appearance of a rather reliable group of adult Catholics at Bagamoyo. These served as godparents for the baptisms of those in the orphanages (or those in danger of death and baptized in extremis) or as witnesses for each other's marriages, roles many had begun to serve at Zanzibar in the 1860s. A smaller number also brought their own children to baptism. The sixty-four marriages recorded represent the best signs of real participation in the mission's life, since many of the 340 baptized were children between eight and twelve from the orphanages. A large number of the others baptized were infants who would soon die.[93] Most of

---

90. For days of work, during many of which there was carrying of stones from the sea for construction, see the Bagamoyo journal in 1872 (May, June, July, August, November) and 1873 (January, February, March, April, May, July). In January the schedule of the mission was changed to increase the hours allotted to work (7i73). In May, there were only two days of school one week, and in July no class for a week (19vii73). Baur complained at the regimen at Bagamoyo, directed by Scheuermann (CSSp 196biii: Baur to Horner, 24x73).

91. Bagamoyo journal, 20x70.

92. BG 9:807. In October 1873, Baur wrote Horner that some fifty African Catholics resided at Zanzibar (CSSp 196biii: Baur to Horner, 24x73). The loss of many of the early sacramental registries along with the mission journals from Zanzibar in those years makes understanding difficult.

93. The ages of the 530 baptized at Bagamoyo between 1870 and 1881 are as follows: 99 under 1 year (who likely died soon thereafter); 20 from 1 to 5 years (many of these also likely died soon); 101 from 6 to 9; 138 from 10 to 14; 78 from 15 to 19; 28 from 20 to 24; 10 from 25 to 30; 20 over 30; and 36 for whom no age was given (Henschel 2000a, 8–9).

those serving as godparents and witnesses for these sacraments had done so ear-lier at Zanzibar, and many had been or remained in the formation programs. Their names for the most part would appear in the historical record in the years ahead too, indicating that Bagamoyo's village supplied active Catholics for decades following.[94]

Horner's annual reports sent to the Propagation of the Faith and the Holy Childhood Society, though they give no names, are also telling, though less reli-able than the sacramental registries. Both reports lumped together the missions at Zanzibar and Bagamoyo to produce a common report, and they counted different things. The Propagation of the Faith sought information on two categories — the numbers of adult conversions and Easter (or paschal) Communions — while the Holy Childhood Society counted children in a number of different categories.

The numbers in benefactor reports are problematic for a number of reasons. In the first place, there are many empty places where the report was left blank. Second, Horner (or Baur, as the case may have been) sometimes counted the total of a category at the mission, other times those added in that category in the year considered. Third, there were other category confusions, such as nursery (*crèche*), which in 1873, for example, had a large number, many of whom were probably not infants. Despite these interpretive difficulties, the reports show a growing mission in most ways, with sizeable increases in Easter Communions through this period.[95]

The sacramental records and Spiritan reports to their benefactors indicated a large mission community at Zanzibar and especially Bagamoyo, with a great deal of sacramental participation. The connection of these African Catholics to the mission from early days at Zanzibar, then to Bagamoyo, and into the 1880s and beyond indicates the emergence of a certain degree of loyalty within them. That loyalty was initiated by the comprehensive program at Zanzibar and then Bagamoyo. Though the Spiritans hardly discussed the villagers in this period, it seems that there arose a sizeable number of people at their missions who thought of themselves as Catholics and behaved within missionary expectations of that identity. They belonged to the mission. They prayed and worked on the land, and possibly also assisted the mission in other ways. The heavy workload after the hurricane might have fallen somewhat upon the villagers as well, who would have had to rebuild their homes and assist in the rebuilding. In any event, the villagers entered the historical record in those years only rarely, for there is little evidence that their work burdened them to the point that they complained about it, something that changed only a few years later. In fact, the absence of Spiritan comments about the villagers through much of this period is the best sign that, for the most part, they pleased the missionaries by their participation in regular devotions as well as by their work on the mission's behalf.[96]

---

94. See Versteijnen 1963.
95. See CSSp 196ax and CSSp 196axii.
96. The missionaries described the fervor of the children for the sacraments as well as the sadness of those not chosen to be baptized. When slave escapees from the other plantations had to be returned

Among the over fifty Christians who appeared more than once in Bagamoyo's sacramental books of those years as sponsors or witnesses were some who married later, before heading off to settle the interior missions in 1878 and afterward. Thus they were probably still in the orphanage before that, since marriage was usually the transitional moment away from the orphanage. But a sizeable number married in the mid-1870s or before, and so resided in the village. These included Charles-Alfred, who already was a leader by virtue of his age and reliability at Zanzibar; Elise and Francesca, two women in the village who once had been in formation to be nuns and who would, with other women, baptize hundreds of children in the 1880s; Almase, who helped return an escapee in December 1873; Joseph Mghindo, who would later demonstrate the mission's effect on him by taking up a preaching ministry outside of missionary control; Léon, a seminarian at this time, whose appeal caused such consternation later in 1882; and Hilarion, who would serve as catechist at the first interior mission in 1877.[97]

Other events at the mission, recorded in the extant journals and correspondence, undo the tranquil view of regular church activity that appears from within the sacramental registries. Bagamoyo's caravans meant the constant comings and goings of large numbers through the area, and Europeans visited the mission regularly. Most importantly for the life of the African Christians at the mission, however, 1873 marked a series of escapes and other misbehavior at the missions of Zanzibar and Bagamoyo. These subsided, but they occasioned considerable Spiritan frustration and commentary. The first recorded escape that year came in August— *"Louis s'est evadé"* — but Baur's letters mentioned earlier troubles at the seminary, then in Zanzibar. Numerous other escapes followed later in 1873, from both the village and the orphanages.[98]

Most of the escapees were not named, and even with names it is difficult to identify who escaped since many of the children shared names. A few named escapees, however, were in all likelihood villagers with long connections to the mission. Thus Louis, the first escapee mentioned in the Bagamoyo journal, was probably baptized at Zanzibar in 1862 on the same day as Casimir. At Zanzibar he also received his first communion and was married in 1867, a husband in one of the first four couples married. When he escaped he was a Christian villager at St. Joseph village at Bagamoyo. He later returned, serving as a baptismal sponsor in 1876.[99] Evidence for connecting the 1873 escapee with the 1867 husband lies in the fact that the journal names him at all. Another escapee, Benoît, may have

to their masters for fear of antagonizing the sultan, the missionaries reported on their profound sadness; the girls had grown used to the life organized by the sisters at the girls' orphanage (BG 9:525; CSSp 196biii: Scheuermann to Horner, 2vi73).

97. On Almase's role, see Bagamoyo journal, 27xii73. The names of the others appeared as sponsors in the mission's baptismal book starting in 1871, when Hilarion himself was baptized not long after he was ransomed.

98. Escapes in Bagamoyo journal: 6viii73, 17viii73, 25x73, 23xii73, 27xii73.

99. Zanzibar sacramental registry, 11v62; Bagamoyo journal, 6viii73; CSSp 196bii: Baur to Horner, 11viii67; Bagamoyo baptismal register, 1876. Later he took up residence with the White Fathers (Bagamoyo journal, 9x83).

been one of the seminarians Duparquet inducted into the confraternity of the Holy Spirit in 1871, a young man who later went to Europe.[100]

Many left never to return, perhaps entering fugitive slave communities near the coast,[101] serving with European caravans, entering Swahili society in some other fashion, or making their own way as cultivators where land was available. Spiritan records indicate that others returned in various ways, some willingly, some forcibly brought back to the mission. Ten years later the missionaries had a prison bloc constructed at Bagamoyo; for the time being, they sought to limit the flights and occasionally administered physical punishments in view of the others to discourage future escapes.[102]

Interpreting Escapes from Bagamoyo in the 1870s

There are difficulties in interpreting these escapes for a variety of reasons. First, the flights from the orphanages and the village, unlike difficulties in the seminary to be discussed below, rarely received elaboration by the missionaries. Usually those fleeing were not named, and in this period the missionaries gave no reasons for the escapes. The loss of the mission journals for several years only increases the difficulty of interpreting these actions, for certain details about them no doubt would have appeared there, as they did later in the journal records of the 1880s. Another interpretive difficulty arises from the fact that, as in 1866 and 1867 — the period when Casimir and Josephine escaped, and Africans first married at the Zanzibar mission — Baur was the acting superior, and thus is the reporter of these events.[103] This raises the question of whether the records of escapes are an effect of his being the reporter, since he might have recorded events that Horner would have ignored or interpreted differently. In addition, one can speculate that Baur's leadership style might have encouraged escapes and other misbehavior. Earlier, Horner had complained that he was inexperienced in dealing with Africans, and later in the early 1880s, he was very strict with the Christian villagers, as we shall see.

Despite such considerations, it seems there was an increase in flight from the mission in 1873, for other correspondence from the period mentions such difficulties, too, while later correspondence does not.[104] Since the missionaries

---

100. CSSp 196biii: Duparquet to Barillec, 17vii71. Perhaps, however, the seminarian sent to Europe was another person named Benoît, since the Spiritans would have been reluctant to send a former escapee.

101. On such communities, see Morton 1990, Glassman 1995, and Deutsch 2003. In a private notebook, or *carnet*, Courmont recorded a visit he made to one such village near the Kenyan coast in 1887 (CSSp 198b: Courmont, 18x87). Otherwise, Spiritan writings show little awareness of *watoro* settlements before 1890, when Le Roy mentioned them in *Les Missions Catholiques* (MC 22 [1890], 462).

102. For a description of the punishment administered to escapees once caught, see Baur's letter: CSSp 196biii: Baur to Horner, 17iv73.

103. Horner left for Europe in February 1873, returning in 1874 (Bagamoyo journal, 13ii73).

104. In 1877, two couples escaped from Bagamoyo and came to Zanzibar, but they returned of their own accord (Zanzibar journal, 16xii77). Other than that there were very few accounts of escapes from

Figure 13. Father Etienne Baur,
CSSp. From the Bagamoyo
Mission Museum. Used with
permission.

offered no explanations, one might ask why escapes from the mission proliferated
at this time. What had attenuated the loyalty of those who fled, so that they chose
to exit rather than remain? What made them feel that the moral economy of the
mission was being violated?

Several factors situate the many decisions to flee in 1873. In the first place,
escape was easier than it had been before the move to the mainland, so that exit
was a more realistic option. Bagamoyo's mission was located in a less confined
setting than Zanzibar, and not only because of the missionary strategies encouraging a more open environment like that at Mettray. As part of a rather rural
mainland it afforded more directions to flee than Zanzibar's urban and island setting. Villages composed of refugee slaves existed within several days' journey.
At Bagamoyo, too, the sultans' power was weaker than at Zanzibar, as shown by
Spiritan difficulties in holding their land and the negotiations the sultans had to
undertake to assure the missionaries' control. If an escaped mission child at Zanzibar was likely to be seen and captured as a fleeing slave, that was less certain
at Bagamoyo. Large groups coming to the mission, especially from British slave
interdictions, also made flight easier. Thirty-six came in June 1871, sixty-three in

---

1873 until 1880, though Horner admits "rare defections" in an 1878 report (CSSp 196axii: Horner
to Holy Childhood Society, *compte-rendu*, 31xii78).

October 1872, and seventy-two a month later. These led to periodic overcrowding at Bagamoyo's orphanages with many new faces, and keeping track of them all would have been difficult for the Spiritans.[105]

Second, the Bagamoyo mission's extensive building to reconstitute itself after the destruction of the hurricane of April 1872 meant rigorous work. It is certainly imaginable that the increased burden made flight a more attractive option for some. In the wake of the hurricane, illnesses also increased at the overcrowded mission, and deaths became quite common at the orphanages in 1873.[106] Those able to recognize the increased danger might have been induced to flee what seemed a disease-ridden environment. The newly arrived numerous freed slaves sent by the British were also less attached to the mission, with a very thin loyalty to the Spiritans. They had little stake in the mission's program, so exit was an easy choice.

A third factor fostering escapes might have been the visit of Sir Bartle Frere in 1872 and 1873, which was widely anticipated by unfreed laborers at the coast. An extensive slave uprising took place in nearby Pangani in 1873, attributed in part to the visit and accompanying rumors of the impending abolition of slavery.[107] Neighboring plantation owners struggled to maintain their slaves in this period, for the Spiritans faced the issue of what to do with those fleeing Arab masters and seeking asylum at the Bagamoyo mission. Scheuermann, who was in charge at Bagamoyo while Horner was in Europe, reluctantly decided that the mission had to return them in order to avoid antagonizing the sultan and other Arabs.[108]

The coincidence of escapes from the Bagamoyo mission with heightened escapes and unrest among slaves at the coast suggests that the Africans at the Bagamoyo mission felt affinities with other unfree workers in the region. Even if the Spiritans sought a self-contained environment, the boundaries between the mission and the broader coastal world were porous. The mission's children no doubt likened their situation to others who labored in the Swahili economy. Certainly the circumstances of those in the orphanages and the village at Bagamoyo bore structural resemblances to such groups, due to their connection to the land and the work they did. No group at the mission was a precise analogue to any other broadly constituted group of unfree laborers, but their situations had suggestive parallels to several.[109] Those in the orphanages at Bagamoyo most resembled

---

105. For accounts of freed slaves handed over to mission in this period, see the following: CSSp 196biii: Horner to Schwindenhammer, 6xi72, 22x74; ibid.: Baur to Schwindenhammer, 10iv74; CSSp 196biv: Zanzibar journal excerpt, 4iv76; ibid.: Horner to Schwindenhammer, 30vi76; Bagamoyo journal, 1vi71, 7viii72, 11x72 (sixty-three children received), 13i73, 7v73; BG 9:522f.

106. CSSp 196biii: Machon to Schwindenhammer, xi73.

107. BG 9:268; CSSp 196biii: Baur to Horner, 4vii73. On the slave revolt in 1873, sometimes called the Makorora rebellion, see Glassman 1995, 109ff; Deutsch 2003, 175. The rebellion also followed from the recent imposition of harsh sugar plantation slavery. The Spiritans reported that some slaves in the area felt that their masters used the 1872 hurricane as a pretext to keep them enslaved, no doubt adding to the unrest.

108. CSSp 196biii: Scheuermann to Horner, 2vi73; BG 9:522ff.

109. Thaddeus Sunseri helpfully notes and seeks to resolve the dichotomy among those who have studied slave protests in eastern Africa. Some, like Glassman, contend that slaves, even when

those designated *shamba* slaves. These slaves, who served as field hands on plantations, were often recently arrived at the coast and new to enslavement. They
were not paid but normally they received small plots of land, *makonde*, upon
which they could grow their own crops. Recall that the fifty boys who first came
to Bagamoyo received such plots, though how long that practice continued at the
mission is unclear, since the number of children must have mitigated against it
as boatloads came from the British.

Such *shamba* slaves often had little stake in coastal society due to their recent
arrival, and thus when they fled, they often did so for good. In the same way,
one can speculate that most of those fleeing the orphanages at Bagamoyo in
this period probably did not return either. Revealingly, the Spiritans rarely gave
their names, a sign of a limited missionary investment. Such young men and
women probably felt the burden of the strict schedule and heavy work. In light of
surrounding circumstances of labor organization and economic life in the region,
those at the orphanages who more strongly assimilated themselves to *shamba*
slaves may have wanted land (or more land, as the case may have been) in order
to be treated to the same possibilities of social reproduction as the *shamba* slaves.
Using Hirschman's categories, they likely chose the exit option because voice —
the ability to use their own agency to change the circumstances in which they
found themselves — was not open to them.

The villagers were a different story. They certainly had land that resembled
makonde — in this they were not like those sometimes called *watumwa*, who
received small wages but usually did not have land. But like the *watumwa*,
who valued Swahili customs and who thus protested or even escaped slavery
in order to rise within Swahili society, the villagers had a stake in the mission,
one predicated on their possession of some land and a more extended exposure
to missionary formation. Few escaped, and the missionaries reported that those
who did usually returned after escaping, like Louis. Even if Louis did not intend
to return when escaping, that he did return suggests a loyalty that was latent
within him.

The villagers' consciousness was certainly not reducible to any simple for-
mula. Their circumstances prior to arriving at the mission varied considerably,
as had the length of time they had been exposed to the coast and the missionary
practices of evangelization. Yet compared to those in the orphanages, they had
a stronger commitment to the mission in which they partook. Thus when they

escaping, usually held a desire to advance according to the hegemonic constructs of social prestige at
the coast. Others, such as Fred Morton, emphasize the brutality of coastal slavery and thus celebrate
the liberative human achievements represented by slave flight and the new life achieved in slave
settlements. Sunseri notes that perhaps the difference between these two perspectives lies in the
kinds of slaves at issue. Glassman, Sunseri observes (in Glassman's 1991 article, at least), focuses
on slaves acculturated to the Swahili coast. They usually worked in close relation to their masters,
in roles long held by slaves in the region. Those like Morton who emphasize the African agency
indicated by slave flight, on the other hand, highlight those who worked on the newer plantations
of eastern Africa, a disproportionate number of whom became *watoro*, or escapees (Glassman 1991;
Morton 1990; Sunseri 1993).

fled, they often returned, and the Spiritans tended to keep better track of them. The villagers' exits, then, usually differed from those of the *watoro* from the mission who escaped never to return. In that sense, their exit was calculated to a certain degree, or moderated by a loyalty to the mission. One might designate such an exit strategic, since it was not simply an effort to leave the mission entirely. Casimir's and Josephine's 1866 flight was of this sort, since both returned and, for a time at least, participated fully once again in the mission's life. In the case of the later Bagamoyo villagers, such loyalty had likely been generated by the practical fact of possessing land and the intangible connections built up over years of common prayer and other practices of evangelization. Those in the orphanages, on the other hand, usually exited with little loyalty and did not look back. They opted for exit that might be designated decisive, since it was not predicated on any such loyalty.

As we shall see in the next chapter, over time this connection to the land in the dual contexts of missionary evangelization and a larger coastal economy generated a collective identity in the villagers that can be discerned. Beginning in the early 1880s, their voices came through in the historical record as they protested in a corporate way against the missionary strategy as it impinged on them as villagers. Before that time, however, the historical record has no such evidence of collective voice from the villagers.

That absence up to this point in the story does not mean that no collective identity had yet emerged. It does mean that the missionaries had not recorded it. In fact, almost certainly the villagers had already developed some common identity before it appeared so clearly, as the names in the sacramental books suggest. After all, Casimir and the other boys at Zanzibar had already spoken with a collective voice in wanting certain children ransomed, and those in the villages had been together longer and shared more interests in common with one another.

One way to think about the delay between the actual formation of collective identity and its appearance in the historical record is to distinguish between what one political scientist, building on Hirschman's concept of voice, calls "horizontal voice" and "vertical voice."[110] Horizontal voice arises when a group of people realizes that they share interests in common, while vertical voice is an articulation of those shared interests directed at those above them. Thus, collective vertical voice depends upon the prior reality of horizontal voice, yet collective horizontal voice can exist long before collective vertical voice finds expression. And even before it finds obvious expression, vertical voice can act through oblique ways that evade the perceptions of the powerful.

The absence of missionary comments about the villagers in this period suggests that horizontal voice indeed remained oblique among African Catholics at Bagamoyo. Given the absence of other evidence, the appearance of escapes,

---

110. Guillermo O'Donnell offers this distinction, reflecting on the experiences of his fellow Argentines under dictatorship (O'Donnell 1986).

therefore, represents an indication that certain villagers — at this point a few only — felt that their ability to improve their circumstances through exercise of their voice toward the missionaries was insufficient to encourage such an attempt. Their loyalty attenuated, their capacity for effective voice seeming limited or difficult, they fled. They perhaps did not flee with the intent to leave forever, but they fled nonetheless.

Life in the Formation Programs

Spiritan writings from the 1870s attended more fully to the Africans who participated in the programs set up for the training of indigenous future priests and nuns than to those at the orphanage or the village. They are obviously the group in whom the Spiritans most eagerly sought signs of loyalty, in Hirschman's terms, and whose disaffection through exit, or self-assertion or complaints through voice, most disturbed the missionaries.

The Spiritans had high hopes for those in formation at the minor seminary in the early 1870s. Horner and the others praised both the boys and the girls who were in specialized formation until the middle of the decade. Duparquet was replaced briefly as director by Father Machon, then for longer by Father Alexandre Thorax, whose approach was much more low-key than his predecessor.[111] Horner continued to claim that the creation of an indigenous clergy represented the principal hope of the mission. Letters described the achievements of the students, celebrated at the seminary's annual day, when the missionaries honored scholastic excellence. The consoling death of one, a former cannibal who had been sold into slavery by his own father, showed the promise in these young African seminarians.[112] In December 1873, the boys numbered twenty-eight, and a few months later Horner considered expansion since the classrooms for their education at Zanzibar were too small. At the end of 1874, there were also twelve women in the program for potential future sisters, which Horner called a novitiate, though he was aware that it had no such canonical status. As late as mid-1875 Horner could write that the seminary in Zanzibar was prospering.[113] Several among the seminarians served regularly as sponsors for baptisms at Bagamoyo.

Yet all was not well, for the 1873 flights from elsewhere in Bagamoyo's mission coincided with difficulties in the seminary. In addition, the archive reveals that the missionaries carried out corporal punishments on the seminarians whose behavior failed to comply with the mission's expectations. As noted earlier, in the wake of trouble among the seminarians in 1873, Baur and Scheuermann, the first director of the minor seminary, had argued about which site, Bagamoyo or Zanzibar, was the source of the difficulties. Their dispute showed the heightened

---

111. CSSp 196biii: Horner to Schwindenhammer, 6xi72; BG 10:450. Unlike Duparquet, Thorax wrote few letters to Paris.

112. Bagamoyo journal, 17viii72, 1ix72; BG 9:512–13.

113. BG 9:511ff; CSSp 196biii: Horner to Schwindenhammer, 3vii72, 2vii74; CSSp 196axii: Horner to Propagation of the Faith, 14iv72; ibid., Horner to Laverriere, 16vii75.

missionary awareness of milieus in relation to the effects of evangelization. Both were keen to blame the other and the other's preferred site of the seminary for the onset of the "restlessness" that led several of the seminarians to seek the company of women in nighttime sorties.

In the midst of their conflict, Baur forced two of the seminarians caught at Zanzibar *in flagrante delit* to confess in public that they had begun the practice of visiting *des mauvaises maisons* ("the evil houses") before returning to Zanzibar. He wrote Horner that Bagamoyo had been a chaotic environment for the seminarians, then lectured Scheuermann about the laxity of his regime, much to the latter's annoyance.[114] Baur had the boys who tried to escape chained up, and the same fate befell those who knew about the escapades but did not alert him.[115] No rationale was offered for these punitive and repressive measures the missionaries took to control their charges. This suggests that in Spiritan eyes no rationale was needed; they were the expected actions to take in light of disobedience.[116] One can only imagine that violence toward those in the orphanage at the agricultural colony and *not* in specialized education for future elite service was even harsher.

Disturbances in the seminary program seem to have eased after 1873. The further unraveling of the seminary program and the formation program for sisters, however, began in the mid-1870s. Unforeseen deaths took the lives of candidates for the Spiritans and the sisters, while the missionaries faced disappointment with those who survived and persevered.

The deaths of the young men did not take place in eastern Africa. Though the 1870 chapter had urged that formation to Spiritan religious life and priesthood take place in the region in order to keep the candidates "simple" and not let them grow accustomed to European luxuries,[117] it had also recognized the need for a period with the congregation in France. Thus several of the most promising pupils went to Europe for their novitiate, one to possibly be a priest, and the others to be Spiritan brothers. The first of the latter group, Ferdinand Mzoako, had accompanied Horner on his 1873 fund-raising and recuperative trip to Europe. He entered the novitiate and took vows in Paris in November 1875, returning to Zanzibar with the religious name Philippe in December 1875.[118]

When Horner returned to Europe in 1875 for the Spiritan general chapter he brought with him two others, Benoît Colossi (possibly the 1871 escapee mentioned above) and Joseph Pari Amontikira. Horner deemed their vocations "ripe"

---

114. CSSp 196biii: Baur to Horner, 8iv73, 11iv73; ibid., Scheuermann to Horner, 8iv73.

115. One of those chained because he did not inform on those who went out in the evenings was François, discussed later in this chapter and chapter 5 (CSSp 196biii: Baur to Horner, 11iv73).

116. A point made by Henry Koren (Koren 1983, 451).

117. CSSp 196axii: Holy Childhood Society to Horner, 20v78; CSSp 196aiv: chapter of 1870; Ricklin 1880, 300f.

118. BG 10:204, 641; Koren 1994, 26. On Philippe and the others in Europe, see Kieran's summary (1966, 134ff) as well as: CSSp 196biii: Horner to Schwindenhammer, 25x73; CSSp 196biii: Horner to Schwindenhammer, 5vi74; CSSp 196axii: Horner to Laverriere, 16vii75. Ferdinand had been baptized at Bagamoyo in 1871, with Léon (who appealed to the French consul in 1883) as his sponsor (Bagamoyo sacramental registry, 1871).

since, he said, they had not swerved from their convictions for eight years. Like Philippe, they entered the process of religious formation that the missionaries themselves had undergone in France. Both died of consumption (tuberculosis) in late 1876 at the Paris novitiate, after having taken the religious names Godfrey and Aureline.[119] Two more had arrived in France in March 1876 for the brothers' novitiate, Julien Livualia and Dieudonné (baptized as Isidore) Madjonda, along with one designated to be a priest, Patrice Akouchouku, whose intellectual gifts had impressed the Spiritans already in the mid-1860s. The deaths of their predecessors led to the return of Julien and Dieudonné to eastern Africa in December 1876. Patrice came back in June 1877.[120]

This group continued in a program designed to prepare them for full membership in the Spiritan community, but after their return the three did not last long within it. Their return coincided with increasing frustrations among the European missionaries with Philippe, the first eastern African Spiritan, once called Ferdinand. Baur characterized him as childish and a total loss, while Horner saw in Philippe evidence that educating Africans in Europe made them headstrong.[121] Philippe's conflicts with the missionaries increased after his move to the new mission at Mhonda in March 1878, yet he, too, like Dieudonné, Julien, and Patrice, remained connected to the Spiritans for many years. We resume their story in the next chapter.

Experiences with the girls who wanted to be sisters also encountered tragedy. A collapsed building at Zanzibar took three of their lives in 1875, along with that of seven workers. Horner sought to hide the cause of the disaster — faulty construction — from his benefactors, blaming heavy rain. He eventually sent three of the surviving sisters' novices, whom he called his nieces, to Réunion in 1877 to pursue their proper novitiate. One was Madeleine, the supposed source for *Suéma*. She died in 1878, and the others were never mentioned again by the Spiritans.[122]

The deaths and the premature return of the others from Europe had a chilling effect on the programs of formation for religious life and priesthood in Zanzibar.[123] If these tragedies did nothing to encourage young Africans to consider a future as a priest or religious, Horner had also grown frustrated with the students at the seminary by early 1876. In February he sent away all but the best students, leaving ten. Soon only six remained. A few months later Horner discontinued Latin entirely, and some of the last students remaining, François and Laurent, became teachers of the other boys in class still at Zanzibar. Those at Zanzibar

---

119. Koren 1994, 45; CSSp 196biii, Baur to Schwindenhammer, 17xi76.
120. Kieran 1966, 139; Zanzibar journal, 10ii76, 10xii76, 28vi77; BG 10:788; BG 11:26–27; CSSp 196aix: Information about postulants and scholastics sent to Europe, 1876.
121. CSSp 196iv: Baur to Schwindenhammer, 17xi76; ibid., Horner to Schwindenhammer, 30i77.
122. CSSp 196biv: Horner to Schwindenhammer, 13xii75, 2/3vi76, 24viii78; BG 10:719; CSSp 196axii: Horner to Holy Childhood, 13xii75; CSSp 196ax: Horner to Propagation of the Faith, 31xii75; MC 8 (1876), 40–41.
123. Baur spoke of the embarrassment suffered by the mission at these events (CSSp 196biv: Baur to Schwindenhammer, 17xi76).

continued to receive a more refined education for their projected future, no longer as clergy or brothers, but as catechists.[124]

After the closing of the seminary program, Horner requested permission from his Paris superiors to open a postulancy program specifically for preparing Holy Ghost brothers in eastern Africa. Permission was granted, and François and Laurent continued in formation while they taught at Zanzibar's school, which now trained only future catechists. Though disappointed with the failure to produce priests, the Spiritans maintained a curriculum similar to that of the *latinistes* but without Latin.[125]

Vivid Loyalty among African Catholics

The 1870s furnished several revealing letters by Africans who were in these elite training programs. Henri Isa, one of the seminarians at Zanzibar and a founding member of Duparquet's confraternity of the Holy Spirit, wrote to Spiritan seminarians at the major seminary at Langonnet in France in early 1876.[126] In the letter, Isa narrated the story of his own enslavement after his family was seized by the Mafitis, an African group with a fierce reputation. He was sold to Arabs for a sack of salt, and after two years as a slave at Zanzibar he was ransomed by Horner, the first European he had ever seen. In the letter, Isa encouraged the European seminarians to come to Africa to save those "plunged in idolatry." He also described the Arabs, Swahilis, and Banians at Zanzibar. The last, he wrote, were especially mired in "superstition," since they believed their parents were found in "the meat on their plate," an apparent reference to Hindu beliefs in reincarnation and taboos about the eating of beef.

A similar embrace of the mission's message appeared in letters written by Madeleine, the young woman who, Horner claimed, narrated *Suéma* from her own experience. At least three letters from Madeleine remain, all addressed to the publisher of *Suéma*, Monsignor Gaume. These letters indicated a similar kind of internalization of the mission's message as Henri Isa's, or at least a careful presentation of what the missionaries would have wanted to hear. Like Isa, what we know about her suggests that she fulfilled the hopes of the missionaries, but her interior life remains hidden. Her discourse, however, like that of Isa, evinces the loyalty the missionaries sought in the former slaves, especially those prepared for elite status.[127]

---

124. CSSp 196biv: Horner to Schwindenhammer, 10ii76; ibid.: Bro. George to Bro. Alexander, 29v76; ibid.: Acker to Schwindenhammer, 8ii76; Zanzibar journal, 26v76, 2vi76, 27vi77, 23viii76; BG 11:702. Horner's reasoning in this decision was never explained, as far as I can tell. Others who had once been in formation to be Spiritans also taught at Bagamoyo's elementary schools.

125. CSSp 196biv: Horner to Schwindenhammer, 15xi77, 24viii77; CSSp 196axii: Horner to Propagation of the Faith, 31xii77; Zanzibar journal, 19i78; CSSp 195ix: Horner to Simeoni, 31xii78.

126. CSSp 196biii: Duparquet to Barillec, 17vii71; CSSp 196aiv: Isa to Langonnet, 3i76. Isa is Arabic and KiSwahili for "Jesus."

127. These letters are described in Moulinet 1998, 117–18.

There are other traces in the Spiritan records pointing toward African experiences of slave evangelization. A few of those who had been in the seminary program apparently taught in the schools before François and Laurent.[128] Another of the former slaves gave the missionaries trouble, and it was suggested that he needed to marry to stop what was called an "infection" at the mission.[129] One former resident at the mission apparently left and ended up dead in Zanzibar's prison, from where he had unsuccessfully requested a Christian burial.[130]

Diverse Responses to Missionary Evangelization

Most of what we know about the experiences of evangelization of all three groups at the missions — those in specialized formation programs, the villagers, and those in the orphanages — comes from the Spiritans. And most of the Spiritan accounts described missionary frustrations, not promising circumstances for clear understanding. Those who escaped, for example, did not speak for themselves except by their flight as reported by the Spiritans, and the seminarians' defiance was interpreted by the missionaries as ingratitude and racial weakness, with no discernible attention to the reasons motivating such action. But there is evidence that helps situate such decisions. This includes growing Spiritan reliance on the labor of the mission's children, reliance that led to greater efforts to control that labor by the missionaries. No doubt the regime was felt onerous by some. Spiritan descriptions as well as likely parallels to similar practices elsewhere suggest that the seminary regime was also strict. In such a setting, one can imagine adolescent boys straining to elude missionary supervision.

---

128. A brief comment of Baur's in 1875 indicates that other Africans collaborated with the missionaries as teachers at the schools. Baur wrote that one of them, Eugene, had left the mission and that the other, Janvier, wanted either a salary increase or dismissal. Janvier was described as a creole from the Seychelles at the time of his death and burial at Zanzibar in 1882. Previously he had been music teacher at the school at Zanzibar. He is almost certainly the same person as the fellow named Janvier LaLove whom Horner met on his way back from France in late 1867. LaLove lived with the Spiritans for a time and taught music at the school in Zanzibar. Horner described him as a former seminarian for the Jesuits who was dismissed for what he claimed were unjust reasons. He joined the Spiritan community for a brief bit before departing in November 1868, though he must have stayed on — or at least returned — as instructor. Later he taught music to the sultan's slaves. The Bagamoyo journal mentions Eugene assisting Horner with the establishment of the new mission in April 1868. He is described as a creole from Réunion. In an 1871 letter from Zanzibar, Horner wrote Duparquet at Bagamoyo, saying that he was sending six chairs to Janvier and Eugene. This suggests that they were instructors in the school at Bagamoyo (CSSp 196bii: Horner to Schwindenhammer, 2ii68, 13ii68, 29xi68; CSSp 196biii: Horner to Duparquet, 27iv71; CSSp 196biv: Baur to Horner, 2vii75; Zanzibar journal, 2vii77, 23vii77, 2vi82; Bagamoyo journal, 13iv68).

129. CSSp 196biii: Horner to Duparquet, 27iv71. This fellow, Constantine, had received his first communion in 1867 (CSSp 196bii, Baur to Schwindenhammer, 11viii67), and he later served as a sponsor for many sacraments at Bagamoyo. Horner claimed that his wife, Genevieve, was a poor cook, and he used her example to inveigh against the service given by the nuns who had educated her (CSSp 196biii: Horner to Schwindenhammer, 12vii71).

130. Zanzibar journal, 1xi76. The account reads, "In the evening the death of Edmond is announced from the sultan's prison. Since he hadn't been coming to Mass for nearly two years, he hadn't rendered his soul to God; [thus] though he had requested the honors of Burial, it was refused, and the care was left to Arab authorities." Like Constantine, Edmond had received his first communion in 1867 (CSSp 196bii, Baur to Schwindenhammer, 11viii67).

The Spiritans certainly recorded defiance of various sorts by the mission's residents, and exit became a common option for a certain period around 1873, especially for those in the orphanages at Bagamoyo. The circumstances leading to escapes — difficult labor, physical punishments of the disobedient, rumors of abolition, suspicion of the missionaries as slaveholders, and marked flight from other plantations in the region — point toward a shared sense of outrage that led many to try and flee.

The timing of the escapes from Bagamoyo suggests that even if the Spiritans did not see themselves as slave owners nor the mission's children as slaves, they could not control perceptions of themselves and others at the mission held by others. Given the circumstances, their missionary practices likely identified the missionaries with slaveholding landowners in Zanzibar and its environs in the eyes of some observers.[131] They likely were seen that way by many of the former slaves who came to the mission, especially the older ones and those more socialized into coastal life. This assimilation of the missionaries with other patrons in the Swahili world was an important part of the former slaves' internally defined and evolving moral economy of the mission, as they developed their own worldview within the dual contexts of the mission and the broader coast.

The children at the mission no doubt saw the differences over time between the missionaries and other slaveholders. Yet their diverse circumstances meant there was no single experience of slave evangelization among these earliest African Christians. Instead, since consciousness results from historically specific conditions and processes, the consciousness of those evangelized in this period varied considerably. Some had been at the mission for years, but large numbers arrived after 1869. Boys and girls stayed in separate dorms, with supervision by priests and brothers on one hand, and the nuns on the other. Between the skilled workers in the workshops at Zanzibar and the agricultural laborers at Bagamoyo, life at the mission appeared quite differently, and the same was true for the ordinary children at the orphanages and those marked out for special formation as priests or nuns for the future, as well as between the Christian villagers and those not yet married or having their own homes. Each of these groups shared in the liturgical life of the mission and received education to some extent. Each also worked at the mission, most on Bagamoyo's plantations. Yet they received different attention from the missionaries, and their daily activities also varied. One can surmise, therefore, that the former slaves' particular locations within the missionary strategy generated different expectations within the evolving moral economy of the mission.

131. Some local political authorities knew that the Spiritans bought children and received them when they were freed by the British, and this led them to treat the missionaries as regular slaveowners at times. For example, the chief who sent his sons to the missionaries shortly after the chapter of 1870 to encourage them to settle in his area, and whose capital they visited in August 1870, treated them as he might have any other slavetrader from the coast who came in search of human cargo. He wanted gunpowder to wage war on his neighbors, and, knowing that they bought children, offered to give them a large number for it (MC 6 [1874], 5). Europeans later had similar suspicions, as we shall see.

In seeking to make sense of these diverse responses to evangelization, one should be wary of isolating any particular type as more "authentic," either in an African or Christian sense, than the others. In particular, the historical convention that views conflict as particularly revealing of agency in those who resist such domination is questionable.[132] Most of the children in the orphanage did not flee, but this does not mean they acquiesced to everything the missionaries desired. Though evidence is slight, it is reasonable to assume that they developed ways to negotiate the mission's demands without sacrificing themselves. At the same time, some of those in the formation programs for elites appeared to receive the missionary message in ways that pleased the missionaries, so much so that the Spiritans preserved their writings. Yet such overtly religious responses to what looks to have been oppression or domination should not be cast as implicitly "colonized" and politically fruitless. Henri Isa, Madeleine, and Philippe were not any less free than the others simply because they apparently cooperated, at least for a period, with the missionary program.

On the other hand, others probably chose different sorts of options that approximated voice and exit, that is, they remained within the missionary program but sought to pursue their interests within it, or they fled temporarily. The nighttime sorties of the seminarians, reacted to so strongly by Baur, did not necessarily indicate a desire to leave, for the seminarians were probably not escaping for good. They point to youthful indiscretion typical of tight regimes such as boarding schools. Others, like Philippe, sought to pursue their interests by joining the missionaries as a member of the Congregation, a decision whose rationale we cannot fully uncover but which made sense given the experience of being ransomed by and raised within the mission. His decision no doubt made sense to him, and it should not be merely dismissed as evidence that he had swallowed the missionary message without understanding it. In the voices of Isa and Madeleine, at least as preserved in texts, we see loyalty most clearly. The genuineness of that loyalty cannot be proven, for Madeleine died attempting to be a nun, and Isa left formation, likely when Horner closed down the program. He married in 1877.[133]

Before the establishment of an interior mission in 1877, the historical record yields traces of agency in those who fled the mission, as well as individual writings and other evidence suggesting complex and mixed loyalties. Other than the letters from Madeleine and Henri Isa, the best evidence of abiding loyalty probably lies in the rather mundane descriptions of life at the missions, and sacramental records. During these years the Spiritans recorded few escapes from their missions except for the large number in 1873, and little other unrest at Bagamoyo or Zanzibar. Through the 1870s, the mission or *colonie agricole* at Bagamoyo continued to grow in size and reputation. The children there, who numbered 354 at the end of 1877, received rudimentary primary education and worked on the

---

132. Others who share the refusal to valorize conflict as particularly revealing of agency include Guha 1988, 79–82; Spivak 1988, 7, 10–11, 14; Asad 1993, 15.

133. Bagamoyo sacramental registry, 25x77.

plantations. The Christian village, also a source of agricultural workers, had one hundred stone houses in August 1878. Four among the villagers composed the first group to colonize the interior in accord with the Spiritans' plan for the evangelization of Africa. They arrived at the new mission of Mhonda in November 5, 1877.[134]

Yet collective identity among African Catholics had not appeared. It is that collective identity — reliant upon missionary practices but not constrained by missionary goals — that the next chapter explores.

---

134. CSSp 196biv: Horner to Schwindenhammer, 24viii78; Mhonda journal, 5xi77.

Chapter Five

The Move to the Interior, 1877–89

Triumph, Crises, and Attempted Reform

Timeline

1877	August: Horner returns ill from Mhonda and enters the hospital.
	October 18: Caravan leaves for Mhonda, mobilized by news of Protestant plans.
	November 5: Arrival at Mhonda of two Spiritans and two African couples.
	December 8: Foundation ceremony at Mhonda.
1878	Propaganda Fide confers interior territories on White Fathers.
	January 23: Machon arrives at Mhonda to lead the mission.
	April 29: White Fathers' caravan planners arrive at Zanzibar; caravan leaves June 11.
1879	May: Horner leaves Zanzibar ill and dies at Cannes in May 1880.
	June 29: Chapel dedicated at Mhonda.
	October 25: Baur named apostolic vice-prefect and superior in Zanguebar.
1880	Mandera chosen as site for new mission.
1881	January: Mandera established.
	Death of Schwindenhammer. Levavasseur becomes superior general until his death in 1882. Emonet follows and will remain as superior general until 1895.
	December: Alexandre Le Roy arrives in Zanzibar.
1882	Mission founded at Morogoro.

1883	Propaganda Fide establishes an apostolic vicariate to replace the prefecture of Zanguebar.
	Spiritan Raoul de Courmont named bishop in November, ordained in December.
1884	Mission founded at Tununguo.
	March: Courmont arrives in Zanzibar with Le Roy and Madame Chevalier.
	September: Chapter meeting at Bagamoyo.
1884–85	Peters expedition lays the basis for German occupation of what becomes Tanganyika.
	Berlin Conference legitimating European division of Africa.
1885	Mission founded at Kondoa (later moved to La Longa, eventually called Ilonga).
1886	November 8: Anglo-German agreement divides influence over Zanzibar's territory.
1888	April 28: German East Africa Company (DOAG) leases coast from sultan for fifty years.
	September 4: Bushiri revolt begins near Pangani, spreads to Bagamoyo on September 8.
1889	May 8: Rebel camp attacked at Bagamoyo, ending revolt.
	December 15: Bushiri hanged at Pangani.
1890	July 1: British extend their protectorate to Zanzibar and Pemba with formal agreement, first with Germans and later with the sultan (November 4).
	August 5: Anglo-French agreement over the Indian Ocean.

African Catholics Asserting Themselves:
The First Catechist and a Eucharistic Dispute

On November 5, 1877, two Spiritans and two married couples arrived at Mhonda, a nine-day journey from the coast, to establish the first Catholic mission station in the interior of eastern Africa. The couples, former slaves, had married six weeks before at the mission at Bagamoyo. There they had spent a decade or so, prepared by the environment and practices of Spiritan evangelization to compose the Catholic nucleus at an interior mission. Upon arriving, the group undertook the arduous work of clearing the land and erecting huts for temporary shelters until more permanent structures were built. On December 8 they held a founding ceremony like the one at Bagamoyo in 1868, claiming the territory for Christ. In June 1879 they dedicated a chapel.[1] The wait was over. Mhonda fulfilled the long-standing Spiritan dream of an interior mission in eastern Africa.

One of the husbands, Hilarion Maruammakoma, quickly distinguished himself. He and his wife Germaine became the first Catholic lay catechists in eastern Africa, teaching the children of other Catholic couples who came from Bagamoyo to populate the village. They also instructed the surrounding peoples drawn to the new settlement by curiosity and other motives.[2] As the mission developed, the Spiritans called Hilarion their "powerful auxiliary," and he became a trusted emissary on many errands and projects. In addition to serving as catechist he helped prepare caravans and negotiated with local chiefs. Later he established his own Christian village, where he ran a catechumenate for locals wanting to join the Catholic Church.

Twenty tumultuous years later, Hilarion was still living near Mhonda, but as a Muslim. The first lay African catechist in eastern Africa, recipient of years of the mission's formation at Zanzibar and then Bagamoyo, coworker with the Spiritans and ally in many of their causes at Mhonda, in the end disappointed the missionaries bitterly. He had opted to exit the mission after years of apparent, though complicated, loyalty.[3]

Another incident that took place soon after Hilarion arrived at Mhonda casts a different but also revealing light on the Africans whom the Spiritans envisioned as their assistants. In March 1878, Horner forbade the frequent reception of communion by the students at Zanzibar, those who, after the closing of the seminary program, were in training to be catechists. The director of their training, Father Acker, had encouraged frequent communion for these boys and girls, whom the missionaries wanted to follow in Hilarion's and Germaine's footsteps. To Horner's mind, however, Acker had exaggerated their spiritual advances out of a misplaced desire to treat them like the children of Europe. Horner mockingly likened this mistake to Duparquet's earlier foolish practice of leaving the seminarians "unsupervised so that they would grow in responsibility." In a reference to the nocturnal escapades of seminarians about which Scheuermann and Baur argued, discussed in the previous chapter, Horner said the consequence of Duparquet's overconfident laxity had been tragic: the larger boys had "visited *les négresses* of the village and been lost." He feared that Acker's indulgence might have similar consequences. *"Les noirs,"* Horner wrote, "can become carried away

---

1. Mhonda journal, 5xi77, 8xii77; BG 11:730ff; Versteijnen and de Jong 1977. Banns for the two Mhonda-bound couples were announced September 23 at Zanzibar, and the weddings took place six days later at Bagamoyo. The journey to found the new mission commenced the next day (Zanzibar journal, 23ix77, 29ix77, 30ix77).

2. BG 11:737. Already in early 1878, Hilarion was instructing a catechumen, Almase, who traveled to Bagamoyo (Mhonda journal, 18ii78). It is unclear if he was ever baptized.

3. MC 10 (1878), 243. For a fuller account of Hilarion's story, see Kollman 2004a. Brief discussions appear in the following: Sahlberg 1986, 93; W. B. Anderson 1977, 12f, 57f (where Hilarion is mistakenly identified as catechist at Mandera in one place, and at Mhonda in the second). The other husband, Marie-Gabriel, was a former seminarian (MC 4 [1871], 77).

and too familiar *with holy things* [like the Eucharist; emphasis in original]," continuing, "The heads of the blacks are hard; they develop only with difficulty." Acker defended himself in his own letter to Paris. He asked whether Horner had the right to interfere in such a matter when Acker himself was the one who heard the children's confessions. In his defense, Acker cited the joy of the children at receiving communion, the dictates of the Council of Trent, and his rights as a confessor.[4]

This chapter examines slave evangelization from 1877 to roughly the end of the 1880s. The world in which the Spiritans pursued their strategy changed irrevocably in those years, as Omani power in the region eroded before European advances. As the Germans approached and, with the British, established colonial control in the region, the Spiritans also expanded their activities. They founded a number of interior missions with the help of former slaves turned Catholics like Hilarion, beginning with Mhonda in 1877. They achieved the goal that had motivated slave evangelization. Each new mission had a village in which to settle couples formed at the coast, the anticipated *noyau* of the new local church.

At the same time, those former slaves whose transformation into Catholics the Spiritans had pursued had also changed. Both Hilarion's evolution and the ways the catechists-in-training could divide the Spiritans suggest the complexities inherent in the emerging new identities of these African Catholics in the era prior to and at the beginning of formal colonial overrule in eastern Africa. Their behavior repeatedly frustrated the missionaries and even led the missionaries to alter their strategy. Sometimes, as with the Zanzibar students eager for Eucharist, the children of the mission found themselves caught between different views of missionary strategy — in this case, divergent views about the frequency of communion, both of which represented European Catholic piety and practice at the time.[5] These students wanted greater participation in the faith life of the mission, and on Acker's terms more than on Horner's, thus exposing Spiritan disagreement. Horner's connection between the laxity of Acker, which led to too-frequent communion for the students, and Duparquet's lack of supervision that had led to earlier escapes and misbehavior, reiterates the Spiritan tendency to trace unacceptable behavior in the mission's children to faulty missionary preaching or mistaken missionary practices. The missionaries had trouble attributing what was perceived as African misbehavior to any agency or achievement by the Africans themselves.

The self-understanding of these early African Catholics still eludes simple categorization over a century later. Yet Catholics they usually were, for the years at Bagamoyo and Zanzibar had helped forge a Catholic identity in them. But the move to the new interior missions created conditions that differed from those

---

4. CSSp 196biv: Acker to Schwindenhammer, 4iii78; ibid.: Horner to Schwindenhammer, 7iii78.
5. R. Gibson 1989, 251ff. A 1905 decree of Pope Pius X made frequent communion the norm for Catholics, ending several centuries of ambiguous teaching.

operative at the coast, not only placing new demands on the missionaries, but also creating new possibilities for African Catholics. In such settings, the former slaves showed their loyalty and their identity as Catholics through various exercises of voice, not all of which the Spiritans could appreciate.

Like Hilarion, many of the evangelized former slaves were little inclined to the simple obedience to missionary expectations that the Spiritans hoped their program would inculcate. Few, however, took Hilarion's option and exited the church entirely, and even his decision to leave took several decades and many twists and turns. If Spiritan desires for obedient Catholics on their own terms went unmet, Spiritan practices nonetheless contributed to a context in which professed and practicing Catholics emerged at their missions. This period thus presents numerous historical windows into both missionary and African experiences of slave evangelization and its aftermath.

The Expansion of Catholic Missions in Eastern Africa

The late 1870s and 1880s occasioned a number of important developments for the Spiritan missions of eastern Africa. Hilarion helped found the third mission at Mhonda in 1877, and in early 1881 a new crop of Bagamoyo Christians founded a fourth at Mandera. The Spiritans established other stations in 1882 at Morogoro, in 1884 at Tununguo, and in 1885 at Kondoa. In each case the Spiritans negotiated for land with local leaders, and then headed off in caravans with Christians from Bagamoyo to clear the earth, then build rudimentary and, later, more permanent shelters. Mhonda was founded by the Spiritans with two married couples, but in all the missions founded afterward, the initial work was carried out by a few Spiritans along with a group of around ten young unmarried men. Once the preliminary work of clearing and erecting temporary shelters was complete, one of the Spiritans accompanied the young men back to Bagamoyo, where they married and returned with their wives to constitute the new Christian village.[6] Bagamoyo remained what the missionaries called the nursery for the entire mission and the site for the formation of the majority of former slaves at the orphanages. It also maintained the large village named after St. Joseph. Meanwhile Zanzibar continued to offer specialized formation for catechists and, for a short period, for potential African Spiritans.

Ecclesiastical decisions from Rome had new consequences for the Spiritans in this period. In 1878, Propaganda Fide began to redraw Catholic boundaries in the region.[7] Such decisions deprived the Spiritans of much of the territory they dreamed of conquering for Christ and conferred it on other Catholic missionary groups. Most prominently, the White Fathers arrived in 1878, surprising the Spiritans and taking charge of the western parts of what would become Tanganyika as well as Uganda and other areas around the Great Lakes of eastern

6. For summaries, see the following: Kieran 1966, 375–78; BG 13:1073f; Versteijnen 1968a, 39.

7. For a summary, see Kieran 1966, 40ff, as well as Koren 1992.

Africa. This ended the Spiritan hope of moving into the interior and meeting their confreres from central Africa. Bitter Spiritan frustration shows that their zeal for missionizing the interior meant that even other Catholics could appear as their rivals. The Spiritans raged against the supposed incompetence of their own confreres in Rome who had been blindsided by Lavigerie's machinations. The colonial presence of the German empire beginning in the mid-1880s facilitated the later arrival of a mostly German Catholic missionary society, the Benedictines of St. Ottilien, who assumed control of Catholic missionary work in the territory south of Bagamoyo in 1887.[8]

If these decisions shrinking their territory frustrated the Spiritans, they drew encouragement from others emanating from Rome. The 1883 Vatican decision to erect an apostolic vicariate from the apostolic prefecture of Zanguebar meant their territory became the equivalent of a diocese. The new bishop, the Spiritan Courmont, arrived in 1884 as unrest in the mission stations seemed unmanageable, leading the missionaries to question their strategy. Under Courmont's leadership the Spiritans reconsidered their efforts, especially the organization of the Christian villages, where there were many problems.[9]

Spiritan mission stations inland from the coast developed while formal European colonialism approached and then consumed eastern Africa. In the wake of the German incursion begun in 1884, the late 1880s and early 1890s witnessed the so-called Bushiri War and other armed struggles as the Arab and African inhabitants of the coast and interior fought German control. When the Germans bombarded the city of Bagamoyo in September 1888, the Spiritan mission served as a sanctuary from violence for thousands of refugees. Later, the Spiritans temporarily abandoned some of their missions in the interior to avoid the fighting.[10]

Fortunately for the Spiritans, their stations rarely became targets in the conflicts between the Germans and those who resisted their occupation. Other missionaries, Catholic and Protestant, were not so fortunate. One of the rebels' raids sacked the first Benedictine mission in Pugu (near Dar es Salaam), where several German Catholic missionaries were killed and others taken hostage. Baur and Courmont, as senior missionary in eastern Africa and Catholic bishop of Zanguebar, respectively, helped free the hostages as well as others taken later from British Protestant missions. Their apparent neutrality made the Spiritans valued intermediaries when the Germans and their Arab and African foes negotiated not only for European hostages but also later when they deliberated over terms of truce or surrender.[11]

---

8. The Zanzibar journal anticipated the Benedictines' arrival (22v87, 24v87, 26v87). For the details of the territorial arrangements, see BG 14:369. See also Kollman 2001, 149 n. 9.

9. BG 12:910. Details about Courmont's appointment can be found in CSSp 195v.

10. For a summary of these events, which have received much attention from historians, see Kieran 1966, 291ff and Kollman 2001, 400f. For a broader perspective, see relevant portions of Bennett 1986 and Glassman 1995.

11. Bushiri, the leader of the rebellion against the Germans until his hanging in December 1889, initially considered the French missionaries exempt from his attacks on Europeans, especially

Despite the relative security of their missions during these conflicts, the antic-ipation and implementation of colonial overrule affected the Spiritan missions. In the first place, the political changes made them beholden to new political au-thorities. They wrestled with their natural French loyalties in light of the German presence on the mainland as well as forthcoming semiofficial British control of Zanzibar.[12] In the face of new realities, Courmont urged Paris to send English- and German-speaking missionaries, and sought repeatedly to be replaced by a German national. He also sought to ensure that Spiritan criticisms of the German presence not be published, trying to shield the mission from the ire of colonial officials. By the early 1890s, most of their mission stations were in German Tan-ganyika, a few were in soon-to-be British Kenya, and the original mission at Zanzibar was officially still under the sultan of Zanzibar, though he was effec-tively controlled by the British. Besides these changes in jurisdiction, the onset of colonialism led the Spiritans to lower their opinions of Islam and the Arab authorities at the coast. After 1889, both became more firmly fixed as foes of the Christian missionary and civilizing enterprise. The mission had sought neu-trality early on in the war and prided itself on maintaining Bushiri's friendship by its refusal of partisan politics. But in 1889 Courmont said that the danger to Christians was only from the Arabs. "Islam," he wrote, "is the enemy."[13]

The Interior Missions

Experiences at the interior stations varied. Usually the Spiritans received a warm initial welcome to settle a new mission from local authorities, but other obstacles invariably arose, small and great. Part of the problem was the unsettled nature of political authority away from the coast, which meant that settlement required ongoing negotiation and generated frequent conflicts. Authorities closest to the proposed mission sites often had patrons above them whom the Spiritans also had to placate, but such relationships were rarely stable.[14] Unlike the coast, where the sultan's power was formidable even if still subject to mediating local authorities, the interior stations arose in frontier-like locales where his reach was

---

Germans (Zanzibar journal, 18xii88; CSSp 197aii: Courmont to Emonet, 11i89). Later Bushiri turned on the French *wapadri* (Swahili for "fathers," a loan word from Portuguese), accusing them of spying on him and otherwise assisting the Germans (CSSp 197aii: Courmont to Emonet, 2ix89; Zanzibar journal, 24vi89, 25viii89; CSSp 197aiii: Courmont to Emonet, 3iii90). For a judicious discussion of the justice of Bushiri's complaints, discussing German as well as missionary sources, see Kieran 1966, 291–96. For more on Spiritan activities in this period, see Tullemans 1982a and 1982b; see also de Jong 2002, 62ff.

12. Kieran 1966, 130; Kieran 1971, 31.

13. For Courmont's concerns in these matters, see the following: CSSp 197aii: Courmont to Emonet, 30xii85, 7vi86, 20xii86, 17viii87, 27viii87, 29ix87, 11vi88; ibid.: Courmont to Barillec, 27vi86. From Paris, Emonet scolded Courmont for his desires to resign and blamed the bishop himself for allowing a story from eastern Africa criticizing the German administration to appear (CSSp 196bi: Emonet to Courmont, 18ii87, 19x87, 14xi87).

14. Such was the case at Mandera, where the local chief, Kingaru, was very welcoming, but he had to bring the missionaries to his overlord, Kolwa, to receive his approval (van den Eeden 1980, 6f).

much more attenuated. Some Spiritan missions developed fortifications because of occasional participation in conflicts among ambitious local leaders. In addition, the missionaries suffered illnesses and early deaths, and at times passionately disagreed among themselves. Most importantly, as we shall see, Hilarion was neither the first nor the last Christian villager who came from Bagamoyo only to frustrate the missionaries at the interior stations.

Partly for these reasons, the evangelization of neighboring peoples usually developed slowly. The Anglican UMCA, in its efforts to establish villages in the interior, sought places where the former slaves from Zanzibar who settled there already knew the language.[15] The Spiritans made no such efforts to build upon the remnant ethnic identities within their Catholics, thus preestablishing potential bridges with local peoples. Whether this would have made the Bagamoyo-based Catholic missionary effort more attractive to local peoples is unclear. Regardless, ongoing local conflicts and the persistence of so-called pagan practices, such as infanticide, polygamy, and the murder of alleged witches, hampered efforts to draw their neighbors to the Spiritan missions.

The interior missions developed different ways to cope with their circumstances. At Mhonda, Father Machon, the longtime superior, became a local power broker to whom many regional chieftains pledged fealty in return for protection from their enemies; some even offered themselves as the mission's slaves. Disagreements with neighboring villages were frequent, and the mission became a regular participant in local disputes, with Hilarion frequently at their center. The catechist figured strongly in a larger such conflict in February 1881, labeled a war by the missionaries. In addition, the ambitious Machon tried to attract the sons of chiefs to the mission, trusting that "*les noirs* follow their chiefs," but few came in the 1880s.[16]

The station at Morogoro, founded in 1882, spent its early days in a struggle to overcome the local chief's reluctance to hand over land initially promised. It also suffered a devastating fire in October 1884. It later became a much-admired station and famous for the cultivation of coffee.[17] Tununguo, founded in 1884, suffered from attacks by a marauding group, the Mafitis, and the early deaths of its missionaries. It never quite flourished and was abandoned periodically in the decades after its founding. Though Tununguo's mission had periods of relative calm in the twentieth century, it is the only one of the stations founded in the

---

15. Small 1980, 35ff.
16. Kieran 1966, 246f. Machon served as superior at Mhonda for most of the years between 1878 and his death in 1898. In his first reports he wrote that he and the few couples from Bagamoyo then at the mission were already considered "big people" by their neighbors (BG 11:738). On Mhonda's first century, see Versteijnen and de Jong 1977. See also: BG 11:730ff; CSSp 196biv: Machon, Notes, 1xii78; Mhonda journal, 13vi79, 8ix79, 16ix80, 6–7x80, 3xi80, 2ii81, 11v84; BG 13:1102f; CSSp 197aii: Courmont to Emonet, 12i87.
17. On Morogoro, see the following: BG 13:95ff; CSSp 198a: Gommenginger, n.d.; MC 15 (1883), 375–76; APF 61 (1889), 59f; Ananias 1949. For praise of Morogoro by an American observer in 1886, see Hassing and Bennett 1962, 145. The first church in Morogoro is now in an area called Kinguranyembe, on the grounds of a teachers' training college.

Figure 14. The first residence for the Spiritans at Mhonda. Photo by author.

1870s and 1880s that no longer serves as an active parish. The Spiritans received the mission founded at Kondoa in 1885 as a gift from the French Committee of the International African Association. By the next year, the Spiritans had discovered its environment too Muslim and moved to La Longa, two hours away, a mission today called Ilonga.[18]

Unlike Mhonda and Tununguo, the mission at Mandera mostly stayed out of local armed conflicts in the years that followed. Its most pressing difficulty lay in the persistent infanticide practiced by the surrounding people. In July 1883, the superior, Fr. Cado Picarda (1854–87), met with thirty of the local chiefs in an attempt to convince them of the folly of the practice. This meeting, recounted in various mission journals, failed to stem the killing of children, but it showed the increasing focus of Spiritan evangelization at such interior stations: missionaries directed their efforts not primarily at ransomed or received ex-slaves, but toward settled peoples in the interior whose cultural practices and characteristics shaped missionary strategies. The Christian villages, composed primarily of former slaves from the coast, receded in Spiritan accounts of their work. Despite the trend, 319 slaves were ransomed at Bagamoyo between 1884 and 1888, and

---

18. On Tununguo, see BG 13:1116f; BG 14:650f; BG 15:738ff; BG 16:750ff; APF 61 (1889), 61f: CSSp 420ai: Le Roy, report on Zanzibar mission. Le Roy wrote that it had been abandoned by the missionaries from 1900 to 1909, but maintained by its chief and catechist, Valerie, only to have it unravel with World War I. On Kondoa (then La Longa, now Ilonga), see BG 13:1130ff; BG 14:655ff; BG 15:742ff; BG 16:781ff; APF 61 (1889), 60–61. For Courmont's accounts of the decision to move from Kondoa to La Longa, see CSSp 198b: Courmont, 19–22x86.

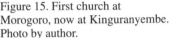
Figure 15. First church at
Morogoro, now at Kinguranyembe.
Photo by author.

a total of 1,580 slaves were taken in between 1884 and 1894 through a variety
of means.[19]

Courmont's Achievements

Bishop Courmont acted decisively in his new post. He arrived at Zanzibar
in March 1884, traveled to Bagamoyo in April, and called a chapter meeting in
September, the major goal of which was to address the difficulties faced at the
Christian villages. Over the next years, he tightened organization in his diocese,
traveled extensively to open new mission stations in the future Tanganyika and
Kenya, and presided over the modification of the evangelizing strategy. During
his tenure as bishop the Spiritans continued to establish Christian villages at
their missions in order to settle those formed at Bagamoyo. They also founded
schools at the interior stations to attract the children from surrounding peoples.

---

19. BG 14:615; LERE. For Picarda's attempt to stop infanticide, see the original account in the
Mandera journal (29vii83), later prepared as a separate document (copied, Picarda said, word for word
from the journal) and reprinted (CSSp 194bv: Picarda 1883; CSSp 194bi: Picarda 1884/5, *Echos des
Missions d'Afrique;* MC 16 [1884] 505–9). For discussion see W. B. Anderson 1977, 52–53. On the
story of the foundation of the mission at Mandera, see BG 13:83f; MC 14 (1882), 368–70; APF 54
(1882), 364f; van den Eeden 1980, 4.

In addition, Courmont had brought with him from France a laywoman, Madame Chevalier, who established a hospital at Zanzibar called *Notre Dame des Anges.* She was joined by a younger Frenchwoman, Mademoiselle Duclos, and together they gained a reputation for unselfish service in Zanzibar. Notre Dame des Anges served the needy, but the Spiritans recognized that it also raised the mission in the eyes of Zanzibar's population.[20]

The new hospital also signaled a new institutional commitment to the zeal for souls. Notre Dame des Anges targeted those dying, hoping to baptize them, a fact admitted by the missionaries: though they recognized the call to be merciful, the care of the injured or ill body was a pretext for obtaining eternal salvation.[21] Such convictions, which had characterized Spiritan missionizing from the beginning, also took expression in an unprecedented energetic campaign of baptisms at Bagamoyo, starting in 1882. Father François Antoine Hirtzlin (1850–89) initiated the mass baptisms, most of which were surreptitious consecrations of Muslim children. Later, stymied by local resentment of his deceit, he began using women from the mission. They operated incognito and thus could enter Muslim homes without attracting notice.[22] These women represented a remarkable example of African Catholic identities emerging in this period, one of many to be discussed later in this chapter.

Courmont's accession led to a number of other developments, as the new bishop sought to organize the growing mission along the lines of congregation-wide expectations. He published clear instructions about the founding of new mission sites, many of which were begun under his authority in the years before he left the position in 1896. Finally, he urged local fund raising through a variety of means, not only the cultivation of crops but also the gathering of plant and animal species for sale to Europeans.[23]

The end of the nineteenth century and beginning of the twentieth witnessed great changes in the Catholic presence in eastern Africa, as European colonialism gripped the region more fully. The Holy Ghost mission, blocked to the west by the White Fathers and to the south by the German Benedictines, expanded with vigor into the region around Mount Kilimanjaro and present-day Kenya, with the most spectacular growth among the Chagga around Kilimanjaro.[24] Famines, possibly related to the impress of colonial overrule, led many to seek asylum at the missions, and others sold their children due to economic and environmental distress. Slavery continued, and Cardinal Lavigerie's abolitionist zeal led the Vatican to mount its own anti-slavery campaign beginning in the late 1880s. In 1896, Bishop Courmont issued a detailed report on slavery in eastern Africa to

---

20. For more on *Notre Dame des Anges*, see the following: Zanzibar journal, 4viii84; MC 17 (1885), 401–5; BG 13:1070.

21. CSSp 194bi: Courmont, *Notre Dame des Anges*, 1886 (which appeared as MC 17 [1885], 378, 389–91, 401–5); BG 13:1070; APF 61 (1889), 52f.

22. BG 13:1077f; BG 14:615ff; AA (1888), 86–93.

23. On Courmont's achievements, see Kieran 1966, 61f and Kollman 2001, 400f.

24. Henschel 2001, 22. On Holy Ghost expansion into Kenya, see especially Njoroge 1999.

assist the campaign and encourage support from Propaganda Fide for the Spiritan missions.[25]

In 1906, Bagamoyo became the seat of a separate diocese, Central *Zanguebar.* This reflected the German control of the mainland that made administration of the missions from British-dominated Zanzibar complicated. Bagamoyo continued to house a large and important mission until well after World War I. Its vitality shrank, however, as that of other missions away from the coast grew, especially because in 1892 the Germans made Dar es Salaam their capital. They consequently laid the railroad from the interior to the coast in such a way as to bypass Bagamoyo.

Successors to Horner

Horner's departure in 1879 due to illness meant the end of his duty as primary reporter on Spiritan evangelization in eastern Africa, a role he had played since 1863. He died in 1880 in France.[26] Baur replaced Horner for the next few years, becoming the superior as well as the main correspondent with congregational authorities in Paris and the missionary support agencies. Compared to Horner, Baur was neither a thorough correspondent nor attentive to finances. This frustrated Holy Ghost superiors and funding agencies alike.[27] Yet his penchant for discussing more openly the difficulties with the African Catholics at the missions in letters to Paris — already evident in the 1860s and 1870s during Horner's absences and continuing in this period — makes our grasp of African experiences of evangelization fuller than it would otherwise be. Baur remained in eastern Africa until his death in 1913, and in that lengthy tenure may have shaped the Spiritan missionary presence more than any other single individual.[28] But Courmont's accession in 1884 ended his role as the primary witness to slave evangelization.

After his arrival as bishop in March 1884, Courmont naturally composed most of the official reports and correspondence from the Spiritan missions. He also kept small personal notebooks, *carnets*, that preserved his observations during his many interior voyages to visit stations and investigate possible new sites.[29] There he often described the African Catholics more intimately than in summary treatments in correspondence and reports. Courmont's often pious writings evince manifold interests, careful observation of African cultures and landscapes,

---

25. On the famines, see CSSp 194xiii: Courmont to Hespers, 24i96, 28ii96; CSSp 195iii: Courmont to Ledochowski, 26i96. Lavigerie's letter introducing his campaign, replete with maps and substantial historical reporting, can be found in MC 20 (1888), 457–62, 469–75, 481–87, 493–99, 517–22. For Courmont's report on slavery, see CSSp 195iii: Courmont to Simeoni, 1896.

26. After the August 1877 visit that chose Mhonda as the new site, Horner entered Zanzibar's hospital and his health never returned. He left eastern Africa in May 1879 and died a year later while convalescing in Cannes (MC 11 [1879], 440; MC 12 [1880], 268, 309ff).

27. On frustrations with Baur's accounts and reports, see CSSp 196bi: Schwindenhammer to Baur, 14xi81; ibid.: Emonet to Courmont, 23v84.

28. On Baur, see the following: CSSp 194bii: Noel 1983; ibid.: Dubourget 1941.

29. These *carnets* are found at the Spiritan archives, catalogued under CSSp 198b.

and a strong classical education. He wrote poetry, too, though rarely for public consumption.

An even more revealing recorder had arrived a few years before Courmont, in December 1881. Introduced in chapter 1, Alexandre Le Roy, whom the Holy Ghost superior in Paris told Baur was "an excellent addition to your mission," later became an archbishop in western Africa, superior general of the Spiritans (from 1896 to 1926), and a prominent figure in the early years of the discipline of the history of religions.[30] He wrote extensive accounts of Spiritan voyages throughout eastern Africa. A remarkable polymath, Le Roy's voluminous writings reveal familiarity with nineteenth-century botany, zoology, geography, geology, linguistics, anthropology, and sociology. Le Roy advised Courmont, and together they represent our most revealing historical sources on slave evangelization in the 1880s.

Le Roy's extensive, detailed, and entertaining reports on his visits to the interior with Baur and later Courmont marked a signal change in Spiritan writings during this period.[31] In addition, he was a talented artist, and his ink and pencil drawings of events on voyages, local faces and features, and animal and plant species filled editions of *Les Missions Catholiques*, which often resembled a late-nineteenth-century precursor of *National Geographic*, though both more pious and sometimes more highbrow. Other Spiritans also described their efforts in the 1880s, though none compared with Le Roy.

Le Roy's writings oscillate between close descriptions of the events and details of his journeys, and reflections of a more philosophical or theological sort. The details revealed his imaginative construal of the African interior and also life on the caravans to and from the coast. The caravans were mostly composed of porters, but trusted Catholics from the Bagamoyo and Zanzibar missions also usually supervised and assisted. Le Roy's descriptions of African customs also represent an important stage in the development of the conceptual category that later became known as "African traditional religion," by which Europeans sought to understand the religious beliefs and practices of the continent's peoples prior to contact with Islam or Christianity. Le Roy described typical features of African religions, such as ancestor veneration and varieties of spirits; religio-cultural practices like sacrifice, funerals, marriage, initiation, and witchcraft accusations; and religious authorities like the so-called witchdoctor or *mganga*.[32]

In his musing reflections on these observations, Le Roy stressed the shared humanity between Africans and Europeans. In examining his discourse on Africans as a whole, however, his attempted evenhandedness rests uncomfortably with the

---

30. CSSp 196bi: Schwindenhammer to Baur, 20viii81. For more on Le Roy's life, see the following: Gittins 1999b, Goré 1952, Ducol 2000a, 2003.

31. Le Roy's works are listed in the bibliography, and many appeared first serially in *Les Missions Catholiques*.

32. Some of Le Roy's ideas prefigured influential twentieth-century studies of the religious beliefs and practices of African peoples, such as those by Godfrey Lienhardt, E. E. Evans-Pritchard, and Edwin Smith. For example, see MC 16 (1884), 45; MC 19 (1887), 308–12.

exoticism inherent in his descriptions of African peoples. To explain the differences between his readers and his subjects, differences that his close descriptions of African customs disclosed, he had recourse to sociological explanations. Le Roy insisted that their social experiences had made Africans "children as long as they live," generating the lower level of civilization on the continent compared to Europe. While this mode of description refused the biological racism that grew in nineteenth-century European descriptions of the world's peoples, it also legitimated the colonial (and thus missionary) project of civilizing Africans. His emphasis on the consequences of socialization also made him wary of freed slaves as a reliable basis for the church, for he believed them often to have been corrupted by their experiences.[33] Not surprisingly, in the early twentieth century Le Roy became a prominent figure in the emerging field of "colonial sociology."[34]

Continuity in Forming the *Noyau*:
Education and Labor in the Late 1870s and 1880s

Bagamoyo remained the largest center of the Holy Ghost missions until well into the twentieth century. There and at Zanzibar the same activities that had taken place before 1877 continued through the 1880s.

The educational efforts of the Spiritans at the coast, for example, continued in the same institutions during this decade. The children remained separated by age and gender, as well as by missionary perceptions of their aptitude for academic study. Bagamoyo maintained its creche for infants and toddlers as well as the large orphanages that served as primary schools for most of those at the mission. In 1882, Baur wrote in gratitude of the generous support given the Spiritans, support that allowed them to have 600 Christians who had been delivered from slavery at their missions. These arrived at differing ages, and beginning at about seven years entered the orphanages, there spending their days at prayer, study, and work on the plantations. Bagamoyo's orphanages housed around 250 children through most of the 1880s, and the education offered remained rudimentary: catechism, simple arithmetic, reading, and writing. Though some European observers questioned the usefulness of educating "descendants of Ham," others expressed astonishment at

---

33. Kieran 1966, 49f. Le Roy's awareness of the damage done by enslavement appeared much more strongly in retrospect, that is, in his later writings than in those that emerged in the 1880s when he worked in eastern Africa (Le Roy 1906a, 2; Le Roy 1934b, 47). There is little evidence for such sociologically informed pessimism when he was implementing slave evangelization, at least in his writings. Libermann had admitted the unfortunate results of slavery, too, but urged zeal nonetheless (Kieran 1966, 98). The UMCA missionaries at Zanzibar also blamed the misbehavior of the African Christians at their mission on their slave backgrounds (UMCA 1883–84, 19ff).

34. See Le Roy 1906a, 1906b. Le Roy's early writings anticipated his later stature in this field. Thus in what would become part of *Au travers Zanguebar*, he discussed African family life, comparing it with European family life. His constant refrain was "It's the same here as everywhere," and he closed by observing, "All people everywhere are the same species, the human species" (MC 16 [1884], 92–93). For a recent examination of the origins of scientific racism in France, see Staum 2003. A work that attempts (unsuccessfully, in my opinion) to present nineteenth-century anthropologists as more enlightened with regard to race is Hecht 2003.

Spiritan achievements.[35] Spiritan reports to the Propagation of the Faith and the Holy Childhood Society in these years, prepared by Horner, Baur, and Courmont, suggested a steadily growing mission:

Spiritan Reports to Propagation of the Faith and the Holy Childhood Society 1878–89[36]

Propagation of the Faith

Year	Adult converts	Easter communions
1878	97	(700 Catholics)
1879	80	200/800 Catholics
1880	166	(1100 Catholics)
1881	150	(1500 Catholics)
1882	153	(1800 Catholics)
1883	208	–
1884	291	(552 total)
1885	173	
1886	151	
1887	–	
1888		
1889		

Holy Childhood Society

Year	Baptized	Surviving	In nursery	In Christian families	At orphanages	At schools	At workshops	On farms
1878		536	72		536	208	37	219
1879	550	397	38		405	119	43	243
1880	545	514	61		51	182	95	228
1881	602	540	67		540	217	98	225
1882	–	–	–		–	–	–	–
1883	802		91		429	151	117	161
1884	843				552	196	143	181
1885	800 baptisms in danger of death							
1886	1080 baptisms in danger of death							
1887	1131 baptisms in danger of death							
1888	1176 baptisms at Bagamoyo, 200 minimum elsewhere							
1889	450 ("War ends work everywhere.")							

---

35. For example, German visitors expressed such sentiments (Bagamoyo journal, 9vii80).

36. These reports can be found in CSSp 196ax, CSSp 196axi, CSSp 196axii, and CSSpaxiii. They depict totals from all the missions, not just Bagamoyo. Horner prepared the reports until 1879, Baur from 1879 to 1883, then Courmont after that. As is clear, the reports are incomplete, with many of the requested categories left blank and other information given in place of that requested by the mission's benefactors. In addition, the Spiritans who prepared them counted those at the mission in ways that changed over time. For instance, the 51 listed at the orphanage in 1880 is obviously wrong. It either should be 514, or Baur decided to list only the new boys and girls who came to the orphanage in the preceding year, rather than the total. Courmont also ended Baur's practice of totaling the number of Catholics at Spiritan missions. He might simply have wanted to avoid what he saw as Baur's past exaggerations. In the mid-1880s, when Hirtzlin was baptizing so many, Courmont's count depicts not the total baptized (as in preceding years), but those baptized in the year indicated. Courmont also decided not to be as thorough in his reports as the others had been. Perhaps the high numbers of those baptized led him to believe that other figures were unnecessary.

Meanwhile the mission at Zanzibar featured specialized educational and formation programs, continuing Horner's onetime hope of creating complete Christian communities for the interior. In the first place, though the end of Latin instruction closed off explicit seminary training in the late 1870s, the missionaries initially maintained hopes for African religious to join Philippe in their community in permanent vows. The three young men who returned from Europe with Horner in 1876 and 1877 (after the deaths of the other two novices in Paris) — Julien, Dieudonné, and Patrice — continued for a little while in the program at Zanzibar. While those three continued in this makeshift novitiate, two others, François Kundjou and Laurent Tousouméné Aulouguéla, remained alongside them in the postulancy program that ostensibly prepared candidates for the novitiate.[37] Ongoing Spiritan frustrations with Philippe, the first eastern African Spiritan, still in temporary vows, influenced missionary approaches to these young men and chastened hope for reliable confreres from among them. This small group represented the remnants of the onetime seminary program.[38]

As part of their training, those in formation to be Spiritans taught in the schools at Zanzibar that continued the specialized education once reserved for seminarians and those preparing to be nuns. Zanzibar housed two schools of thirty students each, one for the boys and the other for the girls whose gifts indicated that they could be catechists or teachers in the future. This was the location of the conflict between Acker and Horner over the frequency of Eucharistic reception, mentioned at the beginning of this chapter. When Zanzibar's workshops moved to Bagamoyo in 1882, Zanzibar's mission focused even more on the specialized training for future catechists and teachers. The workshops themselves henceforth almost exclusively provided services for the Spiritan missions themselves rather than outside clients.[39]

There was both continuity and some important innovation in the formative efforts at the missions in the 1880s. In 1882, the Spiritans mandated KiSwahili as the language for instruction after debating its merits compared to persisting in French.[40] The chapter also set a minimum age at which children were able to leave school and go to work in the fields on a full-time basis. This decision indicated again that the priests present recognized the possibility that African ex-slave labor could merely be exploited, in appearance if not in fact, thus continuing enslavement. Like their confreres at the earlier chapter of 1870, they did not want to be accused of enslaving anyone, an ironic concern given the prevalence of escapes and complaints at the time. No doubt quite aware of the difficulties they faced in maintaining their plantations and villages in the midst of unrest at the mission stations, the chapter's delegates decreed that all children had to

37. On Laurent and François, see Koren 1994, 74. We return to them later in the chapter.
38. The girls who wanted to be nuns had gone to Réunion some years before, and our only record of them is Madeleine/Suéma's death, recounted in chapter 4.
39. CSSp 197aiii: Courmont to Emonet, 1vii91. On the workshops, see Kollman 2001, 406.
40. Bagamoyo journal, 17ix82. On the decision, see Kollman 2001, 405.

complete instruction for their first communion, meaning they remained in school until about the age of twelve.[41]

Meanwhile, Bagamoyo's plantations continued to expand in the next de-' cade. These busied the many children at the orphanages and the Christians in St. Joseph's village, and provided considerable food and income for the mission community. The Spiritans continued to trust the moralizing that came from work in the fields more than classroom education. Outsiders repeated praise of the regime of work at Bagamoyo as well as the beauty and orderliness of the mission's plantations. The Spiritans proudly spoke of their yields from the more than one hundred different species cultivated. Smaller cultivation continued at Zanzibar on the plot called Baobab, and strenuous work clearing land for crops accompanied the founding of each of the new mission stations of the interior.[42]

At Bagamoyo, baptisms took place in large numbers, especially when Hirtzlin's mass campaign was at its peak in the mid-1880s. A steady stream were also married, usually before heading to an interior station to constitute the Christian village. The number of dead often reflected the number of dying children baptized.

Bagamoyo mission's sacramental activity, 1878–90[43]

Year	Baptized	Died at the mission	Married at the mission
1878	96	24	5
1879	34	39	10
1880	32	36	6
1881	81	27	16
1882	154	134	–
1883	169	111	18
1884	491	253	1
1885	1138	276	1
1886	1226	466	25
1887	982	452	7
1888	1063	554	22
1889	122	89	8
1890	172	70	10

The names of the sponsors and godparents serving in baptisms and marriages indicated the persistence of the reliable group associated with the Christian village

41. CSSp 196aiv: chapter of 1884.

42. MC 12 (1880), 310; CSSp 194aii: Mauberge, 2ii83; CSSp 196ax: Le Roy to Propagation of the Faith, 15ix83; APF 56 (1884), 49–50; BG 11:714ff. For examples of ongoing labor, see the following: Zanzibar journal, 3–5 and 12vi79, 29iii80, 11ii81, 4v81, 16–17v81, 5x81, 31x81, 2v82, 26ix82; Mhonda journal, 19iii78; v-vi78, 14vii80 (where "even the women" were working); Mandera journal, 28i81, 1ii81, 9iii81, 19iii81, 18v81.

43. Versteijnen 1963. These figures are derived from Bagamoyo's sacramental registries.

at Bagamoyo, many of them former seminarians. Some of the Spiritans, including the African brother Philippe, also served in such capacities. Of those frequently named in the sacramental books, some later became notorious, but most lived at the villages for the rest of their lives, either at Bagamoyo or an interior mission.

The official Spiritan approach to the villagers stressed their paternal authority over those they had redeemed. In a letter to the Holy Childhood Society in 1877, Horner described how the Africans at Bagamoyo's village gladly accepted punishment from *les blancs*, as long as it was seen as just.[44] A few years later, in a lengthy description of the village appearing in *Les Missions Catholiques*, Acker wrote, "Since we ransomed them from slavery we maintain full authority over them," adding, "They continue to call us their fathers and we love to name them our children." He praised the effect of these paternal ties: "Holding [this] full paternal authority [over them] helps us to powerfully maintain our blacks (*nos noirs*) in piety and fortify in them habits of order and work. We are, for the most part, satisfied with their conduct."[45]

Through the late 1870s and 1880s, the ransoming of slaves continued at Bagamoyo and inland, but sales were sporadic since there were no formal markets as had been at Zanzibar. Usually between forty and one hundred people were ransomed per year.[46] Meanwhile, the British consul sent the Spiritans groups of slaves freed at sea into the early 1880s, usually handing them over to the Zanzibar mission, from where most went to Bagamoyo. The missionaries continued to feel tension between taking those who were young enough to be formed and the need to use the labor of those at the mission, who thus needed to be of a certain age. When the British offered slaves they sometimes gladly took those "not yet in the state of self-sufficiency," and at other times rejoiced to have older ones who could support themselves.[47]

Challenges to the Spiritan Program from Europeans

The late 1870s and 1880s saw new challenges to the Spiritans' coastal missions from several directions. First, the Spiritans expressed more fears that the mission's children might leave the mission to follow European explorers and traders passing into the interior, drawn by promises of adventure and remuneration. Such temptations grew as these harbingers of approaching European colonialism joined Islam and paganism as ongoing sources of potential pollution

---

44. CSSp 196axii: Horner to Holy Childhood, 31xii77.

45. MC 12 (1880), 337, 341; BG 11:718ff.

46. For examples of ransoming, see Bagamoyo journal, 7vi82, 15iii84, 24iii84, 8v84, 3ii85, 27iv85, 28v85, 24vii85, 21i86. A summary of the numbers per year has been given by John Henschel (2000a, 5). See also BG 14:615f and LERE. Ransoming increased with the social upheavals surrounding colonial rule, continuing into the 1890s (CSSp 196axiii: Courmont to Holy Childhood, 8i92), and the increase is reflected in LERE.

47. Bagamoyo journal, 1viii80, 6viii80, 20x81. The UMCA mission in Zanzibar received 155 slaves in 1880 and 36 more in early 1881 (UMCA 1881, 8f). For more details, see Kollman 2001, 340 n. 58.

of the Christian *noyau*, or nucleus. A second challenge came to the Spiritan program when British misgivings about Spiritan strategies both shrank the number of Africans coming to the Catholic missions and led to an investigation. Early in the 1880s, the British consul, John Kirk, ordered a stop to the practice of handing over freed slaves to the Catholic mission, accusing the Spiritans of encouraging the slave trade by their willingness to ransom slaves and of not paying their workers at their missions.[48] Handovers proceeded for a while even after Kirk's decision, but the numbers of those received after being freed at sea fell between 1883 and 1887.

Kirk's concerns were taken seriously by the French government, which in 1882 sent a visitor, Comte Mauberge, to inspect the mission at Bagamoyo. Mauberge issued his report in February 1883. The French observer exonerated the Spiritans of accusations of slaveholding. He suggested that British accusations had been fueled by envy since their similar institution at Freretown had run into trouble. Besides giving his measured support for the work of his fellow Frenchmen, Mauberge's report represents one of the most comprehensive accounts of the mission by an outsider.[49]

For the most part, Mauberge described the accomplishments of the missionaries in glowing terms. He extolled the beauty of the grounds at great length: the shaded walkways, tasteful buildings, and the order and harmony of the fields. He admired the results obtained with the mission's children, who were "moralized, Christianized, and given a taste of work." The industrious and well-organized village had sixty couples.

Mauberge mentioned that the missionaries sought to keep the children from ostentation and vanity, yet he noticed an off-putting sanctimonious allure in them. He questioned one of the priests about this revealing observation. The Spiritan admitted that their efforts to prevent such attitudes from emerging often failed: "It [such an attitude] is hardly compatible with morning work in the field and the afternoon workshop. But these children are a little like monkeys who strive to copy the priests and brothers." Mauberge appreciated the explanation.

Toward the end of the report, Mauberge directly addressed the British complaint that the mission exploited its residents. "The mission does earn profits," he wrote,

> and some complain that they do not pay their workers. But this manner of seeing things is too strict, even erroneous. In truth, [the mission's residents] are not paid in money, but they are fed, dressed and lodged well, and even instructed in the workings of the market. . . . In fact, they have better freedom in this century of mandatory instruction because they are educated. . . .[50] These workers are also remunerated by being removed from

48. Versteijnen 1968a, 22; BG 13:25–26; Kieran 1966, 107; Brown 1971a, 211–12. On Kirk and the Spiritans, see Kollman 2001, 67f and 419, n. 35.

49. CSSp 194aii: Mauberge, 2ii83.

50. It is likely that Mauberge here is playing on a contrast between the words *instruction* and *education* in order to praise the Spiritans for providing the latter, which he saw as the basis of

nothingness and abjection to enter the human family. Their work is exploited, but not for the French — rather for the workers [themselves]. . . . If the exploitation was so bad, the word would spread!

Mauberge's comments show how one French outsider not sharing their religious convictions interpreted the missionaries' evangelizing efforts. Despite his suspicions, he admired their work and placed it within the universalist ideology of a civilizing mission, according to which the mission's children received "better freedom" and were brought within the human family. In his eyes, missionary evangelization, quite apart from its religious goals, fostered self-improvement among the former slaves.

Even though one attack on their missions had been fended off, the missionaries continued to feel the need to defend their regime against accusations of practicing slavery into the mid-1880s.[51] Still, possibly because Freretown had grown controversial, Kirk's successor as British consul in the late 1880s relented on the previous embargo and renewed the handovers as before. Between 1888 and 1890 the Spiritans received 153 freed slaves from the British.[52]

A still more serious challenge than European inspectors and explorers, however, was facing the Spiritans, and this from within the mission itself. It lay in the Africans whom the Spiritans sought to transform into allies and auxiliaries in evangelizing the interior.

Unrest at the Missions in the Early 1880s

Two years before Mauberge's visit, resentment at the strictness of the regime of labor and social control in the village of St. Joseph at Bagamoyo had grown among the villagers, who numbered around seventy households in 1880.[53] Whether or not such unrest served as a background and impetus to Kirk's accusations and the visit sponsored by the French consul is unclear, but by early 1880, discontent was widespread. Baur wrote to Paris of the nightly disorder at the village in Bagamoyo in January 1880. He blamed it on the lack of supervision by the missionaries. In the late 1870s, a hut had been erected to allow a missionary to remain overnight in the village to oversee things. Now Baur asked permission to prevent "*promenades* into town" by placing a priest every evening in the hut, which was situated to see many of the houses and the roads out of the village. If that failed, Baur wrote, he would ask the sultan's local governor (the *liwali*)

---

real freedom. In nineteenth-century French educational debates, the former indicated specialized knowledge or training (which Mauberge says was "mandatory" in the nineteenth century) while the latter connoted a more comprehensive teaching that included character and, for Catholics at least, religious training (Harrigan 1973).

51. Le Roy defended the voluntary nature of the work offered at Bagamoyo and referred to accusations faced by the missionaries (AA 1886, 46–47).

52. BG 15:682; Kieran 1966, 275–84.

53. BG 11:718; Vogt, n.d. The sixty couples Mauberge saw two years later probably reflected the settlement of some from Bagamoyo at Mhonda and Mandera.

to help enforce the mission's rules with his *baton*. He felt himself under "the strictest necessity," lest the Spiritans "lose the fruit of our efforts."[54]

By March 1880, one of the priests, Father Foels, was living full-time in the village, watching those married couples whom the missionaries still designated as children. His presence and the surveillance hut had helped, but troubles remained in the village. Baur recognized that it was overcrowded, with insufficient land for the couples present. In the face of endemic misbehavior, the missionaries could not simply be priests: "[They] must combine ecclesiastical and civil functions; because, with these poor children of Africa, who are children as long as they live, it's not enough to be a priest, one also must be prefect of police and night watchman [*garde-champêtre*]."[55]

Baur emphasized the ill effects on the villagers of a conflict between Foels and Hirtzlin. Baur criticized both. He claimed that Hirtzlin had been negligent in supervising the villagers (not surprisingly, given the idiosyncratic and zealous campaign of mass baptizing in which he would be enmeshed two years later). Much worse in Baur's eyes, however, was Foels's preaching to the children what Baur angrily called "independence." Over the next few years, Foels's influence was often adduced in missionary explanations of the problems with the mission's children. As a consequence of his "baneful encouragements," Baur claimed, the villagers were "bold and corrupt," even laying a hand on a Spiritan brother in a threatening way. Baur also was concerned about his confrere's drinking. Yet Baur also admitted that the oldest of the couples, those with the longest experiences in the mission, were the most disappointing, an admission that little cohered with the blame accorded the single missionary Foels, who had arrived not long before.[56]

The orphanages at Bagamoyo also faced their share of problems. Escapes grew numerous in 1880, and there were also incidents of threats of violence against the missionaries and theft.[57] Machon, the superior at Mhonda, blamed the large number of older boys for the disturbances at the coastal mission. Their unruliness, he believed, stemmed from the fact that they were forced to be celibate within the orphanage. Since the village at Bagamoyo was already filled to capacity, it was incapable of adding households, and new missions — with new villages for married couples — were not being founded quickly enough inland. As a

54. CSSp 197ai: Baur to Schwindenhammer, 10i80. Baur also repeated his earlier complaints about the brothers' failures in supervision discussed in chapter 3 (CSSp 196bii: Baur to Horner, 30iii67).

55. CSSp 197ai: Baur to Schwindenhammer, 8ii80,7iii80, 8iii80, 1vi80; BG 11:719–20; BG 13:49; Versteijnen 1968a, 19.

56. For examples of Spiritans blaming problems on Foels, see the following: CSSp 197ai: Baur to Schwindenhammer, 7iii80, 1vi80, 8iii81; ibid.: Baur to Emonet, 26iv83; ibid.: Courmont to Emonet, 10iv84. On Baur's concerns about Foels's drinking, see CSSp 197ai: Baur to Schwindenhammer, 30iv80. From Paris, Schwindenhammer confirmed Baur's observations regarding Foels's excessive indulgence of the mission's children. He ordered Foels to stop drinking and to overcome his "weakness toward the children" (CSSp 196bi: Schwindenhammer to Baur, 4iii80; ibid.: Schwindenhammer to Foels, 1iv80; ibid.: Schwindenhammer, 22vii80).

57. The Zanzibar journal recorded receiving escapees from Bagamoyo, who were returned by Foels (4–5iv80, 7iv80). See also the Bagamoyo journal, 8viii80, 18viii80, 21viii80, 14–15ix80.

consequence, the young men in the orphanage were "languishing at the coast" instead of colonizing the interior.[58]

Yet overcrowding and stifled sexuality might not have accounted for the unrest. Other conditions might well have led people to consider flight or other resistance. In his 1882 report, Mauberge wrote that he asked one of the priests about the kinds of force by which the missionaries maintained discipline in the orphanages. Though the missionary had been evasive, admitting that they had their small punishments but saying that then "the door was opened," Mauberge had not been satisfied, suspecting some coercive means were regularly used.

Spiritan records justify Mauberge's suspicions that they used coercive force in detaining their charges, and his confidence that the Spiritans could do no real violence seems mistaken.[59] Baur was not afraid to chain mission children in 1873, whether they tried to escape or simply remained silent while others did.[60] The early 1880s saw recourse to more extreme measures. One day in 1880 was ominously called *"la journée de fimbo,"* the day of the stick (*fimbo* being Swahili for "stick"), because of the number beaten for stealing coconuts, refusing to do their work, and assisting escapees who were hiding nearby by bringing them extra clothes. Two received the *bastonade*, and another was beaten for expanding the pockets of his pants, a sure sign he was going to steal. Such physical punishments only became more common in the years following, as missionary frustration at African lack of compliance spilled into violence.[61]

More important than the escapes from the orphanages in this period, however, was the emergence in late 1880 and early 1881 of a collective voice of protest against Spiritan policy from the villagers at Bagamoyo. The residents, led by former seminarians and other prominent villagers, sent delegations to the mission superior, Baur, asking for more land, more freedom, and compensation for labor. This was an unprecedented sign that the Catholic villagers there could act in unison.[62] Horizontal voice had appeared in collective vertical voice, so that the relations between the villagers, forged over years, now appeared in resistance to the missionary program. Baur blamed Foels's preaching for sowing discord, filling the heads of the children with what he felt was idle mischief about "independence." By being "too liberal" with them, Baur thought that the younger man had foolishly and imprudently wanted to win their hearts through his largesse. Now the mission reaped the harvest of that indulgence.

The official response of the mission at Bagamoyo, led by Baur since he and Horner had switched places in the mid-1870s, was to crack down. The leaders,

---

58. CSSp 197ai: Machon to Schwindenhammer, 7iii80; ibid.: Machon to Horner, 1v80.

59. See also Kieran 1969.

60. CSSp 196biii: Baur to Horner, 11iv73.

61. Bagamoyo journal, 18viii80. Notorious cases of violence by Holy Ghost missionaries came later, though, as Kieran points out, never with the negative publicity faced by the Anglican mission at Freretown (Kieran 1966, 100, 252; O'Hare 1969; Strayer 1978).

62. Bagamoyo journal, 3x80, 20ii81 ("Matthieu represented the families"), 11–12ix81 (the three leaders had been in "large" school), 14xi81, 18xi81. See Kieran 1966, 121.

named as Matthieu, Maurice, Eloi, and Thibault — each of whom had been connected to the mission for years — were confined.[63] Baur stridently insisted that the villagers fulfill their obligations, refusing to modify the demands placed on them by the mission. Because the villagers had sufficient time to cultivate their plots for their own subsistence, he wrote, "the rest of the time must be at the disposition of the mission which ransomed them, and there should be no talk that they are free and clear of their obligations to the mission.... One never wins anything by being weak with *les noirs*."[64] Baur won little cooperation by being strong. In September 1881 the villagers repeated their appeal for more liberty and less work.[65]

Bagamoyo's village witnessed such collective complaints first, but similar sentiments soon came from the villages at the stations of the interior, where backbreaking labor accompanied the early years of a new mission. After a few months of unremitting work clearing land and erecting shelters, escapes began in early 1881 among the former Bagamoyo Christians who had helped establish the new mission at Mandera. Four months later, eight men from the Christian village there — about half of the men then at the mission — plotted and fled secretly for Bagamoyo to plead their case before Baur, claiming unfair treatment. Their pleas replicated those of Bagamoyo Christians the year before: *terre et liberté*. Baur did as he had done before, refusing to relent on the mission's demands on the labor of the former slaves and incarcerating the complainers. Three returned to Mandera two weeks later and publicly apologized, while five remained in irons at Bagamoyo.[66]

One of those whose confinement lasted longer, Dominique — called by the Mandera journal writer one of "the most evil-minded" — died of pneumonia at Bagamoyo while in prison. He was unable to confess before dying. The Mandera superior later used the tragedy to remind the couples of the senselessness of their actions; they must not miss, he said, the warning God gave them in the sudden death of one of the ringleaders. The superior apparently felt Dominique's sad death a potent lesson to be adduced to create a more obedient spirit among the Christians of the village. The other four returned to Mandera several weeks later, and after a few months the Spiritans at Mandera reiterated the requirement that

63. CSSp 197ai: Baur to Schwindenhammer, 1vi80, 16xi81; ibid., Baur to vicar general, 30vi81, 28vii81. Thibault had been a seminarian at Zanzibar and Bagamoyo, served several times as a godfather for baptisms, then married in 1878. Matthieu, Maurice, and Eloi had been baptized at Bagamoyo in the early 1870s, served as sponsors for others receiving sacraments, and married later in the decade. Exactly where and how they were confined is unclear (CSSp 196biii: Duparquet to Barillec, 17vii71; MC 4 [1871]:76–77; Bagamoyo sacramental registries; CSSp 198b: Courmont, 1887).

64. ...*que le reste du temps ils doivent être à la disposition de la mission qui les a rachetés: et de ne pas dire qu'ils sont libres et dégages de leurs obligations vis à vis de la mission* (CSSp 197ai: Baur to Schwindenhammer, 7iii80 and 1vi80; see also Kieran 1966, 121). The names come from Vogt, n.d.

65. Bagamoyo journal, 11ix81.

66. On the escapes, complaints, and then punishments of those at Mandera, see the journal: 3vi81, 8vi81, 9x81, 22x81, 31x81, 14–17xi81, 20i82, 12vi82. For the list of the villagers then at Mandera, see van Eeden 1980, 10–11.

Thursday be dedicated to the mission's work. The response from the villagers was not what the missionaries hoped. Soon another villager escaped. Meanwhile, the missionaries at Mandera reaffirmed the "absolute nature" of their "paternal authority," maintaining that *les noirs* were like children, though also "free-thinkers" and thus not without malice.[67]

Spiritan severity and inflexibility, seen both in Baur's response at Bagamoyo and replicated in Mandera, failed to curb the fleeing, which reached epidemic proportions by 1883. Chapter 1 noted the appeal for liberty early in that year directed to the French consul by Léon and his fellow escaping companion from Mhonda, one such episode that was particularly unsettling since it involved authorities external to the missionaries. The Mhonda mission faced other escapes in 1883, while the Christians at Mandera continued to grumble about the burden of work upon them and stole items from the mission.[68] At Mhonda, Machon likened his mission to a prison due to the measures he was taking and placed his hopes on pious associations to improve the holiness of the villagers. He also saw potential in vaccines, which would prove the value of the mission's protection.[69] Facing these difficulties, other Spiritans apparently wanted to relent somewhat on the demands placed on the villagers, but Baur held firm.[70]

Missionary evangelization among local peoples also showed little promise. In response, Spiritan frustration — doubly confirmed among their own villagers and among those in whom their long-term hopes lay — took the form of racist denunciations unprecedented in their sweep and severity. Sometimes the missionaries even linked African identity with demonic possession. The journal at Mandera recorded such frustration in September 1883, after no one had attended a catechetical session: "God, you have spilled your blood for these people, and yet the devil has them in his iron chain." The Bagamoyo journal spoke of the "demon's artifices," called *les noirs* a truly corrupt race, and spoke of the "black brain as vicious, mischievous, and obstinate."[71] Other generalizations about Africans, too, served to explain Spiritan failures: they were easily seduced by the appeal of

67. *Libres-penseurs* (BG 13:91). The Mandera journal throughout 1881 indicates that most days were dedicated to clearing the forest and building tasks. Other missions also worked their villagers. The Mhonda journal admits that "even women" were working in the forest (14vii80). Also see the Morogoro journal, vi84.

68. Machon spoke of the bad spirit in the village at Mhonda (CSSp 197ai: Machon to Baur, 13vi83), and escapes were numerous at Bagamoyo and elsewhere. See Bagamoyo journal: 12i83, 2ii83, 27vi83, 1vii83, 3vii83, 25vii83, 6viii83, 12ix83, 20x83, 22x83, 23x83, 25x83, 27x83, 28xii83, 1i84, 13v84, 16v84, 17viii84; Mhonda journal, 8iii83, 20iii83; Mandera journal, 9ix83, 12–15xii83, 27xii83; CSSp 197ai: Baur to Schwindenhammer, 26iv83.

69. CSSp 197ai: Machon to Emonet, 13vi83; BG 13:80. Machon's words resembled those of an Anglican missionary at a UMCA mission in the interior, who earlier in the 1870s had said he felt "more like a gaoler than a missionary" (Small 1980, 37).

70. Henschel 2000a, 20. Certainly Foels was among those who wanted a less strict regime. Henschel also mentions Charles Sacleux, later a famous expert in KiSwahili, and Hirtzlin. Given Le Roy's later reforms, he may have sympathized with Foels's more open attitude, but there is no such evidence before 1883.

71. Mandera journal, 22–23ix83, 28vii84; Bagamoyo journal, 3vii83, 25x83, 30vii84. Anglican reports from this time showed a similar tendency to use racist language, something not so obvious earlier (UMCA 1883–84, 19ff).

gain or the prospect of easy pleasure, and thus prone to become Protestant (who were wealthier than the Catholics) or Muslim (for Islam did nothing to curb their natural sensuality); they were children even when adult age, and needed frequent scolding. In public writings, the Spiritans stressed the need for patience, comparing their missions to the date-palm, which needed ten or more years of careful tending before bearing any fruit, but in private they complained bitterly.[72] Though the missionaries had hoped to find more docile souls inland, they struggled to attract local people, while the resistance shown by their own villagers surprised and frustrated them.[73]

It was at Bagamoyo's mission that the problems were most severe. The large village there lacked land for expansion and thus often faced overcrowding. The behavior of the several hundred children and adolescents in the orphanages also exasperated the missionaries. As in 1880, one of the mission's boys attempted to strike a missionary in 1883. He was chained and thrown in isolation. The numerous escapes were even more unsettling. In July 1883, the mission's journal lamented that seventeen from the village and the orphanages had fled that year already. It counted twenty more escapes before the end of the year, with many repeat offenders. Children in the orphanages fled in groups or singly; village couples fled together, or with one spouse abandoning the other. Crops (especially coconuts), livestock, and other mission property were often stolen in the midst of flight. Sometimes the Spiritans saw signs of escape before they recognized the absence of the mission's children or villagers: missing geese and turkeys (the poultry were sold in the market and the buyer then fingered the guilty Christians who had offered them for sale; they in turn took the mission's launch and fled via the ocean); a roof cover on the dormitory loosened ("a sure sign of escape"); a slaughtered chicken or pig in the mission's field; and alcohol missing.[74] Baur feared that the villagers' actions could create scandals that would embarrass the church. He tried to hide some of the misbehavior, including the murder via poisoned arrow of one villager's child by another villager.[75] To no avail: by early 1884, the sultan himself complained of the disorder at the mission.[76]

Those escaping faced different experiences. As in 1873, many left no traces, likely making their way to a *watoro* village or some other place outside of historical recording. Local chiefs or the officials of the sultan detained some of the escapees and occasionally returned them to the mission, often in chains. Many *watoro* returned on their own, possibly feeling remorse or finding the life away from the mission less satisfying than they had hoped. Escapees from the mission, as non-Muslim Africans without any patron to shelter them, would have been vulnerable to detention by the sultan's local representatives in much of the

---

72. BG 13:101.

73. BG 13:24, 49, 59; BG 14:616, 622.

74. Bagamoyo journal, 3ii83, 27vi83, 1vii83, 3vii83, 19vii83, 6viii83, 20x83, 2xii83, 19vii84, 19xi84, 28xi84, 2xii83, 3xii84, 11ii85, 16vi85.

75. CSSp 197ai: Baur to Emonet, 26iv83. The murder was at Mhonda (Mhonda journal, 17iii83).

76. Bagamoyo Journal, 10iii84.

coastal region, especially if suspected of being slaves who had fled their masters. Those leaving the mission were often so categorized.[77]

The missionaries also took more direct means in returning the *watoro*, not simply allowing local officials to detain them, or the whim of the escaped to remain the only way back. Two senior members of the Christian village at Baga-moyo, Charles-Alfred and Martial — the former serving as mayor — received responsibility to pursue and apprehend those who fled. These two sometimes brought back the *watoro* after receiving word that the former residents were incarcerated and in the custody of a local Zanzibari official in Dar es Salaam or elsewhere. At other times they located them on their own, seized them, and brought them back to the mission at Bagamoyo. The missionaries also took new measures to prevent escapes, building a surveillance *cabinet* in the orphanage at Bagamoyo. This resembled the hut in the village where a priest could watch for possible escapes, as well as the room for surveillance that had previously existed in the seminarians' dormitory.[78]

No matter the means, if they returned, the escapees were usually punished, something the journal and even sometimes correspondence recorded. Though the means of physical punishment were rarely described, there are ominous lines in the journal: punishment administered "according to their sin" (*selon leur peché*); "to be punished without any pity" (*punis sans pitié aucune*); and "they will be corrected as impossible recidivists" ("back-sliders" or "repeat offenders"; *ils seront corrigés comme recidifs impossibles*). They could be locked up, initially probably in a shed or room on the mission compound, though in July 1884 the missionaries at Bagamoyo felt obliged to lay the foundation for a prison. Even those who appeared to be planning to flee were locked up. They sometimes labored in chains while detained. Those who came back could also be forced to beg forgiveness on their knees in the chapel for their misdeeds. Both the physical punishments and the pleas for forgiveness often took place before the others, part of the missionary attempt to enforce discipline among their children.[79]

In 1884, two more delegations of villagers from internal stations came to Baga-moyo to appeal to Baur about the punishing work regimes and other conditions in the villages where they lived. The first came in May, when five men from Moro-goro arrived to lay before Baur their disaffection with their situation. According

77. For examples of detention by local Omani officials, see Bagamoyo journal, 21xi83, 7iv84, 17v84, 21v84, 8viii84, 18viii84, 30viii84, 17v85. Glassman describes such practices (1995, 106ff).

78. Charles-Alfred had probably been at Zanzibar and was baptized in 1862 (Zanzibar sacramental registry). He was later mayor in Thomasville, the second Christian village established at Bagamoyo (Zanzibar journal, 2iii86) and also helped found another village near Mhonda (Mhonda journal, 12x88, 17xi88). Martial Koumakoulakoula was ransomed and baptized when he was about eighteen years old in 1872, and married two years later (Bagamoyo sacramental registry, 30iii72, 24xi74). For their (and other) efforts to return those imprisoned or to recapture escaped Christians, see Bagamoyo journal, 12viii83, 23x83, 29x83, 3xi83, 20–21xi83, 1i84, 10iii84, 23iii84, 28viii84. On the room for surveillance in the orphanage, see ibid., 9x84.

79. On physical punishments and confinement *en bloc*, see Bagamoyo journal, 12–13i83, 3ii83, 12viii83, 22xi83, 22xii83, 1i84, 21iii84, 14v84, 21v84, 27vi84, 3vii84, 19vii84, 28vii84, 17viii84, 31xii84, 11ii85, 31viii85, 2iii86. On the prison foundation, see ibid.,11vii84.

to the journal account, those who had come to complain were sent back with a letter from Baur. The superior at Morogoro, Father Charles Gommenginger, later wrote that twelve days after leaving they paraded haughtily into the village and defiantly gave him Baur's message. A few days later he expelled them from the village along with their wives. He explained that this "extreme measure" had been forced by the "arrogance" shown since their arrival back from the coast. The journal continued, "The expulsion was carried out before all the children convoked for the occasion. This sufficed to calm heads and no longer was there grumbling or an evil spirit in the children." A few weeks later Gommenginger came to Bagamoyo to organize the resettlement of some of those expelled back at Morogoro. He was glad that the "bad" Christians had been "filtered out."[80]

The same day that the Morogoro superior returned to his mission after relocating his former villagers, a second group arrived at Bagamoyo to request less work, this time from Mandera. The Bagamoyo journal recorded their arrival with great frustration. After describing the departure of the Morogoro superior, the account continued:

Such a sad story! The black brain is devious, proud, whining, treacherous! Someone who does not want to believe it should live with us several years, and the most curious and extraordinary trials will convince them right away! As soon as we have installed our complainers from Morogoro here in our own village, this morning come four children from Mandera.

They came, according to the account, bemoaning lack of food at Mandera, something confirmed by the Mandera journal. Famine had affected the area, and the day before they left for Bagamoyo the Mandera superior, Picarda, had announced that he was distributing money for the last time. Still, the Mandera journal writer condemned them just as fulsomely, seeing diabolical possession in such defiance. The account closed by lauding their imprisonment at Bagamoyo: "May this example teach them to work!"[81]

Though they spent several years rebuffing any calls for revision of their program, the Spiritans eventually acquiesced and faced the implications of the resistance they were facing. Courmont's 1884 arrival occurred a few months before the Mandera and Morogoro delegations visited Bagamoyo, and he had been there himself only a few weeks before on his first visit. In September, a few months later, he summoned the chapter of 1884, where a reconsideration of the Christian villages dominated the agenda. Alexandre Le Roy's proposed new policies for the villages served as the starting point for the discussion.

---

80. CSSp 198a: Gommenginger; Morogoro journal, 19v84, 31v84, 2vi84, 6vi84; Bagamoyo journal, 30vii84; CSSp 197ai: Machon to Emonet, 10vi84; BG 13:1114. The Morogoro fire destroyed the journal written at the time, but Gommenginger rewrote it later.
81. Bagamoyo journal, 30vii84; Mandera journal, 28vii84.

The Spiritan Chapter of 1884

Having arrived in eastern Africa in 1881, Le Roy had returned to France in 1883 suffering from an eye ailment. He recovered and Courmont's appointment in late 1883 meant that Le Roy and the new bishop had several months in Europe as well as the trip to Africa together. They discussed the new diocese often before arriving in March 1884.[82]

Already Le Roy had written about the Spiritan missions in eastern Africa, describing the difficulties in producing vocations to priesthood and religious life, and urging concerted effort at KiSwahili, including new textbooks. He observed that Bagamoyo's orphanage was overcrowded, and that those of age needed to be married soon to avoid great disorders, while the village stood in need of new direction. Courmont asked for other reports from his junior confrere. Meeting with the missionaries in the days after arriving at Zanzibar, the new bishop acknowledged the crisis of the village system and made suggestions reflecting Le Roy's diagnoses.

Courmont wrote Paris that the boys at the Bagamoyo orphanage pretended to be sick in order to sneak into the girls' dormitories. When caught they were put in irons. Seven or eight of the married couples at the villages, he wrote, caused real problems. Echoing Baur, he said that the words of Foels had exposed the villagers to "certain ideals of emancipation that have germinated into complaints of a paternal yoke." Foels's words had given them "a seed of *affranchissement*," though Courmont admitted that others had also contributed to the troublesome spirit in the villages. A consensus had emerged among the Spiritans on the need for reforms at the village to deal with this "whiff of emancipation," as Courmont called the villagers' motivations. All recognized the need for more land. The priests had other ideas, too, like a greater uniformity in dress among the Christians.[83]

The chapter of 1884, like the earlier chapter in 1870, covered many topics.[84] Mindful of the long-standing Spiritan goal, the chapter encouraged the missionaries to evangelize surrounding populations from their interior missions. Picarda, the superior at Mandera, lamented that the need to discipline the Christians who had come from Bagamoyo prevented an external ministry with surrounding peoples, which had been the goal of the ministry to the interior in the first place. Instead, echoing Machon's view of Mhonda (as well as Horner's Mettray-derived label for Bagamoyo), he likened his mission to "an agricultural and penal colony." Recognizing the competing demands on their missionary energy, all agreed on the need to "go after the fish, not let them come to them," and Courmont encouraged the missionaries to go out on tours of preaching and to establish hospitals.

82. For a description of Le Roy's activities while in Europe, see Ducol 2000a, 39ff.
83. CSSp 195v; Le Roy 1883, Notes on Zanguebar; CSSp 197ai: Courmont to Emonet, 10iv84, 10vi84; Bagamoyo journal, 2iv84, 26iv84. Emonet supported the goal of providing adequate land for every villager (CSSp 196bi: Emonet to Courmont, 23v84).
84. CSSp 196aiv: chapter of 1884.

Picarda himself promoted the establishment of schools, a tactic that eventually became a widespread Spiritan strategy. In addition, the delegates reiterated the ongoing need to form the Christians through regular liturgical prayer, even stipulating specific devotions with the hope that such ceremonies and practices might reshape the hearts and minds of the Christians. Reflecting long-standing Spiritan assumptions about the need for comprehensive formation, they admitted that "external commands are not enough." As Le Roy wrote, missionaries must "work to make the Christian life natural, so there is no need to impose it exteriorly."[85]

Le Roy's report on the Christian villages served as the basis for most of the conversations at the chapter. His specific recommendations were meticulous, paying close attention to details such as the necessary equipment and skills to be possessed by the first settlers at the new mission. Our goal, he wrote, has been to establish Christianity and meanwhile to save as many souls as possible, and the villages were the method to establish the church on a firm foundation. Continuing the concern for proper environments demonstrated by Spiritans earlier, he carefully described the desired characteristics of the proper milieu for a new mission: sufficient fertility (water, land for herds and crops), lack of Arabic influence, absence of infanticide (a feature that, Le Roy believed, slowed evangelization for twenty years), welcoming local authority, and the unlikelihood of conflicts with other groups, whether local chiefs, Arabs, or Europeans.

The guidelines relied on the already-operative idea of beginning with young men from Bagamoyo who would build initial dwellings at new stations in the interior. He also stipulated the need to maintain the missionary environment on that trek — as noted in chapter 1 — insisting that "no lapse" should occur in the mission children's "habits of regularity and piety." After the original installation, the young men would head back to the coast to find wives before returning to settle the village at the new station.

Le Roy insisted that the Spiritans organize the choice of spouses so as to respect the freedom of both women and men to find a suitable partner in accord with their wishes. Marital arrangements made prior to the departure of the young men to the new mission were to be respected, but not encouraged.[86] The villages ideally should have no more than fifty households built upon such marriages.

Le Roy urged that immediately upon their return to the interior mission station the Spiritans should read to the new couples the formal contract to be established between them and the mission. The rules for life in the village codified what had been in place at St. Joseph village at Bagamoyo and operative at the other interior stations: common prayer, curfew, punishment of offenses, including imprisonment or expulsion. If the children followed the contract, the missionaries promised to provide all they needed for a "happy and Christian" life, and Le Roy

---

85. CSSp 391a: Le Roy, Christian villages, 1884; Kieran 1966, 123ff.
86. Three young men who had gone to establish the mission at Morogoro returned to Bagamoyo and sought the hand of women too young for missionary approval (Bagamoyo journal, 5ix83).

urged that the contract be formally established with "exterior solemnity, to create a good spirit with [missionary] authority."[87]

The major change in Le Roy's guidelines involved the way labor was conceived. Le Roy saw the villages passing through three stages, each of which gradually lessened the labor owed the mission by the villagers. This progression figured prominently in the contract between the missionaries and the villager-couples. At first the villagers would complete the new mission and their own village, with all their needs supplied by the mission. This period completed, they then would assume their own plots of land, still supplying the mission regularly with labor and receiving support. In the third stage, the mission would end its supplies and the villagers would be granted freedom with their land and their homes, except for a specified number of days' labor per year allotted for general maintenance of the mission property. If the Spiritans wanted the villagers to work on the mission's behalf apart from the days allotted according to the agreement, then the missionaries would have to pay them. Paying them for "free work" would, in Le Roy's opinion, stimulate them to be industrious. Employees of the mission with special responsibilities, such as the schoolmaster, catechist, keeper of the herds, and kitchen managers, were also to be paid.

Le Roy's plan was clearly set up in response to the discontent of the Christians, and he evidently understood some of the reasons for the unrest. He articulated the Spiritans' fear when he wrote that the missionaries must "never create a situation when they [the mission's residents] would envy the lot of slaves, Arabs, or their indigenous neighbors." He recognized that exit was a distinct possibility for the villagers, who looked around them to see other options for life at the coast.

The change in the Christian village concept enacted by Le Roy's proposal represented a new Spiritan approach toward work, further deemphasizing labor's formative role that Horner had envisioned at the mission's outset. Before the 1880s, the Spiritans had seen the villagers' self-sufficiency and nonparticipation in the market economy of the coast as a blessing. As Le Roy himself wrote before implementing his reforms, the Africans at the mission were "easily seduced by material values [and] ... are children as long as they live. ... [In the village, however] without being preoccupied by wealth and without suffering poverty, the first-born of the church of Zanzibar live happily under the law of the Gospel."[88] The Spiritans had been leery of paying their workers, especially the agricultural workers at Bagamoyo on whom they placed so many hopes as future Catholic colonists. In the missionary view, money and the anxiety associated with it were not distractions that this new African Christian colony needed. On the contrary, for the Spiritans — before Le Roy's reforms, at least — wage-labor meant that work was simply an economic exchange and no longer formative, much less a contribution to the mission's livelihood and expansion. Horner, dead four years by the time of the 1884 chapter, would have thought Le Roy's reforms made the

87. CSSp 391a: Le Roy, Christian villages, 1884.
88. BG 13:49; APF 56 (1884), 53–54.

freed slaves into employees, poor preparation to be the vanguards of the future church Horner had once imagined they would embody. Le Roy's willingness to countenance payment of the villagers for their labor thus represented a departure in Spiritan practice: the expressed acceptance of the fact that work was now a commodity in the mission.

The Spiritans first saw labor as formative for their future Catholics, then added its role in regeneration, then increasingly recognized its place as a resource for their mission. In the face of African protests, Le Roy admitted that African labor was a commodity. He felt that paying for work was a realistic appraisal of the circumstances. It offered a chance to salvage the villages by giving the Christians there some satisfaction, while preserving an ongoing Christianizing role for these social arrangements.

Implementing Le Roy's Plan

The chapter approved Le Roy's plan. As they described the implications of the new program to the villagers, the Spiritans sought to encourage acceptance and enthusiasm. Upon his return, Picarda gathered his Mandera villagers and began by reminding them of the four of their number who had gone to Bagamoyo to plead their case a few months before the chapter, the ones who had complained of lack of food. Picarda rebuked those assembled, deploring their foolishness at sending such emissaries. He reminded the villagers of all they had received from the mission and of their responsibility to support the missionaries, since "The one who belongs to the altar must live at the altar." With the new program, Picarda continued, the industrious would be rewarded and the lazy would suffer. Urging them to leave behind their sullen attitudes, he continued:

> Do the right thing, show good will.... If so, I will treat you well. I regard you all as my children. God has confided you to my care and I accept that. Up to now, if I reproach myself for anything, it's having been too indulgent in sparing the stick. The punishment you have received has never been excessive and I've never done any injustice.

Picarda also announced the punishments to be accorded the recent escapees. They had to make up the work they had missed and would receive no guns or meat from the mission for three months.[89]

The announcement, couched in Picarda's paternalistic and pious rhetoric, did little to dissolve the villagers' frustrations. Two weeks after this meeting, Picarda heard grumblings from the escapees about the harshness of their punishment. One of them expressed his displeasure so forcefully that he was, as the mission journal ironically described his confinement, "put away [to have] freedom of reflection."

---

89. Mandera journal, 10x84. Two days later, Picarda also lessened the number of times the villagers were required to join the mission's liturgical prayer (Mandera journal, 12x84).

Four days later he recanted. A few weeks later, however, another villager escaped the mission to seek the services of a local *mganga*, a traditional healer (in
missionary language, a witch-doctor). His subsequent death was described in the
mission journal as "God's will."[90]

Picarda's rhetoric appeared as well in Bishop Courmont's comments during his visits to interior stations in the wake of the chapter meeting. In one
well-documented instance during Courmont's inaugural 1885 visit to the interior
missions, the bishop first arrived at Mandera. In their gathering with him the
villagers requested to be discharged of all their responsibilities for work on the
mission's behalf, an appeal the journal writer called "the same refrain, edited so
many times." Hearing them speak of their rights, Courmont responded that if
they had rights, the missionaries themselves had conferred them. After he had
departed, the mission journal observed that the bishop now had a practical sense
of the daily difficulties connected with Christians ransomed from slavery, who
were still quite affected by that initial condition.[91]

From Mandera the bishop proceeded to Mhonda. In a speech to the villagers,
he alluded to a letter from one of their number complaining about the burdensome
work for the mission. Courmont described this letter as ungracious, and likened
the author's ingratitude to the selfishness shown to a self-sacrificing and generous
father by a thankless son: " 'Now that I am strong,' the son says, 'I no longer
need you. I no longer want to help you.' " Courmont urged the Christians to see
the work required of them as a justifiable recompense offered to the missionaries
who served them. He expressed disappointment that they were not more willing
to work for the spread of the kingdom of God.[92] He had just come from Mandera,
he said, where he had preached a similar message to the children there when they
had asked him that they be discharged of all work owed the mission. Courmont
observed that they only mentioned their rights, not their duties, overlooking the
sacrifices the missionaries had made on their behalf.

Explanations of the new system and promises of eventual payment for their
labor did little to satisfy the villagers' desires. Disgruntled villagers continued to
complain about their work, while they and those in the orphanages at Bagamoyo
fled in a steady stream. Thibault, one of the leaders during the villagers' complaints in the early 1880s, was sent away from Bagamoyo and came to Zanzibar in
February 1885, the Spiritans' forbearance with him apparently exhausted. There
he began to work with the Germans, and he passed through Bagamoyo several
months later. Two years later he was still working with the Germans and visited
with Courmont on one of the bishop's visits to the interior missions.[93] Another
villager, Henri — possibly the Henri Isa who wrote the pious letter to French
Spiritan seminarians in the 1870s, when he was also a seminarian — escaped and
was returned from Zanzibar after imprisonment. At Zanzibar he told the bishop

90. Mandera journal, 24x84, 28x84, 23xi84.
91. Mandera journal 15vi85, 16vi85, 17vi85.
92. Mhonda journal, 28vi85.
93. Bagamoyo journal, 15ii85, 16vi85, 27vi85, 6xii85; CSSp 198b, Courmont, 1887.

that he had been imprisoned naked — whether earlier by the mission or by the sultan is unclear. A month later it was learned that he apparently also had been circumcised and was keeping a concubine. The Spiritans decided to send him away to the new mission at Tununguo. Other longtime Christians were also sent away.[94]

Problems like these plagued the Spiritan missions at Bagamoyo and elsewhere throughout the 1880s and beyond. The completion of Bagamoyo's prison in January 1885 did little to stem the frequent escapes from the largest mission. Some of the *watoro* disappeared, others were seized by the sultan's soldiers or by those sent to bring them back to the mission. Still others fled and begged their way back in, sometimes, the missionaries guessed, simply because the rains were coming. Thefts were also frequent.[95]

In addition to the villagers' and orphans' disturbing behavior, other obstacles also arose to the quick implementation of Le Roy's reforms. The Spiritans at Bagamoyo sought land for a new village to supplement overcrowded St. Joseph's, to allow for expansion and the fresh enactment of the proposals. To their dismay they discovered that Sultan Barghash had ordered an interdiction on selling land to Europeans. After much searching, the missionaries in early 1885 found and obtained a site near the Bagamoyo mission. They distributed plots among the couples who inhabited the new village, Thomasville, where the new policy would be put into practice. The local Zanzibari official was jailed when the sale was announced, evidence of Sultan Barghash's anger that his embargo on selling land to outsiders had been violated.[96]

Still, as was the case again and again, the most formidable challenges to the Spiritan program came from the Christians themselves. Whatever the reason, the missionaries faced new occasions of African Catholic intransigence and truculence besides the reluctance or refusal to work. At Thomasville in April 1886, the villagers refused a Spiritan request to help build a chapel in their village,

94. Bagamoyo journal, 10iv85, 7v85. One named Frederick had been baptized at Zanzibar in 1864, and was sent from Bagamoyo in 1886 along with Stanislaus, who had come to Bagamoyo from Mandera and wanted to found his own village at the coast (Zanzibar sacramental register, 6i64; Bagamoyo journal, 16ix86, 18x86, 22x86).

95. For escapes, imprisonments, complaints about work, and thefts at Bagamoyo, see, for example: Bagamoyo journal, 19xi84, 20xi84, 26xi84, 28xi84, 3xii84, 31xiii84, 11ii85, 15ii85, 20ii85, 20iii85, 10iv85, 17v85 (three escapees now want to return), 16vi85, 10vii85, 11vii85 (a Christian, Gervais, sentenced to prison by the sultan), 31viii85, 13x85, 28x85, 5–6ii86, 2iii86, 28iii86 ("Alphonse, now penitent because of the rains"), 18iv86, 5v86, 28v86, 2–3ix86, 15ix86, 22x86, 1i87, 2i87, 4ii87, 9iii87, 24iv87, 2iii95, 13iii95.
For escapes at Mhonda, Mandera, and Morogoro, see Mhonda journal, 28xi87, 9iv88, 21ix88, 9xi88, 14xii88, 17xi88; Mandera journal, 14ii87, 4vi87, 12ix87, 6–7i89; Morogoro journal, ii86. Machon wrote that his village (at Mhonda) wanted more independence in 1887, and Courmont spoke of similar unrest at Mandera in 1888 (CSSp 197aii: Machon to Emonet, 30x87; ibid.: Courmont to Emonet, 7iv88). At Mhonda, one missionary wrote, *les noirs* dislike "sequestration and hard work" (APF 61 [1889], 56). Similar problems came when the Spiritans moved to present-day Kenya (CSSp 405v).

96. Bagamoyo journal, 8xi84, 25i85; Brown 1971a, 223. This village, in the area called Kimarangombe, took its name from a German priest-benefactor of the mission (CSSp 197aii: Courmont to Emonet, 16ii85). In July 1885, Le Roy blessed the new huts (Bagamoyo journal, 10vii85).

and the priest found himself forced to carry a portable altar to celebrate weekly Eucharist.[97]

In addition, some villagers left to found their own villages. Spiritans were wary of such desires, and early on refused permission. Yet eventually such developments were welcomed under certain conditions. They could relieve the Spiritans of a troublesome villager and also gave scope to sometimes laudable ambition. Thus in 1888, Charles-Alfred, onetime mayor at Bagamoyo and a trusted Christian who helped the Spiritans track down escapees, started a village of his own not far from Mhonda. Such fission was a common feature of society and politics among many African peoples, and in these circumstances it was a way for African Christians to achieve greater autonomy, while maintaining their ties to the mission.[98] For some, on the other hand, it represented a move outside of the mission's authority.

More disturbing still, the villagers themselves kept slaves, a practice the missionaries disliked but allowed in the 1880s. Those holding such slaves tended to be leaders in the village, such as the catechists. Thus, Charles-Alfred, in founding his own village, did so along with his wife and two slaves.[99] Ironically, during this period the missionaries themselves continued to seek to shield themselves from accusations that they trafficked in slaves, and there is evidence of their ongoing discomfort at potential accusations.[100] Not only did this practice disturb some of the Spiritans. It might also have confirmed some observers' suspicions of the missionaries' own labor practices. Perhaps recognizing the incongruity, Courmont declared this practice forbidden in 1892, specifying that young girls held as slaves had to be released at once, a sign that they were seen (and possibly treated) as concubines. The Christian villagers at Mhonda protested this decision in 1895.[101]

The different responses of the villagers in this period reflected a number of factors, especially the fact that they were now landowners away from the coast, a setting where they faced new challenges and opportunities. Yet the missionaries saw their protests only as ungrateful rebellion. Courmont's and Picarda's words at Mandera and Mhonda reinvoked the missionaries' view of the moral economy

---

97. Vogt, n.d.; Bagamoyo journal, 18iv86. Eventually a chapel was built.

98. Mhonda journal, 12x88, 17xi88. Hilarion's desire was the earliest and most significant of these efforts, and it is discussed more fully later (Mhonda journal, 29ix85). At other times the Spiritans resisted a villager's request to start his own village (Bagamoyo journal, x86).

99. See also Bagamoyo journal 9iii87, 27i90; Mandera journal, 4v87; Kieran 1966, 127ff.

100. Already in the early 1880s, Spiritan writings emphasized that interior chiefs knew that the missionaries took neither wives nor slaves (MC 14 [1882], 368–70; APF 54 [1882], 362). Later in 1884, the missionary in charge at Mandera had tried to end the practice of infanticide, and been offered the chance to purchase children condemned to death. Though he would accept them at the mission, he refused to buy such children because, he said, "whites have no slaves." Instead he threatened the people with smallpox and an embargo on guns if they continued to kill their children (CSSp 194bv: Picarda, 1884). At about the same time, a group of non-Christians who were deeply in debt to the mission at Mhonda came secretly to the head of the mission to offer themselves in slavery in lieu of repayment. They were refused, and the superior insisted that the debt would have to be repaid (Mhonda journal, 5vii84).

101. Kieran 1971, 33: CSSp 195vi, Courmont circular letter, 2i92; Mhonda journal, 22xii95.

of the mission, casting it in a paternalistic image where the missionaries were fathers providing for their children.

One abiding feature of this paternalism was the attribution of gratitude and ingratitude to the Africans. This idiom was not new. Already at Zanzibar in the 1860s the Spiritans had presented the thankfulness of the children ransomed as evidence of the good done by the mission. Conversely, later difficulties associated with the labor of the Christian villagers were interpreted in Spiritan discourse as ingratitude. Such entreaties and judgments, however, had little effect. The missionaries could hardly enforce the thirty days of work per year on the mission's behalf that eventually became the standard requirement.[102]

The Spiritans did not appreciate the motivations behind what they saw as African shortcomings and defiance. By spiritualizing and even demonizing African refusals to go along with their evangelizing program, the Spiritans ignored the complexities of the African Catholic identities their practices had helped engender. After all, Thibault, who was sent away from the mission and joined the Germans, regularly came back through and visited the Spiritans. Bagamoyo's journal records in June 1885 that he went to confession at the mission on one such visit, and six months later he and three Germans came to Sunday Mass. His later conversation with Courmont suggested an abiding loyalty and an ongoing connection that contests missionary denigrations.[103] And Thibault was not alone among those once prominent who rebelled, for many of those who most frustrated the Spiritans were the most deeply influenced by their evangelization. Even in the midst of their protests, African Christian villagers continued to attend Mass and confessed their sins.

But the Spiritans did not understand the nature of the changes they had effected and resented the lack of cooperation shown by these new Catholics. Regardless of the missionaries' views, however, former slaves constituted the bulk of the church that was being born.

African Catholics at Spiritan Missions
in the Late 1870s and 1880s

Le Roy himself later attributed the abiding problems at the Christian villages to the corrupted characters of the former slaves, which, despite evangelization, still retained "the old spirit of slavery." But he also admitted missionary shortcomings, as did later Spiritans. One member in the early twentieth century claimed that human beings were not made for the ideals of the Christian utopia held out by the missionaries.[104]

102. Bagamoyo journal, November 1884, July 1885, March/April 1886; Morogoro journal, November 1886; BG 14:604ff.

103. Bagamoyo journal, 27vi85, 3xii85; CSSp 198b: Courmont, 1887.

104. The author in question is not known, but it may have been Le Roy (CSSp 198bviii: The Mission at Zanzibar, n.d.). For Le Roy's later opinions, see Le Roy 1906a; Le Roy 1934b. For negative evaluations of the Christian villages at Spiritan missions, stressing the resistance shown to missionary paternalism, the isolation imposed, and the failures to attract surrounding peoples, see

Without denying the validity of these observations, it is also true that the villages were the setting for more than missionary failure. In particular, the protests of the Christian villagers at Bagamoyo and the interior stations represented a landmark in the history of African Christianity. Such actions certainly led the Spiritans to modify their strategy through Le Roy's reforms. They also signaled an unprecedented collective African Christian identity, notable especially since it did not emerge from within the elite formation programs where the most revealing insights into African experiences of slave evangelization had previously appeared. The villages were the site for the emergence of a Catholic Church not dependent on obedience to missionaries.

Widespread Unrest in the Christian Villages

The escapes, delegations of complaint, and other signs of resistance from the villagers beginning in 1880 indicated their growing sense that the moral economy of the mission — the expectations they had come to hold about how they should be treated — was not being fulfilled. They expressed their dissatisfaction in two primary ways. Many opted to exit, as had previous villagers and numerous young persons from the orphanages of Bagamoyo in the early 1870s. As in the 1870s, not all exited with the same hopes. Some wanted to free themselves of the mission entirely and opted for what was earlier designated "decisive exit."

But others did not exit in this way. Instead they escaped with the hopes of an abiding relationship with the mission, but their own circumstances enhanced. And a larger number still of these Christian villagers came together in the 1880s to act as a group and exercise their collective voice. They felt justified in calling for more of the "land and liberty" that the Spiritans already claimed to be providing as fathers for their children. Such collective acts represented achievements of a new sense of themselves among these African Christians. They were a group with shared interests, interests they could pursue together against the ways they felt the missionaries were constraining them.

It is not easy to make sense of this new visibility of African Catholics acting in concert. The nature of the sources invites speculation, not certainty about such processes. There are no first-person accounts that described such an achievement, and African Catholics at such places today recall next to nothing of those earliest days. Missionary sources are spotty and, as observed above, were prone to belittle such evidence as ungrateful disloyalty.

In addition, it may be that similar previous actions had occurred before but had not been noted by Horner, who had left only in 1879. Rarely did Horner

---

the following: Brown 1971a, 217ff; Kieran 1966, 129ff; O'Hare 1969; Kieran 1971, 25ff; W. B. Anderson 1977, 13; Sahlberg 1986, 47ff; Giblin 1992, 67; Koponen 1994, 358. Some also echo Le Roy's claims of the abiding effects of enslavement, while a few have praised the civilizing roles of the villages (Oliver 1952; J. Baur 1994, 232).

comment on misbehavior among the new Catholics at the Spiritan missions.[105] During Horner's previous absences, Baur's writings had shown more attention than Horner's to African actions, especially those that disturbed missionary expectations. Thus one might expect that once Baur had become the chief witness to slave evangelization, as he was from 1879 until Courmont's accession in 1884, such examples of resistance would feature more prominently in Spiritan writings coming from eastern Africa. Yet other Spiritans, including Le Roy, Acker, Courmont, and Machon, also mentioned the unrest. This suggests that more than Baur's greater sensitivity and willingness to record African resistance explains the evidence of heightened unrest. How then did this new African agency and identity appear?

Collective consciousness like that exhibited by African Catholics in eastern Africa in this period was not simply the product of social authorities like the missionaries. It is best seen as a conceptual achievement by the former slaves who embodied the new awareness. As asserted by practitioners of what is sometimes called "new social history," people have made and continue to make themselves and their world — in France as well as in Africa, in circumstances of proletarianization or colonialism, on slave plantations and within prisons. Coherent and collective voices can emerge in situations of domination of various sorts. No group, no matter how deprived of overt power, is incapable of making its own history, even if those efforts remain hidden.[106] And African Catholic protests in the 1880s did not remain hidden, even if those Africans themselves did not record their own actions.

Acknowledging the achievements of these former slaves does not entail accepting that they unilaterally determined their own history. All human practices and activities, and all achievements of individual or collective identity, are situated within constraints, some obvious and others eluding full self-conscious awareness. At the same time, no circumstances remove all possibility of agency. As Talal Asad says, people are never, no matter how much power they appear to have (or lack), *only* agents (or subjects) within their own history.[107] Thus, while African Catholics were responsible for achieving this collective identity and the agency that came with it, they did not do so in a vacuum. Important factors situating their achievement included the years of common experiences shared by many of the villagers while at the missions, the Spiritans' own divided opinions about missionary strategy, the new social environment of the Christian villages, and the unsettled conditions of the interior of Africa. Such circumstances — both dependent upon missionary decisions and also related to the broader world in which

---

105. In his 1877 report to the Holy Childhood Society, Horner mentioned one villager at Bagamoyo who had been punished for leaving the village at night, but this was unusual (CSSp 196axii: Horner to Holy Childhood, 31xii77). He was much more likely to complain to his Spiritan superiors about his confreres!

106. Sewell 1980, 11f; Atkins 1993, 143ff, passim; James Scott 1990, 136–38, 154.

107. Asad 1993, 4.

these African Catholics lived — created opportunities that Africans in turn exploited. They did so as individuals, but more importantly by coming together and pursuing their common interests.

In the first place, these villagers had been subjected to intense and repetitive social experiences at Zanzibar and Bagamoyo for years, decades in some cases. Even if they knew the larger world of the Swahili coast, even if they were tempted to flee the mission, even if their faith would have been found wanting by the missionaries, they had prayed, worked, and been educated in those places day after day. Their relationships to each other had been formed while undergoing those common practices together. These people thus protested and complained not as disembodied individual agents, but as African Catholics whose identity had been shaped, to a considerable extent, by the mission.

Yet the mission itself was not a single reality, for the Spiritan program never operated from a set blueprint. Instead it took its shape from a partially coherent but also evolving set of assumptions and practices that the missionaries selectively applied. In that very selectivity, African Catholics found occasions for their own improvisations. In this period in particular, the adaptive nature of Spiritan practices led the missionaries to disagree with each other and blame each other for African defiance at their missions. They had held each other accountable for failures before: Horner had accused Baur of overreacting in the 1860s to Casimir's escape, and the two had bitterly criticized each other in the 1870s; Baur blamed the brothers for poor oversight of the mission's children in the 1860s and 1870s; Scheuermann and Baur had blamed each other for the seminarians' misbehavior in the early 1870s. But the differences grew sharper in the late 1870s and early 1880s, with implications affecting more of the mission's children. A number of Spiritans thus blamed African defiance on Foels for encouraging a "spirit of independence" among those at the mission. Other Spiritans questioned Baur's harshness in the early 1880s, while Le Roy's reforms indicated his own second thoughts about Spiritan strategy. This does not mean the Spiritans *caused* the Africans to act the way they did. But one need not directly attribute African consciousness to one Spiritan's own disobedient spirit to appreciate that disagreements among the missionaries themselves allowed the villagers to consider their options more fully.

Evolving Spatial Practices in Slave Evangelization

Most importantly, the new settings in which African Catholics found themselves in the late 1870s created new possibilities for the former slaves. The Spiritans, as we have seen, adapted their missionary strategy to the circumstances in which they found themselves: at Zanzibar, then at Bagamoyo, then at interior stations. In turn, each new setting and missionary strategy created new opportunities for self-assertion and adaptation for those evangelized. At each stage, consequently, these African Catholics developed new capacities and new competencies within the economic and other possibilities available.

Thus in Zanzibar's Muslim and urban environment, the Spiritans obtained slaves and established a setting characterized by enclosure within which they carried out practices designed to form a Christian *noyau* for the interior. There the Africans at the mission had few obvious ways to assert themselves, and activities kept them at the mission nearly all the time. In addition, the confining streets and the sultan's authority meant that unattached Africans easily fell under suspicion as escaped slaves and were subject to seizure. Most at the mission were children, too, whose capacities for self-determination and self-expression were limited anyway. But the shared experiences of evangelization no doubt forged a common identity among them as they underwent schooling, work, and liturgical practices simultaneously. They were exposed together to the rhythms of the mission and a common Christian narrative punctuated with sacramental moments of initiation and celebration. Admittedly, the historical traces of such an identity are few, but they were not absent. Casimir and the other boys at Zanzibar, for example, had requested that the missionaries ransom more children to help lessen the burden of their work. The mission's routines had their effects on him and many others.

Later at Bagamoyo, the Spiritans created a different kind of spatial arrangement. Such more open spatial arrangements were defended by juvenile reformers in Europe as better for internal reforms because they fostered a spirit of self-policing. Though they might have pursued surveillance more vigorously at Bagamoyo, the Spiritans rarely defended Bagamoyo on those grounds. Instead, they saw the mainland mission as better for the formation they sought because it allowed scope for more agricultural labor and less Muslim influence. Spiritan eyes were always on the interior, where they anticipated they would garner larger numbers of Catholics. In the meantime, however, those in the orphanages, villages, seminary, and formation program for sisters had an important role to play in that envisioned future and needed ongoing formation.

At the same time, those subjected to such formative processes grew older, and the large numbers in the orphanages, the village's distance from missionary eyes, and the plantations' expansiveness challenged Spiritan attempts to control their mission's boundaries. Exit became a common option, especially when work was onerous or broader circumstances in the region, like nearby slave unrest in 1873, encouraged flight. Loyalty, too, emerged, in a large number of men and women who cooperated with the Spiritans. A more tangible loyalty appeared among those in preparation for priesthood or religious life.

Bagamoyo in the 1870s, however, saw little evidence of collective voice. Only in 1880 did there appear in the historical record something like a collective identity. Many factors contributed to its appearance, including missionary inclinations to record such expressions. Yet further insights into this appearance of collective African Catholic identity can be gained by comparisons with other processes in Africa where collective identity emerged in particular historical situations.

Emerging Catholic Identity among Villagers

Recent historical analyses of ethnic as well as class-based assignations such as those ascribed to peasants, workers, and the middle class in Africa and elsewhere suggest two things. First, such collective identities are the result of creative action on the part of those who embody the new identity. Second, they also depend on particular circumstances.[108] In the first place, the achievement of group identity should be attributed to those who achieved it. It is commonly recognized that such identities are never simply political or economic consequences of material circumstances, on the one hand, nor only ideological assertions of a cultural and symbolic sort, on the other. Instead the material and symbolic aspects of identity affect, reinforce, and modify each other as humans act to develop their sense of themselves.

At the same time, such identities, as historical achievements, appear within certain situations that encourage them. Of particular importance are almost invariably structural ambiguities created or exacerbated by social changes associated with abolition, colonialism, independence, or other economic and political upheavals. Unsettled situations — which can be actual physical frontiers, or frontier-like circumstances where there are interstices within given identities and forces undoing the assumed nature of social belonging — act as catalysts for those who share interests. Such people act in concert in pursuit of common interests — perhaps to reduce the effects of the circumstances that create their suffering, or to undo situations creating their precariousness or marginalization. Self-conscious aspects of identity such as class, race, ethnicity, religion — even certain forms of gendered identity — thus often originate as strategic avowals, assertions of "This is who we are" that result both from broad structural realities of ambiguity and human action to overcome its consequences. Such an approach takes into account the necessity of human agency in the achievement of identity, while acknowledging the normal (though not inevitable) likelihood that unchosen structural circumstances fostered the ways such identity appears.

This process was true as well among slaves in nineteenth-century eastern Africa. Studies of the collective identities emerging among these unfree workers show that their sense of themselves as a group with common interests emerged from structural ambiguities within which slaves acted as historical agents. The variety of terms used in eastern African slavery points toward such fluidity, as do the diverse idioms — of patronage and kinship, especially — in which a slave relationship was expressed. Categories such as class and ethnicity fail to capture how those enslaved began to think of themselves, either before or

---

108. Anne Norton in her recent work offers as thesis #31: "Identities make interests. Interests make identities" (Norton 2004, 57–58). In a huge literature, the following have been helpful to my own thinking about the emergence of collective identity among Africans subjected to slave evangelization: Ranger 1978; Bernstein 1979; Bundy 1979; Bunker 1987; Kopytoff 1987; Hefner 1990; Vail 1991; Kimambo 1991; Atkins 1993; Harries 1993; Klein 1993 and 1998; Krikler 1993; Isaacman 1996; Maddox, Giblin, and Kimambo 1996; Bravman 1998; Larson 2000; Sunseri 2002; West 2002; Isaacman and Isaacman 2004; Taylor and Spencer 2004.

after abolition. Yet even if slaves were not a class in any meaningful sense,[109] they developed a collective identity over time, in eastern Africa and elsewhere. Building upon the insight of Frederick Cooper that forms of slavery were not fixed structures but interactive processes, Glassman called this slave awareness a collective consciousness that he saw emerging in nineteenth-century slaves at the Swahili coast.[110] George Deutsch agrees, recognizing that "relative personal 'freedom' was an in-built feature of the various forms of pre-colonial slavery." Thus slavery was not a fixed institution with essential elements, but a social process always reworked and often an ongoing social negotiation fraught with conflict.[111] It was not an essential identity but one predicated on relationship. Appreciative of the achievements of slaves in eastern Africa, Deutsch generalizes about similar groups: "... marginalized people are able to confront effectively social, political and economic hegemony ... in their everyday lives without being represented by a formal organization, taking part in concerted militant actions or subscribing to an overarching political ideology."[112]

The confrontation Deutsch mentions, however, depends on the achievement of what might be called an already-extant horizontal voice — a shared identity — that can become vertical, that is, expressed toward social superiors. And the Christian villagers at Spiritan missions in the 1880s showed the effects of just such collective horizontal and vertical voice through their appeals and protests. Such acts suggest that these Christian villagers had developed a consciousness that was new, at least that became new within the historical record. Where did this new identity came from? What we know of the villages, as well as imaginative comparison with similar processes elsewhere, suggests that it derived from collective decisions made in the face of a series of structural ambiguities in which the villagers found themselves. One can speculate that these ambiguities created a series of nested incongruities that helped to foster a particular sort of Catholic identity in the villages at Spiritan missions.

I believe that one set of incongruities came from the place of the Christian villages and their residents within the Spiritan strategy itself. On the one hand, as the anticipated *noyau* for the hoped-for churches of the interior, those who became the first Christian villagers had long been the chief target of Spiritan energy. At Zanzibar and Bagamoyo, they had been the focus of intense missionary interest, and forming them had been the missionaries' most important goal. Particular attention had been paid to those envisioned as future elites: priests, brothers, and sisters.

By the 1880s, nearly all of those once in such programs had left them. They joined the other villagers, often marrying. Yet once in the villages, and especially the villages in the interior, their transitional role became all too clear. Once at the heart of Spiritan strategy, now they became a stage to be passed through.

---

109. Deutsch 2003, 175.
110. Cooper 1979, 105; Glassman 1995. See also Sunseri 1993, 511.
111. Deutsch 2000, 5f.
112. Deutsch 2003, 187.

Their labor remained important, since they had to work very hard to establish the mission. But all that labor was directed at creating a stage for the evangelization of the surrounding peoples. Thus the villagers and their labor were instrumentalized by the missionary strategy that had at an earlier stage put them at its center.

V. Y. Mudimbe has shown how such villages in the Congo existed in a similar contradictory position in relation to Catholic missionary strategy, which he elaborates with reference to literary tropes. In his eyes, Christian villages were on the one hand an attempt at a utopia which he calls a "synechdoche," the literary trope in which a part equals the whole, as when "Washington" stands for the entire United States. At the same time the villagers were what he calls an "asyndeton," a term that refers to a Greek figure of speech indicating the deliberate absence of ordinary coordinating and connecting pieces of a sentence.[113] By referring to the Christian village both as a synechdoche and an asyndeton, Mudimbe emphasizes that the Catholic missionaries he discusses had very high hopes for the villages, but at the same time planned for their effacement as the missionary strategy progressed.

The same could be said for the slaves evangelized by the Spiritans at Zanzibar and Bagamoyo. The consciousness of Christian villagers in eastern Africa, their ability to be at once loyal and obstinate, was, I speculate, partly a response to this rather difficult and ambiguous place of the villages within the missionary strategy of the Holy Ghost missionaries as well. The focus of enormous energies in the short run — they were the *noyau* of the church of the future — the villages were to be eclipsed once the mission among the peoples of the interior was up and running. The villagers' collective reactions to evangelization, therefore, expressed most clearly their awareness that they possessed only temporary and instrumental value in the eyes of the missionaries.

Their incongruity in relation to Spiritan strategy was embodied within the habitual ways the Spiritans labeled them. On the one hand, they were regularly called the "the mission's children." This designation reflected Spiritan paternalism and their sense of responsibility for the former slaves who were now Catholics at the missions, who existed in a filial relation to their fathers. No doubt calling them children in an ongoing way was only reinforced by encroaching colonial circumstances. Yet this label and the relationship it implied sat in rather stark conflict with two other ways that the Spiritans simultaneously considered the villagers. First, the missionaries desired that these Catholic villagers would embody the mature faith purportedly found in European Catholic families: working hard, raising children, giving a good example for surrounding peoples. A second reality, however, was concretized in light of Le Roy's reforms, which had as their expressed purpose a deeper self-reliance among the villagers. The reforms made very clear that the relationship between the mission and the village households approximated patron-client relations elsewhere in the region. Le Roy's ideas invited

---

113. Mudimbe 1994, 136–38.

the Christian villagers to perhaps supplement, perhaps replace their role as children with that of clients of the missionaries, who were quite explicitly envisioned as patrons deserving certain remuneration for their care of their clients.

The villages generated a second set of incongruities in relation to their non-Christian neighbors. The village at Bagamoyo already created new material realities and generated possibilities that had not been available in the orphanages. The reception of land by the villagers in particular cast them in a new position in relation to other unfree laborers at the coast. Some decades later, when slavery was abolished, freed slaves knew that the acquisition of their own property was the first step in the move toward freedom. Likewise the possession of land allowed scope for the Christian villagers to pursue their own interests.[114]

Compared to Bagamoyo, however, the interior stations gave even more chances for the villagers' independent exercise of authority. Land was more available than at the coast, and political authority was correspondingly more fluid. While the coastal region underwent significant political changes in the 1880s, strong authorities — Omani and then European — always laid claim to control and could buttress those claims with force. In the interior, though the sultan claimed authority until the mid-1880s, many others did as well. In fact, the missions themselves often developed as significant power brokers. In such frontier-like contexts, where authority was constantly being negotiated and renegotiated, opportunities for self-assertion and expansion of authority by ambitious villagers were many. African Catholics could aspire to patronal status on their own, forming alliances and taking on clients, as many apparently did. They could seek to found their own village, sometimes even with the mission's permission. These political opportunities also generated economic ones, so that available land could be cultivated and crops sold.

At the same time as the interior expanded the possibilities facing the Christian villagers, it also made clearer the villagers' anomalous place in relationship to the broader coastal economy, which had a number of different roles that their circumstances resembled. No other social role, however, fit the villages' circumstances. Having been evangelized and become Catholics, they did not think of themselves as slaves, and yet in some ways they approximated the slaves held by plantation owners. After all, the Spiritans tried to keep them within a relationship defined by paternalism, an idiom that was often associated with enslavement in the region. Yet even among the group of other unfree laborers at the coast, the villagers had no obvious parallel. Their possession of land and relationship to the missionaries situated them uncomfortably within the variety of types of servility at the coast and the many possible construals of patron-client relations.

For example, the coast had *shamba* slaves who worked plantations and received *makonde*, their own plots of land. It also had *watumwa* of the more traditional sort, either *wazalia* or *wakulia*, that is, those born into slavery or raised in it, and associated with the houses or town. This group did not usually

---

114. Fair 2001, 15, 265.

have its own land, but received small monies from which they paid *ijara*, a rent to their patron. These *watumwa* could eventually accumulate enough to buy their freedom. If the orphanage children — at least those with their own small plots — approximated the coastal category of *shamba* slaves, Christian villagers would have fit uncomfortably within either of these two categories. With Le Roy's reforms, however, they eventually became paid for labor in excess of their mission requirement. Still the parallel with the *watumwa* was inexact, since ordinary *watumwa* did not possess land.

While resembling slaves in some ways, the villagers also bore a similarity to free laborers, whose number grew as the colonial era spread the cash economy and generated labor demands for plantations, mines, railroads, and other institutions.[115] After all, the villagers often worked for a wage on the mission, as Le Roy's reforms envisioned they eventually would. In addition, the skills imparted by their mission education — in language, mathematics, or in agriculture or small industries — would have made them attractive within the emerging colonial economy.

Another potential role from the broader region was that of peasant, and this was the role that best approximated the emerging moral economy of the mission held by the villagers. The social formation of peasants in eastern Africa had already begun by the nineteenth century, and ongoing commoditization associated with colonialism increased it.[116] The villagers' placement on the land as well as in Africa's interior, along with the relations between themselves and the missionaries generated by missionary practices, generally conduced to foster in the villagers a sense of their own interests as landed peasants, with the missionaries as their local patronal authorities. Their identities approximated those of other small landholders who might produce some surplus for sale in local markets. Such people usually existed as clients to a local patron, with varying types of fealty, dependence, and deference operative in those relations.

Yet their identity as peasants was not static, for the moral economy of the mission was not simply a set of traditional and unchanging expectations, an implicit conservatism that resisted any change.[117] From the beginning, the moral economy inculcated through slave evangelization evolved along with the Spiritan program of evangelization and its approach to space and labor. As the mission's children grew older, moved from Zanzibar to the mainland, entered seminary training,

---

115. On free labor in the colonial period in Tanganyika, see Sunseri 2002.

116. On peasantry there is a vast and complex literature. I have found the following helpful for Africanist approaches: Bunker 1987; Glassman 1995, 9–12, 35–54; Kimambo 1991; Bundy 1979; Atkins 1993; Maddox, Giblin, and Kimambo 1996. Ranger (1986) argues that rural resistance to colonialism in Africa can often best be interpreted as the result of incipient agrarian class consciousness. As for a definition of peasants, Glassman's is apt: peasants are " . . . autonomous family farmers whose economic activities were geared primarily toward subsistence and the production of use-values — that is, they grew most of what they ate — yet who yielded a regular surplus to a nonproducing elite" (1995, 45).

117. Randall and Charlesworth 2000, 19. Glassman criticizes what he calls neo-Weberian formulations of the moral economy in which it represents traditional expectations that resist new economic realities, as in the early work of James Scott (Glassman 1995, 14).

married, and assumed new roles within the Spiritan program, they experienced the mission differently. They thus developed distinctive horizons of expectation that represented differing moral economies of the mission. Depending on their particular experiences, they began to possess different interests, developed distinctive ways to think about human thriving, and assimilated themselves to different types of people in eastern Africa.

In turn, many villagers sought to enhance their place, or even to move into a role as a patron with their own clients. Such ambition entailed departure from the mission for some as they established their own households outside missionary authority. Others sought missionary permission to found their own villages. In assuming the patronal role, the villagers emulated the missionaries themselves, especially at places like Mhonda, where the mission's role as local power broker was so obvious. They also no doubt took cues from their neighbors, among whom were some who were accorded status as chiefs. Some of the villagers assumed that status as well. Their slave-keeping practices also displayed their ambition. Slaves could assist in the cultivation on a villager's land and also signaled aspirations toward a patronal role.

The requests and appeals for more land and liberty also indicated this dynamic peasant-like identity, an identity that could evolve into patronal status. The missionaries interpreted such calls in a theological way, as ingratitude, even though they recognized the shortage of land. One can surmise, however, that for the villagers, liberty came not only from the fact of having been ransomed or received after enslavement. It also came with the land given them and the provisions given in exchange for labor. Thus liberty meant more chances to work that land through a lessening of the expectations that they would serve the mission. These Christians sought to expand their prospects for social reproduction by creating conditions in which they themselves could be patrons.

Those who appealed did not opt for decisive exit and flee the mission. They had internalized a sense of themselves that accepted in a fundamental way the definitions of identity sought by missionary evangelization. The directions of their appeals also revealed the nature of the moral economy of the mission within that identity. They first addressed their local superiors at the mission stations, then Baur as superior at Bagamoyo, and later the French consul. After his arrival, they also appealed to Bishop Courmont. This trajectory points toward a further manifestation of the villagers' sense of themselves, which was self-consciously Catholic. These Christians used their voice to appeal following the hierarchical order of authority in which the missionaries situated themselves. They saw the missionaries as landlords of a sort, to whom they owed some fealty and from whom they could expect some redress of their grievances.

Significantly, the villagers did not voice their appeal to the obvious political authority in the region (until the mid-1880s, at least), the sultan of Zanzibar, as did other coastal Africans who felt oppressed by those above them. Slaves in revolt in 1873 had done so, as did those fighting German colonialism in 1888–89 and later in the Maji Maji rebellion beginning in 1905.[118] Instead the Christian villagers appealed to the missionaries when they wanted their conditions bettered, and then in a few cases to the French consul, who seemed because of his national and religious affinities somehow part of the hierarchy of authorities in which they placed themselves. Their voice, as that can be recovered, reveals a developing identity that showed the effects of evangelization, even when it disappointed the missionaries.

The unrest at the villages in the 1880s should therefore be seen as a consequence of developing identities and accompanying interests, pursued by African Catholics within changing circumstances. The villagers' frustrations betrayed an approach to space that differed from that of the Spiritans. The missionaries saw the spaces of evangelization in instrumental and programmatic ways. Each setting was an environment that could be more or less suitable for the formation they sought, and which needed to be shaped in order to effect the changes they wanted. Those they evangelized, on the other hand, took an improvisational approach to their locations, using their settings for the advantages they could gain. More opportunities emerged in the open and legible world of the mainland than at the island of Zanzibar, where enclosure was the missionary strategy. And the village, with its expectations of land stewardship, first at Bagamoyo and then more profoundly in frontier conditions around the interior missions, allowed still more room — literally and figuratively — for Africans to pursue their own interests. In particular, the frontier-like conditions of the interior fostered in the villagers desires for expansion of their own households. The coming of colonialism only increased the opportunities for such ambition, as changing political circumstances created new possibilities for alliances and escape of previous constraints. In this perspective, Spiritan practices at each stage of slave evangelization — at Zanzibar, Bagamoyo, and the interior missions — created new opportunities for self-assertion and self-enhancement among the African Catholics, who took those opportunities with initiative and resourcefulness.

How, then, did African Catholic identity appear in this collective guise? In the first place, though dependent on the circumstances of evangelization as well as other contextualizing factors, the consciousness of the villagers as African Catholics was fundamentally an African achievement deriving from collective practices they carried out. Those practices, however, were enacted in settings and under constraints that were not chosen by them. The missionaries themselves helped produce the settings and constraints that situated this appearance of collective African Catholic identity. The missionaries were also responsible for our capacity to discern that consciousness, for they recorded most of its traces even when they did not appreciate what they were recording. Yet they did not create these African Catholics directly, for that was due to Africans making use of the discourses and practices of Catholic Christianity to which they were exposed. The voices and agency we can discern open a new window on African

---

118. Glassman 1995, 111–13, 267; Iliffe 1979.

experiences under the impact of missionary evangelization in the period prior to formal colonial overrule in nineteenth-century eastern Africa.

•

Important as they were, the collective protests of the villagers did not exhaust important African Catholic experiences at the Spiritan missions in this period, which took a variety of forms. Such collective action cannot be separated completely from the stories of particular individuals who appear distinctively within the historical record. Most were themselves villagers who began at Zanzibar or Bagamoyo. In addition, a small number of men remained in formation programs for membership in the Spiritan community in the 1880s and have left important traces in the historical record. Others cooperated with the missionaries as they pursued their program of evangelization. And certain individuals carved idiosyncratic paths as they received the mission's evangelizing processes. Among those whose peculiar stories are preserved in the historical record were Melchior and Joseph, the "monster" and the *mwalimu*, KiSwahili for "teacher."

Melchior and Joseph

The first notice of Melchior in Bagamoyo's journal recounted his August 1883 return to the mission from Dar es Salaam in the clutches of Charles-Alfred and Martial, the senior Christians at the mission who often went after the *watoro*, or fugitives. That must have been a recapture from the second escape of this boy from Bagamoyo's orphanage, because two months later the journal recorded what it named as his third. In company with another he fled during the night, an expertly slaughtered pig carcass in the field alerting the missionaries to the other escapee, a skilled butcher with whom Melchior had fled.[119]

The next record of Melchior appeared in the journal of the Zanzibar mission, where he had come from the coastal town of Kilwa in order to return to the mission at Bagamoyo. Two days later, the Bagamoyo journal recorded the return of this "rascal of the worst type" who, after numerous escapes, "presents himself as a penitent at Zanzibar," wanting to return. Then, however, the journal recorded startling news (*quelle surprise*): "We learn that Melchior sold Hyacinthe, one of our other fugitives," and now came to Bagamoyo to slip away (*s'echapper*) to avoid punishment. "This monster," the entry continued, "has been put in irons."

---

119. Bagamoyo journal, 12viii83, 20x83. Nine days later the journal recorded that six escapees were reported in the custody of the *liwali* (the sultan's local representative) at Dar es Salaam, but none were named (Bagamoyo journal, 29x83). A few weeks later a rumor that those detained had been sold to Arabs sent shivers through the Christians at Bagamoyo (ibid., 20xi83), but it turned out to be untrue. The next day a group were returned, nine total. They were chained together and set to work digging (ibid., 21–22xi83). A little over a month later, seven of the nine escaped, two having decided to remain. At this point the group was named, and Melchior was not among them (ibid., 28xii83). But he was caught a few days later and the journal took the occasion to say that five of them had escaped four times.

Perhaps he had gone into the prison at the mission, the foundations of which had been dug just three weeks before.[120]

It was but three weeks later, during a liturgical celebration, that this mission-product-*cum*-slave-trader escaped a fourth time, now along with ten others. Most of these eleven were back at the mission within a few weeks. Some came willingly, but Melchior was brought with two others from Dar es Salaam. They were described as having "sold one another" for a pittance. By February 1885, he had apparently escaped and been apprehended a fifth time. After several months in jail he begged to be allowed back into the mission as a "good Christian." Melchior was readmitted but this time with the proviso laid down by the missionaries that this would be the last time. In October 1885 he indeed escaped again along with an unfortunate accomplice named Blaise, whom Melchior promptly sold into slavery.[121]

Melchior was not alone among the mission residents who escaped repeatedly. According to Bagamoyo's baptismal records, he came to the mission around the age of fifteen and was baptized in 1876. He served as a baptismal sponsor in 1878, indicating that he was held in esteem by others at the mission and trusted to some extent by the Spiritans.[122] His later penchant for selling his fellow fugitives, however, left the Spiritans awestruck. Yet escaped slaves in eastern Africa during this period often took to slave trading themselves.[123] This suggests that Melchior's behavior was not "monstrous" so much as strategic, even common for those in his shoes. Though the *watoro* might appear vicious there was a method in their violence. By selling his fellow escapees, Melchior gained money for his own protection in a dangerous environment.

His later behavior points to the difficulty of isolating a shared consciousness among those at the Spiritan mission. Perhaps his previous enslavement until the age of fifteen had hardened him. Perhaps Bagamoyo's regime had contributed to his selfishness. Though he begged his way back into the mission, protesting his loyalty, his strategically modulated voice showed no real internalization of any notion like a moral economy of the mission seen in other African Catholics. In the colonial and proto-colonial circumstances of the 1880s at the eastern African coast, his actions show the most strident pursuit of self-interest and no sense of collective identity for or against the mission or his fellow Africans.

An earlier incident involved an escapee of a less sinister sort who became his own sort of missionary. The full account of the escapades of a boy later identified as Joseph Mghindo appeared in an 1883 report to the Society for the Propagation of the Faith prepared by Le Roy.[124] In the midst of describing the children at the orphanages, Le Roy said that in general they were very well-behaved. Every once in a while, however, they were "taken by strange illusions." Desiring not to

120. Zanzibar journal, 26vii84; Bagamoyo journal, 11vii84, 28vii84.
121. Bagamoyo journal 17viii84, 18viii84, 19viii84, 27viii84, 20ii85, 13x85.
122. Bagamoyo sacramental registries, 24xii76, 20iv78.
123. Morton 1990, 19ff.
124. CSSp 196ax: Le Roy to Propagation of the Faith, 15ix83; APF 56 (1884), 51f; BG 13:51f.

appear as "savages," or perhaps by a desire for more independence, they escaped. Joseph was one such example.

Le Roy narrated how Joseph, nicknamed the *mwalimu*, had wanted "to tempt fortune." Knowing that his skin would not suffice to attract the attention he wanted, he took a choir robe and other liturgical garb from the mission when he fled. For one month he preached in the region, introducing himself as an emissary from "the whites" to convert *les noirs*. He had the habit of "concluding every homily with a touching harangue [*peroraison*] . . . in which he insisted on remuneration. . . . " Everywhere he excited the liveliest admiration, Le Roy wrote, especially when he spoke of the savagery and ignorance of his hearers. Finally, however, one chief, more skeptical than others, seized him and brought him back to the mission. Six months later he was dead, likely not more than fifteen years old.[125]

For Le Roy, Joseph's story was perfect for one of the major benefactors of the mission. It reinforced Spiritan claims that the children at the mission represented promising material for the Christian life even when they also frustrated the missionaries. Reading the description today, however, Joseph reveals the wherewithal and imagination of Africans to take the missionary message — as well as its forms and practices — and use them in a way not imagined by the Spiritans themselves. It may be that Joseph had been a seminarian,[126] and in preaching externally he did something that Spiritans were not doing at that time when he escaped and made his impact. Even if he preached only to make money — a conclusion not warranted by the evidence we have — he had heard the mission's message loudly and clearly, and appropriated it in ways not anticipated by the missionaries themselves. Joseph's voice showed loyalty to the mission even as he pursued a policy of flight or exit from the missionaries' control. Evangelization, and perhaps seminary formation, had forged a profound identity in him.

Former Slaves in Spiritan Formation in the 1870s and 1880s

The missionary program had an even more profound and long-lasting effect on the small number of men who continued to prepare for religious life in the Congregation of the Holy Ghost in the late 1870s and 1880s. Despite the suppression of Latin instruction and the effective end of seminary training in the late 1870s, the missionaries maintained their hopes for indigenous members of their congregation into the 1880s. In the mid-1870s, Philippe had returned in temporary vows and lived in the Spiritan community. Meanwhile Julien, Dieudonné, and Patrice — the three who returned from Europe after the 1876 deaths of the

---

125. Bagamoyo journal, 21viii80: "Joseph Mghindo approaching his end."

126. There was a seminarian who is identified in 1871 as Joseph Kipandji of the people from Ugindo, and it may be that Joseph Mghindo in this story is this same young man, with his second name referring to his ethnicity (CSSp 196biii: Duparquet to Barillec, 17vii71). On the other hand, one of the seminarians who went to France and died was also named Joseph, so the one listed in 1871 may be different than the escapee-turned-missionary. Given his temporary success as a preacher, he must have had some gifts for oratory.

two novices in Paris — initially continued in formation at Zanzibar. Julien, whose musical ability Horner had praised, left soon after he and Dieudonné returned in December 1876. Dieudonné, however, remained, in formation at Zanzibar. Joining him there were François and Laurent, who were designated postulants (a stage in formation prior to the novitiate) while Dieudonné was called a novice. All three assisted in the catechetical school. They also had short conferences each day, given by one of the Spiritans at Zanzibar. This situation persisted until early 1881, when Dieudonné went to Mhonda to assist. Though the Spiritans found him a bit listless, they allowed him to remain until he voluntarily decided not to renew his vows in March 1881. He left the congregation in June, then joined the villagers soon thereafter, retaking his baptismal name, Isidore.[127] He married a woman named Henrietta in July 1882 at Mhonda, and they had a son in 1883.[128]

By the time Dieudonné returned to being Isidore, Patrice and Philippe had already departed the Spiritans as well. Patrice Ambimoyo's intellectual gifts had long been touted by the Spiritans. Though he admitted Patrice's timidity, Horner had high hopes for him, and proposed that he, alone among the Africans from eastern Africa sent to France, prepare for priesthood. Horner also pondered sending him to the Spiritan seminary at Blackrock in Ireland to study in English, the language Horner foresaw as important for the future at Zanzibar. The promising student never reached Ireland, though he began seminary studies at Langonnet in France. After the 1876 deaths of the other two Africans in France, however, he was sent back to Zanzibar shortly after Julien and Dieudonné. Given the education Patrice had received in France, however, there was no further educational or formation program for him to pursue in eastern Africa. He left the formation program and married at Bagamoyo in 1879. He continued to work in the printing press until at least the mid-1880s.[129]

During the late 1870s, the Spiritans grew increasingly frustrated with Philippe, the first eastern African Spiritan. He had taken vows in Paris and returned to Zanzibar in 1875. Of his first few years as a Spiritan brother we know little, though Horner and Baur complained that he lacked a skill to help the mission advance, and Horner complained of his pride.[130] Philippe arrived at Mhonda in

---

127. CSSp 196biv: Horner to Schwindenhammer, 10ii76; Zanzibar journal, 17i78, 13ii78; Mhonda journal, 4ii81, 6iii81, 13iii81, 24vii81; CSSp 197ai: Machon to Schwindenhammer, 25viii80, 9ii81, 25iii81, 23vi81; ibid., Baur to Levavasseur, 4v81; CSSp 196bi: Schwindenhammer to Baur, 30v81; BG 11:703.

128. Isidore had been baptized in 1871 at Bagamoyo, with Patrice as his sponsor (Bagamoyo sacramental registry). The Mhonda sacramental books record a marriage on 24vii82 and the baptism on 26vii83. They had another child in 1886 (Mhonda journal, 1vi86).

129. On Patrice, see the following: CSSp 196aiv: Duparquet to Schwindenhammer, 19ix71; CSSp 196biv: Horner to Schwindenhammer, 12i76, 10ii76; Zanzibar journal, 28vi77. Patrice was married at Bagamoyo in February 1879 (Bagamoyo sacramental registry). In September 1884, the Spiritans debated whether he could work at Zanzibar's hospital with his wife without being exposed to "dangerous contacts," which could mean passing Europeans who would try to hire him (CSSp 405aiv: Le Roy to Courmont, 26ix84). Patrice and his wife returned to Bagamoyo in March 1885 (Bagamoyo journal, 10iii85).

130. CSSp 196biv: Horner to Schwindenhammer, 10ii76, 30i77; ibid., Baur to Schwindenhammer, 17xi76.

March 1878 still in temporary vows. There he worked with his fellow Spiritans and the small group of Catholics there from Bagamoyo to develop the mission. He built an oven and took a sick Spiritan confrere back to Bagamoyo.[131]

Troubles were brewing, however, for Horner reported in May that the African brother had been humiliated in front of the villagers by one of the Spiritan priests. A few months later, Horner relayed a report from Baur that Philippe had mis-behaved with some of the children at Bagamoyo in preparation for their return journey to Mhonda some months before. When some of the children had departed early rather than leave in the caravan as planned, Philippe had defended them before the mission authorities. Then, against Baur's wishes, he brought along for the journey another of the Bagamoyo Christians as his servant. Finally, Baur alleged that Philippe had plotted with a group of mission children to plan an evening away from the mission, during which he had spent money Baur had set aside for another purpose. In light of these accusations, Horner requested per-mission from the mother house that Philippe repeat his novitiate. This request was denied by Spiritan authorities in Paris because it violated their constitutions. Nonetheless, Philippe was allowed to renew his temporary vows. Though the Spiritans claimed that he did not possess great promise, his behavior sufficed for continuing membership in the congregation.[132]

In early 1880, Philippe served the mission as a typical Spiritan brother, over-seeing work in the fields and cooking for all those at the mission.[133] Then in September another incident occurred, and Philippe stood accused of hoarding gunpowder, guns, and cloth in cooperation with Hilarion, the catechist. A follow-up in October led Machon to conduct a search at another site where he suspected Philippe had hidden other stolen items. As the inquiry continued, Philippe also faced accusations that he had been involved with women in the Christian village and found with one in compromising circumstances.[134] The report took the oc-casion to remark that Philippe was "all too free" with the villagers and hardly spoke to the priests at the mission.

The accusations of theft and inappropriate behavior with the local woman led to Philippe's dismissal from the Spiritan congregation. The Spiritan superior at Mhonda, Machon, admitted that, though nothing had been proved, Philippe had certainly been imprudent. Machon regretted what he called the open environment of the Spiritan community at Mhonda, which in his opinion had contributed to

131. Mhonda journal, 19iii78, 22v78, 28vi78, 19viii78, 27viii78.

132. Philippe renewed his vows on November 9, 1879 (Mhonda journal, 9xi79). See also: CSSp 196iv: Baur to Schwindenhammer, 17xi76; ibid.: Horner to Schwindenhammer, 30i77, 24viii78; 6iii79; ibid.: Horner to Laverriere, 5v78; CSSp 196axii: Horner to Laverriere, 6iv78. The child who returned with Philippe from the coast was named Arnulf (Mhonda journal, 27viii78). Apparently Philippe was joined at Mhonda by another Spiritan brother, and Machon was not impressed by the work of either (CSSp 196biv: Machon to Horner, 17ix79). From Paris, the superior general had already complained about the formation environment in eastern Africa (CSSp 196bi: Schwindenhammer to Horner, 9i79).

133. Mhonda journal, 12vi80, 11viii80.

134. Mhonda journal, 10ix80, 13ix80, 16ix80, 6x80, 7x80; CSSp 197ai: Machon to Baur, 22ix80.

the loss of Philippe's vocation to the religious life by exposing him to temptations that led to his misbehavior. Baur concluded that he was a sad child who had not been well-formed. Meanwhile, some Spiritans in Paris apparently felt that their one-time protégé had been treated unfairly. The superior general Schwinden-hammer, however, understood and respected the local missionaries' decision. He also applauded their desire to help Philippe start a new life by giving him a herd of cattle. Philippe was sent to live at the Christian village at Mandera in December 1880.[135]

Philippe's travails highlight the difficulties faced by those Africans at the mission who found themselves the object of missionary hopes and yet who also faced other social and personal pressures. Horner wrote that Philippe was called *noir-blanc* (black/dark-white) by the people, adding that locals were pleased to so call him (*se plaisent à appeler*).[136] It is unclear whether this was a term of derision, or simply descriptive. The label was understandable given Philippe's circumstances and setting, for he no doubt confused the ordinary categories by which people perceived those at the mission. He had been in Europe for two years, no doubt spoke French well, and surely wore the black Spiritan habit, yet he was an African and not European, unlike all but very few of the Spiritans in eastern Africa at the time. The accusations that he was unduly familiar with the mission children, even fomenting trouble among them, suggests that he empathized with Africans despite his formation in Europe and his vows as a Spiritan. Such actions no doubt led to missionary questions about his loyalty to the mission and his vows. Unfortunately no records exist of Philippe's own interpretations of these events.[137]

Reflecting Spiritan disappointment with Julien, Dieudonné, Patrice, and Philippe, Baur blamed "slave roots" for their inability to embody the ideals of clergy. He maintained the hope that it might be possible to get some brothers and catechists from former slaves. Better prospects would come, he believed, from the Christian villages where children untouched by slavery were being born. Mean-while, he defended the decision to cease forming potential priests. Missionary energies, he claimed, should be used at tasks more likely to be successful than making religious out of those unable to fulfill expectations.[138]

Yet Baur's disappointment was not the end of the story, for these men did not cease to be important for the growing Catholic presence in eastern Africa. Though all four left the Spiritan formation program, they remained connected to the Spiritan missions to varying degrees. According to the Mandera journal, Julien

---

135. CSSp 197ai: Machon to Baur, 22ix80; ibid.: Baur to Schwindenhammer, 23ix80; ibid.: Hac-quard to Schwindenhammer, 9x80; CSSp 196i: Schwindenhammer to Baur, 9xii80, 6i81, 1iv81, 30v81. According to Koren, he left vows on November 1, 1880 (1993, 41).

136. CSSp 196axii: Horner to Laverriere, 6iv78; MC 10 (1878), 242.

137. Horner's account of Philippe's earlier humiliation at the hands of the Spiritan priest is also frustratingly vague. He mentioned that the priest might have been drunk and also urged his corre-spondent, the director of the Propagation of the Faith in Lyon, not himself to contact Philippe about it because of the latter's sensitivity (CSSp 196biv: Horner to Laverriere, 5v78).

138. CSSp 196ax: Baur to Propagation of the Faith, 15xi80; BG 11:703.

Figure 16. Photo of Isidore, a former slave and early African aspirant to membership in the Spiritans (d. 1937). Courtesy of the Spiritan photo archives, Paris.

served as a catechist.[139] Isidore remained a prominent member of the Mhonda parish until well into the twentieth century, as the photo here attests, and is still remembered there, having died only in 1937. He taught class until 1887 and also played the harmonium — a type of hand-organ — in church. He was often a sponsor in marriages or baptisms.[140]

Patrice maintained even stronger ties to the Spiritans. He worked in the printing shop at Bagamoyo for years, and the Spiritans were furious when he was unaccountably beaten in 1885 by a local Omani official, possibly accused of collaboration with the Germans. The Spiritans protested his case. Later he served as personal assistant to Courmont on the bishop's journeys to interior missions in the 1880s. Le Roy reported in 1888 that during a hunting trip on one such journey, Patrice had told him the remarkable story of his enslavement and deliverance by the missionaries.[141]

139. Mandera journal, 12ix83. A few months later the journal records that Julien, likely the same fellow, had gone to Bagamoyo in search of his wife, who had fled (Mandera journal, 18iv84, 22v84).

140. Mhonda journal 13vi87. His death appears in Mhonda's register of the dead. According to Christians at Mhonda, Isidore (or Isidori, as his name was Swahili-ized) taught in the school for many years and spoke French with Bishop Aloys Munsch in the early twentieth century. The photo was taken by Father Rault, who arrived in eastern Africa in 1911.

141. On the beating, see Bagamoyo journal, 29/30xi85. For other references to Patrice in years following, see Zanzibar journal, 7xii86: MC 19 (1887), 344; MC 20 (1888), 515. For Patrice's role as

For his part, Philippe returned eventually to the Mhonda mission, where he had served as a Spiritan brother. There he remained for many years, cooperating with the missionaries and the other Christians at the village.[142] In 1884, he accompanied two Spiritans as they looked for a new mission site, indicating an ongoing cooperative relationship. His son was baptized and married at Mhonda's mission. Philippe himself was wounded fighting on the mission's behalf in December 1886 and later joined a few of the men in the village to pursue escapees. Like many of the villagers, he moved away from the mission to help start another Christian village, but he was a godfather at the Mhonda mission up to 1890.[143]

Another Try at Forming African Spiritans: The Agregés

The departures of Julien, Patrice, Dieudonné/Isidore, and Philippe from formation by the early 1880s left only François and Laurent, who continued in the postulancy, the first stage of Spiritan formation. Both former slaves from the Yao people, François and Laurent had been in the seminary program for about a decade hoping to become Spiritans.[144] In 1881 the Spiritans faced the issue of whether or not to admit them to the novitiate. Since this was a formal decision requiring congregational approval, Baur wrote the mother house in Paris on the question. His ambivalent remarks revealed the progressive waning of Spiritan hopes for indigenous religious. They also showed the growing racism within the Spiritans' discourse and their awareness of the limitations of the social circumstances in which they acted.

Baur recommended that they be admitted as *agregés*, something like "associates," so they could wear the habit but not be equal to the other Spiritans. They would in consequence, he thought, be less prone to pride and able to serve in the same capacity as regular brothers. But later, he reasoned, their expected departure would not cause quite the scandal as the others had. In response, the Spiritan council in Paris noted the difficulties of treating Africans the same as Europeans in the current state of affairs, as well as the faint guarantee of their fidelity and perseverance judging from Spiritan experiences in other parts of Africa. They accepted Baur's proposal for this new status within the congregation.[145]

---

assistant to Courmont during the bishop's interior voyages, see the *carnets* as follows: CSSp 198b: Courmont, 8i85, 10vii85, 13x–9xi86, 9i–26ii88. Le Roy's account of Patrice's imprisonment and coming to the mission can be found in Le Roy 1888.

142. Mhonda journal, 13ix82, 13x85, 14iv86, 6xii86, 9vi87, 20ix87.

143. CSSp 198b, Courmont, 28i87; Mhonda journal, 10viii84, 24xii86, 20ix87, 28xi87, 4xii87; baptismal and marriage registries, Mhonda mission. I have found no record of Philippe after 1890, but the registry of the dead at Mhonda only begins in 1910, so he probably died before that.

144. BG 13:25; CSSp 197ai: Machon to Schwindenhammer, 25viii80. Both are named in an 1871 letter enrolling the then-seminarians in the Confraternity of the Holy Spirit (CSSp 196biii: Duparquet to Barillec, 17vii71). Later François was chained up at the order of Baur at the time of escapes and misbehavior by the seminarians in 1873, accused of being "compromised" by those who fled (CSSp 196biii: Schwindenhammer to Horner, 8iv73; ibid.: Baur to Horner, 11iv73).

145. CSSp 196aix: Baur to Paris, 26viii81; CSSp 196bi: Superior General to Baur and Acker, 27iv83.

François and Laurent were frustrated by the long wait in response to their petition and were further disappointed to hear that they would not be received as brothers with regular vows. Laurent wrote the administration in Paris on their behalf, saying that they accepted the decision, "pained by the news . . . but submitting with an open heart." He and François took their qualified vows in October 1882. Acker, in charge of the two, spoke favorably of their progress later that year and in 1883. They seemed to have embraced their status despite the disappointment Laurent expressed. Acker also received another young man into the postulancy in 1882, and it appeared that the *agregé* system might proceed smoothly.[146]

The chapter of 1884 discussed the *agregés* in the context of a more general discussion about the formation of indigenous religious and clergy. The mood of the chapter was to stress that no moral pressure be exerted on young boys or girls to take religious vows unless they themselves asked for them, recognition of both Spiritan frustrations with previous efforts and their growing doubts about African abilities to embrace celibacy despite concerted efforts at their education and training.[147]

As time went on, the *agregé* situation caused frustration for all involved. As a consequence of the chapter's refusal to make a decision, the two Africans continued in their unresolved state, teaching at the Zanzibar schools. François taught first-year French and Laurent the second year, also serving as organist and music director for the students. François wrote Bishop Courmont soon after the 1884 chapter, expressing his perplexity and dejection after fifteen years of seeking to satisfy his interior desires — first for priesthood and now religious life with the Spiritans, all undertaken "for the great glory of God and most certainly my own salvation as well as that of my fellow countrymen." Frustrated by hopes raised and then dashed time and again, François now felt afflicted by "the poison of discouragement and despair." He blamed the shifting demands placed upon him and Laurent, recalling a perverse cycle of encouragement followed by demeaning questions about their readiness from those with certain "so-called prejudices" (*prétendus prejugés*). Now he noted the chapter's decision to end their novitiate but continue with this *agregé* status, the hope being to have a novitiate later, "when we will become the first brothers, seeing that Philippe and Dieudonné have left." Frustrated, he recognized that he and Laurent had been prevented from attaining the same chances and material advantages as Europeans out of fear that they would become proud, stubborn, and demanding. As a consequence, François concluded, the life of the Spiritans, once so attractive, now struck him as insipid, a sad and unfortunate condition in which he was like a convict in a confining

---

146. CSSp 197ai: Laurent to Superior General, 9ii82; CSSp 197ai: Acker to Secretary General, 6iv82, 16x82, 30iii83, 21vii83, 16ix83; BG 13:1058. The new candidate's name was Sylvester Tota, but no mention was made of him again (CSSp 197ai: Acker to Secretary General, 6iv82). Courmont, however, does mention a third *agregé* in 1884, who might have been Sylvester Tota (CSSp 197ai: Courmont to Emonet, 2vii84).

147. CSSp 196aiv, chapter of 1884.

prison. He asked Courmont to assign him to another responsibility in which his discouragement might be assuaged.[148]

Courmont, too, was uncomfortable with the *agregé* system, which represented a two-tier system within the congregation. At the same he also espoused racist convictions that vocations were lacking because of "impure blood." Still, he continued to think that François, at least, remained promising, and from Paris the Holy Ghost authorities accepted a renewal of his vows for another year. They commiserated with Courmont's difficulties, admitting that the question of African brothers was "complex and embarrassing."[149]

Though he recognized the justice in the frustrations of François and Laurent, by early 1886 Courmont also impatiently complained of their growing discontent. He blamed the Spiritan "creoles" — brothers from the Caribbean — rather than the more indicting sentiments François had articulated. As in the case of the Christian villagers, whose discontent was laid at the feet of Father Foels, African protest was again attributed to outside interference rather than locally inspired resentment.

The downward spiral continued. In early 1886, Laurent left the mission without permission several times, then was beaten by Le Roy with the *nerf de hippopatome*, that is, a whip made from hippopotamus hide, in Swahili a *kiboko*, considered a brutal instrument to this day.[150] Courmont commented sadly on the incident, for Laurent was, among other things, a valuable musician: "It is the passion and weakness of will encountered in this race that unite for their loss." A month later Laurent intimated that he sought to leave his *agregé* status, and Courmont planned to send him away. Eventually Laurent was imprisoned, probably for drunkenness, which may have occasioned Le Roy's prior beating. After being released, he begged Courmont for forgiveness in a beautifully written but pathetic letter, full of self-recrimination. Describing himself as a brute who could not bear being castigated without reacting (with violence, one assumes), he expressed his frustration with his status, reasserting his desire to be faithful for life. He swore to avoid the *maudit boisson* (cursed drink) that had led to this state and put himself entirely in Courmont's hands.[151]

Laurent's plea went unheeded. Instead Courmont dismissed him from the *agregé* program after his imprisonment. Soon afterward he married and went to Mhonda, where the first reports from the superior said he was ineffective as a catechist. For his part, François went first to Bagamoyo still an *agregé*. He then

148. BG 11:702; Koren 1996, 74; CSSp 197aii: François, no date.

149. See Kieran 1966, 141. Also: CSSp 197ai, Courmont to Emonet, 19vii84; CSSp 197aii: Courmont to Carrie, 2xii85; ibid.: Courmont to Emonet, 23xi85, 23xii85, 30xii85, 2i86; ibid.: Emonet to Courmont, 26ii86; CSSp 196axiii: Courmont to Holy Childhood Society, 5x84; CSSp 196bi: Emonet to Courmont, 15i86.

150. CSSp 197aii: Courmont to Emonet, 2i86, 7vi86; Zanzibar journal, 26iv86. Emonet, the superior general in Paris, again expressed his sympathy for Courmont's troubles with Laurent (CSSp 196bi: Emonet to Courmont, 31iii86).

151. CSSp 197aii: Courmont to Emonet, 7vi86, 2vii86, 7vii86, 14iii87; ibid.: Laurent to Courmont, 5iv87.

left and married before going to Mandera with his wife. There he replaced the
instructor-catechist, also a onetime slave from Bagamoyo, who had been over-
seeing the school there.[152] The formation of African clergy and religious, despite
occasional attempts to revive it and Spiritan self-recriminations in their reports
to Rome and their superiors, effectively ceased until the twentieth century.[153]

The frustrations expressed by those within the formation programs coincided
with complaints and protests emerging from the Christian villagers. Whether the
villagers connected their own plight with the nearly simultaneous and equally
distressing experiences of Laurent and François in their formation as potential
elites — or vice versa — is unknown. Missionary accounts did not connect the
frustrations of the two groups. It is hard not to do so from this vantage, however,
when the 1880s seem to represent such important years for African Catholics
in eastern Africa. Both the villagers' protests and the letters from François and
Laurent revealed the profound effects of evangelization and African Catholic
frustrations with the missionaries.

But there were differences. François and Laurent felt unfairly judged and
discriminated against, and gave voice to those feelings in eloquent letters full
of overtly Catholic language. Their ability to articulate such sentiments depended upon the fact of missionary evangelization itself. After all, they wrote
in French — and with beautiful handwriting — and reflected on their vocational hopes in ways that expressed a spiritual and theological perspective not
dissimilar to the missionaries' own. While Laurent and François voiced their
discouragement in a theological or religious idiom, mentioning the thwarting of
their vocation, recognizing their own sins but also finding fault with the missionaries, the villagers' complaints to the missionaries, at least as the missionaries
recorded them, lacked specifically religious language for the most part. Their appeals and protests reflected more practical frustrations. They sought to enhance
their circumstances. Both types of complaint reflected the ambitions embodied
within slave evangelization itself, for the Spiritans sought to create new people
from slaves, and a new church where one had not been before.

Though their behavior frustrated and disappointed the missionaries, one suspects that Laurent and François, like most villagers, had profound loyalty to the
mission, generated through years of prayer, study, and labor. In the case of the
former *agregés*, that loyalty was magnified by an ambition to join the Spiritans.
The missionaries were not in a position, however, to hear such voices expressive
of that loyalty. Instead the Spiritans blamed outside agitation or "slave roots" for

152. CSSp 197aii: Courmont to Emonet, 9v87, 12vii87, 14vii87; ibid.: Chevalier to Emonet,
14viii87; Bagamoyo journal, 1vi87, 12vii87, 30x87. Mandera journal, 30vii87, 13viii87, 14ix87;
van den Eeden 1980, 19.
153. Zanzibar journal, 25vii87; Mandera journal, 30vii87, 13viii87; Kieran 1966, 141–42. Courmont in 1890 could still ask the superior general for guidelines on the formation of African brothers
(CSSp 197aiii: Courmont to Emonet, 3v90, 9v90), and he was told to wait until the next generation
(CSSp 196bi: Emonet to Courmont, 11vi90). Thus there was little activity in this area later in the
1890s, only muted expressions of disappointment (CSSp 197bi: Allgeyer to Le Roy, 26iv03; CSSp
195viii: Allgeyer to Gotti, 20x03). See Kieran 1966, 138.

the troubles. In publications for benefactors, they explained the lack of indigenous clergy and religious on essential incapacities among Africans or Islamic tainting, despite the fact that Laurent and François had probably been at the mission for twenty years or more.[154]

Yet, as in the case with the others who had been in formation before them, the subsequent histories of the former *agregés* suggested that the Spiritans underestimated both their impact on these men and their value in their missionary enterprise. François assisted at Mandera for the rest of his life, taking on the role of assistant to the Spiritan superior of the mission. He accompanied the superior on trips into the surrounding regions, including the retrieval of a woman burned as a witch, who was subsequently baptized before her death. Service to the church continued in his progeny. His son Maurice was known at Mandera as *Mwalimu Morisi* (the teacher Maurice) until the 1980s, suggesting a long commitment to the church there and a role as instructor in school.[155]

Catholics at Mhonda mission to this day likewise possess fond memories of Laurent, who lived at the Christian village near the mission with his wife Felicitas, dying only in the 1940s.[156] His children Eliza, Paschali, Magdalene, and Christopher lived long after him at Mhonda, and one granddaughter remained a parishioner at least until June 2004.[157] Many recall that Laurent played the *kinanda* or harmonium in church and taught Gregorian chants that are still sung by the Catholics at Mhonda. His son Seraphim also played the *kinanda* before his own death. Laurent's history as a seminarian and candidate with the Spiritans remains well-known even today; he was, as one parishioner said, "almost a deacon." Later, another recalled, he became blind and spoke French with the Spiritan missionaries well into the twentieth century, when the photo seen here was taken. One claimed that during World War I, when fighting near the mission led to the withdrawal of the Spiritans, he held the Mhonda Catholic community together. As regards his drinking, the *maudit boisson* he promised Courmont he would avoid, opinions were divided.[158]

Despite Spiritan disappointments, the African men who sought to join their congregation ended up contributing a great deal to the beginnings of the Catholic Church in eastern Africa. The Spiritans noted these contributions, but disappointment crowded out their appreciation for what their programs had achieved. They were intent on developing fellow Spiritans from such men in line with expectations within their formal missionary ideology. They were also trapped in their preconceptions about proper religious life and affected by a deepening racism

154. APF 58 (1886), 186ff; APF 61 (1889), 47ff.
155. Mandera journal, 14ix87, 7ix88; van den Eeden 1980, 18.
156. My information on Laurent comes from a number of local interviews at Mhonda in June 2003, including with Emmanuel Teodori, Ferdinandi Nicolas Kabelwa, John Anthony Kangati, and Morisi Alberti Mswemwa.
157. I regret being unable to interview the granddaughter, Felicita Paulo. Her age and my schedule made it difficult.
158. As with that of Isidore, this photo is also attributed to Father Rault.

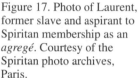

Figure 17. Photo of Laurent, former slave and aspirant to Spiritan membership as an *agregé*. Courtesy of the Spiritan photo archives, Paris.

not unconnected to encroaching colonial overrule. These factors left them ill-prepared to recognize the effects of their evangelization when these did not meet their expectations. Fortunately, sufficient evidence exists within their own records for a better appreciation from our vantage today.

•

Those who participated in the formation programs did not exhaust the significant possible roles played by African Catholics in the 1880s. There were others who also cooperated in the missionary enterprise, assisting the Spiritans in a variety of ways at their missions. The Spiritans in eastern Africa succeeded in creating a broad cadre of collaborators of various sorts, onetime slaves they evangelized who themselves became evangelizers.[159]

The Women Baptizers

One of the most remarkable roles taken by African Catholics in this period was that of *baptiseuse*, a woman baptizer, assumed by a number of women at

---

159. Libermann had foreseen the need for such collaborators and even unsuccessfully requested that catechists be accorded minor orders and thus a formal role in the Catholic hierarchy (Gay 1943, 130; Burke 1998, 64).

Bagamoyo in the 1880s. Several of these women had once been in formation to be sisters and later married, living at the Christian village. Others were wives in the village without the previous history as prospective nuns. The *baptiseuses* emerged out of the idiosyncrasies of Father Antoine Hirtzlin, who embarked on a campaign of mass baptisms beginning in 1882.

Apparently, resentment against his baptisms of non-Christians grew among the local Muslim populace, however, and his visits grew unwelcome in some quarters. In response, Hirtzlin recruited a group of local Christian women, whom he called *baptiseuses*, to assist him. If he was refused admission to a house where a dying person lay, a *baptiseuse* returned in native dress to console the family or assist as a midwife or local healer. But her real task was to baptize surreptitiously. Elise Voulia was a former girl in the formation program for nuns who had married another ex-slave, Martin, in 1874. She was the first such assistant in 1883, and at least seven others followed. They are listed as the baptizing minister in the Bagamoyo baptismal register.[160] Like the men in formation, clearly the time spent in the convent had shaped the identity of Elise and some of the others who followed her lead.

Due to Hirtzlin's work, and especially that of the *baptiseuses*, the number of baptisms per year leapt from double digits to over one thousand.[161] Hirtzlin's baptizing campaign, though useful in representing the progress of the mission in European mission journals, failed to endear him to his Spiritan confreres. Courmont wrote that he discouraged the others and later reported that Hirtzlin claimed to be no longer under his authority. In 1886 the bishop even asked the superior general in Paris to recall the earnest baptizer.[162] His death obviated his removal from eastern Africa.

Regardless of his confreres' frustrations, Hirtzlin's utilization of African *baptiseuses* represents a remarkable nineteenth-century example of African participation in missionary activity, especially participation by women. Horner had dreamed of such a work fifteen years before, and Jacques Laval (1803–64), Libermann's first missionary, used women advisers (*conseilleuses*) in Mauritius in the 1850s.[163] But nothing had been done to enact any official role for women, save the abandoned attempt to form nuns. By the time of Hirtzlin's campaign and collaboration with *baptiseuses*, the official strategy of forming an indigenous clergy

160. Bagamoyo journal, 2vi83; BG 13:1077–78; BG 14:619f; CSSp 196axiii: Courmont to Holy Childhood, 5x84; AA 1888, 86–93. Listed in the register are Elise, Alice, Apollina, Emilia, Francesca, Julienne, Louisa, and Madeleine. This last named might have received her first communion at Zanzibar in 1867 (CSSp 196bii, Baur to Schwindenhammer, 11viii67), but if so then she is not the Madeleine who ostensibly wrote *Suéma* and died in Réunion in formation to be a nun in 1878. Elise and Francesca were among the earliest group of young girls who, with Madeleine/Suéma, had been in formation to be nuns starting in November 1870 (Vogt, n.d.).

161. BG 15:137.

162. CSSp 197aii: Courmont to Emonet, 27ix85, 13ix86, 21xi86, 26xi86. See Kollman 2001, 449ff.

163. CSSp 196ax: Horner to Propagation of the Faith, 28x69. On Laval, see Spindler 1999.

was abandoned and that of forming indigenous religious was soon to follow. In retrospect, Hirtzlin's collaborative mass baptizing campaigns were among the strongest examples of relegation of true responsibility to African Catholics allowed by the Catholic mission before the twentieth century. Though idiosyncratic and dubious on all sorts of grounds, Hirtzlin's practices revealed lay people acting within missionary evangelization in prominent ways not generally seen at the time, in Africa or elsewhere. Unfortunately the *baptiseuses* left no trace in their own voice. Nonetheless, their activity suggests a striking loyalty to the missionary goal of the salvation of souls.

•

Besides the *baptiseuses* and those who had tried to join the Spiritans, others also worked closely with the missionaries in the 1880s. The caravan accounts written by Le Roy and Courmont mentioned others besides Patrice among the mission children who served as porters and personal assistants to the missionaries on the journeys to existing stations and in pursuit of possible new sites. When identified, such men were described as fathers in the Christian village at Bagamoyo, and also as "children" of the mission.[164] Even more prominent in missionary writings were two villagers from Mhonda, Léon and Hilarion, whose stories, already introduced, bear further examination.

Léon

Léon Matelala was one of the two Christians who left Mhonda to complain to the French consul at Zanzibar and ask for freedom in early 1883, an episode discussed in chapter 1 that aroused Spiritan fears. The other was not named, suggesting that Léon was the leader. Certainly he had known the Spiritans for a long time. He was baptized in 1865, when the missionaries estimated that he was seven years old, then was in the seminary program by 1871. He remained in formation with François and Laurent until 1877, but left soon thereafter and did not join them in becoming *agregés* later.[165] From there he apparently went to Bagamoyo as a cook for the mission, likely with a prominent role in the village due to his education. In February 1878, he traveled to Zanzibar with two Spiritans, a sign that he held a trusted position. Eight months later he was married. He and his wife Maria then headed to the newly founded mission at Mhonda, arriving

---

164. These included Antoine, who served as cook during several *safaris*, and Xavier, who was *homme d'affaires* (MC 16 [1884], 17f). Later there appeared Engelbert, who served as Courmont's attendant in 1887 and later, and who was ransomed at Zanzibar; and both Guillaume and Marie-Vincent, who waited upon Baur (CSSp 198b: Courmont, 8i85, 29viii–2ix87; MC 21 [1889], 32; MC 22 [1890], 19).

165. Zanzibar sacramental registry, 17ix65; Zanzibar journal, 1iii78. Judging from two lists of seminarians in 1871, he joined the program after July and before December (CSSp 196biii: Duparquet to Barillec, 17vii71; MC 4 [1871], 76–77).

in October 1878 with another couple, Denis and Odila.[166] They constituted the third and fourth Bagamoyo-trained Catholic couples at Mhonda, joining Hilarion and Germaine, as well as the other couple, Marie-Gabriel and Françoise.[167] At Mhonda, Léon cooperated in the building of huts for the married couples and in other business of the mission.[168] A daughter born to him and his wife in 1880 died a few weeks later, but a later child lived. He weathered a life-threatening illness in April 1882 and helped ransom a child in September. He then fled in December.[169]

The next record comes from the Bagamoyo journal, which records the events of the 1883 appeal to the consul at Zanzibar earlier than the journal at Zanzibar itself, the latter kept less diligently at that time. It alludes to "the sad news of Léon, reclaiming his freedom," received when the boat from Zanzibar brought a Spiritan brother who passed on the news. After this we have Acker's letter describing the event in more detail, written about three weeks later. Acker described the appeal to the consul, its danger for the mission, the baneful "love of liberty" among the mission children, and the fortunate precedent in the consul's decision to disregard the Africans' plea. Acker's description of the escapees, however, mentions also that they were being advised above all by the first children of the mission, who were married and living in Zanzibar.[170] Apparently there was a network of Christians in Zanzibar willing to assist the fugitives.

Other records from a few months later deepen the intrigue with even more information. The Zanzibar journal records that Léon was pardoned for his transgression, crossed over to Bagamoyo, and eventually returned to Mhonda. A few days later, Baur, still the Spiritan superior in eastern Africa since Courmont had not yet arrived, wrote Paris. He indicated his frustration with the Mhonda Christians who, he claimed unsurprisingly, had been spoiled by "the spirit of independence and liberty inculcated by Father Foels." Disastrous effects had ensued, Baur said, describing the appeal to the consul by the two escapees. He continued by relating that the consul himself had been forced to imprison the two, apparently a reversal of his original, more conciliatory approach. Baur wrote that the French consul was "trumped ... [H]e had believed it possible to win them with money and treat them like Europeans, but then saw this was silliness." Baur was

166. Zanzibar journal, 20ii78, 16ix78; Mhonda journal, x78; Versteijnen and de Jong 1977, 3.

167. Denis, too, had a colorful history at Mhonda. In the mid-1880s, he apparently left the mission to work for the Germans, while his wife returned to Bagamoyo (CSSp 198b: Courmont, 1887). Then in 1889 he returned to the mission at Mhonda (Zanzibar journal, 19iv89). Today Catholics at Mhonda remember him well as one of the earliest Christians from Bagamoyo. As an old man he still drove a *piki*, or motorcycle (interviews with Ferdinandi Nicolas Kabelwa and John Anthony Kangati, June 2003).

168. Mhonda journal, 12ix79, 18x79, 24x79, 27v80, 16xii80. He also once misfired his gun, accidentally wounding another of the villagers, Hugues, who recovered (Mhonda journal, 13ix79).

169. Mhonda journal, 3iii80, 16ii80, 27vii81, 19iv82, 29iv82, 3ix82, 15xii82. Another of the villagers, Adrian, fled a week later and returned from Zanzibar in January with a note from Acker (Mhonda journal, 16i83). He may have been Léon's companion in the appeal, and perhaps the note he carried informed the mission at Mhonda of what had transpired at Zanzibar.

170. Bagamoyo journal, 2ii83; CSSp 197ai: Acker to Emonet, 21ii83.

pleased that the consul would no longer live under such illusions; "rather, a firm hand is needed."[171]

Baur's letter importantly indicates, however, that Léon had been right to sense an original openness in the consul to the Africans' appeal. The consul had even given them money. One wonders what had changed this French official's opinion. Regardless, the evidence suggests that at a certain stage in the proceedings Léon and the other villager rightly sensed that the consul had an affinity or sympathy with their interests *against those of the missionaries.* Temporary though that sympathy was, these African Catholics acted under the accurate assumption that the consul shared *their* view of the moral economy of the mission, so that an appeal to him seemed a reasonable way to ameliorate their circumstances and force concessions from the missionaries. That window closed, as Baur's letter indicates, yet why is not clear. What is clear is that possibly Baur and certainly Acker before him feared that the appeal might bring opprobrium on the mission. To their relief, the former slaves' appeal ultimately went unheeded.

The records from this appeal show other things as well. First, the escapees relied upon other Christians in Zanzibar as they made their appeal, suggesting that their frustrations were not unique. There was a group of Catholics there who formed a community of support for them, a community that stretched from Mhonda to Bagamoyo and to Zanzibar. Horizontal voice existed and facilitated the expression of vertical voice, this time over the heads of the Spiritans. Second, the villagers identified their situation with the French consul and his office, seeing it as part of the structure of authority in which they, as mission residents, existed. The direction of their vertical voice indicated a facet of the evolving moral economy of the mission in which the French consul lay within and not outside the mission's authority structure. Third, these two Christian villagers were not attempting to escape the mission permanently, unlike some others who fled the missions at this time. In this they, like earlier villagers who fled, resembled slaves in the period who fled coastal slaveholders not to escape the hegemonic world of the coast, but to insert themselves within it with their status enhanced. Their exit was strategic and not decisive.

In acting this way, Léon and the other escapee expressed a deep loyalty to the mission and a strong sense of identity as Catholics, even though the Spiritans could not see it. They also pursued their own interests generated by their social experiences. These experiences included the missionary environments forming them at Bagamoyo and Zanzibar, as well as the broader Swahili coast. Later, too, their identity evolved at the interior mission of Mhonda, which represented a frontier-like environment in which the sultan's authority was more attenuated. In such an environment their interests approximated those of peasant-like local producers, and their ties to the mission resembled those of a client to a patron. After being rebuffed at the level most near to them (their local superior at Mhonda) and by the superior at Bagamoyo (Baur), they now appealed to another authority —

171. CSSp 197ai: Baur to Emonet, 26iv83.

one possibly parallel to, possibly above the missionaries — namely, the French consul. Their actions thus typified eastern African clientelist behavior, according to which one appealed above various levels of authority until satisfied.[172]

The appeal to the consul might also have shown awareness in Léon and his companion of the vulnerability of the missionary regime to other European ideas. It is difficult to prove this, for an appeal for more liberty from a mission Christian to the French consul could have been to two different senses of France. On the one hand, it was an appeal to the nation with the closest links to that mission. At the same time, it was an appeal to a nation with a complex history of church relations over the concept of liberty. Léon and his partner might have noticed contradictions and discrepancies between these different aspects of France in their appeal. Did these two see the complexity of the relationship between the mission and its French identity? Did they know of rising anticlericalism in the France of the 1880s? Were they aware of Spiritan misgivings about their participation in July 14 (Bastille Day) observances hosted by the consulate, especially in the early 1880s?[173] It is impossible to tell. Yet their appeal to the consul emerged from within an evolving identity that was self-consciously Catholic and thus an effect of missionary evangelization, but which at the same time refused to follow the prescriptions within the official ideology motivating that evangelization.

After his imprisonment, Léon was pardoned and returned to Mhonda, which was his home, after all. He resumed his life as a villager, suffering several thefts from his field, for which he was compensated.[174] Then in March 1885 he became ill. After being anointed a few months later, he died at Mhonda just after being visited by Courmont, who was making his first visit to the interior mission.[175] Nothing certain is known of the companion who appealed with him.[176]

Hilarion

Like Léon, Hilarion had a long connection to the Spiritan mission. He had been baptized at Bagamoyo in 1871, at which time his age was estimated at fifteen. He then received his first communion in 1873, and was a leader among the boys in the orphanage there in the 1870s. Like Léon and many others, he served as a sponsor for the sacraments celebrated at Bagamoyo. At Mhonda, when he would have been in his early twenties, the journal recorded Hilarion's deeds regularly, for the Spiritans relied on him for a variety of tasks. They sent him to find one of their number whose return from the coast had been delayed.

---

172. Glassman 1995, 111.
173. CSSp 197ai: Acker to Vicar General, 7iv81.
174. Mhonda journal, 4v83, 4vi84, 9vi84, 21x84.
175. Mhonda journal, 19iii85, 4vi85, 14vi85, 17vi85, 29vi85; CSSp 198b: Courmont, 29vi85.
176. If this companion was Adrian, then he was back at Mhonda earlier in 1883. Not only did he return in January with a note from Acker at Zanzibar, but he arrived with a caravan in April (Mhonda journal, 4iv83).

He also accompanied the head of the mission at Mhonda, Father Machon, on a futile search for a preferable site for the new Christian colony. Later Hilarion went back to Bagamoyo for wine used at Mass when the mission ran short, tried to make peace on the mission's behalf with a threatening local chieftain, and even took money to ransom some children for the mission.[177]

At the same time, however, Hilarion began to act on his own apart from the mission — that is, as his own independent agent. In May 1879, for example, he ransomed a child from slavery on his own behalf, and in the next month he took two porters on a self-initiated journey, probably for personal trade. Hilarion's first substantial conflict with the mission came in 1880 when he was implicated along with Philippe in the scheme to steal guns and gunpowder from the mission. Exactly what was planned for the guns and powder remained unclear, but a possible explanation emerged in light of the "war," as the missionaries called it, that occurred four months later. Hilarion was instrumental in this conflict with a local leader in February 1881, in which several of the Christians were injured and neighboring villages were burned in retaliation.[178]

This conflict did little at first to change Hilarion's relationship to the mission. He continued to assist the missionaries as messenger, preparer of caravans, and catechist. Yet he also maintained and expanded the pursuit of his own interests — as a landowner, local trader, and purchaser of slaves for his own household. The status of such slaves was never stipulated, but the missionary example likely taught him that even freeing them did not mean that such people could leave his household. In early 1884, however, he began to act independently of the mission in more obvious ways and even began a plan to start his own village apart from the mission. In February he left without permission to spend the night outside the Christian village, taking along with him one of the females whom he had ransomed from slavery. A missionary, commenting on this misbehavior in the mission journal, wrote, "Deliver us, Lord," asking release from Hilarion and such scandals.[179]

---

177. Bagamoyo sacramental registry; Bagamoyo journal 11viii73; Mhonda journal 26vii78, 8xi78, 10vii79, 8ix79, 29x80.

178. Mhonda journal, 11v79, 22vi79. Regarding the so-called war, while the Mhonda journal details the fighting itself (8ii81), a letter from a Spiritan to Paris written shortly after the events narrates the background to the conflict. Hilarion had apparently been robbed and was paid a slave in compensation, which he in turn traded for six sheep. Not having been paid the sheep, he complained and received a gun from the mission in order to strengthen his demand for payment. Rebuffed, Hilarion later took the gun again and seized a youth of the village from where the sheep were supposed to come. That village then attacked the village of the Christians at Mhonda, but the latter were prepared and fought off the assault. The next day the Christians (the missionary uses "we") went back with a friendly chief and burned the offending village, returning with cheers and congratulations at the courage of "the children of the whites." Another letter says that Hilarion had taken the young man as surety for a debt, which was customary in the region. This account also blamed the missionary who had written the first report, Foels, whose liberality with the mission's "children" had only encouraged this independence of spirit. Baur seconded this opinion, also singling out Hilarion for blame (CSSp 197a: Foels to Schwindenhammer, 8ii81; ibid., Machon to Schwindenhammer, 9ii81; ibid., Baur to Superior [in Paris], 8iii81; BG 13:74).

179. Mhonda journal, 19ii84, 20ii84.

A few months later a local non-Christian chief named Baraka visited the mission to ask about the onetime catechist, who was now residing in Baraka's village. The missionaries guessed that Baraka, fearing retaliation for sheltering a runaway Christian like Hilarion, wanted assurances that his village would not be attacked by the mission. The chief also probably wanted to ascertain if he was dealing with a rascal. He promised to bring Hilarion back, bound hand and foot, should the missionaries so desire. The journal writer opined that Baraka might well have been in debt to Hilarion, who "is always in revolt against us." The journal added that the two — Baraka and Hilarion — were "wolves who will devour each other." Over the next months, Hilarion remained away, leaving his wife and family behind at Mhonda. In December, he returned, pleading his submission to Spiritan rule, but a few months later the missionaries felt his submission was not "pure and simple."[180]

Courmont's inaugural 1885 visit to Mhonda led him to address the dissatisfaction at the Christian village there, and Hilarion met with Bishop Courmont to discuss the situation. As a consequence, the catechist received permission to start his own village a day's journey or so from Mhonda, with the understanding that it would remain closely connected to the mission. Later he began to run his own catechumenate at the new village. His wife Germaine joined him there, and for the next year or so relations between the central mission station and the new Christian village remained cordial. In *Les Missions Catholiques*, Courmont described the village called Kilwende, whose chief was "one of our young Christians ... who promised me to catechize his world." Courmont described the esteem in which this chief, presumably Hilarion, was held by his pagan neighbors, as well as his loyalty to the mission. The village had a small chapel where the catechumens and Catholics from Bagamoyo prayed twice daily. Courmont praised the possibilities of what he called "a new mode of evangelization."[181] Hilarion supported the mission when it was threatened, and this support was reciprocated when he felt pressure from hostile neighbors. Machon, the superior, visited Hilarion's village, and in response Hilarion sent the mission a cache of ivory. Machon saw Hilarion again when he was ill, for Hilarion had medical skills and treated the Spiritan. In another "war" around Christmas of 1886, Hilarion joined the mission against its enemies.[182]

In early 1887, Courmont visited Mhonda again, initially recording that Hilarion had been courted by the enemies of the mission but had remained faithful. A few days later the bishop visited the catechist, however, only to find him living with a concubine, his wife gone. Courmont met with the estranged couple in an effort at reconciliation, eventually overcoming Germaine's hesitations to return

---

180. Mhonda journal, 11v84, 29xii84, 9ii85.
181. MC 18 (1886), 595–96.
182. Mhonda journal, 5vii85, 4ix85, 21x85, 14viii85, 22–29ix85, 13x85, 7i86, 22i86, 29vii86, 13vi86, 29vi86, 30xii86; CSSp 198b: Courmont, 2–5vii85.

to her husband. Then some months later there was trouble again when Hilarion seized a woman from a local village which threatened retaliation.[183]

By the early 1890s, after German control over what would become Tanganyika had been more or less achieved, Hilarion and his village drifted further away from Spiritan authority. As the decade progressed, tension in the area only increased as German colonial ambitions encroached on the mission's autonomy. Hilarion's insubordination to the mission emerged ever more strongly in the new situation. In their efforts to create local administrative order over their colonial possessions, the Germans appointed Africans as "headmen" (Swahili, *majumbe*, sing. *jumbe*) in charge of local villages, and Hilarion received this post in 1896. To the dismay of the missionaries, he and his village converted to Islam the following year.

The Spiritans regarded Hilarion's decision as intended to build his alliances with local Muslim chieftains, and also to deepen his friendship with the Germans. The new colonizers now held formal power over an area that had long been nominally under the control of the sultan of Zanzibar, but where missionary authority centered at Mhonda had played a prominent role for nearly two decades. The Spiritans recognized that the Germans tired of the strong personalities of both the missionaries (many of whom were French) and mission-educated African Christians. The latter, with missionary support, often resisted demands for wage laborers and also disputed colonial land claims. Though they understood the reasons behind Hilarion's defection, given the changing political realities in the regions, the Spiritans also regretted what they could only see as a betrayal that had long been coming.[184]

As with previous Spiritan disappointments with their African Catholic elites, however, the historical record resists simply seeing Hilarion's relationship with the mission through Spiritan eyes. To this day, local Mhonda Christians remember him as a superb teacher of the faith who imparted Catholic teaching to many, both young and old. The baptismal books at the mission also indicate that he served as a godfather at least as late as 1895, something he could not have done without at least begrudging missionary approval.[185] He must have remained in their — perhaps halting — good graces until then. Some of his children joined him as an apostate but others remained Christian, as did his wife, Germaine, even after the catechist became Muslim.[186]

183. CSSp 198b: Courmont, 24i87, 30i87.

184. For details on these events, see the discussion in Kieran 1966, 317ff. In admitting the possibility that the missionaries accurately diagnosed Hilarion's reasons for becoming Muslim, one should admit that his conversion was also possibly genuine and sincere (thus W. B. Anderson 1977, 58). Evidence does not exist to judge the reasons for Hilarion's decision, but the missionaries' proximity to the events as witnesses is vitiated by their self-interest in attributing selfish motives to Hilarion.

185. *Liber Baptizorum* I, Mhonda mission, #755.

186. One daughter, Maria Theresia, baptized December 20, 1883, did become an apostate, according to the baptismal registry at the Mhonda mission. Local informants at Mhonda, however, point to others who remained with the mission, including Hilarion's wife, Germaine. Courmont's accounts of his interactions with Hilarion underscored her greater loyalty to the church (CSSp 198b: Courmont, 30i87).

The missionaries detected loyalty and leadership skills in Hilarion, and thus confided a great deal of responsibility in him, beginning in 1877 when he left Bagamoyo. Over time, however, his own evolving interests as a landowner and prospective patron in Mhonda's frontier-like conditions attenuated that loyalty, initiating a long process that eventually culminated in his exit.

Hilarion's slow estrangement from the Spiritans contrasts with Léon's sudden and unexpected exercise of voice through his appeal to the French consul. Both disappointed Mhonda's Spiritans, and yet the missionaries made no obvious connection between them in their records. In retrospect, one can detect a logic in their actions that reflected their circumstances. Léon's appeal to higher authority and Hilarion's pragmatic steps to establish himself as a patron both were common enough strategies for the ambitious in eastern Africa at this time. Léon chose a more decisive act through which to register his frustration, while Hilarion pursued a long-term strategy in which his break was gradual, yet more inexorable. Hilarion chose not to exercise his voice directly against his situation, for the records show no obvious way in which he tried to change Mhonda's rules by complaining or appealing to the missionaries. Instead he acted as he saw fit, forcing the Spiritans themselves to observe and react to his growing self-reliance. Even Courmont went to Hilarion on his interior journeys; Hilarion did not come to see him. And there is no evidence that Hilarion pursued reconciliation with the mission when his actions frustrated the missionaries. Apparently his loyalty did not manifest itself in a sense of dependence on them at all. His sense of himself as a Catholic hardly seemed to need them.

•

Hilarion, Léon, Melchior, Joseph, *les baptiseuses*, and those who vainly persisted in Spiritan formation programs for congregational membership in the 1880s represent some of the different responses to slave evangelization in the early and mid-1880s. The first four all resisted the mission, at least in the eyes of the missionaries. Yet they did so in very different ways. Melchior's slyness, his ability to escape and manipulate his fellow escapees and then beg his way back into the mission, demonstrated little obvious internalization of the mission's message, though it makes sense in light of what we know of the social history of slave escapes in this period. Léon, on the other hand, used language that the missionaries no doubt could have used themselves to appeal to an authority related to but distinct from the mission itself. The extent to which his appeal relied on mission-inspired sentiments cannot be determined with certainty, for the coastal world had long known the strategy he pursued of appealing above the head of immediate authority. But one suspects that Léon, after so many years at the mission, had a strong sense of himself as a Catholic Christian, and that his appeal to the consul was a voice inspired somewhat by loyalty to that identity. He was not simply a rebel.

Joseph Mghindo took the religious and civilizing impulse of the missionaries and made it his own in a preaching venture, clothing himself in authorizing symbols deriving from the mission and speaking with their codes. Though the missionaries likely resented his flight, his preaching showed the impress of the practices of the mission. Hilarion's long service and the trust the missionaries showed him for two decades leads one to resist any quick dismissal of him as a failed missionary project. Yet the pull of his own interests in becoming a patron led him out of the mission's formal boundaries and into another self-chosen religious identity, even though slave evangelization no doubt continued to affect him.

There was no single way to be Catholic at the Spiritan missions. Instead the decades of slave evangelization witnessed many different ways that people internalized the missionary message. The "sanctimonious allure" that the French observer Comte Mauberge noticed among Bagamoyo's children suggests a self-consciousness that the missionaries saw as an unwelcome by-product of their evangelization. But haughtiness was not the only source of missionary discomfort. The diversity of responses to their evangelization underscored that the Spiritans were not in charge of how former slaves decided to become Catholic.

The Aftermath of Slave Evangelization

In the late 1880s, external observers praised the Spiritans as "tireless knights of civilization" for the order of their mission stations and the disciplined work of their children.[187] According to such reports, the Christian villages in particular showed the error of those who saw Africans as incapable. One German admirer praised the Christian villages as "schools of agriculture and the habits of industry." He wrote, "Gone is the legendary laziness and indifference of the blacks."[188] When Le Roy himself recalled the Spiritan reforms of the villages in later years, he claimed that his reforms had caused a revolution that had finally undone the "old spirit of slavery" that had clung to the Christian villagers, ending the desertions, thefts, and "the bad spirit."[189]

The observers did not know the whole story and, like most of us, Le Roy had a selective memory. The villages continued to face problems in the late 1880s and beyond. Residents fled, protested the amount of their work, stole from the mission, sought to found their own villages, bought and kept slaves, and continued to frustrate the Spiritans. In 1888, Courmont and the Spiritans decided to send to Mhonda all of Bagamoyo's residents who were too old for the orphanages and not settled into households in the villages. Machon welcomed them, for the indifference of his neighbors made him feel a need for more adults at his mission. Earlier he even requested adults freed at sea from the British consul, receiving

187. Versteijnen 1968a, 25f; CSSp 194ai: Simonis 1889. As Roland Oliver points out, observers poured accolades on other missionary enclaves in this period as well (1952, 63ff).
188. CSSp 194ai: *Deutsch Reichs-Zeitung*, 6xi88.
189. Le Roy 1906a; Le Roy 1934b.

two groups of forty. Upon arriving at Mhonda, however, the large group from Bagamoyo integrated poorly and most soon fled.[190]

Despite these difficulties, the move away from the strategy of the villages was slow. As long as the Spiritan missions took in slaves they faced the issue of what to do with them. Their control over the mainland led the Germans to hand over slaves they freed from caravans, sometimes large numbers, while the British continued to hand over those freed from slave ships into the 1890s. Other slaves fled to the mission for refuge.[191] In 1896, Bagamoyo received forty slaves, twenty from the Germans, ten from the British, nine through ransoming, and one who fled to the mission.[192] And others came to the missions in similar need, leading the Spiritans to ransom those accused of witchcraft to keep them from being burned alive.[193] Only in 1912 did the bishops of eastern Africa announce an end to their support for the practice of ransoming slaves, and the Spiritans ransomed and received those freed by others into the twentieth century.

Though former slaves resided at all their mission stations, the focus of the Spiritan mission had changed by the late 1880s. Evangelizing slaves did not command Spiritan attention as it had for the previous two and a half decades. The scheme of settling former slaves as a *noyau* for the anticipated church moved away from the center of the Spiritan missionary strategy, in fulfilment of the missionary plan from the beginning.[194] At Mandera, frustrations with the villagers coupled with the persistence of infanticide had led to the foundation of a school for the children among the local peoples in 1885. Other interior missions soon followed suit.[195] Courmont's 1892 circular letter encouraged local superiors to mandate school attendance at their missions, with a particular eye to educating the children of chiefs. In the ensuing decades, the attention given the villages diminished, while schools at the Spiritan missions registered steady growth.

Along with schools, the missionaries also emphasized health care as a way to gather people to the missions. Already in the early 1880s, the missionaries claimed that approaching death was a helpful perspective to encourage people to enter the church. During epidemics the missionaries were not above demanding the destruction of fetishes before vaccines would be administered, recognizing that Africans knew the power of "white magic" against scourges like smallpox. They also handed out religious medals to ward off illness. They gained,

---

190. Kieran 1966, 128; BG 15:720; Mhonda journal, 5ix88, 9ix88, 11x88, 17x88, 9xi88, 14xi88.

191. CSSp 197aii: Courmont to Emonet, 4x89; CSSp 197aiii: Sacleux to Emonet, 3x90; ibid.: Courmont to Emonet, 15viii92; ibid.: Acker to Courmont, 20ii93, 27iv93, 2v93, 9v93; BG 15:719ff; BG 16:683ff; Bagamoyo journal, 2i90, 27ii90, 31iii98; Morogoro journal, 15ii90. For an example of a mission receiving a fleeing slave, see Bagamoyo journal, 10i90. Mandera received twenty-five freed slaves in 1892 from the Germans (van den Eeden 1980, 29).

192. Versteijnen 1968a, 28.

193. The mission at Mhonda had ransomed twenty-two such people by 1888 (BG 14:639).

194. Slavery as a social problem, however, remained prominent in Spiritan descriptions of their work. The Spiritans embraced abolition, joining Cardinal Lavigerie's vigorous and widely known antislavery campaign (AA 1889, 124–42; AA 1892, 4–15).

195. Mandera journal 3v85, 4v85; Mhonda journal, 30x87; BG 13:1098; BG 16:725–26; CSSp 198a: Gommenginger.

sometimes unwittingly, considerable reputations for the Catholic mission by their medicines.[196] Other missionaries wrote of debates with local peoples over the truths of Christianity, something little in evidence when slave evangelization was the Spiritan focus.[197]

While schools and medical care advanced at the interior stations, Christian villages, like plans for African priests and religious, lost their importance. Yet they were not closed, for the Spiritans maintained the villages for decades. In 1895, Bagamoyo had six Christian villages attached to the mission, and the next year there were fifty-two villages linked to the Spiritan missions in eastern Africa.[198] Moreover, some of the villages took on new responsibilities with colonialism. At times the Germans invited the Spiritans to formalize the judicial roles they had played at their interior missions before colonial overrule. At other times they sought to limit what seemed the missionaries' excessive inclination toward theocratic rule.[199]

With colonial rule in place, Spiritan evangelization increasingly took a shape more common in recent Christian missionary activity, in which European missionaries faced the strangeness and stubbornness of the differences between their message and those they sought to evangelize, the kinds of differences often subsumed under the term "culture." Most Spiritans welcomed the changes that came with colonialism. In 1885, Le Roy described the mission's considerable accomplishments in twenty-five years, but also admitted the Spiritans' disappointments. He blamed the omnipresence of Islam, which, he said, had restricted the missionaries to "night-fishing," that is, rather covert evangelizing that targeted only slaves. The coming of the Europeans, though not without its problems, would allow them to "fish" during the day, he believed.[200]

Colonialism did not quickly bear the fruits for which Le Roy hoped. The first decades of colonial rule forced numerous adjustments in missionary practices and slowed the establishment of new missions, except around Mt. Kilimanjaro and in present-day Kenya. In some places, it is true, missionary esteem grew as colonial power made its effects known, but elsewhere resistance to Christianity was linked with resistance to colonialism. Islam also served as a vehicle for anticolonial sentiments. In 1903, the bishop of Zanzibar, Courmont's successor Allgeyer, wrote of his ongoing disappointment that the Catholic Church in eastern Africa had not yet led an entire people to baptism, along with their king, as had missionaries in ages past.[201]

On Courmont's visits to the interior stations in the 1880s and 1890s, he spent time with the Christian villagers there. He counseled others besides Hilarion and Germaine with marital difficulties, visited the new villages established even

---

196. BG 13:53, 74ff; BG 15:724f; CSSp 197ai: Machon to Baur, 13vi83.
197. BG 15:733.
198. Vogt, n.d.; Kieran 1966, 112, 127.
199. Kieran 1966, 246–47, 322: Sahlberg 1986, 86ff; BG 15:718, 723–24.
200. APF 58 (1886), 186ff.
201. CSSp 196axi: Allgeyer to Propagation of the Faith, 26xi03.

when such choices had gone against missionary wishes, and reported on onetime villagers who had left the missions.[202] In his 1892 circular letter to all his missionaries, he spoke of the three goals of their mission stations: first, to work for the missionaries' own sanctification; second, to support and develop the *noyau* of the faithful already present; and third, to convert the pagans in the district. He also reaffirmed the need to get thirty days of work per year for the mission from the villagers. He recommended distributing *pombe* — liquor — to help ease the burden of such labor and encourage awareness in the villagers that remaining in the village was in their interest.[203] Whether this was ever practiced, and how it was received by the villagers, is uncertain.

Eventually Bagamoyo's role in forming young people into Christian couples to start new villages slowed down, since the decrease and then end of slavery meant that Bagamoyo received fewer people through ransoming and European handovers. Still, some Spiritans continued to see the advantages of their previous practices. In 1888, Courmont admitted to dreaming, like his Spiritan predecessors, of receiving small children untainted by anything before their exposure to missionary influences. He wrote the Propagation of the Faith that parents often offered their children to the mission, and he mused about the morality of such purchases with the funds these benefactors provided.[204] Yet in 1901 Le Roy, then superior general, admitted that it was no longer possible to control the mission's children as in the past, and he criticized the strategy of the villages.[205]

Life in these missions thus evolved with two populations of Catholics, quite distinct in the ways they had come to the faith. The villagers originally formed at Bagamoyo maintained a complex relationship with the Spiritans. Both spoke French (though increasingly the missionaries were German) and knew the orderly life of the mission as an embracing world, as had been practiced at Bagamoyo. They were known as *les mariés*, or, as this French term for "the couples" was Swahili-ized, *wamarie*. Those in the villages who remained firmly connected to the mission usually stayed on their original village land nearby the missionaries' own residence, tilling their soil and raising their children. Others drifted away, though the numbers varied from one mission to another, depending on the mission's own history and especially the effects of colonialism. Sometimes they remained connected to the mission, other times they severed the relationship.

The growing population at such missions, however, was composed of those who had not been formed at the coast. Not all were local people. Trade brought some to the area, others fled from conflicts or witchcraft accusations, still others sought protection from the mission. Most, however, were from nearby, drawn to the mission by different desires, some pragmatic, no doubt, others more overtly religious.

---

202. CSSp 198b.
203. CSSp 195vi: Courmont, Circular letter, January 1892.
204. CSSp 196axi: Courmont to Propagation of the Faith, 8vi88.
205. CSSp 196bi: Le Roy to Allgeyer, 10v01.

How these two groups interacted and evolved together at the parishes is not very clear. Parishioners at Mhonda and Mandera today recall the old villagers as amazing their fellow Africans and other visitors alike by their literacy and their familiarity with Catholic lore and liturgical arcana. Some also retained a strong coastal Swahili accent. One local Catholic said that not a few returned to the coast eventually, more comfortable in Bagamoyo's regulated environment (after the upheavals of 1888–89 and World War I) than in the more tumultuous interior.

Whether there was tension between those villagers once subjected to slave evangelization and the newer Catholics is hard to tell, but the distinctions remained well into the twentieth century. Some older Catholics today recall a certain degree of *ubaguzi*, or favoritism shown toward one or the other of the two groups, and also claim that the villagers felt some *aibu*, shame, at their slave roots. Others discount that any such feelings existed. But no one disputes that the villagers were prominent Catholics at the missions of the interior.

Chapter Six

Conclusion

Slave Evangelization and Catholic Identity in Eastern Africa

This book describes the opening chapter in the story of the present-day Catholic Church in eastern Africa. That ongoing saga continues in places where slave evangelization took place, as well as in other Catholic communities. In that story, the disjuncture between those early days and the present appears quite sharp, for the past described seems quite remote from contemporary Catholic concerns. Slavery is over in the region, and those who came to the Spiritan missions as slaves are all deceased. Most Catholic sisters, brothers, and priests in the region are African. Very few are French. African Catholics no longer struggle to negotiate their futures in precolonial or colonial frontier-like situations. Instead — in Tanzania, at least — they live their faith in an independent country whose stability and political culture are the envy of most of the continent. Present-day Tanzanian Catholics do not strive to appropriate religious and political identities imposed from the outside. They instead work to develop styles of faith and citizenship appropriate for African believers of the twenty-first century.

Perhaps because of the perceived remoteness of those origins and the consequent sharpness of the disjuncture between then and now, there has been for some time an inattention to the slave origins of the Catholic Church in eastern Africa. The Spiritans themselves have not always been keen to draw attention to their practices, while the end of slavery in the colonial period meant that the church's energies went elsewhere. As colonialism continued in the twentieth century, those origins became an embarrassing aberration to what was deemed proper missionary activity with African peoples. A 1955 historical summary of the mission at Zanzibar written by the Spiritans mentioned almost nothing about slavery, focusing instead on the "three great races" that formed the church there: Africans, Europeans, and (mostly Goan) Asians.[1] African Catholics themselves have not always wanted to revisit the origins of their church either, which can seem tainted by slave associations and the unfree means by which the earliest Catholics came to the church.

---

1. CSSp 420ai: The Zanzibar mission, 1955.

266

Thus the odd spatial experiences facing visitors to the Catholic parishes in Zanzibar and Bagamoyo — which first struck me, and with which this book began — reflect the uncomfortable place of slave evangelization in the history of the Catholic Church in eastern Africa. The evangelization of slaves first brought the Catholic Church to Zanzibar, and resources flowed in from Catholics elsewhere who were anxious to save souls through ransoming and baptizing. Yet Zanzibar's Catholic effort was even then more visible from distant Europe than it was from within Zanzibar. Like the twin towers of Zanzibar's Catholic cathedral, the evangelization of slaves became less visible the closer one drew toward it. Catholic missionary efforts receded from the view of most of Zanzibar's own population, including the mass of slaves who moved through the port in the nineteenth century. And Bagamoyo's mission, imposing yet often seemingly unfilled, still evokes its role as a place that planned and administered its own effacement. There former slaves were formed as Catholics, then sent to the interior to settle in newer, more promising mission sites. The strategy that focused on Bagamoyo's central formative role led to its diminishment, and the growing colonial economy complied, bypassing what had once been the busiest mainland port in the region.

Conscious continuity with their origins for the churches at Zanzibar and Bagamoyo has been made more difficult by the fact that ethnicity has not been available as a stimulus to memory of those origins, as it has been elsewhere among African churches. The earliest Catholics came from many places, sharing no common ethnic origins. Though they all eventually spoke KiSwahili, the coastal identity associated with the language was fundamentally Islamic and not easily fashioned as a component of Catholic identity. Thus one common attribute to which religious identity has often been linked in Africa and elsewhere — ethnicity or culture — was not available. Inculturation, in the normal missiological sense, has never been an easy option.

In the nineteenth century, the Spiritan goal of building the church shaped their evangelization. They did not try to adapt their message to the cultures of those they evangelized. They enacted practices to make slaves into Catholics who could be members of a hierarchically ordered *societas perfecta*. The organization and nature of the church to be formed thus was not something about which the missionaries speculated. They were helping to establish a church whose essence was considered already erected by Christ's ministry and consequently in no need of reconsideration.

Contemporary Catholics in eastern Africa have no such luxury. Those at Bagamoyo, Zanzibar, and elsewhere need to think about their church, and they are invited to do so by the church's leaders. Part of that process is appropriating their past in relation to their present, and there are signs that Catholics at Bagamoyo and Zanzibar now feel a pull to make sense of those first decades of their existence. The Catholic diocese at Zanzibar will celebrate 150 years in 2010, and plans are underway to celebrate the past with a fuller awareness than was possible in 1955. Bagamoyo, too, has witnessed an increased interest in the earliest African Catholics. At the seafront, a memorial has been erected to mark

Horner's first Mass on the mainland in 1863, while the museum at the mission recently expanded into new quarters. The Catholic mission has also produced videos. One is a film of a play based on the story of Suéma (now Siwema, in the local idiom) and produced in Bagamoyo's national cultural center. The other has the optimistic title "New Hope in the Town of Slaves? Slavery in Bagamoyo Yesterday and Today," and features interviews with current residents descended from former slaves who came to the mission.[2]

This book was not self-consciously crafted to serve those communities as they make sense of their origins. Yet this conclusion will discuss two important insights to be drawn from this story of slave evangelization, each of which has potential value for Catholic self-understanding. In the first place, a historical appreciation for the particularities of Spiritan missionary practices shows the complexity of nineteenth-century European Catholic identities, and also invites a consideration of the morality of such practices. As a historical site of investigation, slave evangelization yields a privileged view into how social forces forming missionaries in Europe in turn helped shape missionary activity in a very different setting. It also serves as an entry point to consider the ethics of mission more generally.

The second lesson has more direct relevance for the Catholic Church in eastern Africa, as well as for other places where Christianity is relatively young. This has to do with locating the missionary role in the appearance of a Christian church, and not merely the appearance of individual Christians, in a certain place. This story suggests that missionary activity may be a necessary factor in the process of creating Christians, but that such practices, no matter how comprehensive, are not sufficient ground for the formation of a church. Instead, African appropriations, especially collective appropriations, of Christian identity constitute the origins of the church in a particular place. That insight is not a new one. What is distinctive here is the absence of the kinds of resources usually contained within the idea of culture. This story, unlike those that highlight the role of culture, underscores the crucial role in those origins played by what I have here called collective vertical voice. Such voice, moving from being merely horizontal to a voice articulated in protest against the missionaries, marked an essential component of the process by which these former slaves became the church. Even if missionary activities formed the ground of possibility for such collective voice, becoming Catholic in the self-conscious way that marked the appearance of a church depended on attaining a religious identity independent of obedience to missionaries.

But first, a few thoughts about Spiritan practices and what they reveal.

The Implications of Spiritan Missionary Practices

The organization of the space of evangelization and the changing role of labor were the most important threads running through Spiritan strategy. Spiritan attempts to form a space in which to enact their missionary practices evolved as

---

2. Holy Ghost Fathers, 2000; Bagamoyo Catholic mission, n.d.

they moved from the island of Zanzibar to the mainland, and then from the coast to the interior. The zeal for enclosure in Zanzibar first gave way to a more open environment believed better for personal reformation enacted at Bagamoyo. Later they sought to order their missions with similar processes around the interior missions. Spiritan missionary desires were thus at once typically evangelistic and also geographic, for their attempts at making Catholics depended upon construction of an environment conducive to that end, and thus meant territorial acquisition and control. Once away from the coast, however, the placement of Catholic households within the frontier-like conditions around Mhonda, Mandera, and the other interior stations made impossible the programmatic and restrictive spatial arrangements available to the missionaries at Zanzibar and Bagamoyo. Perhaps not coincidentally, in this period a collective identity emerged in the historical records about these African Catholics. The conditions for that emergence derived at least in part from the experience of evangelization and the changing approach to labor and space in that strategy as perceived, and reacted to, by Africans.

The place of physical labor also changed in the missionary program, so that its ongoing role in the formation of ex-slaves accommodated a growing function as a resource essential for the mission's financial health. The mission's dependence on labor grew in ways the missionaries did not anticipate from the beginning, inclining the Spiritans toward coercion and violence that were not foreseen. The decision to treat labor as a commodity in the 1880s came in response to the resistance of African Catholics, not because the missionaries themselves grew to appreciate the value of free labor.

Development within the Spiritan strategy is not surprising. The missionaries never claimed to follow any particular program or ideology in their evangelizing efforts. Despite their reliance on techniques they knew from their own formation to religious life and priesthood, as well as from their service in juvenile reformatories, they did not think of themselves as either rectors directing a seminary (except when they were, in fact, acting in that capacity), or as prison officials running a reformatory. They only rarely mentioned those previous experiences. Though they drew upon practices enacted at reformatories, in both the earlier and later Mettray-style regimes, they did not follow everything prescribed in such places, as their recourse to violence shows. In fact, their practices at Bagamoyo and elsewhere borrowed from a number of different places and discourses. They showed great care about the liturgical calendar and connected their missionary strategy with Catholic piety at every turn, while at the same time they attended to the economics of their mission and chose practices deriving from various phases of evolving social interventionism in France.

Evaluating the Spiritan Missionary Strategy

The Spiritans pursued the evangelization of slaves for two reasons. They did so first to begin the church in eastern Africa, targeting former slaves for the formative and educative processes that they thought would make them good Catholics.

Within that strategy also rested the hope that such Catholics-to-be would themselves become evangelists of a sort, either as members of the Congregation of
the Holy Ghost, nuns, or as assistants of another sort in the missionary process.
Formed by slave evangelization in the first sense (as objects of missionary attention), they would, the missionaries hoped, practice slave evangelization (as
former-slave subjects) in the second sense. In retrospect, we can see that the missionaries not only subjected these Africans to complicated formative processes,
but tried by such processes to constitute their subjectivity, in the process projecting upon these Africans their hopes for the future church. The extent to which
those so targeted understood those missionary hopes is not always clear. There
can be no doubt, however, that these Africans were affected by such practices,
and that their reactions often frustrated the missionaries.

There are many reasons for misgivings at what the Spiritans did. The harshness of one's judgment, of course, depends on one's predilections. To those wary
of all missionary activity, the entire project lacked merit. In stressing the newness of Christianity it implicitly denigrated those evangelized.[3] Others object to
strict formative regimes of the sort these missionaries pursued, emphasizing the
coercive practices the Spiritans enacted. A similar shadow would be cast over
other Christian missionaries in the era here considered, Protestant and Catholic,
who carried out similar practices with slaves, subjecting them to regimes in ways
that look very unfree. Missionaries before and since have enacted such processes
with other groups, including peoples on every continent. Yet processes that subject others against their will and thus attempt to create their identity as subjects
are very common. Of course they continue in correctional facilities. They also
occur in the raising of children, in schools, and through many other social processes that we take for granted. Imposing one's own views on others seen as
vulnerable and needy — not to mention those deemed a threat — is, judging from
its ubiquity, an instinct apparently as necessary as it is undoubtedly dangerous.[4]

Turning to theological appropriations of missionary activities like those entailed in slave evangelization, contemporary missiology has no single evaluative
lens for judging missionary practices. Many of those who think about Christian
mission, however, would share misgivings of a nontheological sort. They might
also add other reasons to find the Spiritan evangelization of slaves wanting. In
their recent overview of contemporary theologies of mission, Stephen Bevans

---

3. Burridge 1991.
4. Literary critic Judith Butler contends that proper human selfhood is impossible without subjection to some external authority, and she struggles over how to evaluate that necessary and yet
lamentable process (Butler 1997, 1–30). Adam Seligman, like Butler, recognizes that human subjectivity depends on subjection. Unlike Butler, however, Seligman does not bemoan or question the
ethical basis of that process. On the contrary, he maintains that "modernity's wager" to try and
constitute the self on an autonomous basis has failed, yielding both rootless anomie and hardened
fundamentalism in too many places and peoples. Seligman argues that, "[W]ithout a sacred locus of
self, any attempt to account for action cannot rise beyond the purely calculative, power-orientated
acts of utility maximization." He believes that an autonomous account of the self is insufficient (2000,
x, 1–12). I am in sympathy with Seligman's approach.

and Roger Schroeder present as the best model for missionary activity today a notion of *prophetic dialogue.*[5] Given such a model, the practices here described were very problematic. It is easy to see that the Spiritans were not very prophetic in their approach to slavery, for they dealt with the issue pragmatically rather than confronting its inhumanity. Nor did they attempt any dialogue with the Muslims, who controlled the omnipresent religious context in which their evangelization was carried out.[6]

Other criticisms from a missiological perspective might note the Spiritans' absence of ecumenical effort and their ecclesiocentrism. Despite their over-whelming minority status as Christians in coastal eastern Africa, they showed little energy for cooperation or shared activity with other Christian groups. And so focused were they on forming the church that they failed to emulate Jesus' own preaching, which stressed the in-breaking of the reign of God. Given these criticisms, it is not surprising that many mission scholars join African national-ists in criticizing practices like those of the Spiritans. Such practices are seen to have created artificial enclaves that removed people from the life-giving cultures to which they should properly have belonged.

Yet the slaves evangelized by the Spiritans were already far from those cul-tures. In fact, the focus on slaves, and especially slave children, encouraged the Spiritans to homogenize Africans and overlook the obvious cultural differences among those they evangelized, another aspect of their evangelization that is easy to criticize from a missiological point of view. This occurred because of a com-bination of factors, not all of them equally deplorable. On the one hand, the Spiritans thought of Africans first and foremost as people to be saved and the raw material out of whom to form Catholics, including clergy and religious. Forming the future church composed of African Catholics thus shaped Spiritan approaches to missionary evangelization, and the bulk of their writing and re-flection concerned very practical attempts to shape the environment to effect the changes necessary in those whom they evangelized. These ecclesiological hopes inclined the Spiritans to emphasize African potential for Catholic life against those who discounted such potential.

At the same time, like most other Europeans of the day, the Spiritans usu-ally assumed they were evangelizing people whose social and cultural position was inferior to their own. Operating in a racialized world that reinforced their self-perception of superiority, the Spiritans could not but be affected by the so-cial inequality around them. Whether under Omani or, later, European control,

---

5. Bevans and Schroeder 2004, 348ff.
6. Already in 1889, an Anglican bishop criticized the Spiritans for their refusal to address Islam: "As to the Romanists, we may admire their industry and success in educating the slaves handed over to them by the British agent, but we may look in vain for any successful work done by them among the Mohammedans, Arab or Negro. I am not aware that they even hope for converts from that quarter. I once asked the Superior of their establishment at Bagamoyo if he was able to effect any good among the people of the town. His answer was, 'Oh, our Mission is not for them at all; it is for the interior!' " (Mackay 1889, 23).

Africans had little obvious social power in Zanzibar compared to Arabs or Europeans.[7] This dramatically unequal social situation only reinforced racial bias from their European background. Unsurprisingly, the Spiritans, especially as time went on, shared the typical views of Africans held by Europeans of their day, views that grew more racist in the later nineteenth century as racism gained scientific prestige.[8]

As a consequence of the tension between a European racism reinforced by local social experiences, and their abiding but often thwarted ecclesiological hopes tending toward Christian assimilation, Spiritan views of Africans showed little consistency. But both racism *and* the ecclesiological focus fostered inattentiveness to the distinctive cultural characteristics of those they evangelized. The Spiritans thus resembled other missionaries in this period, who, according to a recent portrayal, "subordinated ethnological discrimination to Christian assimilation."[9] This tendency was only enhanced by the cultural diversity of the former slaves they evangelized, which rendered not only unlikely but practically impossible any real adaptation of the Christian message to African particularities. Their preference for children five and under, whose cultural attributes could easily be overlooked, further enhanced a learned inattentiveness to cultural background. The missionary need for labor and the large numbers who came at once from slave ships beginning in the late 1860s only made such inattentiveness easier still.

Understanding such dynamics at work in slave evangelization suggests that Western stereotypes about African depravity alone fail to explain the missionaries' absence of attention to culture.[10] Locked into seeing missionary strategy as only either "adaptation," typified by the Christian evangelization in Asia, or "civilizing" through direct or indirect conquest, as happened in the Americas, observers often fail to recognize other distinctions among missionary practices. In this case, the Spiritan decision to evangelize slaves profoundly conditioned their strategy, so that in eastern Africa their strategy cannot simply be reduced to a single civilizing model. To do so would be to overlook the changing Spiritan evaluations of Africans, and the obvious missionary ability to differentiate between African peoples on cultural grounds. The Spiritans knew that accommodation to local custom had a long history in Christian missionary activity and

---

7. From the beginning, the Spiritans were well aware of the racialized identities in the world of Zanzibar. Thus Horner was reluctant to have the superior at Réunion send him black brothers, an opinion criticized by his superiors in Paris, who found his refusal to be against the congregation's policy (CSSp 196bii: Horner to Duboin, 1vi64; ibid.: Horner to Levavasseur, 13xii64).

8. On the growth of scientific racism in British and French thought, see A. C. Ross 2003 and W. Cohen 1980, 210ff. Such racial ideologies could take a variety of forms, so that not only French ethnocentrism but also French exoticism could underpin negative stereotypes about Africans. Christianity, with its monogenetic assumptions about the unity of all people, often drew criticism as a naive foil to the "scientific" polygeneticism of Renan, LeBon, Gobineau, and other more explicit racists. But, as Tsvetan Todorov has pointed out, this did not mean that Christians did not share racist assumptions, only that they defined them differently (Todorov 1993, 80ff, 288f).

9. Pels and Salemink 1999, 29.

10. Kieran 1966, 85ff.

that it was mandated by the Vatican and reinforced by Libermann's ideas. It took place later when they began to work with the settled peoples of the interior.[11] The Spiritans did not feel obliged to follow these guidelines initially, however, because they did not think they applied to their situation. While they displayed negative impressions of African peoples, typical of their time, the circumstances of their earliest attempts at evangelization determined their approach as much as these preconceptions.

Not all analyses of missionary activity decry strategies like the Spiritans'. Lamin Sanneh is one scholar who has sought partially to defend such practices. Sanneh is most known for describing the creative cultural practices engendered by Christian missionary biblical translations. He has offered an influential appreciation of the local cultural vitality protected and enhanced by vernacularization of the Bible, thus resisting the blanket condemnations of those who blame missionaries for the destruction of African cultures.[12] Sanneh has a similar counterintuitive appreciation for what he calls "A Plantation of Religion," by which he means missionary strategies like the Spiritans' that targeted the lowly of African society rather than the chiefs. Sanneh's project, as in his study of the implications of translation, is at once historical and also theological. His focus is on western Africa, where he notes that the nineteenth-century Sierra Leone mission that targeted slaves and other marginalized people marked a new approach to evangelization, away from the top-down missionary strategies that had typified missionary work in Africa and elsewhere for centuries. He argues that the abolitionist movement as enacted in mission first in Sierra Leone represents an ethical and historical breakthrough, forging an underlying democratic impulse within African Christianity.[13]

Harder to defend than the decision to evangelize slaves per se are the ways the Spiritans treated those at their missions when they wanted to leave. Ransoming slaves for the purpose of evangelization is one thing; recourse to violent means to keep Africans working at missions is quite another. Such violence was something that Courmont later felt compelled to condemn. Libermann had earlier warned against it.[14] It was also forbidden at Mettray. Was this violence the result of human weakness that led the Spiritans to ignore both the obvious and latent sources of their missionary practices, something to which they were inclined by the proto-colonial and then colonial circumstances in which they acted?

---

11. Schmidlin 1931; Goyau 1948; Burke 1998, 78. A recent study of early evangelization in Mexico, usually seen as the prototype of mission as conquest, underscores the keen desire for cultural awareness that motivated mendicants there in the sixteenth century (Pardo 2004, 9ff, passim).
12. Sanneh 1989.
13. Sanneh 1997. Though he does not draw theological conclusions like Sanneh, Justin Willis has found a similar pattern to have occurred at the Anglican UMCA mission at Bondei, an interior mission founded from Zanzibar. There, he argues, the local hierarchy was inverted at the mission, since former slaves from the coast became prominent as church leaders, while local people who wanted to join assumed the lowliest place (Willis 1993).
14. CSSp 195vi: Courmont, Circular letter, 1892; Burke 1998, 50ff.

Perhaps. But I also believe that Spiritan recourse to violence was fostered by contradictions within slave evangelization itself. These derived from a latent conflict between the nature of the faith that the Spiritans were trying to inculcate, which was a traditional Catholic notion predicated on obedience, and the practices chosen to pursue that faith. Such practices derived from a tradition of social disciplining that quite self-consciously pursued the creation of an internally reflective and self-administering subject who could, in principle, affirm or deny the faith offered, through the exercise of personal choice. This contradiction arguably lies at the heart of a great many religions, which invite their adherents to renounce their freedom at one level in order to gain greater freedom at a deeper level. Such contradictions appeared within the products of the Spiritan program, whose exercises of voice the missionaries often could not recognize as evidence of their evangelizing successes. They also appeared in Spiritan writings, which implicitly espoused views of freedom at odds with their official worldview.

The Theological and the Sociological Sources of Spiritan Practices

It is easy to see that the influences inspiring Spiritan strategy derived from sources both theological and secular. On the one hand, the missionaries sought to form good Catholics as defined by their ecclesiology and their view of the human person. According to that official perspective, the good Catholic was loyal to the institutional church, pious, and obedient — ideals the Spiritans sought to embody in themselves. Thus specific Catholic discourses and practices featured in their missionary program. These included the expectations represented by their liturgical attentiveness, scholastic curricula, and other aspects of their program that marked it as overtly Catholic. Besides the ideal theological values that they espoused when they were at their most self-conscious, Spiritan practices also depended on values whose origins were less directly theological. Prominent among those influences in shaping the practices of slave evangelization were, as we have seen, practices deriving from the juvenile reformatories in which the Spiritans served and from which they took important parts of their missionary strategy.

But it is too simple to contrast only the secular and theological sources drawn upon by the Spiritans. At the same time, they were also immersed in *sociological* streams whose divergences into religious and secular traditions became clearer later. In the first place, their practices with freed slaves derived from what some have called the rise of the disciplinary society or "tutelary complex" in nineteenth-century France and Europe more generally, the trend that led to new forms of social intervention enacted in juvenile reformatories.[15] Gilles Deleuze and Jacques Donzelot have called this widespread tendency "the rise [or invention] of the social."[16] This designation indicates a new awareness of the social

---

15. Foucault 1977; Fuchs 1984, 49f.
16. Deleuze 1979; Donzelot 1984. See also Meyer 1983.

world both as an extraindividual cause of social ills and also a new site for the deployment of state power to combat them.

At the same time, as Catholics they participated in a parallel sociological tradition that came to be known in the 1880s and 1890s as "social Catholicism." Social Catholicism emerged from Catholic responses to the visible social inequalities accompanying the Industrial Revolution in the early nineteenth century. Its forerunners advocated social reform and resisted laissez-faire economics, but many were wary of socialism and respected the hierarchical nature of society. As a consequence, they called for social change, but also emphasized the paternal responsibilities of the wealthy and the rights of the church.[17] By the end of the nineteenth century, this movement was distinguished from — and characterized as reactionary in relation to — the rise of the disciplinary society.

But recent research has questioned the utility of that distinction — between solving immediate needs of those suffering and examining the causes of such distress — at least as operative in the minds of the many Catholic reformers who were later seen as forerunners to social Catholicism. In this perspective, the stark contrast often drawn between these two movements misrepresents nineteenth-century French social thought before the 1880s. Distinctions surely existed between nineteenth-century French Catholic attempts at social reform often characterized as "integralist" or interested in charity, on the one hand, and the rise of social work by "population technicians" associated with the modern nation-state, on the other. Yet there was also considerable overlap. Thus the newspaper article about La Providence, the social institution at Réunion, praised its dual attention to "charity" and "the social question," referring to the two differing emphases. And Mettray's organization epitomized the disciplinary society, yet the language of faith imbued the institution as well.[18]

Most importantly, despite their divergences, both trends in social thought participated in the forging of discursive and conceptual links between efforts to solve social ills in Europe and to assist others far away. Part of that change consisted in the characterization of the Paris proletariat as "savage," both in technical and popular literature. In the early nineteenth century, Anne-Marie Javouhey, the famous French missionary nun and friend of Libermann's, had linked the demoralization and sufferings of African slaves and French workers.[19] Eventually the savage (understood as *le noir*), the barbarian, and the vagrant were assimilated to one

---

17. They also increasingly became Legitimists, interested in reestablishing the French monarchy. For a summary, see Kollman 2001, 195f. See Kale 1992, 140ff for an explanation of the distinctions among socially minded Catholics in the nineteenth century.

18. *The Monitor*, Réunion, 29xi59; see BG 2:98ff, 187ff, 232ff. On Mettray, see Carpenter 1969 and Foucault 1977, 294. On the forerunners of social Catholicism, see Chevalier 1973, 45. These include Albert de Mun and Frederic Ozanam (Dansette 1961, 1:254). Thus Bernard Plongeron has entitled an article "Christian socialists before the age of social Christianity" (1995), while Steven Kale's influential study of French legitimism isolates the rise of what he calls "economic Catholicism" in the 1820s (1992, 140ff). Both argue that there was more complexity in what Plongeron calls "the hiatus between charity and philanthropy [understood as the more socially comprehensive response to social ills]" (1995, 119f).

19. Cornuel 1999, 279.

another in popular culture.[20] Such connections between their overseas missions and the needy closer to home existed in the Spiritan imagination as well. In *Douze Sous*, a play written in 1886 by Le Roy to encourage children to support the missions, one child who is reluctant to contribute to the Catholic missions asks his persistent playmates, "What about our Chinese, our *nègres*"?[21]

Le Roy's reforms, enacted a few years before this play, also drew upon both wings of this increasingly differentiated and contrasted social tradition. This is not surprising, given the range of his interests. But the source upon whom he claimed to have relied as he wrote his reform proposals helps us appreciate the evolving mix of influences that inspired him. In 1896, Le Roy wrote that he had been reading a work of Frédéric Le Play's while he ruminated on the difficulties the Spiritans faced in eastern Africa. Le Roy attributed his ideas to Le Play, recalling that Le Play had said that the commandments of God sufficed for a legal code, a sentiment with which the missionary sympathized.[22]

Le Play (1806–82) was a French sociologist who was an important figure for those later espousing social Catholicism. His conventional placement among later French conservatives is understandable, since his ideas were used to buttress calls for the return of the French monarchy into the twentieth century.[23] But recent analyses have argued that placing his thought squarely within a Catholic reaction advocating social paternalism misrepresents Le Play. Indeed, his work has been adduced to epitomize the tendency to read back into the past strong distinctions between trends in French social thought that operated only later. In this revisionist account, Le Play represents one of those figures in nineteenth-century French history who underscores the difficulty of distinguishing clearly between the secular and religious wings of nineteenth-century French social thought.

In this, Le Play resembles Spiritan slave evangelization, which drew upon secular practices without self-consciously foregoing its theological and religious underpinnings. Seeing Le Play's thought outside the bounds of the previous stereotype yields insights into why he might have been attractive to Le Roy as the missionary pondered the reform of the Christian villages in the early 1880s. Like Le Play's ideas, Le Roy's reforms were not radical in any obvious sense. They envisioned a slow weaning away from direct mission control — to end the monthly distributions of food and supplies and to encourage individual initiative.

---

20. Chevalier 1973, 359ff, 394ff.

21. CSSp 196axiii.

22. Kieran believes the work in question was *"La question sociale au XIXe siècle,"* published in 1879, where Le Play argued that "society was based on two foundations, the Ten Commandments and Paternal Authority" (Kieran 1966, 123).

23. Since Le Play's push for a hierarchical organicism fit comfortably with the political program of later French Legitimists and other European conservatives who sought to reestablish the monarchy, they naturally used his ideas in their intermittent attempted "counterrevolution" against the Republic. Through the later nineteenth and early twentieth century, Le Play's ideas thus found favor among a broad spectrum of conservative Catholics and others who rejected the modern ideals represented by the French Revolution. On Le Play's relation to other French social conservatives, see Duroselle 1951, 672ff; Geiger 1972, 7ff; Kale 1992.

Le Play's influence might also lay behind the very practical methods Le Roy espoused for the villages, with clear guidelines as to stages in building the mission station and a thorough inventory of needed items at the mission. As one of the founders of empiricism in sociology and a rigorous observer of local details, Le Play had a worthy adherent in Le Roy. Le Roy, along with every other Spiritan, also championed the family as the foundation of moral order, as did Le Play. Finally, Le Roy's refusal to be doctrinaire about the villages, his willingness to neither surrender missionary authority nor impose it in perpetuity, strikes the kind of balance one finds in Le Play, at least as he has been interpreted more recently. The missionary and the social reformer both sought to be realistic in their analyses, but both nonetheless had a zeal for reform.

Le Play's approach to the attribute of freedom also might have appealed to Le Roy. Though they rarely discussed the subjective experiences of the mission's children, the Spiritans implicitly sought to internalize proper virtues in the former slaves who had become Christians. They wanted obedient faith and loyalty, not mere adherence to exterior expectations, for these were to be colonizers of the interior. Yet they also tried to create people who would embody what they saw as real freedom, that is, not the freedom they associated with secularism. Le Play, too, saw a role for freedom in proper human thriving, and he, too, resisted the more liberal-style freedom of Republican secularism. At the same time he did not merely embrace the view of freedom as unthinking obedience to authority associated with French Catholic Legitimism in the era of the Dreyfus Affair and afterward. Of Le Play's view of freedom, one commentator has remarked, "Liberty was no mere rhetorical device [for him]," and "[Le Play] repeatedly stressed that individual freedom and initiative was [sic] important." As a consequence, his view of freedom was "[u]nlike Legitimist notions of 'specific' freedoms — those embedded in the traditional usage of a hierarchical and relatively static local community." Instead, "Le Play's [view of freedom] was relatively forward-looking and non-authoritarian."[24]

This reliance on Le Play underscores the fact that Spiritan missionary practices and discourses in this period also negotiated varying approaches to freedom. They were deeply affected by an older view that struck a sharp distinction between "mere" freedom of choice and "true" freedom dependent on grace — a distinction at the foundation of their dominant paternalistic ideology. This approach has a long pedigree in Christian theology. Thus Libermann echoed Augustine in distinguishing between what he calls "true freedom" and "independence":

> Freedom is given to people by the Creator. Independence is contrary to nature and is destructive of every principle of the Christian Faith. The fanatical urge for independence led to Protestantism. It has led, too, to a modern philosophy that promotes egoism to a frightening extent that led to

---

24. Pitt 1998, 80, 78–79. Le Play analyzed a large number of different types of families in various parts of the world with an eye on their economic arrangements. His research with families was very influential in the history of sociology.

the barbarity of the past century. Christianity has come to bring freedom to the world and at the same time to wage war on independence which is totally contrary to the faith and to moral principles.[25]

Yet there was a second and developing approach that softened the strong distinction between liberal and Catholic views of freedom. This second, transitional position is suggested by Le Play's ideas and Le Roy's reforms. In retrospect, one can see that it was a view on its way to that which, in one common interpretation of Catholic theological approaches to human freedom, eventually prevailed at Vatican II in the decree on religious freedom, *Dignitatis Humanae*, and in the contemporary Catholic embrace of democratic governments. Its appearance in Spiritan discourse, however, was profoundly practical. Le Roy's reforms sought to encourage self-sufficiency and a degree of independence for the villagers that was more akin to — though not embracing — the liberal freedom they previously derided. Le Roy remained, however, within the overarching paternalistic framework. At the same time, the villagers' actions that spurred the reforms — as well as their ongoing complaints — indicated that they yearned for something different from what the Spiritans were willing to give.

Despite Le Roy's personal awareness of the villagers' situation, the Spiritan notion of proper human thriving and freedom was never clearly elaborated in discourse. In fact, their language at times appeared self-contradictory. For example, Baur made two claims about the unrest of the 1880s that seem in conflict. The first, often reiterated, was that the missionary Foels's talk of independence had spoiled the Christian villagers and lay at the basis of the troubles. This suggested that notions linked with a derided "modern" view of freedom could only have come from the missionaries themselves, even if they thought them anathema. They could not represent any convictions generated by the Africans themselves.

Baur's second claim was that those who had been at the mission the longest were the most rebellious. This claim, which looks to be supported by the archival records, suggests that the former slaves developed a sense of themselves due to the practices of evangelization that undermined missionary expectations and hopes. Such results cannot simply be laid at the feet of the words or deeds of any one missionary, especially one whose time in the mission was as short as Foels's. On the one hand, Baur sought a scapegoat among the missionaries; on the other he recognized that evangelization itself fostered the problems they faced. Judging from their own analysis, it seems that the longer one was at the mission, the more one was likely to appeal for more land and liberty. The irony is that the missionaries rejected such appeals and saw them as disloyalty, responding with

---

25. ND X, 231: trans. Burke 1998, 71. "Independence" was a vice that the Spiritans were quick to deny in themselves, though it was an accusation thrown when one missionary displeased another. Horner complained of Baur's "slippery independence" (CSSp 196biii: Horner to Schwindenhammer, 15vi70), and often defended himself against the label (ibid.: 9i72, 28i72, 15iv72; CSSp 196biv: Horner to Schwindenhammer, 7iii76), as did Baur (CSSp 196biii: Baur to Schwindenhammer, 15viii72). To be labeled as possessing "airs of liberalism," as were some scholastics at the Spiritan seminaries in France, did not bode well for one's future in the congregation (CSSp 106ai).

racist denigrations and theologically inflected judgments. In fact they might well have shown the very impress of that evangelization itself, and thus represented voices of loyalty and a growing Catholic identity — one that the missionaries could not accept.

The frustrations of the missionaries revealed that they did not appreciate the Africans' own evolving views of human thriving, views that differed from the terms the missionaries thought they were presenting. Almost certainly, however, the Spiritans misconstrued what looked to them like stubborn ingratitude, using Western categories of "independence" to name it and projecting upon still-new African Catholics views more appropriate to nineteenth-century liberal Europeans. Meanwhile, the former slaves could play upon such categories, articulating certain ideals when it was to their advantage.

In fact, neither the missionaries nor these earliest African Catholics were likely enamored of notions of freedom espoused by most abolitionists. To the missionaries such freedom bespoke a tradition inimical to the church and its ideal of proper personhood within the hierarchical ecclesial order. The resistance of the former slaves to such notions, at least as they became socialized into the mission and the Swahili coast, was more implicit. Probably, however, they often sought better lives within hierarchical relationships, whether defined paternalistically or in another idiom, not escape from them. Later, some pursued roles as patrons in ways more typical to the locales in which they found themselves. The actual aims of African Catholics were likely thus more pragmatic than the Spiritans recognized, deriving from their circumstances first at the coast and then after settling at interior stations. Though the missionaries interpreted their charges' complaints as replicating views of freedom that rejected the mission, African Catholics were likely not stating substantive values but deploying strategies in a struggle to enhance their interests. They did so as Catholics, though not on terms the missionaries appreciated.

Spiritan Dramas and Modern Subjectivity

A second piece of writing by Le Roy — in addition to his Le Play–inspired reforms — also indicates the complexity of the sources behind Spiritan practices. While a seminarian in 1875, before he ever reached eastern Africa, the future missionary wrote his first published play. *Andalouma* was eventually published in 1884 in order to be performed by members of the Holy Childhood Society "to interest Christian hearts in the misfortunes of the children of Ham."[26] In his introduction, Le Roy referred to *Suéma*, Horner's previous Spiritan effort at uplifting tale-telling, from which he claimed inspiration.

Set in a non-Islamic area of eastern Africa in 1870, the action of *Andalouma* follows the sufferings and eventual fate of the title character, an African Christian boy whose father, Goma, is a pagan chief. The villain, named Mganga (Swahili

---

26. Goré 1952, 42–44; BG 13:47, 224; CSSp 196axiii; Le Roy 1884, 75.

for "sorcerer," the archetypal enemy of Christianity in the missionary imagination), convinces Goma that a traitor threatens the tribe, then bewitches the chief into an oath to kill the traitor. Lots are cast and, through Mganga's manipulations, Andalouma is identified as the culprit, much to his father's dismay. His father's reluctance to carry out the sentence is overcome by a medal of Mary that Mganga dramatically discovers under the boy's shirt. This becomes evidence, for the Mganga-beguiled chief, of his son's culpability. Implored to renounce his Christian faith, Andalouma refuses his father's pleas, unwilling to deny the truth of his convictions and sad at his father's lack of faith. But he is spared the flames when slave raiders come and take everyone away to the coast for sale. In Zanzibar, a missionary who already knew him purchases Andalouma and together they rescue Goma and the rest of the tribe. Mganga, bound and subject to death, is forgiven and spared by Andalouma, but dies soon thereafter, his heart hardened.

Texts like *Suéma* and *Andalouma* are problematic as windows on the actual experiences of Africans who suffered enslavement and then were evangelized by the Holy Ghost missionaries. Suéma, as already noted, probably did not narrate her story, despite Horner's claims to the contrary. Though Le Roy never asserted that *Andalouma* was historical, when publishing it he asserted its accuracy as a portrayal of the circumstances of eastern Africa. Yet the story's hero is a very unlikely product of Spiritan missionary activity before the 1890s. Le Roy presents Andalouma as somehow exposed to the mission's message without having been enslaved, something that did not happen before 1877 despite the anachronistic 1870 setting of the drama.

These texts do, however, reveal missionary preconceptions, and both young people in these stories represent ideal missionary products in the Spiritan imagination. Suéma, or rather Madeleine, revealed herself a hardworking and pious girl, desiring to become a nun in order to evangelize her brothers and sisters who remained in darkness. Pious Andalouma remains steadfast in his faith before the threat of death, not even letting the tender appeals of his weeping father convince him to renounce his Christianity. Both pray often, especially in difficulty, and both forgive those who have harmed them.

At the same time, however, the portrayals of Andalouma and Suéma hint at the potential contradictions within Spiritan practices. The Spiritans thought of themselves as forming from childhood persons who would be free of what they saw as the polluting notions of paganism, Islam, and even modernity. In practice such a quarantine was impossible, as Spiritan experiences suggested. But prototypical so-called modern aspects of selfhood appeared even in these ideal portraits of the anticipated products of that strategy. Suéma, as we saw, could not be coerced by the sisters to forgive her mother's murderer, but only came to do so after wrenching self-doubt and introspection. Andalouma's portrayal shows even clearer contradictions around the issues of authority and obedience. According to the official missionary ideology, Christian faith created obedient subjects, but Andalouma's deep faith fails to connect him to at least one of the proper authorities in his life, namely his imploring and then condemning father.

Instead, his conversion to Christianity separates him — internally at first, externally later — from his paternalistic social context. As he considers his situation, the play features several interior monologues and dialogues with God, so that Andalouma considers his beliefs as if from a distance and clings to them in a voluntaristic way, against the wishes of his father. His living situation before this crisis also reflects something anomalous in Spiritan strategy before the 1880s, for Andalouma maintains his faith despite living apart from the mission and with his people, something that the missionaries discouraged.

In this respect, the Marian medal Andalouma wears, the finding of which the sorcerer uses to demonstrate the youth's disloyalty to the tribe, points to the portability of faith. Indeed it declares that remaining Catholic did not depend on living within the paternalistic care of the mission. Fingering the medal while listening to the pleas of his father to renounce his faith, Andalouma feels God's strength supporting him. This portrayal, showing a young man disobedient to his father, then showing him strong in faith apart from the mission's highly structured environment, replicates contradictions within the Spiritan strategy with its multiple influences. Their efforts to keep their villagers in the mission — efforts that could be violent and coercive — coexisted with Le Roy's reforms that sought to encourage self-reliance and a real, if limited, independence.

Andalouma's character was laudable, and yet his portrayal is implicitly dangerous for the missionaries, who sought to replace the families of children and keep them at the mission. They did not want children to disobey their new fathers, yet out of obedience to the mission Andalouma disobeyed his proper father. Perhaps Joseph Mghindo, the young man who draped himself in missionary garb and fled to preach in the region around Bagamoyo, felt a similar interior call to disobey the missionaries in order to follow a deeper intuition. Perhaps Léon, who appealed to the consul, likewise felt himself called to represent the interests of the other villagers against missionary directives. Perhaps Hilarion became Muslim not because he stopped believing in Christ, but because belonging to the mission on Spiritan terms in the late 1890s kept him from the patronal role he sought for himself as he grew in local authority and power. Certainly François and Laurent considered their vocations as genuine and resented Spiritan doubts.

Representations of interiorized consciousness in fictional episodes like those in *Suéma* and *Andalouma* revealed explicit missionary hopes for the formation of a private subjective sphere within the self, an aspect of selfhood that some have seen as particular to the modern period.[27] This private subjective sphere indicates the triumph of one central feature of what is often seen as modern Christianity, so that "truth is private" and religion consists of a system of beliefs.[28] This private "self" was not simply Protestant in origin — after all, Augustine's *Confessions* narrated a deep interior conversion before Luther and Ignatius of Loyola's *Spiritual Exercises* seek just that sort of transformation — but its most self-conscious

27. Barker 1995; Luria 1996; van Rooden 1996.
28. Needham 1972; Asad 1993, 1996; Viswanathan 1997; Lopez 1999.

expression in the early modern period has often been associated with the respect for the subjective appropriation of faith emphasized in Reformation theology. Catholic practices such as frequent confession and the annual mandate to bare one's soul before the superior of one's religious order, designed to foster spiritual growth in the Spiritan seminaries of Europe, reflected a similar desire for self-awareness. The Spiritans would replicate such practices in their efforts to form an African clergy, and confession was a frequent practice for the mission's children. But within the possession of self sought by such practices lay the seeds of contradiction for an ideology so bent on fostering obedience to authority.

Spiritan slave evangelization thus reinforces the impression that the stark distinction sometimes drawn between two prototypical ideal notions of self and society — a premodern Catholic version fostering hierarchy and obedience and a modern version with Protestant roots valorizing autonomy and democracy — is far too neat, something other analyses of Western subjectivity, personhood, and selfhood suggest.[29] The complexities become even more apparent when examining how such practices helped create African Catholic identity. The Spiritans attempted to make loyal Catholics, but their efforts to evangelize slaves to that end, in the complex circumstances of eastern Africa, only showed the contradictions at the heart of their efforts. They wanted obedient Catholics who drew their identity from the mission, yet they encouraged European benefactors to establish sponsorship relations with individual slaves. Not only could a European sponsor make an offering for ransoming and subsequent baptism; they could also name the child in question. They wanted seminarians who would do what they were told, yet they trained them in habits of self-reflection and introspection, and gave them academic and linguistic capacities that fostered many options within nineteenth-century eastern Africa rather than dependence on the mission. It is no wonder that the French observer, Mauberge, sensed a sanctimoniousness among the boys at Bagamoyo. They *were* becoming quite distinctive!

These contradictions were exacerbated in the circumstances where slave evangelization was pursued: a slaveholding and increasingly racialized world exposed to new sources of authority articulating abolitionist rhetoric, embodied, for example, in the British consul. In those circumstances, calls for *liberté* were heard differently by the missionaries and those they evangelized. For the missionaries such calls could only be a threat to the Catholic future they strove after. Yet African responses to Spiritan evangelization, including calls for more liberty and appeals to those in authority, showed that the former slaves drew upon missionary discourses and practices of evangelization in their growing sense of themselves,

29. Filtering out the theological roots from other "sources of the self" is not easy, as Max Weber and, more recently, Charles Taylor (1989) and Michel Foucault have recognized. Accounting for this prototypical "modern" self lies beyond the scope of this study. Works that have helped me think about this issue include: Asad 1993; Judith Butler 1997; Carrithers, Collins, and Lukes 1985; Comaroff and Comaroff 1991, 49–85; Deleuze 1979; Donzelot 1979; Dumont 1985; Dupré 1993; Ferguson 2000; Foucault 1977; Greenblatt 1980; Greven 1977; Hirschman 1977; Lienhardt 1961; MacPherson 1962; Marglin 1990; Poovey 1995; Rabinow 1989; Seligman 2000; C. Taylor 1989; J. Taylor 1963; van der Veer 1996a and 1996b.

even when that sense of themselves moved beyond what the missionaries wanted. "Land and liberty" in the mouths of the Christian villagers did not usually represent efforts to depart the mission, despite missionary fears. And the direction of the appeals — toward authorities within the mission rather than outside — points toward a genuine loyalty to the mission. Such appeals indicated not rebellion, but the pursuit of very pragmatic goals, goals that emerged as part of the growing collective consciousness of a group of African Catholics who were responding in logical ways to slave evangelization.

Slave Evangelization and the Emergence of African Catholics

The African Catholics who appeared in the wake of Spiritan slave evangelization had endured the demanding restrictions at Zanzibar and Bagamoyo, the harsh conditions of the interior stations, and the temptations of encroaching colonialism. This group, emerging between 1860 and 1890, took many forms, as we have seen. But a confident grasp of what their becoming and being Catholic meant *to them* remains elusive. Existing sources do not allow the kinds of insights one might want to have about the subjective experiences of undergoing evangelization. Describing African feelings — apart from the stylized forms of *Suéma* and *Andalouma* — was not a Spiritan preoccupation. No early African Catholic wrote an autobiographical account, and no evidence exists of anything like any real friendships between the missionaries and early African Catholics in this period. As a consequence, our insights into what James Scott has called the "hidden transcript" — the many ways that those without obvious social power act strategically outside the awareness of the powerful — of these former slaves who became Christians are few.[30] What records we have of such resistance and/or compliance usually appear in connection with elites being prepared for priesthood or membership in the Spiritans. The acceptance, resignation, discouragement, or subtle resistance of so many others evades the historical record.

According to the Holy Ghost plan for the evangelization of slaves, those the Spiritans received spent between twelve and fifteen years in formation at the coastal missions of Zanzibar or Bagamoyo before becoming colonizers of the interior in Christian villages.[31] The highly differentiated responses to Holy Ghost evangelization preserved in the historical record suggest that being Catholic meant different things to different people. Is it possible to extrapolate from the evidence that exists in order to make reasonable guesses about what was going on in these Africans' hearts and minds? What is the best way to think about the consequences of those years of formation in those carefully constructed environments? If the missionaries worked hard at their formation, what happened to the Africans subjected to slave evangelization? Did these experiences destroy

---

30. James Scott 1990.

31. APF 61 (1889), 47ff. Of course many spent less than that; having arrived older they were sent to the interior after a shorter time at the missions. Others escaped before entering the roles the Spiritans anticipated for them.

their freedom? Are there ways to judge their sincerity and maturity as Catholics? Other related questions naturally arise about the relationship between missionary practices and these new Catholics: Did the former slaves' complex reactions to evangelization derive from the latent contradictions within the Spiritan message and evangelizing practices, since the missionaries idealized a certain view of personhood that their practices perhaps simultaneously undermined? Or do these African Catholics point to how the apparent contradictions could be resolved in practice?

Asking such questions also necessarily raises the issues of just what kind of impact the missionaries had, and how their power determined the identities that emerged within those they evangelized. So far this book has been cautious in invoking notions of power. Without overlooking the occasionally brutal aspects of the missionary regime, the analysis has focused on issues of space, time, labor, and narrative identity. It has not invoked terms often used in the study of colonialism like domination, hegemony, and ideology. Yet such terms are not thereby inappropriate. Did the missionaries have what historian Ranajit Guha calls "dominance without hegemony," that is, overall control of behavior but no ability to orchestrate the consciousness of the former slaves? Or did their efforts to pursue comprehensive formation, especially through the legibility sought at Bagamoyo, allow them to approximate *structural* power? The anthropologist Eric Wolf isolates this as power's most subtle form — the ability not only to impose one's will on another, but to organize people's preferences in a way that they may not even recognize — a power that could be likened to hegemony.[32] What relation, if any, existed between the power of the missionaries, expressed through the practices of evangelization, and the agency and power exhibited by the Africans who were subject to such evangelizing practices?

One study of missionary activity that attempts to take seriously the issue of power as enacted in missionary processes is by South African Graham Duncan. In his book on Lovedale, a large and famous Protestant mission station founded in southern Africa in the 1820s, Duncan analyzes the tightly controlled regime there as a type of total institution in the sense described by Erving Goffman in his famous 1961 work *Asylums.* Duncan claims that in understanding missionary activity in places like Lovedale, sociological approaches to identity formation have more salience than questions usually asked in reference to conversion. This book has made a similar case.

Duncan borrows the concept of coercive agency to describe the effects of Lovedale's environment on the Africans schooled and formed there. By pairing "coercive" with "agency," Duncan attempts to articulate the paradox achieved by total institutions, which shape the behavior and determine the identity of those within them, but without obvious repression. In Duncan's view, the agency of the Africans at the mission was effected through the coercion of others, namely

---

32. Guha 1997; Wolf 1990, 1999, 5f. Echoing Wolf, Anne Norton writes, "The most effective domination is internal" (Norton 2004, 71ff).

the European missionaries who organized the mission's environment and then placed Africans in it.[33]

Duncan's term "coercive agency" is suggestive, and his descriptions of Lovedale have obvious parallels with the Spiritan program, which sought similar goals. Yet his view of human agency emerging from such places, in my opinion, fails to appreciate two things. First, he underestimates the capacity of individuals to make their own what is forced upon them, and thus exceed (and often even undermine) the intentions of those who establish regimes like those at Lovedale. In eastern Africa, in fact, the former slaves' behavior in turn shaped the Spiritan program, as Le Roy's reforms suggest. And many of those evangelized, even in unfree circumstances, acted in ways that transcended the status that missionary activity sought to confer on them.

Second, Duncan posits identity in too univocal a way, imagining that the Africans who emerged from Lovedale only thought of themselves in relation to that institution and the goals of those who established it. The African Catholics emerging from slave evangelization suggest, to the contrary, that people's sense of themselves is not contained by the efforts others put into forming that sense. Hilarion, François, and others also showed that human identities can comprise many different reference points and aspects at once.[34] African Catholics did not merely internalize the Catholic identity that the Spiritans proffered, but developed a sense of themselves from evangelization and other sources, a tendency the Spiritans recognized and sometimes deplored.[35]

Strong Individuals and Slave Evangelization

In a recent description of the Christian villagers formed at Bagamoyo, Bengt Sundkler, the late and eminent historian of African Christianity, says of the ex-slave settlers:

... One should not overemphasize the fact that the groups which built new villages inland were "ransomed slaves." These young men and women were

---

33. Duncan 2003, 10–12, 81ff.

34. Thus Anne Norton writes, "Subjects have multiple identities" (Norton 2004, 47–49). In a recent book, Lamin Sanneh has distinguished between what he calls "world Christianity" and "global Christianity." He defines the first as "the movement of Christianity as it takes form and shape in societies that previously were not Christian, societies that had no bureaucratic tradition with which to domesticate the gospel." He continues, "World Christianity is not one thing, but a variety of indigenous responses through more or less effective local idioms, but in any case without necessarily the European Enlightenment frame." Global Christianity, on the other hand, Sanneh defines as "the faithful replication of Christian forms and patterns developed in Europe," or "religious establishment and the cultural captivity of faith" (Sanneh 2003, 22–23). This is an odd distinction from someone who has done so much to generate an appreciation for Christianity's distinctiveness as manifested in so many locales. I do not believe that global Christianity, as Sanneh defines it, exists. In fact, few people's writings have demonstrated its implausibility as clearly as his. Whether Sanneh's preferred usages will become normative remains to be seen, but I hope not.

35. Duncan's book also suffers from a lack of historical evidence from archival sources, so that his interesting theories often appear more as assertions than arguments.

not keen to remain bound by historical chains of the past. They saw themselves as modernizing "Readers," fortified by several years of schooling at
Bagamoyo.[36]

Sundkler is mistaken to claim that these African Catholics saw themselves as
"Readers." That term was used by Anglicans at Zanzibar and more famously
by early converts to Protestantism in Uganda around this same time. But it was
generally eschewed by Catholics and not used by the Spiritans in this period
at all. Yet Sundkler does rightly highlight the dynamic sense of themselves that
emerged in these Africans under the impact of evangelization.

Enslavement constituted a violation of their dignity. In response, Africans
coming to the Spiritan missions did what they could to overcome its effects, using
whatever means were at their disposal. Such means first of all implied relationships with others that could maintain oneself and create a new life. Those newly
arrived sought advantageous relations to the missionaries, to those who joined
them at the Spiritan orphanages or villages, and probably also with surrounding
peoples.[37] Such relationships helped constitute the new social identities that developed in those subjected to slave evangelization. Most of that process lies beyond
the reach of historical research. Yet even when these men, women, and children
left no written words — as was normally the case — their circumstances do not
remain completely opaque to historical understanding. Of course, as one commentator says, "The most important mental transformations occurred far away
from missionary eyes."[38] But actions discernible to the historical imagination can
yield some insights into those hidden transformations.

The scant evidence that exists, most of it lying within missionary discourse
and requiring particular historical and critical strategies of reading, reveals that
over time the former slaves developed an awareness of themselves as Catholic
Christians. Evangelization also generated, however, a complicated set of interests
and motivations that cannot be reduced to either the failure or success of conversion. When they saw their labor being used for revenue while their education
was set aside — as, for example, when work in the fields replaced time in the
classroom in the wake of the hurricane of 1872 — then a sizeable number of the
former slaves fled. Their loyalty to the mission was tested by the conditions of
the evangelizing strategy, and they chose to exit.

Those marked for special service as elites (some of them, at least) sincerely
and fervently pursued their own spiritual growth and internalized a strong sense

---

36. Sundkler and Steed 2000, 540.
37. Of slaves in Brazil, Joseph Miller writes, "In an age before medical science dreamed of
assuring the integrity of the body, integrity of spirit and of community were the only spheres of life
over which anyone dreamed of asserting control. Pain and death could not be avoided, but one could
seek solace in the company of others. People therefore constructed identities of a primarily social sort,
and the identities in Africa that the slaves had lost through capture and forced removal to the Americas
were — certainly significantly and adequately for purposes of structuring a coherent interpretation
of what they did on the continental scale ... — thinkable, and attainable, through connections with
others" (Miller 2003, 83).
38. Etherington 1996, 217.

of loyalty. Some who advanced toward such status also faced obstacles when their race was held against them and their loyalty rendered suspect. Such resistance from the missionaries generated discouragement — for example, in Philippe, Laurent, and François. The extent to which that discouragement made these men question the truths on which their new religious adherence was based is difficult to determine. The records we have, however, indicate that these elites could distinguish between the Christian message and the practical and personal limitations of the missionaries. As François remarked, they had their "prejudices."

Slave evangelization thus eventuated in some very strong individuals, despite the firm control of the environment the missionaries sought as they established their program at Zanzibar and Bagamoyo. Far from only creating individuals prone to conformity, the regulated environment for the evangelization of slaves generated responses to the missionaries' program indicating acute awareness of their situation, as well as a self-conscious agency that often contradicted missionary hopes. This began only a few months after the Spiritans' arrival in 1863, with Casimir's reluctance to support the ransoming of children too young to work and his resulting plea for larger boys to ease his burden. Later other individuals also left traces in the archive suggesting distinctive character and personality. Such traces allow us some appreciation, for example, of the difficulties facing Philippe, once named Ferdinand, the first Spiritan who had been a slave in eastern Africa, and who struggled to be an African and a missionary; Léon, who represented the Christian villagers in an appeal to the French consul, articulating his disagreement in a way that revealed his belonging to the mission as well as his distance from some of its official expectations; and Hilarion, a vital contributor to Mhonda's mission for two decades who eventually left the church. Decisions to escape by many also no doubt indicated a defiance that depended on self-conscious assertion.

Not all showed their resilience by resisting the Spiritan message, even if such resistance is perhaps its best sign. It took strength of a different sort to make a life within the missionary program, as indeed Casimir, Léon, and Hilarion also did for years. Some of those who showed less obvious recalcitrance, however, also emerged rather sharply in the historical record. Even if she did not narrate *Suéma* herself, Madeleine's voice can be heard in her letters, as can the voices of Henry Isa, François, and Laurent. The surreptitious consecrations by the women baptizers at Bagamoyo indicated their willing cooperation in the mission's goals, a cooperation that typified a good number of the villagers in the 1870s and 1880s. Finally, the complaints of many of those same villagers in the 1880s represented the clearest collective response to slave evangelization.

Collective Identity and Oppositional Consciousness: Forming the Church

Besides the strong individuals who appeared in the historical record of slave evangelization, a collective identity emerged among the Christian villagers and became visible in the 1880s. The previous chapter noted several factors that fostered the appearance of such common identity: the existence of frontier-like conditions around the Christian villages; the obvious differences among the missionaries themselves over their practices and ideologies of evangelization; the shared Christian narrative and common practices to which the freed slaves had been exposed; the increasing presence of colonialism and opportunities it created; and local practices supportive of patronage and the fission of ambitious potential patrons. There I offered an admittedly hypothetical account of how that collective identity might have been fostered by these factors, pointing toward the various incongruities in which the Christian villagers found themselves: in relation to Spiritan strategy as it evolved, and in relation to the broader world of eastern Africa.

One missiological lesson to be drawn from this case is the importance of what has been called here collective voice in the formation of a religious identity that emerges in the wake of missionary activity. Such collective voice among the former slaves who were evangelized indicated the formation of a common identity that was derived from the many practices they underwent together as well as interests they shared. That identity represented a common consciousness about who they were that was historically contingent and dependent upon social circumstances, on the one hand, yet also the result of their own agency. It emerged because of their sense that the moral economy of the mission was being violated, for the missionaries were not living up to these new Catholics' expectations.

Others have called an emerging sense similar to this an oppositional consciousness. By oppositional consciousness, political scientist Jane Mansbridge means an "empowering mental state that prepares members of an oppressed group to act to undermine, reform, or overthrow a system of human domination."[39] Such consciousness, Mansbridge argues, takes a variety of forms, depending upon the nature of the perceived system of domination, yet it arises from within a group that is formed by social processes they do not choose themselves. The members of the group find themselves together subordinated by exercises of power chosen by others. Seeing themselves disadvantaged, they become aware of their plight and then with that awareness they can act to change their circumstances. Oppositional consciousness represents, therefore, the awareness that allows resistance.

Something like that sort of oppositional consciousness no doubt generated large-scale attempts to leave the mission via Hirschman's exit. But more importantly, another form of oppositional consciousness developed that sought the reform, *not* the undermining or overthrowing of the missionary system. This was oppositional consciousness that was loyal, and it helped create the collective horizontal and then vertical voice that indicated the African Catholics had developed a new sense of themselves. The voices that were most important in the 1880s for the history of African Christianity were voices that derived from loyalty in Hirschman's sense. Certainly it was a loyalty that was oppositional inasmuch as it protested aspects of the Spiritan program. But these African Catholics voiced

---

39. Mansbridge 2001a, 4–5, passim. See also Mansbridge 2001b.

a commitment to that Catholic identity, not primarily a desire to leave it. As political scientist Anne Norton writes, "Opposition is productive," and in this case it produced a Catholic identity not dependent upon missionary approval, even though its emergence depended upon missionary practices.[40]

The former slaves' initial belonging to the mission had been enacted by the Spiritans, and then constructed through the practices the missionaries organized. Such practices of prayer, education, and work were identity-producing performances that helped inculcate a sense of belonging to the mission among the former slaves. As the mission moved inland, however, and as villagers pursued their lives as landholders, the contingent and relational basis of that belonging manifested itself very clearly. The missionaries stressed their paternal role, yet their children, like most children, grew up. And some wanted to move away from these parents, others into a different relationship, no longer on the missionaries' terms but also not apart. In relenting and admitting that African Catholics should be paid for their work on behalf of the mission, the Spiritans after Le Roy's reforms acknowledged the limits of the paternalistic metaphor, but they did not thereby abandon their paternal role. Meanwhile the villagers pushed at the limits of what was allowed, showing that their sense of what was right — their internalized moral economy — was being violated. Yet they did so as Catholics.

I suspect that Christian communities that emerge as the result of missionary activity must develop such an oppositional consciousness in order to become a church not dependent on missionaries. They must disobey or otherwise resist those whose practices made their identity possible. In this case, the Spiritans were ill-disposed to see the inherent loyalties within such expressions. They thus viewed as disloyalty what was actually evidence of a complex and yet quite Christian consciousness generated by their evangelization, both in the prospective elites and in the Christian villagers. In retrospect the missionaries look like slaves themselves, slaves to a narrow ecclesiology and to racial attitudes that blinded them to the effects of their own evangelization. Slave evangelization made possible the conditions that allowed there to be Catholics from eastern Africans. Perhaps it did not sufficiently challenge the missionaries who enacted it.

•

In early 2003, the Catholic parish in Mhonda, Tanzania — the first Catholic parish founded in eastern Africa away from the coast of the Indian Ocean, onetime home of former slaves and early African Catholics Léon, Hilarion, Isidore, and Laurent — celebrated its 125th anniversary. The event had originally been scheduled for June 2002, within the actual 125th year since the parish's founding and to coincide with the feast after which the parish was named, the Sacred Heart of Jesus. First it had been rescheduled to a few months later, to accommodate the joyful occasion of the ordination to the priesthood of a young man from the parish. Then, as that day neared, cholera appeared in the area, and a decision

---

40. Norton 2004, 68–69.

was made to postpone again. The next time that Bishop Telesphor Mkude of
Morogoro — the diocese in which Bagamoyo, Mhonda, and all the early Spiritan
missions founded between 1868 and the late 1880s now lie — could come was
January 23, 2003. And so at 10:00 a.m. on that day, the people of Sacred Heart
gathered in joy and thanksgiving to celebrate the life of their church.

The Mass began as Bishop Mkude, many priests, and a long line of other
Christians processed toward the altar, singing and dancing. The Scriptures chosen
for the occasion were most apt. A reader proclaimed the story of the Exodus of
the chosen people. Those present knew that their parish, too, had begun with an
exodus of former slaves, not Hebrews from the fleshpots of Egypt but eastern
Africans who had become Catholic Christians at the coast and then made a long
march to Mhonda. The first four African Catholics came in 1877, and other groups
followed in the next few decades. Then all heard a gospel text depicting Christ's
passion and the suffering he endured, his body spilling blood and water while he
hung on the cross (John 19:31–37). Their parish, too, knew painful suffering. The
cholera outbreak a few months before was only the latest of many epidemics that
had struck the parish and its surroundings since its founding. Other hardships
had also afflicted Mhonda. Only four years after its founding, the local chief,
who had been a good friend to the mission, had been ambushed and died, and
numerous other armed conflicts had raged around the mission prior to German
overrule. Droughts had come, as well as locust swarms, one of which in 1895
had forced the temporary return of the entire parish — then still composed mostly
of freed slaves who had come from the coast — to Bagamoyo. In 1916, during
World War I, the parish had again been abandoned due to nearby fighting, and
the church building suffered bombardment. The yoke of colonialism, the Maji
Maji rebellion of 1905–7, independence, *ujamaa* socialism — all the dramas of
Tanganyika and then Tanzania's history had been felt by Mhonda's parishioners.[41]

But African Catholic Christians had prayed on that site for 125 years, and
that was a reason to celebrate. Yes, the first catechist, Hilarion, had become a
Muslim, but his wife Germaine and some of his offspring had remained Catholic.
And many others from the first generation from Bagamoyo had stayed in the
church. Some of their descendants stood in the crowd. They kept alive the stories
of "the couples," or *wamarie.* Many remembered the first child baptized at the
parish, a daughter of Marie-Gabriel and Françoise, the other couple that had
come to establish Mhonda with two Spiritans along with Hilarion and Germaine
in November 1877. Brigitta Kiota had died only in 1958, after eighty years of life
at Mhonda. In the parish cemetery, overgrown but cleared a bit for the celebration,
stood faded wooden posts on which one could barely read her name and the names
of others among the earliest Catholic pioneers.

Mhonda's jubilee serves as a helpful concluding counterpoint to a view of
slave evangelization that emphasizes the Spiritans' role. Stopping this narrative

41. For these and other details about the first hundred years of Mhonda, see Versteijnen and de
Jong 1977, prepared for the hundred-year anniversary of the parish.

when slave evangelization ceded its place at the center of the Spiritan efforts —
and thereby letting missionary strategy determine both its chronological end-
points — can lend the story the feel of tragedy. In such a view, well-meaning and
zealous missionaries found themselves committing and condoning violence in
the name of establishing a church, likely led in this direction by their dependence
upon the labor of the ex-slaves, increasing racism, and encroaching colonialism.
Their early ideal, with an indigenous clergy leading harmonious villages in the
Christianizing of the interior of Africa, disappeared before their own limitations
and frustrating African responses to their message, not to mention other factors
beyond their control. By the 1880s, their initial approach had played itself out,
and little remained that gave reasons for hope: the Christian villages appeared
doomed to unrest and attempts to form African clergy had ceased, only to be
renewed in the twentieth century. By all appearances, the *noyau* of the future
church they had tried to create from former slaves disappointed them. Even the
emphasis on work's formative role had given way to an acceptance of payment
for labor done on the mission's behalf.

The moral qualms that naturally arise in us as we ponder these missionary
activities of the past can tempt us to question the African Catholic individuals
and communities who emerged from these historical processes. But becoming
Catholic was not only the result of missionary activity; it also reflected African
choices. Never merely passive victims of Spiritan manipulation and coercion,
the former slaves who became Catholic articulated their identities in ways that
allowed them to become African Catholics on terms the missionaries did not
always appreciate.[42]

For this is also the story of Catholic origins, and Catholic communities arose
where the Spiritans founded them. Most persist to this day. Their story represents another aspect of slave evangelization, one no doubt more important
for African Christianity, now and in the future. Keeping African Catholics in
view foregrounds not missionary deeds (or misdeeds) but the complex ways in
which missionary practices, easy in retrospect to judge harshly, eventuated in religious communities that serve contemporary Tanzanians and embody the church's
ongoing mission.

---

42. Elizabeth Elbourne, in her review of the work of Jean and John Comaroff, sees them as
limiting the possibilities available to African Christians: "The Comaroffs . . . cannot bring themselves
to see acceptance of Christianity in its unadulterated mission form as anything other than a defeat
for African converts, who were thereby surrendering positions in the struggles over the colonization
of consciousness. . . . [In fact, conversion] . . . fulfilled a wider and more flexible range of functions
than is suggested by the Comaroffs' reduction of it to a symbolic field of struggle over capitalism.
A reading that focuses too exclusively on Christianity as a language of cultural domination rather
than a language with a multiplicity of possible meanings pays too much attention to the Western
roots of Christianity and not enough to the multiple uses to which Africans quickly put it." She
concludes, "From the very beginning of the activity of Christians in Africa, as elsewhere in the
world, Christianity was out of control, unorthodox, and an available subject for reinterpretation in
light of the needs of its interlocutors. Ironically, in sum, it is not always wise to take missionaries at
their word" (Elbourne 2003, 452–53, 455, 459).

Interviews and Conversations
Listed in chronological order

Barnabas Salvi Mkuku. September 3–4, 1997; June 29, 1998. Zanzibar

Michael Joseph Misheli. August 1, 1998; August 2, 1998. Bagamoyo, Tanzania
Leonia Richardi. August 2, 1998. Bagamoyo, Tanzania
Sofia State. August 2, 1998. Bagamoyo, Tanzania
Ferdinand Petro. August 2, 1998. Bagamoyo, Tanzania
Francis Damas. August 2, 1998. Bagamoyo, Tanzania
Joseph Ignasio. August 3, 1998. Bagamoyo, Tanzania
Faustina Innocent. August 3, 1998. Bagamoyo, Tanzania
Maria Pius. August 3, 1998. Bagamoyo, Tanzania
Louis Innocent. August 3, 1998. Bagamoyo, Tanzania
Peter Naali. August 4, 1998. Bagamoyo, Tanzania
Michael Joseph Kabelewa. August 4, 1998. Bagamoyo, Tanzania

Father Constantine Luhimbo. July 19, 2001. Ilonga, Tanzania
Father Richard Zgorzelak. July 21, 2001. Mandera, Tanzania

Morisi Alberto Msemwa. June 1–2, 2003. Mhonda, Tanzania
Emmanuel Teodori Mdumbe. June 3, 2003. Mhonda, Tanzania
Ferdinandi Nikolas Kabelwa. June 4–6, 2003. Mhonda, Tanzania
John Anthony Kangati. June 6, 2003. Mhonda, Tanzania

Bibliography

I. Primary Sources, Abbreviated Sources, and Archives Consulted

AA   *Annales Apostoliques de la Congrégation du Saint-Esprit et du Saint Coeur de Marie.*

APF   *Les Annales de la Association de la Propagation de la Foi* (later *Annales de la Propagation de la Foi*)

BG   *Bullétin Général de la Congrégation du Saint-Esprit et du Saint Coeur de Marie.*

Paris. Quarterly publication of the Holy Ghost Congregation, distributed to every community, begun in 1857. After the designation of volume will follow the page number, e.g., BG 11:335. Because the sources of the materials in this journal are often not identified, the date of the excerpt cited is difficult to ascertain. The dates of the issues, however, are as follows:

BG 1: 1857–1859	BG 11: 1877–1881
BG 2: 1860–1862	BG 12: 1881–1882
BG 3: 1862–1863	BG 13: 1883–1886
BG 4: 1863–1865	BG 14: 1887–1888
BG 5: 1866–1867	BG 15: 1889–1891
BG 6: 1867–1869	BG 16: 1891–1893
BG 7: 1869–1870	BG 17: 1893–1896
BG 8: 1871–1872	BG 18: 1896–1897
BG 9: 1872–1874	BG 19: 1898–1899
BG 10: 1874–1877	BG 20: 1899–1900

CSSp   Holy Ghost Archives, Chevilly, Paris

Letters and files will be cited with box number, then file number, then writer (and recipient of the letter) if relevant, page number (if relevant), and date, in European-dated format. For example, the reference "CSSp 196bii: Horner to Schwindenhammer, 4ii65" refers to the Holy Ghost Archives, box 196, file bii, Horner to Schwindenhammer, February 4, 1865.

Note: In the late 1990s the archives in Paris adopted another system of cataloguing. I have, except where indicated, used the older system, for that has been the practice in previous literature on the Holy Ghost missionaries in eastern Africa.

Journals of Holy Ghost mission stations in Eastern Africa

>(microfilm, Holy Ghost Archives, Bethel Park, Pennsylvania, USA; except for the Zanzibar and Mandera microfilms, which are only at the Holy Ghost Archives, Chevilly, Paris)
>>Cited by name of the mission and date of the entry:
>>>Bagamoyo
>>>Mandera
>>>Mhonda
>>>Morogoro
>>>Zanzibar

LERE   *Livre des Enfants Rachetés de L'Esclavage.* Bagamoyo mission, 1884–94.

MC   *Les Missions Catholiques* (Lyon)

>Publication of the Society for the Propagation of the Faith

MS   *Mémoire Spiritaine*

>Publication of the Congregation of the Holy Ghost

ND   *Notes et Documents relatives à la Vie et à l'Oeuvre de Vénérable François-Marie-Paul Libermann, Supérieur Genéral de la Congrégation du Saint-Esprit et du Saint Coeur de Marie.* Edited by P. Cabon. Paris: 1929–41. 13 Volumes.

Sacramental registries

>Zanzibar
>Bagamoyo
>Mhonda

TNR   Tanganyika Notes and Records

UMCA   Annual reports of the Universities' Mission to Central Africa, 1860–1900

Zanzibar Archives

II. Secondary Sources

Abbink, Jon, Mirjam de Bruijn, and Klaas van Walraven, eds.
>2003   *Rethinking Resistance: Revolt and Violence in African History.* Leiden and Boston: Brill.

Abdurahman, Muhammed
>1938   "Anthropological Notes from the Zanzibar Protectorate." TNR 8, 59–84.

Abou, Sélim
>1997   (1995) *The Jesuit "Republic" of the Guaranís (1609–1768) and Its Heritage.* New York: Crossroad.

Abungu, George H. O.
  1998   "City States of the East African Coast and Their Maritime Contacts." In
          Connah 1998, 204–18.
Acker, A.
  1908   "Die Erziehung der Eingeborenen zur Arbeit in Deutsch-Ostafrika," *Jahrbuch
          über die Deutschen Kolonien* 1, 117–24.
Actes du Colloque de Lyon
  1984   *Les Réveils Missionnaires en France: Du Moyen Age à nos jours (XIIe–XXe
          siècles).* Paris: Beauchesne.
Adas, Michael
  1993   "High" Imperialism and the "New" History. In *Islamic and European Expan-
          sion: The Forging of a Global Order.* Edited by Michael Adas. Philadelphia:
          Temple University Press, 311–44.
Ajayi, J. F. Ade
  1965   *Christian Missions in Nigeria, 1841–1891: The Making of a New Elite.*
          Evanston, Ill.: Northwestern University Press.
  1989   *Africa in the Nineteenth Century until the 1880s.* General History of Africa,
          vol. 6. Oxford: Heinemann International; Berkeley: University of California
          Press; Paris: Unesco.
Akinola, G. A.
  1972   "Slavery and Slave Revolts in the Sultanate of Zanzibar in the Nineteenth
          Century." *Journal of the Historical Society of Nigeria* 6:2, 215–28.
Alpers, Edward A.
  1967   *The East African Slave Trade.* Nairobi: Historical Association of Tanzania.
  1975   *Ivory and Slaves: Changing Patterns of International Trade in East Central
          Africa to the Later Nineteenth Century.* Berkeley and Los Angeles: University
          of California Press.
  1983   "The Story of Swema: Female Vulnerability in Nineteenth-Century East
          Africa." In Robertson and Klein 1983, 185–219.
  1984   " 'Ordinary Household Chores': Ritual and Power in a Nineteenth-Century
          Swahili Women's Spirit Possession Cult." *International Journal of African
          Historical Studies* 17:4, 677–702.
  2000   "East Central Africa." In Levtzion and Pouwels 2000a, 303–25.
Amory, Deborah Peters
  1994   "The Politics of Identity on Zanzibar." Ph.D. dissertation. Stanford University.
Ananias, Brother
  1949   "Mwanzo wa Misioni ya Morogoro" (Beginning of the Morogoro mission).
          Typed manuscript, Bishop's residence, Morogoro, Tanzania.
Anderson, Gerald, ed.
  1999   *Biographical Dictionary of Christian Missions.* Grand Rapids: Eerdmans.
Anderson, W. B.
  1977   *The Church in East Africa, 1840–1974.* Dodoma: Central Tanganyika Press.
Archer, Léonie, ed.
  1988   *Slavery and Other Forms of Unfree Labour.* London and New York: Routledge.

Archer, Margaret
  1996   *Being Human: The Problem of Agency.* Cambridge: Cambridge University Press.
  2000   *Culture and Agency: The Place of Culture in Social Theory.* Cambridge: Cambridge University Press.
  2003   *Structure, Agency, and the Internal Conversation.* Cambridge: Cambridge University Press.
Archibald, Robert
  1978   *The Economic Aspects of the California Missions.* Washington, D.C.: Academy of American Franciscan History.
Areskough, Anna, and Helena Persson
  1999   *In the Heart of Bagamoyo: The Decoding of a Coastal Town in Tanzania.* Lund, Sweden: Lund Institute of Technology.
Arnold, David, and Robert A. Bickers
  1996   Introduction. In Bickers and Seton 1996, 1–10.
Asad, Talal, ed.
  1973   *Anthropology and the Colonial Encounter.* London: Ithaca Press.
  1993   *Genealogies of Religion: Discipline and Reasons of Power in Christianity and Islam.* Baltimore and London: Johns Hopkins University Press.
  1996   "Comments on Conversion." In van der Veer 1996, 263–73.
Ashcroft, Bill, Gareth Griffiths, and Helen Tiffin, eds.
  1995   *The Post-Colonial Studies Reader.* London: Routledge.
Atkins, Keletso
  1993   *The Moon Is Dead! Give Us Our Money! The Cultural Origins of an African Work Ethic, Natal, South Africa, 1843–1900.* London: James Currey.
Atmore, A. E.
  1985   "Africa on the Eve of Partition." In Oliver and Sanderson 1985, 10–95.
Austen, Ralph
  1989   "The Nineteenth Century Islamic Slave Trade from East Africa (Swahili and Red Sea Coasts): A Tentative Census." In Clarence-Smith 1989a, 21–44.
Avanzini, M., ed.
  1996   *Pédagogue Chrétienne, Pédagogues Chrétiens.* Paris: Éditions Don Bosco.
Axel, Brian Keith, ed.
  2002   *From the Margins: Historical Anthropology and Its Futures.* Durham, N.C., and London: Duke University Press.
Axtell, James
  1985   *The Invasion Within: The Contest of Cultures in Colonial North America.* New York and Oxford: Oxford University Press.
Azumah, John Alembillah
  2001   *The Legacy of Arab-Islam in Africa: A Quest for Inter-Religious Dialogue.* Oxford: Oneworld Publications.
Baëta, C. G., ed.
  1968   *Christianity in Tropical Africa.* London: Oxford University Press.

Bagamoyo Catholic mission

n.d.   *New Hope in the Town of Slaves? Slavery in Bagamoyo Yesterday and Today.* Video Tumaini, Dar es Salaam.

Barker, Francis

1995   (1984) *The Tremulous Private Body: Essays on Subjection.* Ann Arbor: University of Michigan Press.

Barrett, David B., George T. Kurian, and Todd M. Johnson, eds.

2001   *World Christian Encyclopedia: A Comparative Survey of Churches and Religions in the Modern World.* Vol. 1, *The World by Countries: Religionists, Churches, Ministries.* Vol. 2, *The World by Segments: Religions, Peoples, Languages, Cities, Topics.* 2nd ed. New York: Oxford University Press.

Baumont, Jean

1984   *La renaissance de l'idée missionnaire en France au début du XIXe siècle.* In Actes du Colloque du Lyon 1984, 201–22.

Baur, Etienne

1867   *Katekismou Kisouahili na Kifranza tcha Vasouahili no Vatoumoua oua Angoudia na Mrima oua Souahili (Catechisme souahili et français pour les souahili et les noirs de la côte Orientale d'Afrique).* Zanzibar.

1882   *Voyage dans l'Oudoé et l'ouzigoua (Zanguebar).* Lyon.

Baur, John

1994   *2000 Years of Christianity in Africa.* Nairobi: Paulines Publications–Africa.

Bayo, Valentine, and Casimir Nyaki

n.d.   Historical Bagamoyo. (pamphlet) Bagamoyo.

Beachey, R. W.

1976a   *A Collection of Documents on the Slave Trade of Eastern Africa.* New York: Barnes and Noble.

1976b   *The Slave Trade of Eastern Africa.* New York: Barnes and Noble.

Beattie, John

1980   "Representations of the Self in Traditional Africa." *Africa* 50:3, 313–20.

Bedouelle, Guy, Liliane Chauleau, Philippe Delisle, Claude Prudhomme, eds.

1999   *L'Église et l'abolition de l'esclavage.* Paris: Le Centre D'Études du Saulchoir.

Beech, Mervyn W. H.

1916   "Slavery on the East Coast of Africa." *Journal of the African Society* 15:58, 145–49.

Beidelman, T. O.

1962   "A History of Ukaguru: 1857–1916." TNR 58/59, 11–39.

1982a   *Colonial Evangelism.* Bloomington: Indiana University Press.

1982b   "The Organization and Maintenance of Caravans by the Church Missionary Society in Tanzania in the Nineteenth Century." *International Journal of African Historical Studies* 15:4, 601–23.

Beinart, William, and Joann McGregor, eds.

2003   *Social History and African Environments.* Oxford and Athens: James Currey and Ohio University Press.

Bennett, Norman R.

1963a   "The Holy Ghost Mission in East Africa: 1858–1890." In Bennett 1963b, 54–75.

1963b   *Studies in East African History.* Boston: Boston University Press.

1964   "The Church Missionary Society at Mombasa, 1873–1894." In Butler 1964, 157–94.

1966   "Charles de Vienne and the Frere Mission to Zanzibar." In Butler 1966, 109–21.

Bennett, Norman R., ed.

1969   *From Zanzibar to Ujiji: The Journal of Arthur Dodgshun, 1877–1879.* Boston: African Studies Center.

1971   *Mirambo of Tanzania, 1840(?)–1884.* New York: Oxford University Press.

1973   "France and Zanzibar, 1844 to the 1860s." Part 1. *International Journal of African Historical Studies* 6:4, 602–32.

1974   "France and Zanzibar, 1844 to the 1860s." Part 2. *International Journal of African Historical Studies* 7:1, 27–55.

1978   *A History of the Arab State of Zanzibar.* London: Methuen and Co.

1984   *The Arab State of Zanzibar: A Bibliography.* Boston: G. K. Hall and Co.

1986   *Arab versus European: Diplomacy and War in Nineteenth-Century East Central Africa.* New York and London: Africana Publishing Co.

Bernstein, Henry

1979   "African Peasantries: A Theoretical Framework." *Journal of Peasant Studies* 6:4, 421–43.

Bevans, Stephen B., and Roger Schroeder

2004   *Constants in Context: A Theology of Mission for Today.* Maryknoll, N.Y.: Orbis Books.

Bhacker, M. Reda

1991   "Family Strife and Foreign Intervention: Causes in the Separation of Zanzibar from Oman: A Reappraisal." *Bulletin of the School of Oriental and African Studies* 54, 269–80.

1992   *Trade and Empire in Muscat and Zanzibar: Roots of British Domination.* London and New York: Routledge.

Bickers, Robert A., and Rosemary Seton, eds.

1996   *Missionary Encounters: Sources and Issues.* Surrey, England: Curzon Press.

Blais, J.

1916   "Les anciens esclaves à Zanzibar." *Anthropos* 10–11, 504–11.

Boahen, A. Adu

1985   *Africa under Colonial Domination, 1880–1935.* General History of Africa 6. Paris: UNESCO.

Bolt, Christine, and Seymour Drescher, eds.

1980   *Anti-Slavery, Religion, and Reform: Essays in Memory of Roger Anstey.* Kent: Dawson and Sons.

Bonnell, Victoria, and Lynn Hunt, eds.

1999   *Beyond the Cultural Turn: New Directions in the Study of Society and Culture.* Berkeley: University of California Press.

Bouchard, J.

1957   "Les missions d'Afrique." In Delacroix 1957, 297–354.

Bouché, Denise

1968   *Les villages de Liberté en Afrique Noire Française.* Paris: Mouton and Co.

Bourdieu, Pierre

1977   *Outline of a Theory of Practice.* Cambridge: Cambridge University Press.

1990   *The Logic of Practice.* Stanford, Calif.: Stanford University Press.

Brasseur, Paule

1984   "Les religions traditionelles et l'Islam vus par les premiers missionnaires français à la côte d'Afrique." In Actes du Colloque du Lyon 1984, 335–62.

1988   "L'esclavage, les campagnes abolitionnistes et la naissance de l'œuvre de Libermann." In Coulon and Brasseur 1988, 319–32.

1998   "De l'abolition d'esclavage à la colonisation de l'Afrique." *Mémoire Spiritaine* 7, 93–107.

Bravman, Bill

1998   *Making Ethnic Ways: Communities and Their Transformations in Taita, Kenya, 1800–1950.* Portsmouth, N.H.: Heinemann.

Brett, Stephen F.

1994   *Slavery and the Catholic Tradition.* New York: Peter Lang.

Briault, Maurice

1946   *Le Vénérable Père F. M. P. Libermann.* Paris: J. DeGigord.

Bridges, Roy

2000   "Towards the Prelude to the Partition of East Africa." In *Imperialism, Decolonization, and Africa.* Edited by Roy Bridges. New York: St. Martin's Press, 65–113.

Brooks, James F.

2002   *Captives and Cousins: Slavery, Kinship, and Community in the Southwest Borderlands.* Chapel Hill and London: University of North Carolina Press.

Brown, Walter T.

1971a   "A Pre-Colonial History of Bagamoyo: Aspects of the Growth of an East African Coastal Town." Ph.D. thesis, Boston University.

1971b   "The Politics of Business: Relations between Zanzibar and Bagamoyo in the Late Nineteenth Century." *African Historical Studies* 4:3, 631–43.

Brunschwig, Henri

1966   *French Colonialism, 1871–1914.* New York and Washington, D.C.: Praeger.

Buhlmann, Walbert

1979   *The Coming of the Third Church.* Maryknoll, N.Y.: Orbis Books.

Bundy, Colin

1979   *The Rise and Fall of the South African Peasantry.* Berkeley and Los Angeles: University of California Press.

Bunker, Stephen

1987   *Peasants against the State: The Politics of Market Control in Bugisu, Uganda, 1900–1983.* Urbana: University of Illinois Press.

Burke, Christy
  1998   *Morality and Mission: Francis Libermann and Slavery (1840–1850)*. Nairobi: Paulines Publications–Africa.
Burridge, Kenelm
  1991   *In the Way: A Study of Christian Missionary Endeavours*. Vancouver: UBD Press.
Burton, Richard
  1858   "Zanzibar: and Two Months in East Africa." *Blackwood's Magazine* (Edinburgh) 83, 200–224, 276–90, 572–89.
  1872   *Zanzibar: City, Island, and Coast*. London: Tinsley Brothers.
Butler, Jeffrey, ed.
  1964   *Boston University Papers in African History*. Vol. 1. Boston: Boston University Press.
  1966   *Boston University Papers on Africa*. Vol. 2. Boston: Boston University Press.
Butler, Judith P.
  1997   *The Psychic Life of Power: Theories of Subjection*. Stanford, Calif.: Stanford University Press.
Campbell, Gwyn
  1989   "The East African Slave Trade, 1861–1895: The 'Southern' Complex." *International Journal of African Historical Studies* 22:1, 1–26.
Carpenter, Mary
  1969   (1851) *Reformatory Schools for the Children of the Perishing and Dangerous Classes and for Juvenile Offenders*. New York: Kelley.
Carrithers, M., Steven Collins, and Steven Lukes, eds.
  1985   *The Category of the Person*. Cambridge: Cambridge University Press.
Cary, Phillip
  2000   *Augustine's Invention of the Inner Self: The Legacy of a Christian Platonist*. Oxford: Oxford University Press.
Cassinelli, Lee V.
  1987   "Social Construction on the Somali Frontier: Bantu Former Slave Communities in the Nineteenth Century." In Kopytoff 1987, 214–38.
Cave, Basil S.
  1909   "The End of Slavery in Zanzibar and British East Africa." *Journal of the African Society* 9:33, 20–33.
Chande, Abdin
  2000   "Radicalism and Reform in East Africa." In Levtzion and Pouwels 2000a, 349–69.
Charmetant, P.
  1882   *D'Alger à Zanzibar*. Paris: Société Bibliographie.
Chevalier, Louis
  1973   (1958) *Laboring Classes and Dangerous Classes in Paris in the First Half of the Nineteenth Century*. Translated by Frank Jellinek. New York: Howard Fertig.

Cholvy, Gérard

1991 *La religion en France de la fin du XVIIIe à nos jours.* Paris: Hachette.

1997 *Etre Chrétien en France au XIXe siècle, 1790–1914.* Paris: Seuil.

Cholvy, Gérard, ed.

1996 *L'éveil des catholiques français à la dimension internationale de leur foi, 19e et 20e aiècle.* Montpellier: Centre régional d'histoire des mentalités.

Cholvy, Gérard, and Nadine-Josette Chaline, eds.

1995 *L'enseignement catholique en France aux XIXe et XXe siècles.* Paris: Les Éditions du Cerf.

Cholvy, Gérard, and Yves-Marie Hilaire, eds.

1985 *Histoire religieuse de la France contemporaine.* 3 vols. Toulouse: Bibliothèque historique privat.

Chrétien, Jean-Pierre

2003 *The Great Lakes of Africa: Two Thousand Years of History.* Translated by Scott Straus. New York: Zone Books.

Clarence-Smith, William Gervase

1979 *Slaves, Peasants and Capitalists in Southern Angola: 1840–1926.* Cambridge: Cambridge University Press.

1989b "The Economics of the Indian Ocean and Red Sea Slave Trades in the Nineteenth Century: An Overview." In Clarence-Smith 1989a, 1–20.

Clarence-Smith, William Gervase, ed.

1989a *The Economics of the Indian Ocean Slave Trade in the Nineteenth Century.* London: Frank Cass.

Cobbing, Julian

1988 "The *Mfecane* as Alibi: Thoughts on Dithakong and Mbolompo." *Journal of African History* 29, 487–519.

Cohen, David William, and E. S. Atieno Odhiambo

1989 *Siaya: The Historical Anthropology of an African Landscape.* London: James Currey Press.

Cohen, Paul

1997 *Freedom's Moment: An Essay on the French Idea of Liberty from Rousseau to Foucault.* Chicago and London: University of Chicago Press.

Cohen, William B.

1980 *The French Encounter with Africans.* Bloomington: Indiana University Press.

Comaroff, Jean

1985 *Body of Power, Spirit of Resistance.* Chicago: University of Chicago Press.

Comaroff, Jean, and John Comaroff

1991 *Of Revelation and Revolution.* Vol. 1, *Christianity, Colonialism, and Consciousness in South Africa.* Chicago and London: University of Chicago Press.

1992 *Ethnography and the Historical Imagination.* Boulder, Colo.: Westview Press.

1997 *Of Revelation and Revolution.* Vol. 2, *The Dialectics of Modernity on a South African Frontier.* Chicago and London: University of Chicago Press.

2001   "On Personhood: An Anthropological Perspective from Africa." *Social Iden-tities* 7, 267–83.

Comby, Jean
1992   *L'evolution de la formation dans la Société des Missions Africaines de Lyon.* In Spindler and Gadille 1992, 333–39.

Comerford, Frank
1978   "Looking Back: A Brief Synopsis of C.S.Sp. History in East Africa." *Spiritan Papers* 6, 47–55.

Conklin, Alice
1997   *A Mission to Civilize: The Republican Idea of Empire in France and West Africa, 1895–1930.* Stanford, Calif.: Stanford University Press.

Conley, Tom
1996   *The Self-Made Map: Cartographic Writing in Early Modern France.* London and Minneapolis: University of Minnesota Press.

Connah, Graham, ed.
1998   *Transformations in Africa: Essays on Africa's Later Past.* London: Leicester University Press.

Constantin, François
1988   "Charism and the Crisis of Power in East Africa." In Cruise O'Brien and Coulon 1988, 67–90.

Constantin, François, ed.
1987   *Les voies de l'Islam en Afrique Orientale.* Paris: Karthala.

Cooper, Frederick
1977   *Plantation Slavery on the East Coast of Africa.* New Haven, Conn.: Yale University Press.
1979   "The Problem of Slavery in African Studies." *Journal of African History* 20, 103–25.
1980   *From Slaves to Squatters: Plantation Labor and Agriculture in Zanzibar and Coastal Kenya, 1980–1925.* New Haven, Conn., and London: Yale University Press.
1981   "Islam and Cultural Hegemony: The Ideology of Slaveowners on the East African Coast." In Lovejoy 1981a, 270–307.
1994   "Conflict and Connection: Rethinking Colonial African History." *American Historical Review* 99:5, 1516–45.
2000   "Conditions Analogous to Slavery: Imperialism and Free Labor Ideology in Africa." In Cooper, Holt, and Scott 2000, 107–49.

Cooper, Frederick, Thomas Holt, and Rebecca Scott
2000   *Beyond Slavery: Explorations of Race, Labor, and Citizenship in Post-emancipation Societies.* Chapel Hill and London: University of North Carolina Press.

Cornuel, Pascuale
1999   "Mana, un village au carrefour d'un monde en mutation, 1836–1846." In Dorigny 1999, 271–93.

Coulon, Paul

    1988   "Inventaire critique des études historiques sur Libermann (1855–1986)." In Coulon and Brasseur 1988, 133–60.

    1999   *Combats de chefs au Zanguebar: Pentecôte sur le Monde* 783, 24–25.

    2000   Éditorial. MS 12, 3–9.

Coulon, Paul, and Paule Brasseur, eds.

    1988   *Libermann, 1802–1852: Une pensée et une mystique missionnaires.* Paris: Les Édition du Cerf.

Coupland, Reginald

    1933   *The British Anti-Slavery Movement.* London: Thornton Butterworth.

    1938   *East Africa and Its Invaders.* Oxford: Clarendon Press.

    1967   (1939) *The Exploitation of East Africa, 1856–1890: The Slave Trade and the Scramble.* Evanston, Ill.: Northwestern University Press.

Cox, James L., and Gerrie ter Haar, eds.

    2003   *Uniquely African? African Christian Identity from Cultural and Historical Perspectives.* Trenton, N.J., and Asmara, Eritrea: Africa World Press.

Craton, Michael, ed.

    1979   *Roots and Branches: Current Directions in Slave Studies.* Toronto: Pergamon Press.

Cruise O'Brien, Donal B., and Christian Coulon, eds.

    1988   *Charisma and Brotherhood in African Islam.* Oxford: Clarendon Press.

Curtin, Philip D.

    1964   *The Image of Africa: British Ideas and Action, 1780–1850.* Madison: University of Wisconsin Press.

    2000   *The World and the West: The European Challenge and the Overseas Response in the Age of Empire.* Cambridge: Cambridge University Press.

Curtis, Sarah

    2000   *Educating the Faithful: Religion, Schooling, and Society in Nineteenth-Century France.* DeKalb: Northern Illinois University Press.

Curto, José C., and Paul E. Lovejoy, eds.

    2003   *Enslaving Connections: Changing Cultures of Africa and Brazil during the Era of Slavery.* New York: Humanity Books.

Daget, Serge

    1980   "A Model of the French Abolitionist Movement and Its Variations." In Bolt and Drescher 1980, 64–79.

    1989   "The Abolition of the Slave Trade." In Ajayi 1989, 64–89.

Dale, Godfrey

    1969   (1920) *The Peoples of Zanzibar: Their Customs and Religious Beliefs.* New York: Negro Universities Press.

Daniel, E. Randolph

    1975   *The Franciscan Concept of Mission in the High Middle Ages.* Lexington: University Press of Kentucky.

Dansette, Adrien
  1961   (1948) *Religious History of Modern France.* 2 vols. New York: Herder and
          Herder.
Daull, Auguste
  1879   *Grammaire Kisouahili.* Colmar: M. Hoffmann.
Davidson, Basil
  1980   *The African Slave Trade.* Boston and New York: Little, Brown and Co.
de Certeau, Michel
  1984   *The Practice of Everyday Life.* Berkeley: University of California Press.
  1988   *The Writing of History.* New York: Columbia University Press.
de Gruchy, John
  2003   "Who Did They Think They Were?" in Porter 2003a, 213–25.
de Jong, Albert
  2002   "Church, Colonialism and Nationalism in Tanzania." From Wijsen and Nissen
          2002, 61–77.
de Kock, Leon
  1996   *Civilising Barbarians: Missionary Narrative and African Textual Response in
          Nineteenth-Century South Africa.* Johannesburg: Witwatersrand Press.
Delacroix, S., ed.
  1957   *Histoire universelle des missions catholiques.* Vol. 3, *Les missions contempo-
          raines (1800–1957).* Paris: Librairie Grund.
Deleuze, Gilles
  1979   "The Rise of the Social." Foreword to Donzelot 1979, ix–xvii.
Delisle, Philippe
  1995   "Le Monarchie de Juillet, l'eglise de France et l'esclavage." *Mémoire Spiri-
          taine* 2, 59–80.
Delpechin, Jacques
  1991   "The Transition from Slavery, 1873–1914." In Sheriff and Ferguson 1991,
          11–35.
de Lubac, Henri
  1967   (1965) *The Mystery of the Supernatural.* Translated by Rosemary Sheed. New
          York: Herder and Herder.
de Montclos, Xavier
  1984   *La vie spirituelle en France au XIXe siècle et l'élan missionnaire.* In Actes du
          Colloque de Lyon 1984, 321–37.
Dereymez, Jean-William
  1995   *Frédéric Le Play, réformateur chrétien?* In Plongeron and Guillaume 1995,
          145–67.
Desai, Gaurav
  2000   *Subject to Colonialism: African Self-Fashioning and the Colonial Library.*
          Durham, N.C., and London: Duke University Press.
de Ste. Croix, G. E. M.
  1988   "Slavery and Other Forms of Unfree Labour." In L. Archer 1988, 19–32.

Deutsch, Jan-Georg

2000   *Slavery under German Colonial Rule in East Africa, c. 1860–1914. Habilitationsschrift.* Humboldt University at Berlin.

2003   "Absence of Evidence Is No Proof: Slave Resistance under German Colonial Rule in East Africa." In Abbink et al. 2003, 170–87.

de Vienne, Charles

1872   "De Zanzibar à l'Oukami." *Bullétin de la Société Geographie*, 356–69.

Dietrich, Donald J., and Michael J. Himes, eds.

1997   *The Legacy of the Tübingen School: The Relevance of Nineteenth-Century Theology for the Twenty-first Century.* New York: Crossroad Herder.

Din, Gilbert C.

1999   *Spaniards, Planters, and Slaves: The Spanish Regulation of Slavery in Louisiana, 1763–1803.* College Station: Texas A & M Press.

Dirks, Nicholas, ed.

1992   *Colonialism and Culture.* Ann Arbor: University of Michigan Press.

Dodgshun, Arthur

1969   See Bennett 1969.

Donovan, Vincent

1978   *Christianity Rediscovered.* Notre Dame, Ind.: Fides Press.

Donzelot, Jacques

1979   *The Policing of Families.* New York: Pantheon Books.

1984   *L'Invention du social: Essai sur le déclin de passions politiques.* Paris: Fayard.

Dorigny, Marcel, ed.

1999   *Esclavage, résistances et abolitions.* Paris: CTHS.

Drescher, Seymour

1980   "Two Variants of Anti-Slavery: Religious Organization and Social Mobilization in Britain and France, 1780–1870." In Bolt and Drescher 1980, 43–63.

Drescher, Seymour, and Stanley L. Engerman, eds.

1998   *A Historical Guide to World Slavery.* New York and Oxford: Oxford University Press.

Driver, Felix

1990   "Discipline without Frontiers? Representations of the Mettray Reformatory Colony in Britain, 1840–1880." *Journal of Historical Sociology* 3:3, 272–93.

Ducol, Bernard

2000a   "Le père Alexandre Le Roy au Zanguebar (1881–1892)." MS 11, 30–56.

2000b   "Dans la même portion de la vigne: Le père Libermann et la mère Javouhey." MS 12, 10–33.

2003   "Mgr Alexandre Le Roy: Une enfance normande (1854–1874)." MS 18, 73–105.

Duffy, James

1962   *Portugal in Africa.* Cambridge, Mass.: Harvard University Press.

Dumax, V.

1876   Intéressants détails sur la mission de Zanzibar. *Annales de L'Archconfrérie de Notre Dame des Victoires*, 154–62.

Dumont, Louis

 1985   "The Christian Beginnings of Modern Individualism." In Carrithers, Collins, and Lukes 1985, 93–122.

Duncan, Graham A.

 2003   *Lovedale — Coercive Agency: Power and Resistance in Mission Education.* Pietermaritzburg, South Africa: Cluster Publications.

Dupré, Louis

 1993   *Passage to Modernity: An Essay in the Hermeneutics of Nature and Culture.* New Haven, Conn.: Yale University Press.

Durand, L'Abbé

 1874   *Les Missions Catholiques Françaises.* Paris: Delagrave.

Duroselle, Jean-Baptiste

 1951   *Les Débuts du Catholicisme Sociale en France.* Paris: Presses Universitaires de France.

Dussercle, Roger

 1974   *Histoire d'une Fondation: Mère Marie Madeleine de la Croix et la Congréga- tion des Filles de Marie, St. Denis-Réunion.* Réunion.

Eisenberg, Jose Monroe

 1998   "Theology, Political Theory, and Justification in the Jesuit Missions to Brazil, 1549–1610." Ph.D. dissertation, City University of New York.

Elbourne, Elizabeth

 2003   "Word Made Flesh: Christianity, Modernity, and Cultural Colonialism in the Work of Jean and John Comaroff." *American Historical Review* 108:2, 435–59.

Ellis, John Tracy

 1967   *Essays in Seminary Education.* Notre Dame, Ind.: Fides.

Elton, Frederic

 1874   "On the Coast Country of East Africa, South of Zanzibar." *Journal of the Royal Geographical Society*, 227–52.

Engel, Alois

 1932   *Die Missionsmethode der Missionare v. heiligen Geist auf dem afrikanischen Festland.* Knechtsteden.

Ernoult, Jean

 1992   *Les lieux Spiritains en France.* Paris: Congrégation du Saint-Esprit.

 2000   *Histoire de la Province Spiritaine de France.* Paris: Congrégation du Saint- Esprit.

Etherington, Norman

 1996   "Recent Trends in the Historiography of Christianity in Southern Africa." *Journal of Southern African Studies* 22:2, 201–19.

Eve, Prosper

 1999   *Du torchis à la pierre: La Congrégation des Filles de Marie, 1849–1999. Le triomphe de l'Amour.* Réunion: Conseil Général de La Réunion.

Ewald, Janet

 1998   "Africa: East Africa." In Drescher and Engerman 1998, 41–46.

Fair, Laura Jeanne
   1994   "Pastimes and Politics: A Social History of Zanzibar's Ng'ambo Community,
           1890–1950." Ph.D. dissertation, University of Minnesota.
   2001   *Pastimes and Politics: Culture, Community, and Identity in Post-Abolition
           Urban Zanzibar, 1890–1945.* Athens: Ohio University Press.
Fajans, Jane
   1997   *They Make Themselves: Work and Play among the Baining of Papua New
           Guinea.* Chicago and London: University of Chicago Press.
Falola, Toyin, and Paul E. Lovejoy, eds.
   1994   *Pawnship in Africa.* Boulder, Colo.: Westview Press.
Farr, James R.
   1991   "The Pure and Disciplined Body: Hierarchy, Morality, and Symbolism in
           France during the Catholic Reformation." *Journal of Interdisciplinary History*
           21:3, 391–414.
Fava, M. l'Abbé
   1933   "Lettre à Mgr. Maupoint, Éveque de Saint-Denis, 25 juillet 1861." *Revue
           d'Histoire des Missions* 10, 106–21.
Feay, Troy
   2003   " 'Religion Enfranchising the World'? Bishops, Politicians, and the Recruit-
           ment of Missionaries to the French Slave Colonies, 1815–1839." University
           of Notre Dame, unpublished paper.
Federini, Fabienne
   1998   *L'abolition de l'esclavage de 1848.* Paris: L'Harmattan.
Feierman, Steven
   1974   *The Shambaa Kingdom: A History.* Madison: University of Wisconsin Press.
   1995   "Africa in History: The End of Universal Narratives." In Prakash 1995, 40–65.
   1999   "Colonizers, Scholars, and the Creation of Invisible Histories." In Bonnell and
           Hunt 1999, 182–216.
Ferguson, Harvie
   2000   *Modernity and Subjectivity: Body, Soul, and Spirit.* Charlottesville: University
           Press of Virginia.
Fields, Karen
   1985   *Revival and Rebellion in Colonial Central Africa.* Princeton, N.J.: Princeton
           University Press.
Finkelman, Paul, and Joseph C. Miller, eds.
   1998   *Macmillan Encyclopedia of World Slavery.* New York: Macmillan.
Finneran, Niall
   2002   *The Archaeology of Christianity in Africa.* Gloucestershire, UK: Tempus.
Flint, John E., ed.
   1963   "The Wider Background to Partition and Colonial Occupation." In Oliver and
           Mathew 1963, 352–90.
   1976   *The Cambridge History of Africa. Vol. 5, From c. 1790 to c. 1870.* Cambridge:
           Cambridge University Press.

Forde, Darryl, ed.
1954   *African Worlds.* Oxford: Oxford University Press.
Fortes, Meyer, and E. E. Evans-Pritchard, eds.
1940   *African Political Systems.* London: KPI Limited.
Fortes, Meyer, and Robin Horton
1983   *Oedipus and Job in West African Religion.* Cambridge: Cambridge University Press.
Foucault, Michel
1965   *Madness and Civilization: A History of Insanity in the Age of Reason.* New York: Random House.
1971   *The Order of Things: An Archaeology of the Human Sciences.* New York: Pantheon Books.
1972   *The Archaeology of Knowledge and the Discourse on Language.* New York: Pantheon Books.
1973   *The Birth of the Clinic: An Archaeology of Medical Perception.* New York: Vintage Books.
1977   *Discipline and Punish: The Birth of the Prison.* New York: Pantheon Books.
Franklin, John Hope, and Loren Schweninger
1999   *Runaway Slaves: Rebels on the Plantation.* New York and Oxford: Oxford University Press.
Frederickson, George
2000   "The Skeleton in the Closet." *New York Review of Books* 47:17, 61–66.
Freeman-Grenville, G. S. P.
1965   "The Augustinian Missions in East Africa, 1596–1730." *Research Review* (University of Ghana), 36–37.
1988   *The Swahili Coast, Second to Nineteenth Centuries: Islam, Christianity, and Commerce in East Africa.* London: Variorum.
Frere, Sir Bartle
1873   Correspondence concerning the mission of Sir Bartle Frere (found in the Holy Ghost Archives, Paris: CSSp 196bi, #3).
Fuchs, Rachel Ginnis
1984   *Abandoned Children: Foundlings and Child Welfare in Nineteenth-Century France.* Albany: SUNY Press.
Gallay, Alan
2002   *The Indian Slave Trade: The Rise of the English Empire in the American South, 1670–1717.* New Haven, Conn., and London: Yale University Press.
Gann, L. H., and Peter Duignan, eds.
1969   *The History and Politics of Colonialism 1870–1914.* Vol. 1. Cambridge: Cambridge University Press.
Gaume, Monsignor J.
1870   *Suéma: or the Little African Slave Who Was Buried Alive.* Translated by Mary Elizabeth Herbert. London: Burns, Oates, and Co. Originally published as *Suéma, ou La Petite Esclave Africaine enterée vivante: Histoire contemporaine dediée aux jeunes chrétiennes de l'ancien et du nouveau monde.* Paris.

1872   *Voyage à la Côte Orientale d'Afrique pendant l'Année 1866 par le R. P. Horner.* Paris: Gaume Frères.

Gavin, R. J.
1962   "The Bartle Frere Mission to Zanzibar, 1873." *Historical Journal* 5:2, 122–48.

Gay, Mgr. Jean
1943   *La doctrine missionnaire du Vénérable Père Libermann.* Guadeloupe: Imprimerie Catholique.

Geiger, Roger Lewis
1972   "The Development of French Sociology." Ph.D thesis, University of Michigan.

Geoghegan, Arthur Turbitt
1945   *The Attitude towards Labor in Early Christianity and Ancient Culture.* Washington, D.C.: Catholic University of America Press.

Giblin, James
1992   *The Politics of Environmental Control in Northeastern Tanzania, 1840–1940.* Philadelphia: University of Pennsylvania Press.
1996   *The Precolonial Politics of Disease Control in the Lowlands of Northeastern Tanzania.* In Maddox, Giblin, and Kimambo 1996, 127–51.

Gibson, Henry
1886   "Mission of Zanguebar." *The Month* (London) 58, 197–214 (part one) and 564–80 (part two).

Gibson, Ralph
1989   *A Social History of French Catholicism, 1789–1989.* London and New York: Routledge.

Giddens, Anthony
1979   *Central Problems in Social Theory: Action, Structure, and Contradiction in Social Analysis.* Berkeley and Los Angeles: University of California Press.

Gifford, Prosser, and W. R. Louis, eds.
1967   *Britain and Germany in Africa: Imperial Rivalry and Colonial Rule.* New Haven, Conn., and London: Yale University Press.
1971   *France and Britain in Africa: Imperial Rivalry and Colonial Rule.* New Haven, Conn., and London: Yale University Press.

Giglioni, Mgr. Paolo
2001   "Le réveil missionnaire au XIXe siècle: Charismes et congrégations missionnaires: La contribution de l'Église de France." MS 13, 81–96.

Gilbert, Erik
2004   *Dhows and the Colonial Economy of Zanzibar, 1860–1970.* Oxford: James Currey.

Gildea, Robert
1994   *The Past in French History.* New Haven, Conn., and London: Yale University Press.

Gill, Sam
1998   "Territory." In *Critical Terms for Religious Studies.* Edited by Mark Taylor. Chicago and London: University of Chicago Press, 298–313.

Ginzburg, Carlo
    1999   *History, Rhetoric, and Proof.* Hanover, N.H., and London: University Press of
           New England.

Githige, R. M.
    1986   "The Issue of Slavery: Relations between the CMS (Church Missionary Soci-
           ety) and the State on the East African Coast prior to 1895." *Journal of Religion
           in Africa* 16/3, 209–25.

Gittins, Anthony
    1999a   "Duparquet, Charles." In G. Anderson 1999, 189.
    1999b   "Le Roy, Alexandre." In G. Anderson 1999, 396.

Glassman, Jonathon
    1991   "The Bondsman's New Clothes: The Contradictory Consciousness of Slave
           Resistance on the Swahili Coast." *Journal of African History* 32, 277–312.
    1995   *Feasts and Riot: Revelry, Rebellion, and Popular Consciousness on the Swahili
           Coast, 1856–1888.* Portsmouth, N.H.: Heinemann.
    2004   "Slower Than a Massacre: The Multiple Sources of Racial Thought in Colonial
           Africa." *American Historical Review* 109:3, 720–54.

Godlewska, Anne
    1999   *Geography Unbound: French Geographic Science from Cassini to Humboldt.*
           Chicago: University of Chicago Press.

Goffman, Erving
    1961   *Asylums: Essays on the Social Situation of Mental Patients and Other Inmates.*
           New York: Doubleday.

Goldenberg, David M.
    2003   *The Curse of Ham: Race and Slavery in Early Judaism, Christianity, and Islam.*
           Princeton, N.J.: Princeton University Press.

Good, Charles M., Jr.
    2004   *The Steamer Parish: The Rise and Fall of Missionary Medicine on an African
           Frontier.* Chicago and London: University of Chicago Press.

Gordon, Murray
    1989   *Slavery in the Arab World.* New York: New Amsterdam Books.

Goré, R. P. Henri
    1952   *Un Grand Missionnaire: Mgr Alexandre Le Roy.* Paris: Imprimerie des
           Missions.

Goyau, Georges
    1932   *Missions and Missionaries.* Translated by F. M. Dreeves. London: Sands
           and Co.
    1948   *La France missionnaire dans les cinq parties du monde.* Vol. 2. Paris: Société
           de l'Histoire Nationale.

Gray, John M.
    1958   *Early Portuguese Missionaries in East Africa.* London: Macmillan.
    1962   *History of Zanzibar from the Middle Ages to 1856.* London: Oxford University
           Press.

1963   "Zanzibar and the Coastal Belt, 1840–1884." In Oliver and Mathew 1963, 212–51.

1977   "The Hadimu and Tumbatu of Zanzibar." TNR 81/82, 135–53.

Green, Nicholas

1990   *The Spectacle of Nature: Landscape and Bourgeois Culture in Nineteenth-Century France.* Manchester and New York: Manchester University Press.

Greenblatt, Stephen

1980   *Renaissance Self-Fashioning: More to Shakespeare.* Chicago: University of Chicago Press.

Greven, Philip

1977   *The Protestant Temperament: Patterns of Child-Rearing, Religious Experience, and the Self in Early America.* New York: Alfred A. Knopf.

Grew, Raymond

1997   "Liberty and the Catholic Church in Nineteenth-Century Europe." In Helmstadter 1997, 196–232.

Grew, Raymond, and Patrick J. Harrigan, eds.

1991   *School, State, and Society: The Growth of Elementary Schooling in Nineteenth Century France — A Quantitative Analysis.* Ann Arbor: University of Michigan Press.

Gronemeyer, Marianne

1992   "Helping." *The Development Dictionary.* Edited by Wolfgang Sachs. London and Atlantic Highlands, N.J.: Zed Books, 53–69.

Grove, Richard H.

1995   *Green Imperialism: Colonial Expansion, Tropical Island Edens, and the Origins of Environmentalism.* Cambridge: Cambridge University Press.

Groves, C. P.

1948   *The Planting of Christianity in Africa.* 3 vols. London: Lutterworth Press.

Grzybowski, Laurent

2000   "L'espoir renaît à Bagamoyo." *Pentecôte sur le monde* 793, 12–16.

Guha, Ranajit

1988   "The Prose of Counter-Insurgency." In Guha and Spivak 1988, 45–86.

1997   *Dominance without Hegemony: History and Power in Colonial India.* Cambridge, Mass.: Harvard University Press.

Guha, Ranajit, and Gayatri C. Spivak, eds.

1988   *Selected Subaltern Studies.* New York and Oxford: Oxford University Press.

Guillain, Charles

1856   *Documents sur l'histoire, le géographie, et le commerce de l'Afrique Orientale.* Paris: Bertrand.

Hall, Catherine

2002   *Civilising Subjects: Colony and Metropole in the English Imagination, 1830–1867.* Chicago and London: University of Chicago Press.

Hamilton, Genesta

1957   *Princes of Zinj: The Rulers of Zanzibar.* London: Hutchison.

Handelman, Don

   2002   "Postlude: The Interior Sociality of Self-Transformation." In Shulman and
           Stroumsa 2002a, 236–53.

Harries, Lyndon

   1946   "The Missionary on the East African Coast." *International Review of Missions*
           35, 183–86.

Harries, Patrick

   1993   *Work, Culture, and Identity: Migrant Laborers in Mozambique and South
           Africa, c. 1860–1910.* Portsmouth, N.H.: Heinemann.

Harrigan, Patrick J.

   1973   "French Catholics and Classical Education after the Falloux Law." *French
           Historical Studies* 8:2, 155–278.

   1980   *Mobility, Elites, and Education in French Society of the Second Empire.*
           Waterloo, Ont.: Wilfrid Laurier University Press.

Hassing, P., and Bennett, N. R.

   1962   "A Journey across Tanganyika in 1886." TNR 56, 129–47.

Hastings, Adrian

   1994   *The Church in Africa, 1450–1950.* Oxford: Clarendon Press.

   2000   "African Christian Studies: Reflections of an Editor." *Journal of Religion in
           Africa* 30:1, 30–44.

   2003   "The Clash of Nationalism and Universalism within Twentieth-Century Mis-
           sionary Christianity." In Stanley 2003, 5–33.

Hawley, John C., ed.

   1998   *Historicizing Christian Encounters with the Other.* London: Macmillan Press.

Hazareesingh, Sudhir

   1998   *From Subject to Citizen: The Second Empire and the Emergence of Modern
           French Democracy.* Princeton: Princeton University Press.

Hecht, Jennifer Michael

   2003   *The End of the Soul: Scientific Modernity, Atheism, and Anthropology in
           France.* New York: Columbia University Press.

Hefner, Robert W.

   1990   *The Political Economy of Mountain Java: An Interpretive History.* Berkeley:
           University of California Press.

Hefner, Robert W., ed.

   1993   *Conversion to Christianity: Historical and Anthropological Perspectives on a
           Great Transformation.* Berkeley: University of California Press.

Helmstadter, Richard, ed.

   1997   *Freedom and Religion in the Nineteenth Century.* Stanford, Calif.: Stanford
           University Press.

Henschel, John

   n.d.A   *Bagamoyo in 1884.* Bagamoyo, Tanzania.

   n.d.B   *Documents Tell about Slavery from 1900–1915.* Bagamoyo, Tanzania.

   n.d.C   *Missionaries of Bagamoyo.* Bagamoyo, Tanzania.

n.d.D *Tears of Fear, Tears of Joy: The Story of the Slave Girl Siwema.* Bagamoyo, Tanzania.

2000a *Listen to the Story of the Tombs: Bagamoyo Mission, 1870–1930.* Peramiho, Tanzania.

2000b *The Two Worlds: Bagamoyo and Slavery in the 19th Century.* Bagamoyo: Catholic Museum.

2001 *Bagamoyo: Where Cultures Met: History of the Town.* Peramiho, Tanzania: Peramiho Press.

Herbert, Christopher

1991 *Culture and Anomie: Ethnographic Imagination in the Nineteenth Century.* Chicago and London: University of Chicago Press.

Hickey, Raymond

1997 *Two Thousand Years of African Christianity.* Jos, Nigeria: Augustinian Publications.

Himes, Michael J.

1997 *Ongoing Incarnation: Johann Adam Möhler and the Beginnings of Modern Ecclesiology.* New York: Crossroad Herder.

Hirschman, Albert O.

1970 *Exit, Voice, and Loyalty: Responses to Decline in Firms, Organizations, and States.* Cambridge, Mass.: Harvard University Press.

1977 *The Passions and the Interests.* Princeton, N.J.: Princeton University Press.

Hobsbawm, Eric, and Terence Ranger, eds.

1983 *The Invention of Tradition.* Cambridge: Cambridge University Press.

Hofmyer, Isabel

2004 "Studying Missionaries in a Post-National World." (Review of J. D. Y. Peel's *Religious Encounter of the Making of the Yoruba*). *African Studies* 63:1, 119–29.

Hollingsworth, L. W.

1953 *Zanzibar under the Foreign Office, 1890–1913.* London: Macmillan and Co.

Holt, Thomas

1992 *The Problem of Freedom: Race, Labor, and Politics in Jamaica and Britain, 1832–1938.* Baltimore: Johns Hopkins University Press.

Holy Ghost Fathers

2000 *Siwema.* Video Tumaini. Dar es Salaam.

Hoppe, Kirk

1993 "Whose Life Is It, Anyway? Issues of Representation in Life Narrative Texts of African Women." *International Journal of African Historical Studies* 26:3, 623–36.

Horner, Antoine

1873 "De Bagamoyo à l'Oukami." *Bulletin de la Societé de Geographie*, 125–39.

Horton, Mark, and John Middleton

2000 *The Swahili.* London: Blackwell.

Horton, Robin

1967 "African Traditional Thought and Western Science." *Africa* 37,1–2.

1971   "African Conversion." *Africa* 41,2.

1975   "On the Rationality of Conversion." *Africa* 45, 3–4.

Huber, Mary, and Nancy C. Lutkehaus, eds.

1999   *Gendered Missions: Women and Men in Missionary Discourse and Practice.*
        Ann Arbor: University of Michigan Press.

Idowu, E. Bolaji

1968   "The Predicament of the Church in Africa." In Baëta 1968, 417–40.

Iliffe, John

1969   *Tanganyika under German Rule: 1905–1912.* Cambridge: Cambridge Univer-
        sity Press.

1979   *A Modern History of Tanganyika.* Cambridge: Cambridge University Press.

2005   *Honour in African History.* Cambridge: Cambridge University Press.

Ingrams, W. H.

1967   (1931) *Zanzibar: Its History and Its People.* London: Frank Cass.

Isaacman, Allen F.

1996   *Cotton Is the Mother of Poverty: Peasants, Work, and Rural Struggle in
        Colonial Mozambique, 1938–1961.* Portsmouth, N.H.: Heinemann.

Isaacman, Allen F., and Barbara S. Isaacman

2004   *Slavery and Beyond: The Making of Men and Chikunda Ethnic Identities in
        the Unstable World of South-Central Africa, 1750–1920.* Portsmouth, N.H.:
        Heinemann.

Isichei, Elizabeth

1995   *The History of the Christianity in Africa: From Antiquity to the Present.* Grand
        Rapids: Eerdmans.

2002   *Voices of the Poor in Africa.* Rochester, N.Y.: University of Rochester Press.

Jablonski, M.

1866   "Notes sur la géographie de l'île de Zanzibar." *Bulletin de la Société de
        Géographie* 13, 353–70.

James, William

1902   *The Varieties of Religious Experience.* New York: Longmans Green.

Jay, Martin

2005   *Songs of Experience: Modern American and European Variations on a
        Universal Theme.* Berkeley: University of California Press.

Jedin, Hubert, ed.

1981   *The History of the Church.* 10 vols. New York: Crossroad.

Jennings, Lawrence C.

1988   *French Reactions to British Slave Emancipation.* Baton Rouge and London:
        LSU Press.

2000   *French Anti-Slavery: The Movement for the Abolition of Slavery in France,
        1802–1848.* Cambridge: Cambridge University Press.

Johnson, Frederick, and A. C. Madan

1939   *The Standard Swahili/English Dictionary.* Oxford: Oxford University Press.

Jonas, Robert

2000   *France and the Cult of the Sacred Heart.* Berkeley and London: University of California Press.

Joyce, Patrick, ed.

1987   *The Historical Meanings of Work.* Cambridge: Cambridge University Press.

Kale, Steven

1992   *Legitimism and the Reconstruction of French Society.* Baton Rouge and London: LSU Press.

Kaplan, Steven Laurence, and Cynthia J. Koepp, eds.

1986   *Work in France: Representations, Meanings, Organization, and Practice.* Ithaca, N.Y., and London: Cornell University Press.

Kelly, Bernard J.

1955   *The Spiritual Teaching of Venerable Francis Libermann.* Dublin: Clonmore and Reynolds.

Kieran, John A.

1966   "The Holy Ghost Fathers in East Africa, 1863 to 1914." Ph.D. dissertation. University of London.

1968   "The Origins of the Zanzibar Guarantee Treaty of 1862." *Canadian Journal of African Studies* 2, 147–66.

1969   "Some Roman Catholic Missionary Attitudes to Africans in Nineteenth-Century East Africa." *Race* 10:3, 341–59.

1971   "Christian Villages in North Eastern Tanzania." *Transafrican Journal of History* 1, 24–38.

Kimambo, Isaria N.

1989   "The East African Coast and Hinterland, 1845–1880." In Ajayi 1989, 234–89.

1991   *Penetration and Protest in Tanzania: The Impact of the World Economy on the Pare, 1860–1960.* London: James Currey.

Kippenberg, Hans G., Yure B. Kuiper, and Andy F. Sanders, eds.

1990   *Concepts of Person in Religion and Thought.* Berlin: Mouton de Guyter.

Klein, Martin

1998   *Slavery and Colonial Rule in French West Africa.* Cambridge: Cambridge University Press.

Klein, Martin, ed.

1993   *Breaking the Chains: Slavery, Bondage, and Emancipation in Modern Africa and Asia.* Madison: University of Wisconsin Press.

Kollman, Paul V.

1996   "The Roots and Consequences of the Terms *Missio* and Missiology: Studies in Religious Discursive Change." University of Chicago Divinity School.

2001   "Making Catholics: Slave Evangelization and the Origins of the Catholic Church in Nineteenth-Century East Africa." Ph.D. dissertation, University of Chicago Divinity School. Ann Arbor: University of Michigan Dissertation Services.

2004a   "Early Catholic Lay Ministry in Eastern Africa." In *Christianity and Native Cultures: Perspectives from Different Regions of the World*, edited by Cyriac K. Pullapilly et al. South Bend, Ind.: Cross Cultural Publications, 112–32.

2004b   "After Church History? Writing the History of Christianity from a Global Perspective." *Horizons* 31/32, 322–42.

Komonchak, Joseph
1997   "Modernity and the Construction of Roman Catholicism." *Cristianesimo nella storia*, 18, 353–85.

Koponen, Juhani
1994   *Development for Exploitation: German Colonial Policies in Mainland Tanzania, 1884–1914.* Helsinki: Raamatutalo.

Kopytoff, Igor
1979   "Commentary One." In Craton 1979, 62–77.

Kopytoff, Igor, ed.
1987   *The African Frontier: The Reproduction of Traditional African Societies.* Bloomington: Indiana University Press.

Kopytoff, Igor, and Suzanne Miers
1977   "African Slavery as an Institution of Marginality." In Miers and Kopytoff 1977, 3–81.

Koren, Henry J.
1958   *The Spiritans: A History of the Congregation of the Holy Ghost.* Pittsburgh, Pa.: Duquesne University Press.

1983   *To the Ends of the Earth: A General History of the Congregation of the Holy Ghost.* Pittsburgh, Pa.: Duquesne University Press.

1990   *Essays on the Spiritan Charism and on Spiritan History.* Bethel Park, Pa.: Spiritus Press.

1992   "The Evolution of the Church in Africa since the Beginning of the Nineteenth Century." Unpublished manuscript.

1994   *Spiritan East Africa Memorial, 1863–1993.* Bethel Park, Pa.: Spiritus Press.

1995   "Cardinal Lavigerie and Spiritan Missions in the Heart of Africa." *Inter Nos Forum.* Internal publication, Congregation of the Holy Ghost, USA East Province.

1997   *Spiritan West Africa Memorial for Gambia, Sierra Leone, Liberia, and Ghana: 1842–1996.* Bethel Park, Pa.: Spiritus Press.

Koren, Henry, and Henri Littner
1998   "Le cardinal Lavigerie et les missions spiritaines au coeur de l'Afrique." MS 8, 30–49.

Krapf, J. L.
1882   *A Dictionary of the Suaheli Language.* London.

Krikler, Jeremy
1993   *Revolution from Above, Rebellion from Below: The Agrarian Transvaal at the Turn of the Century.* Oxford: Clarendon Press.

Laburthe-Tolra, Philippe
2000   "L'ethnologue Alexandre Le Roy (1854–1938)." MS 12, 62–71.

La Fontaine, J. S.

1985 "Person and Individual: Some Anthropological Reflections." In Carrithers et al. 1985, 123–40.

Lambek, Michael

2000 "The Anthropology of Religion and the Quarrel between Poetry and Philosophy." *Current Anthropology* 41:3, 309–20.

Landau, Paul Stuart

1995 *The Realm of the Word: Language, Gender, and Christianity in a Southern African Kingdom.* London: James Currey.

Lange, Claude

1992 "La formation des missionnaires dans la Société des Missions Etrangères: son evolution, des origines au XXe siècle." In Spindler and Gadille 1992, 341–52.

Langer, Erick D.

1998 Preface. In Hawley 1998, ix–xi.

Larson, Pier M.

1997 " 'Capacities and Modes of Thinking': Intellectual Engagements and Subaltern Hegemony in the Early History of Malagasy Christianity." *Journal of American History* 102:4, 969–1002.

2000 *History and Memory in the Age of Enslavement: Becoming Merina in Highland Madagascar, 1770–1822.* Social History of Africa. Portsmouth, N.H., and Oxford: Heinemann and James Currey.

Latham, H.

1869 "The *Maison Paternelle* at Mettray." *Macmillan's Magazine* 21, 44–50.

Launay, Marcel

1988 *L'Église et l'École en France, XIXe–XXe siècles.* Paris: Desclée.

Lebovics, Herman

1988 *The Alliance of Iron and Wheat in the Third French Republic, 1860–1914.* Baton Rouge and London: LSU Press.

1992 *True France: The Wars over Cultural Identity.* Ithaca, N.Y., and London: Cornell University Press.

Legrain, Michel

2000 "Le Saint-Esprit et le Saint Cœur de Marie après l'union: une fidélité mal comprise." MS 12, 34–55.

Lema, Anza A.

1980 *The Influence of Christian Mission Societies on Education Policies in Tanganyika, 1868–1970.* Hong Kong: Minda Printing.

Le Roy, Alexandre

1884 *A Travers le Zanguebar.* Paris: Congrégation du St.-Esprit.

1888 "Ambimoyo, ou histoire d'un jeune esclave, raconté par lui-même." *Almanach des missions.* Lyon and Paris: Delhomme et Briguet.

1893 *Au Kilima-ndjaro (Afrique Orientale).* Paris: L. de Soye.

1894 *Sur terre et sur l'eau: Voyage d'exploration dans l'Afrique orientale.* Tours: A. Mame.

1899a   *D'Aden à Zanzibar: Un coin de l'Arabie heureuse le long des côtes.* Tours:
         A. Mame.

1899b   "Les maisons de formation." Internal letter. Paris: Congrégation du St.-Esprit
         (CSSp 2C1.2A, new system).

1906a   *L'action sociale des missions catholiques.* Lyon: Publications de la Société
         d'Etudes Historiques et Littéraires.

1906b   "Le rôle scientifique des missionnaires." *Anthropos* 1 (reprinted in MS 12
         [2000], 72–80).

1909   *La religion des primitifs.* Paris: Beauchesne.

1911   *The Evangelization of Africa, 1822–1911.* New York: Society for the Propa-
         gation of the Faith.

1921   *La Congrégation du Saint-Esprit et du Saint Coeur de Marie.* Paris.

1934a   "Le cinquantenaire du vicariat apostolique de Zanguebar." *Revue d'Histoire
         des Missions* XI, 1–4.

1934b   "Mes Souvenirs." Holy Ghost archives, CSSp 56A.

Levtzion, Nehemia

1985   "Slavery and Islamization in Africa." In Willis 1985, 1:182–98.

Levtzion, Nehemia, and Randall L. Pouwels, eds.

2000a   *The History of Islam in Africa.* Athens: Ohio University Press.

2000b   Introduction. In Levtzion and Pouwels 2000a, 1–18.

Libermann, François-Marie-Paul

n.d.   *Lettres spirituelles de Notre Vénérable Père.* Paris: Procure Général de la
         Congrègation.

1874   *Lettres spirituelles du R. P. Libermann.* Paris: Librairie Poussielgue Frères.

Liebowitz, Daniel

1999   *The Physician and the Slave Trade: John Kirk, the Livingstone Expeditions,
         and the Crusade against Slavery in East Africa.* New York: W. H. Freeman
         and Company.

Lienhardt, Godfrey

1961   *Divinity and Experience: The Religion of the Dinka.* Oxford: Oxford University
         Press.

1985   "Self: Public, Private. Some African Representations." In Carrithers, Collins,
         and Lukes 1985, 141–55.

Lincoln, Bruce

1989   *Discourse and the Construction of Society.* New York and London: Oxford
         University Press.

2000   "Culture." In *Guide to the Study of Religion.* Edited by Willi Braun and
         Russell T. McCutcheon. London and New York: Cassell, 409–22.

Locke, Robert R.

1974   *French Legitimists and the Politics of Moral Order in the Early Third Republic.*
         Princeton, N.J.: Princeton University Press.

Lodhi, Abdulaziz Y.

1973   *The Institution of Slavery in Zanzibar and Pemba.* Uppsala: Scandinavian
         Institute of African Studies.

1984   "A Short History of the Arab Period in Zanzibar from the Sultanate to the People's Republic." Unpublished manuscript, Northwestern University library.

Lonsdale, John

1985   "The European Scramble and Conquest in African History." In Oliver and Sanderson 1985, 680–766.

Lopez, Donald

1999   "Belief." In *Critical Terms for Religious Studies.* Edited by Mark Taylor. Chicago and London: University of Chicago Press, 21–35.

Lovejoy, Paul E., ed.

1981a   *The Ideology of Slavery in Africa.* Beverly Hills, Calif.: Sage Publications.

Lovejoy, Paul E.

1979   "Indigenous African Slavery." In Craton 1979, 19–61.

1981b   "Slavery in the Context of Ideology." In Lovejoy 1981a, 1ff.

1988   *Transformations in Slavery: A History of Slavery in Africa.* Cambridge: Cambridge University Press.

Luig, Ute, and Achim von Oppen

1997   "Landscape in Africa: Process and Vision: An Introductory Essay." *Paideuma* 43, 7–45.

Lukes, Steven

1985   "Conclusion." In Carrithers, Collins, and Lukes 1985, 282–301.

Luria, Keith P.

1996   "The Politics of Protestant Conversion to Catholicism in Seventeenth-Century France." In van der Veer 1996, 23–46.

Lutzbetak, Louis

1988   *The Church and Cultures.* Maryknoll, N.Y.: Orbis Books.

Lyne, Robert Nunez

1936   *An Apostle of Empire: Being the Life of Sir Lloyd William Mathews, K.C.M.G.* London: George Allen & Unwin.

1969   (1905) *Zanzibar in Contemporary Times.* New York: Negro Universities Press.

Mackay, A. M.

1889   "Muscat, Zanzibar, and Central Africa." *CMS Intelligencer*, January, 19–24.

Mackenzie, Donald

1895   "Report on Slavery and the Slave-Trade in Zanzibar, Pemba, and the Mainland of the British Protectorates of East Africa." *Anti-Slavery Reporter* (June–August), 69–96.

MacPherson, C. B.

1962   *The Political Theory of Possessive Individualism: Hobbes to Locke.* Oxford: Oxford University Press.

Madan, A. C.

1886   *Kiungani, or Story and History from Central Africa.* Zanzibar.

Maddox, Gregory, James Giblin, and Isaria N. Kimambo, eds.

1996   *Custodians of the Land: Ecology and Culture in the History of Tanzania.* London: James Currey.

Bibliography

Manning, Patrick
   1990   *Slavery and African Life: Occidental, Oriental, and African Slave Trades.*
          Cambridge: Cambridge University Press.
Mansbridge, Jane
   2001a "The Making of Oppositional Consciousness." In Mansbridge and Morris
          2001, 1–19.
   2001b "Complicating Oppositional Consciousness." In Mansbridge and Morris 2001,
          238–64.
Mansbridge, Jane, and Aldon Morris, eds.
   2001   *Oppositional Consciousness: The Subjective Roots of Social Protest.* Chicago
          and London: University of Chicago Press.
Marglin, Frédérique Apffel, and Stephen A. Marglin, eds.
   1990   *Dominating Knowledge: Development, Culture, and Resistance.* Oxford: Clar-
          endon Press.
Marglin, Stephen A.
   1990   "Towards the Decolonization of the Mind." In Marglin and Marglin 1990,
          1–28.
Martin, B. G.
   1976   *Muslim Brotherhoods in Nineteenth-Century Africa.* Cambridge: Cambridge
          University Press.
Maupeou, Henri de
   1932   "Le R. P. Horner et la fondation de la mission du Zanguebar." *Revue d'Histoire
          des Missions* 9, 506–33.
Maurier, Henri
   2000   "L'enseignement de Mgr Le Roy et l'Historie des Religions à l'Institut
          Catholique de Paris (1907–1908)." MS 12, 81–87.
Maxwell, David
   1997   "New Perspectives on the History of African Christianity." *Journal of Southern
          African Studies* 23:1, 141–48.
Maxwell, John Francis
   1975   *Slavery and the Catholic Church.* London: Anti-Slavery Society.
Mazrui, Alamin M., and Ibrahim Noor Shariff
   1994   *The Swahili: Idiom and Identity of an African People.* Trenton, N.J.: Africa
          World Press.
McCaskie, T. C.
   2004   "Cultural Encounters: Britain and Africa in the Nineteenth Century." In *Black
          Experience and the Empire*, ed. Philip D. Morgan and Sean Hawkins. Oxford:
          Oxford University Press, 166–93.
McCool, Gerald
   1977   *Catholic Theology in the Nineteenth Century: The Quest for a Unitary Method.*
          New York: Seabury.
McGreevy, John T.
   2003   *Catholicism and American Freedom: A History.* New York: Norton.

McIntyre, Thomas

    1997   "Changing Religious Establishments and Religious Liberty in France." In Helmstadter 1997, 233–72 (part one), 273–302 (part two).

McManners, John

    1972   *Church and State in France, 1870–1914.* New York: Harper and Row.

Meilaender, Gilbert C., ed.

    2000   *Working: Its Meaning and Its Limits.* Notre Dame, Ind.: University of Notre Dame Press.

Meillassoux, Claude

    1991   (1986) *The Anthropology of Slavery: The Womb of Iron and Gold.* Chicago and London: University of Chicago Press.

Meritt, H. P.

    1978   "Bismarck and the German Interest in East Africa, 1884–1885." *Historical Journal* 21, 97–116.

Meyer, Philippe

    1983   (1979) *The Child and the State: The Intervention of the State in Family Life.* Cambridge: Cambridge University Press.

Middleton, John

    1992   *The World of the Swahili.* New Haven, Conn., and London: Yale University Press.

Middleton, John, and Jane Campbell

    1965   *Zanzibar: Its Society and Its Politics,* London: Oxford University Press.

Miers, Suzanne, and Igor Kopytoff, eds.

    1977   *Slavery in Africa.* Madison and London: University of Wisconsin Press.

Miers, Suzanne, and Richard Roberts, eds.

    1988   *The End of Slavery in Africa.* Madison: University of Wisconsin Press.

Miller, Christopher

    1994   "Unfinished Business: Colonialism in Sub-Saharan Africa and the Ideals of the French Revolution." In *The Global Ramifications of the French Revolution.* Edited by Joseph Klaits and Michael H. Haltzel. Cambridge, Mass.: Woodrow Wilson Center Press, 105–26.

Miller, Joseph

    1998   "Freedom." In Finkelman and Miller 1998, 344–47.

    1999a   "Presidential Address: History and Africa/Africa and History." *American Historical Review* 104:1, 1–32.

    1999b   *Slavery and Slaving in World History: A Bibliography.* 2 vols. Armonk, N.Y., and London: M. E. Sharpe.

    2003   "Retention, Reinvention, and Remembering: Restoring Identities through Enslavement in Africa and under Slavery in Brazil." In Curto and Lovejoy 2003, 81–121.

Miller, Richard Roscoe

    1957   *Slavery and Catholicism.* Durham, N.C.: North State Publishers.

Mills, Kenneth, and Anthony Grafton, eds.
  2003   *Conversion: Old Worlds and New.* Rochester, N.Y.: University of Rochester Press.

Mitchell, Allan
  1984   *Victors and Vanquished: The German Influence on Army and Church in France after 1870.* Chapel Hill and London: University of North Carolina Press.

Mitchell, Timothy
  1988   *Colonising Egypt.* Cambridge: Cambridge University Press.

Morrison, Karl Frederick
  1992a   *Conversion and Text: The Cases of Augustine of Hippo, Herman-Judah, and Constantine Tsatsos.* Charlottesville: University Press of Virginia.
  1992b   *Understanding Conversion.* Charlottesville: University Press of Virginia.

Morton, Fred
  1990   *Children of Ham: Freed Slaves and Fugitive Slaves on the Kenya Coast, 1873 to 1907.* Boulder, Colo.: Westview Press.
  1998   "East Africa: Swahili Region." In Finkelman and Miller 1998, 1:265–66.

Motylewski, Patricia
  1998   *La Société française pour l'abolition de l'esclavage, 1834–1850.* Paris: L'Harmattan.

Moulinet, Daniel
  1998   "Mgr Gaume, l'œuvre apostolique et le rachat des esclaves." MS 7, 108–26.

Mudimbe, V. Y.
  1988   *The Invention of Africa.* London: James Currey Press.
  1994   *The Idea of Africa.* London: James Currey Press.

Murphy, Agnes
  1948   *The Ideology of French Imperialism, 1871–1881.* Washington, D.C: Catholic University Press.

Mutoro, Henry
  1998   "Precolonial Trading Systems of the East African Interior." In Connah 1998, 186–203.

Mwanzi, H. A.
  1985   "African Initiatives and Resistance in East Africa, 1880–1914." In Boahen 1985, 149–68.

Needham, Rodney
  1972   *Belief, Language, and Experience.* Oxford: Blackwell.

Neill, Stephen
  1966   *Colonialism and Christian Missions.* New York: McGraw-Hill.
  1986   (1964) *The History of Christian Missions.* New York: Penguin Books.

Neumann, Roderick P.
  1998   *Imposing Wilderness: Struggles over Livelihood and Nature Preservation in Africa.* Berkeley: University of California Press.

Newitt, Malyn, ed.
  2002   *East Africa.* Aldershot: Ashgate Publishing.

Newman, Henry Stanley
  1898   *Banani: The Transition from Slavery to Freedom in Zanzibar and Pemba.* New York: Negro Universities Press.
Nicholls, C. S.
  1971   *The Swahili Coast: Politics, Diplomacy, and Trade on the East African Littoral, 1798–1856.* London: Allen and Unwin.
Nicolini, Beatrice
  2002   *Il sultanato di Zanzibar nel XIX secolo: Traffici commerciale, relazioni internationale.* Turin: L'Harmattan Italia.
Nieboer, H. J.
  1910   *Slavery as an Industrial System.* The Hague: Martinus Nijhoff.
Niederveen, Jan
  1992   *White on Black: Images of Africa and Blacks in Western Popular Culture.* New Haven, Conn., and London: Yale University Press.
Nimtz, A.
  1980   *Islam and Politics in East Africa: The Sufi Order in Tanzania.* Minneapolis: University of Minnesota Press.
Njoroge, Lawrence
  1999   *A Century of Catholic Endeavour: Holy Ghost and Consolata Missions in Kenya.* Nairobi: Paulines Publications.
Nock, A. D.
  1933   *Conversion.* New York: Oxford University Press.
Noël, Bernard
  1988   "Aloÿs Kobès." In Coulon and Brasseur 1988, 649–57.
Noonan, John T.
  1995   "Development in Moral Doctrine." In *The Context of Casuistry.* Edited by James F. Keenan and Thomas A. Shannon. Washington, D.C.: Georgetown University Press, 188–204.
  2005   *A Church That Can and Cannot Change: The Development of Catholic Moral Teaching.* Notre Dame, Ind.: University of Notre Dame Press.
Norton, Anne
  2004   *95 Theses on Politics, Culture, and Method.* New Haven, Conn., and London: Yale University Press.
Nwulia, Moses D. E.
  1975   "The Role of Missionaries in the Emancipation of Slaves in Zanzibar." *Journal of Negro History* 60:2, 268–87.
  1981   *The History of Slavery in Mauritius and the Seychelles, 1810–1875.* London: Associated University Presses.
Nyaki, Casimir
  n.d.   *Guide to the Historical Museum of Bagamoyo Catholic Mission.* Bagamoyo, Tanzania.
O'Donnell, Guillermo
  1986   "On the Fruitful Convergences of Hirschman's *Exit, Voice, and Loyalty,* and *Shifting Involvements*: Reflections from the Recent Argentine Experience."

Working Paper 58. Notre Dame, Ind.: Kellogg Institute for International Studies.

O'Donohue, James A.

1957   *Tridentine Seminary Legislation: Its Sources and Its Formation.* Louvain: Publications Universitaires de Louvain.

Ofcansky, Thomas, and Rodger Yeager

1997   *Historical Dictionary of Tanzania.* Lanham, Md., and London: Scarecrow Press.

O'Hare, Jacqueline

1969   "The Christian Response: The Work of the Church Missionary Society at Freretown and Congregation of the Holy Ghost at Bagamoyo for the Slaves of East Africa, 1868–1904." Unpublished manuscript.

Okihiro, Gary, ed.

1986   *In Resistance: Studies in African, Caribbean, and Afro-American History.* Amherst: University of Massachusetts Press.

Oliver, Roland

1952   *The Missionary Factor in East Africa.* London: Longmans.

1991   *The African Experience.* New York: Icon Editions.

Oliver, Roland, and Gervase Mathew, eds.

1963   *History of East Africa*, vol. 1. Oxford: Clarendon Press.

Oliver, Roland, and G. N. Sanderson, eds.

1985   *The Cambridge History of Africa, from 1870 to 1905*, vol. 6. Cambridge: Cambridge University Press.

Ollendoroff, R.

1945   "Bagamoyo, 1883–1945." TNR 20, 62–63.

Olsen, Margaret M.

2004   *Slavery and Salvation in Colonial Cartagena de Indias.* Gainesville: University Press of Florida.

O'Meara, Thomas F.

1997   "Beyond 'Hierarchology': Johann Adam Möhler and Yves Congar." In Dietrich and Himes 1997, 173–91.

Omoka, Wanakayi K.

1979   "Strategies and Tactics of Inauguration of African Underdevelopment: The Case of Christian Missionization Violence in East Africa." *Ufahamu* 9:3, 43–64.

Osborne, Michael

1994   *Nature, the Exotic, and the Science of French Colonialism.* Bloomington and Indianapolis: Indiana University Press.

Owtram, Francis

2004   *A Modern History of Oman: Formation of the State since 1920.* London: I. B. Tauris.

Pandey, Gyanendra

2000   "Voices from the Edge: The Struggle to Write Subaltern Histories." In *Mapping Subaltern Studies and the Postcolonial*, ed. Vinayak Chaturvedi. London and New York: Verso, 281–99.

Panikkar, K. M.
1959   (1953) *Asia and Western Dominance.* London: Allen and Unwin.
Panzer, Joel
1996   *The Popes and Slavery.* New York: Alba House.
Papayanis, Nicholas
2004   *Planning Paris before Haussmann.* Baltimore: Johns Hopkins Press.
Pardo, Osvaldo F.
2004   *The Origins of Mexican Catholicism: Nahua Rituals and Christian Sacraments
        in Sixteenth-Century Mexico.* Ann Arbor: University of Michigan Press.
Patterson, Orlando
1982   *Slavery and Social Death.* Cambridge and London: Harvard University Press.
Pearson, Michael N.
1998   *Port Cities and Intruders: The Swahili Coast, India, and Portugal in the Early
        Modern Era.* Baltimore and London: Johns Hopkins University Press.
2000   "The Indian Ocean and the Red Sea." In Levtzion and Pouwels 2000a, 37–59.
Peel, J. D. Y.
1995   "For Who Hath Despised the Day of Small Things? Missionary Narratives
        and Historical Anthropology." *Comparative Studies in Society and History* 37,
        581–607.
1996   "Problems and Opportunities in an Anthropologist's Use of a Missionary
        Archive." In Bickers and Seton 1996, 70–94.
2000   *Religious Encounter and the Making of the Yoruba.* Bloomington: Indiana
        University Press.
Pels, Peter
1997   "The Anthropology of Colonialism: Culture, History, and the Emergence of
        Western Governmentality." *Annual Review of Anthropology* 26, 163–83.
1999   *A Politics of Presence: Contacts between Missionaries and Waluguru in Late
        Colonial Tanganyika.* Amsterdam: Harwood Academic Publishers.
Pels, Peter, and Oscar Salemink
1999   *Colonial Subjects: Essays on the Practical History of Anthropology.* Ann
        Arbor: University of Michigan Press.
Penn Monthly
1881   "Colonie agricole de Mettray." Vol. 12, 478–80.
Perrot, Michelle, ed.
1990   *A History of Private Life.* Vol. 4, *From the Fires of Revolution to the Great
        War.* Cambridge and London: Harvard University Press.
Petersen, Derek, and Jean Allman
1999   "Introduction: New Directions in the History of Missions in Africa." *Journal
        of Religious History in Africa* 23:1, 1–7.
Petit, Jacques-Guy
1990   *Ces peines obscures: La prison penale en France, 1780–1875.* Paris: Fayard.
Pétré-Grenouilleau, Olivier, ed.
2004a   *From Slave Trade to Empire: Europe and the Colonisation of Black Africa,
        1780s–1880s.* New York: Routledge.

Pétré-Grenouilleau, Olivier
   2004b   "Cultural Systems of Representation, Economic Interests, and French Penetration into Black Africa." In Pétré-Grenouilleau 2004a, 157–84.
Pettifer, Julian, and Richard Bradley
   1990   *Missionaries*. London: BBC Books.
Pierrard, Pierre
   1986a   *Histoire des curés de campagne de 1789 à nos jours*. Paris: Plon.
   1986b   *Du prêtre français au XIXe siècle, 1801–1905*. Paris: Plon.
   1988   *L'Église et la revolution*. Paris: Nouvelle Cité.
Pieterse, Jan Nederveen, and Bhikhu Parekh, eds.
   1995   *The Decolonization of the Imagination: Culture, Knowledge and Power.* London: Zed Books.
Pitt, Alan
   1998   "Frèdèric Le Play and the Family: Paternalism and Freedom in the French Debates of the 1870s." *French History* 12:1, 67–89.
Plongeron, Bernard
   1995   *Des socialistes chrétiens avant l'âge du christianisme sociale*. In Plongeron and Guillaume 1995, 109–13.
Plongeron, Bernard, and Pierre Guillaume, eds.
   1995   *De la charité à l'action sociale: Religion et société*. Paris: Editions du CTHS.
Poinsatte, Charles, and Anne Marie Poinsatte
   1984   "Augustin Cochin's *L'Abolition de l'esclavage* and the Emancipation Proclamation." *Review of Politics* 46:3, 410–27.
Poole, Stafford
   1965   *Seminary in Crisis*. New York: Herder and Herder.
Poovey, Mary
   1995   *Making a Social Body: British Cultural Formation, 1830–1864*. Chicago and London: University of Chicago Press.
Porter, Andrew, ed.
   2003a   *The Imperial Horizons of British Protestant Missions, 1880–1914*. Grand Rapids: Eerdmans.
Porter, Andrew
   2003b   "The Universities' Mission to Central Africa: Anglo-Catholicism and the Twentieth-Century Colonial Encounter." In B. Stanley 2003, 79–107.
Pouwels, Randall L.
   2000   "The East African Coast, c. 780 to 1900 C.E." In Levtzion and Pouwels 2000a, 251–71.
Prakash, Gyan, ed.
   1995   *After Colonialism: Imperial Histories and Postcolonial Displacements*. Princeton, N.J.: Princeton University Press.
Pratt, Mary Louise
   1992   *Imperial Eyes: Travel Writing and Transculturation*. London: Routledge.

Prestholdt, Jeremy
  2004   "On the Global Repercussions of East African Consumerism." *American Historical Review* 109:3, 755–81.
Procacci, Giovanna
  1994   "Governing Poverty: Sources of the Social Question in Nineteenth-Century France." In *Foucault and the Writing of History.* Edited by Jan Goldstein. Oxford: Blackwell, 206–19.
Prudhomme, Claude
  1984   "L'île de la Réunion et le réveil missionnaire au début du XIXe siècle." In *Actes du Colloque de Lyon* 1984, 235–47.
  1994   *Stratégie missionnaire du Saint-Siège sous Léon XIII (1878–1903).* Rome: École Française de Rome.
  1996   "Aux sources du réveil missionnaire catholique du XIXe siècle: France, pays de missionnaires." In Cholvy 1996, 7–21.
  1999a   "La papauté facc à l'esclavage: Quelle condamnation?" MS 9, 135–60.
  1999b   "L'église catholique et l'esclavage: Une aussi longue attente." In Bedouelle et al., eds. 1999, 9–20.
Quarterly Review
  1856   "Reformatory Schools." 99:195, 32–65.
Rabinow, Paul
  1989   *French Modern: Norms and Forms of the Social Environment.* Chicago and London: University of Chicago Press.
Rafael, Vicente L.
  1988   *Contracting Colonialism: Translation and Christian Conversion in Tagalog Society under Early Spanish Rule.* Ithaca, N.Y., and London: Cornell University Press.
Rahner, Karl
  1979   "Towards a Fundamental Theological Interpretation of Vatican II." *Theological Studies* 40, 716–27.
Rambo, Lewis R.
  1993   *Understanding Religious Conversion.* New Haven, Conn., and London: Yale University Press.
Ramsland, John
  1989   "*La maison paternelle*: 'A College of Repression' for Wayward Bourgeois Adolescents in Nineteenth and Early Twentieth Century France." *History of Education* 18:1, 47–55.
  1990   "Mettray: A Corrective Institution for Delinquent Youth in France, 1840–1937." *Journal of Educational Administration and History* 22:1, 30–46.
Randall, Adrian, and Andrew Charlesworth, eds.
  2000   *Moral Economy and Popular Protest.* London: Macmillan Press.
Ranger, T. O.
  1978   "Growing from the Roots: Reflections on Peasant Research in Central and Southern Africa." *Journal of Southern African Studies* 5:1, 99–133.

1985   "African Initiatives and Resistance in the Face of Partition and Conquest." In Boahen 1985, 45–63.

1986   "Resistance in Africa: From Nationalist Revolt to Agrarian Protest." In Okihiro 1986, 32–52.

1987   "Taking Hold of the Land: Holy Places and Pilgrimages in Twentieth-Century Zimbabwe." *Past and Present* 117, 158–94.

1999   *Voices from the Rocks: Nature, Culture, and History in the Matopo Hills of Zimbabwe.* Oxford: James Currey.

Ranger, T. O., and I. N. Kimambo, eds.

1972   *The Historical Study of African Religions.* Berkeley: University of California Press.

Rappaport, Roy A.

1999   *Ritual and Religion in the Making of Humanity.* Cambridge: Cambridge University Press.

Rea, William Francis

1976   *The Economics of the Zambezi Mission: 1580–1759.* Rome: Institutum Historicum S.I.

Reed, Colin

1997   *Pastors, Partners, and Pastoralists: African Church Leaders and Western Missionaries in the Anglican Church in Kenya, 1850–1900.* Leiden: Brill.

Reid, Anthony, ed.

1983a   *Slavery, Bondage, and Dependency in Southeast Asia.* New York: St. Martin's Press.

Reid, Anthony

1983b   "Introduction: Slavery and Bondage in Southeast Asian History." In Reid 1983a, 1–43.

Renault, François

1989   "The Structures of the Slave Trade in Central Africa in the 19th Century." In Clarence-Smith 1989a, 146–65.

1994   *Cardinal Lavigerie: Churchman, Prophet, and Missionary.* Atlantic Highlands, N.J.: Athlone Press.

1995   "Aux origines de la lettre apostolique de Grégoire XVI, *In Supremo* (1839)." MS 2, 143–49.

Rhodes, Lorna A.

2001   Toward an Anthropology of Prisons. *Annual Review of Anthropology* 30, 65–83.

Ricklin, L. A.

1880   *La Mission Catholique du Zanguebar: Travaux et voyages du R. P. Horner.* Paris: Gaume.

Ricoeur, Paul

1984   *Time and Narrative.* Vol. 1. Chicago and London: University of Chicago Press.

1992   *Oneself as Another.* Chicago and London: University of Chicago Press.

Risso, Patricia

1986   *Oman and Muscat: An Early Modern History.* New York: St. Martin's Press.

1995   *Merchants and Faith: Muslim Commerce and Culture in the Indian Ocean.* Boulder, Colo.: Westview Press.

Roberts, Richard

1996   *Two Worlds of Cotton: Colonialism and the Regional Economy in the French Soudan, 1800–1946.* Stanford, Calif.: Stanford University Press.

Roberts, Richard, and Suzanne Miers

1988   "Introduction." In Miers and Roberts 1988, 3–68.

Robertson, Claire, and Martin Klein, eds.

1983   *Women and Slavery in Africa.* Madison: University of Wisconsin Press.

Robinson, Ronald, and John Gallagher, with Alice Denny

1961   *Africa and the Victorians.* London: St. Martin's Press.

Rochmann, Marie-Christine, ed.

2000   *Esclavage et abolitions: Mémoires et systèmes de représentation.* Paris: Karthala.

Rockel, Stephen J.

1995   "Wage Labor and the Culture of Porterage in Nineteenth-Century Tanzania." *Comparative Studies of South Asia, the Middle East, and Africa* 15:2, 14–24.

2000   " 'A Nation of Porters': The Nyamwezi and the Labour Market in Nineteenth-Century Tanzania." *Journal of African History* 41:2, 173–95.

Rodriguez, Junius P., ed.

1997   *The Historical Encyclopedia of World Slavery.*, 2 vols. Santa Barbara, Denver, and Oxford: ABC-CLIO.

Ross, Andrew C.

2003   "Christian Missions and the Mid-Nineteenth-Century Change in Attitudes to Race: The African Experience." In Porter 2003a, 85–105.

Ross, Robert

1997   "The *Kulturkampf:* Restrictions and Controls on the Practice of Religion in Bismarck's Germany." In Helmstadter 1997, 172–95.

Rotberg, Robert

1964   *Christian Missionaries and the Creation of Northern Rhodesia, 1880–1924.* Princeton, N.J.: Princeton University Press.

Ruiz de Montoya, Antonio

1993   (1639) *The Spiritual Conquest Accomplished by the Religious of the Society of Jesus.* St. Louis: Institute of Jesuit Sources.

Russell, Mrs. Charles

1935   *General Rigby, Zanzibar and the Slave Trade.* London: George Allen & Unwin.

Rweyemamu, S., and T. Msambure

1989   *The Catholic Church in Tanzania.* Peramiho, Tanzania: Benedictine Publications.

Ryan, Alan

1979   *The Idea of Freedom: Essays in Honour of Isaiah Berlin.* Oxford: Oxford University Press.

Sacleux, Charles

1939–41 *Dictionnaire Swahili-Français.* Paris.

Sahlberg, Carl-Erik
  1986   *From Krapf to Rugambwa — A Church History of Tanzania.* Nairobi: Evangel
          Publishing House.
Sahlins, Marshall
  1968   *Tribesmen.* Englewood Cliffs, N.J.: Prentice-Hall.
  1985   *Islands of History.* Chicago: University of Chicago Press.
Said, Edward
  1993   *Culture and Imperialism.* New York: Random House.
Sangu, Askofu (Bishop) James D.
  1979   *Wamisionari wa Tanzania: majibu kwa shutumu mbalimbali zitolewazo juu
          yawamisionari* (Missionaries of Tanzania: answers to various reproaches
          leveled against missionaries). Tabora, Tanzania: TMP Book Department.
Sanneh, Lamin
  1989   *Translating the Message: The Missionary Impact on Culture.* Maryknoll, N.Y.:
          Orbis Books.
  1997   " 'A Plantation of Religion' and the Enterprise Culture of Africa: History,
          Ex-Slaves and Religious Inevitability." *Journal of Religion in Africa* 27:1,
          15–49.
  2003   *Whose Religion Is Christianity? The Gospel beyond the West.* Grand Rapids:
          Eerdmans.
Scarr, Deryck
  1998   *Slaving and Slavery in the Indian Ocean.* London: Macmillan.
Schafer, Sylvia
  1997   *Children in Moral Danger and the Problem of Government in Third Republic
          France.* Princeton, N.J.: Princeton University Press.
Schama, Simon
  1995   *Landscape and Memory.* New York: Knopf.
Schmidlin, Joseph
  1931   *Catholic Mission Theory.* Techny, Ill.: Mission Press.
Schmidt, Nelly
  2000   *Abolitionnistes de l'esclavage et réformateurs des colonies, 1820–1851:
          Analyse et documents.* Paris: Karthala.
Schoffeleers, Matthew
  1992   *Rivers of Blood: The Genesis of a Martyr Cult in Southern Malawi, c. A.D. 1600.*
          Madison: University of Wisconsin Press.
Schreiter, Robert
  1985   *Constructing Local Theologies.* Maryknoll, N.Y.: Orbis Books.
Schwartz, Stuart B., ed.
  1994   *Implicit Understandings: Observing, Reporting, and Reflecting on the En-
          counters between Europeans and Other Peoples in the Early Modern Era.*
          Cambridge: Cambridge University Press.
Scott, James
  1990   *Domination and the Arts of Resistance: Hidden Transcripts.* New Haven,
          Conn., and London: Yale University Press.

1998   *Seeing Like a State: How Certain Schemes to Improve the Human Condition Have Failed.* New Haven, Conn., and London: Yale University Press.

Scott, Joan

1991   "The Evidence of Experience." *Critical Inquiry* 17, 773–97.

Scott, William Henry

1982   *Cracks in the Parchment Curtain and Other Essays in Philippine History.* Quezon City, Philippines: New Day Publishers.

Segal, Ronald

2001   *Islam's Black Slaves: The Other Black Diaspora.* New York: Farrar, Straus and Giroux.

Seligman, Adam

2000   *Modernity's Wager: Authority, the Self, and Transcendence.* Princeton, N.J.: Princeton University Press.

Sewell, William H.

1980   *Work and Revolution in France: The Language of Labor from the Old Regime to 1848.* Cambridge: Cambridge University Press.

1998   "Language and Practice in Cultural History: Backing Away from the Edge of the Cliff." *French Historical Studies* 21:2, 241–64.

1999   "The Concept(s) of Culture." In Bonnell and Hunt 1999, 35–61.

Shenk, Wilbert R.

1996   "Toward a Global Church History." *International Bulletin of Missionary Research* 20:2, 50–57.

Sheriff, Abdul

1985   "The Slave Mode of Production along the East African Coast, 1810–1873." In J. R. Willis 1985, 2:161–81.

1987   *Slaves, Spices, and Ivory in Zanzibar.* London: James Currey.

1989   "Localisation and Social Composition of the East African Slave Trade, 1858–1873." In Clarence-Smith 1989a, 131–45.

1995   *The History and Conservation of Zanzibar Stone Town.* London: James Currey.

Sheriff, Abdul, and Ed Ferguson, eds.

1991   *Zanzibar under Colonial Rule.* London: James Currey.

Shorter, Aylward

2000   *Religious Obedience in Africa.* Nairobi: Paulines Publications Africa.

Shulman, David, and Guy G. Stroumsa, eds.

2002a   *Self and Self-Transformation in the History of Religions.* Oxford: Oxford University Press.

Shulman, David, and Guy Stroumsa

2002b   "Introduction: Persons, Passages, and Shifting Cultural Space." In Shulman and Stroumsa 2002a, 3–16.

Silver, Catherine Bodard, ed.

1982   *Frédéric Le Play: On Family, Work, and Social Change.* Chicago and London: University of Chicago Press.

Silverman, Dan P.
  1972   *Reluctant Union: Alsace-Lorraine and Imperial Germany, 1871–1918.* University Park and London: Penn State University Press.
Slemon, Stephen
  1990   "Unsettling the Empire: Resistance Theory for the Second World." In Ashcroft, Griffiths, and Tiffin 1995, 104–10.
Small, N. J.
  1980   "UMCA (Universities Mission to Central Africa): The Early Work in Education, 1876–1905." TNR 86–87, 35–55.
Smith, Anthony
  1963   "The Missionary Contribution to Education (Tanganyika) to 1914." TNR 60, 91–109.
Smith, Wilfred Cantwell
  1978   *The Meaning and End of Religion.* New York: Harper and Row.
Soul, Joseph
  1936   "Monseigneur Maupoint et la fondation des missions de l'Afrique Orientale." *Revue d'Histoire des Missions* 13, 44–52.
Southall, Aidan
  1970   "The Illusion of Tribe." *Journal of African and Asian Studies* 5, 28–50.
Spear, Thomas
  1999   "Toward the History of African Christianity." In Spear and Kimambo 1999, 3–24.
Spear, Thomas, and Isaria N. Kimambo, eds.
  1999   *East African Expressions of Christianity.* Oxford: James Currey Press.
Spear, Thomas, and Richard Waller, eds.
  1993   *Being Maasai.* London: James Currey.
Sperling, David C.
  2000   "The Coastal Hinterland and Interior of East Africa." In Levtzion and Pouwels 2000a, 273–302.
Spindler, Marc
  1999   "Jacques Désiré Laval." In G. Anderson 1999, 386–87.
Spindler, Marc, and Jacques Gadille, eds.
  1992   *Science de la mission et formation missionnaire au XXe siècle.* Lyon and Bologna: CNRS.
Spivak, Gayatri C.
  1988   "Subaltern Studies: Deconstructing Historiography." In Guha and Spivak 1988, 3–32.
Stanley, Brian, ed.
  2003   *Missions, Nationalism, and the End of Empire.* Grand Rapids: Eerdmans.
Stanley, Henry Morton
  1872   *How I Found Livingstone.* New York: Scribner, Armstrong and Co.
  1878   *Through the Dark Continent.* 2 vols. New York: Harper and Bros.
  1890   *In Darkest Africa.* 2 vols. New York: Charles Scribner's Sons.

Staum, Martin S.
  2003   *Labeling People: French Scholars on Society, Race, and Empire, 1815–1848.* Montreal and Ithaca: McGill-Queen's University Press.
Steere, Edward
  1870   *A Handbook of the Swahili Language as Spoken at Zanzibar.* London.
Stein, Robert Louis
  1979   *The French Slave Trade in the Eighteenth Century.* Madison and London: University of Wisconsin Press.
Steiner, F.
  n.d.   "A Comparative Study of the Forms of Slavery." D.Phil. thesis, Oxford University.
Stock, Eugene
  1899   *The History of the Church Mission Society.* 3 vols. London: CMS.
Stoler, Ann Laura
  2002   *Carnal Knowledge and Imperial Power: Race and the Intimate in Colonial Rule.* Berkeley: University of California Press.
Stone, Judith
  1985   *The Search for Social Peace: Reform Legislation in France, 1890–1914.* Albany: SUNY Press.
Strandes, Justus
  1961   (1899) *The Portuguese Period in East Africa.* Nairobi: East African Literature Bureau.
Strayer, Robert W.
  1976   "Mission History in Africa: New Perspectives on an Encounter." *African Studies Review* 19, 1–15.
  1978   *The Making of Mission Communities in East Africa: Anglicans and Africans in Colonial Kenya, 1875–1935.* London: Heinemann.
Strenski, Ivan
  1993   *Religion in Relation: Method, Application, and Moral Location.* Studies in Comparative Religion. Columbia: University of South Carolina Press; Basingstoke, U.K.: Macmillan.
  2002   *Contesting Sacrifice: Religion, Nationalism, and Social Thought in France.* Chicago and London: University of Chicago Press.
Sundkler, Bengt, and Christopher Steed
  2000   *A History of the Church in Africa.* Cambridge, Mass.: Cambridge University Press.
Sunseri, Thaddeus
  1993   "Slave Ransoming in German East Africa, 1885–1922." *International Journal of African Historical Studies* 26, 481–511.
  1996   "Labour Migration in Colonial Tanzania and the Hegemony of South African Historiography." *African Affairs* 95, 581–96.
  2002   *Vilimani: Labor Migration and Rural Change in Early Colonial Tanzania.* Portsmouth, N.H.: Heinemann.

Swantz, Marja Liisa

2002   *Beyond the Forestline: The Life and Letters of Bengt Sundkler.* Herefordshire, U.K.: Gracewing.

Swedish International Development Agency

2002   "Summary of Conference Proceedings: Bagamoyo, a World Heritage, September 9–12." Bagamoyo, Tanzania.

Taylor, Charles

1989   *Sources of the Self.* Cambridge: Harvard University Press.

2004   *Modern Social Imaginaries.* Durham, N.C.: Duke University Press.

Taylor, Gary, and Steve Spencer, eds.

2004   *Social Identities: Multidisciplinary Approaches.* London: Routledge.

Taylor, John V.

1963   *The Primal Vision: Christian Presence amid African Religion.* Philadelphia: Fortress Press.

Taylor, Robert H., ed.

2002   *The Idea of Freedom in Asia and Africa.* Stanford, Calif.: Stanford University Press.

Temu, A. J.

1972   *British Protestant Missions.* London: Longmans.

Thomas, Nicholas

1994   *Colonialism's Culture: Anthropology, Travel, and Government.* Princeton, N.J.: Princeton University Press.

Thompson, E. P.

1968   *The Making of the English Working Class.* 2nd ed. Harmondsworth: Pelican.

1971   "The Moral Economy of the English Crowd in the Eighteenth Century." *Past and Present* 50.

1991   *Customs in Common.* New York: Norton.

Thompson, William M., ed.

1989   *Bérulle and the French School: Selected Writings.* New York: Paulist Press.

Todd, Emmanuel

1991   (1987) *The Making of Modern France.* Translated by Anthony and Betty Forster. Oxford: Basil Blackwell.

Todorov, Tsvetan

1984   *The Conquest of America.* New York: Harper and Row.

1993   *On Human Diversity: Nationalism, Racism, and Exoticism in French Thought.* Cambridge and London: Harvard University Press.

Toru, Miura, and John Edward Philips, eds.

2000   *Slave Elites in the Middle East and Africa: A Comparative Study.* London and New York: Kegan Paul International.

Tripp, Aili Mari, and Crawford Young

2001   "The Accommodation of Cultural Diversity in Tanzania." In *Ethnopolitical Warfare: Causes, Consequences and Possible Solutions.* Edited by Daniel Chirot and Martin E. P. Seligman. Washington, D.C.: American Psychological Association, 259–74.

Tsugitaka, Sato
2000   "Slave Elites in Islamic History." In Toru and Philips 2000, 1ff.
Tuck, Patrick J. N.
1987   *French Catholic Missionaries and the Politics of Imperialism in Vietnam,*
        1857–1914: A Documentary Survey. Liverpool: Liverpool University Press.
Tucker, Neely
1997   "Descendants Hold to Ex-Slaves' Dream." *Detroit Free Press.* Available at
        www.freep.com/news/nw/qslave5.htm.
Tullemans, H. G. M.
1982a   *Père Etienne Baur en de Arabische Opstand van 1888–1889.* Dissertation.
        Catholic University of Nijmegen.
1982b   "Transcripted Letters and Documents of the Bagamoyo Mission during the
        Arab Revolt, 1888–1889." Appendix to Tullemans 1982a.
Unomah, A. C., and J. B. Webster
1976   "East Africa: The Expansion of Commerce." In Flint 1976, 270–318.
Vail, Leroy, ed.
1991   (1989) *The Creation of Tribalism in Southern Africa.* Berkeley and Los
        Angeles: University of California Press.
Valey, Valérie
2004   "The Place and Role of the Players in Colonial Expansion: France and East
        Africa in the Nineteenth Century." In Pétré-Grenouilleau 2004a, 185–208.
Van Beek, Walter E. A., and Thomas D. Blakey
1994   "Introduction." In *Religion in Africa.* Edited by Thomas D. Blakey, Walter
        E. A. van Beek, and Dennis L. Thomson. London: James Currey.
Van den Eeden, William
1980   *Misioni Mandera Mwaka Mia* (One hundred years of the Mandera Mission).
        Peramiho, Tanzania: Peramiho Printing Press.
Van der Geest, Sjaak, and Jon P. Kirby
1992   "The Absence of the Missionary in African Ethnography, 1930–65." *African*
        Studies Review 35:3, 59–103.
Van der Veer, Peter
1996a   "Introduction." In van der Veer 1996b, 1–21.
Van der Veer, Peter, ed.
1996b   *Conversion to Modernities: The Globalization of Christianity.* New York and
        London: Routledge.
Van Kaam, Adrian
1959   *A Light to the Gentiles.* Milwaukee: Bruce Publishing Co.
Van Rooden, Peter
1996   "Nineteenth-Century Representations of Missionary Conversion and the Trans-
        formation of Western Christianity." In van der Veer 1996b, 65–87.
Van Walraven, Klaas, and Jon Abbink
2003   "Rethinking Resistance in African History: An Introduction." In Abbink et al.
        2003, 1–40.

Vaughan, Megan
    1991   *Curing Their Ills: Colonial Power and African Illness.* Stanford, Calif.:
              Stanford University Press.
Verne, Jules
    1911   (1873) *The Exploration of the World.* New York and London: Vincent Parke
              and Co.
    1926   (1863) *Five Weeks in a Balloon.* Translated by Arthur Chambers. London:
              Dent and Sons.
Versteijnen, Frits
    1963   "Bagamoyo." Unpublished collection of documents and notes, edited by
              Theodore Winkelmolen.
    1968a   *The Catholic Mission of Bagamoyo.* 1991 reprint by A. K. Zuber and COD
              Saarbrucken.
    1968b   "Pioneer Days in East Africa." *African Ecclesiastical Review* 10:4, 362–66.
Versteijnen, Frits, and Albert de Jong
    1977   *Kanisa la Mhonda, 1877–1977* (Mhonda Church, 1877–1977). Holy Ghost
              Fathers, District of Bagamoyo, Tanzania.
Viollis, Andrée
    2000   "Interview de Mgr. Le Roy dans *Le Petit Parisien* du Lundi 4 Mars 1929."
              MS 12, 56–61.
Viswanathan, Gauri
    1997   *Outside the Fold: Conversions, Modernity, and Belief.* Princeton, N.J.: Prince-
              ton University Press.
Vogt, François Xavier
    n.d.   *Bagamoyo: Resumé des Journaux, 1868–1928.* Morogoro Diocesan Archives,
              Morogoro, Tanzania (also CSSp 391a).
von Aix, Jeffrey, ed.
    1998   *Varieties of Ultramontanism.* Washington, D.C.: Catholic University of Amer-
              ica Press.
Walker, Reginald
    1933   *The Holy Ghost Fathers in Africa: A Century of Missionary Effort.* Dublin.
Walls, Andrew F.
    1996   *The Missionary Movement in Christian History.* Maryknoll, N.Y.: Orbis Books.
    2002   *The Cross-Cultural Process in Christian History.* Maryknoll, N.Y.: Orbis
              Books.
Weiss, Brad
    1996   *The Making and Unmaking of the Haya Lived World.* Durham, N.C., and
              London: Duke University Press.
Werner, A.
    1916   "The Wahadimu of Zanzibar." *Journal of the African Society* 15:60, 356–60.
West, Michael O.
    2002   *The Rise of an African Middle Class: Colonial Zimbabwe, 1898–1965.*
              Bloomington: Indiana University Press.

White, Luise, Stephan F. Miescher, and David William Cohen, eds.

2001   *African Words, African Voices: Critical Practices in Oral History.* Bloomington and London: Indiana University Press.

White, Nicholas

1999   *The Family Crisis in Late Nineteenth-Century French Fiction.* Cambridge: Cambridge University Press.

Wijsen, Frans, and Peter Nissen, eds.

2002   *"Mission Is a Must": Intercultural Theology and the Mission of the Church.* New York and Amsterdam: Rodopi.

Willinsky, John

1999   *Learning to Divide the World: Education at Empire's End.* Minneapolis and London: University of Minnesota Press.

Willis, John Ralph, ed.

1985   *Slaves and Slavery in Muslim Africa.* Vol. 1: *Islam and the Ideology of Slavery*; vol. 2: *The Servile State.* London: Frank Cass.

Willis, Justin

1993   "The Nature of a Mission Community: The Universities' Mission to Central Africa in Bonde." *Past and Present* 140, 127–54.

1996   "The Nature of a Mission Community: The Universities' Mission to Central Africa in Bonde." In Bickers and Seton 1996, 128–52.

1998   "Plantations: Zanzibar and the Swahili Coast." In Finkelman and Miller 1998, 2:730–31.

Wilson, George Herbert

1936   *The History of the Universities' Mission to Central Africa.* London: UMCA.

Wirz, Albert, and Andreas Eckert

2004   "The Scramble for Africa: Icon and Idiom of Modernity." In Pétré-Grenouilleau 2004a, 133–53.

Wolf, Eric

1982   *Europe and the Peoples without History.* Berkeley, Los Angeles, and London: University of California Press.

1990   *Freedom and Freedoms: Anthropological Perspectives.* Cape Town: University of Cape Town.

1999   *Envisioning Power: Ideologies of Dominance and Crisis.* Berkeley, Los Angeles, and London: University of California Press.

Woloch, Isser, ed.

1996   *Revolution and the Meanings of Freedom in the Nineteenth Century.* Stanford, Calif.: Stanford University Press.

Wright, Marcia

1971   *German Missions in Tanganyika, 1891–1941: Lutherans and Moravians in the Southern Highlands.* Oxford: Clarendon Press.

1985   "East Africa, 1870–1905." In Oliver and Sanderson 1985, 539–91.

1993   *Strategies of Slaves and Women: Life-Stories from East/Central Africa.* London: James Currey Press.

Young, Crawford
    2002   "Itineraries of Ideas of Freedom in Africa: Precolonial to Postcolonial." In
            R. H. Taylor 2002, 9–39.

Zeldin, Theodore, ed.
    1970   *Conflicts in French Society: Anticlericalism, Education and Morals in the
            Nineteenth Century.* London: George Allen.

Zorn, J. S. F.
    1992   *L'école des missions de la Société des Missions, 1822–1971.* In Spindler and
            Gadille 1992, 283–98.

Index

Page references in *italics* indicate figures.

339

Bagamoyo mission, *146*
  adult Catholics at, 177–78
  ages of baptized, 177n.94
  agricultural colony of, 144–45
  approach to labor at, 166–70
  Baur and Horner's dispute over, 159–60
  boundaries at, 149–50
  campaign of baptisms at, 203
  careful deployment of labor at, 168
  conflicts with neighbors over land use, 149–50
  continuing unrest after chapter of 1884, 225
  daily schedule, 145
  difficulties in seminary, 185–86
  eclipsing Zanzibar mission in size, 142
  envisioned as self-supporting, 160
  escapes from, 177, 181–85
  evolving spatial practices at, 231
  expanding plantations at, 209
  experiences of evangelization at, 174–75
  groups of people at, 175
  growing in size and reputation through the 1870s, 191–92
  hurricane's effect on, 154, 165, 170, 182
  illnesses suffered at, 176n.88
  increasing unrest at, 212–17
  as *jardin d'acclimation,* 158
  liturgy at, 148–49
  minor seminary at, 145–48
  move to, catalyzing Spiritan disagreements, 150
  move to, evolution in Spiritan activities, 143
  new approach to space at, 157, 160–66
  nursery for eastern Africa mission in 1880s, 197
  orphanages at, 206–7, 213–14, 220
  porousness of, related to outside environment, 174–75
  prison bloc constructed at, 180
  sacramental activity at, 209
  sisters with the sick, *89*
  slaves kept at, question of, 170–73
  special educational program at, 147–48

Bagamoyo mission (*continued*)
  Spiritan strategy at, 156–73
  St. Joseph village, 152–53
  work eclipsing education at, 170
  workshops at, *116*
baptiseuses, 251–53
baptisms
  campaign at Bagamoyo, 203
  of the dying, 48, 91–92, 203
  of mission children, 111
  Spiritans celebrating, 112
Barghash (sultan). *See* bin Said, Barghash
Baur, Etienne, 58, 59n.65, *181*
  addressing new Catholics' misbehavior, 229
  on Africans' intelligence, 105
  arriving at Zanzibar, 90–91
  changing local name to *Père* Etienne, 96
  communicating with Paris in Horner's absence, 135
  concern about children's nighttime sorties, 110n.66
  conflicts with Horner over Spiritan strategy, 131n.112
  contesting Horner's story about *Suéma,* 131
  crackdown at Bagamoyo, 214
  disappointment with villagers' outcomes, 244
  discipline for seminarians, 186
  dispute with Horner over merits of Zanzibar and Bagamoyo, 159–60
  exploratory journey to Bagamoyo, 132
  on first communion of mission's children, 125
  frustration with Mhonda Christians, 254
  gathering children from streets and cemeteries, 91
  helping free hostages taken during Bushiri War, 198
  inspecting Bagamoyo property, 99
  leadership style, 180
  negotiating French-British-local relations, 154–55
  participation in chapter of 1870, 150

Previously published in
the American Society of Missiology Series